The Rise of Talmud

THE BIBLE AND THE HUMANITIES

General Editors
Hindy Najman Elizabeth Solopova Kirk Wetters
This series consists of scholarly monographs that re-integrate
Biblical Studies into the Humanities by encouraging channels of
communication from Biblical Studies into other Humanistic disciplines,
and by bringing current theoretical developments to bear on biblical
texts and traditions.

The Rise of Talmud

MOULIE VIDAS

OXFORD
UNIVERSITY PRESS

Great Clarendon Street, Oxford, OX2 6DP,
United Kingdom

Oxford University Press is a department of the University of Oxford.
It furthers the University's objective of excellence in research, scholarship,
and education by publishing worldwide. Oxford is a registered trade mark of
Oxford University Press in the UK and in certain other countries

© Moulie Vidas 2025

The moral rights of the author have been asserted

All rights reserved. No part of this publication may be reproduced, stored in a retrieval
system, transmitted, used for text and data mining, or used for training artificial
intelligence, in any form or by any means, for commercial purposes, without the
prior permission in writing of Oxford University Press, or as expressly permitted by law,
by licence or under terms agreed with the appropriate reprographics rights organization.
Enquiries concerning reproduction outside the scope of the above should be sent to
the Rights Department, Oxford University Press, at the address above.

You must not circulate this work in any other form
and you must impose this same condition on any acquirer

Published in the United States of America by Oxford University Press
198 Madison Avenue, New York, NY 10016, United States of America

British Library Cataloguing in Publication Data
Data available
Library of Congress Control Number: 2024950427
ISBN 9780198915027
DOI: 10.1093/9780198915058.001.0001

Printed and bound by
CPI Group (UK) Ltd, Croydon, CR0 4YY

The manufacturer's authorised representative in the EU for product safety is Oxford
University Press España S.A. of El Parque Empresarial San Fernando de Henares,
Avenida de Castilla, 2 – 28830 Madrid
(www.oup.es/en or product.safety@oup.com). OUP España S.A. also
acts as importer into Spain of products made by the manufacturer.

Contents

Acknowledgments	vii
Texts, Translations, and Citations	ix
Introduction	1

I. INDIVIDUATION

Introduction to Part I	21
1. Who Is Speaking? Identification of Anonymous Teachings	35
2. The Sages, Opinionated: *De'ah* and Individual Inclination	77
3. The Switched Line: *Shita* and Reading for Consistency	98
4. Lip-Synching in the Grave: Narratives and Images of Attribution	130

II. IMPERFECTION

Introduction to Part II	169
5. The Scattered Torah: The Problem of Textual Knowledge	176
6. *Variae Recitationes*: Comparison of Divergent Texts	202
7. It's Not Here: Emendations	242
8. Needy, Lost, and Kind of Divine: Intertextuality, Necessity, and Recontextualization	264
Conclusion: The More Humane Letters	304
Bibliography	313
General Index	329
Index of Rabbinic Terms and Phrases	335
Index of Halakhic Subjects	337
Index Locorum	339

Acknowledgments

Ishay Rosen-Zvi and Mira Balberg read the manuscript very closely and made dozens of sharp, encouraging, and challenging comments. Hindy Najman stimulated and supported this project from the moment we discovered our shared enthusiasm for Nietzsche's inaugural lecture. Yaacob Dweck uplifted my spirits and the text's clarity. Their insight, critical engagement, and above all their friendship made this book a lot better, and writing it much more rewarding.

Leib Moscovitz, whose scholarship is foundational for the type of inquiry undertaken in this book, also commented on the manuscript with generosity, acuity, and erudition, and shared with me the forthcoming second part of his work on the Yerushalmi's terminology.

In more indirect but undeniable ways, this book has been shaped by close friendship and intellectual exchange with Yair Lipshitz, Wallace Best, Casey Lew-Williams, Todd Berzon, Daniel Heller-Roazen, James Redfield, and Elaine Pagels. The earliest stages of writing benefited greatly from Carey Seal's care and wisdom.

The teachings of Vered Noam and Peter Schäfer fill these pages, much more than is evident in the footnotes, because, as R. Yohanan says, "everyone knows R. Meir is a student of R. Aqiva" (see Chapter 4).

Tom Perridge and Cathryn Steele of Oxford University Press and Vinothini Thiruvannamalai from NewGen shepherded my manuscript on its path to becoming this book. Tim DeBold expertly prepared the indices.

For making Princeton a fantastic place for teaching and writing, I am grateful to my colleagues in the subfield of Religions of Mediterranean Antiquity, Martha Himmelfarb, AnneMarie Luijendijk, and newcomers Liane Feldman and Yedidah Koren; to other members of the Department of Religion, Andrew Chignell, Gabriel Citron, Jonathan Gold, Eric Gregory, Bryan Lowe, Shaun Marmon, Seth Perry, Garry Sparks, Stephen Teiser, Tehseen Thaver, Nicole Turner, and Qasim Zaman; to colleagues in the Program in Judaic Studies, Jonathan Gribetz, Eve Krakowski, Martina Rustow, and Esther Schor; to co-teachers and friends across campus, Joshua Billings, Zahid Chaudhary, Tom Hare, Maya Kronfeld, Carolina Mangone, and Caroline Yerkes; and to Mary Kay Bodnar, Florian Fues, and Kerry Smith, who run the Department smoothly and gracefully. I thank Judith Weisenfeld and Leora Batnitzky for their stewardship of the Department and the Program.

The students I had the privilege of teaching while writing this book have taught me a great deal. I am particularly grateful to former and current graduate students—Ari Lamm, A. J. Berkovitz, Elena Dugan, Madeleine Brown, Mark Letteney, Yitz Landes, Eliav Grossman, Adina Goldman, and Shira Mogil, and formidable former undergraduates—Ayelet Wenger, Yossi Quint, Tali Pelts, and Michah Newberger.

This project has benefited from conversations with many friends and colleagues, including Mika Ahuvia, Carol Bakhos, Michal Bar-Asher Siegal, Hallel Baitner, Adam Becker, Beth Berkowitz, Daniel Boyarin, Jonathan Boyarin, Peter Brown, Elizabeth Castelli, Mike Chin, Sergey Dolgopolski, Emanuel Fiano, Gregg Gardner, Richard Hidary, Sarit Kattan Gribetz, Reuven Kiperwasser, Derek Krueger, Rafael Neis, Annette Reed, Jeremy Schott, Seth Schwartz, Shai Secunda, David Stern, Alex Weintraub, Haim Weiss, and Holger Zellentin. I am particularly grateful to fellow Yerushalmi scholars—Eliashiv Cherlow, Menachem Katz, Maren Niehoff, Yakov Mayer, and Hanan Mazeh, for sharing with me ideas and unpublished work.

To Daniel Ewert, Seth Williams, and Allen Gillers, my gratitude for the best times at Riis, the Pines, and Maspeth.

I am grateful to Kathleen, Rob, Samara, and Phil Spitzer for welcoming me to their family.

Tiki and Avi Vidas continue to inspire me and support me with their relentless energy, creativity, and love. My Friday check-ins with them and Ori and Nir make me feel at home no matter where I am.

Harry Spitzer accompanied the writing of this book in its most intensive stages, from Athens to Zipolite. He helped me untangle argumentative knots on long walks and hikes; cheered me up on days plagued by frustrating *sugiyot* or footnotes; and taught me to celebrate every milestone of writing. I cannot express enough gratitude for his partnership and all the riches that he shares with me.

Texts, Translations, and Citations

The base text of the Talmud Yerushalmi used in this book is the Leiden manuscript (Scaliger no. 3, Or. 4720) as it is transcribed in *Ma'agarim*, the database of the Academy of Hebrew Language. The text I present reflects the later corrections recorded in the manuscript, which I do not normally mark. I note when I use other textual witnesses. Texts of Genizah fragments are also copied from *Ma'agarim*; for MS Vatican of the Yerushalmi, I consulted Schäfer and Becker's *Synopse*. My presentation of the text includes punctuation added for legibility. I make emendations when I judge that they are required for the text to make sense, but I do not try, for example, to standardize the Yerushalmi's grammar and spelling or correct forms that are affected by Babylonian Aramaic. When emendations are straightforward (e.g. because they are minor or because the corrected text is documented in a parallel or another manuscript), I note them in a footnote to the text. In the few places where I make major emendations on interpretive grounds, I also note them in the translation. Most other rabbinic texts are cited according to *Ma'agarim* with similar principles; for the Mishnah, for example, I quote the transcription in that database of the Kaufmann manuscript. Quotations from the Babylonian Talmud are copied from the Friedberg Project Talmud Bavli Variants database, noting the manuscript.

Passages in the Yerushalmi are identified as they are in *Ma'agarim*: tractate, chapter, Mishnah unit (according to the Mishnah's printed edition), along with the pagination in the Venice edition. While the reference to Mishnah units does not reflect the division of the Yerushalmi itself, I use it since *Ma'agarim* and its printed equivalent, the Academy of Hebrew Language edition, are the most widely used texts. References to fragments note library shelf numbers and page numbers in Sussmann, *Ginze Yerushalmi*. Rabbinic compilations other than the Yerushalmi are cited with the following abbreviations before the tractate name: *m.* for Mishnah; *t.* for Tosefta; and *b.* for Bavli. I use standard abbreviations for tractates in the notes. References to Midrashim use full titles.

For the Hebrew Bible, I consulted the *New Revised Standard Version* but made modifications to clarify the way the rabbis read thet text. Translations of rabbinic sources are generally my own, but for the Mishnah, I often adopted translations from the *Oxford Annotated Mishnah*. Names of sages appear in simplified transliteration, except biblical names that have common English equivalents (Jacob and Joshua, not Ya'aqov and Yehoshua). When the Yerushalmi drops the vowel in the beginning of the name, I use the full name in English (Eleazar, Abba, or Hila—not Leazar, Ba, or La). Our versions of the Yerushalmi present various spellings of the same name. My translations refer to Simeon b. Laqish even when the text has Reish Laqish, and R. Yose even when the text has Yasa or Asi; the Tannaitic R. Judah is always R. Judah, even when the Yerushalmi refers to him as R. Yudan; but the Amoraic R. Yudan is always R. Yudan. The sage the Talmud refers to as "Rabbi" appears in my translations as "Rabbi Judah the Patriarch," but in the discussion I sometimes use the abbreviated "Judah" or "the Patriarch" (but never "R. Judah").

Texts marked with *TLG* were consulted through the *Thesaurus Linguae Graecae* (*TLG*) database of the University of California. Texts indicated with *LCL* were consulted via the *Loeb Classical Library* website. In both cases, I note the name of the editor or translator. I reproduce the Greek text only where I offer my own translation.

I refer to the following commentators and commentaries now included in traditional editions of the Yerushalmi: Solomon Sirilio; Elijah of Fulda; *Penei Moshe* (= *PM*) by Moses Margolies; *Qorban ha-'Edah* (= *QE*) and *Sheyarey Qorban* (= *SQ*) by David Fränkel; Elijah of Vilna; and Yaakov David Wilovsky (= Ridbaz). The reference is *ad loc.* unless otherwise noted. Yerushalmi citations in medieval works were consulted through the Netanya College Talmud Yerushalmi Citation Database except when a specific reference is given.

On the Cover

The image on the cover was painted by Navot Miller following the author's guidance. It illustrates the Talmudic story, discussed in Chapter 4, about Rabbi Yohanan, Rabbi Jacob, and Rabbi Eleazar (*Mo'ed Qattan* 3:7 83c, par. *Berakhot* 2:1 4b).

Introduction

The rabbinic sages of antiquity have acquired a reputation as sophisticated readers and experts in texts, established largely on Midrash, their interpretation of Scripture. But beginning in the third century CE, these sages also took on extensive commentary on a different kind of text: the growing body of rabbinic teachings. This book examines the first collection of this type of commentary, the Palestinian Talmud or Talmud Yerushalmi, compiled in the late fourth century in Tiberias,[1] tracing the interpretive concepts and practices that set this endeavor apart from earlier rabbinic projects. It argues that the development of a branch of scholarship dedicated to texts which were construed, in contrast with Scripture, as the product of human teachers, introduced a wide-ranging transformation of the rabbinic intellectual landscape and a new conception of Torah or Jewish knowledge.

According to traditional Jewish historiography, when Rabbi Judah the Patriarch collected the teachings of the preceding generations in the Mishnah (circa 200 CE), the "Tannaitic" period concluded and the "Amoraic" period began. Some suggested that the very name of the latter period indicates that its sages were "interpreters," *amora'im*, of their predecessors' words, and even those who offered other etymologies have defined it as an era of commentary.[2] But while this interpretive turn has long been recognized, the degree to which it reflected the innovative approach of Amoraic scholars has been underestimated, and the distinctive character of the commentary they produced remains understudied.

Medieval authors saw in this commentary a compelling but straightforward elucidation of the Mishnah and other teachings, and precisely for this reason did not theorize its emergence or approach.[3] Modern accounts have recognized that this commentary employed a particular interpretive framework, but they have emphasized its similarity to Midrash, showing how Amoraic scholars applied to rabbinic teachings the same approaches that their predecessors developed in relation to Scripture.[4] These accounts pointed to practices common in both realms

---

[1] Moscovitz, "Formation and Character," 665–6; see also Leibner, "Settlement Patterns," 283–7; Sussmann, "Ve-shuv," 132–3 n. 187. Kraemer, *History*, 109, suggests the "turn of the fifth century or later."

[2] On "*amora'im*" as interpreters, see Rapoport, *Erech Millin*, 117, adopted e.g. in Melamed, *Introduction*, 47. The word *amora* in the sense of "interpreter" who communicates the sage's words is attested in the Talmud (e.g. *Ber.* 4:1 7c), but it does not define sages chronologically. Goldberg, "Palestinian Talmud," 303, adopts a different etymology but still defines the period as one of commentary.

[3] Gafni, *The Mishnah's Plain Sense*, 37–42; see more in the next section.

[4] The analogy with Midrash was not, at first, articulated to describe the Talmuds' interpretive practices. It was conceived to defend the authority of the sages to read the Mishnah as they wished (see Gafni, ibid., 53–72, on Elijah of Vilna's students), and subsequently to claim that Amoraic scholars did

of commentary, such as the derivation of significance from minute textual details, and noted that in both cases interpretation served to ground new positions in authoritative texts.[5] But while such overlaps are considerable, explaining Amoraic commentary on rabbinic teachings primarily as an extension of Midrashic approaches misses its defining features and the transformative significance of its development.

The central aim of this book is to establish the unique character and impact of Amoraic commentary by tracing how it diverged both from earlier approaches to the rabbinic tradition and from the sages' commentary on Scripture. Part I argues that Amoraic scholars introduced a new individuated understanding of rabbinic teachings; they developed a sophisticated set of interpretive practices which were premised on the idea that these teachings were shaped by the sages to whom they were attributed and reflected their individual characteristics. Part II argues that these scholars construed rabbinic teachings as fragmentary or imperfect attestations of the rabbinic tradition; it demonstrates that pervasive patterns in the Talmud presented the transmission and composition of these teachings as subject to contingency, variance, and error.

These approaches to rabbinic teachings were decidedly not Midrashic. Both Tannaitic and Amoraic sages read Scripture as reflecting a singular divine voice rather than different human authors and portrayed the text of Scripture as faithfully and uniformly transmitted. To pursue these new questions about rabbinic teachings, Amoraic scholarship developed new interpretive practices which were rare or absent in Midrash, such as the attribution of anonymous texts and comparison of textual versions. At the same time, these aspects of Amoraic commentary did not simply reflect the fact that rabbinic teachings were conceived differently than Scripture. They presented a new perspective on the nature of these teachings and therefore a broad reconceptualization of the tradition. It is not just that Tannaitic sages did not comment on the way teachings were shaped by individuals or the contingencies of transmission; they negotiated these teachings as positions which transcended textual form and individual contribution. The Amoraic turn expanded Torah study to include commentary on rabbinic teachings as texts; but

---

not aim to interpret the Mishnah but merely used it as support for their own rulings. Zacharias Frankel, one of the founders of modern Talmudic scholarship, makes this comparison to explain his omission of the Talmuds from his survey of the Mishnah's interpreters (*Hodegetica*, 317; see Gafni, ibid., 251–2). As far as I know, the explicit analogy first appears in the early modern period: scholars sometimes cite in this context a comment by the medieval Talmudist Isaiah di Trani (Wertheimer and Lis, *Piske ha-rid*, 229), but that comment does not concern exegetical approaches or methods.

[5] An early influential account is Weiss, *Dor Dor we-Dorschaw*, 3.10–16; though Weiss shares Frankel's approach to some degree (see previous note), his account also employs the comparison to argue for substantial similarity in interpretive practices. More recent studies include Jaffee, "Aspects"; Hayes, *Talmuds*, 105–6, 223–4; Alexander, *Transmitting Mishnah*, 77–116; Stern, "Canonization," 243–50; Kraemer, *History*, 90–1, 95–6; Brenner, *Okimta*, 26–7, 44, 157. The argument is often cited in introductions and surveys, e.g. Elon, *Jewish Law*, 407–9; Satlow, *Creating Judaism*, 133–4.

rather than merely applying to these texts approaches which were previously developed in the study of Scripture, this expansion engaged new ideas and strategies which transformed both the practice of Torah study and the very conception of the texts which constitute Torah.

The significance of these aspects of Amoraic commentary has been missed by different strands of modern scholarship for different, even opposite, reasons. Scholars working in the tradition of modern Talmudic philology showed a great interest in Amoraic comments about attribution, composition, and transmission, but they did not probe these comments for their underlying concepts of text and interpretation because, to some degree, they shared these concepts and took them for granted. Much of modern philology, too, is premised on the notion that texts reflect and originate with specific individuals or that extant texts are imperfect attestations of other texts. These scholars therefore approached these Amoraic comments as natural responses to rabbinic texts or even as precedents for their own philological practices, rather than as a reflection of distinct interpretive positions. Other scholars, particularly in the last few decades, criticized uncritical applications of modern notions to rabbinic literature, but in contrasting modern and rabbinic approaches, they often posited an overly uniform and static view of rabbinic textuality and hermeneutics. The insight that rabbinic literature does not present a modern concept of authorship, for example, has led to the claim that the sages did not conceive of textuality in individuated terms at all; the recognition that the sages' interpretive strategies should not be judged from the perspective of modern historicist attempts to reconstruct the text's "original" meaning has led to a description of rabbinic hermeneutics almost exclusively in Midrashic terms. Consequently, the types of comments examined in this book have been ignored or written off as aberrations and exceptions.

It is when we recognize the centrality of these aspects of Amoraic commentary and the fact that they presented a distinct hermeneutic approach that we can clearly see how this commentary reshaped rabbinic scholarship and reconceptualized the rabbinic tradition. This recognition also significantly enriches our picture of rabbinic hermeneutics with a new set of interpretive practices just as sophisticated and creative as those which the sages developed in their reading of Scripture. In turn, tracing this broader diversity in rabbinic scholarship allows for a more nuanced and generative comparison with other traditions of scholarship, both ancient and modern.

The Talmud Yerushalmi has long been eclipsed by a similar collection, the Babylonian Talmud or Talmud Bavli, which took on something like its current form about two centuries after the Yerushalmi, in what is now Iraq.[6] It was the Bavli that became the central text of the traditional Jewish curriculum, while centuries

---

[6] On dating the Bavli, see Gross, "Editorial Material."

of relative neglect have left the Yerushalmi poorly documented and understood.[7] Modern scholarship has gone a long way to counter this traditional emphasis, but the story of what we now call "Talmud"[8]—as a branch of rabbinic knowledge or as a genre of commentary—is still often defined in terms of the Bavli. The idea that Amoraic scholars read rabbinic teachings in the same way they read Scripture was primarily based on the later Talmud, in which Midrash-like exegesis applies to such teachings more frequently.[9] More important, the very turn to studying and commenting on rabbinic teachings, and the distinctive characteristics of that project, were given a secondary role. Instead, modern accounts have tended to focus on other processes, more evident in the Bavli, such as the increased emphasis on dialectical argumentation and the formation of the elaborate literary units which present it. The Yerushalmi has been regularly assigned to a "less developed" point in this teleological narrative.[10] By focusing on the first Talmud, this book aims both to describe its interpretive practices on their own terms and to center the rise of textual scholarship on rabbinic teachings as a pivotal development in Jewish intellectual history.

The Amoraic Turn and the Mishnah

While the following chapters examine the distinctive nature of Amoraic scholarship on rabbinic teachings, this section addresses the conditions that led to its emergence. Amoraic scholars were not the first to study rabbinic teachings; but more than their predecessors, they approached these teachings as texts, and took on the study of these texts as an end in itself. By texts, I do not mean written sources. Rabbinic literature distinguishes between Scripture, "the Written Torah," and the words of the sages, "the Oral Torah," and the evidence from both Tannaitic and Amoraic compilations suggests that throughout antiquity, the sages studied rabbinic teachings in oral form, by hearing, memorizing, and reciting them.[11]

---

[7] On the Yerushalmi's reception, see Ginzberg, *Commentary I*, xli–lxiv (in English) and *88–*132 (more extensively, in Hebrew). But the standard narrative may be overly lachrymose. Rustow, *Heresy*, 20–3, offers a reassessment of the "Babylonian 'triumph'" in the early Middle Ages. See also studies of the history of the Yerushalmi's text, including the production of manuscripts and the first edition: Sussmann, "Introduction"; idem, "Masoret limud"; Mayer, "Vatican Ebr. 133"; idem, *Editio Princeps*.
[8] On this term, see the discussion at the end of this Introduction.
[9] See Alexander, *Transmitting Mishnah*, 83, 104, and Hayes, *Talmuds*, 106, 180, who speak of the Yerushalmi as presenting a "less developed" or "nascent" instance of this approach; see also the discussion in Chapter 8, Section 2.
[10] See the acknowledgment of the problem in Kraemer, *History*, 124, and the detailed discussion in the Conclusion.
[11] The major statement on this subject is Sussmann, *Oral Law*, who argues for absolute orality, especially (though not only) with respect to the Mishnah. For a reassessment, see Stern, "Publication," who does not deny the predominance of oral instruction but posits that writing was involved in the composition, initial circulation, and private study of the Mishnah.

There are several references to rabbinic writing, and scholars have pointed to other considerations which suggest that written circulation existed alongside oral study,[12] but orality seems to have been predominant.[13] We tend to associate orality with fluidity and writing with fixed verbal form, and there is indeed plenty of evidence that orality enabled such fluid transmission of rabbinic teachings.[14] But we also find evidence that the sages aimed to transmit rabbinic teachings verbatim and commented on their wording even in oral form. It is not that orality made no difference; but if our sources point to a predominantly oral study culture, they also undermine determinist assumptions about orality and textuality. There is no evidence for a major shift to writing rabbinic teachings in the Amoraic period,[15] but there is evidence that the Amoraic period saw a significant textualization of the engagement with these teachings, in the sense that scholars more often cited and commented on their wording.

Tannaitic sages, for the most part, state their positions directly on the issue at hand, without citing a justification. When they do offer support for their positions, it is usually with inferential reasoning or Scripture rather than the citation of earlier rabbinic teachings. Commentary on such teachings rarely appears.[16] This is not because Tannaitic sages did not preserve the words of previous generations or study them; it is because of how they approached these words. Scholars have shown that we can distinguish different layers in the Mishnah and other Tannaitic compilations which betray chronological development and suggest preservation of earlier textual sequences. The same reconstructions, however, also show that the interpretive engagement with these earlier texts, while crucial for the development of the tradition, was usually done not through explicit commentary but through compositional adaptation that was not thematized in the text. When Tannaitic sages wanted to explain, qualify, or expand the rabbinic texts they inherited,

---

[12] For a list of passages which mention writing see Stern, "Publication," 449 n. 20. Naeh, "Scrolls," suggests evidence for transmission of the *Sifra* in writing, at least in Babylonia, and supports a hybrid model more generally, though again emphasizing Babylonia. For arguments supporting a hybrid model in Palestine see Jaffee, *Torah in the Mouth*, 100–25; Alexander, "Orality," 53–5; Stern, ibid. As Furstenberg, "Invention of the Ban," shows, the ban on writing rabbinic teachings appears only in a late passage in the Bavli.

[13] Different explanations have been offered for this emphasis on orality: that it preserved the privileged status of Scripture (Sussmann, *Oral Law*, 344–5); that it centered rabbinic study on the living relationship between master and disciple (Jaffee, *Torah in the Mouth*, 126–52; and see below, the conclusion to Chapter 4); that it was a form of differentiation from Christians (Yuval, "Oral Law") or Romans (Dohrmann, "Jewish Books"); that it allowed for controlled circulation (Stern, "Publication," 466–9); and that it was more practical and economical given the vast size of the text (Landes, "Transmission," 51, addressing the Mishnah specifically).

[14] Sussmann, *Oral Law*, 266–79 (while also stressing the stability of the Mishnah itself, 342–3); Alexander, *Transmitting Mishnah*, 35–76, and Rosenthal, "History of the Text," on the transmission of the Bavli in a much later period.

[15] This point is made repeatedly in Sussmann, *Oral Law*, e.g. 307.

[16] Weiss, *Amoraim*, 8; Halivni, *Midrash*, 69 (and see ibid., 58, on lack of justification as the "hallmark" of the Mishnaic form); Henshke, *Original Mishnah*, 1; Rosen-Zvi, *Mishnah and Midrash*, 37 (on general lack of justifications) and 52 (on infrequency of marked commentary). On relative lack of citations, see also the discussion below in the Introduction to Part I.

they did so normally by reformulating them, interpolating glosses into them, or embedding them in new literary structures.[17] Even where we do find late Tannaitic sages discussing their predecessors' positions, we can often observe how they formulated these positions based on their own conceptual considerations rather than on the interpretation of words attributed to these earlier sages.[18]

All of this suggests that the aim of Tannaitic engagement with rabbinic teachings was not to interpret these teachings, but rather to understand the issue at hand—normally the analysis of Halakhah, the rabbinic system of legal and ritual norms, though not necessarily Halakhic ruling. The activity of formulation, collection, and juxtaposition of rabbinic teachings that resulted in the Tannaitic compilations constituted a rich engagement with these teachings. Below, I consider how the emergence of these compilations as defined texts already indicates a different approach to rabbinic textuality. But as a rule, neither the statements appearing in these compilations nor their editorial frameworks take commentary on the sages' words as their primary objective.

This approach shifts in the third century CE. Traditional rabbinic historiography posits that commentary on the Mishnah began immediately upon its publication, which inaugurated the Amoraic period.[19] More recent scholarship has shown that the turn was not so immediate. Statements attributed in the Talmud to the first generation of sages following the Mishnah's compilation look mostly like statements of Tannaitic sages. But beginning with statements attributed to the following generation, in the middle of the third century, we can observe a significant increase in statements commenting on and citing earlier rabbinic teachings: first the Mishnah and other Tannaitic teachings, and then also the growing body of Amoraic teachings.[20]

This rise of commentary on rabbinic teachings has been understood as a product of the Mishnah's promulgation or canonization, which is reasonable given that the Mishnah is central to this commentary and that this turn occurs shortly after the Mishnah's compilation. But explaining this process in more detail presents some challenges. Ancient sources do not offer a narrative of how the Mishnah became a central text or how Amoraic commentary began.[21] Moreover,

---

[17] Henshke, *Original Mishnah*, 195–6; Rosen-Zvi, *Mishnah and Midrash*, 40–60; Furstenberg, "Literary Evolution," 110–23.

[18] See the discussion below in the Introduction to Part I, as well as Chapter 1, Section 5.

[19] See Maimonides' account in Shilat, *Hakdamot*, 51 and Sherira's in Lewin, *ISG*, 30 and 51–3.

[20] Lapin, "Institutionalization," and Be'eri, *Exploring Ta'aniot*, 58–61, each relying on quantitative classifications of statements in specific tractates of the Yerushalmi. The Bavli may tell a different story; see Bokser, *Post-Mishnaic Judaism*, who argues based on the Bavli that the teachings of Samuel already show intensive interest in Mishnah commentary. The Bavli, too, presents continuities between first-generation Amora'im and their Tannaitic predecessors, but in a different way. See Weiss, *Amoraim*, 8–14; Kraemer, *Mind*, 30–4; Safrai, "Oral Torah," 82.

[21] A discussion that is preserved in the Yerushalmi at *Hor.* 3:8 48c (par. *Shab.* 16:1 15c) and in the Bavli at *b. B. M.* 33a–b has frequently been taken to refer to this process. But as Neah ("Three Comments," 211) and Assis (*Concordance*, 1094 n. 1742) argued, the Yerushalmi does not refer to a historical development involving the Mishnah, but rather the educational development of a student. The

we have very few indicators of the reception of the Mishnah outside this commentary, which makes it difficult to separate them as cause and effect, as sequential developments, or even as analytically distinct phenomena. Several scholars have therefore taken a different approach, arguing that the Mishnah and its canonical status are as much a product of Amoraic commentary as they are its premise: it is through this commentary that the Mishnah was generated as a canonical or even a stable text (as opposed to a framework for varying oral performances).[22] The "self-reinforcing circle"[23] posited by this approach—Amoraic commentary responds to the Mishnah and its canonical status, while this canonical status, or even the Mishnah itself, is produced by Amoraic commentary—fairly captures the mutually constitutive relationship between canonical texts and their interpretation; but it leaves us poorly equipped to understand the conditions that engendered the Mishnah's centrality or the Amoraic turn to commentary. It also runs the risk of a teleological narrative, according to which the Mishnah only became central through the Talmudic paradigm which eventually became dominant. The Tosefta, which is structured as a companion to the Mishnah,[24] and the Aqivan Midrashim, which assume their audience has detailed knowledge of its text,[25] show that responding to the Mishnah as a foundational text did not necessarily result in the type of commentary we find in the Talmud.

Even if we take the centrality of the Mishnah as a fact, the path to an extensive scholarly commentary is not as straightforward as it might at first seem, and explanations of how one led to the other normally suggest additional factors. For accounts that assume Amoraic scholars simply meant to elucidate the Mishnah or defer to its authority, explaining the rise of commentary was particularly problematic. The tenth-century *Letter of Rav Sherira*, the earliest history of rabbinic literature, posits that when the Mishnah's compiler, R. Judah the Patriarch, died, there was also a decline in the intellectual capacity of sages, and therefore the lesser sages needed explanations of things which were clear to the earlier sages.[26] But there is no evidence that Amoraic scholars themselves saw the rise of commentary or the periodic turn in this way or that they posited an intellectual decline in this period (let alone that such a decline took place).[27] Solomon Rapoport, one

---

Bavli passage too does not address so much the question of commentary as different modes of study (see Amit, "Homilies"; and Vidas, *Tradition*, 118–32).

[22] Stern, "Canonization," 243; Alexander, *Transmitting Mishnah*, 77.
[23] Kraemer, *History*, 96.
[24] Goldberg, "Tosefta"; Mandel, "Tosefta." On teachings included in the Tosefta that are earlier than the Mishnah see Friedman, *Tosefta atiqta*. For the view that the Tosefta as a compilation predates the Mishnah, see Hauptman, *Rereading the Mishnah*.
[25] Kahana, "Abbreviators" and "Relations."
[26] Lewin, *ISG*, 50–69. On the traditionalism of this account see Blidstein, "Concept," 13–16.
[27] The *Letter* cites *b. Sot.* 49b, but while that passage, like similar passages at *m. Sot.* 9:9–15 and *t. Sot.* 15:4, associates various kinds of decline with the deaths of different sages, the one associated with Judah the Patriarch in the Mishnah (ironically?) is that after his death there was no longer humility. We do find statements about intellectual or spiritual decline in the Yerushalmi (e.g. *Sheq.* 5:1 48c–d), but they

of the founders of the modern study of Judaism, explained that the interpretation of rabbinic teachings became a major occupation for Amoraic scholars because they were distant chronologically, and in Babylonia also geographically, from these teachings' origins.[28] But Amoraic commentary rises shortly after the compilation of the Mishnah, and in the same Galilean region in which Mishnaic sages taught. Shalom Albeck's *Introduction to Jewish Law* suggests that Amoraic scholars came from a humbler social background, which meant also that they were humbler in character, and therefore did not consider themselves worthy of contradicting Tannaitic sages but only of interpreting their words.[29]

Those who were willing to attribute to Amoraic scholars more than humble deference to the Mishnah could account for the rise of commentary in terms of these scholars' approaches and aims. For David Halivni, the reason Amoraic scholars became "interpreters, rather than imitators" of the Mishnah was that the Mishnaic apodictic form was not "indigenous" to Judaism and Amoraic scholars sought to return to a deliberative approach to the law by offering justification and reasoning in their commentary.[30] The most current explanation, as I have mentioned, relies on the model of Midrash. Amoraic commentary was motivated by, and enacted, the Scripture-like authority of the Mishnah and its binding legal status, both in the sense that it justified new positions through (often ingenious) interpretation of the Mishnah[31] and in the sense that it lavished on its text the same kind of exegetical attention the sages lavished on Scripture.[32] There is much that is true in that model, but the rest of this book argues that this focus on "Scripturalization" misses the distinctive features of Amoraic commentary. Furthermore, the question of commentary should be separated from the question of legal status and even, to some degree, authority: those were certainly important factors, but Amoraic scholars commented on Mishnaic and other teachings whether they considered them legally binding or not, and even, we shall see, when they thought they were erroneous.

In order to assess the role of the Mishnah in the rise of Amoraic commentary, we should first determine the nature of its canonization. The Mishnah is the earliest

---

do not point to that generation and are not used to explain the rise of commentary or the authority of Tannaitic teachings. On the idea of decline in rabbinic literature more broadly see Kellner, *Decline*.

[28] Rapoport, *Erech Millin*, 116–17.
[29] Albeck, *Introduction to Jewish Law*, 81–2.
[30] Halivni, *Midrash*, 73.
[31] See Frankel's statement cited above, n. 4; Weinberg, *Seride 'esh*, 4.237–41; De Vries, *Development*, 46; Florsheim, "Rav Hisda." While in these accounts, "interpretation" and "Halakhic innovation" seem to stand in tension or even opposition (with the assumption that true interpretation is only interpretation which aims at the "plain sense" or "original intention" of the text), more recent works make a similar point but with a hermeneutic framework that recognizes a wider variety of legitimate interpretations and therefore do not make such oppositions. See Jaffee, "Oral Torah"; Kraemer, *History*, 91–2; Brenner, *Okimta*, 40–8.
[32] Weiss, *Dor*, 10; Jaffee, "Oral Torah"; Stern, "Canonization," 243–50; Alexander, *Transmitting Mishnah*, 77–116 (who uses the term "Scripturalization" in this context); Kraemer, *History*, 95–6.

surviving rabbinic compilation. For some scholars, this fact indicates that it was the first attempt to offer a comprehensive account of rabbinic teachings; others posit that the Mishnah was not so unprecedented, that it was a relatively conservative effort reworking existing collections; still others take some position in between.[33] The noun *mishnah*, which means "recitation" of the tradition, appears in the Tannaitic corpus, but none of its occurrences point to a collection of teachings, at least not unambiguously.[34] In the Talmud, the noun does point to such collections, including the Mishnah itself, but these collections are attributed to sages from the same period as the compilation of the Mishnah.[35] We do have evidence, as I have mentioned above, for composite sequences of rabbinic teachings that predate the Mishnah.[36] But since no such composition survives independently, it is difficult to assess their scope or nature, and therefore which characteristics, if any, made the Mishnah distinct.

There is, however, a way to account for the Mishnah's distinction not in terms of its inherent features or unprecedented scope, but rather in terms of the agents who promoted it, as Yitz Landes argued extensively in a recent dissertation.[37] The Talmuds associate the Mishnah with R. Judah the Patriarch.[38] Judah was not only a brilliant sage; he was also the head of a dynasty which, at least beginning with the third century, acquired considerable resources and power, resulting in what became the institution of the Patriarchate.[39] The promulgation of Judah's *mishnah* as "the Mishnah" reflects the emergence of this institution. The patriarchs used their power to disseminate the Mishnah and other rabbinic texts. This standardization of the rabbinic curriculum asserted their authority, promoted their version of the rabbinic tradition, and contributed to their centralization and institutionalization of the community of sages by providing a shared textual foundation which projected cohesion and interconnectivity.

There are other indications of institutionalization from this period, albeit on a relatively modest scale. Scholars have shown, for example, that late layers of Tannaitic literature indicate a change in the meaning of the term "study house" (*beit ha-midrash*): whereas in the Mishnah the term more commonly signifies a

---

[33] For these positions, see Furstenberg, "Literary Evolution."

[34] See critiques of earlier scholarship in Rosen-Zvi, *Mishnah and Midrash*, 45, on "the first *mishnah*," and Yadin-Israel, "Canonicity," 437, on the "*mishnah* of R. Aqiva," and see the analysis below, Chapter 1, Section 5.

[35] See *Hor.* 3:8 48c, "these are the great *mishnayot*, like the *mishnah* of R. Hiyya, the *mishnah* of R. Hoshaya, and the *mishnah* of Bar Qappara" ("Hiyya" represents an emendation; the text reads Huna). Versions of this teaching outside the Yerushalmi add the "*mishnah* of R. Aqiva" (see some of the manuscrpits for *Ecclesiastes Rabbah*, 2.8.1). The Yerushalmi's introductory formula "Rabbi so-and-so recited" (תני ר׳ פלוני) frequently refers, in addition to the sages who appear in *Hor.*, also to the pre-Mishnaic R. Ishmael and R. Simeon b. Yohai.

[36] See n. 17 above.

[37] Landes, "Transmission," 23–52; earlier statements include Lapin, *Rabbis as Romans*, 59.

[38] See Chapter 1, Section 2.

[39] On the Patriarchate, see Jacobs, *Institution*; Levine, "Status"; Stern, "Rabbi"; Schwartz, *Imperialism*, 110–28.

study session, the Tosefta, the Tannaitic Midrashim, and the Yerushalmi feature more instances in which it designates a building where such sessions were held.[40] Sources from this period also begin to speak about rabbinic "appointments."[41] The promulgation of the Patriarch's Mishnah, as well as the production of other Tannaitic compilations, both reflected and contributed to this centralization and institutionalization.[42] As Hayim Lapin argued, the self-referentiality evident in Amoraic commentary on and citations of rabbinic teachings similarly attests to these processes.[43]

Traditional accounts posited that the Mishnah was accepted as a legally binding document immediately upon its publication.[44] More recent studies noted that Amoraic scholars routinely adopted legal positions different from the Mishnah's,[45] and still other studies argued that the Mishnah was not even intended as a legally binding document but was construed as such by some Amoraic scholars.[46] In considering the development of commentary, however, the very organization of the curriculum around a specific "recitation" or formulation of rabbinic teachings is more fundamental than the question of legal status. It is this new configuration of rabbinic study culture that resulted in textual engagement. Interpretation was now presented in the form of commentary rather than adaptation since, by definition, the recitation would change if it were adapted. Commentary addressed not only Halakhic and other positions, but how such positions were conveyed in specific strings of words. As Elizabeth Shanks Alexander emphasized, the absence or at least marginality of written transmission means that this feature of Amoraic commentary did not merely respond to a stable text of the Mishnah: it was one instrument through which the Mishnah became a defined text with specific wording.[47] But it would be an exaggeration to say that the Mishnah *only* became a stable text through Amoraic commentary; there are other attestations to its crystallization.[48]

---

[40] Shapira, "Beit Hamidrash," 48–51.
[41] Cohen, "The Rabbi"; Lapin, *Rabbis as Romans*, 77–83. On the question of funding, see Dalton, "Rabbis as Recipients of Charity."
[42] At the same time, not all of these compilations share the vision of the rabbinic tradition on which the Mishnah is predicated: see Yadin-Israel, "Canonicity."
[43] Lapin, "Institutionalization."
[44] See the accounts of Maimonides and Sherira, above n. 19.
[45] See e.g. Halivni, "Reception."
[46] Goldberg, "Palestinian Talmud," 309; Brandes, "Canonization," 150–1. Both attribute this construction to R. Yohanan, which would make it concurrent with the rise of Amoraic commentary, but I think there are good reasons to date that construction later, to R. Yohanan's students and their students. See below, Chapter 1, Section 2.
[47] Alexander, *Transmitting Mishnah*, 77–116. While Alexander associates this process with what she calls the "Scripturalization" of the Mishnah and the Midrash-like attribution of textual economy to the Mishnah (which in my opinion are more specific developments), she also describes her argument as applying to textual fixity and authority (see e.g. 29). See also Kraemer, *History*, 90–1.
[48] See on the Halakhic Midrashim, above n. 25. Early third-century crystallization is also suggested by the fact that while the later Tosefta includes many statements attributed to sages from the generation of Rabbi Judah the Patriarch, such attributions rarely appear in the Mishnah itself (Goldberg, *Tosefta Bava Kamma*, 29–30).

While the Mishnah was uniquely central to Amoraic scholars—they refer to it as "our Mishnah"[49]—they lavished similar interpretive attention on other Tannaitic teachings, often without much differentiation between teachings included in the Mishnah and those which were not.[50] The more important line drawn by Amoraic commentary is the line between what we now call the Tannaitic and Amoraic periods. The Yerushalmi does not present the distinction we find in later sources between "Tanna'im" and "Amora'im" as chronological groups of sages.[51] But it does designate certain teachings as "recited" (*matnita* in Aramaic, *mishnah* in Hebrew), and that designation has chronological and hierarchical implications: recited teachings mention only sages who lived in the period that concluded with the Mishnah (though these teachings may be attributed to later sages), while post-Mishnaic sages do not formally contradict a recited teaching unless they can support their position with another recited teaching.[52]

The Talmud never spells out this approach to recited teachings or explains how it came about. If one sees in the compilation of the Mishnah the first large-scale formulation of rabbinic teachings, one could posit that this compilation also produced the Tannaitic past, sealing an era by presenting an anthology of its teachings.[53] On the view that the Mishnah was not so unprecedented, this approach may have reflected the new study culture of which the dissemination of the Mishnah was a part: a curriculum increasingly organized around defined texts. While the greater authority accorded to recited teachings may imply that Amoraic scholars saw themselves as inferior, that implication should be taken with a grain of salt: the sages also do not contradict Scripture, and yet it is clear to us that they claim a great deal of authority as the arbiters of its meaning; as David Kraemer argued, the same can be said with respect to Amoraic commentary on the Mishnah and other Tannaitic teachings.[54]

The turn to commenting on rather than composing recited teachings was not absolute. Recent scholarship has shown that certain teachings marked as recited in the Talmuds, and even teachings included in the Tosefta, are derived from Amoraic-era statements.[55] In other words, the production of recited teachings by at least some Amoraic-era sages persisted alongside the practice of commentary.

---

[49] "מתניתן"; see Moscovitz, *Secondary Terms*, s.v. מתניתא. On the possible distinction between "our Mishnah" and the Patriarch's Mishnah, see Chapter 6, n. 34.

[50] There are scores of examples of such analysis in this book. The Yerushalmi only rarely distinguishes terminologically between the Mishnah and other Tannaitic teachings; they are both *mishnah* or *matnita*. See below, Chapter 1, n. 50.

[51] Amir, *Titles and Institutions*, 176–8 (who considers this to be the case in the Bavli as well); Vidas, "What Is a *Tannay*," 54–7.

[52] See Havlin, "'Al ha-ḥatimah," on traditional interpretations of this rule. On exceptions, see e.g. Albeck, *Studies*, 20–1 (concerning a subset of recited teachings attributed to Amoraic figures), and see more below on the continued composition of recited teachings in the Amoraic period.

[53] Thus Havlin, ibid.

[54] Kraemer, *History*, 96–7.

[55] Mazeh, "Demai," 20–46; Schremer and Katzoff, "Inseparable Considerations."

Given that some recited teachings are explicitly attributed to early Amoraic figures and that many mention no sages at all,[56] this continued composition may tell us that the marking of a teaching as "recited" did not necessarily claim that the teaching was composed in the Tannaitic period, but rather that it was perceived as representing the position of Tannaitic sages (or even the *mishnah* in the sense of the oral tradition). As a rule, though, recited teachings were not approached as adaptable sources: Amoraic scholars routinely comment on the specific wording of such teachings to argue in support of their positions. But even if the continued composition of recited teachings was the exception rather than the rule, it is significant because it shows us that the rule itself was a discursive practice, a reflection of a particular approach gradually adopted by the sages rather than a definitive and inevitable periodic change.

The model of commentary focused on texts did not remain limited to recited teachings; it was also applied, in subsequent generations, to the growing body of Amoraic teachings. While there is some difference in the comments Amoraic scholars make on those teachings and the comments they make on recited teachings, there is also a significant overlap.[57] The origins of textual engagement with rabbinic teachings may have been the compilation of the Mishnah or a study culture that was first focused on Tannaitic teachings, but eventually, what is reflected in the Talmuds is, as David Stern emphasized, the canonization of the rabbinic tradition as a whole.[58]

The foregoing discussion traced how the increased centralization among the community of sages, and the standardization of the curriculum through which it was realized, created the conditions for, and was reflected in, a new type of textual engagement with rabbinic teachings, resulting in increased citation and commentary. The interpretive practices studied in this book are premised on, and enact, this textual engagement: they attend to the wording and form of rabbinic teachings, prioritize statements that are textually supported by such teachings, interrogate their sources and their transmission, and compare different formulations of them. But textual engagement itself did not inevitably lead to these specific interpretive practices. Rabbinic teachings could have been, and indeed were, read in other ways, and we will see, throughout this book, how the application of these practices reflected specific interpretive choices and ideas about these teachings. In the Conclusion, I suggest that what gave this commentary its shape were the interests of Amoraic scholars in the new possibilities that this commentary opened for them: new modes of analysis, new kinds of authority,

---

[56] Albeck, *Studies*, 15–43, 48–60.
[57] Chapters 1, 6, and 7 below address types of commentary that apply only to recited teachings; Chapters 2 and 3 address comments that apply with identical terminology to recited and Amoraic teachings; and Chapters 5 and 8 discuss interpretive practices that apply, sometimes in different forms and with different terms, to both kinds of teachings.
[58] Stern, "Canonization"; Jaffee, "Oral Torah," 394.

and new visions of Torah. The following chapters are dedicated to tracing these distinctive possibilities.

Method

Rabbinic literature does not usually state its principles of interpretation or notions of text.[59] The discussion below reconstructs such hermeneutic positions by examining Amoraic scholarly practices as they are represented in the Talmud. Most chapters examine a type of argument or comment that is central to ancient Talmudic scholarship, or alternatively, a set of related types of such arguments and comments. Centrality is demonstrated both quantitatively and qualitatively. These types of arguments or comments appear in dozens, often hundreds of passages in the Talmud (while the Yerushalmi contains many duplicate passages, quantitative assessments are based on unique instances). Examining the function of these comments and arguments shows how they play diverse roles in the Talmud, supporting different kinds of interpretation, structuring different kinds of discussions, and often defining the purpose of Talmudic inquiry.

To establish that Amoraic approaches to rabbinic teachings were new and distinctive, this book engages in comparative discussions of Midrash and the Tannaitic compilations. Because most of these approaches differ dramatically from what we find in the rabbinic study of Scripture, the discussion of Midrash is short and confined largely to the introductions to each part of the book; the exception is Chapter 8, which addresses interpretive practices that more closely overlap with Midrash. The comparison between these Amoraic approaches and the representation of rabbinic teachings in the Tannaitic compilations presents subtler differences, as well as precedents or apparent precedents, which are discussed in detail. These comparative discussions aim to avoid simplistic contrasts, rarely positing absolute distinctions of "never" and "always." Still, these comparisons demonstrate substantial reconfiguration and restructuring: what is marginal, rare, or incidental in Midrash or the Tannaitic corpus becomes central, frequent, and definitive in the Amoraic commentary on rabbinic teachings.

This book is not intended as a comparative study of Amoraic scholarship in its Greco-Roman context, but it engages in such analysis at critical junctures, both to illuminate aspects of Amoraic scholarly practice and to demonstrate how the consideration of rabbinic scholarship beyond Midrash furthers our understanding of the sages in the context of the broader scholarly culture of their time. Recent studies have shown that Midrash shares goals, methods, and even

---

[59] On this issue in Midrash, see the discussion in the beginning of Chapter 8 below; and see Brenner, *Okimta*, 33–9, on the lack of hermeneutic self-reflection in the Bavli's interpretation of rabbinic teachings.

terminology with ancient Homeric scholarship.[60] Other studies have demonstrated that rabbinic and Christian scriptural commentary are similar in structure and content and posited that they shaped each other through exchange and polemic.[61] But the focus on Midrash in these comparative examinations of the sages' textual scholarship can lead to contrasts—on issues such as attribution to individuals and textual criticism—which are significantly qualified once we consider the sages' commentary on rabbinic teachings. The comparative discussions below consider a broad range of ancient scholars, but they center on Christian scholars working in Palestine. Origen, Eusebius, Jerome, and Epiphanius were among the most philologically oriented Christian authors in antiquity.[62] The fact that their scholarship is relatively well preserved and well studied offers us an opportunity to read Amoraic commentary alongside work produced in close geographical and temporal proximity by scholars who had documented contact with Jewish sages.[63]

Much of this book focuses on terminology. Rabbinic literature is formulaic, frequently employing a relatively narrow set of terms and phrases to mark specific discursive procedures. This formulaic nature allows us to make several kinds of claims. By gathering all the passages which present phrases associated with a particular type of comment or argument, we can establish relatively well-defined and wide-ranging datasets; these in turn allow us to examine how such arguments or comments are used and what they achieve, and also to offer a certain quantification and assessment of their importance. By looking at the wording of these terms and phrases, we can also get a sense of how Amoraic scholars perceived and presented their interpretive practices. And by tracing the history of terms and phrases—identifying when they first appear or how their meaning changes—we can follow the development of new practices or ideas. The terminology of the Palestinian Talmud is particularly well served with path-breaking reference works by Moshe Kosovsky, Moshe Assis, and Leib Moscovitz, to which the present study is indebted.[64]

---

[60] Moss, "Noblest Obelus"; Paz, *Scribes to Scholars*.

[61] Hirshman, *A Rivalry of Genius*; Bar-Asher Siegal, *Jewish-Christian Dialogues*; Bakhos, "Rabbinic and Patristic Interpretations." On the impact of Christianity on the rabbis see more broadly Boyarin, *Border Lines*; and Schäfer, *The Jewish Jesus*.

[62] On Origen, see Neuschäfer, *Origenes als Philologe*; and Martens, *Origen and Scripture*; on the broader Caesarean tradition, including also Pamphilus and Eusebius, see Grafton and Williams, *Christianity*; on Jerome, see Williams, *The Monk and the Book*; on Epiphanius, see Jacobs, *Epiphanius*. To be sure, there were also non-Christian scholars in the Greco-Roman philological tradition in Palestine; but the state of preservation of their work, as well as scholarship on them, does not allow for comparative reading on the same resolution. On Greek intellectuals in Palestine, see Geiger, *Tents of Japheth*.

[63] On Origen, see De Lange, *Origen and the Jews*. On Jerome, see Newman, "Jerome and the Jews"; Williams, *The Monk and the Book*, 89–95; and Berzon, "Double Bind," 459–67. For a survey of what Christian authors knew about the rabbis, see Newman, "Patristic Perspective."

[64] Kosovsky, *Concordance*; Assis, *Concordance*; Moscovitz, *Terminology* and *Secondary Terms*. A foundational treatment of rabbinic terminology in general is Bacher, *Exegetische Terminologie*.

The formulaic nature of the evidence also poses challenges. On the one hand, we find in much of the Yerushalmi a considerable homogeneity in terminology across hundreds of statements attributed to different sages living in different places over the course of two centuries. On the other hand, the Babylonian Talmud, and even one of the Yerushalmi's tractates, *Neziqin*, attribute to the same sages different, and equally homogeneous, sets of terms and formulae.[65] This suggests that the standard terminology in our sources reflects, to a large degree, not uniformity among the sages to whom the use of these terms is attributed, but a later standardization by those who compiled and transmitted these different compilations.[66] At least the wording of the terms, or its pervasive use, may therefore represent only a particular stage in the development of Amoraic scholarship or the text's transmission. A related challenge is that uniformity of terminology does not indicate uniformity of function: broadly speaking, the evidence suggests diverse, and sometimes even imprecise, usage of terms and phrases, as well as phenomena such as stylistic variegation and homogenization that often prevent pressing the terminology too hard.[67] While the chapters below do draw conclusions from the wording of terms and phrases, these are always supplemented with detailed examinations of how these terms and phrases function in large sets of passages.

The possibility of a late standardized terminology is part of a more general challenge presented by rabbinic compilations: determining the degree to which they reflect multiple voices, beyond the voice of the compilers. Many studies have questioned, in particular, the reliability of attributions.[68] In part because I share this skepticism, this book focuses on the general characteristics of Amoraic scholarship as it is represented in the Yerushalmi, without denying, of course, that Amoraic scholars could have diverse approaches alongside these broadly attested characteristics. I only rarely make distinctions among individual sages or different generations within the Amoraic period.[69]

At the same time, I do not think that the observations made in this book apply *only* at the level of compilation.[70] The Talmud does not attribute the same kind of scholarship consistently to all generations of sages. Most Tannaitic sources cited in the Talmud are of a piece with what we see in Tannaitic compilations; and as noted above, statements the Talmud attributes to the first generation of Amoraic scholars show considerably less interest in commentary on rabbinic teachings and less

---

[65] On *Neziqin*, see Lieberman, *Talmud of Caesarea*, 7–9; Sussmann, "Ve-shuv," 60 n. 27.
[66] Sussmann, *Oral Law*, 338–9 n. 39; Epstein, *IMT*, 441 (speaking of a specific example, but noting it is "usually the case in these matters").
[67] Sussmann, ibid.; Moscovitz, *Terminology*, 12–18.
[68] See the discussion below, Introduction to Part I.
[69] The traditional division of Amoraic sages to generations is particularly problematic when it comes to Palestine (see Sussmann, "Ve-shuv," 98 n. 178a); I generally avoided assigning sages to specific generations.
[70] For the view that we can only speak of the Yerushalmi as a final document, see Neusner, *Judaism in Society*, 13–19.

frequent engagement with the scholarly practices discussed in this book. This suggests that the pervasive presentation of subsequent Amoraic scholars as engaging in these practices is not only the result of later homogenization. The Yerushalmi is certainly not a transparent or raw archive of the sages' words. As Amoraic scholars occasionally noted themselves, and as modern scholarship demonstrated extensively, complex processes of transmission and composition shaped both the individual teachings presented in the Talmud and the often artfully produced discussions in which they are embedded.[71] But this emphasis on reformulation and literary creativity is different from, and can even oppose, the position that the text can tell us only about a presumed singular point of composition.

I have not regularly used evidence from the Babylonian Talmud, even though it attributes many statements to the same Amoraic scholars whose work is discussed in this book. I do not doubt that the Bavli contains materials which date to the third and fourth centuries, but many studies have demonstrated that when there are significant differences between the Talmuds, the Yerushalmi usually preserves the material in an earlier form, and the Bavli often reflects later developments.[72] Generally speaking, all aspects of Amoraic commentary that are analyzed here are also attested in the Bavli, even though they may take a different form and significance in that Talmud.

In the title of this book, I use the term Talmud, without the definite article, to refer to the rabbinic study of rabbinic teachings (as opposed to "the Talmud," which is normally used to refer to the Bavli and which I use to refer to the Yerushalmi). This meaning of the term is not attested in the classical rabbinic corpus itself.[73]

---

[71] On composition of individual teachings, see Albeck, *Talmud*, 452–522, focusing on the Bavli, but with frequent discussions of the Yerushalmi. Even scholars who believed the Yerushalmi did not result from a "final redaction" or processing and therefore presents a raw or "precise transmission" recognized that parallel passages reveal different arrangements and formulations of the material (Epstein, *IAL*, 273–90). More recent scholarship on composition and literary structure posited higher degrees of design or dynamic reformulation; see e.g. Becker, *Sammelwerke Palästinas*; Be'eri, *Exploring Ta'aniot*; Benovitz, "Transferred 'Sugyot'"; Hezser, *Form*; Katz, "Division"; Kretzmer-Raziel, "Talmudic stam"; Mazeh, "Demai"; Meir, "Questions or Answers"; Moscovitz, "Aggadic 'Foreign Bodies,'" "Parallel Sugiot," "Sugyot Muḥlafot"; Rubenstein, "Structural Patterns." On Amoraic comments on transmission and composition, see below Chapter 8, Section 3.

[72] See Sussmann, "Ve-shuv," 96–114; Friedman, *Talmudic Studies*, 40–7; Rubenstein, "Criteria."

[73] Some of the instances of the term *talmud* designate, already in the Tannaitic corpus, a particular kind of expertise or study (when it does not refer to Torah study more broadly), but it is difficult to define it precisely. Scholars noted that *talmud* and *midrash* seem to be interchangeable or parallel terms. They appear as variants of each other in the manuscripts (Rosenthal, "Torah," 464 n. 48). Passages which list kinds of Torah knowledge almost never feature both terms, and they place them similarly: both, for example, appear after *mishnah* and *miqra* (*Sifre Deuteronomy* §161 for *talmud*, ibid., §306, for *midrash*). But this does not indicate that *talmud* means *midrash* in the sense of the interpretation of Scripture, since *midrash* was not yet restricted to Scripture in this sense (see n. 75 below). Rather, both terms seem to refer to advanced forms of Torah study (perhaps differing in context), which could focus on but were not defined by analysis of Scripture (Shapira, "Beit Hamidrash," 47). This picture does not change much in the Yerushalmi. A passage at *Hor.* 3:8 48c offers some more specific characterization, including an association of the distinction between *talmud* and *mishnah* with a distinction between students strong in analysis and erudition, and a homily which posits that the master of *talmud* is the sole beneficiary of the labor of all other types of Torah scholars, as he is the only one who can issue rulings. On the term in the Bavli, see Vidas, *Tradition*, 115–49, and Secunda, "The Talmud of Babylonia."

There is no indication in the Talmud that it is specifically connected with the type of Torah knowledge called in rabbinic sources *talmud*, other than the title, which may post-date the work (the same is true for the Babylonian term *gemara*). The connection between *talmud* and the Talmuds, as well as instances of that word which refer clearly and specifically to the interpretation of rabbinic teachings, appear first in medieval texts.[74] But the fact that the rabbinic corpus does not have a specific term for the sages' interpretation of rabbinic teachings does not preclude discussion of the distinctive features of this interpretive undertaking. The term *midrash*, similarly, did not refer exclusively to the study or interpretation of Scripture for much of the classical rabbinic period, even after the emergence of the form of interpretation now called Midrash.[75] Still, I chose not to use the term "Talmud" in my discussion here so as not to give the impression that there was an emic ancient rabbinic term for the realm of scholarship studied in this book.

---

[74] See the *Letter of R. Sherira*, Lewin, *ISG*, 51–2 and Rashi on *b. Suk.* 28a and *b. B.M.* 33a (in standard editions of the Bavli). The *Letter* offers another definition of *talmud* that emphasizes analysis and logical derivation as well as Midrashic principles (*ISG*, 48–9); and while that definition functions to support the argument that *talmud* existed even before there was a Mishnah to interpret, it is in continuity with Talmudic sources (see previous note).

[75] Mandel, *Origins*, 222–80, traces the emergence of the term as we know it now, noting the process begins in the end of the Tannaitic period (259), but that even well into the Amoraic period, the term is not restricted to interpretation of Scripture (268).

I
INDIVIDUATION

Introduction to Part I

Rabbinic literature routinely presents teachings attributed to individual sages: "Rabban Gamaliel says: Each day, a person must pray the Eighteen [Benedictions]. Rabbi Joshua says: A summary of the Eighteen" (*m. Berakhot* 4:3); "Rabbi Yose says: Let your fellow's property be as precious to you as your own" (*m. Avot* 2:12). Our intuition might be to see in these attributions an invitation to read the teaching in light of the name, and posit questions like: Why does this particular sage rule, or think, in this specific way? How does this teaching relate to other teachings by this sage? How does this teaching reflect his personal worldview, inclinations, and interests?

Scholarship from the past few decades has argued that such questions go against the sages' own ideas about what these attributions mean because they are premised on a notion of individual authorship that is distinctively modern. This type of question assumes that much like the appearance of the name "Jane Austen" on the cover of *Emma* intends to communicate that Austen is the author of *Emma*, so does the attribution of a teaching to, say, Rabbi Joshua, intend to communicate that the teaching originated with Rabbi Joshua. They also assume that much like the *Genealogy of Morals* or *Jazz* reflect the mental world and situation of the individuals who authored them, Nietzsche and Morrison, so does a given rabbinic teaching reflect the particular thought, methodology, or situation of the sage to whom it is attributed. Such assumptions, Martin Jaffee argued in an influential essay, were not shared by the sages themselves. Jaffee posited that the sages viewed rabbinic teachings as drawn from a timeless chain of transmitters with origins in an unspecified past or even a distant divine revelation; consequently, the attribution of a teaching to an individual meant he was "merely the latest one to pass it on, at best its transmitter ('tradent' in academese)."[1] While not all scholars share, we shall see, this particular reconstruction of rabbinic ideology, Jaffee's critique of the authorship model represents a consensus.

This part of the book argues, in contrast, that Amoraic scholarship construed rabbinic teachings precisely in such individuated terms. The following chapters show how Amoraic scholars developed a sophisticated set of interpretive practices,

---

[1] Martin Jaffee, "Authorship," 22. A similar but more nuanced account is offered by Sacha Stern, who recognizes that the Bavli oscillates "between tradition and creativity, individual authorship and collective anonymity" ("Concept," 195) but concludes that the sages gave "ontological priority" to the latter (ibid., 188) and that the individual sage "would always be seen as the bearer and tradent of his masters' teachings and of other, earlier traditions" ("Attribution," 51).

articulated ideas about attribution and citation, and engaged in compositional practices premised on the notion that rabbinic teachings were shaped by individual sages and reflected their individual characteristics. This construction of rabbinic teachings was new, departing from the way they were negotiated in Tannaitic compilations. And while it was produced through the new textualized study of such teachings, discussed in the Introduction, it was not an inevitable outcome of textualization: it reflected a particular interpretive approach even as other options were available.

The opposition scholars such as Jaffee and Sacha Stern have drawn between the rabbinic notions of knowledge and texts and the modern Western view of authorship is certainly justified: this view resulted from specific technological, ideological, economic, and religious factors of modernity. As Jaffee and Stern recognize, though, the concept of individual authorship itself is not exclusively modern.[2] Their historicization of the modern concept relies mainly on the works of Michel Foucault and Roland Barthes.[3] But even Foucault, the theorist most associated with the claim that "the author" is a construct, argued that the definition of the author in modern literary criticism was "directly derived" from early Christian discourses of author authentication, pointing specifically to Jerome's *On Illustrious Men*.[4] As we shall see in Chapter 1, the scholarly techniques that Foucault discusses in this context were developed long before Jerome and were employed widely in the ancient world;[5] but the fact that his essay, which has been central for the contrast between "modern" and "rabbinic" notions of authorship, locates the origin of the "modern" notion in a work written in Bethlehem in the fifth century—very close to Amoraic scholars in time and place—should give us pause. Ancient ideas and practices relating to text production certainly do not emphasize originality and autonomy as much as the construction of authorship which prevailed for much of the modern period;[6] and the chapters below explore significant differences between Amoraic and Greco-Roman scholars in the construction of attribution and texts. But the fact that Amoraic scholars configured the relationship between individuals and texts in a distinctive way does not mean that this relationship was not central to their scholarship.

Foucault's essay argues that the "author" is a function of discourse that is projected on texts through practices that associate texts with individuals and define

---

[2] Stern points out that Christian and other Greco-Roman works tend to have named authors while rabbinic compilations are anonymous ("Attribution," 49; "Concept," 193; see more below, Chapter 1, Section 6). Jaffee mentions that the sages knew books authored by individuals, referring to Homer and Aesop, biblical authors, and Jewish authors writing in Greek ("Authorship," 21).

[3] See Jaffee, "Authorship," 18–20, and the citation of Foucault at 35 n. 2; Stern cites Barthes's "Death of an Author" at 185 n. 8, criticizing the essay but also agreeing with Barthes's point on modern Western individualism. Bregman, "Pseudepigraphy," 36 n. 47, uses Foucault and Barthes in a similar way.

[4] Foucault, "What Is an Author," 110–11.

[5] See Vessey, "The Forging of Orthodoxy," 508, on Foucault's over-estimation of Jerome's singularity, and Wilson, "Foucault," 350 and 352, on the tension between Foucault's claim for historical specificity and trans-historical characteristics and his ambiguity on whether the "author function" was one phenomenon or several.

[6] For a survey of scholarship tracing the emergence of this notion, see Haynes, "Reassessing 'Genius.'"

how texts are organized and read; it is a construction that is historically and culturally conditioned and varies as it is applied to different types of texts.[7] Above all, his essay demands that we do not take this function of discourse for granted, but rather examine how it is developed by specific agents through specific practices. The following chapters aim to do just that for Amoraic scholarship. Precisely because Amoraic associations between teachings and individual sages represented an interpretive construction, we should not expect it to conform to our own reconstruction of the way rabbinic teachings were composed. One factor that led modern scholars of rabbinic literature to de-emphasize individual authorship has been well-informed skepticism about the historical reliability of rabbinic attributions. Building on work that has shown that attributions vary greatly, that they were sometimes later additions, and that teachings were often reformulated, late twentieth-century scholarship criticized earlier attempts to explain rabbinic teachings in light of the figures who purportedly produced them.[8] This critique and the ensuing avoidance of such readings are certainly justified. But as we shall see, such attribution-informed readings played a significant role in Amoraic hermeneutics, and that is important regardless of their failure in terms of our standards of historical proof. Foucault argues that "Hermes Trismegistus did not exist, nor did Hippocrates—in the sense that Balzac existed—but the fact that several texts have been placed under the same name indicates there has been established among them a relationship of homogeneity, filiation, authentication of some texts by the use of others, reciprocal explication, or concomitant utilization."[9] We can similarly say that while R. Aqiva and R. Judah b. Ilay may not have said what rabbinic compilations attributed to them, Amoraic scholars used their names precisely in the same way, to construct homogeneity among "their" teachings, to attribute other teachings to them, and to explicate teachings in light of each other.

Underscoring the constructed and interpretive nature of Amoraic approaches to attribution also means recognizing that they are selective in terms of agents and compositional activity. Since the production of texts is normally a collective enterprise, the attribution of texts to individuals privileges certain agents, often in ways that reflect social hierarchies and power dynamics. As Candida Moss and Mika Ahuvia have recently argued regarding ancient Christian and Jewish texts, respectively, attributions marginalize—though they do not necessarily erase—the contributions of other individuals who participated in the shaping of texts, such as enslaved persons and women.[10] Relatedly, attribution also focuses on certain features of the text: for Greco-Roman scholars, connection between individuals and texts was primarily understood in terms of style or aesthetic quality;[11] Amoraic

---

[7] Foucault, "What Is an Author," 110. See Wilson, "Foucault," 350–4, on Foucault's inconsistency on this question.
[8] Stern, "Attribution," 49; Green, "What's in a Name," 88.
[9] Foucault, "What Is an Author," 107.
[10] Moss, "Secretary"; Ahuvia, "Reimagining."
[11] Peirano, "Authenticity"; see more in Chapter 1, Section 6.

scholars focused on Halakhic position. Neither style nor position is necessarily indicative of individual footprint and neither exhausts the features of the text, but for scholars working in these respective traditions, they played a definitive role.

While modern notions of authorship tend to emphasize originality and autonomy, the Amoraic discussions examined here present a different range of approaches even as they are interested in individual contribution. Amoraic scholars use the terminology of "recitation," inherited from their predecessors, to refer to certain types of literary production. This terminology, we shall see, implies both the transmission of existing material and its reformulation. The attribution of a recited teaching to a certain sage did not amount to the claim that the teaching wholly originated with him, but it was often taken to mean that the particular form of that teaching was shaped by that sage and reflected his opinion or inclination. Similarly, attribution is rarely invoked in discussions of chronological development, and sometimes the importance of chronology is dismissed. And while modern constructions often imagine the author as having absolute and final control of the text, Amoraic scholars occasionally considered how a teaching may be changed by individuals other than the sage to whom the teaching is attributed, by noting other "reciters" who formulated the teaching subsequently.[12] These features of Amoraic discourse of attribution do not, however, diminish the significance of the connection Amoraic scholars posited between texts and individuals: they present the specific form in which that connection was configured.

The re-orientation posited here was not absolute or all-encompassing. In terms of composition, practices of collective authorship persisted. The only Jewish compositions from late antiquity with self-identifying individual authors are the liturgical poems known as *piyyutim*.[13] The Talmud itself is an anonymous compilation, and it presents both anonymous materials and teachings attributed to many individuals; modern analysis has shown that Talmudic composition continued to feature fluid textuality, as sages shaped the text without consistently distinguishing what they received and what they added. The picture is also heterogeneous when we look at Amoraic hermeneutics, where Tannaitic-era patterns persisted alongside new conceptions and practices. The overall picture, however, shows that new attention to individual agency and the significance of attribution were central to the method and aims of ancient Talmudic interpretation.

Individual authorship in the rabbinic interpretation of Scripture

The sages' engagement with Scripture, generally speaking, construes it as a unity representing a single voice. Midrash is the interpretation of "verses, not books,"

---

[12] On recitations, see more in Chapter 6; on chronological discussions, see Chapter 4, n. 95; on multiple reciters, see Chapter 1, n. 16 and Chapter 8, Section 3.
[13] On authorship in *piyyutim*, see Münz-Manor, "Performance of Identity," 391–3.

and one of its distinctive features is that any verse can refer to and illuminate any other verse in Scripture.[14] The attribution of the biblical books to various "authors" therefore plays a limited role; but we do find, in the vast and diverse world of Midrash, discussions where it becomes more significant. The Torah, the most important scriptural text for the sages, is regularly presented as the word of God; quotations from it are introduced with such phrases as "the Merciful One wrote," and there are passages which describe it as having been written before any human being was created.[15] At the same time, the Torah itself already suggests an association with an individual, Moses.[16] While the sages sometimes deny Moses any role except writing exactly what God dictated to him, there are a few passages which suggest individual verses may reflect Moses' own contributions.[17] But such comments are rare, and the most recent study of them concludes that Moses' involvement in the composition of the Torah did not seem to be a particularly engaging issue for the sages.[18]

The other figure associated with the Torah is Ezra, whom several ancient authors present as the Torah's second giver, receiving it for the second time or restoring it after it was lost.[19] The rabbinic engagement with this narrative tradition is comparatively limited. It appears in a passage that discusses the change of the Torah's script from paleo-Hebrew (which the rabbis call *da'aẓ*) to the Aramaic square script (which the rabbis call *ashuri*, "Assyrian") still used today.[20] The passage presents three positions. R. Yose says that Ezra was "given" both the new Aramaic script of the Torah and its language. R. Judah the Patriarch argues that the Torah was originally given in the Aramaic script, that Israel's sins caused the script to change to the Hebrew script, and that "in the days of Ezra" the script was restored to its original. R. Eleazar Ha-Moda'i argues no change happened at all. Only the first of these teachings gives Ezra himself a role in this change (through revelation), and even then, the process is limited to a change in script and "language"—which may mean that the teaching directs this narrative tradition away from the text of the Torah, positing Ezra was given only its Aramaic translation, the Targum.[21] As several scholars have noted, the passage seems to be designed specifically to deny the idea that the Torah was lost and to limit Ezra's contributions.[22]

---

[14] See Boyarin, *Intertextuality*; the quote is from Kugel, "Two Introductions," 145. More on this approach in Chapter 8.
[15] *Genesis Rabbah* 1; see Urbach, *Sages*, 175–8.
[16] On ancient approaches to Mosaic authorship, see Najman, *Seconding Sinai*.
[17] See *b. Shab.* 87a and *b. Meg.* 31b.
[18] Viezel, "Moses' Role," 49. See also Fraade, "Moses and the Commandments."
[19] Naeh, "Script of the Torah"; Wollenberg, "The Book that Changed."
[20] The passage appears at *t. San.* 4:7, *Meg.* 1:8 71b–c, and *b. San.* 21b–22a. Schremer and Katzoff, "Inseparable Considerations," argue that the Tosefta passage adapts the sequence of teachings from the Yerushalmi.
[21] Naeh, "Script," 136; Wollenberg, *Closed Book*, 33–4, sees here a reference to the language, that is, the formulation, of the Torah itself.
[22] Naeh, "Script"; Balberg, *Fractured Tables*, 216.

The limited scope of the activities the sages attribute to Ezra is particularly evident in comparison with Christian sources which attribute to him considerable editorial agency, suggesting he re-composed a lost text either from fragments or from his own memory.[23] As Rebecca Wollenberg noted, this passage complicates simplistic accounts of the rabbinic perception of Scripture.[24] But while Rabbi Yose's teaching can be read as attributing to Ezra an important role in shaping the biblical text, as far as I know such option is never taken up in the sages' exegetical practice: in contrast with medieval Jewish exegesis,[25] Midrash does not employ the notion of Ezran authorship in interpreting Scripture. One teaching which seems to consider Ezra as the scribe who copied the text as we know it attributes to him the addition of the dots over ten phrases in Scripture; other than that, the sages do not identify Ezran interventions in the text of the Torah.[26]

The Babylonian Talmud dedicates a long passage to the question of who "wrote" the biblical books.[27] It is not clear whether writing here means "composing" or "transcribing," or if the passage is at all interested in making these distinctions. In the discussion of Moses' writing, one of the opinions understands writing as transcribing God's dictation; the discussion of the time in which Job lived includes a suggestion based on a specific word that appears in the book, which could imply human contribution to the book's formulation, but there are other ways to read this suggestion and in any event it is rejected. No other distinctions in style or position are made among the different books. Identification of the figures who wrote them is based on scriptural ascriptions or chronological considerations. The Bavli raises, for example, the question of whether Moses, Joshua, or Samuel could write the passages about their own death; it attributes the writing of the books of Judges and Ruth to Samuel, and Kings and Lamentations to Jeremiah, based on chronological information (sometimes derived from Scripture, at other times apparently traditional). The interpretive upshot that is mentioned in the passage is also chronological: the identity of the writer of the Book of Job is connected to the question of the time in which Job lived; the fact that Ezra wrote the book bearing his name is linked to a teaching which posits that Ezra undertook his genealogical work before leaving Babylonia. While the passage as a whole shows that the sages thought in complicated ways about the question of writing,[28] it is unique and limited in scope. As Louis Jacobs wrote, "all the indications go to show that the rabbis were not particularly interested in who wrote the Biblical books."[29]

---

[23] See the sources adduced by Wollenberg, "The Book that Changed," 148–9.
[24] Wollenberg, *Closed Book*, 33–4.
[25] On medieval appeals to Ezra's editorial role, see Steiner, "Theory."
[26] See *Avot de-Rabbi Nathan*, Version A 34.25 and Version B 37.28.
[27] b. B. B. 14b–15a, with a partial parallel at *Sot.* 5:5 20d.
[28] Wollenberg, "A King and a Scribe."
[29] Jacobs, *Structure and Form*, 32.

Other rabbinic discussions of human involvement in the shaping of Scripture respond to features of the scriptural text. The similarity between the prophecies in Jeremiah 49 and Obadiah 1 leads R. Isaac to comment that prophets may receive a single communication from God but differ in the way they relay it to their audience (*b. Sanhedrin* 89a). A. J. Berkovitz has shown that the authorial superscriptions of the Psalms function in rabbinic interpretation "as a marker that encourages the exegete to reflect on the identity and compositional choices of the Psalmist."[30] He points, among other discussions, to a passage comparing the way Jeremiah, Isaiah, and Asaph, the singer of Psalm 79, describe the destruction of the Temple in a different key and in different terms, clearly ascribing agency to each of these figures.[31]

The sages also employed techniques of differentiating characters speaking in Scripture which resemble the ways they distinguish the voices of different sages in rabbinic teachings.[32] While recognizing different speakers in a text is different from recognizing the individuals who shaped it, the distinction between "characters" and "authors" is not always so clear. The sages interpreted the prophecies of Jeremiah, for example, in light of his biography, an approach which Ishay Rosen-Zvi described as "almost inevitable" in the case of "the most biographical prophetic book in the Hebrew Bible," where "prophecy is inextricably intertwined with narrative."[33] Still, this interpretation coexisted with reading Jeremiah's words as channeling a divine voice. The *Pesiqta de-Rav Kahana* presents a series of reflections on the authorial superscription of the Book of Jeremiah ("these are the words of Jeremiah," Jeremiah 1:1), many of which rely on the harsh quality of his prophecies. One comment centers on Proverbs 1:23, in which Wisdom cries out, "Give heed to my reproof, I will pour out my thoughts to you and I will make my words known to you." The *Pesiqta* reads the doubling ("thoughts," "words") as two different kinds of speech, belonging to different prophets, and links them to the "reproof": "if 'you turn at my reproof', I will 'pour out my thoughts to you,' through Ezekiel, and if you do not [repent], 'I will make my words known to you,' through Jeremiah."[34] As Rosen-Zvi writes, this homily contrasts Ezekiel, whose prophecies show hope, with Jeremiah's prophecies of destruction, when all is lost for the unrepenting Israel.[35] Both prophets, however, express the same divine voice which is also speaking in the Book of Proverbs.

The sages showed occasional interest in the attributions of biblical texts and in deriving meaning from those attributions; but they did so rarely and the significance they derived was often limited or suggested rather than spelled out. These

---

[30] Berkovitz, "Beyond Attribution," 60.
[31] Berkovitz, ibid., 60–1, discussing *Lamentations Rabbah* 5:2.
[32] Mazeh, "Speaker-Splitting Technique," describes this method as "unusual." This method resembles the Talmudic method of positing "two reciters" for Tannaitic materials, as Mazeh points out on 18 n. 66; on that technique, see below in Chapter 8, Section 3.
[33] Rosen-Zvi, "Like a Priest," 572–4.
[34] *Pesiqta de-Rav Kahana*, 13.2, 226–7.
[35] Rosen-Zvi, ibid., 585.

rabbinic engagements with the biblical authors do not challenge the unity of Scripture, but they nonetheless point in a different direction than the dominant mode of reading in Midrash. The particularity of the sages' approach is accentuated by the fact that among Christian scholars, we find an emphasis, alongside the idea that the scriptures are divinely inspired, on the individual human authors of biblical books.[36]

Attribution and authorship between the Tannaitic and Amoraic periods

The idea that rabbinic teachings are drawn from an ancestral tradition, which is sometimes traced to Moses, appears already in the Tannaitic compilations, and the sages seem to have inherited it from the Pharisees.[37] One version of this idea indeed presents the sages, as Jaffee argues, to be mere "tradents": Tannaitic compilations tell us that R. Eliezer "never said something he has not heard from his teacher," or present R. Joshua as sticking only with what "he has heard."[38] Even if such passages are hyperbolic or ideological, they indicate that when the same compilations attribute a teaching to R. Eliezer or R. Joshua, they mean that at least in some sense that teaching is traditional, that it did not originate with these sages, and that it does not necessarily reflect their personal thought (regardless of how much these sages actually shaped these teachings—a separate question from how rabbinic texts perceived and represented their contributions).

Yet this emphasis on tradition and its faithful transmission is not representative of the Tannaitic corpus as a whole.[39] A number of scholars have argued that in the first half of the second century CE there was a decisive, if not absolute, move away from this emphasis. Menahem Kahana and Ishay Rosen-Zvi pointed to an increase in argumentation based on Scripture and logical inference; while such arguments could be used to sustain tradition (as they seemed to have been in the case of Rabbi Aqiva), they nonetheless show that justification by tradition alone was no longer sufficient.[40] Yair Furstenberg argued that the commonplace structure of dispute, "Rabbi so-and-so prohibits and Rabbi such-and-such permits" (and similar phrases), designed first to preserve conflicting traditions, subsequently replaced the traditionalist emphasis on the tradition or the *shemu'a*: these disputes were

---

[36] See Krueger, *Writing and Holiness*, 46–7, and the literature cited there.
[37] Novick, "Tradition." For an early example of the claim that the entirety of Torah knowledge was given at Sinai, see *Sifra, Be-har*, 1:1 105a.
[38] R. Eliezer: *t. Yev.* 3:31, R: Joshua: *m. Par.* 1:1 and *m. Nid.* 1:3.
[39] In addition to studies that posit a historical development, see Schremer, "*Avot* Reconsidered" and Yadin-Israel, "Concepts," who argue that the emphasis on extra-scriptural traditions represents the approaches of particular strands in the rabbinic movement. See also Hayes, *Divine Law*, 166–370, who shows how Tannaitic sages present the law as dynamic and subject to human authority.
[40] Kahana, "Dispute"; Rosen-Zvi, "Dust."

understood to present different positions, not traditions; this textual structure was increasingly used not to accurately transmit the words of earlier sages, but to reformulate and even generate positions attributed to them in light of shifting understandings of the issues at hand; and the study of these disputes became one of the central modes through which rabbinic teachings developed.[41]

These developments certainly contributed to the process of individuation that is studied in this book. The move away from presenting the sages as mere tradents, the increased reliance on argumentation, and the centrality of disputes could, and eventually did, lend themselves to interest in individual contribution and to individuated notions of rabbinic teachings. The following chapters argue, however, that the Tannaitic compilations themselves do not show such conceptions, at least not on a general and structural level. In part, this is because, as Furstenberg emphasizes, the Tannaitic turn to argumentation and innovation was implicated in a move from punctilious transmission to creative transmission. As E. S. Rosenthal argued, this creative transmission was premised on a unity of tradition and innovation which de-emphasized distinctions between old and new and which was interested in Halakhah, not its history.[42]

A key passage for this description of Tannaitic innovation appears in *m. Pesaḥim* 1:6. It presents a particular genre of teachings, testimonies on the practices of authoritative figures in the past. In this case, Hananiah, the prefect of the priests, offers a testimony on how the priests handled burning impurities during the time the Jerusalem Temple was still standing. The Mishnah then says that R. Aqiva "added" another detail about this practice of the priests. Rosenthal and Furstenberg argued that R. Aqiva's additional testimony is not an "authentic" testimony: his addition explicates the principles about purity laws that are already evident in Hananiah's testimony, and it displays the same approach apparent in one of R. Aqiva's other rulings. This passage shows us the process by which testimonies about earlier practice or more broadly legal traditions—which until that point the sages aimed to transmit conservatively—became open sources, reformulated and readapted in the creative process of expanding the law. For our purpose here, what is important is that R. Aqiva's addition is also formulated as a statement of tradition, that it is presented as an account of what the priests did in the past rather than an analytical comment on Hanania's teaching. Neither R. Aqiva nor the Mishnah necessarily deny that there is an innovation here; still, they present innovation not only as the true meaning of the tradition, but as indistinguishable from it.[43] The same passage, however, also records a different kind of note: R. Meir's comment that we can learn or derive further significance from the words of Hanania and Aqiva. This comment is explicitly interpretive, but such comments are rare in the Tannaitic corpus,

---

[41] Furstenberg, "Tradition to Controversy."
[42] Rosenthal, "Tradition and Innovation."
[43] Rosenthal, ibid., 351–9; Furstenberg, ibid., 619–20.

and even this comment is interested in the law, not in reconstructing R. Aqiva's or Hananiah's opinion.[44]

One of the most common types of passage in which Tannaitic sages discuss their predecessors is debates about the scope of disputes between earlier sages. At *m. Karetot* 4:2–3, for example, R. Yose as well as R. Simeon and R. Simeon of Shezor offer different accounts of a dispute between R. Joshua and R. Eliezer about inadvertent transgressions. These later sages do not present their arguments as interpretation of words attributed to these earlier sages or as alternative tradition reports of what these sages said; rather, they each simply recast the dispute, using the phrase typical of such passages: "they did not dispute concerning *this*... rather, concerning what did they dispute? concerning *that*."[45] The positions that result from the new version of the dispute are not presented as stemming from the later sages: they are clearly attributed to the earlier sages. But the flexibility with which the particulars of the dispute vary—and openly so—shows that what is at stake is not in any strict way an account of what the earlier sages said or meant. This passage is not about the words R. Eliezer and R. Joshua, but it is also not about how R. Yose and R. Simeon interpreted them. In the terms introduced above, R. Yose and R. Simeon are not "authors," as the positions they present are attributed to R. Eliezer and R. Joshua; but they are also not "tradents," since the passage does not claim that they transmit the words of these earlier sages. Such passages are interested in defining different positions as part of the systematic analysis of Halakhah, rather than in any specific historical and individual formulations of these positions.[46] The author function rises in the Talmud, we shall see, precisely when such a particular formulation becomes the object of interpretation.

What is an attribution?

We can observe the same characteristics on a much larger scale, when we compare the way attribution formulae function in the Tannaitic corpus and the Talmud. I begin not with attributions on the level of the compilation's framing—that is, when the Mishnah or the Talmud report to us what "Rabbi so-and-so said," but rather, with instances in which named sages cite other named sages, for which the most common citation formula is "Rabbi so-and-so in the name of Rabbi such-and-such." An investigation of all instances of this formula in the Tannaitic corpus,[47]

---

[44] So much so that the Talmud suggests it is not clear whether R. Meir refers to these sages or to R. Eliezer and R. Joshua, cited later in the passage. See the discussion below in Chapter 8, Section 3.

[45] "לא נחלקו על ... ועל מה נחלקו? על"; see e.g. *m. M. S.* 3:6, *m. Tem.* 3:1, *t. Ber.* 5:30, *t. Shab.* 15:9, *t. Pes.* 5:4, *t. Ket.* 12:4. Many of these instances address the disputes between the Houses of Hillel and Shammai, a major subject of Tannaitic interpretive effort. See Furstenberg, ibid.

[46] I discuss a similar passage in detail in Chapter 1, Section 5.

[47] I thank Ayelet Wenger, who worked as my research assistant and compiled an analytical list of these Tannaitic citations.

and a comparison of these instances with those found in the Talmud, shows that the meaning of such citations has changed over time. In Tannaitic literature this formula represents transmission: it portrays the teaching as having been taught, directly, from the cited sage to the citing sage. In the Talmud, this formula can also represent what we have termed authorship—the cited sage is the sage with whom the teaching is distinctively associated, the sage with whom the teaching originated or whose opinion the teaching reflects, regardless of the process of transmission.

In the Tannaitic corpus, almost without exception, the citing sages are close enough in time to the cited sages that they could have known them personally. Very often, the formula is used when a student cites his teacher.[48] In the Talmud, in contrast, this formula also introduces citations which cannot or do not indicate face-to-face transmission. First, we find sages citing sages they could not have known.[49] More important, we know that this formula does not imply face-to-face transmission from passages in the Talmud which explicitly ask about the transmission of the teaching. A number of passages associated with R. Mana and his circle raise the question of the identity of a teaching's transmitter, showing us that the original citation did not indicate who actually transmitted the teaching to the citing sage:[50]

Yevamot 4:10 6a (par. *Nid.* 1:4 49b)

ר' ברכיה בשם שמואל: לעולם אין האשה יולדת אלא[51] למאתים ושבעים ואחד או למאתים ושבעים ושנים או למאתים ושבעים ושלשה או למאתים ושבעים וארבעה. אמ' ליה ר' מנא: מנן שמע ר' הדא מילתא? אמ' ליה: מן ר' בא.

R. Barachia [said] in the name of Samuel: A woman always gives birth on the 271st, 272nd, 273d, or 274th day [of pregnancy].

R. Mana said to him: From whom did you[52] hear this thing?

He said to him: From R. Abba.

R. Barachia cites Samuel, though he has never heard the teaching from Samuel; he heard it from R. Abba, but did not indicate it in his citation, as we know from

---

[48] There are very few exceptions; once in the Mishnah, in the unusual tractate *Avot* (*m. Av.* 2:5) and a few times in the Tosefta, including *t. Ter.* 10:2 (but see Lieberman, *TK*, 1.465), *t. Shab.* 9:13, *t. Shab.* 14:16, *t. Pes.* 3:8, and *t. Meg.* 1:6. On the frequency of students citing their teachers in the Tannaitic corpus, see Bacher, *Tradition*, 82.

[49] Amoraic sages might even cite long-gone Tannaitic sages: "R. Yohanan [said] in the name of R. Simeon b. Yohai" (e.g. *Ber.* 1:2 3b, *Ter.* 11:2 47d, *Qid.* 3:12 64d), "R. Simeon b. Laqish [said] in the name of R. Meir" (as part of a longer chain; *Shab.* 2:3 4d). For more examples see Melamed, *Introduction*, 294–6.

[50] In addition to the passage quoted above, see *Dem.* 1:3 22b (par. *Qid.* 2:8 63a—where unlike the three other instances, R. Mana is approving), *Pes.* 5:4 32b (par. *Bez.* 1:1 60b), and *Yev.* 4:10 6a (par. *Nid.* 1:4 49b), right before the instance quoted above.

[51] Correcting או, with *Nid.*

[52] In both this and the next passage cited, the Aramaic takes the polite form, "From whom did the master hear," "Does the master know Bar Pedaya."

R. Mana's question. Note that there is no critique implied in R. Mana's question, and in fact earlier in the same *sugiya*, he himself cites a teaching in the name of Samuel without even remembering how he has come to know it. In contrast to these passages, there is a passage which criticizes such transmissions, which we will explore in detail in Chapter 4; but even that passage indicates that Amoraic scholars did just that:

y. *Shabbat* 1:2 3a (par. *Shab.* 14:4 15a, *Qid.* 1:7 61a)

אמ' ר' זעירא לר' יסא: חכים ר' לבר פדיה דאת אמר שמועתא מן שמיה? אמ' ליה: ר' יוחנן אמרן משמו. אמר ר' זעירא לר' בא בר זבדא: חכים ר' לרב דאת אמר שמועתא מן שמיה? אמ' ליה: רב אדא בר אהבה אמרן משמו.

Said R. Ze'ira to R. Yose: "Do you know Bar Pedaya, that you say teachings in his name?" He said to him, "R. Yohanan said them in his name." Said R. Ze'ira to R. Abba b. Zavda, "Do you know Rav, that you say teachings in his name?" He said to him, "Rav Ada b. Ahava said them in his name."

Twice in this passage R. Ze'ira questions the practice of certain sages to cite teachings in the name of teachers they have never met. In both cases, the unruly citers answer that they have heard these teachings through a reliable sage.

While in these cases the intermediary has not been named, we also see in the Yerushalmi an increase in the use of long chains of transmission consisting of three or more sages. In the Yerushalmi, such chains are very common;[53] in the Tannaitic corpus, they are very rare.[54] Long chains are presumably intended as reports or claims of transmission, naming the sage from whom the citing sage heard the teaching; but they depart from the Tannaitic model by going beyond face-to-face transmission and tracing the teaching further back.

These differences, I argue, reflect an expansion of the function of citation. In the Tannaitic period, citation identified the person from whom the citing sage heard the teaching, in order to establish a reliable authority for that teaching. In the Amoraic period, citation was also used to associate permanently a particular sage with a particular teaching, regardless of who transmitted the teaching to the citing sage. It is unlikely that Tannaitic citations were meant to function in the same way: if the intention of Tannaitic sages was to indicate the sage with whom the teaching originated, it is not clear why they would cite almost exclusively their contemporaries. And if it was the sole intention of Amoraic sages to offer a credible source of

---

[53] There are, for example, about forty such chains in *Ber.* and fifty in *Shab.*

[54] *t. Dem.* 3:1, *t. 'Or.* 1:8, *t. B. Q.* 9:31, *t. San.* 4:8, and *t. Neg.* 1:2. Even when we go beyond this specific formula, multiple stages in the transmission are rare: see *t. Naz.* 5:1 and *t. Oh.* 4:14, as well as the instances in which the tradition is traced to a "tradition to Moses from Sinai," at *m. Pe'ah* 2:6, *m. 'Ed.* 8:7, and *m. Yad.* 4:3 (with *t. Yad.* 2:16).

their teachings, they would not have skipped the most crucial step of the transmission chain, the one right before the citing sage.

This development coheres with several other developments studied in this part of the book. We shall see that Amoraic scholars thought that teachings are associated with individuals, and that the attribution of a teaching became significant to the way they understood and used that teaching. The fact that citation practices now included the identification of the teachings' "authorship" thus reflects both Amoraic notions of these teachings' production and the importance of attributions in Amoraic hermeneutics.

What, then, about the commonplace attributions that we find in the Tannaitic compilations—"R. so-and-so said," "these are the words of R. so-and-so"? Because these attributions themselves are unattributed, we cannot subject them to the same analysis as we did with citations; we do not know who introduced the teaching "on each day a person must pray the Eighteen" with the attribution "Rabban Gamaliel says," and therefore we cannot know whether that person knew Rabban Gamaliel or not. More important: once the attribution is fixed in this way in a stable text, there is a permanent association between Rabban Gamaliel and that teaching which endures long after his death. Recited in subsequent generations, this attribution can no longer communicate face-to-face transmission. This means it could suggest the sage as the origin of the teaching. Was this the intention behind Tannaitic attributions?

Here it is important to note that while there is a substantial number of instances in which Tannaitic sages cite other Tannaitic sages, they are far less common in comparison with instances in which Amoraic sages cite their predecessors—broadly speaking, it is much more common for Tannaitic sages to simply state their position without citing anyone else.[55] If we assume that attribution indicates the origin of the teaching unless the sage also cites a predecessor, we find ourselves with a very unlikely picture in which Tannaitic compilations only rarely understood sages as relying on their teachers. The opposite solution, that these teachings were never perceived to be the result of original thought, that these attributions merely indicate tradents, as Jaffee argued, is also unlikely, given that Tannaitic compilations are forthcoming about the way sages derive laws based on argumentation.

The most reasonable conclusion is that using the terms "tradent" and "author" in a mutually exclusive way is not appropriate, for the most part, in the case of Tannaitic literature. These texts connected teachings to different sages in order to legitimate (sometimes contradictory) teachings by showing they were endorsed by known sages; the authority of these sages was grounded, variously, in their faithfulness to tradition and in their ability to produce sound derivations

---

[55] See already Bacher, *Tradition*, 72, who concludes, based on this picture, that Tannaitic literature presents only authors, not tradents: "Die in den tannaitischen Traditionssammlungen mit Nennung des Autors sich findenden Aussprüche erscheinen in der Regel ohne Nennung eines die Urheberschaft bezeugenden Tradenten."

and interpretations, but Tannaitic texts were not normally interested in distinguishing these elements. The reformulation or expansion of a teaching in light of new argumentation was a legitimate part of its transmission. To be sure, we may be interested in whether a Tannaitic sage is merely passing on something he heard or presenting his own new ruling, and we may be able to come up with an answer based on analysis of the sources; but such a distinction is not central to the presentation and construction of rabbinic teachings in the Tannaitic compilations. In the Talmud, this distinction becomes important. We have already seen how it is operative in the form and significance of Talmudic attributions. Some comments in the Talmud differentiate between what a sage "says in his own name" and what he says in the name of another.[56] Most important, for our purposes, is that this distinction is one of several elements in the Amoraic individuation of rabbinic teachings, evident in many other patterns of analysis and representation. The following chapters explore these patterns in detail.

---

[56] See e.g. *Kil.* 2:5 27d and see Assis, *Concordance*, 256 for a list of other instances. See also Chapter 3, Section 4.

1
Who Is Speaking?
Identification of Anonymous Teachings

The anonymity of so much of rabbinic literature gives it "an almost transcendent quality," William Green writes in a classical essay on the subject of rabbinic attributions; it "creates the sense that the document, or the tradition, is speaking for itself, independent of any individual mind."[1] Amoraic scholars chose a different path in their reading of anonymous teachings: they sought precisely to identify the individual minds behind the anonymity and in doing so, broke through or refused this apparent transcendence of the text; they did not let tradition speak for itself, but rather raised the question, again and again: Who is speaking? This chapter examines in detail the premise, procedures, and functions of Talmudic identifications of anonymous teachings to show how they played a significant role in the individuation of rabbinic scholarship. The penultimate section addresses identifications and similar phenomena in the Tannaitic corpus, demonstrating the degree to which Amoraic scholars departed from their predecessors; and the final section discusses comparable phenomena in Greek and Latin scholarship.

1. Identifications and their significance

I use the term "identifications" to refer to comments which identify a teaching, that is at first presented anonymously, as the words of a particular sage, in contrast with "attributions," which are presented initially alongside the teaching ("Rabbi so-and-so said"). Identifications of this sort are among the most common exercises Amoraic scholars undertake in addressing recited teachings.[2] They appear in hundreds of unique passages throughout the Talmud,[3] often as the very first comment on the Mishnaic passage at hand.[4] Identifications may function to determine

---

[1] Green, "What's in a Name?," 80.
[2] The Talmud also presents a significant number of identifications of Amoraic teachings, but these are rarer and differ from identifications of Tannaitic teachings in terminology, configuration, and purpose. Nonetheless, those identifications also demonstrate an interest in individual attribution and employ some of the same methods discussed in this chapter. See e.g. *Pe'ah* 1:1 15b, *Dem.* 2:4 23a, *Kil.* 2:10 28b, *Ter.* 8:4 45c, *Shab.* 1:6 4a, *'Er.* 10:7 26b.
[3] There are about 125 unique instances of the most common identification term, *de-rabbi* {name} *hi*; dozens of instances of each of the identification terms next in frequency, *matnita de-rabbi* {name} and *man tanna* {statement} {name}; and various other less common phrases and non-formulaic identifications.
[4] e.g. *Dem.* 3:2 23b, *Ter.* 9:7 46d, *'Er.* 3:1 20c, *Pes.* 9:11 37a, *Ḥag.* 2:1 77a.

whether a teaching is legally binding or not, to interpret its precise meaning or the reasoning behind it, or to solve various difficulties or challenges.[5] Despite their dominant presence in both Talmuds, these identifications have not received much attention in modern scholarship.[6] The most extensive treatment is in Jacob N. Epstein's *Introduction to the Mishnaic Text*, but Epstein does not address the hermeneutic positions and interpretive dynamics of these identifications, because, to some degree, he shares them: his own project also aims at identifying the sages behind anonymous texts, and he is interested more in what identifications can tell us about the Mishnah's sources and less in what they tell us about the Amoraic scholars who proposed them.[7]

Most identifications introduce the name of the sage with one of three common phrases—"it is R. so-and-so's," "the recited teaching is Rabbi so-and-so's," "who recited this? R. so-and-so"—normally followed by a citation of or an allusion to an attributed teaching which demonstrates the identification, whether because it presents the exact same position or even words of the anonymous teaching or because it shares a conceptual feature or inclination with it. The following example is a particularly good point of departure for our investigation of Amoraic interpretation since its subject matter is the role of intention in interpreting utterances:

m. *Nedarim* 8:7 (the passage with the anonymous teaching)

היו מסרבים בו לשאת את בת אחותו וא', "קונס שהיא נהנת לי לעולם", וכן המגרש את אשתו, אמ', "קונם אשתי נהנת לי"—הרי אלו מותרות מליהנות לו, שלא נתכוון זה אלא לשם אישות.

[Like most of tractate *Nedarim*, the following teaching examines whether certain vows are valid and obligate the person, and, if they are found to be valid, in what precise obligations they result.]

If they were urging him to marry his sister's daughter, and he said, "*qonas*[8] that she ever derives any benefit from me," and likewise someone who divorces his wife, if he said, "*qonam* that my wife ever derives benefit from me"—they [the women] are in fact permitted to derive benefit from him [even after the divorce or the refusal to marry], since he only intended [the vows] to concern marital relations [and not actually to prohibit them any benefit from him or his property].

---

[5] For a survey of functions, see Moscovitz, *Terminology*, on the relevant terms: *de-rabbi peloni hi*, 139–41; *man tanna*, 382–5; and *matnita de-rabbi peloni*, 468–71.

[6] Melamed, *Introduction*, 381–3, classifies identifications in the Bavli (usually by formulation or tradent) but offers no other analysis; Moscovitz, *Terminology* (see previous note) presents a foundational treatment of the most common identification terms; Stern, "Concept," 193–4, provides a brief but important conceptual analysis of identifications in the Bavli.

[7] Epstein, *IMT*, e.g. 240–3, 287–8, 1141–6.

[8] *Qonas* or *qonam* are words used to refer to sacrifices in vow formulations; see m. *Ned.* 1:2. The intention of the vow is to prohibit or avoid whatever follows these words.

Nedarim 8:7 41a (the identification)

אמ' ר' יוסי: דר' יודה היא. דר' יודה אמ': "הכל לפי הנדר".

Said R. Yose: It is R. Judah's. For Rabbi Judah said: "Everything is according to [the intention of] the one making the vow."

m. *Nedarim* 7:3 (the passage with the attributed teaching)

הנודר מן הכסות מותר בשק ובירועה ובחמילה. אמר: "קונס צמר עולה עלי", מותר לכסות בגיזי צמר; "פשתן עולה עלי", מותר לכסות באניצי פשתן. ר' יהודה או': הכל לפי הנדר. טען והזיע והיה ריחו קשה. אמ', "קונס צמר ופשתים עולין עלי". מותר לכסות ואסור להפשיל אחריו.

One who vows [to abstain] from clothing is permitted [to wear] sackcloth, tent-cloth, or a blanket. If he said, "*qonas* that wool will come on me," he is permitted to cover himself with woolen fleeces; "That linen will come on me"—he is permitted to cover himself with flaxen stalks. R. Judah says: Everything is according to [the intention of] the one making the vow. If he was carrying a load [of wool and linen], and he was sweating and he[9] had bad odor, and he said, "*qonas* that wool or linen will come on me," he is permitted to cover himself [with wool or linen], but prohibited to throw [it, as a load,] over his back.

An anonymous teaching in the Mishnah rules that if a man vowed that he will not allow his wife, whom he was divorcing, or his niece,[10] whom he was refusing to marry, to derive any benefit from him, the vow does not actually bind him, and he may allow them to derive such benefit, since he only uttered the vow in the particular contexts of divorce or marriage, intending it only as a rejection of marriage with these women. The Talmud records R. Yose's claim that this anonymous teaching is R. Judah's.[11] A quotation of another teaching from the same tractate follows as a demonstration of this claim. In *Nedarim* 7:3, the Mishnah discusses vows of abstention from different kinds of clothing. The anonymous teachings in that passage rule that different outcomes of the vow follow from the specific words the vower used. R. Judah adds, perhaps in dissent, that we should consider not just the language of the vow but also its context and therefore the intention of the person making the vow. He offers as an example someone who was uncomfortable as he was carrying a load of wool, and vowed that wool should not come upon him. Even though normally this language would be interpreted as a vow to abstain from wearing wool, in this case, R. Judah rules, the vower is only bound to abstain from *carrying* wool, since it was the discomfort of carrying that led him to make the

---

[9] Alternatively: "or it," i.e. the load of wool.
[10] Albeck (*Shisha sidre mishnah*, 3.174): "Not necessarily [his niece], but just an example, for it was their custom to marry the sister's daughter."
[11] MS Leiden records here two separate identifications, one for each scenario; Epstein *IMT*, 1049, argues this doubling is a scribal error.

vow. Both the ruling in *Nedarim* 7:3 and the ruling in *Nedarim* 8:7 thus consider the vower's intention in context rather than the wording of the vow; and since the former is attributed to R. Judah, R. Yose argues, the latter must be R. Judah's as well.

Talmudic identifications assert that the teaching in question was shaped by a particular sage and reflects his distinctive approach. They are not merely claims of congruity, "associations," aiming to show that the anonymous teaching is similar to the attributed teaching or that the anonymous teaching adopts a similar approach. Such associations are found in the Talmud, but identifications are distinguished from them in terminology and configuration. Associations are introduced with phrases such as "it goes like [or: according to] R. so-and-so" or even simply "like R. so-and-so."[12] We will see below, in Section 4, that once a teaching has been identified, that teaching may be used to shed light on that sage's other teachings. This type of interpretive consequence would not work if the claim was only that the anonymous teaching adopts a similar position to the one espoused in the attributed teaching. Similarly, we find instances where identified teachings are expected to be consistent with the sage's teachings as a whole.[13] In one passage, R. Yohanan identifies a teaching in *m. Terumot* 2:6 as R. Judah's, since it requires the priest's-share alternative be provided from the choicest produce, as is R. Judah's opinion in *m. Terumot* 2:4; but then R. Yohanan objects that R. Judah is inconsistent, since that now-identified teaching implies that cooked wine is worse than uncooked wine, and R. Judah says in another teaching, at *m. Terumot* 11:1, that cooking wine improves its quality.[14] This objection only works if the intention of the identification is that *m. Terumot* 2:6 actually presents R. Judah's words. Occasionally, the Talmud makes an explicit distinction between the claim that a teaching is from a certain sage and the claim that the teaching is from "the sages, [teaching] in R. so-and-so's line."[15]

Given that there is a large number of identifications and that they vary in function, textual contexts, and the sages to whom they are attributed, we can accept considerable diversity in their nature. And while the distinctive formulation of identification terminology generally separates them from other types of association, the context of identifications does not often allow for a clear separation

---

[12] אתיא כר׳ פלוני; כר׳ פלוני.

[13] In addition to the example discussed above, see also e.g. *Kil.* 1:9 27d (par. *Shab.* 3:3 6a; the identification, but not the objection to it, is also found at *Shab.* 3:6 6c and *Bez.* 2:10 61d), with the emendation by Lieberman, *YK*, 79.

[14] *Ter.* 2:6 41d. The text is somewhat confusing, since the quote from *m. Ter.* 11:1 appears to be the proof for the identification, whereas it is more likely that the identification is relying on *m. Ter.* 2:4 (not cited since it is nearby), and *m. Ter.* 11:1 is the basis for the statement about the contradiction.

[15] חכמים שהן בשיטת ר׳ פלוני, in five unique instances: *Dem.* 3:4 23c, *Pes.* 7:6 34c (modifying an identification to answer an objection; see the emendation in Lieberman, *YK*, 483–4), *M. Q.* 2:1 81a (also modifying an identification to answer an objection; see the emendation in Lieberman, *YK*, 11 n. 3 and the emendation by Lieberman of Lieberman ibid., 542), *Hor.* 1:5 46b (where the contrast is with a *ke-* association), and *Nid.* 2:3 49d. In two instances the term seems to appear without such an explicit contrast—see *Shab.* 1:1 2c and *Git.* 2:4 44b. See the analysis of '*Or.* 2:11 62b–c in Section 4 below.

between these different functions. But among the hundreds of identifications I have examined, I have not found an instance which cannot be interpreted as a claim that the teaching reflects the words of the named sage, and there are, as we have seen, significant reasons to posit that this is generally the intention behind them. To be clear, identifications did not amount to the claim that the creation of the teaching began and ended with the named individual. As I have noted in the Introduction to this part of the book, the language of recitation implied transmission of early materials as well, and we find interest in how teachings continued to be shaped by sages other than the sage whom attributions and identifications name.[16] But identifications named an individual definitively associated with the teaching. Their pervasive use demonstrates the development of an individuated conception of rabbinic teachings in the Amoraic period.

2. The premise of identifications: the Mishnah, anonymity, and the law

The majority of teachings presented in the Mishnah and in Tannaitic compilations more broadly are anonymous; these anonymous teachings are also frequently accompanied by teachings attributed to particular sages: "If someone read out the *Shema* but did not make it audible to himself, he has fulfilled his obligation; R. Yose says: he has not fulfilled his obligation" (*m. Ber.* 2:3). Tannaitic compilations do not explain the significance of anonymity and its relation to attributed teachings; the development of a term for unattributed teachings is Amoraic, itself an indication of the attention to textual features of rabbinic teachings and an increased interest in attribution.[17] There are, however, a few Tannaitic statements which distinguish the teachings of "individual" sages and those of the "many" or the majority, explaining the importance of preserving individuals' teachings even though the law follows the majority.[18] It seems likely that already in the Tannaitic period this distinction between the words of the majority and those of dissenting individuals referred not just to cases where individual and majority are explicitly contrasted (e.g. when a teaching attributed to an individual is followed by what "the sages say"), but also to cases where the majority position was expressed anonymously and presented alongside dissenting attributed teachings.[19] As we shall see below, in Section 5, there are

---

[16] On recitation, see also Section 5 below and the discussion in Chapter 6. On reformulation, see e.g. *Pe'ah* 5:2 18d, where two reciters are posited for a teaching that is identified as R. Yose's.
[17] The term *stam* (סתם; literally "unspecified") never signifies anonymous teachings in Tannaitic texts. It points to other kinds of absent specifications, mostly in legally relevant speech (e.g. vows, *m. Ned.* 2:4), and even on the rare occasions it refers to teachings, it is not to lack of attributions (e.g. *m. Par.* 1:1).
[18] *m. 'Ed.* 1:4–6 and *t. 'Ed.* 1:4; see Furstenberg, "Tradition to Controversy," 610–13.
[19] Frankel, *Hodegetica*, 268–73; Rosen-Zvi, "Introduction," 49–50.

also a couple of Tannaitic texts which posit that the anonymous position reflects the position of the sage who formulated the text. These two ideas, that anonymity reflects the words of the majority and that it reflects what the sage behind the teaching considered the accepted law, certainly cohere; but they also stand in tension, especially when we are faced with positions that are presented anonymously in one teaching and attributed in another.

While the rest of the chapter explores the practice of identifications in the Talmud, this section explores Amoraic statements that are more explicit about the significance of anonymity and identifications. Most of these statements are drawn from a single passage in tractate *Yevamot*. I divide the passage into two parts, each representing a different set of concerns and, at least in terms of the Talmud's attributions, different chronological stages (appearing in reverse order). The first part presents statements attributed to scholars from the later part of the Amoraic period about the legal status of anonymous passages in "our" Mishnah and their relationship to other recitations; the second part presents a debate between two earlier Amoraic scholars, R. Yohanan and R. Simeon b. Laqish, on the nature of anonymous teachings in general. Both parts of the passage, I argue, attest to an individuated understanding of rabbinic teachings, and both provide us with a framework for understanding the practice of identifications in the Talmud.

Later Amoraic scholars on anonymity and the Mishnah

The Mishnah in *Yevamot* 4:10 presents an anonymous teaching which rules that women must wait three months following divorce, death of husband, and so forth, before re-marrying, to rule out doubts about paternity. It also records two dissenting opinions, by R. Judah and R. Yose; the latter allows immediate betrothal for all women, except widows. The Talmud's discussion of this passage opens with a ruling by R. Yohanan:

Yevamot 4:10 6b (par. *Megillah* 1:3 70d, *Ta'anit* 2:8 66a)

שמעון בר בא אמ': אתא עובדא קומי ר' יוחנן והורי כר' יוסי. והוה ר' לעזר מצטער.

אמ': שבקין סתמא ועבדין כיחידייא!

אשכח תני לה ר' חייה בשם ר' מאיר.

כד שמע[20] דתני לה ר' חייה בשם ר' מאיר אמ': יאות סבא ידע פירקי גרמה.[21]

---

[20] Correcting בר' שמעון שמע לה, with both parallels.
[21] Correcting גיטא, with both parallels, as well as the Darmstadt's fragment (Darmstadt, HLH, HS 507; Sussmann, *Ginze Yerushalmi*, 467) for the next appearance of the word in *Yevamot*.

Simeon b. Abba said: A case came before R. Yohanan, and he ruled in accordance with R. Yose. And R. Eleazar was troubled. He said: They abandon the anonymous [position] and act according to the individual [sage]!

It was found that R. Hiyya recited it [the anonymous teaching] in the name of R. Meir.

When he [R. Eleazar] heard that R. Hiyya recited it in the name of R. Meir, he said: How well the old man [R. Yohanan] knows his chapters on his own.

R. Yohanan permitted a woman to be betrothed to another man prior to three months after her previous connection ended, following R. Yose's view in the Mishnah. R. Eleazar found the ruling upsetting. How could R. Yohanan rule in accordance with the position of R. Yose, if that position disputes what is presented as an anonymous position in the Mishnah? This expectation that the law should follow the anonymous ruling, again, may already be implied in the Mishnah itself, and it is found in many other Talmudic passages.[22] We then hear of a twist in the plot: another recited teaching, drawn from R. Hiyya's *mishnah*,[23] is discovered, and that teaching attributes to R. Meir the position which appears anonymously in the Mishnah. This development is not unusual in the Talmud. We will examine, in Chapter 5, such discoveries of recited teachings, and in Chapters 6 and 8, how the Mishnah is compared with parallel *mishnayot* such as R. Hiyya's.

In the context of our story, what is important is that this discovery appeases R. Eleazar, who then remarks admiringly that R. Yohanan knew on his own, before the discovery of this teaching, that the anonymous position was also an individual's position. The implication is that a ruling which appears in the Mishnah anonymously may be transmitted in a different version as the ruling of an individual, and therefore may not be necessarily binding.

This part of our passage raises a few questions. Why would a teaching circulate both in anonymous and attributed forms, and what is the relationship between these forms? And if the Mishnah signals, with anonymity, that a certain ruling presents the accepted law, what does it mean about the authority of the Mishnah if a different version of a teaching can lead to a different ruling? The next section addresses these questions with a long series of teachings:

---

[22] There are only a few other instances of the term "anonymous" (e.g. *Ber.* 2:3 4d, which, like our passage, includes a parallel tradition from R. Hiyya) or when attributed positions are called "individual" (see *'Or.* 2:11 62c); but the assumption is evident, for example, in many passages which contrast identifications with the words of "the sages": e.g. *Dem.* 5:1 24c, *Shab.* 7:1 9b, and *Meg.* 1:7 71b.

[23] The Talmud does not understand this teaching as a version of the Mishnah itself, but rather as another *mishnah* which records the same material; otherwise, it could not posit that the anonymous formulation is of R. Judah the Patriarch's whereas the attributed teaching is recited by "another."

Yevamot 4:10 6b (par. *Megillah* 1:3 70d,[24] *Ta'anit* 2:8 66a)

ר׳ מנא בעא קומי ר׳ יודן: לא כן[25] אמ׳ ר׳ חזקיה ר׳ אבהו בשם ר׳ לעזר, "כל מקום ששנה ר׳ מחלוקת וחזר ושנה סתם הל׳ כסתם משנה", והכא את אמר הכין?

אמ׳ ליה: לא ר׳, דילמא חורן אמ׳?

מה אין הן[26] דשנה ר׳ מתני׳ מחלוקת וחזר ושנה סתם הל׳ כסתם, אתר[27] דלא אשכח ר׳ מתני׳ מחלוקת אלא אחרים שנו מחלוקת ור׳ שנה סתם לא כל שכן תהא הל׳ כסתם?

אתא ר׳ חזקיה ר׳ יעקב בר אחא ר׳[28] שמעון בר אבא בשם ר׳ לעזר: ואפילו שנו אחרים מחלוקת ור׳ שנה סתם הל׳ כסתם.

ולמה הוא מורי ליה כיחידייא?

ר׳ שמואל בר איניא בשם ר׳ אחא: הדא דתימר בשאין מחלוקת אצל סתם, אבל אם יש מחלוקת אצל סתם לא בדא הל׳ כסתם.

ר׳ יוסי ביר׳ בון בשם ר׳ אחא: הדא דתימר ביחיד אצל יחיד, אבל ביחיד אצל חכמ׳ לא בדא הל׳ כסתם.

R. Mana asked before R. Yudan: But did not R. Hezekiah [say that] R. Abbahu [said] in the name of R. Eleazar, "Every place in which Rabbi [Judah the Patriarch] recited a dispute, and then went back and recited anonymously, the law is according to the anonymous Mishnah"—and here you say thus?

He said to him: But it is not Rabbi [Judah the Patriarch], but perhaps another who said so?

But if where Rabbi [Judah the Patriarch] recited the teaching in dispute and then went back and recited it anonymously the law is according to the anonymous Mishnah, where it was not found that Rabbi [Judah the Patriarch] recited the tradition in dispute, but rather others recited a dispute and R. [Judah the Patriarch] recited anonymously, is it not all the more so the case that the law should be according to the anonymous [Mishnah]?

Came R. Hezekiah [who said that] R. Jacob b. Aha [said that] R. Simeon b. Abba [said] in the name of R. Eleazar: And even if others recited a dispute and R. [Judah the Patriarch] recited anonymously, the law is according to the anonymous [Mishnah].

---

[24] The parallel in *Meg.* lacks the last teaching; this is probably an omission by error, as the last two teachings end with the same words, but see n. 31 below.
[25] Correcting תמן, with parallels. Moscovitz, "Parallel Sugiot," 547, suggests "there" was copied here because of *Sot.* 6:1 20d, for which see below.
[26] Reading the base Leiden text prior to its correction, with Assis, *Concordance*, 929 n. 335.
[27] Correcting אתאי, with parallels.
[28] Correcting ור׳, with parallels.

Why then, does he [R. Yohanan] rule according to the individual [position]? R. Samuel b. Inaya [said] in the name of R. Aha: This [the guideline from R. Eleazar] you say when there is no dispute [stated] with the anonymous [teaching]. But if there is a dispute [stated] with the anonymous [teaching]—in that [case,] the law is not according to the anonymous [position].

R. Yose b. R. Abbin [said] in the name of R. Aha: This you say where there are two individual [teachings]. But when there is an individual [teaching] with the [teaching of] the sages—in such [a case,] the law is not according to the anonymous [position].

R. Mana points to an apparent contradiction: on the one hand, R. Eleazar praises R. Yohanan's ruling against the anonymous Mishnah; on the other hand, we have a general guideline, attributed to the same R. Eleazar, which says that anonymous teachings in the Mishnah are authoritative. But when we look at the guideline itself, the contradiction is not straightforward. We know R. Eleazar's guideline from three other unique instances in the Yerushalmi. In those instances, the guideline is applied to cases where the same teaching appears twice *within* the Mishnah: in one place, the teaching appears attributed and contested, whereas later on, the same teaching appears anonymously.[29] The point of the guideline seems to be that what is presented later is the "final word" of the compiler, R. Judah the Patriarch, and therefore represents the position endorsed by him.[30] In our passage, since we are speaking not of two teachings within the Mishnah but rather of two versions of the same teaching, one from the Patriarch's Mishnah and the other from R. Hiyya's, we cannot place them in a sequence in this way.

The next step in the Yerushalmi addresses this question. R. Yudan responds to R. Mana that R. Eleazar's guideline cannot apply here, since we learned that the anonymous teaching at *m. Yevamot* 4:10 was R. Meir's from the *mishnah* of "another." This answer itself is challenged: if teachings the Patriarch presented anonymously take precedence over teachings he himself presented as contested, is it not even more reasonable that teachings the Patriarch presented anonymously should take precedence over teachings which others presented as contested?

The next teaching presents a particular kind of teaching, which we will examine in Chapter 5: arrival statements in the Talmud often revise or elaborate on earlier statements in light of objections or questions, and here too such a statement offers

---

[29] '*Or.* 2:1 61d suggests that the disputed position attributed to R. Eliezer in *m. Ter.* 4:7 is the anonymous position in *m. 'Or.* 2:1 (this suggestion is rejected using an emendation of the Mishnah); *Pes.* 3:3 30b suggests that the disputed position attributed to R. Judah b. Betera in *m. Pes.* 3:3 appears anonymously in *m. Pes.* 3:4 (see Lieberman, *YK*, 422–3, though that text remains unclear); *Sot.* 6:1 20d seems to argue that what is disputed in *m. Sot.* 6:1 is stated anonymously in *m. Sot.* 6:3 (see Epstein, *IMT*, 85 n. 3).

[30] See *b. B. Q.* 102a (par. *b. 'A. Z.* 7a), which connects the Babylonian version of this guideline to the question of the order of tractates. On the Bavli's version see Brandes, "Rules," 306–16.

a teaching attributed to R. Eleazar to answer the question about his guideline, confirming the interpretation that even when the version in which the teaching is disputed is not from the Patriarch's Mishnah, the law nonetheless follows the anonymous Mishnah. R. Mana's initial objections seem to stand, then, and the question about R. Yohanan's ruling resumes. In response, the Talmud adduces two versions of a teaching by R. Aha which qualify R. Eleazar's guideline: the law follows the anonymous formulation in the Mishnah only when it appears without dissenting opinions, or when it is disputed by another individual (as opposed to the sages).[31]

While the discussion raises several issues, and is not without textual problems,[32] I focus here on what it might tell us about Amoraic understandings of textual anonymity. This passage seems to posit that anonymous teachings may have originated as attributed teachings, but they were *anonymized* by the Mishnah's compiler, Judah the Patriarch, because he accepted them.[33] In its other instances, R. Eleazar's guideline is used to account for cases where Judah knew an attributed version of the position, which he reproduced in one passage in the Mishnah, but then chose to present it anonymously, as the accepted position, in a later passage. Here, the implication is that the anonymous form presents a similar process of selection, even though we do not have evidence in the Mishnah itself that the Patriarch knew the teaching in an attributed form.

There is another passage in the Talmud which similarly claims that an anonymous teaching in the Mishnah reflects Judah's adoption of an attributed position. This position concerns grain offerings that must be brought by certain transgressors. Normally, as with any grain offering, a handful is taken and sacrificed on the altar, while the priests eat the remainders which are left after the handful was taken. But if the transgressor is a priest, the remainders may not be eaten since priests may not consume offerings brought by priests (Leviticus 16:16). The sages therefore rule that in this case, not only a handful but rather the entire offering is sacrificed on the altar. R. Simeon dissents: he agrees that the entire offering is sacrificed, but rules that a handful is nonetheless taken, and that

---

[31] This last teaching cannot answer the question which it ostensibly comes to answer here, about R. Yohanan's ruling, since neither of the Mishnah passages to which the story about that ruling is appended attributes a position to the sages (Assis, "Even," 66).

[32] Some of the problems relate to what we may judge as glosses (in R. Yudan's response, the reference is to "another" when we know it is R. Hiyya; the resumptive question, "why does he rule as an individual," changes the focus from R. Eleazar to R. Yohanan; the explanation that follows "not in this" functions differently than it does elsewhere—see Assis, ibid.); but there are also issues with the building blocks of the passage, including the unusual use of R. Eleazar's guideline and R. Aha's final teaching (see previous note).

[33] My account here differs from Brandes, "Rules," 289: "even in the place where the Yerushalmi says explicitly that 'Rabbi recited anonymously,' the intention is not that Rabbi is the one who changed the formulation from individual to anonymous, but that in the source before him the position was taught anonymously . . . it is clear from the discussion that Rabbi also 'found and taught' and not 'anonymized.'" But our passage never says that Judah "found" the teaching already anonymous—the "finding" is not the Patriarch's finding but the "finding" by the interpreters.

the handful and remainders are sacrificed separately. R. Eleazar, his son, presents yet a third opinion: the handful is sacrificed on the altar, but the remainders are burned and scattered on the Temple's ash heap.[34] A similar issue is discussed in Tractate *Sotah* in the Mishnah, in the context of the grain offering which a woman suspected of adultery must bring as part of her ordeal. If the woman is married to a priest, her grain offering's remainders may also not be consumed by the priests and the Mishnah presents an anonymous ruling that the offering must be burned. The passage in the Talmud comments on the way this ruling relates to the dispute about the transgressor's grain offering:

Sotah 3:6 19b

אמ' ר' יוסי: ראה רבי[35] דעתו שלר' אלעזר ביר' שמעון ושנה כיוצא בו.

ר' בא בר כהן בעי קומי ר' יוסי: ולמה לי כר' לעזר ביר' שמעון? אפי' כר' שמעון אביו. אמ' ליה: איכול בראש המזבח ואין שריפה בראש המזבח.

התיב ר' חנינה קומי ר' מנא: והא תני ר' חייה ופליג, "ליקרב כליל אינה יכולה מפני שותפותה שלאשה. להיאכל אינה יכולה מפני שותפותו של איש". אמ' ליה: ר' ראה דעתו שלר' אלעזר ביר' שמעון, ור' חייה רובה ראה דעתו שלר' שמעון אביו.

Said R. Yose: Rabbi [Judah the Patriarch] preferred the opinion of R. Eleazar b. R. Simeon and recited similarly.

R. Abba b. Cohen asked before R. Yose: And why would I [say Judah specifically taught] as R. Eleazar b. R. Simeon? It could even be [that he taught] as R. Simeon, his father. He said to him: "consumption" is on top of the altar, there is no "burning" on top of the altar.

R. Hanina objected before R. Mana: But R. Hiyya recited and disputed, "it cannot be sacrificed completely because of the wife's part, but it cannot be eaten because of the man's part. [The handful is sacrificed on its own and the remains are sacrificed on their own]."[36] He said to him: R. [Judah the Patriarch] preferred the opinion of R. Eleazar b. R. Simeon, and R. Hiyya the Great preferred the opinion of R. Simeon his father.

R. Yose says that the Mishnah's ruling in *Sotah* reflects R. Judah the Patriarch's choice of the opinion of R. Eleazar, the son of R. Simeon, who ruled that the remainders of a grain offering of a transgressing priest are scattered on the ash heap. R. Abba asks R. Yose why he argues specifically that the Mishnah adopts R. Eleazar's position,

---

[34] In addition to the citation of these opinions earlier in the Yerushalmi, see *m. Men.* 6:1 and *t. Men.* 8:3–4.

[35] Correcting "רבו," with MS Vatican.

[36] The Yerushalmi here cites this teaching in abbreviation, and I am completing it for legibility based on its full citation at *Sot.* 2:1 17d; the sentence omitted here is: הקומץ קרב לעצמו והשיירים קרבים לעצמן. See also *t. Sot.* 2:6.

rather than R. Simeon's position, and R. Yose responds that the Mishnah's use of the word "burned" makes it clear that the remainders are not sacrificed on the altar, as they would be under R. Simeon's opinion. In the second stage of the discussion, R. Hanina adduces a recited teaching, attributed to R. Hiyya, which says explicitly that the remainders are sacrificed. R. Mana responds that indeed, R. Hiyya preferred the opinion of R. Simeon, and the Patriarch preferred the opinion of R. Eleazar, his son, and each of their recitations reflects that preference.[37] These comments reflect a particularly individuated reading of rabbinic teachings. R. Yose could have construed the Mishnah's anonymous ruling as the opinion of the sages, which shows similarity to R. Eleazar's opinion on the priestly transgressor's grain offerings; instead, his comment construes this teaching as doubly individuated: first, it originated in R. Eleazar's opinion; second, it reflects R. Judah the Patriarch's adoption of that opinion in the case of the woman suspected of adultery. The same can be said of R. Mana's comment on R. Hiyya's teaching. The comparison between the Patriarch's and R. Hiyya's *mishnah* both here and in the passage we have examined from *Yevamot* shows us how the interpretation of multiple recitations was part of the motivation for this individuated understanding.

These passages provide us a plausible framework within which the broad Amoraic practice of identifications may be understood. While identifications are normally silent about how the teachings they identify came to be circulated anonymously, these passages suggest that they may have been predicated on the same idea: that teachings which were shaped by individual sages, and which were transmitted with the names of these sages, were subsequently anonymized by the sages responsible for the "recitations" of teachings now extant—the Mishnah and other *mishnayot*.

These passages are also some of the most valuable sources for reconstructing the Talmud's understanding of the Mishnah's compilation, and they show us how such understanding was bound with a new interest in authorship or individual contribution. The extent to which R. Judah the Patriarch shaped the Mishnah has been a subject of debate among modern scholars. Chanoch Albeck claimed Judah "did not change, switch around, or abbreviate the material," but rather included it in the Mishnah as he received it.[38] Epstein argued that while Judah left many of his sources unchanged, his contributions and adaptations can nonetheless be identified throughout the text.[39] In particular, he argued, Judah changed or omitted attributions for the purpose of Halakhic ruling.[40] Much of Epstein's argument was based on the way the Mishnah is understood in the Talmuds, in passages like ours

---

[37] See Lieberman, *TK*, 8.632.
[38] Albeck, *Introduction to the Mishnah*, 102 and 270–83.
[39] Epstein, *Tannaitic Literature*, 200–26.
[40] Epstein, *IMT*, 1141–6. Epstein assumed that the personal guidelines for decisions existed in the Tannaitic period, but the evidence indicates they emerged later; see Brandes, "Rules," 154. Changes between anonymous and attributed formulations, in contrast, do not necessitate an early date for the guidelines, and understanding them as Epstein does is reasonable. See also more below on the guidelines and Epstein's interpretation of Talmudic identifications.

which present the Patriarch as actively shaping the Mishnah according to his preferences. Abraham Goldberg justifiably warned against uncritically accepting such Talmudic representations as facts about the Mishnah's compilation; they present the perspective of Amoraic-era scholars.[41]

This, however, is precisely what makes such representations interesting for our purposes. Regardless of how accurately they depict the Mishnah's composition, they depart from how Tannaitic compilations represent it. The Mishnah has no first-person authorial voice. The Tannaitic corpus does attribute to Judah a significant number of comments which present preference or decision among disputing teachings; but these comments are not bound with the Mishnah's compilation, and they are not attributed only to him.[42] The Tosefta, in its many comments on anonymous Mishnaic teachings, never finds in them traces of adaptation by Judah (and only very rarely, we shall see below, by others). The appeal to Judah in the Amoraic interpretation of the Mishnah reflects Amoraic interest in the way rabbinic teachings were shaped by individuals.[43]

While this association of the Mishnah and Judah is reflected in a number of passages in the Yerushalmi, and while it has been very influential in subsequent perceptions of the Mishnah, it appears relatively infrequently in the Yerushalmi, and it functions very differently from other identifications. Unlike most identifications, it is neither demonstrated nor asserted—we encounter it as an assumption or a premise. Furthermore, we find statements that certain rulings in the Mishnah contradict Judah's own position,[44] and, perhaps even more strikingly, identifications which argue certain teachings in the Mishnah *are* Judah's or according to his position.[45] The Yerushalmi routinely identifies other sages as the sources of Mishnaic teachings, and even when it speaks of the act of literary formulation it prefers to speak of anonymous reciters or "whoever arranged the *mishnah*."[46] It is possible that all this suggests that the association between the Mishnah and Judah the Patriarch represents a late or relatively uncommon perspective among

---

[41] Goldberg, "Purpose and Method," 261.

[42] The phrase "I see the words of R. so-and-so [as preferable]" appears most commonly with Judah the Patriarch, e.g. *m. 'Ar.* 8:5, *t. Dem.* 1:9, *t. Shevi.* 8:3, *t. M. S.* 4:5, *t. Sot.* 15:1. But it also appears with other sages: Rabban Gamaliel (*m. Ket.* 13:3–5, *m. B. B.* 9:1, and *m. Shevu.* 6:3), R. Yose (*t. M. S.* 4:6, *t. Men.* 4:5, and *t. Me'il.* 1:20), R. Aqiva (*m. Sheq.* 4:7), R. Ishmael (*t. Yev.* 13:4), R. Eliezer b. Jacob (*t. Kil.* 3:10), and R. Eleazar b. R. Simeon (*Sifre Deuteronomy* §38).

[43] See also Brenner, *Okimta*, 112 and 118–19, who argues that the Yerushalmi's comment on *Qid.* 3:6 64b demonstrates the notion of the author (R. Judah the Patriarch) as sovereign of the text, in contrast with the Bavli's emphasis, at *b. Qid.* 63a–b, on the interpreter's sovereignty in its solution to the same problem. Brenner's observation about the role R. Judah the Patriarch plays in this passage is similar to the argument made here, but his interpretation of the Yerushalmi passage seems to me too influenced by the Bavli parallel. See also below, Chapter 8, n. 97.

[44] See e.g. *Bik.* 2:11 65c and Epstein, *Tannaitic Literature*, 200–1; Epstein connects this phenomenon to the idea that even Judah sometimes preferred his colleagues' words to his own—see *m. Kil.* 2:11.

[45] See e.g. *Shevi.* 2:3 33d, *Ter.* 3:1 42a, *Ter.* 11:1 47c, *Ma'as.* 3:1 50b, *Shab.* 11:1 14d, *Beẓ.* 1:4 60c (par. *M. S.* 4:12 55b).

[46] מי ששדר את המשנה, *Meg.* 1:1 70b (par. *Pes.* 4:1 30d). On anonymous reciters, see Chapter 6 and Chapter 8, Section 3.

Amoraic scholars; but it is also possible that it was a different kind of attribution, one which saw Judah as a compiler and a decider but not the main or exclusive shaper of Mishnaic teachings. Our passage in *Sotah*, for example, suggests that the anonymous teaching originated with R. Eleazar and was then anonymized by Judah. Incidentally, modern scholarship landed in a similar place: the Mishnah's sources may reflect intensive adaptations of still earlier sources, but the final compilation seems to have been relatively conservative.[47]

R. Yohanan and R. Simeon on anonymous teachings

Back in our passage in *Yevamot*, the next part of the discussion addresses anonymity from a different perspective:

Yevamot 4:10 6b

אמ' ר' יוחנן: כל[48] סתם משניות דרבנן עד שיפרש לו רבו.

ר' שמעון בן לקיש אומר: כל סתם משניו' דר' מאיר עד שיפרש לו רבו.

א'ר זעירא קומי ר' יוסי: לא דר' שמעון בן לקיש פליג אלא דו חמי רוב סתם משניות דר' מאיר.

Said R. Yohanan: All anonymous recited teachings are the rabbis', until his teacher specifies for him [that a teaching is an individual's].

R. Simeon b. Laqish says: All anonymous recited teachings are R. Meir's, until his teacher specifies for him [that it is not R. Meir's].

Said R. Ze'ira before R. Yose: It is not that R. Simeon b. Laqish disputes [R. Yohanan's statement], but rather that he sees the majority of anonymous recited teachings as R. Meir's.

My translation above departs from earlier interpretations of this passage, which considered the issue at hand to be anonymous teachings in the Mishnah of R. Judah the Patriarch.[49] The term the Yerushalmi uses here, *mishnayot*, means "recitations" or "recited teachings" and is never limited to Judah's Mishnah: none

---

[47] Epstein, *Tannaitic Literature*, 204; and more recently, Rosen-Zvi, *Mishnah and Midrash*, 90–108, on the "revolutionary approach" of the schools which reshaped traditional materials and the "relative editorial conservatism" with which Judah compiled the products of these schools. Lieberman considered Judah to be the Mishnah's "editor" in the sense of producing an edition of its text, employing the Greek term διορθωτής, "corrector" (*Hellenism*, 88). Despite the implication of his discussion, the Yerushalmi does not use the root תקן with reference to Judah (and when it applies it to R. Aqiva, it is not in reference to *mishnah*, see ibid., 91). But for our purpose again, what is most important is that Lieberman's characterization, too, relies on the Talmuds (ibid., 97).

[48] Deleting the words "מקום ששנה," with the Darmstadt fragment (Sussmann, *Ginze Yerushalmi*, 467); they were erroneously copied here from above (כל מקום ששנה ר').

[49] See, in addition to traditional commentaries, Halevy, *Dorot Harischonim*, 112–14; Epstein, *Tannaitic Literature*, 98; Baumgarten, "R. Yohanan and Resh Lakish"; Brandes, "Rules," 286–7.

of the instances of this plural form refer specifically to the Mishnah,[50] and the singular form can refer to any recited teaching, whether it was included in the Mishnah or not.[51] One reason scholars interpreted the passage in this way is that Judah's involvement in shaping the Mishnah was the subject of the Talmud's discussion until this point. This part of the discussion, however, does not mention him at all, and there are good reasons to think it was originally an independent unit: it is absent in the parallels, and it stands, I argue below, in tension with earlier parts of the discussion.[52] Another reason behind the traditional interpretation is that in the Bavli (*b. San.* 86a), something like these teachings does refer specifically to the Mishnah;[53] but that is not how they appear in the Yerushalmi.

R. Yohanan and R. Simeon's statements are formulated as guidelines for students. R. Yohanan says that a student should consider anonymous recited teachings as "the rabbis," that is, representing the majority, unless his teacher specifies to him otherwise. R. Simeon b. Laqish, on the other hand, says that by default, anonymous teachings should be viewed as R. Meir's. The fact that these are guidelines for students might explain why they do not anticipate obvious problems such as the existence of teachings in both attributed and unattributed forms and contradictions among anonymous teachings; those are all cases which can be explained to the student by the teacher.

R. Yohanan's statement is largely in continuity with the Tannaitic practice, in which anonymity marks the accepted law and the words of the majority. But it presents an explicit articulation of this function of anonymity which we never find in the Tannaitic texts themselves, reflecting the Amoraic interest in formulated literary sources and properties such as anonymity. His statement also adds a possibility which is barely present in the Tannaitic compilations: the idea that in some cases, anonymous teachings may be identified as stemming from individuals. Identifications under this approach have inherent legal significance. If anonymity indicates that teachings are the words of the majority and, therefore, are legally binding, then attaching a name to an anonymous teaching means it no longer necessarily represents the accepted law.

---

[50] This is certainly the case with the reference to the *mishnayot* of R. Hiyya and Bar Qappara at *Hor.* 3:8 48c; it is also the case with the reference to the vow formulations of *mishnayot* at *Naz.* 1:1 51a which include those outside the Mishnah (see Epstein, *IMT*, 805); the first instance in *Hor.* 3:8 48c (par. *Shab.* 16:1 15c) seems at first to mention Judah the Patriarch, but as Naeh ("Three Comments," 211) and Assis (*Concordance*, 1094 n. 1742) argued, the reference is not to Judah (רבי) but to one's teacher (רבו), much like it is in the teachings here.

[51] Frankel, *Einleitung*, 12a; Epstein, *IMT*, 22 n. 5. See the lists in Assis, *Concordance*, 1093–5 and 1105–8.

[52] Though the teachings cited in this part certainly address the question of anonymity, they were attached to the discussion of R. Yohanan's ruling primarily because of the story about R. Eleazar's approval of R. Yohanan, with which our passage opens. In the final part of the passage, which I did not cite here, the story is used to illustrate which "teacher" is referred to in these teachings by R. Yohanan and R. Simeon.

[53] See *b. San.* 86a and the passages cited below, n. 54.

This statement is premised on a different configuration of legal authority than the one we have seen in the previous part of the discussion. Whereas R. Yohanan accords legal authority to the majority, the previous part accorded legal authority to the Patriarch's Mishnah. It is true that even that section begins with R. Eleazar's critique, which is based on a contrast between "individual" and anonymous or majority teachings; but almost immediately, it turns to discussing the Mishnah as the indicator of legal status: anonymous teachings in the Mishnah represent the binding law even if they were originally attributed, as long as the Mishnah presents them in a certain way. For R. Yohanan, anonymous teachings represent the majority position and binding law except when we learn that they represent an individual's position. Alongside the more expansive meaning of the term *mishnayot* noted above, the significance of the distinction between "the rabbis" and "individual" shows that R. Yohanan's statement has a different perspective on the issue of anonymity. If the Mishnah's authority is paramount, that distinction is of secondary importance—what matters is the representation in the Mishnah. This is why the version of R. Yohanan's guideline in the Bavli, which *does* apply to the Mishnah, is formulated differently: "the law follows the anonymous Mishnah,"[54] without mentioning "the rabbis." While it is certainly possible that this guideline does not actually go back to R. Yohanan, it is also worth noting that there is no indication elsewhere in the Yerushalmi that R. Yohanan considered the Mishnah in general as more authoritative than other recited teachings, and he routinely uses such teachings as the foundation for his ruling.[55] This teaching seems to reflect either a stage or a position under which Judah's Mishnah did not have a superior legal status, in contrast with the previous passage, which approaches the Mishnah as a binding legal text.

The passage next cites R. Simeon's guideline that anonymous teachings should be considered as R. Meir's by default. It is unlikely that this guideline means that anonymous teachings never or rarely represent the majority position: after all, most things are not in dispute.[56] For the same reason, it is unlikely that the exception to the rule, the non-default option, is that an anonymous teaching represents the majority. Rather, R. Simeon's guideline seems to operate outside the distinction between majority and individual positions. All teachings have been formulated, at some point, by individuals, and anonymous teachings, generally speaking, go back to R. Meir, whose recitation serves the basis of most *mishnayot*.

Because R. Simeon's guideline divorces the function of attribution from the distinction between majority and individual positions, it also detaches identifications

---

[54] *b. Shab.* 46a, *b. Yev.* 16b, and *b. Yev.* 42b.
[55] Epstein, *IMT*, 243–4. The Bavli knows these sources too and contends with them by positing that there are conflicting reports about R. Yohanan's position; see e.g. *b. Yev.* 15b and Brandes, "Rules," 292.
[56] Elsewhere in the Yerushalmi, the same R. Simeon explicitly says teachings are "everybody's": *Pe'ah* 4:11 18c, *Ket.* 6:1 30c (according to one transmission).

from direct legal consequence. Neither the general rule that anonymous teachings are R. Meir's nor any identification that presents an exception to that rule has a direct effect on the legal status of a teaching. This also means that this guideline conforms more readily with the Mishnah-centered model presented in the previous stage of the passage, since it allows for legal status to be determined by the way the ruling is presented in the Mishnah rather than by the attribution to an individual. Modern commentators argued that when, in the next statement in the passage, R. Ze'ira claims that R. Simeon does not dispute R. Yohanan, he means that these two guidelines address different aspects of anonymous teachings: R. Yohanan refers to their legal status, whereas R. Simeon is addressing their sources.[57] While I do not think this is a convincing interpretation of R. Ze'ira's words,[58] it does capture the difference between R. Yohanan and R. Simeon on the legal significance of identifications.

At the same time, the symmetrical formulation of these guidelines suggests they do dispute each other. The conflict seems to concern the nature of anonymous recited teachings. R. Yohanan's rule, continuing Tannaitic approaches, construes such teachings in general as collectively transmitted and shaped by the sages; it is only when we are instructed otherwise that we should view them as shaped by individuals. R. Simeon's rule, on the other hand, views anonymous teachings as the product of individuals, even if they may be accepted as law by the majority of the sages.

The difference in the legal significance of identifications between R. Yohanan and R. Simeon b. Laqish is paralleled by identifications in the Yerushalmi more broadly. There are indeed many identifications which amount to legal rejections of anonymous teachings. They are often formulated in a way that brings out the contrast between individual and majority opinion. We find phrases such as "this [teaching] is the words of R. so-and-so, but the sages say . . .";[59] "[this teaching] is R. so-and-so's, but according to the sages . . .";[60] or "I recite [this teaching] in the

---

[57] R. Ze'ira's comment has puzzled scholars (see e.g. Lieberman, "Emendations," 111; Epstein, "To 'Emendations,'" 241; and Baumgarten, "R. Yohanan and Reish Lakish"). The dominant interpretation cited above was first proposed by Frankel, *Mishnah*, 212 n. 7, and variations of it appear e.g. in Halevy, *Dorot Harischonim*, 112–14; and Epstein, *Tannaitic Literature*, 98.

[58] R. Ze'ira's comment does not distinguish between legal rulings and sources, though it could have made such a distinction (e.g. by using the phrase "the sages according to the line of R. so-and-so"). My translation above reflects what is explicit in the statement: R. Ze'ira says R. Simeon does not dispute R. Yohanan and changes "all" in R. Simeon's teaching to "majority." According to R. Ze'ira, R. Simeon adds to R. Yohanan's statement, that in most cases where the teacher specifies the individual behind anonymous teaching, it would be R. Meir. While this interpretation does not fit the wording of R. Simeon's teaching (since it refers to the default rather than the specification, and since it is formulated symmetrically with R. Yohanan's in a way which suggests dispute), it seems to me a better interpretation R. Ze'ira's comment itself.

[59] See Assis, *Concordance*, 617, for a list of instances; and see the discussion in Epstein, *IMT*, 1141–6.

[60] e.g. *Meg.* 1:7 71b, *Meg.* 3:1 73d, *Ket.* 3:8 27d.

52   THE RISE OF TALMUD

name of an individual."[61] Even without employing such phrases, other passages imply that identifying a teaching amounts to rejecting its legal validity.[62]

Most identifications, however, do not have a direct legal outcome. We have already seen in the previous stage of our passage in *Yevamot* how an identification might not mean that the law is not to be followed, since the primary question is how the teaching is presented in the Mishnah. In other passages, we find that the point of the identification is that one *should* follow the anonymous position that has now been identified.[63] Even more important, the large majority of identifications in the Yerushalmi simply has no immediate legal function indicated in the text. Epstein thought identifications were connected to the guidelines for adjudicating Halakhic disputes found in the Yerushalmi and the Bavli, such as "[when there is a dispute between] R. Meir and R. Simeon, the law is according to R. Simeon";[64] Since the law follows particular sages, Epstein reasoned, it was important to determine which sage said what.[65] These guidelines, however, appear on only a handful of occasions with respect to identifications and do not seem to have been a major driving force behind them.[66] This is not to say that identifications do not have a Halakhic implication that can be drawn out by commentators; but the primary function of most of them is identifying the sage who shaped the teaching and whose opinion the teaching reflects, which seems to have been an intellectual end in its own right, needing no further justification.[67] As we shall see, such identifications also often carried further interpretive, rather than legal, implications.

3. Demonstrating identifications

Identifications in the Talmud are normally demonstrated, which means that they are arguments based on the demonstrations they offer. At the same time, there is evidence that suggests identifications were sometimes conceived not as arguments, but as reports of alternative transmissions in which the teaching was attributed. A non-negligible number of identifications are not accompanied by a citation of an attributed teaching. In some of these cases, the attributed teaching which would

---

[61] *Ter.* 4:3 42d, *Bik.* 1:7 64b.
[62] See R. Eleazar's assumption, in the opening our passage, that the revelation that the anonymous teaching is R. Meir's legitimates R. Yohanan's ruling against it; see also *Ber.* 2:3 4d, *Ma'as.* 1:8 49b, and *'Or.* 2:11 62c (par. *'A. Z.* 5:8 45a).
[63] See e.g. *Ter.* 3:1 42a, and in a different way *'Er.* 6:8 23d.
[64] *Ter.* 3:1 42a: ר׳ מאיר ור׳ שמעון הל׳ כר׳ שמעון. On the guidelines see Brandes, "Rules," 231–84; Hidary, *Dispute*, 43–80; and see Letteney, *Christianization*, 217–24, for a reading of these guidelines' emergence in the context of Theodosian interpretive practices.
[65] See above n. 40.
[66] *Ber.* 2:3 4d, *Shevi.* 8:7 38b, *Ter.* 3:1 42a (itself the most importance source for the rules in the Palestinian Talmud), and *Ma'as.* 1:8 49b.
[67] Moscovitz, *Terminology*, 139.

demonstrate the identification is cited close by, so it is likely that it was not repeated for the sake of economy;[68] but there are cases where it is not possible to offer such an explanation.[69] We also find Amoraic scholars adding a demonstration to an identification that did not originally have one.[70] Furthermore, there are several teachings which the Talmud presents as identified through interpretive argument, but which the Tosefta already presents attributed to the same sage named by the Talmud.[71] As with other cases where the Tosefta presents, without argumentation, a position that the Talmud presents as the result of an argument, it is difficult to know whether the Talmud provides an argument to support an existing tradition or that the Tosefta itself reflects the conclusion of a similar interpretive process, perhaps even the Amoraic interpretation that we find in the Talmud.[72] Still, most identifications were either made as arguments or construed as the results of arguments early on. The number of cases where no demonstration is offered is relatively small. Many identifications are contested, both by early and late Amoraic scholars. Very often, the argument against an identification targets the interpretive argument accompanying it, which assumes the argument is the foundation of the identification.[73]

We can distinguish two types of demonstrations in the Talmud.[74] Both are predicated on the view that rabbinic teachings are shaped by individuals. The first is documentary demonstrations. These support identifications with a reference to or quotation of an attributed teaching which presents the very same words or ruling as the anonymous teaching. At least with respect to the most common identification term, "it is R. so-and-so's," this kind of demonstration is less common than the conceptual demonstrations explored below.[75] We have already seen an example of such demonstration, in the passage about *m. Yevamot* 4:10 that told us

---

[68] See e.g. *Meg.* 2:4 73b (par. *Ber.* 2:3 4d and *Ter.* 1:2 40c), discussed above, and *Ket.* 1:4 25c (par. *Yev.* 13:12 14a).

[69] See e.g. *Ter.* 3:1 42a (but something similar appears in *t. Ter.*), *Ma'as.* 1:8 49b, *M. S.* 1:7 53a, *Yom.* 2:3 39d (while a contradiction between the Mishnaic descriptions is demonstrated, the specific attribution is not), and *Git.* 9:4 50b.

[70] See e.g. *Bik.* 1:5 64a and *'Or.* 2:1 61d (see Chapter 2).

[71] See *Sheq.* 1:6 46b, *t. Sheq.* 1:8, *Dem.* 2:4 23a, and *t. Dem.* 3:10–11 (see Mazeh, "Demai," 127–33), *Ket.* 3:8 27d, and *t. Ket.* 3:8, for which see below, n. 87. There are of course many more parallels in the Tosefta for those cases where the Yerushalmi employs what I termed "documentary" demonstrations, but such cases do not raise the same problem since the identification is not based on an interpretive argument.

[72] See above, Introduction, n. 55.

[73] e.g. *Ber.* 6:2 10b (discussed below), *Pe'ah* 4:11 18c, *Dem.* 3:2 23b, *Shab.* 6:3 8b, *Sot.* 8:2 22d, *Git.* 3:7 45a.

[74] Cf. Moscovitz, *Terminology*, 140 nn. 134–5.

[75] The distinction between these and conceptual demonstrations is not always clear, since when the anonymous and attributed teachings present the same ruling but not verbal identity it is difficult to decide whether interpretive steps are required to get from one to the other. Instances of very close similarity or identity include *Ter.* 11:1 47c, *'Or.* 3:9 63b, *'Er.* 3:1 20c, *Pes.* 5:1 31d, *Meg.* 1:7 71b, *Yev.* 8:1 8d (with *t. B. M.* 10:4, though note the irregularity in the identified teaching), *B. Q.* 1:4 2c (par. *B. Q.* 2:5 3a); for cases where the teachings present the same position, but the identification requires some interpretation, see e.g. *Bik.* 1:5 64a, *Shab.* 7:2 10b (par. *Bez.* 1:8 60d), *Ket.* 3:8 27d (par. *San.* 7:9 25c).

that the anonymous position in the Mishnah was found recited, by R. Hiyya, in the name of R. Meir. Normally this kind of demonstration offers a full quotation:

m. Shabbat 8:1

המוציא יין כדי מזיגת הכוס. חלב כדי גמייה.

[According to *m. Shab.* 7:3, one is only liable for transporting an item from one domain to another on the Sabbath if the quantity transported is enough to be considered useful or valuable for that specific item. The Mishnah identifies various *minima* for various items according to their common use, in this case, liquids:]

One who takes out wine [only becomes liable if it is] enough for mixing a cup; milk, enough for one gulp.

Shabbat 8:1 11a (par. *Pesaḥim* 10:1 37a)

ר' יוסה בר' בון בשם ר' יוחנן: דר' יהודה היא. דתני, "מים כדי גמייה. ר' יודה או': כדי מזיגת הכוס. יין כדי גמייה. ר' יודה או': כדי מזיגת הכוס."

R. Yose b. R. Abbin [said] in the name of R. Yohanan: It [the teaching about wine in the Mishnah] is R. Judah's. For we have recited, "Water—sufficient for one gulp; R. Judah says: sufficient for mixing a cup. Wine—sufficient for one gulp. R. Judah says: sufficient for mixing a cup."

The words of the Mishnah are precisely paralleled in the recited teaching adduced by R. Yohanan, which is also preserved in *t. Shabbat* 8:10. Whereas in the Mishnah these words are unattributed, in the other recited teaching they are attributed to R. Judah. At first, this kind of identification may seem straightforward, but if we take it to be a claim about the individual who shaped the teaching, and if the quotation of the attributed teaching is meant to demonstrate that claim, then the identification rests on a particular understanding or assumption. The relationship between these teachings could be interpreted in a different way: that R. Judah merely adopted a wide-spread ruling, which he himself learned anonymously, and that whoever formulated the attributed teaching cited it in the name of R. Judah since he, that formulator, accepted the opposite position. But that is not how R. Yohanan sees it: his identification assumes the priority of individual origins.

The other common mode of demonstrating an identification is conceptual, adducing an attributed teaching which purportedly reflects the same concept or position as the anonymous teaching. The identification of R. Judah's contextual interpretation of vows, which we have seen above, presents one example. In that passage the concept was explicit in the attributed teaching. Very often, the concept is derived or produced through interpretation:

m. Berakhot 6:2

בירך על פירות האילן "בורא פרי האדמה", יצא.

If one recited, over produce of tree, the blessing, "Creator of the produce of the earth," he has fulfilled his obligation.

Berakhot 6:2 10b (par. *Bikkurim* 1:6 64b)

ר׳ חזקיה בשם ר׳ יעקב בר אחא: דר׳ יודה היא. דר׳ יודא עביד את האילנות כקשים.[76] אמ׳ ר׳ יוסי: דברי הכל היא. פירות האילן בכלל פירות האדמה, ואין פירות האדמה בכלל פירות העץ.

R. Hezekiah [said] in the name of R. Jacob b. Aha: It [the anonymous position in *m. Ber.* 6:2] is R. Judah's. For R. Judah treats trees like stalks. R. Yose said: It is the words of everyone. [The sages think that] the produce of trees is included among the produce of the earth, whereas the produce of the earth is not included among the produce of trees.

m. Bikkurim 1:6 (the attributed text to which the passage alludes)

יבש המעיין, ניקצץ האילן - מביא ואינו קורא. ר׳ יהודה או׳: מביא וקורא.

[The offering of first fruits generally involves an obligation to recite Deut 26:3–10 at the Temple courtyard. The Mishnah rules that some people should not make the recitation, since parts of the text do not apply to their situation.]

If the spring [watering the field from which the first fruits are being brought] dried up, or the tree [from which the first fruits are being brought] was cut down, he brings [the offering] but does not recite [the declaration; since that declaration includes a gratitude to God for the "land which you have given me," but the land is now infertile]. R. Judah says: He brings [the offering] and recites [the declaration].

The anonymous teaching at *m. Berakhot* 6:2 rules that if a person about to consume tree produce recited the blessing for produce of the earth instead of the appropriate blessing for tree produce, the obligation to recite a blessing has been nonetheless fulfilled. R. Jacob b. Aha identifies this ruling as R. Judah's, alluding to a teaching presented in his name in *m. Bikkurim* 1:6. The Mishnah there addresses the obligation to recite the declaration of the first fruit offering. It presents an anonymous ruling that if the tree from which the offered fruits were taken was cut, the person making the offering should not recite the declaration, since the tree counts as "the land" on which the produce grows, and because the tree no longer exists the person cannot recite the words of gratitude for the land. R. Judah disputes this ruling, saying that the person may recite the declaration. The Talmud

---

[76] Correcting בקשים.

understands his opinion as treating the trees as inessential, merely a conductor; therefore, even if the tree was cut, the essential source of the produce—the land—remains.[77] This interpretation of R. Judah's ruling on first fruits allows R. Jacob to identify the anonymous ruling in *Berakhot* about the blessings: since R. Judah believes that even tree produce essentially grows from the earth, he must be the one who holds that the recitation of the blessing for produce of the earth upon consuming tree produce is valid. R. Yose objects to R. Jacob's identification, arguing that the blessing for produce of the earth is accepted not because trees are treated as inessential stalks, but because tree produce are classified among produce of the earth and not vice versa.[78]

What is important for our purposes is that this kind of demonstration is premised on what Foucault called an author function, in this case because it reflects the notion that texts attributed to the same individual express consistent and distinctive inclinations. R. Jacob assumes that R. Judah has a distinctive view about the nature of trees which would be evident throughout his various rulings; therefore, if a teaching can be shown to express that view of trees, it must be R. Judah's. Conversely, demonstrating that the teaching can be understood even according to people who disagree with that view, as R. Yose argues here, means that the identification has no basis.

In a number of instances, the demonstration appeals to the teaching's precise formulation:

m. Sukkah 5:1

החליל חמשה וששה — זה חליל של בית השואבה שאינו דוחה לא את השבת ולא את יום טוב.

[Describing the drawing of the water for the libations during the holiday of Sukkot:] The flute [is played on] five or six [days]—this is the flute of the Place of Water-Drawing, which does not take precedence, neither over the Sabbath nor over the festival day.

Sukkah 5:1 55a

הא שלקרבן דוחה. מתנית' דר' יוסה ביר' יודה. דתני: "חליל שלקרבן דוחה את השבת", דברי ר' יוסי ביר' יהודה. וחכמ' אומ', "אינו דוחה לא את השבת ולא את יום טוב."

[Implying,] then, that the [flute] of the offering does take precedence [over the Sabbath]. The *mishnah* is R. Yose b. R. Judah's. For it was recited: "The flute of the offering takes precedence over the Sabbath"—the words of R. Yose b. R. Judah. And the sages say, "It takes precedence neither over the Sabbath nor over the festival day."

---

[77] See Elijah of Fulda on the passage in *Berakhot*.
[78] The latter part of R. Yose's argument refers to the second part of the Mishnah's ruling, not cited here.

Like the bulk of chapters 4–5 of tractate *Sukkah*, this passage is a gloss on *m. Sukkah* 4:1, which lists the number of days in which different rituals of the Sukkot festival take place. In that list, the flute-playing which accompanies the drawing of the water libations is said to take place on either five or six days. The Mishnah here explains that this is because the flute is not played on the Sabbath or the principal festival days—on a year in which the seven-day festival does not begin on the Sabbath, the intermediate days of the holiday will include a Sabbath, and the flute will thus be played only on five days. The Yerushalmi's first comment on this passage focuses on its particular formulation: the Mishnah does not simply say that "the flute does not take precedence over the Sabbath," but specifies *which* flute, "the flute of the place of water-drawing." The Yerushalmi argues that this specification must imply a distinction between the flute-playing which accompanies the water-drawing and the flute-playing which accompanies the offerings on certain days (see *m. 'Arakhin* 2:3). Furthermore, since the specification appears in the statement that the water-drawing flute is not played on the Sabbath, the Mishnah implies that the offering flute-playing *does* occur on the Sabbath. The identification of this clause in the Mishnah relies on this elucidation. The Yerushalmi proposes that this anonymous ruling is R. Judah b. R. Yose's, adducing a teaching which shows us that, contrary to the majority of sages, he believes that the flute accompanying the offering is played on the Sabbath.[79] What is interesting about this kind of identification is that it does not mean that the majority of sages would disagree with the ruling in the Mishnah, or that this ruling is only valid according to an individual sage; the majority also holds that the flute of water-drawing is not played on the Sabbath. Rather, the Yerushalmi uses its exegetical inference to detect the individual footprint in the anonymous teaching based on its particular language choices. We find a number of such identifications in the Talmud.[80]

4. Interpreting with identifications

Identifications functioned in an interpretive discourse which was informed by authorial identity in its means and its ends. Amoraic scholars often interpreted teachings by comparing them to other teachings by the same sage; identifications, like attributions, delineated which teachings could be compared to which teachings. The object of interpretation was frequently, and sometimes explicitly, the approach of the individual sage, independently of whether this approach affected the law or whether reconstructing that approach was necessary for understanding the teachings in which this approach is evident.

---

[79] Versions of this teaching appear in *t. Suk.* 4:14 and *t. 'Ar.* 1:13; see Lieberman, *TK*, 4.899–900.
[80] See e.g. *'Er.* 6:8 23d and *Yev.* 15:9 15b.

The following passage provides a good example:

m. Megillah 2:4

הכל כשירים לקרוא את המגילה חוץ מחרש שוטה וקטן.

Everyone is qualified to read out the [Esther] scroll [to others, discharging themselves and others from the obligation to recite the scroll], except for the deaf, the mentally incapacitated, and the minor.

Megillah 2:4 73b (par. *Berakhot* 2:3 4d and *Terumot* 1:2 40c)

אמ' רב מתנה: דר' יוסי היא. אמ' ר' יוסה: הוינן סברין מימר, מה פליגין ר' יוסה ורבנן? בשמע, דכת' בה "שמע". הא שאר כל המצוות לא. מן מה דרב מתנה אמ', "דר' יוסי היא", הדא אמרה היא שמע היא שאר כל המצוות. ומה טע' דר' יוסה? "והאזנת למצותיו". שמע אזניך מה שפיך מדבר.

Said Rav Mattena: It is R. Yose's [who in *m. Ber.* 2:3 rules that if one reads out the Shema but not loud enough to hear himself, he has not discharged himself of the obligation to recite it].

Said R. Yose: We would have thought to say, [with respect to] what do the rabbis and R. Yose dispute? With respect to the Shema [only], because it is written regarding it "Hear" (Deut 6:4)—so with respect to the rest of the commandments [they do] not [dispute]. From that which Rav Mattena said, "It is R. Yose's," this implies that it is same with respect to the Shema as it is with all other commandments. What is the reason of R. Yose [to make this requirement with respect to all commandments]? "And you shall listen to his commandments" (Ex 15:26)—[meaning,] let your ear hear what your mouth speaks.

Rav Mattena identifies the Mishnah's anonymous ruling that deaf people are not qualified to read out the Esther Scroll as R. Yose's. There is no explicit demonstration here, but from later stages in the discussion it is evident that this identification alludes to *m. Berakhot* 2:3, where R. Yose rules, with respect to the Shema, that unless one "makes [his reading out of the Shema] audible to his own ears" one has not fulfilled the obligation to read it out. Both rulings require that the people reading out the text also hear it. Since in *Berakhot* that requirement is attributed to R. Yose, here too it must be from R. Yose.

R. Yose (the Amoraic-era sage—not to be confused with the Tannaitic-era sage by that name whose rulings are the subject of this passage) builds another argument on this identification. He uses the anonymous teaching in *m. Megillah* 2:4, now attributed to R. Yose, to argue that it teaches us something about R. Yose's approach that we could not have derived from *m. Berakhot* 2:3 alone. If our only source for R. Yose's approach was the teaching explicitly attributed to him, we would have erroneously concluded that his requirement for hearing is limited to the Shema recitation, and that his reasoning for that requirement is that the first verse of the recitation, the one which

WHO IS SPEAKING? 59

has given it its name—"Hear (*shema*) Israel"—mentions hearing specifically. But if, as R. Mattena suggests, R. Yose applied that requirement to the Esther Scroll as well, then his position is certainly broader, and as it cannot be based on the particular language of the Shema commandment, it must be based on Exodus 15:26, which requires hearing with respect to all commandments.[81] Two additional passages in the Talmud follow the very same procedure: first, an anonymous passage in the Mishnah is identified; then, R. Yose argues that this identification changes our assumption about the scope of the sage's teaching on the issue.[82]

Other passages which employ identifications signal in their structure that their aim is to interpret the individual sage's approach. One passage, for example, raises the question of how a sage might rule in an alternative case. The Mishnah in *'Orlah* 2:11 tells us that if two small pieces of leaven, one consecrated and one unconsecrated, fell into a priest's-share dough and fermented it, the mixture is still permitted since the unconsecrated piece was not sufficient to ferment the dough on its own; R. Eliezer, however, prohibits the fermented dough as long as that unconsecrated piece was the last to fall. The Talmud asks what R. Eliezer might say if the pieces fell into the dough not sequentially, but simultaneously. In another passage, the question is defined more broadly, focusing on the sage's general approach. We know R. Meir rules that in case a man married, against the law, a woman who was pregnant with or nursing another man's child, he must divorce her and never return to her again; the Talmud asks if R. Meir is similarly strict in all cases of illegal unions.

In both passages, the Talmud answers the question following a similar procedure. An anonymous teaching concerning a different case is adduced, and identified, respectively, as the words of R. Eliezer and R. Meir. Those teachings provide an answer to the questions raised earlier. R. Meir recognizes unions in at least one case where the law was not perfectly followed; R. Eliezer, we learn from a teaching concerning leaven baked by Samaritans, would prohibit the fermented dough even if the pieces fell simultaneously.[83]

The purpose of these passages is to reconstruct the sage's position in a way that transcends the specific case, either narrowly or broadly. The scholars who shaped them achieve that aim by expanding the sage's body of teachings through identifications of anonymous teachings, which allow them to address interpretive questions that arise from, but are not answered by, teachings attributed to him. We also find in the Talmud the other side of the coin: passages which use identifications to argue that the identified teaching cannot answer the question, because the question is about another sage or about the opinion of the majority of sages.[84] Just like the assumption of authorial consistency and distinctiveness allows us to interpret

---

[81] Henshke, "Reciting Shema," offers a full analysis of this passage and its Babylonian parallels.
[82] *Dem.* 7:6 26b and *Shab.* 3:6 6c (par. *Shab.* 16:5 15d).
[83] R. Meir: *Sot.* 4:3 19c (the identification itself repeats in other contexts: *Yev.* 4:1 5c, *Yev.* 12:4 12d, and *Yev.* 13:11 14a); R. Eliezer: *'Or.* 2:11 62b–c (par. *'A. Z.* 5:8 45a). Other passages which follow the same procedure, and are particularly similar to the latter passage, include *Pe'ah* 3:5 17c and *B. Q.* 4:4 4b.
[84] e.g. *Ber.* 2:8 5d, *Dem.* 5:1 24c, *Shevi.* 7:1 37b, *'Or.* 1:5 61a, *Shab.* 7:2 10b (par. *Beẓ.* 1:8 60d).

the rulings of a specific sage in light of each other, the same assumption can lead us away from using the rulings of one sage to interpret those of another or of the majority.

The conclusion of the passage about R. Eliezer's ruling on fermenting pieces underscores that in order to be usable for reconstructing the sage's position, the identified teaching must be specifically linked to him, rather than merely reflect his approach. The passage first relies on R. Simeon b. Laqish's identification of R. Eliezer as the reciter of the teaching on Samaritan leaven; but then we learn of a different version of R. Simeon's teaching:

'Orlah 2:11 62c (par. 'Avodah Zarah 5:8 45a)

ואמ' ר' יוסי לר' חנינא ענתונייא: נהור אתית אמר את ור' ירמיה בשם ר' שמעון בן לקיש, "מאן תנא חמיצן שלכותים? ר' ליעזר"? ואנן לי נן אמרין כן, אלא ר' הילא בשם ר' שמעון בן לקיש, "ירדו לחמיצן שלכותין כר' ליעזר".

And R. Yose said to R. Hanina Anatoniya: Remember that you and R. Jeremiah said in the name of R. Simeon b. Laqish, "Who recited [the teaching about] the leaven of Samaritans? R. Eliezer"? We do not say so but rather that R. Hila [said] in the name of R. Simeon Laqish, "They [the sages] approached the leaven of Samaritans according to R. Eliezer."

In R. Hila's version, R. Simeon did not say that the teaching goes back to R. Eliezer himself; rather, that teaching reflects an adoption by the sages, in the case of Samaritan leaven, of the approach R. Eliezer takes in his ruling on the pieces that fell into the priest's-share dough. The phrase used here appears in a few other places.[85] It is a type of association, and in two of these cases, it is used in contrast with identifications.[86] The distinction, as I mentioned above, was important to Amoraic scholars. Identifications argue a teaching was shaped by the named sage, even if it now circulates in anonymous form; associations of the type we see here argue that the teaching was merely inspired by the sage in question. Since according to R. Hila's version, R. Eliezer himself is not behind the Samaritan leaven teaching, we cannot use this teaching to learn about his position in 'Orlah. The next stage of the discussion argues that since several Amoraic scholars have ruled according to the teaching on Samaritan leaven, it must indeed represent the words

---

[85] Also in its fuller form, ירדו לה בשיטת רבי, literally "they came down towards it (approached it) in R. so-and-so's line," employing the term *shita*, examined in Chapter 3 below. See *Ḥal.* 3:1 59a, *Shab.* 2:1 4c (par. *Pes.* 7:10 35a), *'Er.* 3:5 21b (*Qid.* 3:4 64a), *Naz.* 7:2 56c.

[86] Moscovitz, *Terminology*, 248. For Moscovitz, the difference between *yaredu la* and identification terms is that the former points only to partial correspondence. But the formulation and different functions of these terms point to a difference in the attribution they suggest. Identification terms imply attribution of the teaching to the sage, whereas *yaredu la*, as the plural implies, attributes the teaching to the sages who followed his approach. This difference in attribution allows, in turn, for the difference in the extent of the correspondence.

of the sages rather than R. Eliezer's position. This comment combines the Halakhic and interpretive functions of identifications which we have observed throughout this chapter. On the one hand, identifying a teaching may operate on the majority/individual axis to render its position binding or not binding; on the other hand, in the context of this passage, concluding from the teaching's legal validity that it represents the majority of sages also renders the teaching unusable for the purpose for which it was cited in the passage in the first place—the reconstruction of the position of an individual sage.

5. Attributions and identifications in Tannaitic compilations

The identifications we have seen in this chapter are a distinctive Amoraic development. Attributions like "R. so-and-so said" and "these are the words of R. so-and-so" are essential to the structure of Tannaitic compilations, but these attributions differ from the identifications we have seen in the Talmud. In the most basic sense, these attributions are not presented as arguments about anonymous teachings, but as facts transmitted alongside teachings. It is true that Tannaitic literature only rarely records argumentation alongside its rulings, and we could have argued that just as we know that such rulings are the results of argumentation that is not textually expressed, attributions too were the result of interpretive identification of anonymous teachings.[87] But this seems unlikely: while Tannaitic sages frequently contest their colleagues' rulings, they never contest attributions, and they never do so on interpretive grounds.[88] It is hard to imagine that attributions presented interpretations of anonymous teachings in an environment where so much is a matter of dispute but were rarely disputed in themselves. This does not mean that attributions were always simply a matter of tradition. But the Tannaitic passages that do present variation in attributions, revealing the degree to which attributions were the product of intellectual activity, show us that these attributions were part of the composition of the teaching itself and the assignment of positions to different sages, rather than the result of interpreting anonymous teachings. This process differs fundamentally, in premise and end, from Amoraic identifications.

---

[87] Above, n. 71, I mentioned cases where the Tosefta presents attributions that in the Talmud are the result of interpretive argument; while these cases may tell us that identifications originated as tradition statements, or that the Tosefta in these cases reflects an Amoraic-era argument, they may also support the claim that Tannaitic attributions too resulted from interpretation. Consider the similarity between Ket. 3:8 27d and t. Ket. 3:8: the way the Tosefta connects the two teachings with the words "for R. Meir would say" could be interpreted to mean that the second teaching justifies the attribution ("these are the words of R. Meir"). But it is more likely that this phrase is used here as it is elsewhere in Tannaitic literature, to explain the reasoning behind the teaching.

[88] In addition to the types of passages presented below, see, for example, the three occasions in which the phrase "the words are reversed" (*ḥiluf ha-devarim*), normally used to present alternative rulings, is used to indicate that attributions in a dispute should be reversed (*m. Shevi.* 4:2, *t. Kel. B. M.* 4:15, and *t. Kel. B. M.* 11:3).

The following passage from the Tosefta offers a good example, both because it illustrates this process and because, in its conclusion, it shows us a Tannaitic statement that is closer to Amoraic identifications.[89] The first part presents two accounts of a dispute between the Houses of Hillel and Shammai about vetches in the status of priest's share:

t. Ma'aser Sheni 2:1[90]

ושל תרומה - "בית שמאי אומ': שורין ושפין בטהרה ומאכילין בטומאה, ובית הילל אומ': שורין בטהרה, שפין ומאכילין בטומאה", דברי ר' יהודה.

ר' מאיר אומ': בית שמאי אומ', "שורין בטהרה, שפין ומאכילין בטומאה", ובית הילל אומ', "כל מעשיהן[91] בטומאה".

[Produce for consumption which has been dedicated as priest's share must be handled by individuals in a state of purity; vetches[92] have a liminal status because they are eaten by humans rarely and otherwise used as animal fodder.]

"[Vetches in the status] of priest's share—the House of Shammai say, they must be soaked and rubbed in a state of purity [since this is how they are prepared for human consumption], but may be fed [to animals] in a state of impurity; and the House of Hillel say, they must be soaked in a state of purity, but may be rubbed and fed in a state of impurity"—these are the words of R. Judah.

R. Meir says: The House of Shammai say, "they must be soaked in a state of purity, but may be rubbed and fed in a state of impurity"; and the House of Hillel say, "All their preparation may be done in a state of impurity."

According to R. Judah, the Houses agree that soaking vetches must be done in a state of purity, and that feeding them to animals may be done in a state of impurity, but they disagree about rubbing them (for the purpose of peeling them): the House of Shammai require that rubbing be done in a state of purity while the House of Hillel do not. R. Meir presents a more lenient range of possibilities: the House of Hillel hold that any preparation of vetches, including soaking, may be done in a

---

[89] My analysis conforms with the analysis of the passage in Furstenberg, "Tradition to Controversy," 629–33, but it emphasizes the contrast with Amoraic identifications.
[90] According to MS Erfurt, copied from the Henkind database, with corrections noted. MS Vienna and the Venice edition record a more unusual (but perhaps, on this account, a more reliable) version: in the words of R. Judah, it has reversed attributions to the Houses so that the House of Shammai is lenient, while in the words of R. Meir it presents a wider gap between the positions. For the purpose of my analysis, these differences are of secondary importance. See Furstenberg, "Tradition to Controversy," 630 n. 148.
[91] Correcting מעשיה, with the other versions.
[92] כרשינין; Lieberman, TK, 1.204, identifies the species as Vicia Ervilia, following Löw's Flora der Juden.

state of impurity, while the House of Shammai hold only that soaking them must be done in a state of purity.

The dispute between R. Meir and R. Judah here and in similar passages[93] reveals what is usually hidden by the anonymity of attributions in Tannaitic literature: that at least sometimes the assignment of positions to earlier sages was a matter of perspective. This dispute concerns the precise scope of an earlier dispute, and it is very similar to the passages employing the phrase "they did not dispute about this," discussed above, which also often concern disputes between the Houses.[94] Like those passages, this one too is not explicit on how, exactly, R. Meir and R. Judah assign the different positions to the Houses. These later sages are not explicitly claiming to have heard alternative traditions on the matter. But they are also not interpreting anonymous or attributed words. If this passage presents attribution as a matter of intellectual activity, it seems to indicate that R. Meir and R. Judah each began with the notion that the Houses are disputed about the case of vetches, and that one is stricter than the other; these later sages then assigned specific positions to the Houses based on what each of them, R. Meir and R. Judah, believed to be the range of positions possible in this case. The Mishnah presents a more detailed range in our case: the strictest position is Shammai himself, followed by the House of Shammai, the House of Hillel, and, most leniently, R. Aqiva.[95] While the Mishnaic passage does not present its account of the positions as contested, the dispute in the Tosefta suggests that the account in the Mishnah too resulted from a similar process of assignment.

The fact that the assignment of positions is not bound or supported by interpretation of words seems to indicate that these claims are not concerned with historical statements attributed to the Houses. The aim here, instead, is to present the legitimate range of positions on the case in question, and to draw our attention to Halakhic distinctions between different types of activities (soaking, rubbing, feeding). R. Meir and R. Judah are also not employing an authorial construct, attributing to the Houses positions based on what we know of them from other teachings (other than, very generally, that the House of Hillel is more lenient— though that is not enough to inform the specific positions).[96]

But it is not just that this passage is not concerned with who said what: it reveals a process of attribution that deeply defies such an interest. The passage does not allow any simple distinction between agents or drawing clear boundaries between

---

[93] See the similar dispute earlier in the same passage in the Tosefta; as well as *t. Shab.* 2:13 and *t. Kel. B. M.* 4:5.

[94] See Introduction to Part I, n. 45.

[95] *m. M. S.* 2:4 (par. *m. 'Ed.* 1:8). The relationship between the Mishnah and the Tosefta is more complicated in the version preserved by MS Vienna and the Venice edition, see above n. 90.

[96] The fact that in MS Vienna and the Venice edition the House of Shammai is more lenient according to R. Judah may respond to a more specific tradition about this case, since it is an exception to the rule of Hillelite leniency; at the same time, in that case, the authorial construct applies even less.

their positions. We cannot say that any of the positions here reflect or originate with the Houses, since their positions are clearly mediated by later sages in different ways; but we also cannot say that these positions originate with or reflect the opinions of R. Meir and R. Judah, since each of these later sages presents his words as a direct account of the positions of earlier sages. Attributions function here not so much as statements about the origins of utterances received from the past, but rather as labels that mark positions produced through jurisprudential analysis.

The next statement in this passage in the Tosefta, in contrast, is closer to Amoraic identifications:

t. Ma'aser Sheni 2:1

א׳ ר׳ יוסי: זו משנת ר׳ עקיבא. לפיכך הוא אומ׳, "ינתנו"[97] לכל כהן". וחכמ׳[98] לא הודו לו.

> Said R. Yose: This [R. Meir's version of the dispute, in which the House of Hillel does not require any preparation of vetches to be done in a state of impurity] is the *mishnah* of R. Aqiva. Therefore he says [in *m. Ḥallah* 4:9], "They [such vetches] shall be given to any priest [even a priest who is not scrupulous about purity]." But the sages did not agree with him.

This comment is one of several comments attributed to R. Yose, mostly in the Tosefta, which concern the attribution or re-attribution of teachings. In a few of these comments, he attributes anonymous positions to the House of Shammai, one of which also includes an attribution to the House of Hillel;[99] in another comment, he attributes a position to R. Hanina b. Gamaliel.[100] In two other passages, he states, like in our passage, that a certain teaching presents the *mishnah* or recitation of R. Aqiva.[101] Unlike Amoraic identifications, these statements are not demonstrated, and, with the exception of our passage, no interpretive consequences follow from them.

There are two ways to understand R. Yose's comment in our passage. Under one interpretation, R. Yose argues that this teaching is the *mishnah* that R. Aqiva has learned from his teachers. Since in this recitation, the House of Hillel, whom the law generally follows, say that all treatment of priest's-share vetches may be done in a state of impurity, he ruled accordingly that such vetches may be given to any priest, even a priest who is not scrupulous about purity laws. R. Yose makes an

---

[97] Correcting ונתנו, with MS Vienna.

[98] Deleting אומ׳, which the scribe added out of habit; it does not appear in MS Vienna or the Venice edition.

[99] *t. Pes.* 1:7 (with the House of Hillel, see more below), *t. Sheq.* 3:9, *t. Par.* 12:18. At *t. Ned.* 6:3–4, a similar identification seems to be made by R. Nathan, but note that the phrase R. Nathan uses—*hen hen*—is elsewhere used not for attribution but for equating the words of different sages (see *t. Sheq.* 2:10).

[100] *t. Neg.* 2:11.

[101] See next note.

argument of this sort at *t. Pesaḥim* 1:7, where he says that the position attributed to R. Aqiva presents the words of the House of Hillel, and R. Aqiva decided the law according to them.

It is more likely, however, that in this case R. Yose makes a different kind of argument: that the version of the dispute attributed to R. Meir was shaped by R. Aqiva, who posited there was no distinction between different preparational activities of vetches and therefore formulated the position of the House of Hillel in a way which reflects his position. This interpretation of R. Yose's identification is supported by the fact that in the two other times that R. Yose identifies a teaching as "the *mishnah* of R. Aqiva," including in another passage that presents alternative versions of disputes between the Houses, R. Yose contrasts "the *mishnah* of R. Aqiva" with an "earlier *mishnah*," which implies R. Aqiva changed the earlier recitation.[102] If we read our passage in light of these and other passages which present R. Aqiva as a modifier of earlier teachings,[103] R. Yose is saying that R. Aqiva shaped the version of the dispute and the ruling in *Ḥallah* according to his own approach, but the rest of the sages did not agree with him. The comment here by R. Yose, then, is similar to what we find in the Talmud.[104] It identifies R. Aqiva as the origin of the position and traces clear lines between him and the House of Hillel (the subject of the teaching) and R. Meir (who is merely transmitting R. Aqiva's *mishnah*).

At the same time, this comment is different from Amoraic identifications. First, it does not address, strictly speaking, an anonymous teaching: it is a comment on a version of the dispute already attributed to R. Meir. More important, it is not demonstrated through an authorial construct. The purpose of the association with the teaching in *Ḥallah* is not to demonstrate that R. Meir's teaching about vetches is R. Aqiva's *mishnah*. None of the other statements R. Yose makes about the "*mishnah* of R. Aqiva" are demonstrated; and here too, the directionality of the causation indicated by the word "therefore"[105] suggests the association does not explain the identification, but rather points to the correlation between the two teachings to explain why R. Aqiva ruled as he did in *Ḥallah*. Finally, the bottom line of the identification concerns the Halakhic status of R. Aqiva's position: "the sages did not agree with him."

---

[102] *m. San.* 3:4, *t. M. S.* 2:12 (par. *t. ʿAr.* 5:15).

[103] We find passages contrasting the "earlier *mishnah*" and what "R. Aqiva says" (*m. Ned.* 6:1), and what "they said . . . until R. Aqiva came and taught" otherwise (*m. Ned.* 9:6, *m. M. S.* 5:8, *t. Pes.* 1:7, *t. M. Q.* 2:10, 14, *t. Ned.* 5:1, and *Sifra Zavim* 5:3 79c). Also relevant are reports of R. Aqiva's "adding" to previous traditions: *m. Kil.* 1:3 (par. *t. Kil.* 1:2), *m. Pes.* 1:6 (par. *m. ʿEd.* 2:1), *m. ʿEd.* 8:1.

[104] The Talmud (*Ḥal.* 4:9 60b) presents a parallel to R. Yose's correlation (of which it does not seem to be aware) between R. Aqiva's position in *m. Ḥal.* 4:9 and his position on priests-share vetches. But since the position on vetches is explicitly attributed to R. Aqiva in the Mishnah, that correlation does not need to go through an identification; it is of the *ke-daʿateh* type discussed in the next chapter.

[105] On the direction of causality of this word, see Azar, "Lepikak."

A Tannaitic reference to the *mishnah* of an individual sage also appears in the following story:

t. Zevaḥim 2:17

אמ' ר': פעם אחת היינו יושבים לפני ר' לעזר והיה איסי הבבלי יושב לפניו וחביב עליו. אמ' לו: ר'. השוחט את הזבח לאכל אמוריו ולהקטי' בשרו, מהו? אמ' לו, "כשר". "להניח את דמו ואת אמוריו למחר או להוציאן לחוץ, מהו?". אמ' לו, "כשר. אלא שר' ליעזר פוסל ור' יהושע מכשיר". אמ' לו: שנה לי את הדבר. ושנה לו.

למנחה בא אצלו. אמ' לו: שנה לי את הדבר. ושנה לו. למחרת בא אצלו, אמר לו: ר' שנה לי את הדבר, ושנה לו.[106] אמ' לו, "מה זה יוסי, שמא לא כיונת שמועתך?" אמ' לו, "הן ר'. אלא שר' יהודה שנה לנו. פסול. וחיזרתי על כל חביריי ולא מצאתי לו חבר. סבור שמא טעות הוא בידי. עכשיו שאמרת לי דבר משם ר' ליעזר החזרת לי את אבדתי".

זלגו דמעיו[107] ואמ': אשריכם צדיקים שאתם מחבבים את התורה. לקיים מה שנ' "מה אהבתי תורתך" וג'. מפני שיהודה בנו של ר' אלעאי ואלעאי תלמידו של ר' אליעזר, לפיכך הוא שונה משנתו של ר' ליעזר.

Rabbi [Judah the Patriarch] said: We were once sitting before R. Eleazar and Issi the Babylonian was sitting before him, and he was dear to him. He [Issi] said to him [R. Eleazar]: "Master, if one slaughtered an offering [with the intention] to eat its sacrificial parts and burn its meat, what is the law?" He said to him, "It is valid." "What [is the law if his intention was] to leave its blood and sacrificial parts for tomorrow or take them out?" He said to him, "It is valid. But R. Eliezer disqualifies it, and R. Joshua declares it valid." He [Issi] said to him, "Recite [or: repeat] this teaching to me," and he recited it.

In the afternoon, he came to him and said to him, "Recite this teaching to me"—and he recited it. The next day, he came to him and said to him, "Recite this teaching to me"—and he recited it. He [R. Eleazar] said to him: "What is it Yose [i.e. Issi]? Perhaps you did not prepare your tradition?" He said to him, "Indeed, my master. But R. Judah said to us it is disqualified, and I searched among all my peers and I did not find a counterpart[108] [confirming this teaching]. I thought that perhaps I was mistaken. But now when you told me this in the name of R. Eliezer you returned my lost object to me."

His [R. Eleazar's] tears were flowing, and he said: Blessed are you, righteous ones, that you love the Torah, to fulfill that which is said, "Oh how I love your Torah!" (Ps 119:97). Because Judah is the son of R. Ilay, and Ilay is the student of R. Eliezer—therefore he recites the *mishnah* of R. Eliezer.

---

[106] This sentence ("The next day..."), omitted in error in MS Vienna, is completed here according to MS Erfurt.
[107] Reading with MS Erfurt, which Ma'agarim adopts; but Friedman, "Zacharias Frankel," 78, suggests this detail was added under the Bavli's influence, as Tannaitic sages do not shed tears of joy.
[108] The Hebrew employs the same word, *ḥaver*, to describe Issi's peers and the missing counterpart teaching.

In the final scene of this story, R. Eleazar offers a genealogy of the teaching Issi has heard. He explains that Issi's teacher, R. Judah, must have received this teaching from his father, R. Ilay, who was a student of R. Eliezer. This response presents something like an identification as well as an explanation based on attribution. None of the links in this chain are, strictly speaking, anonymous: R. Eleazar himself had already presented this teaching as attributed to R. Eliezer; and he hears it again from Issi, who says he heard it from R. Judah. But R. Judah must have taught the teaching to Issi without noting that there is a dispute on the matter, and therefore without any attribution; per the Tannaitic conventions discussed above, he taught it to him anonymously, as "the words of the many." R. Eleazar then identifies this teaching as "the *mishnah* of R. Eliezer." The genealogy he offers does not function to demonstrate the identification, as R. Eleazar already knew the teaching as R. Eliezer's before Issi's predicament was revealed. Rather, it aims to explain why R. Judah would teach the law according to R. Eliezer's recitation, by noting that R. Judah is the son of R. Ilay, who is the student of R. Eliezer. This argument confirms that Issi's tradition is reliable, and goes back several generations, but by delineating its genealogy it identifies it as representing a position which has been rejected.[109]

The passages examined in this section are exceptional: normally, Tannaitic compilations do not present attributions as a matter of perspective or a subject of inquiry. The debate between R. Meir and R. Judah may give us a glimpse into the "backstage" of Tannaitic attributions, but at the same time, in contrast with Amoraic identifications, it shows little interest in tracing particular words to particular individuals; instead, it demonstrates how the process of attribution, which assigned a range of positions to different sages, served the analysis of Halakhic concepts.

R. Yose's references to "the *mishnah* of R. Aqiva" and R. Eleazar's reference to "the *mishnah* of R. Eliezer" are also exceptional—they are the only Tannaitic instances in which a teaching is identified as the *mishnah* of an individual sage. They are more similar to our Amoraic identifications, in form and aim: they are presented as separate comments on teachings that have first been presented without these attributions, and they focus on the identity of the sage behind the teaching. In both examples analyzed here, the attribution does not identify an anonymous teaching, but rather adds another attribution to a teaching that was already associated with a sage. This use of *mishnah* shows us that, already at this point, this term could refer not only to the event or activity of recitation, but also to recitation as a more-or-less fixed teaching that is passed through generations— from Eliezer to Ilay to Judah to Issy. That is also what allows the distinction between different *mishnayot*, such as "the first *mishnah*" and R. Aqiva's *mishnah*. But even these passages do not present the method, premise, or significance of identifications we find in the Talmud: neither of these passages uses an authorial

---

[109] Furstenberg, "Tradition to Controversy," 602-4, reads the passage in the context of Tannaitic approaches to preserving rejected positions.

construct to identify the teaching, and neither uses the identity of the sage to interpret the teaching; both draw on attribution primarily as a signifier of the teaching's Halakhic status.

6. Attribution and interpretation between the Talmud and Greek and Latin scholarship

Ancient scholarship in Greek and Latin differed from Amoraic scholarship on rabbinic teachings in broad and fundamental ways. The former examined written, long-form works in multiple genres; the latter centered on orally-transmitted, short-form teachings largely dealing with Halakhah. These broad differences relate to some of the significant and illuminating differences we find in these traditions' engagement with attributions. At the same time, the existence of a long-standing and developed interest in attribution among Greek and Latin scholars suggests structural similarity with Talmudic identifications and even that the latter may present a rabbinic adoption and adaptation of this established scholarly tradition. The second part of this section argues that the comparison with Greco-Roman scholarship is most helpful in illuminating the hermeneutic significance of the move towards attribution-based interpretation which we find in the Talmud.

Classicists trace the critical examination of attributions back to early authors like Herodotus and Aristotle;[110] the Ptolemaic critic Callimachus is sometimes credited with its systematization.[111] By the Roman period, it has become a cornerstone of philological scholarship in several genres. An essay by the Augustan critic Dionysius of Halicarnassus on the Attic orator Dinarchus, for example, presented sophisticated criteria for assessing authorship, a critique of the methods of earlier scholars on the subject, and the first attestation of the word *"pseudepigraphon,"* which he uses to refer to misattributed speeches.[112] When Aulus Gellius (second century CE) discussed the authorship of plays attributed to Plautus, he could already cite a long tradition of criticism on the subject.[113] Late ancient philosophical commentaries regularly addressed questions of authenticity and authorship in introducing the work under investigation.[114] Galen engages these questions in his commentaries on the Hippocratic corpus.[115] And the reason that Foucault traced

---

[110] Compare their comments on the *Cypria*: Herodotus (*Histories*, 2.117; Godley, *LCL*) writes it cannot be by Homer because it contradicts a narrative detail in the *Iliad*, whereas Aristotle (*Poetics* 1459a–b; Halliwell, *LCL*) contrasts the lesser storytelling abilities of whoever may have written it with Homer's superior talent.

[111] Pfeiffer, *History of Classical Scholarship*, 123–51; Blum, *Kallimachos*.

[112] Dionysius of Halicarnassus' *On Dinarchus* in *Critical Essays* (Usher, *LCL*); on "pseudepigraphon" see Peirano, *Roman Fake*, 2 n. 2.

[113] Aulus Gellius, *Attic Nights*, 3.3.1–14 (Rolfe, *LCL*); Zetzel, *Critics*, 27–8.

[114] Mansfeld, *Prolegomena*; Hoffmann, "What Was Commentary"; Sorabji, *Philosophy of the Commentators*, 47, provides a bibliography.

[115] Bröcker, "Die Methoden Galens"; Hanson, "Galen"; Flemming, "Commentary," 341–2.

the definition of authorship in modern literary criticism to early Christian scholars was that they, too, participated in this Greco-Roman scholarly tradition.[116] These discussions present a great variety, whether in historical context or literary genre, but a comparison between them and the identifications analyzed in this chapter allows for some general observations.

While Amoraic identifications responded to the commonplace anonymity of Tannaitic teachings, Greek and Latin scholars found most of the texts they studied already attributed.[117] Their discussions of authorial identity addressed the possibility that the work was misattributed, erroneously or deliberately, or that a line was interpolated. This meant that such discussions normally concerned authenticity: a successful attribution to a well-known author saved the text from the charge that it was written by a lesser figure or that it was a deliberate forgery.[118] Christian scholars deployed such discussions in a new discourse that equated canonicity with authentic attribution in ways that continue to shape scholarly assumptions about "pseudepigraphic" texts.[119] Amoraic identifications, in contrast, never authenticate a teaching: a *mishnah* is a *mishnah*, regardless of who formulated it. The possibility of spurious recited teachings is raised only rarely.[120] Anonymity is not a reason for suspicion; it is often, as we have seen, the mark of legal authority. Amoraic scholars rarely argue that attributions are false or inaccurate. When they do so, they claim they have not heard such a teaching, not that the attribution must be false based on the sort of interpretive arguments they make to demonstrate identifications,[121] though they sometimes changed attributions in light of perceived inconsistencies.[122]

Discussions of attribution in Greek and Latin normally addressed composition rather than adaptation. But sometimes, they did point to or conjure more complicated compositional histories involving multiple agents. Aulus Gellius' discussion of Plautus, for example, speaks about plays that were originally written by earlier poets, but because they were revised by Plautus, they now feature his unmistakable style.[123] Origen posited that the Epistle to the Hebrews was composed by a student

---

[116] On Christian discourse of attribution and authenticity, see Baum, *Pseudepigraphie*, 21–30; Ehrman, *Forgery and Counterforgery*, 85–92 and 137–45. On Foucault, see the Introduction to Part I.

[117] Peirano, *Roman Fake*, 38–9; Speyer, *Literarische Fälschung*, 40. See also the reference to Williamowitz's notion of "*horror vacui*" there.

[118] For overviews of ancient discussions of authenticity see Speyer, *Literarische Fälschung*, 112–28; Peirano, *Roman Fake*, 36–73; and see n. 116 above on Christian discussions. As Peirano shows (both in the end of that chapter and in the rest of the book), the rigid construction of authorship in *Echtheitskritik* was not the only option, even among educated Romans. For a survey of the issue across European history, see Grafton, *Forgers and Critics*.

[119] Reed, "Pseudepigraphy"; Najman, "Vitality."

[120] See e.g. *'Er.* 1:6 19b, where R. Simeon refer to *mishnayot* that were "not admitted" and therefore should not be relied upon; or when the Yerushalmi has R. Judah the Patriarch refer to "R. Isaac the Great, whose entire recitation I had examined" (*M. S.* 5:1 55d).

[121] e.g. *Sot.* 9:15 24c (par. *Pe'ah* 1:1 15c), *Yev.* 4:10 6a (par. *Nid.* 1:4 49b).

[122] See Chapter 3, Section 4; and Chapter 7, Section 3.

[123] *Attic Nights*, 3.3.13.

of Paul using notes from Paul's teaching, which is why in some sense it may be attributed to Paul even if it was not written by him.[124] Discussions of interpolations, by nature, involved activities like patching and expanding.[125] Analysis of the ways texts were shaped by individuals did not, even in the Greco-Roman context, need to be defined by the idea that texts wholly originated with these individuals.

Some Greek and Latin arguments to support or reject attributions are similar to those which support Amoraic identifications. We find claims that the text agrees or disagrees with positions known from other texts to be held by the author,[126] or that the text is found attributed to someone else.[127] But the paramount criterion was style. Occasionally, comments on style note similar use of vocabulary.[128] More regularly, they focused on broad stylistic features, blending observations of the author's characteristic merits with general judgments of quality;[129] they often bound authenticity with aesthetic value.[130] This criterion applied broadly, even beyond what we might consider belletristic texts.[131] In the Talmud, in contrast, not a single identification is

---

[124] Apud Eusebius, *Ecclesiastical History*, 6.25.11–4 (Oulton, LCL). See more below, n. 126 and n. 130.

[125] A particularly interesting discussion of a text "cobbled together" from many sources is in Galen's commentary on *On the Nature of Man*; see Hankinson, "Galen," 150–3.

[126] See e.g. Boethius' rehearsing of the defense by Alexander of Aphrodisias (early third century CE) of Aristotle's authorship of *On Interpretation*, which combines stylistic and conceptual arguments: "For example: what is said here agrees with Aristotle's views elsewhere on the statement-making sentence; the style which is compressed through terseness is not at odds with Aristotle's [normal] obscurity" (Smith, *Boethius: On Aristotle on Interpretation*, 11.31–12.2, 20). Origen's argument (see above), that while Paul did not write the Epistle to the Hebrews it nonetheless represents his "thoughts" (νοήματα), may have been based on the agreement between them and Paul's known positions. Epiphanius argues that the Ebionites' forgery of a book under Clement's name is indicated by disagreements in positions on celibacy and the Old Testament prophets (*Panarion*, 30.15.3, trans. Williams, 131). On the question of "orthodoxy" and "heresy" in Christian discussions of attribution, see Ehrman, *Forgery and Counterforgery*, 141–2; and see below on Rufinus and Origen.

[127] Diogenes Laertius, for example, notes in his discussion of Plato's dialogues that Favorinus "declares that nearly the whole of the Republic is to be found in a work of Protagoras entitled Controversies"; *Lives of the Philosophers*, 3.57, Hicks, LCL).

[128] See e.g. Schironi, *Best of the Grammarians*, 628–9, on the claims of the "separatists" that the *Iliad* and *Odyssey* were composed by different authors since they use the same words differently, and Aristarchus's defense against these claims. See also Jerome's comments, suggesting that Clement of Rome is the author of the Epistle to the Hebrews, as one of Clement's own epistles uses the same expressions and even word order (*On Illustrious Men* 15, trans. Halton, 31).

[129] See already Aristotle's comment on the *Cypria* (above n. 110); a particularly instructive example of stylistic constructs and aesthetic judgment is Dionysius' *On Dinarchus*, which argues that each of the great orators is recognizable by unique and consistent style, but Dinarchus' style can be identified by the mediocrity with which he imitates these orators—even if he is the best of the imitators; see also Gellius' discussion of Plautus (above n. 113). Such judgments appear several times in Jerome. He notes, for example, that certain commentaries ascribed to Theophilus of Antioch appear not to match the "elegance and style" of his other writings (*On Illustrious Men*, 25, trans. Halton, 48).

[130] Peirano, "Authenticity"; Speyer, *Fälschung*, 124. Discussions of the authorship of Hebrews provide an illuminating exception. Origen (above n. 124), for example, argued that Paul did not write the epistle, as anyone able to discern differences in style will recognize that it has "better Greek" than the "rudeness in speech" which characterizes Paul's writing. Jerome notes the same problem but offers different solutions (above n. 128).

[131] In scientific literature, see Börno and Coughlin, "Galen on Bad Style" (though they note Galen is unique in applying it also to textual criticism of that genre); for an example from philosophy, see above n. 126; and see the quote from Jerome, above n. 129, concerning Theophilius's biblical commentaries.

supported by stylistic analysis. Amoraic scholars attributed teachings to sages based on perceived similarity in Halakhic position, though as we have seen, sometimes that similarity was reconstructed by examining specific choices in wording. This difference stems in part from the generic homogeneity of the materials, what Martin Jaffee aptly called the rabbis' "stereotypical stylistic meat grinder."[132]

At the same time, there is a similarity in premise and conceptual structure even between stylistic discussions of attributions and Amoraic identifications. In both cases, the identity of the person who shaped a text is determined by comparing that text to others known to be by the individual, using an authorial construct which encodes that individual's characteristics: Gellius points to Plautus' entertaining use of archaisms to describe harlots, Dionysius points to the typical rhetorical strengths of each of the great orators, and R. Yose and R. Jacob point to R. Judah's views of trees or his approach to intentionality in vows. The argument centers on particular properties of the text, excluding others, and assumes that these textual properties point to the agent behind the text. While the focus on style in Greco-Roman scholarship may intuitively seem more indicative of authorship to us, it is, as Irene Peirano argues, just as constructed: "the close relationship between authenticity and aesthetics is not an inescapable necessity," but reflects the way that claims about authenticity were intimately bound with the process of "creating and defending a canon of works deemed superior."[133] Claims about attributions, in both traditions, were made using modes of analysis that broadly characterize these traditions, such as aesthetic criticism and Halakhic conceptualization, and in both cases, such claims served broader scholarly aims. But this embeddedness does not diminish the significance of discussions of attributions.

It is on this issue, of the hermeneutic significance of attribution, that the comparison with Greek and Latin scholarship is even more illuminating. Recent scholarship has pointed to the similarity between the sages' use of Scripture to interpret Scripture and the Alexandrian interpretive practice encapsulated by the phrase "*Homerum ex Homero*," "interpreting Homer with Homer."[134] The phrase itself is sometimes presented as a description of the method employed by Aristarchus, a Homeric scholar working in the second century BCE; it has a complicated history, and modern scholars have associated it with a diverse set of ancient interpreters and practices.[135] Here, I want to focus on a subset of these practices which does

---

[132] Jaffee, "Rabbinic Authorship," 22.
[133] Peirano, "Authenticity," 217.
[134] Paz, *From Scribes to Scholars*, 43–54. Alexander, "'Homer the Prophet," 138, writes that the principle is "commonsensical," but as Novick ("Scripture as Rhetor," 59 n. 68) observes, "the notion that Scripture interprets itself can hardly be characterized as simply commonsensical, and still less as universally held."
[135] On the history of the phrase, which appears for the first time in Porphyry's *Homeric Questions*, see Mansfield, *Prolegomena*, 204–5. For analysis of different interpretive practices that have been associated with the phrase, see Porter, "Hermeneutic Lines"; Nunlüst, "Aristarchus"; and Neuschäfer, *Origines*, 276–85.

72   THE RISE OF TALMUD

not fit so easily with rabbinic scriptural exegesis but which does share fundamental hermeneutic positions with the Amoraic practices examined in this chapter.

In his commentary on Hippocrates' *Prognostication*, Galen discusses a reference Hippocrates makes to the divine element in the cause of disease, *theion*. Earlier commentators, he tells us, have understood this word to refer to divine anger. The problem with that interpretation, Galen says, is not that it is implausible as a description of the cause of disease, but rather:

> They do not show whether Hippocrates shared this opinion, which is the task of good exegetes. For we are enjoined not simply to state in our exegeses that which seems true to us, but also that which accords with the meaning of the author, even if it is false.[136]

While in other passages Galen uses the authorial construct as a method of interpretation,[137] here his point is that the principle, that the author's work interprets itself, should also inform the aim or significance of interpretation. Interpreters must say what *Hippocrates* thought about the causes of disease regardless of whether what he thought was correct or not; it is for this reason that interpreters must compare statements from different parts of the author's corpus and identify which statements are authentically his. The resulting interpretation ends up saying something not about the subject matter ("that which seems true to us") but about the author's opinion.[138] This principle of interpretation shifts the usual emphasis in the well-known maxim about Homer: from "interpreting Hippocrates *with Hippocrates* (and not other authors)" to "interpreting *Hippocrates* (and not the subject at hand) with Hippocrates."

It is in this sense that this approach shares more with rabbinic hermeneutics of rabbinic teachings than it does with rabbinic hermeneutics of Scripture. Scripture, for the sages, does not merely represent the opinion of its author; there is no distinction between tracing the truth and interpreting the meaning of the divine text.[139] Furthermore, the approach we find in Galen fits a corpus that is personally differentiated, in which the "law of interpretation" is "interpreting each of the men out of himself."[140] While the sage's scriptural interpretation does not normally hinge on the attributions of the text to individuals, Talmudic interpretation

---

[136] Galen, *In Hippocratis Prognosticum*, 1:4 (Kühn v. 18b, 17–18, *CMG* 9,2 206.5–9, ed. Heeg, *TLG*). Translation from Flemming, "Commentary," 339.

[137] See e.g. *In Hippocratis Epidemiarum* III, 1.4, Kühn 17a 507, and the quote from *De dignoscendibus pulsibus* below; Hanson, "Galen," 47.

[138] Though Galen himself seems not to have been consistent on this point; see the passage discussed by Hankinson, "Galen," 149.

[139] See Halbertal, *People of the Book*, esp. 24–40.

[140] Galen, *De dignoscendibus pulsibus* 4 (ed. Kühn v. 8, 958): "this for me is a rule of interpretation, to interpret each of these men out of himself"; Greek, *TLG*: καὶ γάρ μοι καὶ νόμος οὗτος ἐξηγήσεως, ἕκαστον τῶν ἀνδρῶν ἐξ ἑαυτοῦ σαφηνίζεσθαι.

of rabbinic teachings not only responded to a corpus which contained attributions to different sages but also further construed that corpus as stemming from different individuals, orienting interpretation around a given sage's opinion or position.

The late ancient development and construction of a corpus of Christian authors alongside the texts Christians held to be scriptural raised a similar set of questions and problems on the connection between authority, truth, and individual-bound interpretation.[141] Mike Chin has shown that Rufinus and Jerome offered visions of the Christian literary corpus which differed precisely on the issue of individual authors. Jerome's *On Famous Men* celebrated the individual, "illustrious," Christian author; Rufinus' translations, of which he disavowed his own authorial name, presented "an alternative to Jerome. . . . The dream of the library without authors, that is, of a freestanding expansive knowledge that exists independently of human creation."[142]

The debate between Jerome and Rufinus on the translation of Origen, especially, illuminates how the purpose of textual engagement was bound with notions of text and authorship. Jerome and Rufinus agreed that there are passages in Origen's works which contradict "orthodoxy." Rufinus' translation of these works into Latin aimed to solve the problem in two ways. The first was to suggest that Origen's work has been contaminated by "heretics"; the second was to offer a Latin translation which very much revises Origen's Greek and brings it to conform with "orthodox" doctrine. It was this latter strategy which Jerome attacked:

> I wish to know who gave you permission to cut out a number of passages from the work you were translating? You were asked to turn a Greek book into Latin, not to correct it; to draw out another man's words, not to write a book of your own . . . . I will take an example, from which men may judge of the rest. In the first book of the Περὶ Ἀρχῶν, where Origen had uttered that impious blasphemy, that the Son does not see the Father, you supply the reasons for this, as if in the name of the author, and translate the note [σχόλιον] of Didymus, in which he makes a fruitless effort to defend another man's error, trying to prove that Origen spoke rightly.[143]

---

[141] On the emergence of the so-called "Patristic Argument," the citation of the "Church Fathers" alongside or instead of Scripture, see Vessey, "Forging of Orthodoxy"; and Rebillard, "A New Style of Argument." While the phenomenon itself certainly suggests comparison with the turn to citation and interpretation of rabbinic teachings in the Amoraic period, it occurs later (Morlet, "Aux origines," argues that while it formally appears first with Athanasius, it can be traced in some sense to Eusebius); it differs phenomenologically (see Fiano, *Three Powers*, 151–70, for a comparison between Christian and rabbinic citation practices which focuses on the Bavli but which is also applicable to the Yerushalmi); and was connected with literary practices that in the rabbinic tradition were not distinctively Amoraic (Letteney, *Christianization*, 87–124, identifies as part of this new form of argument an aggregation of interpretations which is similar to what we find already in the Halakhic Midrashim).

[142] Chin, "Rufinus," 624.

[143] Jerome, *Adversus Rufinus*, 2.11 (Lardet, *Jérôme*, 128–30). Trans. from Richardson, "Jerome's Apology."

What bothered Jerome was precisely that Rufinus' translation blurs the boundaries between Origen the author, Didymus the commentator, and Rufinus the translator—while Jerome believes that each of these voices should be distinguished by name. Much like Galen, he insists on the distinction between "that which seems true to us" and interpreting each author's words according to each author's intention—to read Origen out of Origen. Chin discusses a passage from Rufinus' translation of Origen's commentary on Romans which offers the other side of this debate:

> [My detractors] say to me: Since, in what you write, there is a great deal of your own in his works, use a title with your own name, and write, for example, "Rufinus's Commentary on the letter to the Romans" [. . .]. I, however, give more weight to my conscience than to my name; and even if I seem to have added some things or left things out, or to have shortened what was too long, I do not think it would be right for the title to be stolen from the one who laid the foundation for the work and provided the materials for constructing the building.[144]

Note that for Rufinus, too, attribution is important: he defends the attribution of the work to the person who laid its foundations. But he also posits a view of textuality which is less bound to individuals and allows for a collective shaping of texts. This debate between Jerome and Rufinus provides a more explicit articulation of hermeneutic premises which may illuminate the different practices of attribution we find in rabbinic texts. Much like Rufinus' translation, the Tannaitic process of attribution observed above resists rigid distinctions between the different individuals which have shaped rabbinic teachings, since its aim is not understanding words uttered by specific individuals, but rather offering the best account of the issues at hand. Amoraic identifications, on the other hand, fit more with the interpretive agenda set by Jerome here: the purpose of interpretation is to "draw out *another's* words." Jeremy Schott has shown that an earlier stage of this debate about Origen's works, in fourth-century Palestine, was connected with another hermeneutic contrast that is relevant for us. Pamphilus defended himself against the charge that he was treating Origen's work like Scripture, that is, that he approached Origen's words as authoritative sources of the truth; Pamphilus responded that he could read the text critically, distinguishing between the truth and the text's meaning.[145]

While scholars have justifiably criticized the application of a modern notion of authorship to rabbinic texts, we must also appreciate how attribution and authors

---

[144] Rufinus, *Origen's Commentary on the Epistle of the Romans*, epilogue. Translation from Chin, "Rufinus," 627, my omissions.
[145] Schott, "Plotinus's Portrait," 340–3.

mattered in antiquity—not only for establishing the authority of a text, but also in shaping its study. Attribution could determine the corpus to be interpreted, the method of interpretation, and the aim of interpretation. This significance may seem intuitive to us, and we may therefore think of the similarity between Talmudic and other ancient scholars on this question to be not specific enough, even banal. But there were other ways to approach textual scholarship: attribution-based interpretation is central neither in the Tannaitic engagement with rabbinic teachings nor in Midrash. Even within the Greco-Roman tradition, the approach discussed here may have been dominant but far from exclusive: Aristarchus, Galen, and Jerome formulated their principles polemically, against other frameworks and methods.

Conclusion

It is almost tautological to say that the Amoraic introduction of identifications into rabbinic scholarly practice demonstrates an increased interest in the way that rabbinic teachings were shaped by individuals. This chapter examined how these identifications and discussions of anonymity attested to an individuated notion of rabbinic teachings, and played a part in a hermeneutic framework in which attribution was central. Amoraic scholars construed anonymity itself as reflecting the preferences of individual sages, who anonymized teachings in their *mishnayot*. They demonstrated identifications by positing individual patterns of ruling. They employed identifications to define the sage's body of teachings as part of inquiries that aimed to understand each sage on his own terms. Tannaitic compilations, in contrast, rarely presented attribution as an intellectual practice or a matter of perspective; but even when they did, their aim was not, with few exceptions, tracing positions to individuals. Amoraic identifications bear some similarity to discussions of attribution in Greek and Latin, even if they differ in method and purpose. More important, the arguments examined here from Galen and Jerome spell out the hermeneutic principles underlying the practice of interpreting individuals on their own terms, offering us an ancient context with which to consider the Amoraic reorientation of rabbinic interpretation.

Identifications reflect the textualization of the study of rabbinic teachings examined in the Introduction to this book; the very discussion of textual anonymity stems from an interest in the literary form of rabbinic teachings, and the tracing of different words or positions to individuals assumes a transmission of rabbinic teachings in particular formulation rather than constant reformulation by multiple sages. At the same time, identifications were not an inevitable consequence of textualization: we have seen how Amoraic scholars brought a particular perspective to bear on these texts, choosing to read them as the words of individuals even when there were other options available. What makes identifications a particularly good phenomenon with which to think about the Amoraic individuation of rabbinic teachings is that they show how much Amoraic scholars wanted and needed their sources to be attributed. This individuation did not merely respond to the fact that some Tannaitic teachings were attributed; it was central enough to Amoraic commentary that it read individuals even into texts in which they were absent or hidden.

2
The Sages, Opinionated
Deʿah and Individual Inclination

It is customary in scholarship to speak about the teachings of the sages as their "opinions." This term is not trivial. It implies views about the source and nature of these teachings. In English, for example, the word "opinion" points to subjective thoughts; when we say something is "a matter of opinion" we mean it is disputed and that different positions reflect personal inclinations or calculations. This chapter argues that it was only in the Amoraic period that the sages began referring to their teachings with the Hebrew and Aramaic words *deʿah* and *daʿat*, which similarly point to subjectivity and personal inclination.

This development is part of our story about individuation in two ways. First, the shift from "words" to "opinions" of the sages presents their teachings as the expression of individual thought. More specifically, this chapter centers on one of the most important attribution-based scholarly practices in the Talmud, the claim that a sage said a teaching "according to his opinion" (*ke-daʿateh*). Amoraic scholars employed this phrase to identify distinctive patterns and inclinations in the sage's teachings. The frequency of such comments demonstrates an active, conscious Amoraic interest in the way rabbinic teachings were shaped by individuals with consistent positions, personal leanings, and sometimes even biographies and bodies.

1. The history of "opinion"

Deʿah or *daʿat* have the primary sense of "knowledge" in Biblical Hebrew.[1] In rabbinic literature, these words take on several related meanings. In Halakhic contexts, they are used, for example, to indicate the lack or presence of the intellectual capacity required for a person to perform a certain action, especially with respect to minors, individuals with disability, and other categories of agents perceived by the sages as incapacitated.[2] The most common meaning of *daʿat* in the Tannaitic corpus is knowledge in the sense of consent, will, or intention by a party in a legal situation: *m. Bava Meẓiʿa* 8:9, for example, rules that if a rented house collapsed,

---

[1] On the near identity between *deʿah* and *daʿat* in Biblical, Rabbinic, and liturgical Hebrew see Gluska, "Leshon tefilat ha-ʿamidah," 107.
[2] See e.g. *m. Pes.* 10:4, *m. Suk.* 3:15, *m. Git.* 2:6, and *Mekhilta de-Rabbi Ishmael, Shabbata* §1.

the owner must provide the renter with a new house, and that any significant difference in features between the old and new houses must be agreed upon by both parties—"on the *da'at* of both of them."[3]

Other, less common uses of *de'ah* in Tannaitic compilations similarly refer to personal inclinations, preferences, or character traits.[4] A teaching in *m. Avot* 5:11 lists "four kinds of temperament (*de'ot*): easy to anger and easy to appease ... difficult to anger and hard to appease ..."; when R. Meir presents the way that men vary in their reactions to their wives' behavior, he says that "just as there are [different] preferences (*de'ot*) with respect to food so there are [different] preferences (*de'ot*) with respect to women" (*t. Sotah* 5:9); the Tosefta records the ruling that one should not give a cup that one just drank from to another person, because "people do not have the same preferences (*de'ot*)" with respect to drinking from other people's cups (*t. Berakhot* 5:9); on two occasions, the Mishnah describes people who are not easily disgusted by certain kinds of food as having good or strong "disposition" (*da'atan yafa*); a homily in *Sifre* on Numbers (§101) emphasizes that when Numbers 12:3 says Moses was humble, it means "humble in character (*be-da'ato*)," not in terms of wealth or stature; teachings at *t. Berakhot* 6:2 and *t. Sanhedrin* 8:6 liken the difference in *de'ot* among people to their differences in appearance or sound; and in *m. Kellim* 17:6, *de'ah* marks an individual's subjective judgment as opposed to a standardized procedure. Finally, to say someone is performing an action from or by his own *de'ah* can mean that the action is done independently, without guidance or directives from God or a teacher.[5]

These connotations of *de'ah* point to individual inclination in the idiosyncratic, independent, not necessarily rational, and sometimes even capricious sense. This might explain why Tannaitic sages only rarely use these words in connection to the sages' teachings. I could find only two passages in the entire Tannaitic corpus which use the word in the sense of a sage's position or legal ruling, and in both contexts the point is that the ruling is a lone, particular position.[6] Tannaitic

---

[3] Other examples include *m. Er.* 7:11, *m. Ned.* 4:3, and *m. B. B.* 1:2, *m. Bek.* 5:3, and *m. Kel.* 5:4.

[4] The only place where *de'ah* seems to mean "reason" is *t. Ḥul.* 7:1, "reason decides (*ha-da'at makhra'at*)," a phrase that is also taken up at *Yev.* 10:3 10d.

[5] *Sifre Numbers* §46 comments that, when giving the wagons and the oxen to the Levites (Num 6–9), Moses determined how much each family should get "on his own mind" (*le-fi da'ato*) contrasting Moses's actions here with the times he acted under God's guidance (Kahana, *Sifre on Numbers*, 367 n. 4). See also *Mekhilta de-Rabbi Ishmael, Kaspa* §20.

[6] *m. Av.* 4:7: "Do not judge alone ... and do not tell [your colleagues], 'accept my opinion!'"; *t. San.* 5:1: "we have only your opinion." There are other times where the word is used in connection with sages, though not with respect to their positions, but rather in line with the Tannaitic usage discussed above: *m. Ḥag.* 2:1 (in the sense of intellectual capacity), *m. Kin.* 3:6 (where the "settled mind" of older sages is contrasted with the "unsettled" mind of older non-sages), *Sifre Numbers* §134 (the Torah gave sages the "mind" to interpret, perhaps drawing on the sense of independent capacity), *t. Sot.* 7:12 ("lest someone say in his mind ..."), *t. San.* 3:8 ("say what is on your mind"), *t. San.* 7:6 (too many responses will upset your colleague's mind), and *t. San.* 7:9 (in the sense of intention but also disposition).

compilations normally refer to the sage's positions not as their opinions, but as their "words."[7]

In contrast, there are hundreds of passages in the Talmud in which *de'ah* refers to the positions and rulings of sages; the word appears in this sense in several recurring terms that are foundational to Talmudic discourse.[8] This terminological shift, from "words" to "opinions," is not trivial. We can observe its significance not just in the contrast between the Talmud and the Tannaitic compilations, but also in the way that *de'ah* functions in the Talmud itself. Drawing on the word's sense of independence, mentioned above, the Yerushalmi uses *de'ah* to mark a position that is not based in tradition:

Megillah 3:4 74a–b

חל להיות בערב שבת, במה קורין? ר׳ זעורה אמ׳: קורין לשעבר. ר׳ אילא ר׳ אבהו בשם ר׳ יוחנן: קורין לבא. והוה ר׳ זעורה מסתכל ביה. אמ׳ ליה: מה את מסתכל בי? אנא אמר מן שמועה ואת אמר מן דיעה ואת מסתכל בי?

[*m. Meg.* 3:4 stipulates that if the new moon of the month of Adar falls on the Sabbath, the congregation reads on that Sabbath the Torah portion of *sheqalim*; if Adar begins during the week, they move that reading up to the previous Sabbath.]

If it falls on Sabbath eve, when do they read? R. Ze'ira said: They read it in the previous one. R. Hila [said that] R. Abbahu [said] in the name of R. Yohanan: They read it in the next one. R. Ze'ira was staring at him. He said to him: Why are you staring at me? I say from tradition [*shemu'ah*] and you say from opinion [*de'ah*], and *you* are staring at *me*?"

R. Ze'ira and R. Hila offer different answers to the question at hand; R. Hila quotes a ruling on the subject which is attributed to R. Yohanan and was transmitted by R. Abbahu; R. Ze'ira does not offer any pedigree for his answer. When R. Ze'ira stares at R. Hila—staring often communicates disapproval in the Talmud[9]—the latter complains: it should be him, R. Hila, who disapproves of R. Ze'ira, given that R. Hila's answer is based on tradition and R. Ze'ira's is not. We are not told why R. Ze'ira ruled as he did; the only indication that his ruling was merely his opinion, besides R. Hila's marking of his answer as *de'ah*, is that he does not cite anyone else (though the Yerushalmi later adduces Tannaitic traditions supporting each

---

[7] Phrases like "the words of R. so-and-so" are commonplace in Tannaitic literature, whereas references to *de'ah* of a particular sage simply do not appear. We can also observe the shift in the passage analyzed in the previous chapter from *Sot.* 3:6 19b, which employs "Rabbi so-and-so saw the *opinion* [דעתו] of Rabbi such-and-such [as preferrable]," whereas the Tannaitic phrase is to "see the *words*" of a sage as preferable (see Chapter 1, n. 42).

[8] In addition to *ke-da'ateh*, analyzed in detail below, see also *hi da'ateh* or the very common *'al da'ateh*; Moscovitz, *Terminology*, 192–5 and 512–17 respectively.

[9] Lieberman, *YK*, 289 n. 2.

80 THE RISE OF TALMUD

of these positions). In two passages in tractate ʿEruvin, deʿah appears in a similar contrast: they tell us that one scholar offered a ruling based on *ulpan*, received instruction, whereas the other offered it based on *deʿah* (ʿEruvin 3:7 21b and 4:1 21d). In yet another passage, R. Zeʿira states that a ruling by R. Yose was "not based on his opinion (*la min daʿateh*), but on [the words] of R. Yohanan and R. Simeon b. Laqish" (*Sheviʿit* 5:1 35d).

The fact that *deʿah* is used in Tannaitic compilations to refer to personal preferences and dispositions rather than statements of sages, and the fact that in the Yerushalmi, this word is also used to mark what is not traditional, both shed light on the pervasive use of *deʿah* in the Yerushalmi to refer to the sages' teachings. This terminological change reflects a shift towards describing rabbinic knowledge in individual terms, the expression of subjective leanings and preferences—as opinions.

2. Ke-daʿateh

The phrase "*rabbi...ke-daʿateh*" (henceforth: *ke-daʿateh*) can be translated, "Rabbi so-and-so [said this][10] according to his opinion," and it appears in around ninety-five unique instances in the Talmud.[11] I first consider the accepted interpretation of this phrase, as formulated by Leib Moscovitz, according to which the primary function of *ke-daʿateh* is to associate two similar teachings attributed to the same sage; I proceed to offer a different interpretation of the phrase, arguing it makes the claim that the teaching reflects the sage's personal inclination. Under both interpretations, the pervasive use of *ke-daʿateh* demonstrates the importance of attribution in Amoraic scholarship; but if the interpretation offered here is correct, this phrase shows more clearly that attribution-based interpretation was also bound with a view of the nature of rabbinic teachings as grounded in individual inclinations.

Moscovitz defines *ke-daʿateh* as a phrase which associates two teachings attributed to the same sage in order to point out the similarity between them. He writes that the similarity varies greatly: the phrase associates teachings that are nearly identical, teachings which share a substantial conceptual similarity, and teachings that have only a "formal and flimsy" connection. The purpose of these associations might be the association itself, an explanation of the teaching's underlying logic, or a solution to problems raised in the passage.[12] To make things

---

[10] In one instance examined below, *Shab*. 14:3 14c, the term appears with the word "said (אמר)"; Moscovitz, *Terminology*, 254 n. 27 argues the text should be emended according to the parallel in *Leviticus Rabbah*; but even if "said" is not part of the original formulation, "said" may be implied in the phrase (much like we read the citation formulation "in the name of" as "[said] in the name of").

[11] I did not count instances which merely preface the comment, but when the same unit makes two different claims, I counted them as two. In cases of the common structure, "This one [sage] *ke-daʿateh* and that one [sage] *ke-daʿateh*; R. so-and-so *ke-daʿateh* ... R. such-and-such *ke-daʿateh* ...," I counted two instances, rather than four or one.

[12] Moscovitz, *Terminology*, 253–5.

concrete, I offer one of the two examples Moscovitz uses to illustrate the phrase's function:

Shabbat 3:3 5d (par. *Terumot* 10:2 47a,[13] *Ḥallah* 1:1 57a, and *Pesaḥim* 2:5 29b)

תמן תנינן: תפוח שריסקו ונתנו לתוך העיסה וחימיצה הרי זו אסורה. תני: ר׳ יוסי מתיר. [...] ר׳ יוסי כדעתיה. כמה דו אמר תמן אין חימוצו ברור, כן הוא אמ׳ הכא, אין תבשילו תבשיל ברור.

[*m. Shab.* 3:3 prohibits placing an egg near a kettle or wrapping it in hot cloths so that it may cook on the Sabbath; it cites R. Yose's dissenting opinion which permits this kind of cooking.][14]

We recited there [*m. Ter.* 10:2]: An apple [of priest's share] that was chopped and placed in [unconsecrated] dough, and [the dough] rose, [the dough] is prohibited [to non-priests; i.e. since the dough was so affected by the apple, it has also acquired its priest's-share status]. It was recited: R. Yose permits [the dough; according to him, it does not acquire the apple's status]. [...]

R. Yose [said this] according to his opinion. Just as he says there [concerning *m. Ter.* 10:2] that its fermentation is not definite, so he says here [at *m. Shab.* 3:3] that its cooking is not definite cooking.

This passage argues that there is a similarity between two rulings by R. Yose: cooking or baking in a method that is not fully effective, such as indirect heating or making dough rise with an apple, is not legally significant, and therefore it neither counts as a transgression of the Sabbath law nor transfers the priest's-share status. Moscovitz writes that since "there is obviously no necessary or even probable logical connection between the different rulings associated here... the Talmud's claim... seems to reflect surface similarity rather than a bona-fide shared principle," a claim which he sees as motivated by "the natural tendency to associate like with like."[15]

Even under this interpretation, the pervasive use of *ke-daʿateh* fits well within the process posited by this part of the book. This new Amoraic interpretive practice highlights or produces connections between disparate teachings attributed to the same individual. If we accept Moscovitz's distinction between "conceptual" and more "superficial" connections, the significance of these patterns varies: in some cases, they reveal the principles or concepts underlying the sages' rulings;[16] at other times, they may simply point to similarity. The phrase shows us a practice of reading rabbinic teachings that is oriented around the identity of the sage

---

[13] Though without *ke-daʿateh*.
[14] At least under the Talmud's interpretation, R. Yose permits in both cases; Goldberg, *Shabbat*, 63.
[15] Moscovitz, *Talmudic Reasoning*, 284; idem, "Ameru Davar Eḥad," 131–3.
[16] See similarly the analysis by Rubenstein, "Talmudic Expression" of the similar Bavli phrase, ר׳ פלוני לטעמיה דאמר. See also n. 30 below.

to whom they are attributed. But there is a possibility that the phrase tells us even more about how Amoraic scholars construed rabbinic teachings.

I suggest that *ke-da'ateh* claims draw on the meaning of *de'ah* explored above to argue that the teaching in question reflects the sage's individual inclination or perspective: "Rabbi so-and-so said this teaching according to his *de'ah*." Since *de'ah* refers to a variety of personal inclinations, the phrase may point to patterns that some may judge "flimsy" alongside conceptual patterns, and in any event it seems that Amoraic scholars did not make such distinctions. Like all phrases in the Talmud, *ke-da'ateh* may be used with considerable diversity; and *ke-da'ateh* claims have simultaneous functions, such as solving difficulties or answering questions. But the formulation of the phrase as well as pervasive patterns in the way it is deployed suggest that its specific and unique function is to mark a teaching as reflecting the sage's individual inclination.[17]

Under this interpretation, the purpose of citing the second teaching is not to associate the two teachings, but to demonstrate the claim that the first teaching is grounded in the sage's perspective by showing that there is a pattern in his teachings. Amoraic scholars were certainly interested in association and conceptualization in general: this is apparent in connections made throughout the Yerushalmi between teachings attributed to different sages or anonymous teachings, using general association terms. But in the case of *ke-da'ateh* claims, association and conceptualization are the instruments through which the claim is demonstrated rather than the purpose of the claim.

The difference between these interpretations of *ke-da'ateh* can be illustrated in the way the phrase is translated. Baruch Bokser, in his translation of Yerushalmi *Pesaḥim*—the best English translation of any tractate of the Talmud—renders the phrase, "R. so-and-so is in accord with his view [elsewhere]."[18] The "elsewhere" in this translation must be supplied because the "view" is necessarily the view that is expressed elsewhere; the point of the claim, under this interpretation, is that the two teachings are consistent. Under the interpretation I propose, "elsewhere" is not necessary. The "opinion" is the opinion expressed in both teachings. The point of the claim is that the first teaching expresses the sage's individual inclination, and the second teaching is adduced to demonstrate this claim.

A comparison with the identifications examined in the previous chapter illustrates this instrumental function of association in *ke-da'ateh* claims. The primary function of identifications, we have seen, is to name the sage behind an anonymous teaching; while such identifications regularly refer to another teaching by the same sage, the purpose of the reference is to demonstrate or illustrate the pattern that

---

[17] Other phrases involving *de'ah* do not mark the teaching as *de'ah*, so their use of the term might not be as strong or precise; for example, in the phrase *'al da'ateh* the emphasis is not on the teaching discussed but on deriving from it another ruling. Furthermore, particular features of *ke-da'ateh* that support my interpretation here are absent with the other phrases. One feature discussed below, for example, is that *ke-da'ateh* does not apply to citations; but *'al da'ateh* does (see e.g. *Ter.* 4:11 43b, *Shab.* 1:1 2b, and *Qid.* 4:6 65d).

[18] Bokser and Schiffman, *Yerushalmi Pesaḥim*, 90.

allows us to identify the anonymous teaching. This is also the case with *ke-da'ateh*. Consider the similarity between the following passages:

Pesaḥim 1:7 28a	*'Orlah* 2:1 61d
אמ' ר' אבין: ר' מאיר כדעתיה. דר' מאיר מחמיר בדבריהם כדברי תורה. אן אשכחן דר' מאיר מחמיר בדבריהן כדברי תורה? אמ' ר' חיננה: כיי דתנינן תמן, "הרואה כתם הרי זו מקולקלת וחוששת משום זוב. דברי ר' מאיר. וחכמ' אומרי'. אין בכתמים משום זוב".	מאן תנא "תרומת מעשר שלדמאי"? ר' מאיר. דר' מאיר מחמיר בדבריהן כדברי תורה. אן [19] אשכחן דר' מאיר מחמיר בדבריהן כדברי תורה? אמ' ר' חנינה: ההיא דתנינן תמן, "הרואה כתם הרי זו מקולקלת וחוששת משום זוב. דברי ר' מאיר. וחכמ' אומ'. אין בכתמין משום זוב".
[In *m. Pes.* 1:7, R. Meir says that we derive from testimonies by Hananiah, the prefect of the priests, and R. Aqiva that on the eve of Passover, one may burn pure leavened priest's-share food with impure one; because the leavened priest's-share food is about to become prohibited, it no longer requires protection from impurity.]	[*m. 'Or.* 2:1 mentions the priest's share of the tithe of doubtful produce, which is only rabbinically mandated, among sanctified foods which require a hundred measures of non-sanctified food to become permissible to non-priests].
Said R. Abbin: "**R. Meir [said this] according to his opinion.** For R. Meir is as strict about their [i.e. the sages'] words as [he is about] the words of the Torah."	Who recited that "the priest's share of the tithe of doubtful produce"? R. Meir. For R. Meir is as strict about their [i.e. the sages'] words as [he is about] the words of the Torah.
Where do we find that R. Meir is as strict about their words as [he is about] the words of the Torah?	And where do we find that R. Meir is as strict about their words as [he is about] the words of the Torah?
Said R. Hanina: As that which we recite there [*m. Nid.* 6:13]: "If she saw a stain, she is in disorder [with respect to calculating the onset of her menstruation period as well as the eleven intermediate days], and she must be concerned about discharge—the words of R. Meir. And the sages say, spots are not [reason for concern] regarding a discharge."	Said R. Hanina: That which we recite there [*m. Nid.* 6:13]: "If she saw a stain, she is in disorder [with respect to calculating the onset of her menstruation period as well as the eleven intermediate days], and she must be concerned about discharge—the words of R. Meir. And the sages say, spots are not [reason for concern] regarding a discharge."

Without going into the details of these passages or the way they relate to each other, we can observe that they have a similar structure. In *'Orlah*, an anonymous teaching is identified as R. Meir's, because it rules as strictly in rabbinic law as it does with scriptural law, an approach known to be held by R. Meir. In *Pesaḥim*, a teaching by R. Meir is said to represent R. Meir's perspective because it displays the same equivalence. The question of how we know that this approach is characteristic of R. Meir is raised and answered with a reference to *m. Niddah* 6:13. The comparison between the two passages allows us to see the function of this reference. Much like

---

[19] Correcting "הא," with the parallel in *Pes.*

the purpose of the passage in *'Orlah* is to identify the anonymous teaching, the purpose of R. Abbin's statement in *Pesaḥim* is to argue that R. Meir's statement is grounded in R. Meir's personal perspective. In both cases, the reference to the additional teaching supports the argument rather than constitutes it.

3. The distinctiveness and scope of *ke-da'ateh*

The very fact that the Talmud employs a specific phrase for the association of teachings attributed to the same sage supports the suggestion that this phrase does more than just association. The Talmud could have used, in these cases, the same terminology it applies for other associations. There is one instance where the most common association phrase, "it goes as (*atya ke-*)," associates two teachings from the same sage. There is nothing less economical or awkward about that instance, and it only stands out because the fact that the two teachings are attributed to the same sage makes us expect that *ke-da'ateh* will be used.[20] The noun *de'ah* is never used in the Yerushalmi to associate statements attributed to different sages. While such associations usually do not employ a noun at all (e.g. "and [the statement] of R. Simeon goes as [the statement of] R. Eleazar"),[21] when they do so it is not *de'ah* but *shita*, the scholar's "line" of ruling, to which the next chapter is dedicated. This is the case with the phrase "they went down in the line of R. so-and-so," which connects Tannaitic positions attributed to different sages,[22] as well as comments that a sage is teaching something similar to his father or teacher.[23] The Yerushalmi uses *shita* to connect positively the teachings of a single sage only very rarely, and only alongside another association of teachings by different sages.[24]

Another feature of *ke-da'ateh* comments which conforms with the suggestion that they make a claim about the nature of the teaching is that the Talmud never says that a sage is stating something "according to his opinion" when that sage is quoting another sage.[25] When *ke-da'ateh* claims comment on cited teachings, they

---

[20] See *Pes.* 8:8 36b: "ר׳ יוחנן אמ׳. משלחין אותו לדרך רחוקה. ואתיא כיי דמר ר׳ יוחנן ניטמא בטומאת בית פרס משלחין אותו דרך רחוקה." See also Moscovitz, *Terminology*, 108, n. 584, for cases where *atya* connects disputes between the same pair of sages.

[21] אתייא דר׳ שמעון כר׳ אלעזר. *Git.*1:5 43d (par. *Git.* 2:2 44b), and many other places.

[22] Moscovitz, *Terminology*, 247–9; see the discussion in the previous chapter, Section 4.

[23] See e.g. *Yoma* 2:1 39c ("his father"), *Ket.* 3:6 27d ("his teacher").

[24] See *Shevi.* 2:10 34b, *Dem.* 4:6 24c, *Pes.* 9:6 37a, and *Qid.* 1:6 60d.

[25] While there are no exceptions to this rule, there are two cases which complicate it. In *Pe'ah* 1:1 15b and *Meg.* 2:1 73a, *ke-da'ateh* applies to recited teachings attributed to R. Hoshaya and Samuel respectively. While these are not instances of sages quoting other sages, they might seem at first as instances of sages relying on traditional sources. But there is evidence throughout the Yerushalmi that recited teachings attributed to Amoraic scholars were sometimes seen just like other types of statements attributed to these scholars. See Albeck, *Studies*, 23–4, who discusses the passage from *Meg.*, and the discussion above in the Introduction, near notes 55–6.

are directed at the cited sage rather than the citing sage. This property is consistent with the contrast we have seen above. Much like the anecdote about R. Zeira distinguishes between opinion (*de'ah*) and tradition (*shemu'a*), the many occurrences of *ke-da'ateh* draw on the same contrast to mark statements that are not grounded in tradition as *de'ah*.

On the other side of the phrase, i.e. the teachings that come after *ke-da'ateh*, we do find a few examples where the sage quotes another sage.[26] These, however, are not the teachings to which the *ke-da'ateh* claims apply, the teachings marked as *de'ah*, but rather the teachings which demonstrate *ke-da'ateh* claims. The same association of *ke-da'ateh* with the contrast between opinion and tradition applies here too if we understand it to argue that the scholar indeed had a tradition regarding that *other* case, the subject of the second teaching, and that allowed him to rule in the teaching marked as *de'ah* without having a specific tradition on the case it addresses.[27]

The Yerushalmi employs a special phrase for connecting teachings by the same sage where it could have used generic association terminology. The phrase is never used to associate teachings by two different sages, and phrases that are used for association between different sages are never used to connect teachings from the same sage. The phrase employs the word *de'ah*, which, as we have seen, connotes an individual's disposition or inclination. *Ke-da'ateh* claims are never applied to a sage who transmits another sage's teaching, but only to a teaching that is traced to that sage himself. All these considerations suggest that the phrase was used not only to associate teachings. When Amoraic scholars saw patterns in the teaching of a given sage, they used these patterns to make a claim about the nature of the teaching: that it represents the sage's *de'ah* or personal inclination.

4. Demonstrating personal inclination

The passages in which this function of *ke-da'ateh* is most strikingly evident are passages where it connects a teaching not with another teaching by the same sage, but with a biographical detail about that sage. The following passage makes two such claims with respect to two sages and their places of residence:

---

[26] The number of these instances depends on whether we count recited teachings attributed to Amoraic scholars (see previous note). There are six instances of Amoraic scholars quoting other Amoraic scholars (*Kil.* 1:9 27b, *Kil.* 5:7 30a—with partial parallels at *Ter.* 7:7 45a and *'Or.* 1:1 60d, *Ḥal.* 3:5 59c, *Shab.* 1:4 3c, *'Er.* 2:1 20a, *Ned.* 4:3 38c) and three instances of Amoraic scholars quoting recited teachings, the first of which is attributed by the Amoraic R. Jonah to the Tannaitic R. Simeon, and the rest are anonymous (*Ḥal.* 2:2 58c, *Pes.* 5:7 32c, *Ned.* 2:1 37b).

[27] But see possible exceptions at *Kil.* 1:9 27b and *Ḥal.* 3:5 59c.

Shabbat 14:3 14c

רב ור׳ חייה רבה תריהון אמרין: תשעים ותשעה מתים בעין ואחד בידי שמים.[28] ר׳ חנינה ושמואל תריהון אמרין: תשעים ותשעה מתים בצינה ואחד בידי שמים. רב אמ׳ כדעתיה ור׳ חנינא אמ׳ כדעתיה. רב, על ידי דהוה שרי תמן, דעיינא בישא שכיחא תמן, הוה אמ׳ תשעים ותשעה מתים בעיינה ואחד בידי שמים. ר׳ חנינה, על דהוה שרי בצפרין, דצינתה תמן, הוה אמ׳ תשעים ותשעה מתים בצינה ואחד בידי שמים.

Rav and R. Hiyya the Great both say: Ninety-nine [people] die because of the [evil] eye and one dies at the hands of heaven. R. Hanina and Samuel both say: Ninety-nine [people] die because of the cold and one dies at the hands of heaven.

Rav said this[29] according to his opinion, and R. Hanina said this according to his opinion. Rav, because he was living there [= Babylonia], where the evil eye is common, said that ninety-nine [people] die because of the eye and one at the hands of heaven. R. Hanina, because he was living in Sepphoris, where it is cold, said that ninety-nine [people] die because of the cold and one dies at the hands of heaven.

The statements in this passage offer different positions on the question of the most common cause of death. The first pair of sages contends it is the evil eye; the second contends that it is the cold. An anonymous comment then tells us that Rav and R. Hanina each offered their teachings on this matter according to their opinion. But what follows this statement is not other teachings attributed to these scholars. Rather, the *ke-da'ateh* claim here provides the reason behind the difference in their opinion—they live in different locations. Rav believes the evil eye is the most common cause because the evil eye, apparently, is prevalent in Babylonia, where he lives; R. Hanina believes that it is the cold because Sepphoris, his town, is cold.

What exactly does this comment mean? It does not mean that Rav only meant to describe Babylonia whereas R. Hanina only meant to describe Sepphoris. The Talmud would have used a different formulation if that is what it wanted to say (e.g. "this one in Babylonia and that one in Sepphoris"). Nor is this passage saying that living in these places *necessarily* leads to these particular opinions—Rav and Samuel both lived in Babylonia, and yet they disagree on this matter here. Rather, the passage is saying that these two statements reflect the subjective perspective of the individuals to whom they are attributed, shaped by the place in which they live.

---

[28] MS Leiden presents here two more opinions, which the first corrector believed should be presented after the *ke-da'ateh* comment. This seems right (both the first unit and the *ke-da'ateh* comment end with the same words), but either way this issue does not affect the interpretation of the passage I offer here.

[29] See above, n. 10.

We find a similar claim in a decidedly Halakhic context:

Pesaḥim 10:1 37c (par. *Sheqalim* 3:2 47c, *Shabbat* 8:1 11a)

מהו לצאת ביין מבושל? ר' יונה אמ': יוצאין ביין מבושל. ר' יונה כדעתיה.[30] דר' יונה שתי ארבעתי כסוי דלילי פסחא וחזיק רישיה עד עצרתא.[31]

> What is [the law] on discharging [the four cup drinking requirement on Passover] with cooked wine? R. Jonah said, "One discharges with cooked wine." R. Jonah [said this] according to his opinion. For R. Jonah drank the four cups of Passover night and had his head wrapped until Pentecost.

R. Jonah states that one may fulfill the obligation to drink four cups of wine on Passover night with cooked wine, which is less intoxicating. An anonymous comment tells us that R. Jonah offers this ruling according to his opinion, but here too this comment does not introduce a teaching by the same scholar. Rather, it introduces a story about how R. Jonah once drank the four cups and became so intoxicated he had to have his head wrapped for seven weeks. The story does not illustrate how R. Jonah followed his own ruling. It is cited, rather, to suggest that the sage's low alcohol tolerance is the reason he ruled that one may fulfill the obligation with weaker wine. This claim, again, argues that rabbinic statements reflect individual attributes—here the physical constitution—of their utterers.

The final example in this series comes from a discussion on infant epistemology:

Ketubbot 5:5 30a

נתגרשה אין כופין אותה. במה דברים אמורים? בזמן שאינו מכירה. אבל אם היה מכיר אותה כופין אותה ונותנין לה שכרה שתניק את בנה. כמה יהא לו ויהא מכירה? ר' ירמיה בשם רב: שלשה חדשים. והוה ר' זעירא מסתכל ביה. אמ' ליה: מה את מסתכל בי? נימר לך מן ההיא דשמואל, דאמ' שמואל, "ג' ימים". שמואל כדעתיה. שמואל אמ': חכים אנא לחייתא דילדין לי. ר' יהושע בן לוי אמ': חכים אנא לגזורה דגזרין לי. ר' יוחנן אמ': חכים אנא לנשייא דצבתין עם אימא.

> [The Mishnah lists nursing a child as one of the labors a woman is obligated to perform for her husband. The Talmud discusses what happens in case of divorce:]
>
> If she was divorced, she is not forced [to nurse]. In what cases does this statement apply? When he [the child] does not recognize her. But if he recognized her, she is forced and given wages to nurse her son.
>
> At what age does he begin to recognize her? R. Jeremiah [said] in the name of Rav: Three months. And R. Ze'ira was staring at him. He said to him: Why are you staring at me? I'll tell you from that teaching of Samuel, as Samuel said, "Three days."

---

[30] The parallel in *Sheq.* has "according to his reason (לטעמיה)," a Bavli term (Assis, "Sheqalim," 148 n. 34), as typical in *Sheqalim*.

[31] The parallel in *Sheq.* reads "until Sukkot (עד חגא)," but this is because the scribe there skipped to the end of the next story, about R. Judah. Some medieval authorities may have had before them the seemingly Babylonian formulation (cf. *b. Pes.* 42b), "from Passover until Pentecost (מן דבחא עד עצרתא)" (e.g. *Sefer Ra'avyah* 2.514).

Samuel [said this] according to his opinion, [for] Samuel said: I know the midwife who delivered me. R. Joshua b. Levi said: I know the circumciser who circumcised me. R. Yohanan said: I know the women who were together with my mother.

The passage presents the ruling that after divorce, the mother is no longer obligated to nurse her child; in case the infant recognizes her—*t. Niddah* 5:2 spells out the concern that the child may refuse to be nursed by others and therefore may be in danger—she is compelled by the court to nurse, but she is also paid for nursing since she is no longer bound by her marital duties. The question is from what age can we consider the child to have the capacity for that recognition. R. Jeremiah cites Rav's ruling that the age is three months. R. Ze'ira finds that ruling astonishing and stares at R. Jeremiah. The latter responds to the stare with another teaching, this time by Samuel, which sets the age of recognition at three days. An anonymous *ke-da'ateh* comment follows, introducing a statement by Samuel that he remembers his midwife from birth. We also hear statements from other Amoraic scholars who remember figures from the very beginning of their lives.[32] Here, *ke-da'ateh* introduces an autobiographical comment, and here too, the Talmud is suggesting that a ruling is grounded in personal experience. Samuel concluded, based on his memory of the midwife who helped deliver him, that infants can remember and recognize persons in those early days of their lives.

These three examples are exceptional: normally, Amoraic scholars were interested in individual patterns as they related to a sage's teachings, not their location, body, or early childhood memories. Still, these examples confirm and highlight broadly attested features of *ke-da'ateh* which we have already discussed, in that they emphasize the individual inclination apparent in rabbinic teachings.

We can say something similar about a more pervasive pattern among the teachings used to support *ke-da'ateh* claims. Moscovitz has observed that associations in the Yerushalmi often have an explanatory function. In his treatment of the phrase "they said the same thing (*ameru davar ehad*)," he notes a distinct kind of interpretive association, in which "casuistic" teachings (i.e. specific case-based rulings) are associated with statements of principle or teachings which are explicit about their legal reasoning. Such associations use teachings in which the principles or reasoning supporting the law are explicit in order to illuminate teachings where they are not. Moscovitz notes that with respect to that phrase, this phenomenon is the exception.[33]

---

[32] In this as well as the previous passage, about R. Jonah, *ke-da'ateh* also serves a redactional function that connects a Halakhic discussion to a set of narrative sources.

[33] Moscovitz, "Ameru Davar Ehad," 132, 103 n. 5; at 109 n. 27, he offers four cases in which rulings are associated with principles through the phrase "they said the same thing" (which itself appears in over thirty unique passages).

This kind of association is more common among *ke-daʿateh* claims. Moreover, it follows a particular pattern that divides the two sides of the phrase, the teaching on which the claim is made ("side A") and the teaching which supports the claim ("side B"). In a large number of cases, we find, on side A, specific laws or rulings, whereas on side B we find general statements, broad principles, laws with explanation clauses (that are therefore generative), non-legal general viewpoints, and scriptural exegesis. This pattern can be observed clearly in twenty-six instances of *ke-daʿateh*, and more ambiguously in others.[34] There are only two cases where the pattern is reversed.[35]

This pattern can be understood in light of the broader phenomenon of explanatory associations in the Yerushalmi. But in light of the interpretation suggested above of the phrase's function, this pattern may have a more specific significance when it appears with *ke-daʿateh*. The implication of the juxtaposition between a specific teaching and a broad principle, when it is used with the word *deʿah*—which indicates, as we have seen, personal inclination and non-traditionality—is that the sage based his specific ruling cited on side A on the broad principle, perspective or reason cited on side B. When such associations connect teachings by different sages, the implication may be that these are parallel teachings, that each sage adopted the same principle or reasoning, one explicitly and one implicitly. When such associations connect teachings by the same sage, using the term *deʿah*, they imply a genealogical or causal connection between the two. Let me offer some examples:

Side A	Side B
1–2. *Berakhot* 1:2 3b (specific ruling vs. non-Halakhic broad statements)	
R. Yohanan [said] in the name of R. Simeon b. Yohai: Those like us who are occupied with the study of Torah do not break off even for the recitation of the Shema.	R. Yohanan [said this] according to his opinion, for R. Yohanan said: Oh that we might [be able] to pray all the day long! Why? Prayer never loses its value. R. Simeon b. Yohai [said this] according to his opinion, for R. Simeon b. Yohai said: Had I been at Mount Sinai when the Torah was given to Israel, I would have asked God to give man two mouths, one to toil in Torah, and one to use for all his other needs.
R. Yohanan said about himself: Those like us who are not occupied with the study of Torah [as much must] break off [our activities, including our study] even for the [Amidah] prayer.	

---

[34] In addition to the twelve instances appearing in the table below, I count *Ber.* 1:2 3b (the third instance); *Dem.* 2:1 22d, *Dem.* 6:6 25c, *Ḥal.* 2:2 58c (the second instance), *Pes.* 1:1 27a, *Pes.* 5:4 32c, *Suk.* 1:4 52b, *M. Q.* 3:1 81c, *Naz.* 4:3 53b, *Git.* 8:9 49c–d (both instances), *Shevuʿot* 3:4 34c (both instances), and *Nid.* 3:2 50d. More ambiguous cases include e.g. *Ḥal* 4:9 60b, *ʿEr.* 1:1 18d, *Pes.* 5:7 32c, and *ʿA. Z.* 4:4 44a.

[35] *Ter.* 5:2 43c (R. Eliezer offers his reasoning in *m. Ter.* 5:2 which is on side A) and *ʿEr.* 2:1 20a (the ruling on side A has the explanation clause—"that an *ʿeruv* does not make them one," which the Talmud construes as the reason behind the teaching on side B).

3. *Pe'ah* 1:1 15b (specific statement vs. general statement)

For R. Yohanan said: The [required *minima* of] one *maah* of silver [for the festal offering] and two *maah* of silver [for the pilgrimage offering] are words of the Torah.	R. Yohanan [said this] according to his opinion. For R. Yohanan said: All [required] amounts are tradition given to Moses at Sinai.

4. *Kil'ayim* 4:7 29c (specific law vs. broad principle)

[The teaching, not cited by the Yerushalmi, is presumably *m. Kil.* 2:7: "If his field was of wheat and his fellow's field was of wheat, he is permitted to place alongside it a single furrow of flax, but not a furrow of another kind. R. Simeon says, It is the same with respect to flax as all other kinds."]³⁶	R. Samuel [said] in the name of R. Ze'ira: R. Simeon [said this] according to his opinion, for R. Simeon said: "One cannot render prohibited that which is not his" (*m. Kil.* 7:4).

5. *Hallah* 2:2 58c (law vs. law with explanation)

Dirt from outside the land that was brought on a boat to the land is liable for tithing and sabbatical year obligations. Said R. Judah: In what cases? When the boat touches the land.	R. Judah [said this] according to his opinion. For "R. Judah exempts in the case of water, because it is not substantial" (*m. Beẓ* 5:4).

6. *'Orlah* 1:1 60c (specific law vs. definition relating to the natural world)

[The Mishnah exempts from *'Orlah* requirements trees that were planted for purposes other than food consumption.] It was recited in the name of R. Meir: All kinds of trees can come under an intention that would render them exempt [i.e. all can be planted with an intention other than food consumption], except the olive tree and the fig tree.	R. Meir [said this] according to his opinion. For he said, "All trees are [considered] barren except the olive tree and the fig tree." [This is a close paraphrase of R. Meir's words in *m. Kil.* 6:5.]

7. *Bikkurim* 1:5 64a (specific law vs. broader position)

A man may bring first-born offerings from the property of his wife and recite [the offering declaration]. R. Simeon b. Laqish said, "After [her] death," so not if [she was] alive.	R. Simeon b. Laqish [said this] according to his opinion. For. R. Simeon b. Laqish said, "A man does not inherit his wife according to the Torah."

---

³⁶ This reconstruction is based in part on the content and in part on the parallel at *Kil.* 2:7 27d, where the statement does not have *ke-da'ateh* but rather the identification term *de-rabbi hi*. If the statement is meant to explain R. Simeon's opinion at *m. Kil.* 2:7, then *ke-da'ateh*, which does appear in *Kil.* 4:7 29c, seems more likely, since the Mishnah names R. Simeon.

8. *Pesaḥim* 1:6 27d (ostensible testimony vs. scriptural exegesis)

R. Aqiva added to this and said: In the days of the priests, they did not refrain from burning oil made invalid by one who immersed on that day in a lamp that has been made unclean by corpse uncleanness, even though they were [thus] increasing its impurity (*m. Pes.* 1:6).

Said R. Mana in the presence of R. Yose: R. Aqiva [said this] according to his opinion. For R. Aqiva said, "'*ytm*' (Lev 11:13)—it shall render [other things] unclean, by scriptural law."

[This is a reference to R. Aqiva's scriptural proof, in *m. Sot.* 5:2, that food that became impure in the second degree can also impart impurity to other food].

9. *Mo'ed Qattan* 3:5 82b (specific law vs. broad, possibly non-Halakhic,[37] statement)

[On the prohibition for a mourner to work:]
If he has nothing to eat, on the first day and the second [day of mourning], he does not work, but on the third, he may work discreetly [...]. Bar Qappara said: Even on the third he may not work at all.

Bar Qappara [said this] according to his opinion. For Bar Qappara said: The height of mourning is [the first] three days.

10–11. *Ketubbot* 9:2 33a (ruling on a specific case vs. broad jurisprudential principle)

[The Mishnah discusses a deceased who was survived by wife, heirs, and a creditor, and who is also owed a deposit or a loan by someone else. R. Tarfon says that this deposit or loan should be returned to the most disadvantaged of the aforementioned interested parties. R. Aqiva disagrees.]

A relative of R. Samuel b. Abba was given [the deposit or loan] on account of the "disadvantaged" reason. R. Simeon b. Laqish brought the slaves of R. Judah the Patriarch and took it out of her possession [forcefully]. R. Yohanan was leaning on R. Simeon b. Abba. He told him, "What was done with that poor woman?" He said to him, R. Simeon b. Laqish brought the slaves of R. Judah the Patriarch and took it out of her possession." [R. Yohanan replied,] "Was this a good thing to do?!"

R. Yohanan [said this] according to his opinion, and R. Simeon b. Laqish [said this] according to his opinion. For they were disputed: Everyone agrees that if judges erred in judgment they do not revert [to how it was before their decision]. If they erred in words of Torah they do revert. What is the dispute? In an error of *mishnah*, where R. Yohanan said: An error of *mishnah* is an error of judgment; R. Simeon b. Laqish said, an error of *mishnah* is [an error in] the words of Torah.

---

[37] For the non-Halakhic sense, see the parallel in *Genesis Rabbah* 100:10, which does not employ *ke-da'ateh*.

12. *Nedarim* 2:1 37b (specific law vs. broad reasoning)

One who said to his wife, "*Qonam*, that I do not have sexual intercourse with you"—Rav said he is bound [by his vow] and Samuel said he is not bound.	Rav [said this] according to his opinion. For it was recited, by the House of Rav, in contradiction: What is the scriptural source for vows that are not binding by heaven, but people act with them as binding, so that you would not be vowing and nullifying? The teaching says, "He shall not break [*yaḥel*] his word" (Num 30:2)—he should not make his words profane [*ḥulin*; i.e. they made these vows bindings so people would not utter grave vows that have no effect; cf. *t. Ned.* 4:6].

Example 3 above implies that R. Yohanan's opinion on the origin of the minimum amounts of the festal and pilgrimage offerings is merely an application of his general opinion on minimum amounts; example 6 implies that R. Meir's ruling on the kind of trees that cannot be planted with an intention that exempts them from *'Orlah* laws stems from his general definition of what trees count as "barren." The possibility of causal explanation is even more striking when the associated statement is a value judgment or non-Halakhic principle. Examples 1–2 imply that the rulings by R. Simeon and R. Yohanan on a specific liturgical issue follow from their general valuing of Torah study and prayer respectively. Example 8 argues that R. Aqiva's account on the practice at the Temple is based on his scriptural exegesis. These passages interrogate how specific rulings may be grounded in the perspective, values, or reasoning of individual sages.

5. Attribution-based associations in the Tannaitic corpus

In comparison with the Talmud, Tannaitic compilations present very few associations between teachings in general, and still fewer associations between teachings by the same sage. We do find on occasion the identity of the sage as an organizing principle of a collection of teachings attributed to him. This is the case with much of the unusual Mishnaic tractate *'Eduyot*, which groups rulings by attribution: *m. 'Eduyot* 2:8, for example, transmits "three things which R. Aqiva said, and they [the sages] agreed on two [of them]," and the next two units continue to present teachings by R. Aqiva; *m. 'Eduyot* 3:10 presents "three things with which R. Gamaliel is as strict as the words of the House of Shammai." We find similar collections in other places.

While such collections do not necessarily point to a pattern in the sage's teachings, other Tannaitic associations do seem to point to such patterns. On five occasions, we find the generic association term *ka-yoẓe bo* ("similarly") connecting teachings like the Talmud's *ke-da'ateh* claims:[38]

m. Bava Batra 10:7

המלוה את חבירו על ידי ערב לא ייפרע מן הערב. אם אמ', "על מנת שאיפרע מימי שארצה,", יפרע מן הערב. רבן שמעון בן גמליא' אומ': אם יש נכסים ללווה. בין כך ובין כך לא יפרע מן הערב. כיוצא בו אמ' רבן שמעון בן גמליא': אף הערב לאשה בכתובתה והיה בעלה מגרשה. ידיר הנייה שמא יעשו קינונייא על נכסיו של זה ויחזיר את אשתו.

One who lends his fellow [and the loan terms include a guarantee] by a guarantor may not exact his payment from the guarantor. If he said, [upon making the arrangements, that the loan is] "on condition that I can exact payment from whomever I want," he may exact payment from the guarantor.

Rabban Simeon b. Gamaliel says: If the borrower has property, in neither case may he [the lender] exact payment from the guarantor.

And similarly, Rabban Simeon b. Gamaliel says: Even[39] [in the case of] a guarantor for a wife, for her marriage contract, whose husband was divorcing her, he [the guarantor] should prevent her by a vow from gaining benefit [from his property], lest they [the husband and the wife] conspire for his property, and [the husband] takes back his wife.

These associations are introduced through the same term which is used, much more often in Tannaitic texts, for other kinds of associations, between two different anonymous teachings or between two teachings attributed to different sages.[40] Unlike *ke-da'ateh* claims, then, these passages do not mark specifically a connection between teachings of the same individual or patterns which point to individual inclinations.

There are other ways in which associations of this sort are affected in Tannaitic literature. An editorial note in Mishnah *Sotah*, for example, draws our attention to a correlation between two teachings by the same sage:

---

[38] See, in addition to the example given above, *m. B. B.* 9:7, *m. Par.* 1:1, *Sifra, Nedava* 11:1 10d and Ḥova 2:5 20a.
[39] "Even" here seems to indicate some kind of literary seam.
[40] See e.g. *m. Shevi.* 10:8, *m. Shab.* 1:3, *m. Kel.* 5:5, *Sifre Numbers* §115, *t. Dem.* 2:22–4.

m. Sotah 2:2

היה מביא פיילי של חרס חדשה ונותן לתוכה חצי לוג מים מן הכיור. ר׳ יהודה או׳: רביעית. כשם שהוא ממעט בכתב כך הוא ממעט במים.

He [the priest] would bring a new earthenware bowl and put in it a half-*log* of water from the laver. R. Judah says: A quarter-*log*. Just as he reduces with respect to writing, he reduces with respect to water.

The passage discusses the preparation for the ordeal of the bitter water. R. Judah stipulates half the amount of water of the anonymous opinion. In the next unit in the Mishnah, which stipulates what the priest should write in the scroll that is then erased with the water, R. Judah mandates a text that is shorter than the one required according to the anonymous opinion. The Mishnah notes the correlation between these two rulings—R. Judah's ruling that less writing is required is consistent with his ruling that less water is required to erase the writing. The Yerushalmi makes the same connection with a *ke-da'ateh* claim (*Sotah* 2:2 18a). In another passage, we find the Mishnah connecting different teachings by the same sage in several realms of law (though note that it is possible that the last connection was made by the sage himself):

m. 'Eruvin 3:7–8

ר׳ יהודה או׳: ראש השנה שהיה ירא שמא תתעבר אדם מערב שני עירובים ואו׳, "עירובי הראשון למזרח והשיני למערב", "הראשון למערב והשיני למזרח", "עירובי הראשון והשיני כבני עירי", "עירובי השיני והראשון כבני עירי". ולא הודו לו חכמ׳. ועוד אמ׳ ר׳ יהודה: מתנה אדם על הכלכלה ביום טוב הראשון ואוכלה בשיני. וכן ביצה שנולדה ביום טוב הראשון תאכל בשיני. ולא הודו לו חכמ׳.

R. Judah says: If one worried during the New Year holiday that it might be intercalated, one may prepare two *'eruvim* and say, "My *'eruv* for the first day is towards the east, and for the second, towards the west"; [or] "for the first day is towards the west, and the second, towards the east"; [or] "my *'eruv* [is for] the first, but for the second [I shall be] as the [other] residents of my town"; [or] "my *'eruv* [is for] the second, but for the first [I shall be] as the [other] residents of my town." But the sages did not agree with him.

And R. Judah further said: A person may make conditions regarding a basket [of untithed produce] on a first holiday and eat it on the second. And so an egg that was laid on the first holiday may be eaten on the second. But the sages did not agree with him.

While these examples are not exhaustive, they are representative: Tannaitic associations of teachings by the same sage are infrequent, they employ general associative terminology, and they are of limited scope. Furthermore: unlike *ke-da'ateh* claims, they do not play a central role in the discussion: they are not contested, they are not used to resolve or make objections, and no consequences are derived from them.

It is not that the idea that sages have positions which are consistent across cases is itself not central to the Tannaitic compilations; rather, this idea is used differently, in passages which do different work than our *ke-da'ateh* passages, and which therefore have different aim and significance. A common formal pattern that engages this idea in Tannaitic compilations is the consistent dispute: we find a number of passages which present one or more sages as expressing a consistent position (that is not necessarily formulated through a principle) through a number of rulings across cases with different details (see e.g. *m. Terumot* 8, *m. Shabbat* 10:5–6, *m. Yevamot* 15:6–7, *m. Karetot* 5:4–8). In some of these passages, we also find the statement that a certain sage concedes to or agrees with another sage on a particular case.[41] Such statements come to dispel our expectation that the first sage would disagree with the second sage about this case, an expectation that is premised on the notion that the sages' positions are consistent and apply to a broad set of cases.

A good example is the series of disputes between R. Joshua, on one side, and Rabban Gamaliel and R. Eliezer, on the other, in Mishnah *Ketubbot*. The disputes concern claims regarding the personal status of a woman which may determine her marriage settlement; R. Eliezer and Rabban Gamaliel consistently rule that a woman should be believed about her own personal status, whereas R. Joshua consistently requires that women bring further evidence to support their claims or else accept lesser settlements. Here are the first two of these cases:

m. Ketubbot 1:6–7

והנושא את האשה ולא מצא לה בתולים, היא אומרת, "משארסתני נאנסתי. נסתחפה שדך", והוא אומ', "לא כי אלא עד שלא אירסתיך והיה מקחי מקח טעות". רבן גמליא' ור' אליעזר אומ': נאמנת. ור' יהושע או': אינה נאמנת ולא מפיה אנו חיים. אלא הרי זו בחזקת בעולה עד שלא תתארס. הטעתו. עד שתביא ראייה לדבריה.

היא אומרת, "מוכת עץ אני". והוא אומ' "לא כי אלא דרוסת איש את". רבן גמליא' ור' אליעז' אומ' נאמנת. ור' יהושע אומ': לא מפיה אנו חיים. אלא הרי זו בחזקת דרוסת איש עד שתביא ראייה לדבריה.

And one who marries a woman and did not find virginity signs—she says, "After you betrothed me, I was raped. Your field has been flooded [after you have purchased it, and therefore you must pay for its original price]"; and he says, "No, it was before I betrothed you, and my purchase was a misinformed purchase." Rabban Gamaliel and R. Eliezer say she is believed. But R. Joshua says: She is

---

[41] There are about twenty-five cases in the Mishnah where individual sages "concede"; the phrase is much more common with the collective "the sages" or with the Houses of Hillel and Shammai. For examples with individual sages, see e.g. *m. Dem.* 3:6, *m. 'Er.* 4:5, *m. Ket.* 2:2, *m. B. B.* 9:2, *m. Men.* 2:1, *m. Nid.* 10:5.

not believed, and it is not from her mouth that we live. Rather, until she brings evidence for her words, she is presumed to have lost her virginity before she was betrothed, and to have misled him.

She says, "I have been injured by a piece of wood," and he says "No, you have been trodden by a man." Rabban Gamaliel and R. Eliezer say she is believed. But R. Joshua says, "It is not from her mouth that we live. Rather, until she brings evidence for her words, she is presumed to have been trodden by a man."

Later on, the Mishnah tells us about a case in which R. Joshua agrees with the other sages:

m. Ketubbot 2:2

מודה ר' יהושע באומר לחבירו. שדה זה של אביך היית ולקחתיה ממנו. נאמן. שהפה שאסר הוא הפה שהיתיר.

R. Joshua agrees in [the case] of one who says to his fellow: "This field used to be your father's, and I have bought it from him," that he is believed. For the mouth that prohibited it is the mouth which permitted it [—since the fellow only knew that the field was his family's at some point from the person who now possesses it, we must believe that person also when he says he has acquired it in a legitimate way].

By pointing out this limit to his approach, the Mishnah assumes that R. Joshua has such an approach; we also see that this approach is not confined to rulings on women and marriage settlements but applies also in laws of evidence relating to property. This connection between different legal realms appears already in the formulation of the very first case, with the woman equating her body to a field that was flooded after its sale, and the man equating his marriage to a misinformed purchase.

To appreciate how these Tannaitic passages differ from *ke-da'ateh* passages we can begin with the recognition that they do not merely record debates by the sages or collect their utterances: they are the result of literary composition, one which may be based on a historical teaching by the named sage but which expands and reformulates this teaching through different iterations and cases.[42] It follows that whoever is composing these teachings is not trying to discover or demonstrate that existing teachings result from a sage's inclination; consistency is the starting point, rather than the end point. The composition of passages in which the position of a sage is explored through different cases is grounded in the idea that this position reflects a consistent principle that can be applied to a number of cases. While in *ke-da'ateh* claims, inclination is observed critically by an interpreter, here, consistency is inherent in the position itself. This difference is evident in the different

---

[42] On such expansions in general, see Albeck, *Untersuchungen*, e.g. 5–10.

forms of these passages: *ke-daʿateh* claims are formulated as interpretations of the sages' words; here, consistent rulings are presented as the words of the sages themselves. The goal of such passages is to show how the position in question results in similar or different rulings when it is met with different cases—just as the Mishnah does with unattributed teachings, exploring the nature of the law by examining it through cases with different details.[43] They present a conceptual analysis of the position rather than make a claim about its source: consistent rulings may stem from the sage's opinion, but they may also reflect a faithful application of tradition or represent the necessary logical unfolding of a principle. *Ke-daʿateh* claims, in contrast, argue that similar rulings stem from the sage's *deʿah*.

Conclusion

The Talmud regularly refers to the sages' teachings as representing their *deʿah*, a term which carries connotations of personal preference and inclination both within and beyond the range captured by the English word "opinion." The pervasive application of this term to rabbinic teachings in the Amoraic period was unprecedented and reflects the broader process in which these teachings came to be understood as the product of individual sages. This chapter centered on one of the prominent applications of this new sense of *deʿah*, the claims we find throughout the Talmud that a sage taught "*ke-daʿateh*," "according to his opinion," which normally connects two teachings attributed to the same sage. At the very least, the existence of distinct terminology for connecting teachings from the same individual as well as the frequency of such connections illustrate the significant role attributions played in Amoraic scholarship. But this chapter argued that *ke-daʿateh* attests to the Amoraic individuation of rabbinic teachings in an even stronger sense. It suggested that Amoraic scholars employed this phrase not only to associate teachings, but more specifically to argue that a teaching reflects the sage's personal inclination, his *deʿah*. Under this interpretation, the use of this phrase shows us that uncovering personal characteristics in the sages' teachings was one of the aims of Amoraic commentary. While *deʿah* is not a value-neutral word, and while it is possible that Tannaitic sages did not use it to describe their teachings because it seemed inappropriately belittling, *ke-daʿateh* claims are not intended as negative judgments on these teachings: they are never used to reject teachings and they are rarely themselves contested, which we would expect if they were critical in a negative sense. Instead, *ke-daʿateh* claims seem to have embraced and perhaps even celebrated the way that individual principles, ideas, preferences, and sometimes bodies manifested in the teachings of the sages.

---

[43] Alexander, *Transmitting Mishnah*, 117–73.

3

The Switched Line

Shita and Reading for Consistency

If the previous chapters examined types of commentary which observe or establish patterns among the teachings attributed to an individual sage, this chapter examines Talmudic discussions of cases in which such patterns seem to break down. I trace the development of the term *shita*, which Amoraic sages used to refer to these patterns, and argue that its literal meaning, "line" or "row," illuminates the original function of the term and perhaps also its historical context. The larger part of the chapter centers on passages in the Talmud which make the claim, or objection, that a sage is inconsistent, that his "line is switched." I show, by examining these objections and the discussions that follow, that rather than simply responding to inconsistency, these passages reflect an effort to find inconsistency that was predicated on, and reinforced, the notion that sages have distinctive individual profiles of teaching. I also explore how such discussions engaged concepts of composition and transmission. The final section explores Tannaitic precedents to the discourse examined in this chapter, while maintaining that a broad comparison of Tannaitic and Talmudic discussions shows us how consistency became individuated in Amoraic scholarship.

1. The term *shita*

In Modern Hebrew, the noun *shita* commonly means "method," "system," "theory," and the adjective "*shitati*" means "methodical" or "systematic" in the sense of consistent and coherent.[1] This sense of *shita* is derived from Amoraic scholarship. In Tannaitic literature, where the word *shita* appears rarely, it means a "line" or "row," either of hair (not in the sense of a single hair, but in a sense of a horizontal row of hairs on a balding head)[2] or the line of a written document on a page: "if one placed the [signatures of] the witnesses two full lines [*shitin*] after the [body of] writing, [the bill of divorce] is invalid."[3]

---

[1] Even-Shoshan, *Milon*, 1881.
[2] *m. Bek.* 7:2, *m. Neg.* 10:6–7.
[3] *t. Git.* 7:11 (par. *t. B. B.* 11:10).

In the Talmud, where the word appears hundreds of times, *shita* maintains this sense, but it also acquires a different sense—a sage's "line" of teaching, his approach to a particular matter.[4] The single most common use of *shita* in the Talmud is in the recurring phrase "the line (*shita*) of R. so-and-so is switched," which points out discrepancies between two teachings attributed to the same sage, his teachings being, as it were, in different, "switched" lines; later sections of this chapter examine this phrase closely. More broadly, *shita* is used to refer to the sage's position beyond teachings that are directly attributed to him. It is employed, as we have seen, to speak about teachings the sages formulated "following the line of R. so-and-so";[5] that two teachings by different sages follow the same "line," meaning their rulings are similar ("the teaching of R. so-and-so comes in the line of R. such-and-such")[6]—especially when one sage is the student or son of the other, and thus continues his "line"; that one sage adopted the premise of another sage merely to respond to his interlocutor on his own terms ("he responded to him in his line");[7] and, in a couple of instances, to differentiate between teachings that the sage himself uttered, on the one hand, and teachings that were derived "from" or "in" his line, on the other ("did you learn this explicitly from Rabbi Yohanan, or from his line?").[8]

This figurative use of "line" may seem straightforward. In Modern English, too, a "line of thought" refers to an individual's characteristic thinking, connecting several discrete thoughts; and to be "in line" with something is to be similar to or consistent with it. That is the case in Greek, too, where the verb στοιχέω means to line up, agree with something, be consistent, or even order in a system.[9] The image of the line suggests continuities or consistencies because it evokes a straight line or ordering something in a series which proceeds with predictability, much like letters on the page. It may be that this is all we need to know to understand why the Talmud uses *shita* to speak about connections and consistencies among sages' teachings. In the following, however, I suggest the term may evoke a more specific image.

---

[4] Kosman, "Shitta," 103, characterizes the term differently: "the term *shita* is used in the Talmud to show identity between the rulings of different sages (two or more) and putting them under one group." This characterization is based on the use of the term in the Bavli though Kosman projects to Palestine as well, and the equivalent phrases that Kosman adduces from the Yerushalmi do not employ the term *shita*. *Shita* is certainly used to compare teachings of different sages, but that comparison draws on the way the term constructs the consistent line of each individual sage. In the Yerushalmi, it is always the *shita* of a specific individual (or groups such as "the House of Hillel").

[5] See Chapter 1, n. 15.

[6] See the lists in Assis, *Concordance*, 196, 198–9.

[7] See the lists in Assis, *Concordance*, 225–6 and see below, n. 33.

[8] 'Or. 1:5 61a (cf. 'Or. 1:1 60d). See Chapter 8, Section 3.

[9] Liddell-Scott-Jones, *Greek-English Lexicon* (*TLG*); Lampe, *Patristic Greek Lexicon*, 1261.

There is a somewhat different sense of *shita* which is much less frequent, but which may point to the significance of the more common uses of the term. *Genesis Rabbah*[10] tells us that R. Hama b. Hinana offered six "lines" (*shitin*)[11] of interpretation to the verse at Genesis 29:2–3: "As he looked, he saw a well in the field and three flocks of sheep lying there beside it; for out of that well the flocks were watered. The stone on the well's mouth was large, and when all the flocks were gathered there, the shepherds would roll the stone from the mouth of the well, and water the sheep, and put the stone back in its place on the mouth of the well." The Midrash goes on to detail these six "lines," which respond to each element in the verse and thus create six different interpretations: the first interpretation reads in it a reference to the wandering of Israel in the desert, the second to the Temple festivals, the fourth to the history of empires, and so forth (see the table below). In contrast with more common figurative uses of *shita*, this and similar passages—included in the Talmud itself[12]—are not concerned with consistency and they accept that multiple "lines" may be taught by a single sage.

What *shita* invokes in these passages, I argue, is a tabular image in which information is placed in rows and divided into columns. The most common non-figurative use of *shita* in Amoraic literature is, after all, the lines on a page of a written document, which in antiquity were normally divided into columns. The figurative use of *shita* in these contexts derives from this sense of the word. The Midrashic technique in which different interpretations of the verse are all keyed to the verse's elements appears already in Tannaitic compilation (e.g. *Sifre Deuteronomy* §317). But using the term *shita* to introduce such interpretations projects a table in which we can visualize how these interpretations are keyed to the discrete parts of the biblical text; it allows us to compare the different *shitin*—the rows or lines—as well as appreciate the coherence of each line on its own. Consider this tabular representation of the passage from *Genesis Rabbah*:

---

[10] *Genesis Rabbah* 70:8.

[11] In almost all manuscripts, e.g. MS Vatican 30: ר׳ חמא ביר׳ חנינה פתר ביה שת שיטין; the British Museum manuscript adds in the margin another version: שיתא אפין, "six faces," i.e. six aspects or manners.

[12] See e.g. *Ber.* 9:1 13a, where R. Isaac develops a parable in six "lines," versions of a parable with parallel elements; *Leviticus Rabbah* 2:6; *Ecclesiastes Rabbah* 3:11:2. There are other instances where *shita* may be implied, e.g. *Genesis Rabbah* 20:5; but cf. *Genesis Rabbah* 44:4.

shita	A well in the field	And three flocks of sheep	Out of that well the flocks were watered	The stone on the well's mouth was large	And when all the flocks were gathered there,	The shepherds would roll the stone to water the sheep	And put the stone back
1: Desert wandering	The desert well	Moses, Aaron, and Miriam	From there each one drew water to his banner, tribe, and family	(Said R. Hanina: A sieve-full.)	In times of camping	From there each one drew water to his banner, tribe, and family	In times of journeying
2: Temple festivals	Zion (Jerusalem)	The three pilgrimage festivals	From there they draw the holy spirit	The celebration of the water-drawing house	From the entrance of Hammat to the brook of Egypt (1 Kings 8)	From there they draw the holy spirit	Left for the next festival
3: The court system	Zion (Jerusalem)	The three courts of law	From there they hear the judgment	The great court in the Chamber of Hewn Stone	Other courts in the Land of Israel	From there they hear the law	They give-and-take until there is a true judgment
4: Israel among empires	Zion (Jerusalem)	The three early empires	Which looted the Temple's *sancta*	Israel's ancestral merit	Rome, which recruits troops from all nations	Which looted the Temple's *sancta*	But in the future the ancestral merit shall prevail
5: The Sanhedrin	The Sanhedrin	The three rows of students sitting before them	From there they hear the law	The distinguished judge	Students in the Land of Israel	From there they hear the law	They give-and-take until the law is precisely known
6: Reading the Torah in the synagogue	Synagogue	The three readers of the Torah	From there they hear the Torah	The evil inclination	The public	From there they hear the Torah	When they leave, the evil inclination returns

In the early medieval Masoretic commentary tradition, which presents marginal comments focusing on lexical and orthographical issues on the Hebrew Bible, we find the term *shitata* referring to lists of unusual words presenting a certain pattern. Consider the following example:[13]

The comment on the right margin reads: "From the list [*shitata*] of [words] appearing once with *ve-lo* and in all [other] verses [with] *lo*," noting the irregularity of the way negation phrases appear in these verses. While the list does not represent a table, strictly speaking, it is arranged visually in a way that creates vertical parallels between the negation phrase, the sign for indicating that the usage is unique (ל), and the following words of the verse. Whereas in the Midrashic use, we are presented with several lines of interpretation, here, all lines present the same pattern. But in this case, too, we find *shita* relating to the organization and presentation of scholarly information in rows and columns.

My suggestion is that the pervasive use of *shita* in the Talmud, in the sense of the patterns emerging from the sage's teachings, is similarly linked with the commonplace meaning of the noun as a written line on the page. With respect to these patterns, too, *shita* might evoke a tabular image: the *shita* is the line or row in which the sage's teachings are listed, and the columns are the different cases, words being interpreted, and so forth. The table allows a comparison along two axes. It allows us to compare how different sages ruled on the same case or interpreted the same word; but it also allows us to compare the teachings of the same sages and see whether a consistent pattern emerges. This is why we find references to deriving a ruling from a sage's line—that is, by observing the patterns which emerge in his row of rulings; and it is also why when a sage seems to rule differently on two similar subjects—especially when we would expect such a ruling from one of his disputants—Amoraic scholars say his line or row is "switched." Shlomo Naeh suggested that a key component of rabbinic study culture was a visualization of textual data to aid its memorization and analysis. If the interpretation offered here of *shita* is correct, the organization of the sages' positions in imagined tables presents us with an amply documented practice of visualization.[14]

This tabular interpretation might explain a functional distinction between *shita* and the term *de'ah* studied in the previous chapter. The two most common phrases

---

[13] See the so-called Damascus Pentateuch, MS Jerusalem 24.5702, National Library of Israel, p. 378 (relating to Deut 4:2 on p. 379), for which see the image, from the Library's *Ketiv* website. An additional example is on p. 31 of that codex. These instances are cited in Sokoloff, *DJPA*, 547, and discussed by Shashar, "Jerusalem Manuscript," 308–9. On lists of the "collative Masorah" more generally, see Yeivin, *Tiberian Masorah*, 78–80.

[14] Naeh, "Omanut."

associated with these terms, *ke-da'ateh* and *mehalefa shitateh* respectively, are used for diametrically opposite functions: *ke-da'ateh* points to consistencies, whereas *mehalefa shitateh* indicates inconsistencies; there are several passages where the terms explicitly appear as opposite possibilities.[15] But this opposition raises the question: why could not *shita* and *de'ah* be used interchangeably? In other words, why not connote consistency with "*ke-shitateh*," "the sage is following his own line" (as indeed later rabbinic texts do), or inconsistency with something like "his opinion is switched," *mehalefa da'ateh*? The tabular understanding underscores the fact that *shita* is used almost exclusively in cases of *comparison* between two sages, whereas *de'ah* is normally used where the positions of a single sage are considered.[16] This is clearly the case when we talk about consistency and inconsistency: *ke-da'ateh* comments claim that two teachings reflect the same pattern or position; *mehalefa shitateh* comments object that the two teachings reflect different lines. But it is also the case where *shita* is used to show correlation between two sages.

This tabular interpretation also raises the possibility that the development and frequent use of the term *shita* might partake in broader trends of the scholarly culture of late ancient Palestine. Tables were rare in the Greco-Roman world, where they were used mostly for numerical data or showing equivalences between Latin and Greek.[17] For Eusebius and Origen, two Christian scholars working close in time and place to Amoraic scholars, tables became an important tool for correlating textual scholarly data. Origen's *Hexapla* was a massive enterprise, comparing the Hebrew text of the Bible to several Greek versions (and perhaps also the Samaritan text of the Pentateuch) in tabular form, with six columns representing each of the versions, and the rows used to juxtapose the way each of these versions renders a particular word.[18] Eusebius, greatly influenced by Origen in many ways, was even further involved in the making of tables. His *Chronicle* correlated Babylonian, Egyptian, Jewish, Greek, and Roman histories in tabular form; his *Psalm Lists* classified one hundred and fifty Psalms according to their authors, also appearing in the form of a table; and most important, his Gospel *Tables*, allowed for comparisons across the four gospels: the columns indicate the gospel authors, and the cells in each row contained a number which referred to Eusebius' numeration of gospel passages.[19]

---

[15] See *Ḥal.* 2:2 58c, *Ḥal.* 4:9 60b, *Yev.* 10:3 10d. See also *Ta'an.* 1:1 63a, where the Talmud points out that according to one source, one sage is consistent in two places whereas the other is inconsistent—*de'ah* is used to express the first idea, *shita* the second: "היא דעתיה דר׳ ליעזר קדמייתא היא דעתיה אחרייתא. מחלפא שיטתיה דר׳ יהושע."

[16] Even in those rare instances where *shita* is used to point out the sage's consistent teaching, it is in phrases which compare two other sages with each other: "[the teaching] of R. Huna goes in the line of R. Yohanan, and of R. Eleazar in his own line" (*Qid.* 1:6 60d, and similarly *Dem.* 4:6 24b and *Shevi.* 2:10 34b). The same principle may also explain why at *B. Q.* 3:3 3c the Yerushalmi has "R. Hoshaya recited according to his opinion [*ke-da'ateh*]" but at *Pes.* 9:6 37a we have "R. Eleazar's [teaching] goes in the line of R. [Judah the Patriarch] and Samuel recited according to his own line [*ke-shitateh*]" (accepting the emendation by Shapira, *NY*, with Epstein, *IMT*, 214). But here too the evidence is not fully consistent: we also find "R. Judah's goes in the line of R. Yose and R. Meir's according to his opinion" (*M. S.* 5:14 56d).

[17] Riggsby, *Mosaics of Knowledge*, 42–82.

[18] Grafton and Williams, *Christianity*, 86–132.

[19] Crawford, *The Eusebian Canon Tables*, 74–81; Grafton and Williams, *Christianity*, 133–232; and Coogan, *Eusebius*.

The imagined tables which, I have suggested, are behind the figurative uses of *shita*, differ from these Christian tables considerably. The most important difference is that the Christian tables were in fact drawn out and were bound with a particular materiality of written form, while the Talmudic tables were an evoked feature of a predominantly oral discourse, even if my interpretation is correct. At the same time, the term *shita* is certainly drawn from the world of writing. Furthermore, the main feature of materiality which scholars have emphasized with respect to Christian tables is that the codex, as opposed to the scroll, increased the opportunity for non-linear reading;[20] the material form of rabbinic teachings—oral recitations of discrete teachings—also allowed for such non-linear reading: claims such as *ke-da'ateh* and *meḥalefa shitateh* often compare teachings from distant parts of the Mishnah.

While there are many other differences in function and configuration, the variety of the Christian scholarly tables indicates that tabular scholarship was not limited to a specific configuration or even function of tables. The fact that tables became prominent in textual scholarship among Christians in late ancient Palestine in a way that, to our knowledge, was unprecedented in the Greco-Roman world, and that several of these tables involve comparing different versions or authors, point to the possibility that the term *shita* too was an instance—actualized or at least evoked—of the new scholarly use of tables in that place and time.[21] Regardless, however, of the significance and context of the particular use of line imagery, the development and extensive use of a term to signify the distinctive pattern which emerges from the teachings of an individual sage is part of the individuated hermeneutics explored in this part of the book.

2. The rise of inconsistency objections: the phrase *meḥalefa shitateh de-rabbi*

There are about a hundred and fifty unique instances in the Talmud of the phrase "*meḥalefa shitateh de-rabbi* ...," "the line of R. so-and-so is switched," contrasting two teachings and making the objection that they appear discrepant. There are several cases in which such objections are made about anonymous teachings or teachings attributed to "the sages," but in all but three of those cases,[22] they are

---

[20] Crawford, ibid., 75.
[21] For additional comparative reflections on the Talmud's *shita* and the Eusebian tables based on the interpretation of *shita* proposed here, see Coogan, "Tabular Thinking."
[22] See *Meg.* 1:9 72a, *Yev.* 6:4 7c, and *Sot.* 9:2 23c. We would have expected a more general objection term here, such as: "here you say this and there you say that?" (the parallel to the *Meg.* passage at *Hor.* 3:4 47c indeed employs that phrase instead). These passages seem connected: they all address an inconsistency in interpreting a biblical word in two contexts with respect to inclusion or exclusion. In two of these passages, the same solution is offered by the same sage using the same wording ("Said R. Ilay: each interpretation according to its matter"). The passage at *Sot.* may be derived from the passage at *Pe'ah* 6:2 19d (par. *B. Q.* 6:5 5c). Another example may be added if we accept Lieberman's emendation (YK, 177) of *Shab.* 12:5 13d; cf. Rabinovitz, *STEI*, 180.

accompanied with a *meḥalefa* objection that applies to the teaching of a named sage,[23] which allows the anonymous position to function as if it were attributed, "the sages" functioning, as a named group, like individuals. *Meḥalefa* objections are attributed to sages as early as R. Yohanan, though they are much more often presented anonymously.[24] They are not evenly distributed throughout the Talmud, though I have not found a meaningful pattern in their distribution.[25]

The familiarity of these objections to any student of the Talmud, and the fact that we moderns also associate the consistency of an individual approach with its validity, may obscure from us the distinct development that these objections present. It becomes visible when we consider that Tannaitic compilations very rarely present comments or arguments about individual inconsistency. At first, this difference may seem to relate to two more general differences between the Talmud and the Tannaitic compilations: the latter have much less argumentative and dialectical materials; and they engage less in conceptual comparison between different cases or realms of the law.[26] But the argumentative and dialectical sections we do find in Tannaitic compilations frequently criticize inconsistency in inferences between cases, even across realms of the law; in those cases, what is at stake is inconsistency with the principles of the law in general, not inconsistency within the sage's own teachings. Such passages object to inferences from one case to another, using phrases like "no, if you said in [case x], can you say it in [case y]," "let [this case] be inferred from [that case]," *minore ad maius* arguments, and so forth.[27] The last section of this chapter explores some specific Tannaitic precedents to the Amoraic interest in individual inconsistency but shows that they are few and different in character.

The Talmud clearly marks the possibility that the line is switched as a difficulty,[28] though there are a couple of instances which seem to posit that the line is "switched," but for justified reasons.[29] The objection is refuted in the large majority

---

[23] See Pe'ah 5:3 19a, Pe'ah 6:2 19d (par. B. Q. 6:5 5c), 'Or. 1:2 61a, Shab. 1:3 3b (par. Shab. 6:3 8b), Shab. 13:5 14a (par. Beẓ. 3:1 61d), 'Er. 10:15 26d, Beẓ. 4:7 62d, Sot. 1:5 17a (par. San. 6:3 23c).

[24] I counted twenty-three attributed objections.

[25] For example, the relatively long tractate *Ma'aser Sheni* has only one instance, and even that one may derive from a parallel in *Qiddushin*; in contrast, there are five instances in the short tractate of *Ḥallah*, and three such objections in a row in the first chapter of *'Orlah*. There is only one such instance in the three-part tractate *Neziqin*, which is otherwise known for its distinctive nature.

[26] Moscovitz, *Talmudic Reasoning*.

[27] Such comments are pervasive, but to give at least one example from each order of the Mishnah, see m. M. S. 3:10, m. Pes. 6:1–2, m. Yev. 8:3, m. 'Ed. 6:2, m. Kar. 3:10, and m. Yad. 4:3. In the Tannaitic Midrashim, inferences and criticism of inferences come up very frequently.

[28] Instances of "difficulty" language with *meḥalefa* claims: Sheq. 7:6 50d, Pes. 7:11 35a–b (par. San. 8:2 26a), Yev. 3:4 4d, Ned. 8:2 40d (par. Qid. 3:9 64b), Git. 7:4 48d. We also find *meḥalefa* objections commonly introduced with the term בעי ("ask" or "raise a difficulty") see e.g. 'Or. 1:2 60d, Shab. 7:2 10b, Yev. 12:2 12d. Sometimes, the response to the claim is introduced with *tipater*, "let it be solved," see Ḥal. 1:2 57c, 'Or. 1:2 61a (second instance), Shab. 1:1 2c, Shab. 1:3 3b (par. Shab. 6:3 8b).

[29] See Ḥal. 4:9 60b, where R. Yose responds to a *ke-da'ateh* claim about R. Aqiva, saying, "even if you say his line is switched, it is different here because . . ."; see also Ḥal. 2:2 58c and Yev. 10:3 10d. Two of these are in tractate *Ḥallah* and two are attributed to R. Yose.

of cases, sometimes explicitly saying that the line is not switched,[30] though in some passages there is no response to the claim.[31] Most commonly, the Talmud seeks to demonstrate that the teachings are not incongruent, either by showing that the teachings address issues that are sufficiently different to warrant a different response or by offering a new understanding of one of the teachings. There are other types of solutions. Section 4 of this chapter explores solutions that appeal to the teaching's transmission, offering a correction to the text or claiming that the sage merely transmitted the incongruent statement but did not espouse it. There are three passages in which the Talmud posits the sage's thought on the matter has changed.[32] Another set of three passages solves the difficulty by positing that the inconsistency is due to the sage answering another sage "in his [i.e. the interlocutor's] *shita*"; that is, the sage's words are not consistent with another statement by him because he was, in this instance, replying to another sage according to that sage's premise.[33] In one passage, the Talmud suggests that the sage *acted* not in accordance with his teaching because he was forced by another sage to do so;[34] in another passage it suggests a sage instructed against his own leaning in deference to the opinion of other sages;[35] and still another passage argues each of the two teachings was instructed following another sage.[36] What emerges from these different types of answers is that the Talmud is less bothered by the possibility that a sage *acted* inconsistently, *spoke* inconsistently, or even changed his mind—as long as in terms of the record as we have it now, the sage's own position remains consistent.

One of the striking features of *meḥalefa* passages is that they rarely contrast more than two teachings.[37] While identifications and *ke-da'ateh* arguments also normally rely only on a couple of teachings, here the use of two has an important implication: it means that while *meḥalefa* passages do demonstrate that there is no inconsistency, they do not amount to demonstrations of consistency. A *meḥalefa* passage may demonstrate that a sage who seems at first to be inconsistent has a good reason to rule

---

[30] *Ter.* 2:6 41d (par. *Ter.* 11:1 47d and *'A. Z.* 2:4 41c), *'Er.* 2:4 20a, *Yev.* 11:7 12b, *Ned.* 8:2 40d (par. *Qid.* 3:9 64b).

[31] *Shevi.* 9:1 38d (par. *'Er.* 3:7 21b, *Beẓ.* 1:1 60a), *Ḥal.* 1:2 57c, *Shab.* 8:6 11b, *'Er.* 8:6 25a, *Pes.* 1:3 27c, *Ta'an.* 1:1 63d (second instance), *Ta'an.* 1:2 64a, *Shevu.* 2:5 34a (see *PM*).

[32] *Dem.* 7:4 26b and *Shevu.* 8:3 38d, both relating to instances where the Yerushalmi considers the sage to have asked a question about something in one instance and offered a decision in another. See also *Shevu.* 6:2 37a (with *PM* and Epstein, *IMT*, 227; cf. Nahmanides). *PM* posits that a similar solution is offered at *Suk.* 2:7 53a, but Henshke, "Eimatay," 100, offers a more plausible interpretation of that passage.

[33] *Pe'ah* 5:2 19a, *Shab.* 12:5 13d, *Shevu.* 3:1 34b.

[34] *'Er.* 1:1 18c.

[35] *Beẓ.* 1:7 60d, first solution.

[36] *Ber.* 7:2 11b (par. *Naz.* 5:4 54b).

[37] One exception is at *Yev.* 7:5 8b; see also *Giṭ.* 7:4 48d under the interpretation offered by Ridbaz and *QE* (while the discussion in *Yoma* seems to support *QE*'s interpretation, it does not actually mention m. *Giṭ.* 7:4 but m. *Giṭ.* 3:3). The passage at *'Or.* 1:2 60d may seem like an exception since it refers to multiple examples of R. Ishmael's exegetical principle. But it seems likely that these examples were not collected for this purpose by R. Jonah, who asks the *meḥalefa* question there, but rather were already a part of a single teaching attributed at some point to R. Ishmael. See *Sifre Numbers* §23 for a similar series.

differently in two cases, but because such passages never adduce another ruling by that sage that is similar to one of the rulings already cited, there is never a demonstration that the sage presented the assumed pattern of ruling beyond that one teaching. There are cases where a third teaching is readily available and might even stand in the background of the passage, but the Talmud does not mention it.[38]

3. What is the problem?

What precisely do the sages in the Yerushalmi argue when they say a sage's line is switched? Moscovitz's *Terminology* defines the phrase using another Talmudic term, *rumya*, which the Bavli generally employs to object to one teaching by citing another. This broad definition reflects the diversity of claims made through the phrase. This section describes more specifically the types of problems that *meḥalefa* arguments address or construct in order to identify what is at stake in these arguments.

There are a few *meḥalefa* passages that address what we normally call contradiction:

Sotah 5:5 20c–d

אימתי היה איוב? ר' שמעון בן לקיש בשם בר קפרא: בימי אברהם אבינו הית [...]. ר'
אבא אמ': בימי אבינו יעקב [...]. ר' לוי אמ': בימי השבטים היה. [...]. ר' יוסי בן חלפתא
אמ': בירידתן למצרים היה ובעלייתן מת. [...]. ר' שמעון בן לקיש אמ': איוב לא היה ולא
עתיד לחיות.

מחלפא שיטתיה דר' שמעון בן לקיש. תמן אמ' ר' שמעון בן לקיש בשם בר קפרא: בימי
אברהם אבינו היה. והכא הוא אמ' הכין? אלא הוא היה ויסורין לא היו. ולמה נכתבו עליו?
אלא לומ' שאילולי באו עליו היה יכול לעמוד בהן.

In which period did Job live? R. Simeon b. Laqish [said] in the name of Bar Qappara: He lived in the days of Abraham, our father [...].[39] R. Abba said: In the time of our father, Jacob [...]. R. Levi said: He lived during the days of the tribes [...]. R. Yose b. Ḥalafta said: He lived when they went down to Egypt and when they came up he died [...]. R. Simeon b. Laqish said: Job did not live and is not going to live in the future.

The line of R. Simeon b. Laqish is switched! There R. Simeon b. Laqish said in the name of Bar Qappara, "He lived in the days of Abraham, our father," and here he says this? Rather, he lived, but his sufferings did not [occur]. Why then were they

---

[38] Compare for example *Ḥal.* 2:2 58c and *'Er.* 8:6 25a, each contrasting a teaching of R. Judah with his teaching at *m. Beẓ.* 5:4 but not with each other; see similarly *Pe'ah* 6:2 19d (par. *B. Q.* 6:5 5c) and *Sot.* 9:2 23c, though in this case, the latter passage may derive from the former. There are also cases in which a third teaching is mentioned nearby but it is unclear whether those two parts of the text are of the same cloth: *Shevi.* 8:5 38b (par. *Ned.* 11:1 42c), *Yev.* 12:2 12d, *Git.* 7:1 48c.

[39] I omitted the scriptural quotations throughout the passage.

written concerning him? To say that if they had come upon him, he would have been able to withstand them.

Two teachings attributed to R. Simeon b. Laqish[40] clearly contradict one another—one states that Job lived during the time of Abraham, the other that he never lived at all (and the book tells a tale). An anonymous comment points that contradiction out, and the solution offers a new interpretation of the second statement: R. Simeon b. Laqish did not mean to say that Job did not exist at all, but rather that his sufferings—the *story* of Job—did not in fact occur and were written up to make a point about his upstanding character.

This passage addresses a contradiction between apparently mutually exclusive options: either R. Simeon b. Laqish thought Job existed, or he thought Job did not exist. In this sense, this passage is not very typical of *meḥalefa* passages, which do not usually address such outright contradictions. If we limit ourselves to what philosophers call "explicit contradictions," in which one statement explicitly negates the position expressed in another statement, this passage about Job is the only example: the verb that is used in R. Simeon's first teaching (*haya*, "existed") is negated in the second (*lo haya*, "did not exist"). There are a few more instances which address less explicit types of contradiction. In several passages, the sage gives different answers to the same question;[41] in a somewhat larger set of passages, a teaching by a sage is contrasted with an anecdote from which it appears that his position on the same issue was different;[42] in another set of passages the Talmud derives, through interpretation, contradictory positions on the same case by the same sage.[43]

While the contradictions addressed in these passages are not explicit, they are, at least according to the premise of the objections, contradictions nonetheless: in a case where a husband threw the bill of divorce at his wife instead of giving it to her, and the divorce is only valid if the bill fell close to her—it is either that Rav believes that "close" means four cubits, as one teaching would have it, or that he believes it means within an arm's stretch, as another teaching would have it;[44] in a case where a litigant supports his claim with possession of the property as well as a writ of ownership—it is either that R. Judah the Patriarch believes the case should be decided based on the validity of the writ, as a teaching attributed to him has it, or that he believes it can also be established based on the possession of property,

---

[40] One of these teachings is transmitted by R. Simeon in the name of Bar Qappara. In similar cases, the Talmud resolves the discrepancy by positing that the tradent does not agree with what he transmits (see next section); that solution is not taken up here despite its availability.

[41] *Ta'an.* 1:2 64a (as the question is perceived by the Yerushalmi), *Git.* 8:2 49b, *Sheq.* 7:6 50d.

[42] *Ber.* 4:1 7c (par. *Ta'an.* 4:1 67c), *Dem.* 5:9 24d, *'Er.* 1:1 18c, *Git.* 1:1 43b, *Git.* 6:1 48a, *Qid.* 3:12 64d, and *Shevu.* 6:2 37a.

[43] *Ber.* 5:1 8d, *Shevi.* 8:5 38a, *Ḥal.* 2:3 58c, *Shab.* 12:3 13d (see Lieberman, *YK*, 176), *Suk.* 2:7 53a, *Yev.* 8:4 9d.

[44] *Git.* 8:2 49b.

as he ruled in a specific instance;[45] it is either that R. Eliezer believes a congenital eunuch is subject to the ritual of *ḥaliza*, as the Mishnah records him teaching explicitly, or that he believes such a eunuch is not subject to that ritual, as the Talmud initially infers from another statement he makes about the age in which one is determined to be a eunuch.[46] In all these cases, following the law according to these sages would require a choice between two mutually exclusive positions.

Another type of claim contrasts broad statements or principles with teachings that make a specific point that, according to the Yerushalmi, does not conform with the broad statement. Consider the following example:

Beẓah 5:2 63a (par. *Taʿanit* 1:7 64d, *Taʿanit* 4:6 69b, *Ketubbot* 1:1 24d)

שמואל אמ': אפי' בתשעה באב יארס, שלא יקדמנו אחר. מחלפא שיטתיה דשמואל. תמן הוא אמ': "מושיב יחידים ביתה" "במאזנים לעלות המה מהבל יחד", והכא הוא אמ' הכין? שלא יקדמנו אחר בתפילה.

Samuel said: Even on [the mourning fast day of] the Ninth of Av, [a man] may betroth [a woman], lest another [man] precede him [in betrothing the woman he desires].

The line of Samuel is switched! There he says: "God gives the desolate a home to live in" (Ps 68:6), "Placed on a scale together, they weigh even less than a breath" (Ps 62:9), and here he says this? [Samuel meant:] Lest another [man] precede him in prayer.

Samuel rules that despite the Ninth of Av being a mourning day, a man may perform the merry act of betrothing a woman, lest another man betroth the woman he desires before him. The Talmud objects that Samuel is also known to have cited two biblical verses which, we know from other passages,[47] were taken to imply that matches are made in heaven. If matches are determined by God, how can Samuel be concerned that another man might betroth the chosen woman? The solution offers a new interpretation of Samuel's first teaching, saying he meant another man might pray to God for the woman's affections; this solution seems to be rejected.[48] In this kind of passage, even though the two teachings do not refer to the very same case or issue, they can be considered contradictory since the Yerushalmi takes one as an explicit principle that the other teaching contradicts.[49]

---

[45] *Shevu.* 6:2 37a, accepting the emendation in Lieberman, *On the Yerushalmi*, 8.
[46] *Yev.* 8:4 9d.
[47] See *b. M. Q.* 18b, which also contrasts a similar ruling by Samuel with a (more explicitly formulated) position on divine matches (and see the manuscripts there). Cf. *b. San.* 22a. Palestinian compilations record this exegesis with differences in form and attribution; see *Genesis Rabbah* 65:2, 68:4; *Leviticus Rabbah* 8:1, 29:8. See for full treatment Schremer, "What God Has Joined Together," 147–51. My translation of Ps 62:9 follows Schremer's reconstruction of how the sages read the verse.
[48] Beʾeri, *Exploring Taʿaniot*, 117–19.
[49] Other examples include *Ber.* 4:1 7b (par. *Taʿan.* 4:1 67c), *Kil.* 1:7 27a, the second instance on *Shab.* 1:3 3b (par. *Shab.* 6:3 8b), *Taʿan.* 1:1 63d, *Shevu.* 2:5 34a.

Most *meḥalefa* passages concern not contradictions, but what we may call inconsistencies. These passages compare two teachings that address different issues or cases. The comparison between the teachings responds to or constructs a similarity between the cases which allows for the expectation that the sage will teach similarly in both. I offer first an example where the two cases are relatively close:

Sotah 1:5 17a (par. *Sanhedrin* 6:3 23c)

מחלפה שיטתיה דר' יודן. תמן הוא אמ', "האיש מכסין אותו מלפניו והאשה מלפניה ומלאחריה", והכא הוא אמ' הכין? תמן מכל מקום למיתה היא מתוקנת, ברם הכא שמא תימצא טהורה ויתגרו בה פירחי כהונה.

מחלפה שיטתהון דרבנן. תמן אינון אמרין, "האיש נסקל ערום ואין האשה נסקלת ערומה", והכא אינון אמרין הכין? תמן "ואהבת לרעך כמוך". יבור לו מיתה קלה שבקלות. ברם הכא, "וניוסרו כל הנש' ולא תעשינה כזימתכינה".

[On *m. Sot.* 1:5, which addresses the ordeal of the woman suspected by her husband of adultery: "And a priest would hold her garments—if they were torn let them be torn; if they ripped at the seam let them be ripped at the seam—to the extent that he uncovers her bosom and loosens her hair. R. Judah says: If her bosom were attractive, he would not uncover it; if her hair were attractive, he would not loosen it."]

The line of R. Judah is switched! There he says, [concerning execution procedures, "Four cubits away from the place of stoning, they would undress him]. A man would be covered in the front, and a woman both front and behind" (*m. San.* 6:3), and here he says this [that the woman suspected of adultery may be uncovered from the front as long as her bosom is not attractive]?

There, at any event, she is already set to be killed. But here [she must be covered up] lest, in case she is found to be pure [i.e. not to have committed adultery], the young priests will lust for her.

The line of the sages is switched! There they say, "A man is to be stoned naked, but a woman is not to be stoned naked" (*m. San.* 6:3), and here they say this [that the bosom of the woman suspected of adultery is uncovered]?

There [concerning execution, the sages apply the following exegesis:] "but you shall love your neighbor as yourself" (Lev 19:18), [which means] choose for him the easiest of easy deaths, but here, "so that all women may take warning and not commit lewdness as you have done" (Ezek 23:48).

The similarity between the cases—both dealing with public stripping in punitive contexts—allows for a contrast between them. In the case of the ordeal for a woman suspected of adultery, R. Judah specifies that the woman's chest should not be revealed if it is attractive; in the case of general execution procedures, he seems to allow uncovering of the chest without such further specification. The sages who dispute R. Judah rule that the woman should not be undressed at all in the case of execution, while in the case of the ordeal they too permit uncovering her breast. The Talmud's objection is that both sides of the debate are inconsistent in their approach to female nudity and public stripping. In contrast with the examples we have seen above, in which it was not possible to follow both teachings, one could follow the teachings of R. Judah or the sages in both cases; but that would be, according to the Talmud's objection, inconsistent.

Objections to inconsistencies can receive different solutions than those offered for objections to contradictions. In the contradiction examples we have seen above, the Talmud's solution was to offer a new interpretation of one of the teachings so that it does not contradict the other. With inconsistencies between two cases, however, the Talmud has another solution available, which is to justify the different ruling by pointing out the difference between the two cases. In our example, the solution is that R. Judah ruled differently in these cases because of the different possible fates of these women: the woman who is being executed is surely going to die, and therefore there is no reason to guard against the possibility that men will find her bosom attractive and transgress with her; the woman suspected of adultery, in contrast, may be found not guilty through the ordeal, and therefore we must guard against the possibility that the young priests present during the ordeal will come to lust for her and transgress later on. A similar move is made with the inconsistency in the ruling of the sages, centering on the different principles that govern each of the procedures: the law stipulates executions should be as painless as possible, whereas the purpose of the ordeal is to deter women in the audience from committing adultery.[50] This type of solution is the most common solution offered in *meḥalefa* passages.

In a number of such passages, the cases compared are almost identical.[51] But more usually they are distant enough that a common denominator needs to be supplied for the comparison to work, sometimes one that suggests itself readily and in other times one that takes quite a bit of imagination. Several passages compare cases where a sage appears to rule leniently and strictly on uncertain or borderline cases, even though the two cases can be in very disparate areas of the law. In one such passage, explored in detail below, the Talmud claims the line of R. Yose is switched because in a case of an '*Eruv* which may or may not be valid he rules leniently, that the '*Eruv* is valid, whereas in a case of a purifying immersion which may or may not have been valid, he rules strictly, that the person is impure.[52] Another

---

[50] See Rosen-Zvi, *Mishnaic Sotah Ritual*, 75 and n. 33.
[51] See e.g. *Shab.* 10:6 12c, *Shab.* 12:5 13d., *Shab.* 13:5 14a (par. *Beẓ.* 3:1 61d), *Naz.* 2:9 52a, *Naz.* 3:5 52c, *B. Q.* 2:2 3a.
[52] '*Er.* 21a 3:4, and see below; for other examples, see *Ter.* 7:5 44d, *Yev.* 11:7 12b, and *Shevu.* 2:1 33d (par. *Hor.* 3:3 47b).

frequently appearing common denominator is a biblical word that is interpreted differently in two contexts; in one passage, the Talmud infers from a ruling by R. Judah concerning circumcision of an androgynous person on the Sabbath that he believes the word "male" in Genesis 17:10 includes androgynous people; but that results in an inconsistency, since the Talmud also infers from another ruling of R. Judah, concerning the pilgrimage to the Temple, that the word "male" in Exodus 23:17 excludes androgynous people.[53]

Sometimes the Talmud establishes the contrast between the cases through underlying assumptions that are not legal. One passage tells us that a ruling by R. Judah concerning the time in which one is supposed to stop making leaven is based on his belief that people easily confuse the fifth hour of the day with the seventh, whereas his position on the admissibility of testimonies, the Talmud infers, reflects the view that these times of day cannot be easily confused; R. Yose there offers the solution that in the case of testimony, the court is vigilant and prevents confusion, whereas in the case of leaven, the matter is given to women (since they are in charge of the kitchen), and "women are sluggish."[54] In another passage, the Talmud reasons that R. Judah's ruling regarding offerings of women who have given birth reflects a belief that "death is common," that is, that we should always take into account the possibility someone might die, and yet, again according to the Talmud, his ruling in a particular case of contingent divorce is based on the assumption that death is not common.[55]

The construction of the similarity between the cases is typical of Talmudic comparisons in general. As Louis Ginzberg observed, such comparisons are often based on what he called "external" or "superficial" similarity—or in a more neutral way, "saying things are similar even though they are similar only with respect to one point."[56] In the case of *meḥalefa* claims, this feature of Talmudic comparison means that it is difficult to describe the target of the Talmud's objection as inconsistency of principle. Consider the following example:

Yevamot 12:2 12d

ר' יוחנן בעי: מחלפא שיטתיה דר' ליעזר? תמן הוא אמ', הימנית מעכבת, והכא הוא אמ', אין הימנית מעכבת.

אמ' ר' יוסי: תמן דכת' "ימנית" הימנית מעכבת. ברם הכא דלית כת' "ימנית" אין הימנית מעכבת.

---

[53] *Shab.* 19:3 17b (par. *Ḥag.* 1:1 76a, *Yev.* 8:1 9a). See also: *Yoma* 2:1 39c, *Yev.* 6:4 7c, *Sot.* 9:2 23c, *Qid.* 1:1 58c (par. *Shevu.* 6:1 36d).
[54] *Pes.* 1:4 27c (the second instance; par. *San.* 5:3 22d).
[55] *Git.* 7:4 48d.
[56] Ginzberg, *Commentary I*, 81.

[The anonymous position in the Mishnah rules that in the *ḥaliza* ceremony, described in Deut 25:7–10, if the woman took off the shoe from the *left* foot of her brother-in-law as opposed to his right foot, the ceremony is invalid; R. Eliezer rules that it is valid.]

R. Yoḥanan asked:[57] Is the line of R. Eliezer switched? There [at *m. Neg.* 14:9, concerning the case of a leper who did not have a right ear, thumb, or toe, the places on which his purification blood would normally be applied,] he said the right one is essential [as R. Eliezer there rules that the blood must be applied to the place of the right ear, etc., as opposed to R. Simeon who says it may be applied to the left], and here he said the right one is not essential [because he ruled the *ḥaliza* ceremony valid despite it being done on the left].

Said R. Yose: There, [concerning the leper] where "right" is written [see Lev 14:14], the right one is essential, but here, where "right" is not written, the right one is not essential.[58]

Both teachings the Talmud compares concern a ceremony which, the law specifies, must be performed with the right side of the body; but there are significant differences between them, far beyond the one R. Yose points out. In the leprosy case, the law requires applying material to a certain place; in the levirate case, the law stipulates a shoe is removed in order to humiliate the levir. In the leprosy case, the procedure cannot take place as directed because the leper in question lacks the right ear, thumb, or toe; in the levirate case, the woman could have, but did not, execute the procedure properly. In the leprosy case, R. Eliezer can insist on "the right" because the right side of the body (or head or hand or foot) remains; no such substitution exists in the case of the levirate.

If R. Eliezer had ruled the opposite, deeming the *ḥaliza* procedure invalid unless it is done with the right foot, he would be insisting that the procedure is only valid if it is done the way it was supposed to be done. We would *not* be able to say, then, that such a ruling reflects the same principle as his leper ruling, since in that ruling R. Eliezer actually accommodates a change in the procedure, in contrast with the anonymous position of the Mishnah which rules that a leper of this sort can never be purified. What we *could* say, had R. Eliezer ruled that way, is what we have seen with identifications and *ke-da'ateh* claims: the similarity does not necessarily prove principled consistency of a position, but rather a tendency, a disposition, that a sage might have; it demonstrates the presence of his footprint.

The claim that the line of a sage is switched, in those cases, amounts to the claim that we cannot find such a projected tendency across a sage's teachings. It is an exercise of the Talmud's comparative reading that is based on the failure, rather than

---

[57] Here and elsewhere with *meḥalefa shitateh*, "ask" can also mean "posed a difficulty."
[58] For the rest of the passage, see the discussion in n. 70 below.

success, of comparison. But the absence of such patterns, unlike contradictions or inconsistencies of principles, would only bother us if we were *looking* for patterns; they are not problems in trying to have a coherent understanding of the teachings themselves, or even in following the rulings in practice. What the solutions to these problems defend, then, is not so much the principled coherence of the sage, but rather the premise that reading for distinctive patterns is productive, and that a failure in comparison is due to a particular reason, usually a bad comparison.

In contrast with teachings which are contradictory, teachings which are merely inconsistent are not, strictly speaking, mutually exclusive—whether the comparison between them is founded on a significant similarity or a more limited one. One could hold inconsistent teachings at the same time, and again, both can be followed in practice. It is true that the more essential the similarity, the more a different response is arbitrary or problematic; but even in those cases, as the responses to *meḥalefa* show, there could be good reasons that a different course might be taken. In other words, *meḥalefa* passages are premised on setting up positions as mutually exclusive even if they are not necessarily so. In one exceptional passage, the Talmud concedes this itself:

Nazir 2:1 51d

אמ' ר' יוחנן: טע' דבית שמי משום שהוציא נזירות מפיו. ר' שמע' בן לקיש אמ': משום כינויי כינויין.

ר' עוקבה בעא קומי ר' מנא: מחלפה שיטתיה דר' שמעון בן לקיש? דתנינן תמן, "הרי עלי מנחה מן השעורין", יביא מן החיטים", ומר ר' אבהו בשם ר' שמעון בן לקיש: שהוציא מנחה מתוך פיו. וכא הוא אמ' אכן?

אית ליה הכין ואית ליה הכין. אית ליה משום שהוציא נזיריא מפיו, ואית ליה משום כינויי כינויין. תדע לך שהוא כן, דתנינן: אמ', "אמרה פרה זו". כלום אמרת?[59] לא משום שהוציא נזירות מתוך פיו. וכא. משום שהוציא נזירות מתוך פיו.

[In *m. Naz.* 2:1, the House of Shammai obligate someone who said "I am a Nazirite from dried dates and pressed figs" to be a Nazirite, even though these are permitted to Nazirites, and the vow therefore makes no sense].

Said R. Yohanan: The reason of the House of Shammai is that Naziriteship came out of his mouth [i.e. he is obligated because he uttered "Nazirite," regardless of the rest of his vow]. R. Simeon b. Laqish said: [Their reason is] on account of aliases of aliases. [That is, "figs" could count as an indirect alias for grapes, which are indeed prohibited to Nazirites.] [...]

R. Uqva asked before R. Mana: Is the line of R. Simeon b. Laqish switched? For we have recited there, "[If someone said,] 'I pledge a grain offering of barley'—he

---

[59] Deleting an extra "אמ'," with the Academy edition.

should bring a grain offering of wheat" [even though a grain offering cannot be brought from barley, his vow is valid and he must offer it properly; *m. Men.* 12:3], and R. Abbahu said in the name of R. Simeon b. Laqish: [he is obligated despite the senseless vow,] because [the word] "grain offering" came out of his mouth [thus using an explanation similar to R. Yohanan's in the case of the Naziriteship].

He [R. Simeon b. Laqish] holds this [principle] and he holds that [principle]. He holds "because Naziriteship came out of his mouth" and he holds "because of aliases of aliases." Know that this is so, for we have recited [in the passage in the Mishnah which immediately follows]: If he said, "if this cow declared ['I am a Nazirite if I stand,']" the house of Shammai declare him to be a Nazirite; *m. Naz.* 2:2]. Now did it [the cow] say it? Rather,[60] [he is obligated to become a Nazirite] because Naziriteship came out of his mouth [and even R. Simeon would concede that]. Here, too, [the obligation is incurred] because Naziriteship[61] came out of his mouth.

Like many other *mehalefa* passages, this one creates a sense of mutually exclusive possibilities. It is either, the Talmud implies, that R. Simeon b. Laqish should explain the validity of the vow at *m. Menahot* 12:3 with appeal to the idea of "aliases of aliases," as he does at *m. Nazir* 1:2 in contrast with R. Yohanan, or he should agree with R. Yohanan that the reasoning of the House of Shammai at *m. Nazir* 1:2 is that the mere mention of the Nazirite vow makes the vow valid. Otherwise, his line would be switched. As with other *mehalefa* passages, mutual exclusivity is produced by two elements: a dispute and a comparison. The dispute allows us to imagine one position ("aliases of aliases") as the opposite of another position ("mere mention"), and the comparison between the two cases allows us to expect that the sage that supported one position in one case will support the same position in the compared case. Where this passage departs from other *mehalefa* passages is that the solution it offers acknowledges that the two principles can be held at the same time, and it does so *without* offering a particular reason why in each case R. Simeon chooses to follow one of these explanations. This answer undermines the premise of many of the *mehalefa* claims dealing with inconsistencies: if sages can be informed by different ideas in similar cases without a particular reason to differentiate between them, there is no reason to object to "switched lines."

The analysis above shows that the majority of *mehalefa* objections point not to contradictions but to inconsistencies. Given the significant number of *mehalefa* passages that do point to contradictions, we cannot explain that fact by appeal to a deference towards rabbinic teachings of the kind that scholars have identified in

---

[60] On לא as אלא here and elsewhere see Assis, *Concordance*, *251.

[61] *PM* suggests emending "Naziriteship" to "grain offering," since the reference seems to be to R. Simeon's explanation of *m. Men.* 12:3; but it is possible that the Talmud is using "Naziriteship" deliberately to equate the principle behind the rulings.

biblical exegesis.[62] What the prominence of these inconsistency-focused passages does show us is the considerable scholarly energy spent in *constructing* or at least *looking for* discrepancies that are far from self-evident. The constructed nature of these inconsistencies is even more apparent in the fact that these objections normally only address two teachings, which means that the pattern that is supposedly broken is only identified in the hypothetical opposite teaching the commentary conjures. The premise of mutual exclusivity evident in these objections further contributes to their construction of distinctive profiles for individual sages. The objection that the sage's "line is switched," then, presents both the attempt to find a pattern and an explanation of its failure, sustaining a scholarly attention to individual patterns even when they are absent.

4. Consistency and textuality

In our own intellectual culture, our sources for an author's thought are primarily their own writing or speech, and even though those often involve contributions from editors or copyeditors, we take the final version to reflect the author's control. The teachings of the sages cited in the Talmud, in contrast, were mediated and selected by the people who transmitted them, often long after the death of the sage. The Talmud itself appeals to this mediation to address inconsistency, either implicitly or explicitly. Consider the following example:

'Eruvin 7:2 24b

לא היה רחב ארבעה. ר' בא בשם רב: אסור לכאן ולכאן. ר' זעירא בשם רב: מותר לכאן ולכאן. מחלפא שיטתיה דר' בא. תמן אמ' ר' בא רב יהודה בשם שמואל, "זרקה ונחה על ראשי מחיצות חייב", וכא אמ' הכין?

[The Mishnah rules that if there was a wall between two courtyards that was ten handbreadths high and ten cubits wide, and there was fruit on top of it, residents of either courtyard may come up to the wall and eat the fruit without transgressing the Sabbath laws.]

What if [the wall] was not four [cubits] wide?

R. Abba [said] in the name of Rav: It is prohibited for here and for there.

R. Ze'ira [said] in the name of Rav: It is permitted for here and for there.

The line of R. Abba is switched. There, R. Abba said R. Judah [said] in the name of Samuel, "If one threw [an object] and it landed on top of partitions, he is liable [for transporting between domains on the Sabbath]," and here he says this? [R. Abba's

---

[62] Rosen-Zvi and Rosen-Zvi, "Tannaitic Halakhic and Aggadic Methodology," 211–16.

first ruling implies the top of the wall has the status of both domains, whereas his second ruling implies the top of a wall constitutes a different domain].

The passage records two teachings attributed to Rav that are contradictory in an immediately apparent way: one permits, the other prohibits, the same action in the same situation. And yet the passage records no objection to this contradiction, because the presentation of the teachings already indicates they might differ: one teaching is transmitted by R. Abba and the other by R. Ze'ira. The implication is not that Rav made two contradictory statements, but rather that R. Abba and R. Ze'ira present different reports or interpretations of Rav's position. There are several passages in the Talmud that similarly present clearly contradictory statements by the same sage, each transmitted by a different tradent, and these passages similarly do not record an objection to that contradiction.[63] This passage is particularly instructive because it does record a *mehalefa* objection, but not to this outright contradiction between these two teachings attributed to Rav.[64] It is rare for *mehalefa* objections to apply to cases where the two teachings are transmitted by different tradents.[65] This section focuses on instances in which the Talmud resolves a *mehalefa* objection by appealing to the process of transmission as the source of inconsistency.

Consistency and text-critical questions

In a significant number of passages, *mehalefa* objections are resolved by appeal to alternative versions of teachings or emendations. In some cases, the version or correction concerns the attribution of the statement.[66] In one passage, R. Eleazar argues that in a certain dispute between R. Meir and R. Yose in *Qiddushin*, each of these sages takes up the line he has opposed in a dispute in *Nedarim*—their lines are switched. Rabbi Yohanan answers that "it is not the line that is switched; it is the recited teaching [*matnita*] that is switched": the attributions in the recitation

---

[63] See e.g. *Kil.* 4:9 29c, *'Er.* 1:5 19a, and *Git.* 6:6 48b.

[64] For a similar example involving the same tradents, see *Git.* 9:6 50c.

[65] If we limit ourselves to passages where each of the teachings are cited by a different tradent, I can find only one or two such cases: the second instance on *'A. Z.* 3:7 43b (accepting *PM*'s emendation), and perhaps also *Sot.* 5:2 20a, depending on how one interprets the passage. There are eleven cases where only one of the teachings is transmitted through a tradent and the other teaching is directly attributed to the sage about whom the objection is made. See *Sheq.* 4:5 48a, *Yev.* 4:10 6a (par. *Nid.* 1:4 49b), *Git.* 4:4 45d, *Git.* 8:2 49b, *Naz.* 2:1 51a, *Qid.* 3:12 64d, *Shevu.* 6:2 37a, *Shevu.* 8:3 38d (the second instance), *'A. Z.* 3:7 43b (the first instance), *'A. Z.* 4:4 44a, and *Nid.* 3:2 50c. See also *Ta'an.* 1:1 63a, where the Yerushalmi seems to hypothesize different tradents.

[66] In addition to the case from *Nedarim*, see *'Er.* 10:3 26b, *Pes.* 7:11 35a-b (par. *San.* 8:2 26a), *M. Q.* 2:1 81a (the second solution replaces the identification of the teaching as R. Yose's with an attribution to sages who generally follow his *shita*), and the passage reproduced below from *Gittin*. See also Lieberman's interpretation of *Shab.* 1:1 2c (*YK*, 10), which argues that the discussion features a similar solution to the *M. Q.* passage mentioned above. QE argues that the Yerushalmi offers an attribution alternative as a solution at *Yev.* 4:10 6a but this interpretation is untenable in light of the parallels at *Nid.* 1:4 49b and *Genesis Rabbah* 20:6.

are wrong and should be reversed, resolving the contradiction.[67] In other cases, it is the position rather than attribution that is emended or is said to have another version.[68] When R. Ze'ira adduces a story about R. Joshua b. Levi in which he says something that appears to be in contradiction with one of his rulings, R. Abba b. Zemina responds with a version of the story which does not stand in contradiction with that ruling; the words attributed to R. Joshua in the two versions of the story sound alike, suggesting the two versions were created because the story was heard differently by different people.[69] On a couple of occasions, the Talmud responds to *meḥalefa* objections by positing that there are "two recitations" or "two reciters" with conflicting reports on the sage's position.[70] In one case, the Talmud raises the possibility that the sage did not make the statement at all.[71]

While it is possible and even likely that emendations and alternative formulations were motivated by the desire to harmonize contradictory teachings, the Talmud does not usually present harmonization as the explicit motivator for the emendation. In one instance, the resolution of the contradiction is presented almost as a by-product of the alternative version: "whoever switches [the attributions] does not have those [aforementioned] difficulties."[72] If the ostensible purpose of switching the attributions was to solve the difficulties, then that statement would be redundant. There is one passage where the Talmud presents the resolution of contradiction explicitly as the purpose of an emendation:

Gittin 7:1 48c (partial par. *Horayot* 1:2 45d)

ר' יעקב בר אחא אמ': איתפלגון ר' יוחנן וריש-לקיש. ר' יוחנן אמ', "עודהו קורדייקוס עליו כותבין גט ונותנין לאשתו". ריש-לקיש אמ', "לכשישתפה".

מחלפה שיטתיה דריש-לקיש. דאיתפלגון: נתחרש או נשתטה או נשתמד או שהורו בית דין לאכול חלב - ר' יוחנן אמ', "נדחית חטאתו". ריש-לקיש אמ', "לא נדחית חטאתו".

ר' יוסי ביר' בון אמ': ר' אחא[73] מיחלף שמועתא, דלא תהא מילתיה דר' יוחנן פליגא על מילתיה. דמר ר' שמואל בר אבא בשם ר' יוחנן: הגוסס זורקין עליו מדם חטאתו ומדם אשמו.

רבנין דקיסרין אמרין: ר' חייה ור' יסא - חד כהדין וחד כהדין.

---

[67] *Ned.* 8:2 40d–41a (par. *Qid.* 3:9 64b): לית היא מחלפה מתניתֿ היא מחלפה. See Epstein, *IMT*, 68 and 248.

[68] See *'Or.* 1:6 61b (the second solution); *Beẓ.* 1:7 60d (the second solution), which is striking for the auditory resemblance of the proposed alternative formulation; and, if one accepts the emendation by QE (which seems plausible to me), also *Naz.* 3:5 52c.

[69] *Dem.* 5:9 24d.

[70] See *Yev.* 12:2 12d (and Epstein, *IMT*, 248–9), where the Yerushalmi argues two recited teachings transmit contradictory teachings in the name of R. Eliezer regarding the foot with which the *ḥaliẓa* ritual is performed, though that argument relates only indirectly to the *meḥalefa* objection there (discussed in the previous section). See also *'Or.* 1:2 61a, where the second resolution to the objection invokes a mediating reciter. More on "two reciters" arguments in Chapter 8, Section 3.

[71] *Ber.* 4:1 7b (par. *Ta'an.* 4:1 67c).

[72] *Pes.* 7:11 35a–b (par. *San.* 8:2 26a). See more below, n. 75.

[73] Following the parallel in *Hor.* Here in *Git.*: R. Yohanan.

[The Mishnah rules that if a husband suffers from delirium and asks a bill of divorce to be written and given to his wife, his instruction is invalid; if he retracted his words while suffering from delirium, his retraction is also invalid. The Yerushalmi presents a dispute about a case where the husband gave the instruction and then became mentally incapacitated.]

R. Jacob b. Aha said: R. Yohanan and R. Simeon b. Laqish were disputed. R. Yohanan said, "even while the delirium affects him, they write the bill of divorce and give it to his wife." R. Simeon b. Laqish said, "[they may only do so] once he recovers."

The line of R. Simeon b. Laqish is switched! For they disputed: [If a person became liable for an offering because of a transgression, and, after designating the offering] became deaf or insane or an apostate [and therefore ineligible to offer sacrifices], or if the court has instructed him to eat ḥelev [and thus he is no longer liable]— R. Yohanan says: his purification offering is rejected [since his new status invalidates the offering]; R. Simeon b. Laqish says: his purification offering is not rejected.

R. Yose b. R. Abbin said: R. Aha switches the traditions, so that the statement of R. Yohanan will not dispute [another] statement of his. For Samuel b. Abba said in the name of R. Yohanan: A dying person—they sprinkle for him from the blood of his purification offering and from the blood of his reparation offering.

The Rabbis of Caesarea say: R. Hiyya [and] R. Yose [were disputed]—one [taught] like this and one [taught] like that.

R. Yohanan rules that even though the husband is now mentally incapacitated, the divorce may still be written since he was of sound mind when he gave the instruction; R. Simeon b. Laqish rules that the divorce bill may only be served when the husband recovers. An anonymous comment suggests that R. Simeon is being inconsistent here.[74] In the case of a person who became liable to make an offering, but was subsequently rendered ineligible to make offerings, R. Simeon rules that the offering is accepted and R. Yohanan rules it should be rejected. In the case of divorce bills, R. Simeon rules based on the agents' original status and R. Yohanan rules based on their current status; in the case of offerings, the reverse is true.

The passage proceeds with R. Yose b. R. Abbin's report that R. Aha would switch the attributions "so that the statement of R. Yohanan would not dispute [another]

---

[74] Ostensibly, the same can be said about R. Yohanan; it is possible that a statement to that effect originally appeared here (compare the parallel passages in *Ned.* 8:2 40d and *Qid.* 3:9 64b—the latter has a double statement, the former only one; see Epstein, *IMT*, 68 and n. 2).

statement of his." Here we see an emendation of the attribution with the explicit purpose of maintaining consistency. But the contradiction R. Yose and R. Aha have in mind is not the one we have just analyzed, between R. Yohanan's rulings in the case of divorce bills and the case of offerings eligibility, but rather a contradiction between the latter ruling and yet another ruling attributed to R. Yohanan which implies the offering of a dying person is accepted.[75] R. Yose b. R. Abbin implies that R. Aha thought that if R. Yohanan accepts the offering of a dying person, he should also accept an offering from a person who has become ineligible to make offerings after his liability had been incurred, and therefore switched the attributions in the dispute. While R. Aha's emendation also resolves the contradiction pointed out with *meḥalefa shitateh*, that is not its ostensible purpose. It may be important that the contradiction which is resolved by the emendation is less ambitious conceptually, comparing two teachings in the same area rather than across disparate legal realms.

Consistency and citation

One striking type of resolution we find for consistency objections in the Talmud is the explicit separation between the sage's role as a tradent and his role as a teacher of his own rulings.[76] In these passages, the Talmud explains the inconsistency by arguing that since one of the teachings quotes another sage, it does not reflect the quoting sage's own approach to the matter:

m. *'Eruvin* 3:4

ר׳ יוסה ור׳ שמעון או׳ שספק העירוב כשר. אמ׳ ר׳ יוסה: העיד אבטלס משום חמשה זקנים שספק העירוב כשר.

R. Yose and R. Simeon say that a doubtful case of *'Eruv* is valid. Said R. Yose: Abtolemos testified in the name of five elders that a doubtful case of *'Eruv* is valid.

---

[75] It is true that in *Hor.*, the passage concludes with the statement that whoever switches the attribution does not have those *difficulties*, in the plural (מאן דמחלף לית ליה באילין קישואייה), but that formulation presents the solution as a byproduct of the emendation rather than its purpose. Moreover, since the issue of the divorce bill is not mentioned or assumed by the passage in *Hor.*, it is possible that this sentence was erroneously copied here on the model of the passage in *Pes.* 7:11 35a–b (*San.* 8:2 26a) where there are indeed multiple difficulties noted. The fact that that statement does not appear in *Git.* supports this conjecture.

[76] There are ten unique passages of this kind in the Yerushalmi. In addition to the two passages analyzed above, see also *Ter.* 7:5 44d, *M. S.* 1:2 52c (par. *Qid.* 2:8 62d–63a), *'Or.* 1:2 61a (the anonymous solution), *'Or.* 1:6 61b, *Yev.* 7:5 8b, *Git.* 9:6 50c, and *B. Q.* 2:2 3a; in *Pes.* 2:1 28c, a similar solution is offered in response to a consistency objection presented without *meḥalefa shitateh*.

'Eruvin 3:4 21a

תמן תנינן: "ספיקו טהור. ר' יוסי מטמא". [...] מחלפה שיטתיה דר' יוסה. דתנינן: "אמ' ר' יוסה. העיד אבטולס בשם חמשה זקינים שספק העירוב כשר", וכא את אמר הכין? תמן בשם גרמיה, ברם הכא בשם חמשה זקנים.

We recited there [*m. Miqva'ot* 2:2, with respect to a person who contracted "light" impurity,] "in a case of doubt [whether or not he immersed in the purification pool, whether or not the pool satisfied the legal standards, etc.], he is pure. R. Yose renders him impure." [...]

R. Yose's line is switched! For we recited, "Said R. Yose: Abtolemos testified in the name of five elders that a doubtful *'Eruv* is valid," and here [in *Miqva'ot*] you say this? There [in *Miqva'ot*], [he teaches] in his own name, but here [he teaches] in the name of five elders.

In the Mishnah, we hear that R. Yose and R. Simeon say that an uncertain *'Eruv*—an *'Eruv* which may have been invalidated—is treated as valid. We also hear that R. Yose quoted Abtolemos' testimony in the name of five elders that indeed such an *'Eruv* is valid. The Talmud's discussion opens with a quotation of a Mishnaic teaching from tractate *Miqva'ot*. Like our passage in *'Eruvin*, that teaching deals with a case that is unclear, this time regarding purifying immersions. The Talmud points out that there, R. Yose takes a different approach to uncertainty: whereas in *'Eruvin* he rules leniently that the *'Eruv* is valid, in the case of immersion he rules strictly that it is not valid. The solution the Talmud offers is that in the *Miqva'ot* passage R. Yose's ruling expresses his own opinion, and here in *'Eruvin* he merely transmits the teaching of the five elders.

There are two ways to read the Talmud's argument here. The first is that while R. Yose's general approach to matters of doubt is strict, here he had to rule in opposition to his own approach because he had a tradition from the five elders that an uncertain *'Eruv* is treated as valid. According to this reading, the Talmud concedes that R. Yose indeed ruled inconsistently, but it explains that this inconsistency in *ruling* does not imply an inconsistency in thinking or approach. The second way to read the Talmud's statement is that R. Yose did not, in fact, rule that an uncertain *'Eruv* is valid; that he is merely transmitting here the words of the five elders, which he does not himself support. David Fränkel, who espoused this interpretation, also addressed an obvious problem with it: the Mishnah, immediately before R. Yose's citation of Abtolemos' testimony, also has R. Yose state himself, without quoting anyone else, the same position: "R. Yose and R. Simeon say that a doubtful case of *'Eruv* is valid."[77] This and other difficulties with this reading may lead us to prefer the first reading of the Yerushalmi's argument—but the second reading is consistent with the way this argument is made elsewhere in the Talmud.

---

[77] *SQ* suggests the first statement is a quotation as well. See similarly Goldberg, *Eruvin*, 79 n. 57.

In several passages of this type, it is clear that the Yerushalmi is suggesting that the sage disagrees with the ruling he quotes;[78] consider the following passage:

m. Ta'anit 1:2

אין שואלים גשמים אלא סמוך לגשמים. ר' יהודה אומ'. העובר לפני התיבה ביום טוב האחרון של חג—האחרון מזכיר והראשון אינו מזכיר. וביום טוב הראשון שלפסח—הראשון מזכיר והאחרון אינו מזכיר. עד אמתי שואלין? ר' יהודה אומ': עד שיעבור הפסח. ר' מאיר אומ': עד שיצא ניסן.

One must not ask for rain [in the Amidah Prayer] unless it is close [in time] to the rain [season]. R. Judah says: The one passing before the ark on the last holiday of the [Sukkot] festival—the last one mentions [the rain] but the first one does not mention [the rain]; and on the first holiday of Passover—the first one mentions [the rain] but the last one does not mention [the rain]. Until when does one ask [for the rain]? R. Judah says: Until Passover has passed. R. Meir says: Until [the month of] Nissan is out.

Ta'anit 1:2 64a

מחלפה שיטתיה דר' יודה. תמן הוא אמ', "העובר לפני התיבה ביום טוב האחרון שלחג— האחרון מזכיר והראשון אינו מזכיר", והכא הוא אמ' הכין? חדא בשם גרמיה, וחדא בשם ר' יודה בן בתירה.

The line of R. Judah is switched! There he says, "The one passing before the ark on the last holiday of the [Sukkot] festival—the last one mentions [the rain] but the first one does not mention [the rain; and on the first holiday of Passover—the first one mentions, the last one does not mention]," and here he says this [that one asks for rain "until Passover has passed"]?

One [teaching] is in his own name, and one [teaching] is in the name of R. Judah b. Betera.

During the rainy months of the year, the Mishnah tells us, there are additions concerning rain to the Amidah Prayer. R. Judah specifies the cut-off prayers which begin and end this period: on the last day of Sukkot, in the fall, the leader of the first morning prayer still does not mention rain, but the leader of the additional prayer after it should mention it; on the last day of Passover, in the spring, the leader of the first morning prayer still mentions rain, but the leader of the following prayer does not mention it. The Mishnah then asks until when one may request God for rain, and adduces two answers: R. Judah's, which stipulates one may pray for rain until Passover passes, and R. Meir's, which extends such requests through the month of

---

[78] In addition to the passage analyzed here, see *M. S.* 1:2 52c (par. *Qid.* 2:8 62d–63a) and *Git.* 9:6 50c.

Nissan. The Yerushalmi perceives a contradiction in the words of R. Judah: on the one hand, he says that the second prayer on the last day of Passover is already outside the period in which rain should be mentioned, but on the other hand he says that one should continue to ask for rain until Passover ends, which would include that prayer.

The resolution the Talmud offers is that R. Judah said only one of these teachings in his own name, whereas the other he said in the name of R. Judah b. Betera.[79] In contrast with the previous text we have examined, where the argument that R. Yose's teaching derived from the five elders was based on the Mishnah's explicit attribution of the testimony to them, here the Mishnah does not mention R. Judah b. Betera; the argument that one of the rulings is derived from him seems to be based either on R. Yohanan's statement, quoted earlier in the passage, which attributes one of the teachings to R. Judah b. Betera,[80] or on a recited teaching which presented such a transmission chain and which has been omitted in the Yerushalmi.[81] In this case, it seems clear the Yerushalmi does not mean that R. Judah ruled against his own opinion. At least in the Talmud's understanding, the teachings directly oppose each other—it is either that that prayer includes a reference to rain or it does not—and therefore cannot be held at the same time. The Yerushalmi's resolution seems to posit that whereas R. Judah ruled one way, he also transmitted from R. Judah b. Betera a ruling with which he disagreed.

These arguments should not be seen as last resort solutions in the absence of other options. In both cases we examined as well as others, the Yerushalmi offers alternative solutions which are either adopted or rejected;[82] in one instance, it presents a solution of this type as one of two valid alternatives.[83] Rather, these arguments tell us something significant about the way Amoraic scholars approached consistency, transmission, and authorship. The first, "weaker" sense of the argument, which has the sage rule against his inclination, accepts that a sage may rule against his general approach, but nonetheless is predicated on the idea that the sage has such an approach—even if he may deviate from it in his rulings because he follows a tradition from another sage. The second, "stronger" sense of the argument, which has the sage merely transmitting a teaching, accepts no inconsistent ruling. It breaks away from the broadly attested rabbinic assumption that citation

---

[79] At this stage of the discussion, the Yerushalmi does not explicitly identify which teaching is transmitted and which is R. Judah's own—it later concludes that the first one is R. Judah b. Beteira's (see the emendation suggested by *PM*).

[80] אמ' ר' יוחנן. הל' כר' יודה שאמ' משם ר' יודה בן בתירה.

[81] But something like it is found in *b. Ta'an.* 2b; see Epstein, *IMT*, 251.

[82] In *Ta'an.* the alternative solution, which is rejected, concerns the distinction between "mentioning" the rain (i.e. the description of God as a rain-maker added to the second blessing) and "asking" for rain (i.e. the petition for rain added to the ninth blessing). In *'Er.*, it is the assumption that the two cases are comparable which is rejected, with alternative solutions offered before and after.

[83] See *M. S.* 1:2 52c (par *Qid.* 2:8 63a): מחלפא שיטתיה דר' יודה בר פזי. תמן הוא אמ'. בין חי בין שחוט. והכא הוא אמ'. חי ולא שחוט. תמן בשם גרמיה. והכא בשם ר' יהושע בן לוי. אפילו תימר. כאן וכאן בשם גרמיה. במקדש בחי ובראוי ליפול לו ולאחר שחיטה.

amounts to assent, an assumption that is evident even in our passages (otherwise, there would be no apparent contradiction to be pointed out).

While the distinction between "author" and "tradent" underlies several literary and interpretive phenomena in the Talmud, it rarely appears as sharply and explicitly as it does in this set of passages.[84] The fact that this distinction is made expressly and even relatively often in discussions of consistency is not a coincidence. The new Amoraic interpretive framework, which posited that individual sages teach according to distinct and consistent approaches, required an increased separation between the teachings that represented their own positions and what they transmitted from others.

5. From *middah* to *shita*

While the term *shita* is never used in its Talmudic sense in the Tannaitic corpus, there is a small set of Tannaitic passages which are terminologically linked to the Talmudic discourse explored in this chapter. These passages employ the term *middah* in a way which seems to be the antecedent of the Yerushalmi's term *shita*. But even in these passages, the configuration of consistency is quite different from what we see in the Yerushalmi.

The word *middah* is common in the Tannaitic corpus. It has the primary sense of a measurement, a measuring tool, or container, and because measures are standards, it also has the sense of a constant property or a rule through which various things are assessed.[85] There are a few passages which use *middah* to describe the approach of an individual sage. The Mishnah at *Menaḥot* 3:4 discusses a grain offering, from which the part to be offered on the altar has been already taken, but the remainders of which were burned, contaminated, or lost before the offering on the altar was made. It tells us that "according to the *middah* of R. Eliezer, it [the offering] is fit; but according to the *middah* of R. Joshua, it is disqualified."[86] If the Mishnah was attributing positions to these sages, it would have used a more standard formulation, like: "'It is fit'—the words of R. Eliezer, but R. Joshua disqualifies." The term the Mishnah uses here signals that these positions are derived

---

[84] See e.g. other passages which use the word גרמיה: "R. Jacob b. Aha [said] in the name of R. Isaac b. Nahman .... R. Jacob [said] in his own name" (*Kil.* 2:5 27d); "R. Joshua said it from tradition while R. Simeon said it in his own name" (*Shevi.* 7:6 37c). See also the contrast between *de'ah* and tradition discussed in the previous chapter.

[85] Elitzur, "*Middah*," argues the term also means a unit of received text or tradition. His conclusion is based in part on references in Amoraic compilations to *middah* as an object of recitation, but I have not found that meaning in the Tannaitic corpus. Several texts Elitzur adduces indicate, in my opinion, the opposite: in *m. Pes.* 1:7, for example, the phrase "this is not the *middah*" does not seem to mean "this is not the text that we learned from our masters," as Elitzur understands it (ibid., 24), since R. Meir presents his ruling as an innovation derived from words which did not state it (Friedman, *Tosefta*, 130–3).

[86] ניטמו שירים. נישרפו שירים. אבדו שירים. כמדת ר' אליעזר. כשירה. וכמדת ר' יהושע. פסולה.

from the approaches of these sages in another set of cases, in which R. Eliezer and R. Joshua dispute the *sine qua non* of sacrifices. In that dispute, R. Eliezer holds that blood alone is essential, and so even if the flesh is damaged the sacrifice is acceptable as long as the blood can be poured on the altar; R. Joshua disqualifies the sacrifice even if the blood is intact and only the flesh is damaged.[87] In our passage, the Mishnah applies this dispute in the case of grain offerings: R. Eliezer would accept the offering since the part to be offered on the altar is still intact, whereas R. Joshua would rule it inadmissible since the remainders have been damaged.[88] It is possible that whoever formulated this passage avoided the normal form of attribution because they wanted to emphasize that these rulings are analogical with R. Eliezer and R. Joshua's positions rather than inherent in them. Be that as it may, the term *middah* here refers to the "measuring instrument" through which the sage arrived at his ruling, which can be applied to further cases and realms of the law.[89]

Three passages which employ *middah* address individual consistency head on, with the sages praised or challenged about the consistent application of their *middah*. All of these passages, just like the passage we have just discussed, involve the teachings of R. Eliezer and R. Joshua (the third also involves R. Nehunia), which may tell us something about the limited use of *middah* in this sense. The first passage addresses a case in which a person dedicated his property to the Temple, and the property included animals that were fit for sacrifice. R. Eliezer rules that both male and female animals are sold, and the proceeds go to the maintenance of the Temple. R. Joshua's ruling makes more distinctions: male animals are offered, females are sold; proceeds from selling the female animals go to make whole-burnt offerings, whereas other property is given to the maintenance of the Temple. R. Aqiva says he prefers R. Eliezer's ruling because he "equated" his *middah* whereas R. Joshua "divided" it.[90]

In the second passage, the same sages dispute the status of a union involving a man and a female minor. R. Eliezer says that the union has no validity, "she is not his wife for any purpose," and both the man and girl may state they refuse the union to dissolve it rather than go through the normal divorce procedure. R. Joshua rules that the minor is indeed the man's wife, except that unlike in a normal marriage, the minor can dissolve the union by refusing it (whereas the man would still need to go through the usual divorce procedure).[91] Again R. Eliezer is praised, this time by R. Ishmael: "I have reviewed all the *middot* of the sages and I did not find a man whose *middah* is equal with respect to minors, except for R. Eliezer; and I see the

---

[87] *t. Zev.* 4:1.
[88] See Balberg, *Blood for Thought*, 75–7 on the dispute concerning blood, and 100–3 on its application to grain offerings.
[89] For a similar use of *middah*, see *m. Ḥul.* 2:6.
[90] *m.* אמ' ר' עקיבה. רואה אני את דברי ר' אליעזר מדברי ר' יהושע. שר' אליעזר הישווה את מידתו ור' יהושע חלק *Sheq.* 4:7.
[91] Shemesh and Halbertal, "The Me'un," 386 n. 43.

words of R. Eliezer [as more reasonable] than the words of R. Joshua, for R. Eliezer equated his *middah*, and R. Joshua divided [it]."[92]

The final passage in this set is a discussion on the impurity of small bits of body separated from the limbs of living people (*m. Eduyot* 6:3). If the bit was flesh, R. Eliezer rules it pure and R. Nehunia rules it impure. If the bit was bone, R. Nehunia rules it pure and R. Eliezer rules it impure. R. Joshua, however, rules in both cases it is impure. The Mishnah presents a lengthy give-and-take on these positions, which include confronting R. Nehunia and R. Eliezer for "dividing" their *middah*, that is, ruling differently in each of the cases; the discussion favors R. Joshua's uniform ruling.[93] R. Eliezer and R. Nehunia both offer good reasons, from their perspectives, for the different ruling, though they do not deny that their *middah* is divided.

These passages employ *middah*, much like *shita*, to invoke consistency or inconsistency in the rulings of an individual sage. At the same time, they present somewhat different interests: what is at stake is neither contradiction nor the sage's distinct profile, but rather a preference for uniformity, putting the onus of proof on a sage who makes distinctions between apparently similar cases or components of the same case. Therefore, unlike in the Talmud, where the possibility that the sage's line is "switched" is a problem, one that requires and normally receives a solution which shows that the line is "not switched,"[94] in these passages *middah* may be divided for a good reason.

We find in the Talmud two passages which cement the terminological connection between the Tannaitic *middah* and Amoraic *shita*. The first involves a discussion on inadvertent, or partially inadvertent, defilement of the Temple or its *sancta* (e.g. by entering the Temple while impure):

m. Shevu'ot 1:4

ועל שאין בה ידיעה לא בתחילה ולא בסוף, שעירי רגלים ושעירי ראשי חדשים מכפרים—דב"ר' יודה. ר' שמעון אומ': שעירי רגלים מכפרים אבל לא שעירי ראשי חדשים. ועל מה שעירי ראשי חדשים מכפרים? על טהור שאכל טמא. ר' מאיר או': כל השעירים כפרתן שווה על טומאת מקדש וקדשיו.

[The previous units of the Mishnah stipulated that cases of defilement with partial inadvertence are atoned by goats offered on the Day of Atonement].

If there was no awareness [of the defilement at all], neither in the beginning nor in the end, the goats of the pilgrimage festivals and of the beginnings of the

---

[92] *t. Yev.* 13:4: אמ' ר' ישמעאל חיזרתי על כל מדת חכמים ולא מצאתי אדם שמדתו שוה בקטנות חוץ מר' ליעזר. וראה אני את דברי ר' ליעזר מדברי ר' יהושע. שר' ליעזר השוה את מדתו ור' יהושע חלק. The reading "*middot* of the sages" follows MS Erfurt; the singular appears in MS Vienna and T-S AS 91.420.

[93] Kahana, "Dispute," 67–71, argues that the passage as whole was designed to support R. Joshua.

[94] While this phrase appears relatively rarely (see n. 30 above), the negation may be inferred.

month atone [for the defilement]—the words of R. Judah. R. Simeon says: The goats of the pilgrimage festivals atone [for such a defilement] but not the goats of the beginnings of months. And what do the goats of the beginnings of months atone for? For [someone who was] pure who consumed [something] impure. R. Meir says: All goats have equal atonement, for the defiling of the Temple and its holy things.

Shevu'ot 1:4 33a

אמ' ר' יוסיביר' בון: ר' יודה חלק שיטת ר' מאיר. ר' שמעון חלק שיטת ר' יודן.

Said R. Yose b. R. Abbin: R. Judah divided the line of R. Meir. R. Simeon divided the line of R. Judah.

R. Yose summarizes the rulings in the Mishnah and the relationships between them: For R. Meir, all goats offered perform the same atonement; R. Judah makes a division among the goats, into two groups, saying that those offered on the Day of Atonement perform a different atonement than those offered on pilgrimage festivals and beginnings of months; and R. Simeon makes a further division, between goats offered on pilgrimage festivals and those offered in the beginnings of months. Like in the passages we have seen in the Mishnah, ruling differently with respect to different cases is described here with the verb "divide" (*ḥ. l. q.*), except here the object of the verb is not *middah* but *shita*.

While the use of the verb "divide" here is likely carried over from its use with *middah*, it may also have made sense to R. Yose (or whoever formulated the utterance) given the tabular sense of *shita* postulated above. Under this interpretation, R. Yose offers a visualization of the different sages, a diagram; in this visualization, R. Judah divides the line of R. Meir, and R. Simeon divides the line of R. Judah:

R. Meir	All goat offerings atone for all instances of inadvertent defilement		
R. Judah	Goats offered on the Day of Atonement atone for defilement instances of partial inadvertence	Goats offered on pilgrimage festivals and beginnings of month atone for defilement instances of full inadvertence	
R. Simeon	Goats offered on the Day of Atonement atone for instances of partial inadvertence	Goats offered on pilgrimage festivals atone for defilement instances of full inadvertence	Goats offered on beginnings of month atone for a pure person who consumed impure food

The other passage that shows the terminological continuity between *middah* and *shita* concerns the opposite of the divided *middah*, the *middah* which is "equated" or "equal." When R. Huna asked R. Mana to join his signature to the former's verdict in a certain case of divorce, R. Mana said: "equate your line and

I shall sign"[95]—and then alluded to a teaching by R. Huna that contradicted his present ruling. The Yerushalmi adduces the story to show that R. Huna retracted his original teaching, that is, that he indeed equated his line. While the verbs "divide" and "equate" appear in many contexts throughout rabbinic literature, it is only in *middah* and *shita* passages that we find them as transitive verbs applying to the sage's approach.[96] This terminological similarity adds to the functional similarity between the two terms.

The Tannaitic term *middah* was sometimes used like the Talmudic term *shita*, to discuss similarities and differences in the sage's approach across different cases. There are, however, great differences. First, whereas *middah* in this sense appears in a handful of passages in the Tannaitic corpus, *shita* appears in hundreds of passages in the Talmud. Second, whereas *middah* is a broad term that is only occasionally used to refer to individual approaches, *shita* is a term specifically designated for this purpose. We find in Tannaitic literature passages in which sages criticize other sages' logical derivations by telling them "this is not *the* [proper] *middah*," using *middah* to refer to a common standard rather than that sage's approach;[97] *Shita* could not replace *middah* here since the point of the term is that each sage has his own *shita*. Finally, the shift from *middah* to *shita* also entailed a shift in perspective: *middah* is a rule or measuring tool which the sage himself uses to assess cases; *shita* is the line or pattern observed by the *interpreter* of rabbinic teachings through comparisons. These differences are consistent with the observations made above. The idea that sages had consistent positions is central to Tannaitic composition;[98] but when consistency is the subject of explicit discussion, it is—apart from this small set of passages employing *middah*—consistency with the general principles of the law, not consistency among the teachings of an individual sage.[99] It is in part the interpretive perspective which generates the construction of and search for distinctive individual profiles which we have observed in this chapter.

Conclusion

Amoraic scholars gave a new meaning to the word *shita* to enable a comparative reading across the various teachings of a given sage and between the corpora of different sages. This term and this reading may reflect the tabular imagination of late ancient scholarship. We have seen how passages answering objections about

---

[95] אשוי שיטתך ונה חתים, *Ket.* 1:2 25b (correcting "ובה" in MS Leiden, per the citation in Nahmanides, *Novellae, Ket.* 110b).
[96] Normally we find the verbs indicting dispute or agreement without a grammatical object; transitively, these verbs take the object of the case in question, see e.g. *Shevu.* 8:1 38c and *B. Q.* 2:1 2d.
[97] See *m. Pes.* 1:7 and *m. Sheq.* 4:6, and see Friedman's discussion, n. 85 above.
[98] See Chapter 2, Section 5.
[99] See the discussion above, Section 2.

the sages' "switched line" individuate rabbinic analysis of consistency: whereas Tannaitic sages primarily addressed inconsistency with the general principles of the law, Talmudic discussions seek also to establish the validity of a sage's teaching within his own corpus. It is true that *meḥalefa* objections perform a variety of functions, from introducing interpretations to providing a rhetorical structure for an entire *sugiya*; but this does not lessen the significance of their focus on individuated comparisons. On the contrary: the fact that the Talmud pursues these different goals through this device is an indication of the integral role attribution-based interpretation plays in Amoraic scholarship.

As we have seen, the claim that the line of a sage is switched was also the claim that teachings of individual sages, in general, could be understood along such lines, that they present distinctive patterns which may be found through careful study. *Meḥalefa* objections were predicated on hypothetical comparative reading which construed a similarity between one teaching and the teaching that *should have been*. In other words, they projected patterns into the corpus of the sage's teachings even when such patterns were absent, by expecting them and explaining their absence. While this comparative reading emphasized consistency among the teachings of the same sage, it also underscored the inconsistency among different sages by attributing to them mutually exclusive and distinctive profiles of ruling.

It is common to attribute an apologetic motive to consistency-establishing interpretation, to read it as defending the authority of the text. In our case too, we could approach Talmudic discussions of rabbinic consistency as attempts to bolster the authority of rabbinic teaching. But the details of these passages suggest that they are doing something different. We have seen that there is a significant number of solutions to *meḥalefa* objections which undermine or at least do not serve to bolster the authority of the teachings which they address: they posit that the Mishnah or other rabbinic teachings are not reliable testimonies of rabbinic statements, that sages ruled against the tradition they inherited, that they changed their mind or even acted in a way which contradicted their own teachings. We have also seen that these passages are not reluctant responses to perceived inconsistencies, but rather construct apparent inconsistencies or contradictions through considerable interpretive effort. What seems to be defended in these passages, then, is not the authority which stems from the consistency of the rabbinic tradition or the teachings of a given sage, but rather the very act of comparative reading which these passages undertake.

4

Lip-Synching in the Grave

Narratives and Images of Attribution

While the previous chapters examined scholarly practices, this chapter examines passages in which the sages themselves reflect on the significance and ethics of attribution. These passages do not present a single ideological approach, but rather a lively conversation with opposing views, and yet we can observe, through the questions they raise and the range of answers they offer, the same move towards individuation which we have observed in Amoraic scholarly practice. I organized the discussion around two primary passages, which, though separate, are related enough that they also appear as part of a single composite passage in late versions of the Yerushalmi.[1] Other Yerushalmi passages are analyzed in the course of discussing these primary passages.

1. Passage I: R. Yohanan, R. Eleazar, and Eternal Glory

Our first passage presents the most elaborate treatment of citation in the classical rabbinic corpus. The fact that this passage addresses this issue in a higher register and in more detail than any rabbinic text before or after it may suggest that it was composed in a time when the significance of citation was changing or contentious. It appears in two contexts in the Yerushalmi, both addressing the proper greeting that a disciple owes his teacher. The discussion begins with a story about a failure of a student to offer such a greeting. R. Yohanan was walking with his student R. Jacob, and another student, R. Eleazar, was hiding from them. R. Yohanan complained to R. Jacob b. Iddi that R. Eleazar failed to greet him properly, and also that he failed to cite him properly when he taught what he learned from R. Yohanan. R. Jacob cooks up two ingenious responses to appease his teacher. After the story concludes, the passage proceeds to discuss the significance of citation, drawing on a widely attested ancient trope of literary or textual immortality. The following analysis aims to show how the various elements of this composite text richly engage

---

[1] In printed editions and some manuscripts (including the Bologna fragment), at *Sheq.* 2:5 47a. That composite passage is late and, like the rest of the version of tractate *Sheqalim* which was grafted into the printed edition, it is influenced by the Bavli (*b. Yev.* 96b–97a); see Sussmann, "Masoret-limud," 48. The long passage is missing in the Genizah fragment of *Sheq.* (T-S F17.24 Fragment 4v, Sussmann, *Ginze Yerushalmi*, 284).

ideas about attribution and how they articulate a newly individuated notion of rabbinic teachings.

Leaning on the shoulders of disciples

One of the ways the story brings the themes of citation and attribution to the fore is through playful reversals of hierarchies between teachers and students. This play appears already in the very first line of the story:

Mo'ed Qattan 3:7 83c (second copy)[2] (par. *Berakhot* 2:1 4b)

ר׳ יוחנן הוה מיסתמיך על ר׳ יעקב בר אידי והוה ר׳ לעזר חמי ליה ומיטמר מן קומוי.

R. Yohanan was leaning on R. Jacob b. Iddi and R. Eleazar was seeing him and hiding from him.

As Uri Ehrlich has shown, there are a number of stories which, like this one, tell us about a third- or fourth-century student lending a shoulder to his master while walking. The significance of this practice, Ehrlich argued, went beyond the physical assistance it offered. Rather, this bodily gesture had a two-fold symbolic function: the master expressed intimacy and familiarity with the student by touching him; but he also expressed his authority and dominance by literally imposing his weight on his student.[3] In our story, it also immediately draws a contrast between R. Jacob b. Iddi, who walks up close with R. Yohanan, and R. Eleazar, who is hiding from him.

This image may also serve as a reversal of sorts of the relationship between master and disciple. The word used here, "lean," is the same word that is used throughout rabbinic literature for relying on an authoritative teaching or instruction of a teacher. But if in that context, the intention is that the younger are "leaning" on the words of their seniors, in our image, it is the older who are "leaning" on the younger. The significance of this contrast becomes clearer when we consider that the majority of these stories about leaning masters explicitly thematize not only the intellectual dependence of the student on the master but also, more distinctively, the master's desire for that dependence. Our story tells us how the leaning master, R. Yohanan, wanted to be cited by his student, R. Eleazar. Another passage, discussed in detail later on in this chapter, opens with a story of a leaning master, R. Hiyya b. Abba, who stops his bath because, he says, it is particularly important to hear one's grandson read the Torah—which, after all, the grandson learned from

---

[2] The last pages of tractate *Mo'ed Qattan* were copied twice by the scribe of MS Leiden. See Feintuch, *Versions and Traditions*, 55–9.
[3] Ehrlich, "Lending a Shoulder."

him, directly or through his son; that passage, like ours, follows the story with a discussion of the ethics of citation.[4] A third passage tells us that in the moment in which ben ha-Qappar voted differently from his master, R. Ishmael b. R. Yose, the latter stopped leaning on him and expressed his dismay at his student's new independence.[5] Finally, a story about a leaning master is included in a passage which attempts to define what makes a teacher one's primary teacher. In that story, R. Hanina learns from the disciple upon whom he was leaning that one of his other disciples, R. Yohanan, has become the most popular preacher in town; he boasts that he had taught R. Yohanan "everything in the field of Aggadah, except Proverbs and Ecclesiastes."[6] The image of the old physically leaning on the young, then, is an appropriate illustration of the theme of inter-dependence between master and disciple in these stories. In the case of our story, it may have had its origin in a more specific narrative function, which I explore below; but its prominence in stories and discussions about the dependence of and on disciples makes it likely that it also carries this symbolic function.

Citation and honor

Our story next sets up the conflict:

Mo'ed Qattan 3:7 83c (par. *Berakhot* 2:1 4b)

ר' יוחנן הוה מיסתמיך על ר' יעקב בר אידי והוה ר' לעזר חמי ליה ומיטמר מן קומוי. אמ': הא תרתין מילין הדין בבלייא עבד לי. חדא דלא שאל בשלמי, וחדא דלא אמ' שמועתא מן שמי.

R. Yohanan was leaning on R. Jacob b. Iddi and R. Eleazar was seeing him and hiding from him. He [R. Yohanan] said: So it is two things that this Babylonian has done to me. One, that he did not greet[7] me. And one [other], that he did not say teachings[8] in my name.

The two complaints that R. Yohanan lodges against R. Eleazar make a nice pair: Eleazar was hiding from R. Yohanan instead of greeting him[9] but he was also hiding R. Yohanan as the source of his teachings. The very association between these two wrongdoings reveals a distinct feature of the text's construction of the

---

[4] *Shabbat* 1:2 3a (par. *Qid.* 1:7 61a), see below.
[5] *Shevi.* 6:1 36c (par. *Yev.* 7:3 8a). The Tannaitic version at *t. Oh.* 18:18 lacks the leaning motif.
[6] *B. M.* 2:11 8d (par. *Hor.* 3:7 48b).
[7] Literally here and later, "inquired after my well-being."
[8] The word "שמועתא" is in the determinative rather than plural form, but the context suggests it should be plural. There are other cases where this form occurs and clearly refers to the plural—see e.g. *Shevi.* 3:3 34c and *B. Q.* 5:1 4d, and *Shab.* 1:2 3a (discussed later in this chapter).
[9] For another example of a disciple hiding from his teacher, see the story in *Pe'ah* 1:1 15d, where R. Ze'ira is hiding from R. Samuel b. Isaac because he finds his behavior embarrassing.

significance of citation: it binds citation with personal honor. R. Yohanan's first complaint reflects the expectation, broadly attested in rabbinic texts, that a disciple should show his teacher some deference when he happens to see him, and even actively pursue seeing him by visiting him.[10] The discussion in *Berakhot* in which our story is embedded includes a teaching that permits a person to disrupt his recitation of the *Shema* in order to offer a greeting to his teacher or someone "greater than him in Torah," and an anonymous comment concludes from that teaching that such a greeting is obligatory when one is not praying. According to these teachings, these greetings are tokens of honor or deference, while avoiding them is disrespectful and amounts to a personal offense against the teacher. That is the case with our story as well. When R. Jacob tries to appease R. Yohanan, he uses a verse from Job that discusses expressions of honor and deference, and later on in the passage a re-definition of avoidance as a form of "giving honor" is used to justify R. Eleazar. The issue throughout, then, is R. Yohanan's honor.

The idea that lack of citation constitutes a personal offense is evident not just in the association between the two wrongdoings, but also in the way citation is spoken about throughout the passage. When R. Yohanan makes the complaint, he says, "two things this Babylonian has done *to me*." Later in the story, R. Jacob tries to appease R. Yohanan by telling him that everyone knows that R. Eleazar's teachings originate with him, so credit is given to him anyway. And beyond the story, the passage explicitly raises the question of the personal benefit a scholar derives from being cited.

From our perspective, it is clear why being cited (at least approvingly) amounts to being honored, and why not being cited properly amounts to personal offense. But that view is tied with our specific notions of knowledge production. It is because we see arguments and interpretations as the product of individual labor that we conceive of citing authors by name as a form of honoring them; it is because we see such intellectual products as the property of the individuals who produced them that we see the lack of proper citation as a form of theft and offense against those individuals. But these notions of knowledge production are not universal. As noted above, several scholars believe the sages saw it differently. If the production of Torah is part of a collective enterprise, then a teaching never belongs to a specific scholar, and citation is not a matter of honor. As we shall see below, even the few Tannaitic texts that do speak about citation do not speak about it in terms of honor or personal benefit to the person being cited.

There are two possibilities for interpreting R. Yohanan's complaint. Under the first interpretation, R. Yohanan considers himself mostly as a bearer of rabbinic tradition, a "tradent" in the terms discussed in the Introduction to this part of the book. His complaint is that R. Eleazar teaches what he transmitted to him but does not acknowledge his act of teaching and transmission. Under the second

---

[10] Neis, *Sense of Sight*, 211–12 and 231–9.

interpretation, R. Yohanan thinks of himself as the *origin* of these teachings that R. Eleazar does not cite in his name, that he is their "author," and thus stating these teachings without his name amounts to a personal offense close to what we might consider an infraction of intellectual property.

Later, I show that the final stages of the Talmud's discussion support the latter understanding. But some considerations in favor of this understanding can be raised even at this point. The first is theoretical. It is more plausible that a view of citation that emphasizes individual benefit will be connected with a view that emphasizes individual production of knowledge or text; the more we posit an exclusive association between a sage and his teachings, the more his name can be attached to them in this privileged way, the more we can imagine citation as an issue which concerns individual honor or offense.

The second consideration concerns the kind of teachings R. Eleazar did not cite in the name of R. Yohanan.[11] Our passage does not record them, but we do hear of two such teachings in passages which, in the midst of the Talmudic give-and-take, cite the same complaint by R. Yohanan against R. Eleazar. In both passages, a teaching attributed to R. Eleazar is followed by a statement from R. Yohanan: "If R. Eleazar said this, it was from me that he heard it and said it."[12] It is difficult to determine whether or not these passages have some kind of genealogical connection to our story, though the fact that they are applied to very specific teachings seems to indicate that they represent an early memory, if not the actual words, of R. Yohanan, and that our storyteller, who knew this statement, merged it into an elaborate narrative.

In both of these other passages, the teaching R. Yohanan wants to be cited in his name is not a ruling or a tradition, but an *argument*. In one passage, the teaching solves a problem concerning a Mishnaic teaching by identifying it as R. Meir's and arguing that it reflects a particular principle associated with him;[13] in the other passage, the teaching argues that a contradiction between the testimonies of two wives about the death of their husbands should be treated differently than other contradictions between two witnesses in a given case.[14] If these were legal rulings

---

[11] R. Yohanan refers to the teachings R. Eleazar does not cite in his name with the term *shemu'a*. While this term can be distinguished from what the sage says on his own opinion, that does not mean that R. Yohanan says these teachings were traditions that he himself learned: he describes the teaching as *shemu'a* when he talks about them in relation to R. Eleazar, who indeed learned them from R. Yohanan. See *Pe'ah* 1:1 15d (par. *Qid.* 1:7 61c), where we hear that R. Jonathan "formulated a *shemu'a*" in the name of R. Yannai" (see Katz, *Qiddushin*, 106), and then R. Yose's statement that this *shemu'a* is one of the clearest of his (= R. Yose's) *shemu'ot*. For R. Yannai, it is not a *shemu'a* (he did not formulate a teaching, but rather instructed a litigant in particular way); for R. Jonathan, there is a *shemu'a* in the name of R. Yannai; and R. Yose's statement shows us that *shemu'ot* are what you receive, not what you formulate yourself—since otherwise, his *shemu'ot* could not be unclear to him. The Amoraic sense of the term differs from its Tannaitic function as designating ancient traditions.

[12] "אמ' ר' יוחנן אם אמרה ר' לעזר מני שמעה ואמרה," *Yev.* 3:9 5a (par. *Yev.* 10:9 11b), and *Yev.* 15:5 15a (par. *San.* 5:2 22d).

[13] *Yev.* 3:9 5a (par. *Yev.* 10:9 11b). On identifications as arguments, see Chapter 1, Section 3.

[14] *Yev.* 15:5 15a (par. *San.* 5:2 22d).

or historical anecdotes, we could have said that R. Yohanan was merely the transmitter of these teachings, and that his complaint is that R. Eleazar did not indicate him as the person who transmitted to him. The fact that they are arguments, however, makes it more likely that R. Yohanan considered the teaching as originating with him. Admittedly, there is no necessary connection between our texts and these passages; but they do give us an indication about how R. Yohanan's complaint was remembered in Amoraic circles, and below we will see more support in our passage for the interpretation offered here of his complaint. Still the other interpretation, that R. Yohanan was upset about being left out as a tradent, cannot be ruled out; it seems to be the idea behind a similar complaint by R. Hoshaya.[15] Either way, these complaints about lack of citation present a stronger connection between sage and teaching, and a wish to be the subject of attribution, that we do not find anywhere in Tannaitic literature.

Our story's coupling of the issue of citing one's teacher and honoring one's teacher is paralleled by another set of stories in the Yerushalmi. Those stories also involve R. Yohanan, except in the role of the disciple rather than the master:

'*Eruvin* 5:1 22b

[The Mishnah speaks of setting up '*Eruvin* for cities. The Talmud presents a dispute between Rav and Samuel: Rav says that the verb for this action should be spelled with an *aleph*, *me'abrin*, and Samuel says that it should be spelled with an '*ayin*, *me'abrin*. An anonymous etymology is adduced to support each spelling. The etymology in support of Rav is then repeated by R. Yohanan:]

ר' יוחנן בשם ר' הושעיה: מוסיפין לה אבר. תלה עינויי ואיסתכל ביה. אמ' ליה: "למה את מסתכל בי? "צרך לך צחק לך. לא צרך לך הפליג עליך". תלת-עשר שנין עבד[16] עליל קומי רביה דלא צריך. ר' שמואל בשם ר' זעירא. אילולא דייו אלא שהיה מקבל פני רבו. שכל המקביל פני רבו כאילו מקבל פני שכינה.

R. Yohanan [said] in the name of R. Hoshaya: They add a limb ('*ever*) to it [the city, and so the verb should be spelled with an *aleph*, like '*ever*].

He [R. Hoshaya] raised his eyes and stared at him [R. Yohanan]. He [R. Yohanan] said to him: Why are you staring at me?

[R. Hoshaya said:] "When he needs you, he smiles at you; when he does not need you, he disregards you."

For thirteen years he [R. Yohanan] would go visit his teacher [R. Hoshaya], even though he did not need him. R. Samuel [said] in the name of R. Ze'ira: It would have been enough for him [and he would have stopped going], but he was

---

[15] *B. B.* 3:6 14b.
[16] Correcting "עבר," with *San.*

receiving the face of his teacher [and that, rather than instruction, was what he was seeking with R. Hoshaya]. For anyone who receives the face of his master, it is as if he receives the face of the divine presence.

Sanhedrin 11:3 30b

ר' בא ר' יוחנן בשם ר' הושעיה: אינו חייב עד שיורה בדבר שעיקרו מדברי תורה ופירושו מדברי סופרים. [...] זחלין אפוי דרב הושעיה. אמ' ליה, "צריך לך שחק לך. לא צריך לך הפליג עלך". תלת-עשרי שנין עבד עליל קומי רביה דלא צריך ליה [...].

R. Abba [said] R. Yohanan [said] in the name of R. Hoshaya: He [the rebellious elder, who instructs against the court] is not liable [for punishment] until he instructs something that has its roots in the words of Torah and its interpretation in the words of the scribes [...].[17]

The face of R. Hoshaya lit up. He said to him: "When he needs you, he smiles at you. When he does not need you he disregards you."

For thirteen years he [R. Yohanan] would go visit his teacher [R. Hoshaya], even though he did not need him [...].[18]

Both passages record an emotional response by R. Hoshaya to the fact that his disciple, R. Yohanan, was citing him. In *'Eruvin*, the master angrily stares at R. Yohanan; in *Sanhedrin*, he is elated. Lieberman has shown that these passages use a proverb that is also found in the Book of Ben Sira, 13:6–7, which opines that when someone is in need of you, he smiles at you, but when he does not, he ignores you.[19] Lieberman considered these two stories to present a sequence of events: first R. Hoshaya was happy (as recounted in *Sanhedrin*) and at another time he was upset (as recounted in *'Eruvin*); R. Yohanan commented, in the second of these episodes, about the change in R. Hoshaya's reaction (this interpretation requires erasing the proverb from the passage in *Sanhedrin*).[20] I suggest instead that they are two versions of the same story about R. Hoshaya's response to R. Yohanan citing him. It is R. Hoshaya who utters the statement, "when he needs you, he smiles at you; when he does not need you, he disregards you." The need here is the need of which we learn in the sentence immediately following this one, which tells us that R. Yohanan would visit R. Hoshaya even though he no longer needed him. R. Hoshaya's point in both versions is that R. Yohanan only cites him when he

---

[17] Skipping here a teaching from R. Ze'ira which comments on R. Hoshaya's teaching but which is not relevant to my discussion.

[18] The passage proceeds to quote the same teaching from R. Samuel which appears at the end of the passage from *'Er*.

[19] Lieberman, *YK*, 289; see Kister, "Ben Sira," 318 and n. 36.

[20] There are several problems with this interpretation. First, the emendation has no documentary foundation. Second, the proverb from Ben Sira does not distinguish between happiness and anger but between fawning and ignoring (see Kister, "Ben Sira," 318). Third, there is no indication in the text that the *'Eruvin* story takes place after the incident from *Sanhedrin*.

needs him, which is not often (that R. Yohanan does not need R. Hoshaya is clear in the Yerushalmi, but even more so in the Bavli, where R. Yohanan tells us that after spending eighteen days with R. Hoshaya he only learned from him that one thing about the spelling of the word in the Mishnah).[21] The difference between the two versions is that one imagines R. Hoshaya's response as happiness at being cited at least this once, whereas the other posits he was angry at R. Yohanan's general intellectual disregard of him.

There are important differences between these stories about R. Hoshaya and our story about R. Yohanan and R. Eleazar. In the latter, R. Yohanan is angry because R. Eleazar teaches his teachings without acknowledging their source. R. Hoshaya, in contrast, seems to be upset because R. Yohanan does not need his teachings at all. It is perhaps this difference, or maybe also a somewhat different approach to citation, which leads to another difference between the stories. While in the story about R. Yohanan and R. Eleazar citation is equated with the disciple's obligation to show deference, the stories about R. Hoshaya and R. Yohanan differentiate these two issues: R. Yohanan continues to show deference to R. Hoshaya by visiting him, but he does not cite him. Nevertheless, in both stories citing is something that the cited sage takes personally, and in both the issue of citation is bound with the issue of the sage's honor. These stories too, then, are a testament to an individuation of Torah in the Amoraic period.

R. Jacob's first answer to R. Yohanan is that R. Eleazar was merely following his local custom in Babylonia; while the answer relates to R. Yohanan's first complaint, about the lack of greeting, its formulation may also shed light on the second complaint, about the lack of citation:

Mo'ed Qattan 3:7 83c (par. *Berakhot* 2:1 4b)

אמ' ליה: כן אינון נהגין גבון. זעירא לא שאיל בשלמיה דרבה, דאינון מקיימין "ראוני נערים ונחבאו וישישים קמו עמדו".

He [R. Jacob] said to him: This is how they usually treat each other. The junior [sage] does not greet the senior [sage], for they fulfill [the verse, Job 29:8] "the young men saw me and hid, and the aged rose up and stood."

The word used here for junior, *za'ira*, is not very common in the Yerushalmi; it applies to sages only six other times in the entire Talmud.[22] Three of these instances address the question of citation: two of the passages, unsurprisingly, raise

---

[21] b. 'Er. 53a: "אמר ר' יוחנן שמנה-עשר ימים גדלתי אצל ר' אושעיא ולא למדתי ממנו אלא דבר אחד במשנתנו. כאי-זה-צד מאברין את הערים. באלף".
[22] Kosovsky, *Concordance*, 150 (I am not counting here instances where *ze'ira* is a name or part of a name, as in the case of R. Ze'ira or "R. Abuna the younger"). In addition to the sources noted below, see *Ber.* 2:6 5b (par. *M. Q.* 3:5 82d), *Kil.* 9:4 32b (par. *Ket* 12:3 35a), *B. B.* 9:6 17a.

suspicions about learning from "minor persons";[23] the third passage, however, is less predictable:

Shevi'it 7:4 37c (par. *Sanhedrin* 3:3 21a–b)

ר׳ בא בר זבדא ר׳ אבהו בשם ר׳ אלעזר: הל׳ כר׳ יודה דמתניתן. אקלס ר׳ בא בר זבדא, דמר שמועה בשם זעיר מיניה.

R. Abba b. Zavda [said] R. Abbahu [said] in the name of R. Eleazar: The law follows R. Judah in our Mishnah.

R. Abba b. Zavda was praised, for he said a teaching in the name of someone who is his junior.

In this passage, R. Abba b. Zavda cites R. Abbahu's teaching in the name of R. Eleazar; we then hear that he was praised for citing his junior colleague. If it is noble to cite one's juniors, our story may underscore the hierarchy between "juniors" and "seniors" to cast an unflattering spotlight on R. Yohanan's anger that his juniors do not cite him.

An Amoraic view of Tannaitic citation practices

R. Jacob's second response to R. Yohanan centers on the question of citation:

Mo'ed Qattan 3:7 83c (par. *Berakhot* 2:1 4b)

מי מהלכין חמי ליה חד בית מדרש. אמ׳ ליה: הכין הוה ר׳ מאיר יתיב ודרש, ואמ׳ שמועתא מן שמיה דר׳ ישמעאל ולא אמ׳ שמועתא מן שמיה דר׳ עקיבה. אמ׳ ליה: כל עמא ידעין דר׳ מאיר תלמידיה דר׳ עקיבה. אמ׳ ליה: וכל עמא ידעין דר׳ לעזר תלמידיה דר׳ יוחנן!

As they were walking, he [R. Jacob] showed him a certain house of study. He said: Here R. Meir was sitting and expounding, and he said teachings in the name of R. Ishmael and he did not say teachings in the name of R. Aqiva. He [R. Yohanan] said to him: Everyone knows that R. Meir is the student of R. Aqiva. He said to him: And everyone knows that R. Eleazar is the student of R. Yohanan!

R. Jacob points out a house of study to R. Yohanan and notes that R. Meir taught there statements that he explicitly attributed to R. Ishmael, but not to R. Aqiva. R. Yohanan responds that everyone knows that R. Meir was R. Aqiva's student; there was no need for R. Meir to cite R. Aqiva by name since people would recognize R. Aqiva as the source of the teachings. R. Jacob replies that this logic also applies in the case that troubled R. Yohanan: everyone knows that R. Eleazar is R. Yohanan's student, and therefore just like R. Meir's teachings are recognized

---

[23] *M Q.* 3:5 82b, *Yev.* 8:2 9a.

as R. Aqiva's even if his name is not mentioned, so are R. Eleazar's teachings recognized as R. Yohanan's even if his name is not mentioned. As we shall see later, R. Yohanan seems to be pleased with this explanation.

The premise of this dialogue, that a student does not (or might not) cite his teacher, seems to be shared by another Yerushalmi passage:[24]

Rosh Ha-Shanah 4:4 59b

[*m. Rosh Ha-Shanah* 4:4 tells us about a legal change: the law used to be that testimonies of sighting of the new moon, which established that the new year has begun, were accepted throughout the day on the last day of the last month of the year; but one time the witnesses were late to come, and the uncertainty about whether or not the holiday has begun made the Levites confused about whether or not to sing the holiday song, and so from then on witnesses were accepted only before the time of the afternoon offering.]

אמ' ר' שמואל בר נחמן: מפני מעשה שאירע. פעם אחת נפלה הברה בעיר ובאו סרקיים ונטלום ונתקלקלו הלוים בשיר. אמ' ר' אחא בר פפא קומי ר' זעורה: חברייא בעון קומי ר' שמואל בר נחמן, "בשם מן ר' אמ' לה?" אמ' לון: דכוותכון דאית לכון רבבין סגיך? בשם ר' יהושע בן לוי אמ' ליה.

Said R. Samuel b. Nahman: It [the witnesses' delay] was because of an event that happened. Once a rumor dropped in town that Saracens came and took them [the witnesses] away, and the Levites were disordered in the song.

Said R. Aha b. Papa before R. Ze'ira: The colleagues asked before R. Samuel b. Nahman, "In whose name did you[25] say this?" He said to them, "[Am I] like you, who have so many masters? I said it in the name of R. Joshua b. Levi."

R. Samuel b. Nahman's answer to the colleagues implies that since he only has one teacher (unlike those colleagues), it should be clear that the source of his teachings is R. Joshua b. Levi. It is difficult to know from this passage if R. Samuel invokes a well-known principle (which is not recorded elsewhere) or simply provides a snarky response ("who do you think it's from?"). It is also unclear whether it is true that R. Samuel b. Nahman indeed had one prominent teacher,[26] and it is even less clear that the same pattern of a single prominent master can apply to the relationship between R. Eleazar and R. Yohanan.[27]

---

[24] Assis, "Fragment," 53.
[25] Literally, "the master" or "our master," using the polite form as is usual for students addressing their teacher; PM implausibly suggests that "ר'" stands for "רבי," R. Judah the Patriarch, and that the question goes back to the Mishnah.
[26] Boch, *RH*, 242, suggests the passage should be about R. Isaac b. Nahman.
[27] As Assis notes ("Fragment," 53), other passages present R. Eleazar not simply as R. Yohanan's student but also as a peer (*San.* 1:1 18b) and even have R. Yohanan address him with *rabbi* (*Meg.* 1:10 72c).

There is a significant difference between the kind of teaching that is at stake in the passages about R. Eleazar and R. Yohanan and this passage about R. Samuel. In the latter passage, the colleagues have a good reason to assume that R. Samuel is offering a tradition he had received rather than his own interpretation of the Mishnah, since he refers to a historical event with some very specific details (Saracens!). As we have seen, in the passages which provide the teachings about which R. Yohanan complained, the teachings are not historical anecdotes transmitted across generations, but rather interpretive arguments which R. Yohanan presumably considered his own. The significance and ethics of citation is therefore different in the two incidents. In the passage in *Rosh ha-Shanah*, R. Samuel b. Nahman is merely transmitting something, and citation is therefore an indication of authority—not credit; after all, even R. Joshua b. Levi must have heard it from someone else, since the tradition ostensibly goes back to the time of the Temple. In our passage, R. Yohanan is angry at R. Eleazar precisely because he is stealing "his" teachings and does not acknowledge his unique contribution. While the dialogue between R. Yohanan and R. Jacob may reflect an existing Amoraic practice, then, the story already diverges from the logic underpinning that practice.

A similar combination of continuity and break applies to the passage's reference to R. Meir's citation of R. Ishmael and not of R. Aqiva. It is true that, in the Mishnah, on one occasion, R. Meir quotes a teaching "in the name of R. Ishmael"[28] and we never find him quoting R. Aqiva. Epstein suggested that our story reflects this presentation of R. Meir's teachings in the Mishnah.[29] But the Tosefta changes the picture: it includes several passages in which R. Meir quotes R. Aqiva, and no passages in which he quotes R. Ishmael.[30] There are, therefore, more instances of R. Meir quoting R. Aqiva than instances of him quoting R. Ishmael, contrary to R. Jacob's point here that R. Meir would only cite R. Ishmael (while it is possible that our storyteller was unaware of these instances in the Tosefta, at least one of these instances seemed to have been known to a late Amoraic scholar).[31]

Simply counting these instances, however, can be misleading. The reason that R. Meir's citation practices in the Mishnah differ from those recorded in the Tosefta has to do with the difference between these compilations, not with R. Meir's practices themselves. The lack of citation of R. Aqiva in the Mishnah goes beyond R. Meir: there is, in fact, no instance in the entire Mishnah where a named sage is teaching "in the name of R. Aqiva"; in the Tosefta, however, there are around twenty such citations.[32] R. Ishmael, in contrast, has teachings quoted in his name more

---

[28] *m. Kil.* 3:7.
[29] Epstein, *Tannaitic Literature*, 81.
[30] *t. Meg.* 3:16, *t. Yev.* 11:6, 11:8–9, and *t. Git.* 5:7–9.
[31] See *Yev.* 10:3 11a (par. *Git.* 8:7 49c).
[32] *t. Ma'as.* 2:20, *t. Shab.* 15:17, *t. Meg.* 3:16, *t. Yev.* 11:6, 8, 9, 12:15, *t. Git.* 2:6, 6:6, 7, 9, *t. B. Q.* 6:21 (twice), *t. B. B.* 5:7, *t. San.* 12:10, *t. Zev.* 9:5, *t. Kel. B. Q.* 6:15, *B. M.* 6:7, *t. Oh.* 14:4, *t. Neg.* 1:2, 5:3. Many of these are by R. Meir—see below.

evenly throughout the Tannaitic corpus.[33] These differences reflect what was observed by the Mishnah's earliest readers: that the Mishnah reflects traditions that emerged from R. Aqiva and his students, and in particular R. Meir.[34] Epstein developed this observation and demonstrated it systematically, showing that teachings by R. Aqiva were often recorded anonymously in the Mishnah.[35] The Toseftan passages which indicate when R. Meir quoted R. Aqiva may not have been shaped by the same Aqivan circles; several of them appear anonymously in the Mishnah, without any attribution.[36] We have seen a similar process highlighted in the story about R. Issi, who cited the *mishnah* of his teacher's teacher, R. Eliezer, without knowing so because the teaching was not attributed to R. Eliezer.[37] In this sense, R. Jacob is right: when R. Meir was teaching, he probably did not cite R. Aqiva, precisely because he was teaching *the* Torah, as he had learned it from R. Aqiva. For Tannaitic sages, anonymity, in general, indicates acceptance; attribution indicates dissent or variance.

But while our story captures faithfully certain aspects of Tannaitic citation practices, it reframes them in a way that breaks with their premises. For R. Yohanan and R. Jacob, as they are represented in our story, attribution is an honor that is given as appropriate acknowledgment. R. Yohanan says that R. Meir does not have to cite R. Aqiva because such acknowledgment could be taken for granted: everyone *knows* that the teachings are from R. Aqiva. But from what we can learn from Tannaitic literature itself, R. Meir was not recorded as citing R. Aqiva because those who were recording the teachings did not see them as "R. Aqiva's" or "R. Meir's," but as the accepted teaching or the opinion of the majority—as we have also seen in the rule about anonymous teachings attributed to R. Yohanan himself.[38] If reciting a teaching anonymously indicates its acceptance, it does not amount to dishonor or personal offense.

Quotation, idols, and God

The final scene of the story goes back to the question of R. Eleazar's hiding from R. Yohanan:

Mo'ed Qattan 3:7 83c (first copy) (par. *Berakhot* 2:1 4b)

ומהו מיעבור קומי אדורא צלמא? אמ' ליה: ומה אפליג ליה אוקר? עבור קומוי ואסמי עינוי.
אמ' ליה: יאות ר' לעזר עבד לך דלא עבר קומך. אמ' ליה: ר' יעקב בר אידי, יודע את לפייס!

---

[33] "In the name of R. Ishmael" appears in three passages in the Mishnah (*m. Kil.* 3:7—by two sages), *m. 'Er.* 1:2, and *m. Miq.* 9:6, once in *Mek d. R. I.* (*Pisḥa* §16), once in *Sifre Numbers* (§31) and three times in the Tosefta (*t. B. Q.* 6:18, *t. Bek.* 4:16, *t. Par.* 3:3, and *t. Miq.* 6:14).
[34] See *b. San.* 86a, and the discussion of the Yerushalmi antecedents in Chapter 1, Section 2 above.
[35] Epstein, *Tannaitic Literature*, 81–7; he cites our story on 81.
[36] See Epstein, ibid., 82 nn. 81–2.
[37] Chapter 1, Section 5.
[38] Chapter 1, Section 2.

[R. Jacob asked:] What is [the law about] passing before the idol of Adori?[39]

He [R. Yohanan] said to him: Why are you honoring it? Pass before it and ignore it.[40]

He [R. Jacob] said to him: R. Eleazar has behaved appropriately with you, then, when he did not pass before you.

He [R. Yohanan] said to him: R. Jacob b. Iddi, you know how to appease!

Just as he did earlier, R. Jacob tricks R. Yohanan into admitting that R. Eleazar's actions were appropriate. We can see in this scene more clearly the play on the roles of teacher and student. Ostensibly, R. Jacob is asking the question and R. Yohanan is providing the answer. But R. Jacob really knows the answer. He asks it to appease R. Yohanan and guide him to the correct answer just as he guides him physically. The specific question is in the domain of laws relating to idolatry. When R. Jacob asks R. Yohanan whether they should avoid a cultic fixture, R. Yohanan says that avoiding it would be giving it undeserved honor. R. Jacob replies that if that is the case, then R. Eleazar's avoidance of R. Yohanan was an act of deference.

While there was a pervasive rabbinic prohibition on viewing certain cult statues,[41] we find several anecdotes in which Amoraic scholars permitted passing before them:

'Avodah Zarah 3:8 43b

גמליאל זוגא הוה מיסתמיך בר׳ שמעון בן לקיש. מטון בהו תבניתא. אמ׳ ליה: מהו ניעבור קומוי? אמ׳ ליה: עבור קומוי וסמי עיניה.

ר׳ יצחק בר מתנה הוה מיסתמיך בר׳ יוחנן. מטון צלמא דבולי. אמ׳ ליה: מהו ניעבור קומוי? אמ׳ ליה: עבור קומוי וסמי עיניה.

ר׳ יעקב בר אידי הוה מיסתמיך בר׳ יהושע בן לוי. מטון לאדורי צלמא. אמ׳ ליה: נחום איש קודש קדשים עבר ואת לית את עבר? עבור קומוי וסמי עיניה.

Gamaliel Zugga was leaning on R. Simeon b. Laqish. They arrived at a certain stele. He [R. Simeon] said to him, "What is [the law]? May we pass before it?" He [Gamaliel Zugga] said to him, "Pass before it and ignore it."

R. Isaac b. Mattena was leaning on R. Yohanan. They arrived at the idol of the *Boule*. He said to him, "What is [the law]? May we pass before it?" He said to him, "Pass before it and ignore it."

---

[39] Despite various attempts, scholarship has not yet been able to identify this cult object conclusively; see Schwartz, *Were the Jews*, 136 n. 68.

[40] Literally, here and in the passage from 'A. Z. below: "blind its eye." Translation follows Sokoloff, *DJPA*, 381; see Neis, *Sense of Sight*, 187–90, for an exploration of this phrase, and the suggestion that it may refer instead to a disrespectful gaze at the idol.

[41] Neis, *Sense of Sight*, 170–201.

R. Jacob b. Iddi was leaning on R. Joshua b. Levi. They arrived at the idol of Adori. He said to him, "Nahum, the man of the holy of holies, passed before it, and you would not pass? Pass before it and ignore it."

While the differences and similarities between our story and the set of anecdotes presented here do not allow for a simple model of literary dependence,[42] the similarities are too great to ignore. It seems likely that our storyteller was relying on this genre of stories, if not necessarily on a specific anecdote involving R. Jacob or R. Yohanan. Those brief stories have a specific design that stems from the legal point they are meant to convey. The leaning of the master on the disciple serves a straightforward function here: it is because of that leaning that the student was leading the way, and therefore had to ask the question about passing before the idol. The reason that these stories have the students initiate the question rather than the master simply instructing the law may be found in some of the responses: the very question whether or not to pass before these idols was problematic, either because it suggested a holier-than-thou approach (per R. Joshua b. Levi in 'Avodah Zarah) or because changing course on account of the idol was treating it with more importance than it deserves (per R. Yohanan in our story). Our storyteller chose this story type to set up the fantastic analogy between ignoring the statue and the disciple avoiding his master.

Both our story and the passages quoted above about R. Hoshaya and R. Yohanan construe the honoring presence a disciple owes his master in terms of the latter's divine-like status. In the story about R. Hoshaya, the association of the master with the divine is explicit and positive: the passage concludes with the statement that "anyone who receives the face of his master, it is as if he receives the face of the divine presence." Our story, in contrast, sets up a trickier association. As scholars have noted, it implicitly compares R. Yohanan and an idol. Seth Schwartz argued that this comparison "contains a hint of a reproach of what [the storyteller] may see as the rabbi's self-aggrandizement";[43] Rafael Neis wrote that it casts R. Yohanan "as an icon of sorts to whom visual piety is due, in contrast to the disrespectful treatment that an idol deserves."[44] These interpretations are not mutually exclusive: as we shall see below, the passage may be critical of R. Yohanan's self-aggrandizement while at the same time legitimating it.

In both stories, the analogy with God or idol concerns the question of sight: in the story about R. Hoshaya, beholding the master is like beholding God's presence; in our story, ignoring the idol would be, like ignoring R. Yohanan, a sign of deference. But it is possible that the analogy also relates to our story's exploration of the significance of citation. As I have mentioned above, the Amoraic period saw an

---

[42] Moscovitz, "Sugyot Muḥlafot," 28–30.
[43] Schwartz, *Were the Jews*, 137 n. 68.
[44] Neis, *Sense of Sight*, 190.

increase in citation of rabbinic teachings, giving these teachings a function which had been largely reserved for Scripture. If we accept Schwartz's and Neis's suggestions that the image of the idol functions as an analogy—critical or positive—with R. Yohanan, can we also say that the sage's desire to be quoted is a desire for a God-like status? The passage never says anything close to that explicitly. But the fact that the units which follow the story in our passage address quotation and immortality, another divine prerogative, is suggestive.

Quotation and immortality

The story about R. Yohanan and his students is followed in the Talmud by a discussion which opens with a question about R. Yohanan's conduct:

Mo'ed Qattan 3:7 83c (first copy) (par. Berakhot 2:1 4b)

ור׳ יוחנן בעי דיימרון שמועתא מן שמיה? אף דוד ביקש עליה רחמים. אמ׳, "אגורה באהלך עולמים". ר׳ פינחס ר׳ ירמיה בשם ר׳ יוחנן: וכי עלת על לב דוד שהוא חייה לעולם? אלא כך אמ׳: אזכה שיהו דבריי נאמרים בבתי כניסיות ובבתי מדרשות.

And did R. Yohanan want teachings to be said in his name?

David too prayed for this. He said, "Let me live in your tent forever" (Ps 61:5). R. Phinehas [said] R. Jeremiah [said] in the name of R. Yohanan: And did David actually think that he would live forever? Rather, this is what he was saying: May I be so rewarded, that my words will be said[45] in synagogues and houses of study.

The question itself shows us how this passage stands at a certain juncture in the history of rabbinic citation practices. Modern academics might take for granted that scholars would want their work to be cited. The story which appears before this question also seems to take for granted that R. Yohanan would want to be cited: R. Jacob does not question the importance of people knowing that R. Eleazar's teachings are from R. Yohanan, he just argues that it is already well known. But the discussion which follows the story questions that very desire, in a way which implies at least bewilderment, perhaps even critique (Schwartz's translation captures these overtones: "and why was R. Yohanan so insistent that they report teachings in his name?").[46]

---

[45] MS Leiden for Ber. adds here: "in my name" (על שמי), which emphasizes the point; but the addition is not necessary, and these words are missing also in a Genizah fragment for Ber. (Ox. Heb. d. 45, 4–5 [2674.3]; Sussmann, Ginze Yerushalmi, 17).

[46] Schwartz, Were the Jews, 55.

The anonymous answer to this question argues that even the great King David desired, like R. Yohanan, to be cited. The demonstration of this claim offers a reason for the wish to be cited, through an interpretation of Psalm 61:5 attributed to R. Yohanan. The composer of the passage must have been at least aware of the suitability of answering the question, "why R. Yohanan wanted to be cited," with a citation of R. Yohanan, and it is possible the attribution was concocted precisely for that reason. The interpretation of the verse argues that when the Psalmist asks to reside in God's tent forever, he cannot possibly mean to ask for eternal life. Rather, what David requested from God was that his words—*the Psalms*—would be said in houses of worship and study, God's tents, forever, as generations recite and study the Psalter *in David's name*,[47] referring to the Davidic superscripts of the Psalms ("A Psalm of David"; Psalms 3:1, 4:1, etc.).

In the story about R. Yohanan and R. Eleazar, the desire for citation too is understood as a desire for renown, but fame might be limited to one's lifetime, if R. Yohanan only seeks to be recognized by R. Eleazar in his contemporary study environment. The comparison between R. Yohanan and King David, however, understands the benefits of citation in terms of everlasting mention of their names—a form of immortality.

It is this move towards eternity which, I think, removes any doubt that our passage sees the sage to whom a teaching is attributed as the unique and distinctive figure behind the teaching rather than one of its many tradents. R. Yohanan cannot expect to be remembered forever if his role is simply to transmit a teaching to R. Eleazar—for even if R. Eleazar should cite R. Yohanan by name, and even if R. Eleazar's student would cite his teacher's teacher—surely at some point R. Yohanan's name would have to give way to other masters (I discuss such transmission chains later on in this chapter). An eternal association between a teaching and a sage does not make sense if the sage only has a temporary role in transmitting the teaching; rather, it stems from a view that the teaching, in some sense, belongs to that individual. It also implies a certain textual fixity of the attribution itself, removed as it were from any particular instructional context: that is, much like David's name is inscribed in the Psalms and that inscription is transmitted alongside the Psalms in written form, this passage must imagine that R. Yohanan's name will be attached to his teachings in a fixed way, even if they are transmitted in oral form.

This explanation of the desire for citation with a desire for everlasting recognition participates in a well-documented trope spanning literary cultures in various periods and places; I will return to it later. The Talmud, however, is not quite satisfied with this explanation. It asks what concrete benefit—the word used here is the same term used in Halakhic discourse for deriving financial benefit—R. Yohanan derives from such quotation:

---

[47] See above, n. 45.

Mo'ed Qattan 3:7 83c (par. *Berakhot* 2:1 4b)

מה הנייה[48] ליה? לוי בר נזירא[49] אמ': האו' שמועה משם אומרה שפתותיו רוחשות עימו[50] בקבר. מה טע'? "דובב שפתי ישינים", ככומר זה שלענבים שהוא זב מאיליו. ר' חיננא בר פפא ור' סימון—חד אמ': כהן דשתי קונדיטון, וחורנה אמ': כהן דשתי חמר עתיק. אע״ג דהוא שתי ליה טעמיה בפומיה.

And what is the benefit for him [when his words are cited forever in his name]?

Levi b. Nazira said: Anyone who says a teaching in the name of the one who said it, his [the latter's] lips are moving with him in the grave. What is the proof? ["Like the best wine that goes down to my lover smoothly,] making the lips of the dead move" (Song 7:10). Just like a heap of grapes [shrunk by sun exposure], which oozes [the juice of the grapes] on its own.

R. Hanina b. Papa and R. Simon [disputed]. One said, it is like someone who drinks spiced wine, and the other said it is like someone who drinks old wine. Even though he [already] drank it, its taste is [still] in his mouth.

The question is answered with a teaching from R. Levi b. Nazira; in a passage that is all about attributions, we can probably assume that there was an irony intended in attributing the first among several teachings about wine to a sage whose name evokes the Nazirite, a person who vows to abstain from wine (Numbers 6).[51] The teaching itself presents one of the most striking images in the Talmud. It argues that citation physically affects the cited dead: as the citing living say their words in their name, the dead's lips are moving alongside them in the grave, whispering the same teaching.[52] This claim is supported by a difficult verse from the Song of Songs: the "wine" in the verse is understood, expectedly, as a symbol for Torah; this wine is said in the verse to perform a certain action with the "lips of those who are asleep," an action which is described with the *hapax legomenon* "*dovev*," and which the sages could have understood in relation to verbs which mean "move slowly" or "make speak." The Targum for this verse interprets it as relating to resurrection through prophecy.[53] Like the previous teaching about David, this teaching too posits that quotation overcomes death, but here this overcoming is achieved not through eternal fame but with a physical animation of the body.

---

[48] Correcting אנים, with *Ber.* (spelling with the Oxford fragment).

[49] Reading with *Ber.*; in Leiden here, "Levi" was dropped, probably on account of the ליה, and the first two letters of נזירא were erroneously joined to become ט.

[50] Adding עמו, with *Ber.*

[51] On similar connections, often humorous, between teachings and attributions in rabbinic literature, see Friedman, "Ha-shem gorem."

[52] It is likely that some sound is involved; in *Ber.* 4:1 7a, the same root, *r. ḥ. š.*, is used where sound is implied.

[53] וביחזקאל בר בוזי כהנא דנבבואת פומיה אתערו מיתיא דבקעת דורא. Text from the *Comprehensive Aramaic Lexicon* database.

The next few lines offer images related to wine, which illustrate how this process works. In the first image, the dead sages are likened to grapes from which the juice—the Torah—flows out on its own, with no need for treading. R. Hanina and R. Simon offer an alternative comparison: just like the taste of very flavorful wine stays in one's mouth long after one drank it, so the words of the Torah continue to be in the sages' mouth long after they spoke them, indeed even after their death. These two sages differ in the kind of wine that is given as an example of flavorful wine, one offering old wine, the other spiced wine. What is at stake in this dispute might be the aspect of Torah study that makes it everlasting:[54] old wine might stand here for the faithful transmission of old traditions; spiced wine, which was prepared in part with peppers, might stand for the innovative, sharp reasoning in Torah study which Amoraic scholars called "peppered."[55]

There are certain indications that our passage had a complicated process of composition. The fact that the question "what benefit does he derive" appears after the comment on David's quest for everlasting glory is a bit odd. Perhaps whoever composed the passage did not consider everlasting glory a sufficient benefit, but the passage does not explain why it is insufficient; it is as if the teaching about David was never there. The teaching about the lips in the grave, which is adduced as an answer to this second question, has nothing to do with David or the Psalms—it talks about quoting a *shemu'a*, rabbinic teaching, which serves as a good answer to a question about R. Yohanan, not David. It is possible, then, that originally, this teaching was an answer to the first question about R. Yohanan ("and does R. Yohanan want teachings to be said in his name?"); and that someone added the teaching about David in between. The question "what benefit does he derive?" was added where the original text resumed. This sequencing occurred early enough that already the late ancient compilation *Pesiqta Rabbati* presents a smoother version of our passage without the seams.[56]

We should consider, then, what these discrete teachings may have meant independently of their current context, and how their sequencing in the Talmud affected their meaning. The teaching about the lips in the grave does not mention eternity, nor does it apply to eternity necessarily. It does speak about quoting a teaching beyond the life of the person who said it, but unlike what is implied in the passage as a whole, that does not necessarily mean a person uniquely and permanently associated with a teaching; it could simply refer to the person from whom the sage heard the teaching. In contrast, the teaching about David does imply, I argued, a permanent connection between the cited teaching and the figure whose name is

---

[54] Ashkenazi, *Yefe mar'eh*, 13a.
[55] On old wine, cf. m. *Avot* 4:20; on spiced wine, containing peppers, as a metaphor for Torah, see *Pesiqta de-Rav Kahana*, 12.5, 208. On "peppered" as a term for the sharp and innovative aspects of Torah study, see *Hor.* 3:8 48c. See also the similar dispute by the same sages in *Lamentations Rabbah* 2:16.
[56] *Pesiqta Rabbati* §2.

invoked. While the *derashah* about the tents does not have death physically defied, the teaching about the lips in the grave implies we can limit the physical effects of death. The teaching about David concerns attribution that is fixed in a written text, the Psalms; the teaching about the lips in the grave concerns sages. The sequencing of these teachings together produces the idea that if a sage quotes a teaching in the name of another sage, with whom that teaching is permanently associated, the quoting sage gives the quoted sage a type of immortality, both in the sense of a bit of life in the grave and in the sense of constant presence in the study house.

The final unit in our discussion returns to David:

Mo'ed Qattan 3:7 83c–d (par. *Berakhot* 2:1 4b)

ואין דור שאין בו ליצנים. ומה היו פריצי הדור עושין? היו מהלכין אצל חלונותיו שלדוד ואומ': "דוד! אימתי יבנה בית המקדש? אימתי בית י"י נלך? והוא או': אע"פ שהן מתכוונין להכעיסיני יבוא עלי שאני שמח בליבי. "שמחתי באומרים לי בית י"י נלך".

"והיה כי ימלאו ימיך ללכת עם אבותיך". אמ' ר' שמואל בר נחמן: אמ' הקב'ה לדוד, "דוד, ימים מליאים אני מונה לך. אין אני מונה לך ימים חסירים. כלום שלמה בנך בונה בית המקדש לא להקריב בתוכו קרבנות? חביב עלי משפט וצדקה שאת עושה יותר מן הקרבנות". מה טע'? "עשה צדקה ומשפט נבחר לי"י מזבח".

And there is no generation in which there are no scoffers. And what would the shameless people of that generation do? They would walk to David's windows and say, "David! When will the Temple be built? When can we go to the House of the Lord?" And he [David] answered: "Even though they intend to anger me, I swear that I am happy in my heart." "[A song of ascents of David.] I was glad when they said to me, Let us go to the House of the Lord (Ps 122:1–2)."

"When your days are full to go to be with your ancestors, [I will raise up your offspring.... He shall build a house for me; 1 Chron 17:11–12]." Said R. Samuel b. Nahman: The Holy One, blessed be He, said to David: "David, I count full days for you, and I do not count for you lacking days. Is not your son, Solomon, building the Temple only to offer sacrifices in it? The [acts of] justice and righteousness that you do are dearer to me than the sacrifices." What is the proof? "To do righteousness and justice is more acceptable to the Lord than sacrifice (Prov 21:3)."[57]

This two-part unit addresses God's choice to have King David's son Solomon, rather than David himself, build the Temple. It first tells us that scoffers would taunt David, expressing their impatience with the wait for the Temple. They not only mock David for the fact that he was passed over for the task of building God's house;

---

[57] The *derashah* might be vocalizing the verb forms in this verse differently, which would result in this translation: "The doer of righteousness and justice is dearer to the Lord than the one offering sacrifices."

since God explicitly says the Temple would only be built after David dies, these scoffers also tell the king how much they look forward to his death. The second part begins with the observation that God allowed David's life to run its full course. R. Samuel b. Nahman interprets this as the result of God's preferences: Solomon may build the Temple, but it is the acts of "righteousness and justice" which David has done—relying on 2 Samuel 8:15 without citing it—that is preferable to God.

At first glance, it may seem that this unit only appears here because David was mentioned earlier, that it has little to do with the themes our passage explores. It is likely that it was composed independently of our passage. But once it was incorporated here, it gained a new meaning that does address the passage's central concerns. Schwartz convincingly argued that the unit is "setting up an antithesis between two modes of memorialization, monumental-material and moral-cognitive."[58] In other words, the preference which in this unit itself only results in a longer life for David, becomes in the context of the passage a preference that gives him everlasting life through his memorialization. While Schwartz focuses, with the unit's language, on the memory of David's "righteous behavior," we should keep in mind that in the context of the passage, what is remembered is David's words, not deeds—it is the Psalms that are still recited, even after the destruction of the Temple, and it is the Psalms, which, as we have seen, gain David everlasting fame. In this sense, this unit too becomes part of the discussion about citation.

This move from deeds to words in the context of memorialization also appears in another important intertext for our passage, one which is so close to it that it has inspired an early medieval scribe to copy a version of our passage right after it:

Sheqalim 2:5 47a

תני: רשב״ג או׳, "אין עושין נפשות לצדיקים. דבריהן הן זכרונן".

> It was recited: Rabban Simeon b. Gamaliel says, "One does not make monuments for the righteous. Their words [alt. deeds] are their commemoration."

This teaching—ostensibly Tannaitic, though it appears nowhere else in the classical rabbinic corpus[59]—argues that the righteous are not remembered through elaborate physical monuments, but through their words. The idea that great men are remembered by recounting their deeds is expressed by many ancient writers. But for the purpose of our investigation into notions of citation, it is important again to distinguish between remembering the dead by recalling their deeds through others' words, and remembering the dead by citing and reciting their own words. Here, the righteous are remembered by their *devarim*, which commonly means "words," but could also mean "deeds." The teaching speaks about

---

[58] Schwartz, *Were the Jews*, 139.
[59] Printed editions of *Genesis Rabbah* record a parallel at 82:10, but see the critical apparatus in Theodor and Albeck, *Bereschit Rabba*, 988.

"righteous" people—not sages—and righteous people in rabbinic literature are distinguished by their deeds, not words. We rarely find references to the "words of the righteous,"[60] but the "deeds of the righteous" are mentioned in many places.[61] We also find in the Tannaitic corpus the idea that good deeds give the righteous everlasting fame through inscription in texts. The Tosefta in *Ta'anit* 3:8, for example, explains that the families mentioned in 1 Chronicle 2:54 merited that everlasting reputation for their good deeds. We do not, however, find in Tannaitic literature a statement about remembering the dead by citing them.

It is possible that this teaching by Rabban Simeon b. Gamaliel is indeed Tannaitic, as it is presented. It is also possible that a Tannaitic teaching saw in the words of the righteous their memorial. But it is more likely, if the teaching is indeed Tannaitic, that it celebrates the deeds of the righteous rather than their words. Furthermore, the fact that the teaching appears nowhere else in the classical rabbinic corpus, and that it conforms with Amoraic-era teachings about memory and citation, may indicate that in its current form it belongs in that later period. The odd pairing of "righteous" and "words" may have been influenced by Proverb 10:7's reference to the memory of the righteous, but it may also indicate that the teaching had some Tannaitic original, which spoke of righteous and their deeds, and was subsequently revised in the Amoraic period.

"Useful in the grave is a name on people's mouth"

The trope of textual or literary immortality which we find in these three teachings—the teaching about David, the teaching about the lips in the grave, and the teachings about the monuments of the righteous—is found in many other cultural contexts. I focus here only on the specific idea that the person to whom the text is attributed receives immortality through the reading, recitation, or study of the text, as opposed to the broader idea that literary works immortalize the people depicted in them. In an essay which posits the tomb as the *vorschule* of Egyptian written literature, Jan Assmann writes that the connection between funerary inscriptions and literature explains the rise of the concept of authorship in Ancient Egypt.[62] He cites a school text from around 1200 BCE which encourages students to join the scribal profession:

> Be a scribe, take it to heart,
> That your name become as theirs [= previous sages].

---

[60] See e.g. *Sifre Deuteronomy* §38, but even there it does not refer to their teachings but to their promises.
[61] See e.g. *Sifre Deuteronomy* §324, *Mekhilta de-Rabbi Ishmael Pisḥa* §16, and *Genesis Rabbah* 2:5.
[62] Assmann, "Schrift, Tod, und Identität."

> Better is a book than a graven stela,
> Than a solid tomb-enclosure.
> They [= the books] act as chapels and tombs
> In the heart of him who speaks their name;
> Surely useful in the graveyard
> Is a name in people's mouth!
> Man decays, his corpse is dust,
> All his kin have perished;
> But a book makes him remembered
> Through the mouth of its reciter.
> Better is a book than a well-built house,
> Than tomb-chapels in the west;
>
> Better than a solid mansion,
> Than a stela in the temple!
> Is there one here like Hardedef?
> Is there another like Imhotep?
> None of our kin is like Neferti,
> Or Khety, the foremost among them [...].
> Death made their names forgotten
> But books made them remembered![63]

This text bears some striking similarities to our Talmudic passage. As Assmann notes, it deals with sages, the figures—some real, some fictitious—to whom wisdom literature was attributed. Much like in our passage, where David and R. Yohanan gain everlasting life through the recitation of words attributed to them, the sage described here is remembered, after his body became dust, when his book is recited. While our passage is more specific when it contends that the sage "derives benefit" by being cited since his lips are murmuring in the grave, it is not so far from the assertion here, "Surely useful in the graveyard, is a name in people's mouth." And much like the Talmudic text contrasts Solomon's building of the Temple with the words of David and the sages, this passage contrasts the books of the wise with Temple stela and tomb-chapels.

We find similar ideas in the Greco-Roman tradition. Isocrates writes in his *Antidosis* that he hopes the work would "serve both as the best means of making known the truth about me and, at the same time, as a monument, after my death, more noble than statues of bronze."[64] Horace writes that he has "finished a monument more everlasting than bronze and more conspicuous than the pyramids.... A large part of me will survive, and my fame will grow as long as the pontifex

---

[63] Lichtheim, *Ancient Egyptian Literature*, 177–8. I removed sigla and added the bracketed glosses following context or Lichtheim's notes.
[64] *Isocrates* (Norlin, LCL).

and vestal ascend the Capitol. I shall be proclaimed in Apulia as the first to have brought Aeolian verse-forms to Italian poetry."[65] Ovid writes that while the labors of warriors or politicians are "soon forgotten," he became a poet to seek the "perennial fame" achieved by other poets: "While clustering grapes still ripen and wheat still falls to the scythe, Hesiod's works will be studied. The verse of Callimachus—weak in imagination, strong on technique—has a worldwide readership.... While cupid's armoury still consists of bow and arrows, Tibullus' elegant verses will always be quoted." He concludes the poem by asserting that he too will achieve such fame: "So when the final flames have devoured my body, I shall survive, and my better part live on."[66] Cicero refers to literary works as "monuments" of their authors.[67] This tradition is carried not too far from our *dramatis personae*, in late fourth-century Bethlehem, by Jerome, who likewise refers to the books of his "illustrious men" as their "monuments."[68]

The rabbinic teachings examined in this chapter employ this motif in a way that, as far as I know, was unprecedented in the Jewish tradition. In pre-rabbinic texts, we do find the trope of literary immortality, but it is normally implied rather than spelled out. Samuel Thomas noted that it is not coincidental that figures associated with writing—Enoch, Moses, Elijah, Ezra—are also figures who have, "in one way or another," eluded death.[69] Writing is often presented as a way of transcending time, ensuring the survival of knowledge and speaking to future generations; as Annette Reed has shown, this motif is essential for the development of testamentary literature.[70] The clearest manifestation of the trope in ancient Jewish literature appears in Ben Sira's praise of the scribe, which has been shown to follow Egyptian traditions in other ways.[71] Much like the Egyptian text cited above, Ben Sira notes eternal fame as one of the profession's unique benefits: "Unfading will be his memory, through all generations his name will live; the congregation will speak of his wisdom, and the assembly will declare his praise" (Sirach 39:9-10).[72] The idea was important enough for Ben Sira that he repeats it, almost verbatim, in the prologue to his "hymn in honor of our ancestors": "Their bodies are buried in peace, but their name lives on and on. At gatherings their wisdom is retold and the assembly declares their praises" (Sirach 44:14–15).[73] The verb which Di Lella translates here as "retold" is,

---

[65] Horace, *Odes*, 3:30, 1–2 and 6–13 (trans. Nisbet and Rudd, *Horace: Odes*, 364).
[66] Ovid, *Amores*, 1.15 (trans. Green, *Ovid*, 109–10).
[67] e.g. *De officiis*, 3.4 (Miller, *LCL*).
[68] Jerome, *On Illustrious Men*, 11, 64 (trans. Halton, 24, 92).
[69] Thomas, "Eternal Writing."
[70] See e.g. *1 Enoch* 92:1 and see Reed, "Textuality."
[71] Rollston, "Ben Sira."
[72] Translation of this and the next quotation from Skehan and Di Lella, *Wisdom*. No Hebrew survives for these verses. The Greek reads: οὐκ ἀποστήσεται τὸ μνημόσυνον αὐτοῦ, καὶ ὄνομα αὐτοῦ ζήσεται εἰς γενεὰς γενεῶν. τὴν σοφίαν αὐτοῦ διηγήσονται ἔθνη, καὶ τὸν ἔπαινον αὐτοῦ ἐξαγγελεῖ ἐκκλησία. While the Greek has the nations (ἔθνη) praise the scribe, the Hebrew for 44:15 as well as the parallelism suggest that "congregation" may have been the original Hebrew.
[73] "וגויתם בשלום נאספה. ושמם חי מדור לדור. [חכמתם תשנ]ה עדה. ותהלתם יספר קהל." Masada 1H, with completion from the Genizah fragment (per Ma'agarim). I thank Ishay Rosen-Zvi for directing me to this passage and emphasizing the potential importance of "reciting".

in the Hebrew fragment, "*tishene*," that is, the same verb of recitation which we have seen rabbinic texts use throughout this book. While Di Lella's translation is certainly fair, and seems to be corroborated by the parallelism, it might also indicate that there is a more specific allusion here to the activity of reciting the sages' words or the scribe's texts. Ben Sira deploys this idea for a broader kind of memorialization of different kinds of ancestors, but the appearance of the same verse in his praise of the scribe, and the similarity between that chapter and earlier Egyptian models, might indicate that he is drawing on the idea of literary immortality more specifically. After the teachings explored in this chapter, the next Jewish engagement with this trope is in the use of acrostic authorial signatures, a broad ancient poetical practice adopted by *piyyut* authors in the sixth century.[74]

There are differences, of course, among these texts and between them and the Talmud. Perhaps the most important one is that while our passage speaks of teachings that are transmitted orally, these texts are speaking about *written* literary production. For Assmann, writing is essential: he uses the passage we have seen above to show how a specifically written literature emerged in the context of funerary practices in Egypt. Similar observations have been made in other contexts, about how, through writing, one can speak beyond one's death.[75] At the same time, several of these texts seem to emphasize the living engagement with the written document rather than the document itself, including references to oral performance: the Egyptian text refers to the "reciter" of the sages' writings; Ben Sira may be speaking of the community "reciting" the scribes' wisdom; Ovid writes about the way texts will be studied or quoted. What the Talmudic passage shows us is how the same post-mortem communication could be achieved without the medium of writing at all, through the technique of attribution. Above all, the comparative exploration of this trope underscores how it is in the ultimate absence of the teacher—his death—that he is transformed into the figure of an author; I explore this point further in the conclusion of the chapter.

Tannaitic teachings on the ethics of quotations

We can appreciate the degree to which our passage departs from Tannaitic approaches to quotation and attribution by looking at Tannaitic teachings which similarly reflect on the ethics of quotations. I offer here two examples. The first addresses misattribution:

Sifre Deuteronomy §188

מנ' למחליף דב' ר' אליעזר בדברי ר' יהושע ודברי ר' יהושע[76] בדברי ר' אליעזר, לומר על טמא טהור ועל טהור טמא, שהוא עובר בלא תעשה? ת'ל "לא תסיג גבול רעך".

---

[74] Münz-Manor, "Liturgical Performance," 392. On name acrostics in Greek, see Krueger, *Writing*, 169.

[75] Assmann, "Schrift"; and see, Inowlocki-Meister, "From Text to Relics," on the development of "textual relics" in late ancient Christianity.

[76] Adding ודברי ר' יהושע, which appear in MS Oxford, with Ma'agarim.

From where [do we learn] that someone who substitutes the words of R. Eliezer with the words of R. Joshua and the words of R. Joshua with the words of R. Eliezer, saying[77] about the impure "pure" and about the pure "impure," that he transgresses a negative commandment? Scripture teaches, saying, "You must not move your neighbor's boundary marker [set up by former generations"; Deut 19:14].

The argument that a mistake in attribution constitutes a violation of a Torah commandment shows us Tannaitic sages took attribution seriously. The passage also creates a strong connection between statements and the sages to whom they are attributed by equating attributions with markers of private property: just as boundary-markers were set up by earlier generations to delineate someone's portion in the land, so were attributions recorded by the sages to indicate the proper assignment, or even ownership, of a particular position. At the same time, this concern for attribution seems to be dependent on a concern for proper presentation of the law. Epstein reads the second clause of this passage as a purpose clause, "in order to say about the impure 'pure.'" He argues that the passage warns against a deliberate re-alignment of attributions in light of ruling conventions: since R. Eliezer's rulings have been generally rejected, someone who supports a position attributed to R. Eliezer may want to recite it in the name of R. Joshua, and it is that conduct which this passage forbids.[78] It is also possible that this clause suggests the result rather than the purpose of the forbidden switch in attribution. Be that as it may, the passage binds the two issues together. It is unclear whether its author would consider a switch in attribution that has no legal motive or consequence to be a violation of the commandment as well.

The next example concerns Numbers 31:21, which reports that Eleazar the Priest communicated a certain precept to the troops with the introduction: "This is the statute of the law that the Lord has commanded Moses." Given that Moses normally delivers the word of God to the people directly, the Midrash offers a couple of explanations for why, in this case, Moses delegated that task to Eleazar:

Sifre Numbers §157

ויש אומ': משה נתן לו רשות לאלעזר לדבר, שכשיפטר מן העו' לא יהו אומ' לו, אם בחיי רבך לא היית מדבר, עכשיו אתה מדבר? ד"א: שיהא או' דבר משום אומרו. שנ' "ותאמר אסתר למלך" וגומ'.

---

[77] Finkelstein, *Sifre on Deuteronomy*, 227, chooses the reading "ולאומר," "and to the one saying," which has the passage refer to two actions: switching attributions *and* switching rulings; he is followed by Hammer's translation (*Sifre Deuteronomy*, 208). But this reading has less documentary support, and it is unclear how Halakhic errors transgress Deut 19:14.

[78] Epstein, *IMT*, 6 and n. 2.

And there are those who say, Moses gave Eleazar permission to speak, so that when he [Moses] dies they will not tell him [Eleazar], "During the life of your teacher you did not speak; now you speak!"

Another interpretation: [Moses gave him permission] so that he should say a statement in the name of the one who said it. As it was said, "And Esther told the king [in the name of Mordecai"; Es 2:22].

The first explanation argues that Moses was establishing Eleazar's authority, so that after Moses' death, the people will be assured that Eleazar is teaching with Moses' consent; a similar explanation is offered for Joshua's investiture by Moses in the same compilation.[79] The second explanation, which refers to Eleazar's evocation of Moses in the verse, directly addresses the issue of quotation and attribution. According to this explanation, Moses asked Eleazar to speak to the people so that he would "say a statement in the name of the one who said it," that is, so that he would quote someone, or even "to teach him that one should say a statement in the name of the one who said it."[80] A verse from Esther is adduced to support this explanation, showing the benefit of quotation: had Esther not reported the conspiracy to the king in the name of Mordecai, the king would not have been so favorable to him, and the Jews would not have been saved.

This notion that it is good to "say a teaching in the name of the one who said it" has become synonymous with the rabbinic ideology of citation; this is its earliest appearance in rabbinic literature, and its only appearance in the Tannaitic corpus. In later compilations, the phrase reads "anyone who says a statement in the name of the one who said it brings redemption to the world."[81] Some of these later passages present a contrast between quotation, which is praised, and bad conduct—either stating something without acknowledging its source[82] or stating something that "the sages did not teach."[83] The difference between these two conducts with which quotation is contrasted reveals an ambiguity in this rabbinic praise of quotation. Does it emphasize proper attribution, positing that if I say something I heard or learned from someone else, I should acknowledge my source? Or does it emphasize that what I say must include the words of my teachers or those who came before me? Under the first interpretation, I only need to cite if I am saying something

---

[79] See *Sifre Numbers* §140 and the comments by Kahana, *Sifre on Numbers*, 1169.
[80] Kahana, *Sifre on Numbers*, 1283.
[81] See e.g. *b. Meg.* 15a (BL 400): כל האומ׳ דבר בשם אומרו מביא גאולה לעולם.
[82] Two of the Bavli occurrences, at *b. Ḥul.* 104b and *b. Nid.* 19b, are concerned with proper attribution of an anonymous source—in both of them, the anonymous teaching in the Mishnah is identified with a position attributed to R. Yose later on in the same Mishnah, and so the Bavli argues that the Mishnah therefore teaches us that attribution is important (a third Bavli occurrence, at *b. Meg.* 15a, is in the context of the Esther Midrash). *Tanḥuma, ba-midbar* §22, and *Numbers Rabbah* 5:2, are similar in their concerns and also reproduce the story about R. Yohanan's desire to be cited.
[83] *Kallah* §25.

I have learned from previous sages; under the second interpretation, quotation is something I should pursue in its own right.

In the earliest context in which the notion appears, the explanation of Moses' permission to Eleazar to speak on his behalf, it is difficult to posit that Moses wanted to be given proper acknowledgment as the source of Eleazar's teaching—after all, he would have received such acknowledgment even if he said it himself. It is possible then, that the Midrash means that quotation is meritorious on its own, regardless of the question of credit. If we consider the first interpretation offered in the Midrash, which spoke of Eleazar's teaching after Moses' death, then the other explanation of the merit of quotation can also apply: Moses was training Eleazar to quote him appropriately, so that after his death he would transmit the law in his name. Whether it emphasizes proper credit or the very engagement with the words of the sages, this teaching does not conceive of quotation in the individualist terms with which we have seen it conceived in the story above. The Tannaitic Moses, in contrast with the Talmud's David and R. Yohanan, is not seeking eternal glory.

2. Passage II: Echoes from Sinai

The second Talmudic passage I analyze in this chapter begins with a story about R. Joshua b. Levi which concerns teaching the Torah to one's grandsons; a verse that is cited in that story connects it to a sequence of teachings about attribution and citation. These teachings present a range of ideas about these topics, but overall, they de-emphasize or even negate individual contributions. Even in this passage, however, we can find traces of the new individuated discourse about the rabbinic tradition.

From R. Joshua's bath to Sinai

The passage opens with an interrupted bath:

Shabbat 1:2 3a (par. *Qiddushin* 1:7 61a)

ר' יהושע בן לוי הוה יליף שמע פרשתה מן בר בריה בכל ערובת שובא. חד זמן אינשי ועאל מיסחי בההן דימוסין דטיבריא. והוה מסתמיך על כתפתיה דר' חייא בר בא. אינהר דלא שמע פרשתיה מן בר בריה וחזר ונפק ליה [...]. [..].

אמ' ליה ר' חייא בר אבא: ולא כן אלפן ר', "אם התחילו אין מפסיקין"?

אמ' ליה: חייא בני, קלה היא בעיניך? שכל השומע פרשה מן בן בנו כאילו הוא שומעה מהר סיני. ומה טע'? "והודעתם לבניך ולבני בניך יום אשר עמדת לפני יי אלהיך בחורב", כיום אשר עמדת לפני יי אלהיך בחורב.[84]

---

[84] MS Leiden omits the last sentence here erroneously; it appears in *Qid*.

R. Joshua b. Levi used to hear the [Torah] portion from his grandson on every Sabbath eve. One time he forgot, and went to bathe in the public baths of Tiberias, and he was leaning on the shoulder of R. Hiyya b. Abba. He remembered that he had not heard the portion from his grandson, turned back and came out [...].[85]

Said to him R. Hiyya b. Abba: And did you[86] not teach us [from *m. Shab.* 1:2] that [close to the time of the afternoon prayer one should not begin bathing or other similar activities, "but] if one [already] started [such activities earlier], one does not [have to] stop"?

He said to him: Hiyya, my son, is it trivial for you? For anyone who hears the [Torah] portion from his grandson, it is as if he had heard it from Mount Sinai. And what is the proof? "And you shall make them known to your children and your children's children—the day you stood before the Lord your God at Horeb" (Deut 4:9–10). Just like the day in which you stood before the Lord your God at Horeb.

Like the previous passage, this one also involves a scene in which the master leans on his disciple, and like our previous passage, this one, too, speaks about citation practices and highlights the inter-dependency of students and teachers. Already in the opening sentence, we hear that R. Joshua b. Levi, the distinguished scholar, would regularly go to hear the portion of the Torah from someone many years his junior whom he had taught Torah himself. The point becomes both clearer and more significant when we examine the verse that R. Joshua adduces to support his contention that hearing the Torah from one's grandson is like hearing it at Mount Sinai. Deuteronomy 4:9 speaks about Torah and grandchildren and Deuteronomy 4:10 speaks about the revelation at Mount Sinai; connecting these two adjacent verses is not a big interpretive leap. But the problem is that while R. Joshua wants to demonstrate that *hearing* the Torah from one's grandson is like hearing it at Mount Sinai, the verse speaks clearly about *teaching* the Torah to one's grandchildren. The Bavli's version avoids the problem by stating: "R. Joshua b. Levi said, 'Anyone who teaches his son Torah, Scripture counts it for him as if he received it from Mount Sinai.' "[87] But this is not what the Yerushalmi says and cannot be what it means since the story is clearly about R. Joshua going to hear, not teach, his grandson.

R. Joshua's argument, I suggest, is this: Deuteronomy 4:9–10 can be read as equating the Torah one teaches to one's grandchildren with the moment of revelation at Sinai (as the Bavli has it); this also implies, though, that if one's legacy of

---

[85] I am skipping here a discussion, interjected in the middle of the story, about the stage of bathing at which R. Hiyya stopped, which is important for the context in *Shab.*
[86] Lit., "the master."
[87] *b. Qid.* 30a (MS Oxford), with the prooftext: "א״ר יהושע בן לוי כל המלמד את בנו תורה כאלו קבלה מהר׳ סיני׳ והודעתם לבניך ולבני בניך וסמיך ליה יום אשר עמדת לפני יי אלהיך בחרב". For similar statements, see Kahana, *Sifre Zuta*, 150 (though the Tannaitic statement relies on another verse).

teaching successfully carried over to the grandchildren's generation, then hearing it back from them is like hearing the revelation at Sinai. The grandfather is hearing his own Torah, in a sense, but he is dependent on it being passed through his son and then grandson for this hearing to be likened to the Torah on the day it was given. This *derashah* gives a theological grounding to the natural pleasure one takes in hearing one's student doing well, but it also highlights how this pleasure involves listening to the results of one's own teaching.

There is enough similarity here to the passage explored above that a few productive contrasts emerge already at this stage. That passage showed us a sage who wanted to be acknowledged in name to achieve everlasting fame. Our story, too, operates on a broad temporal axis when it describes the instruction of Torah from generation to generation, but in this story, there is no place for named individuals and their original contributions. R. Hiyya is simply delighted to hear his grandson read the Torah, an activity which would not necessarily occasion citation of rabbinic contributions. The emphasis is on continuity: in hearing his grandson, R. Hiyya is partaking in the perpetual transmission of Torah, from Mount Sinai to the Friday service which has cut his bath short. While one could argue that the reason for this difference between the passages is that they deal with different issues—there, the innovative, advanced scholarship of the sages, and here, the basic instruction offered to children—the next part of our passage extends this view to the teachings of the sages themselves.

Attribution and Sinaitic revelation

Following the story, the Talmud presents a teaching attributed to R. Yohanan that draws on the same verse:

Shabbat 1:2 3a (par. *Qiddushin* 1:7 61a)

ר׳ חזקיה ר׳ ירמיה ר׳ חייא בשם ר׳ יוחנן: אם יכול את לשלשל את השמועה עד משה שלשלה, ואם לאו, תפוש או ראשון ראשון או אחרון אחרון. מה טעמ׳? "והודעתם לבניך ולבני בניך יום אשר עמדת"—עד יום אשר עמדת לפני י״י אלהיך בחורב.

R. Hezekiah [said] R. Jeremiah [said] R. Hiyya [said] in the name of R. Yohanan: If you can trace a teaching up to Moses, trace it; if not, seize either the first or the last [tradent at any given time].[88] What is the proof? "And you shall make them

---

[88] The Hebrew original doubles the words "first" and "last": "first first or last last." Such doubling can mean various things, but in all places in which it appears in the Yerushalmi (sometimes, like here, with the verb "seize"), it means "one at a time." At *Dem.* 7:6 26b, this formulation appears several times to refer to the opinion that if a person makes several statements with legal consequences, only one of them—the first—can apply at any given time. See also *Ma'as.* 1:5 49a and *Ket.* 11:5 34c. These instances double "first"; *b. Qid.* 58a offers an instance of doubling "last" with the same meaning.

known to your children and your children's children, the day you stood [before the Lord your God at Horeb; Deut 4:9–10]." Up to the day in which you stood before the Lord your God at Horeb.

This guideline offers two options for citing a rabbinic teaching. If it is possible to trace—literally "link"—the tradents of the teaching all the way to Moses, one should do so; if not, one should use either the most recent link in the chain or the earliest (known) link. Since it rarely happens that one can offer a complete genealogy of the teaching up to Sinai, the effect of this guideline is restrictive: in most cases, one should not bother with more than a single name. This is why the quotation from Deuteronomy appears not only to support the possibility of tracing the teaching to Sinai, but also to justify the instruction to name only the first or last link when such tracing is not available. It is perhaps in deliberate irony that whoever included this teaching here introduced it with a transmission chain of four names,[89] exceeding not only the guideline's restriction but even the Yerushalmi's common norm of two or three names.

This restrictive approach to attribution may rely on Tannaitic citation practices as we find them in the Mishnah. As I mentioned in the Introduction to this part of the book, Tannaitic compilations do not feature many citation chains; when they do, they are short. We do find elaborate chains occasionally; and on three occasions, strikingly, they indeed go all the way back to Sinai:[90]

m. Pe'ah 2:6

מעשה שזרע ר׳ שמעון איש המצפה לפני רבן גמליא׳, ועלו ללשכת הגזית ושאלו. אמר נחום הליבלר: מקובל אני מרבי מיישא, שקיבל מאבא, שקיבל מן הזוגות, שקיבלו מן הנביאים, הלכה למשה מסיני. הזורע את שדיהו שני מיני חיטים, אם עשאן גורן אחת נותן פיאה אחת. שתי גרנות, נותן שתי פיאות.

It once happened that R. Simeon, a man of Mizpah, sowed [his field with two kinds of wheat and came] before R. Gamaliel [to ask about the laws of designating *pe'ah*]. And they went up to the Chamber of Hewn Stone and asked [the court]. Said Nahum the Scribe: I received [this tradition] from my teacher Me'asha, who received it from his father [or: Abba], who received it from the pairs, who received it from the prophets, a tradition [given] to Moses at Sinai. One who sowed his field with two kinds of wheat, if he made of them one granary, he designates one *pe'ah*; two granaries, two *pe'ot*.

---

[89] The chain in *Qid.* lists three, mistakenly joining two of the names into "R. Hezekiah b. R. Jeremiah." See Lieberman, *YK*, 20.
[90] In addition to *m. Pe'ah* 2:6, see also *m. 'Ed.* 8:7 and *m. Yad.* 4:3. For the few other long chains in Tannaitic literature, see n. 48 in the Introduction to this part of the book.

R. Yohanan's rule may be inspired by this practice in the Mishnah: in the rare cases where a full genealogy up to Sinai is available, one should deploy it; otherwise, there is no need for lengthy chains of transmission.[91]

R. Yohanan not only advises that one name should be used in the absence of such a chain; he also does not insist on citing the earliest or the latest name: one may seize either the first or the last.[92] This "either/or" logic reveals the notion of attribution which underlies this rule. The earliest name can tell us how far back the teaching is documented, and the last name can tell us who most recently transmitted it, but these are merely bookmarks in the teaching's story, not its beginning or end. No attribution has a necessary or permanent association with the teaching, since each link is only that: merely one link in a long chain of transmission.

This view is also apparent in the Sinaitic emphasis of R. Yohanan's rule.[93] The rule does not invoke Sinai because of the idea that specific teachings are transmitted from Sinai; if this were the case, it could have said "when the teaching is from Sinai, trace it to Sinai, and when it is not, trace it to the first person who said it." Nor does it conceive the sages merely as transmitters of a static body of knowledge that they heard from their teachers, and their teachers from theirs, all the way up to Sinai. Other claims to Sinaitic origins in the Yerushalmi make that clear. In one famous passage, R. Joshua b. Levi says that "even what a distinguished student will teach before his teacher was already said to Moses in Sinai": the student clearly did not learn that teaching from his own teacher but rather came up with it on his own; but the teaching is still imagined to derive from Sinaitic revelation.[94] Another passage stipulates that when a rabbinic court really devotes themselves to a matter, it is established just as it was said in Sinai, and proceeds to praise the biblical figures of Bezalel and Joshua for following even details of God's commandments which their teacher, Moses, did not actually command them—figuring it out on their own independent knowledge (*de'ah*, see Chapter 2).[95] In Rabbi Yohanan's rule, like these other teachings, Sinai is invoked to describe Torah teaching as a

---

[91] I thank Ishay Rosen-Zvi for this point.

[92] The rule might even mean that one can switch attributions at any particular instruction of the teaching. See above, n. 88. QE's emendation, "the first *and* the last" (but skipping the "middle" tradent) is based on *b. Naz.* 66b and is not corroborated by any textual witness of the Yerushalmi. See Lieberman, *YK*, 20.

[93] On Sinaitic claims in rabbinic literature see Rosenthal, "Tradition and Innovation"; Sommer, *Revelation and Authority*; Fraade, "Hearing and Seeing."

[94] *Pe'ah* 2:6 17a (par. Ḥag. 1:7 76d).

[95] *Pe'ah* 1:1 15b, *Shevi.* 1:6 33b (par. *Suk.* 4:1 54b), and *Shab.* 1:4 3d (par. *Ket.* 8:8 32c). For a different reading of the passage see Hayes, "Halakhah le-Moshe Mi-Sinai," 102–4. The sequence of teachings about the court, Bezalel, and Joshua appears in the context of contradictory attributions of legal developments (to give the example of *Pe'ah*: who established the limit on charitable giving and when?), but the passages undermine the importance of such questions, pointing out that ultimately everything is derived from Sinai. R. Joshua b. Levi's teaching appears in a discussion of another guideline attributed to R. Yohanan, that we should be careful with rulings whose origins we do not know, as *halakhot* that were given to Moses at Sinai are now embedded with other materials, and since these *halakhot* may present exceptions to the law one should not derive new laws from them; in this context, R. Joshua b. Levi's teaching undermines questions about the "origins" of teachings in general.

dynamic, living tradition that stretches up to the revelation to Moses, but which may continuously transform and evolve even as it maintains its unity. While it is possible to perceive certain moments in these evolutions, these are moments in the continuous life of Torah rather than fixed points of departure.[96]

Though R. Yohanan's rule downplays individual contribution, its formulation indicates that it addressed an audience aware of other options, a scholarly world in which the citation practice it advocated and the view with which such practice is implicated were contested. This is not just because of the truism that rules do not state what is obvious and accepted by everyone. It is also because the instruction to use only the earliest or latest name indicates that more extensive documentation of transmission was available; one does not instruct people to avoid using information which they do not have.

"He must see the master of the teaching"

The passage continues with another rule about citation:

Shabbat 1:2 3a (par. *Qiddushin* 1:7 61a)

גידול אמ': כל האומ' שמועה מפי אומרה יהא רואה בעל השמועה כאילו הוא עומד כנגדו. ומה טע'? "אך בצלם יתהלך איש".

Gidol said: Anyone who says a teaching in the name of the one who said it must see the master of the teaching as if he is standing in front of him. What is the proof? "Only through an image can one walk" (Ps 39:7).

This rule requires the tradent of a teaching to visualize the "master of the teaching" when he is pronouncing it. It is one of several teachings in the rabbinic corpus which emphasize the importance of visual encounter with the sage;[97] here, this encounter is pursued through imagination. The support from Psalms 39:7 may rely on a pun of sorts: the word "walk" (*yithalekh*) has the same root as the word for "tradition" (*halakhah*), and so the verse can read: "only through an image can one transmit a tradition."[98]

The Hebrew phrase "master of the teaching" or "master of the tradition" (*ba'al ha-shemu'a*), attested only in our passage,[99] may at first seem to be a reference to the teaching's "author." If this were the case, this rule would make a fairly strong statement about the importance of individual authorship. But three unique

---

[96] For the notion of texts as part of a living process, see Najman, *Scriptural Vitality*.
[97] Neis, *Sense of Sight*, 202–52.
[98] Lieberman, *YK*, 20, citing Margulies. For an alternative account, emphasizing the *derashah*'s divinizing overtones, see Neis, *Sense of Sight*, 215.
[99] We do find in the Bavli the form *ba'al shemu'ot*, "a master of traditions," but it refers to something quite different—a master specializing in the transmission of traditions as opposed to other aspects of Torah study. See b. Ḥag. 14a and especially b. B. B. 145b; it may be the equivalent of *ba'al halakhot* (t. Naz. 5:1).

instances in the Palestinian Talmud of the phrase's Aramaic equivalent, *mara de-shemu'ata*, seem to rule out this interpretation, to the extent that we can shed light from them on this passage. In those instances, the term refers to a certain scholar as the "master" of a certain teaching even though that scholar transmits that teaching in the name of another scholar. In one of the passages, the Talmud wonders how the "master of the teaching" can ask a question about the teaching he himself uttered, and answers that he must have dozed off in the lesson in which he heard it.[100]

At the same time, in comparison with R. Yohanan's rule, Gidol's rule offers a stronger association between teachings and the sages to whom they are attributed. It not only relies on the idea that there is an individual who could be described as the "master of the teaching," it also mandates that the tradent focuses on that individual to ensure proper transmission of that teaching. A scholar trying to follow both R. Yohanan's and Gidol's rules would have a hard time deciding whom to imagine—the first? the last? all the tradents up to Sinai? Gidol's rule requires a certain accountability to and focus on a particular individual, and the juxtaposition of these two teachings may have been meant to highlight the difference between them.

The visualization R. Gidol's rule mandates and its focus on transmission may suggest that it is connected to memorization techniques, and in another passage in the Yerushalmi, we find the same verse which occupied the passage so far—Deuteronomy 4:9—supporting an argument for textual visualization as a memory aid.[101] Another possibility, which is supported by the material which appears after Gidol's rule, is that visualization is a way for the tradent to ensure he got the transmission and attribution right, that he indeed heard *this* teaching from *this* person. The passage continues:

Shabbat 1:2 3a (par. *Qiddushin* 1:7 61a)

כת׳: "רב אדם יקרא איש חסדו ואיש אמונים"[102] מי ימצא". "רב אדם יקרא איש חסדו". זה שאר כל אדם. "ואיש אמונים מי ימצא". זה ר׳ זעירא. דמר ר׳ זעירא: לית אנן צריכין חששין לשמועתיה דרב ששת דהוא גברא מפתחה.

אמ׳ ר׳ זעירא לר׳ יסא: חכים ר׳ לבר פדיה דאת אמר שמועתא מן שמיה? אמ׳ ליה: ר׳ יוחנן אמרן משמו. אמר ר׳ זעירא לר׳ בא בר זבדא: חכים ר׳ לרב דאת אמר שמועתא מן שמיה? אמ׳ ליה: רב אדא בר אהבה אמרן משמו.

---

[100] *Ter.* 8:5 45d (par. *'A. Z.* 2:3 41a); the other two passages are *Ter.* 8:5 45c (par. *'A. Z.* 2:3 41a) and *San.* 1:2 18c (par. *R. H.* 2:7 58b). Note the proximity between the *Ter.* instances.
[101] See *Ber.* 5:1 9a and the discussion in Naeh, "Omanut," 557–61. For a different approach to Gidol's teaching, see Neis, *Sense of Sight*, 213–15.
[102] Correcting "אמונות," with the parallel in *Qid.* as well as the next occurrence of the word here and MT.

It is written: "Many proclaim a person faithful, but who can find one worthy of trust (Prov 20:6)." "Many proclaim themselves faithful"—this is everyone else. "But who can find one worthy of trust"—this is R. Ze'ira.

For R. Ze'ira said: We do not need to concern ourselves with the traditions of Rav Sheshet, for he is a blind man.[103]

Said R. Ze'ira to R. Yose: "Do you know Bar Pedaya, that you say teachings in his name?" He said to him, "R. Yohanan said them in his name." Said R. Ze'ira to R. Abba b. Zavda, "Do you know Rav, that you say teachings in his name?" He said to him, "Rav Ada b. Ahava said them in his name."

This passage opens by alluding to Proverbs 20:6 in order to praise R. Ze'ira's transmission practices. Most people, we hear, uncritically trust transmitters; but R. Ze'ira more rigorously identifies the reliable ones: he is the person who "can find one worthy of trust." He establishes reliability not by examining the content of teachings, but by considering their attribution. This is evident already in the first statement that demonstrates R. Ze'ira's rigor. He says that R. Sheshet's traditions should not be trusted ("they should not be a concern"—i.e. they do not matter) because he is a blind person. Blindness would not prevent someone from hearing accurately rabbinic teachings; but if a blind person does not recognize the voice of the person who is speaking, they might err in identifying the speaker even if they transmit the content correctly. This passage thus also attests to the increased Amoraic emphasis on proper attribution.[104]

The second example of R. Ze'ira's rigor is even more demonstrative of the changes in citation conventions in this period. We hear two anecdotes in which R. Ze'ira challenges scholars for transmitting teachings in the name of scholars whom they did not know personally. On both occasions, the scholars defend themselves by saying that while they have indeed not heard the teaching personally from the scholar to whom it is attributed, they did hear it from someone who did know that scholar personally.

In the Introduction to this part of the book, we have seen that in the Amoraic period, attribution was used to associate uniquely between a sage and a teaching rather than merely indicate face-to-face transmission; I argued that this function reflects a scholarly culture in which delineating individual contribution became important. But the rise of such new practices of citation was not uncontested. R. Ze'ira expects attribution to indicate face-to-face transmission and therefore guarantee authenticity. R. Yose and R. Abba b. Zavda both use it to identify the teaching's original source, not the person from whom they have heard it. Even

---

[103] Literally "open [eyed?] man," used here euphemistically.
[104] On the representation of such concerns in the Bavli (with reference to the Yerushalmi), see Halivni, "Safke."

though R. Yose heard the teaching from R. Yohanan, he attributes it to Bar Pedaya; even though R. Abba b. Zavda heard the teaching from R. Ada b. Ahava, he attributes it to Rav (another passage in the Talmud offers a concrete example of such citation).[105] R. Ze'ira's challenges seem to stand in tension with R. Yohanan's rule of citation. Whereas according to that rule either the first or last link may be named, R. Ze'ira stresses the most recent link and expects it to be acknowledged.

Conclusion: beyond the master-disciple relationship

The passages explored in this chapter present different ideas and conflicting positions about the significance of attribution. The story of R. Yohanan and his students binds quotation with personal honor, and the discussion which follows it considers quotation as a vehicle for everlasting fame and personal memorialization, suggesting that attribution indicates a unique and permanent connection between the teaching and the sage it names. This passage provides an ideological articulation for the individuated notion of rabbinic teachings which underlies the practices studied in previous chapters of this book. The opposition to this view is most evident in the rule of citation attributed, in the other passage examined in this chapter, to the same R. Yohanan: since all teachings draw from a long tradition that goes back to Moses, no teaching is definitively connected with an individual sage. Other statements from that passage, I argued, present similar ideas.

Alongside this diversity, we find thematic unity. The primary passages we explored both center on engaging with the words of dead or absent teachers. The Talmud's discussion about R. Yohanan's desire to be quoted compares it to David's bid for immortality and descends to the graves of scholars, where it finds their lips moving as they are quoted by the living. R. Yohanan's rule of citation responds to those who attempt to trace teachings several generations back. Gidol's guideline urges the quoter to summon the figure of the quoted teacher to one's imagination, precisely because the teacher is not physically present. R. Ze'ira rebukes those who quote sages whom they had not known and whose teachings they have learned despite their absence. These various statements reflect the development in the function of attribution explored in the Introduction to this part of the book: from an indication of face-to-face transmission to tracing particular words to individual sages.

The association between notions of authorship and the death or absence of the author has been well known to historians and theorists of literature, but it has usually been connected with writing.[106] The presence of this association in rabbinic

---

[105] *Shab.* 14:4 15a.
[106] See e.g. Foucault, "What Is an Author," 206; Derrida, "Signature, Event, Context," 8.

constructions of the connection between individual sages and their teachings, in connection with oral teachings rather than writing, points to a particular development in the history of the community of sages and to one of the factors that affected the rise of the author function in rabbinic hermeneutics. Scholars have stressed the centrality of face-to-face instruction in rabbinic culture.[107] Martin Jaffee, in particular, argued that in the Amoraic period, sages framed the Tannaitic notion of "oral Torah" in an ideology of discipleship in which such personal instruction and the living model of the sage were essential for the study of Torah and sustaining Israel's covenant; "for Torah to be present, the Sage must be present."[108] Jaffee is certainly correct to emphasize these aspects of rabbinic culture. But while both Tannaitic and Amoraic compilations illustrate the significance of the master-disciple relationship, the references in the texts examined here to the absence or death of the teacher and to permanence achieved through attribution push beyond this model.[109]

These texts reflect or project an intellectual community which extends through time and space, where knowledge is acquired not only through encounter with living and present sages, but also through engagement with the words of sages long dead or far away. It is from this extension that the rabbinic author function rises. In the relationship between teacher and disciple, the sage is encountered through his presence, recognized for the knowledge and authority of Torah which he embodies. When he is quoted, after his death or in his absence, the sage is known through attribution, with a name that labels his teachings and distinguishes them from the teachings of other sages; he is now recognized not in the totality of Torah he teaches or embodies, but through the distinctive contributions and arguments evident in those teachings. To some degree, this expansive community is present in the Tannaitic compilations, which bring together teachings of sages from many generations. But the fact that it is first in the Yerushalmi that we find the articulation of the ideas and mechanisms of quotation which produce this expansion reflects the broad developments outlined in the previous chapters: the Amoraic turn to studying the sages' words, and the development of interpretive practices which trace the sages' individual profiles. It is in this type of engagement that the words of the sages become their monuments, and the image of those who said them can be summoned.

---

[107] Other than Jaffee, see e.g. Alexander, "Orality," 41; Hezser, *Social Structure*; Neis, *Sense of Sight*; Schofer, *Making of a Sage*, 31–2; Hirshman, *Stabilization*, 16.
[108] Jaffee, *Torah*, 151–2.
[109] Jaffee, ibid., 149, writes about the image of post-mortem citation: "The disciple in this world keeps his master's teachings in his mouth ... the life of the study circle, at the center of which stands the Sage, is extended to him after his death by the very students to whom he gave the eternal life of torah." But as we have seen, the sequencing in the passage produces the effect that R. Yohanan is linked not just to his students, but to people who never met him or his students, for eternity.

II
IMPERFECTION

Introduction to Part II

Ancient Talmudic scholarship was intensely interested in raising and solving textual problems: access to or knowledge of texts, the existence of multiple versions, textual errors, incompleteness, and faults arising in the process of composition and transmission. Like the attribution-based interpretations examined above, discussions of such problems and their resolution have been central to modern scholarship, and they may therefore appear to us as hermeneutically transparent, naturally responding to facts about texts and their transmission; but like any reading, they are premised on specific notions of text and interpretation. In the Talmud, as well as certain strands of Greco-Roman and modern philology, the engagement with these questions construes extant textual knowledge in fragmentary and imperfect terms: extant texts present a fragment of a corpus which is imperfectly or variedly known due to the contingencies of transmission; these texts represent only a version of the tradition or ruling in question, giving us only a partial view; these texts may contain errors or lacunae, or they may be circulating in misleading contexts. One of the main aims of scholarship, in this view, is to overcome these fragmentary or imperfect forms.

Discussions of such problems were not central in the rabbinic engagement with Scripture. Midrash often problematizes Scripture's meaning; but the scriptural text itself is generally unproblematic: issues of textual access, multiformity, error, or corruption are rare or absent. Rabbinic literature presents the sages as having perfect knowledge of Scripture: we get the impression that they all have it ready to be cited, that they know it uniformly and completely by heart.[1] There is no record of the sages making emendations of the biblical text.[2] We do find occasional discussions of variant texts of Scripture. One passage tells us about three Torah scrolls which were kept in the Temple, each presenting a textual variant which was rejected because it was not attested in the other two.[3] And while that passage presents matters already decided in the sages' distant past, others address contemporary variations. On several occasions, the sages discuss different vocalization or vowels of certain words in Scripture;[4] and a handful of passages refer to variants found in R. Meir's copies of the Torah or the Book of Isaiah.[5] But such direct discussions are rare.

---

[1] Lieberman, *Hellenism*, 52.
[2] Lieberman, ibid., 47.
[3] *Sifre Deuteronomy* §356, appearing also at *Ta'an.* 4:2 68a and later compilations.
[4] e.g. *m. 'A. Z.* 2:5, *Kil.* 3:1 28c. On the issue of whether tannaitic homilies are based on alternative vocalizations, see Naeh, "Did the Tannaim."
[5] *Genesis Rabbah* 9:5, 20:12, 94:9; *Ta'an.* 1:1 64a. See Lange, "Rabbi Meir."

This is not because the sages were not aware of such variants. David Rosenthal argued that the primary form in which the sages addressed or preserved variant readings of Scripture was not through explicit reference, but rather by including the interpretive possibilities that arise from such variants in homilies and rulings.[6] Moshe Zipor showed that while extant variants are occasionally in the background of passages which employ the common phrase "do not read x but y," addressing these extant variants was not the primary purpose of these passages: they never mention such variants explicitly, and their primary purpose is exploring potential interpretations deriving from similarly spelled words.[7] Rabbinic discussions of the Septuagint recognize that it diverges from the Hebrew text, but they present such divergences not as attesting to variants in the original but rather as changes made deliberately by the translators.[8] As Menachem Kahana argued, the sages' awareness of scriptural variants only underscores the significance of their general reluctance to address or debate them directly.[9]

The marginality or absence of such textual problems sets the rabbinic study of Scripture apart from other ancient scholarly traditions, where the problem of access to books, the collation and comparison of different versions or editions, and the correction of texts played a central role.[10] The difference is even more striking when we consider that contemporary Christian scholars did engage with these problems and practices in the study of their Scripture, including the Hebrew Bible and its translations.[11]

David Stern argued that the sages primarily knew the Bible as a memorized and recited text rather than from books.[12] Rebecca Wollenberg suggested that it was this memorized, recited version of Scripture that was sacred for the sages precisely because written transmission could be so problematic.[13] But the lack of engagement with the textual problems mentioned above cannot be explained only in terms of this orality of Scripture: the following chapters show how central such problems were for rabbinic scholarship on rabbinic teachings, which was even

---

[6] Rosenthal, "'Al derekh tipulam."

[7] Zipor, *Tradition and Transmission*, 173–82.

[8] *Meg.* 1:8 71d, *b. Meg.* 9a, and other places. See Veltri, *Tora*, 21–112; and Simon-Shoshan, "Tasks," 11–23.

[9] Kahana, "Halakhic Midrashim," 12–13.

[10] See Reynolds and Wilson, *Scribes and Scholars*; Montanari et al. (ed.), *Ancient Greek Scholarship*; Johnson, *Readers and Reading Culture*; Zetzel, *Critics*. For a comparison between Alexandrian scholarly practices and their rabbinic counterparts see Lieberman, *Hellenism*, 47–67; Moss, "Rabbinic Appropriations"; and especially Paz, *Scribes to Scholars*. Niehoff, *Jewish Exegesis and Homeric Scholarship*, 112–30, shows Philo's works reflect the practice of textual criticism of Scripture among Alexandrian Jews.

[11] See e.g. the foundational study of Origen in Neuschäfer, *Origenes als Philologe*, and the recent, broad account in Grafton and Williams, *Christianity*; more below in Chapter 6, Section 5.

[12] Stern, "Jewish Books." See more below, Chapter 8.

[13] Wollenberg, *The Closed Book*, 119–92.

more defined by orality.[14] The sages' avoidance of these issues with the scriptural text—whether written or memorized—was part of a hermeneutic approach that emphasized the perfection of the scriptural text and its transmission; and conversely, the centrality of these issues in the study of rabbinic teachings reflected an understanding of these teachings as fragmentary or imperfect. The striking effect was that the sages, who in the study of the written Torah did not engage many of the practices typically associated with Greco-Roman book culture, developed their most "bookish" practices in a realm where books were marginal or absent.[15]

Textual interpretation in the Tannaitic compilations

As we have seen, Tannaitic sages do not normally use earlier teachings in support of their positions, do not aim to interpret their meaning, and rarely engage with their wording.[16] As a result, they also do not frequently engage the textual problems discussed in this part of the book. One major exception is the early Tannaitic discourse concerning *shemu'ot*, which we have had the chance to encounter above. *Shemu'ot* or "heard" traditions are distinct from other rabbinic teachings. The so-called "protocol" of the Yavneh sages portrays these traditions as having an official authoritative status in deliberations about the law.[17] The sages considered them inherited, and they are presented with special terminology, including verbs of hearing and receiving.[18] *Shemu'ot* were not as freely adapted as other teachings. Rabbinic statements emphasize the importance of their precise verbal reproduction. Some sages opposed the application of principles derived from *shemu'ot* to other cases, and even some of those who were willing to make such inferences separated the inference from the tradition itself.[19] In the next chapter, I show how this discourse of *shemu'ot* presented a concern with loss, discovery, or access to knowledge similar to that which is found in the Talmud concerning rabbinic teachings. Here, I discuss a more fundamental way in which the Tannaitic engagement with *shemu'ot* anticipated Talmudic discourse.

Because the very words of *shemu'ot* were authoritative, and because the sages aimed to reproduce them accurately, they transmitted them in fixed form even when they did not understand them. Consider the following:

---

[14] On the oral transmission and study of rabbinic teachings in antiquity, see the Introduction.
[15] Dohrmann, "Jewish Books," draws some broad contrasts between rabbinic textuality and Roman book culture, focusing on the Tannaitic period and on Midrash. By including Amoraic commentary on rabbinic teachings, some (though certainly not all) of these contrasts are qualified.
[16] See the Introduction.
[17] *t. San.* 7:4–5. For analysis see Rosenthal, "Tradition and Innovation," 335–6, and see more broadly on this passage, Rosen-Zvi, "Protocol."
[18] Furstenberg, "Tradition to Controversy," 617–18.
[19] See e.g. *m. Kar.* 3:7–9.

m. Parah 1:1

ר' אליעזר אומ': עגלה בת שנתה ופרה בת שתים. וחכמ' אומ': עגלה בת שתים ופרה בת שלוש או בת ארבע.... אמ' ר' יהושע: לא שמעתי אלא שלשית. אמרו לו: מה הלשון שלשית? אמ' להם: כך שמעתי סתם. אמ' בן עזיי: אני אפריש. אם אומ' אתה שלישית, לאחרות במניין. וכשאתה אומ' שלשית, בת שלוש שנים.

R. Eliezer says: The heifer [prescribed by Deut 21:3 must be] one year old, and the cow [prescribed by Num 19:2 must be] two years old. But the sages say: The heifer [must be] two years old, and the cow three or four years old....[20]

R. Joshua said: I have only heard *shelashit*.[21] They asked him: What does this formulation *shelashit* [mean]? He said to them: This is what I have heard without specification. Said Ben Azzai: I will specify. If you say *shelishit*, [it means third] with respect to others in a count; but if you say *shelashit*, [it means] three years old.

R. Joshua heard about the red cow that it should be *shelashit*, but he does not know what that means. Ben Azzai, R. Joshua's junior, says he can explain this word as referring to the age of the cow: unlike the common word *shelishit*, the ordinal number "third," *shelashit* means "of three [years]." The Mishnah proceeds to adduce several similar cases (not quoted here) in which Ben Azzai interpreted unclear teachings transmitted by R. Joshua.

Written texts often become unclear because they are transmitted, in specific formulation, separately from the person who produced them, and their producer may not be there to explain their meaning. We may imagine that oral transmission would present a different dynamic: whoever is presenting the teaching would be able to explain it if there are any questions asked; and whoever is memorizing the teaching to further transmit it would do so in their own words. Here, however, we can see how the emphasis on verbatim transmission produced a result similar to written transmission: R. Joshua "heard" the word *shelashit*; the teacher from whom he heard it may not have understood it himself, and in any event he did not explain it to R. Joshua—but they both transmitted this word anyway. This verbal reproduction abstracts the words of the teaching from their original moment of instruction and indeed from a necessary relationship between understanding them and transmitting them. These teachings function more like a written text, and their meaning, like that of Scripture, is in need of explanation: this is what enables Ben Azzai's contribution.

But the way the passage presents that explanation differs from the way the sages normally present their commentary on Scripture. The verb Ben Azzai uses to describe his activity of specification or interpretation is *afaresh*, which means "I shall specify." It would become a common verb for interpretation in later Hebrew. In

---

[20] Skipping here R. Meir's opinion, which is not relevant for our purposes.
[21] Vocalization according to MS Kaufmann.

early rabbinic literature, when this verb describes a sage specifying a text, the text is always a rabbinic teaching and never a verse from Scripture.[22] This is particularly significant since the verb is used very frequently to describe what Scripture itself does: it is Scripture itself, not the sages, which, through other verses, explains what may be unclear to us.[23] In other words, it is only with respect to rabbinic teachings that the sages present themselves as adding something that is otherwise lacking in the text. I will return in the Conclusion to what this suggests more generally about the different rhetoric of interpretation that is used with respect to these corpora. For our purposes here, what is important is that some of these rare presentations of early textual engagements imply that these teachings or traditions are lacking in a way that Scripture is not.

Another example, involving different members of the same two generations of sages, presents even more strongly the problematic nature of teachings and the way the sages can overcome this problematic nature:

m. Oholot 16:1

כל המיטלטלין מביאין את הטומאה בעובי המרדע.

אמ' ר' טרפון: אקפח את בניי שזו הלכה מקופחת. ששמע השומע וטעה. שהאיכר עובר והמרדע על כתיפו והאהיל צידו אחד על הקבר וטימוהו משם כלים המאהילים על המת.

אמ' ר' עקיבה: אני אתקין שיהוא דב' חכמ' קיימין. יהוא כל המיטלטלין מביאין את הטומאה על אדן הנושאין בעובי המרדע. ועל עצמן בכל שהן. ועל שאר אדם וכלים בפותח טפח.

All movable objects convey impurity if their thickness is [at least] as an ox-goad.

R. Tarfon said: May I ruin my sons if this is not a ruined tradition (*halakhah*), that someone heard and mistook [the following]: When a plougher passes by with the ox-goad over his shoulder, and one end of it overshadowed the tomb, they declared it [or: him] impure because of objects overshadowing a corpse.

R. Aqiva said: I will amend it so that the words of the sages shall be sustained. All movable objects bring impurity upon the person who carries them, if their thickness is as an ox-goad; and on themselves in whichever [thickness], and to other men and vessels if they are a handbreadth wide.

R. Tarfon says that whoever formulated the ruling with which this passage opens must have understood wrongly a tradition which he proceeds to cite. The intention of the original tradition, R. Tarfon argues, was that the sages "declared *it*"—i.e. the ox-goad, "impure"; but the word *tim'uhu* could also mean "they declared *him*," that

---

[22] See especially *m. Pes.* 9:6, *m. Yev.* 8:4, *m. Yom.* 1:1, *t. Zev.* 1:8 (which is similar to the text from *Oholot* below), *t. Nid.* 3:6, *t. Toh.* 7:7.

[23] See e.g. *Mekhilta de-Rabbi Ishmael Pisḥa* §14, *Sifre Numbers* §139, §140, *Sifre Deuteronomy* §48, *t. Hor.* 2:1. See Heinemann, "Technical Terms."

is, the plougher who was using the ox-goad, impure; and that is how it was erroneously understood by the person who formulated the teaching with which the passage opens. R. Aqiva is able to defend the teaching by re-interpreting it, which is consistent with his other activities in defense of extra-scriptural traditions, as Azzan Yadin-Israel has shown.[24]

Here too we see how the verbatim transmission of a teaching, abstracted from the explanation of a teacher, can lead to its misunderstanding, and even to the composition of an "erroneous" teaching. What enables Rabbi Tarfon's comment, R. Aqiva's comment, and our own exposure to this discussion, is that the erroneous teaching too was transmitted verbatim, rather than being presented, from the beginning, as R. Aqiva interpreted it. In other words, it is the erroneous form which gives the opportunity for R. Aqiva to right the wrong through interpretation. Note that R. Aqiva does not deny R. Tarfon's argument that the teaching is erroneous. He offers a correction of the teaching's meaning to sustain the *wording* of the teaching itself, positing that the word "convey" has two different references (objects and persons) depending on the case. Explicit marking of a teaching as erroneously formulated is not common in the Tannaitic corpus, though the Tosefta associated with this passage proceeds to offer other instances of faulty inferences.[25]

This type of engagement is relatively confined in Tannaitic compilations to discussions of *shemu'ot*. As Yair Furstenberg has shown, the importance of *shemu'ot* gradually receded: the emphasis on tradition and verbal transmission gave way to an emphasis on analysis and active reformulation of teachings.[26] Interpretive activities which correct erroneous teachings or explain misunderstood words may have continued, as sages passed on teachings from one generation to the next; but they appear less explicitly in Tannaitic texts because the misunderstood, erroneous forms of the teachings were not preserved and because what was important was the different positions on the issue rather than the words through which these positions had been expressed. Late Tannaitic sages approach the statements attributed to their predecessors not as strings of words, which may therefore be subject to misunderstanding or error, but rather as transparent or adaptable vessels of the positions they articulated.

Amoraic scholars, in contrast, approach and construct the teachings they study in terms more bound with specific formulations. It is not that adaptation and reformulation ended—the Talmud itself, we shall see, recognizes that they occurred. But structurally, the discussion in the Talmud takes on the specific wording of rabbinic teachings. In the Introduction to this book, I connected this feature to the standardization of the curriculum in the early third century, and in the intervening chapters we have seen other textualizing features of Amoraic study culture, such as

---

[24] Yadin-Israel, *Scripture and Tradition*, 105–6.
[25] *t. Oh.* 15:12–13.
[26] Furstenberg, "Tradition to Controversy," 614.

the expansion of instruction beyond the master-disciple circle and the function of attributions beyond the indication of face-to-face transmissions.

This textualization of rabbinic teachings created the conditions for the discourse of textual problems which we find in the Talmud, as the wording of teachings became subject to analysis. Elizabeth Shanks Alexander interpreted the textualization of the Mishnah in terms of its Scripturalization, the process by which it became treated like Scripture, a precise text with nothing accidental in it.[27] While I agree that this description captures significant aspects of Amoraic commentary, the following chapters show how the same process of textualization, as we can reconstruct it from the Yerushalmi, was also bound with ideas which are markedly different than those evident in Midrash.

Still, textualization does not inherently lead to the types of analysis and patterns of representation studied in this part of the book. The sages did not study Scripture in this way, even though they surely approached it as a text. And the Mishnah too, could be imagined and indeed was imagined in other ways. Sherira's *Letter* certainly speaks of the Mishnah as a text, but it emphasizes how it was uniformly known by all, and how it was transmitted faithfully and perfectly through the generations.[28] The Talmud's discussions of textual problems constituted a particular hermeneutics of imperfection. The following chapters show how Amoraic scholars pursued such discussions even when other options were available, and how they employed them generatively for a variety of aims.

---

[27] Alexander, *Transmitting Mishnah*, 77–116.
[28] Lewin, *ISG* e.g. 21–4.

5

The Scattered Torah
The Problem of Textual Knowledge

The Talmud follows the story about R. Jonah's long hangover, which we have seen in Chapter 2, with a story about R. Judah b. Ilay, who once experienced an even longer hangover. We are told that, on a different occasion, a certain lady observed that his glowing face suggests he may be drunk (or perhaps a money-lender or a pig farmer). R. Judah angrily curses the lady and cites a verse from Ecclesiastes to make the point that it is "wisdom," not booze, which "makes one's face shine." The citation of this verse provides an opportunity for the Talmud to tell a story that beautifully exemplifies the discourse of textual access discussed in this chapter:

> *Pesaḥim* 10:1 37c (par. *Shab.* 8:1 11a; cf. *Sheq.* 3:2 47c)
>
> ר׳ אבהו אתא לטיבריא. חמוניה תלמידוי דר׳ יוחנן אפוי נהירין. אמרון קומיה דר׳ יוחנן: אשכח ר׳ אבהו סימא. אמ׳ לון: למה? אמ׳ ליה: אפוי נהירין. אמ׳ לון: דילמא אוריתא חדתא שמע. סלק לגביה. אמ׳ ליה: מה אורייא חדתא שמעת? אמ׳ ליה: תוספתא עתיקתא. וקרא עלוי "חכמת אדם תאיר פניו".

> R. Abbahu came to Tiberias. The students of R. Yohanan saw him with his face shining. They said before R. Yohanan: R. Abbahu found a treasure. He said to them: Why [do you say this]? They said to him: His face is shining. He said to them: Perhaps he heard a new piece of Torah. He came to him and said: What new piece of Torah have you heard? He said to him: An ancient addition. So he read, concerning him, "Wisdom makes one's face shine" (Eccl. 8:1).

Both the students and R. Yohanan get something wrong and something right when they explain R. Abbahu's glowing face. The students get something wrong, since R. Abbahu did not find a treasure, or at least not a treasure like precious stones; but they get something right, since learning something is, in a sense, like finding a treasure. R. Yohanan also gets something wrong: when he asks R. Abbahu what *new* piece of Torah he has heard, R. Abbahu replies that he heard something *ancient*. Still, R. Yohanan is also right: this piece of Torah is new. At least for R. Abbahu, it was a discovery: he seems never to have heard it before, though it may have been known to the locals in Tiberias. We do not know what this discovered text is about: we know that it is "ancient," that it is an "addition,"[1] and that apparently it was not part of the common curriculum in R. Abbahu's Caesarea.

Our own discovery, at the end of the story, that what R. Abbahu found was an ancient text, offers us a new perspective on the students' earlier claim that he found a treasure. The contrast between monetary and intellectual riches is common in ancient literature, but it works particularly well in our passage because, much like treasures, ancient texts can be discovered, are not accessible to everyone, and are located in specific places. That is why the story begins with travel—"R. Abbahu came to Tiberias" from his hometown of Caesarea—and that is why it implies that he could find this ancient text only in Tiberias.

Stories about the discovery of texts were frequently told in antiquity.[2] The fourth-century Christian scholar Epiphanius tells us such a story about the very same city, in about the same period. In his discussion of the Ebionite sect, he mentions that Jewish converts have reported to him that there is a Hebrew translation of the Gospel of John stored in the "treasuries" of Tiberias.[3] He proceeds to tell the story of one of those converts, Joseph of Tiberias,[4] and eventually returns to the moment in which Joseph discovered the Hebrew gospels:

> Now there was a "gazophylacium" there which was sealed—"gaza" means "treasure" in Hebrew. As many had different notions about this treasury because of its seal, Josephus plucked up the courage to open it unobserved—and found no money, but books money could not buy. Browsing through them he found the Gospel of John translated from Greek to Hebrew, as I said, and the Acts of the Apostles—and Matthew's Gospel moreover, which is actually Hebrew. After reading from them he was once more distressed in mind, for he was somehow troubled over the faith of Christ.[5]

There are, to be sure, some profound differences between Epiphanius' story about Joseph and the Talmud's story about R. Abbahu. Still, both feature a Jewish sage discovering an ancient text in Tiberias to great emotional effect; both stories begin with the assumption that some material treasure has been or was about to be discovered, only to conclude that what was in fact discovered was a different kind of precious.[6]

---

[1] The term *tosafot* or *hosafot*, "additions," appears alongside *halakhot* and *haggadot* as an element of Torah knowledge in *Pe'ah* 2:6 17b (par. *Ḥag.* 1:8 76d) and *Hor.* 3:8 48c. Since the Yerushalmi regularly uses *matnita* for a recited teaching whether it is included in the Mishnah or not, there is no reason to think that *tosefta* here necessarily refers to a teaching additional to "our" Mishnah. It might refer to teachings explicitly introducing additions, with phrases like, "R. so-and-so added ..." (e.g. *m. Pes.* 1:6), which the Yerushalmi calls "a language of addition" (*Sot.* 8:5 23a).

[2] Speyer, *Bücherfunde*; Dilley, "Christian Tradition"; Mroczek, "Truth and Doubt."

[3] Epiphanius, *Panarion*, 30 3.8–4.1. Translation from Williams, *Panarion*, 133.

[4] On this episode, see Jacobs, *Remains of the Jews*, 48–53.

[5] Epiphanius, *Panarion*, 30 6.7–9 (ed. Holl; *TLG*). Translation from Williams, *Panarion*, 136.

[6] See another note of discovery by Jerome (*On Illustrious Men*, 75; trans. Halton, 107), speaking of Pamphilus, of Abbahu's Caesarea: "But I have discovered, written by his own hand, twenty-five

R. Abbahu discovers an oral teaching rather than bound books: R. Yohanan refers to him "hearing" a word of Torah. But that seems to make little difference. The story could have told us the circumstances in which R. Abbahu learned of this passage—an encounter with a learned person, for example—but it does not. It speaks almost as if that teaching was a book, waiting in Tiberias to be discovered by the visiting scholar.

This story about R. Abbahu's discovery is not simply a celebration of the study of Torah but also a specific portrayal of Torah and its study. First, it shows us a study culture centered around rabbinic *texts*, rather than around learning from teachers or the analysis of the system of Halakhah. Second, the way that it configures textual knowledge is different from how rabbinic literature configures knowledge of the scriptural text. Whereas Scripture is presented as available and perfectly known, this story projects an image of a fragmentary rabbinic Torah, scattered across different locations. Access to this Torah is incomplete and unequal: not everyone knows everything, and not everyone knows the same things. At the same time, the story celebrates a moment of discovery: knowledge of this scattered Torah develops and changes as people and teachings move from one place to another.

This chapter argues that this approach is central to the scholarly give-and-take of the Talmud. Amoraic discussions center on knowledge of rabbinic texts, but this knowledge is presented as fragmentary. Frequently-occurring phrases and rhetorical structures highlight the discovery of old-new teachings while at the same time emphasizing that even the greatest scholars do not know pertinent teachings; and the recognition that knowledge is subject to contingencies of individual access and geography is employed in passages that explain that certain teachings resulted from limited access to texts.

1. Recited teachings transported and discovered

I start with a small set of examples. They concern the *matnita* or "recitation" of Bar Qappara, a large collection or compilation of recited teachings which the Talmud mentions elsewhere.[7] Three unique passages introduce a recited teaching as coming from that collection with the phrase "R. Hoshaya brought the *matnita* of Bar Qappara from the South and recited...":

1. *Shevi'it* 5:3 35d

אמ' ר' ירמיה: בעלי לוף שוטה היא מתנית'. אייתי רב הושעיה מתני' דבר קפרא מן דרומא
ותני: עלי לוף ועלי בצלים. אית לך מימר, עלי בצלים השוטין?

volumes of the Commentaries of Origen *On the Twelve Prophets*, which I embrace and hold on to with such joy that I believe I am in possession of the riches of Croesus."

[7] See *Hor.* 3:8 48c, where it is numbered alongside other "great recitations," those of R. Hiyya and Hoshaya.

[*m. Shevi'it* 5:3 discusses "an arum plant upon which the sabbatical year has passed" and states that the leaves of such arum plants may be consumed by the poor; this is problematic, given the general prohibition on consuming sabbatical year after-growth.]

Said R. Jeremiah: The recited teaching speaks about leaves of wild arum [the after-growth of which is not prohibited—see *m. Shevi'it* 7:1].

R. Hoshaya brought the *matnita* of Bar Qappara from the South and recited, "the leaves of arum and the leaves of onion" [i.e. the law applies not just to arum but also to onion].

But can you say this [teaching concerns] the leaves of wild onion? [Leaves of wild onion are not eaten, and so it is unlikely that the law refers to wild onion; this undermines R. Jeremiah's interpretation that the law refers to wild arum].[8]

2. *Yoma* 1:1 38d (par. *Megillah* 1:9 72b and *Horayot* 3:4 47d)

מניין שהוא נשאל בשמונה? ר' חייה בשם ר' יוחנן: "ובגדי הקדש אשר לאהרן יהיו לבניו אחריו". מה ת"ל "אחריו"? אלא לגדולה שלאחריו.

ומניין שהוא עובד בשמונה? ר' ירמיה בשם ר' יוחנן: "ובגדי הקדש אשר לאהרן". מה ת"ל "אחריו"? לקדושה שלאחריו.

אמ' ליה ר' יונה: עמך הייתי. לא אמ' עובד אלא נשאל.[9]

אייתי רב הושעיה מתניתא דבר קפרא מן דרומא ותנא: וחכמ' אומ', "אינו עובד[10] לא בשמונה של כהן גדול ולא בארבעה שלכהן הדיוט".

Where from [do we know] that he [the priest anointed for war] receives [the divinatory] inquiries in eight [garments, like the high priest]? R. Hiyya [said] in the name of R. Yohanan: "The sacred vestments of Aaron shall be passed on to his sons following him" (Ex. 29:29). What is being taught by saying "after him" [since obviously Aaron's descendants follow him]? For [those] following him in greatness [thus including the priest anointed for war].

Where from [do we know] that he serves [at the altar] in eight [garments]? R. Jeremiah [said] in the name of R. Yohanan: "The sacred vestments of Aaron" (Ex 29:29). What is being taught by saying "after him"? For [those] following him in sanctity [thus including the priest anointed to war].

---

[8] Felix, *Shevi'it*, 326–7.
[9] In MS Leiden, the words "ובמה נשאל" were added by the corrector after R. Jonah's objection. They also appear in MS Leiden for *Meg.* and *Hor.* but are missing in the Genizah fragment for *Yom.* (T-S F 17.49; Sussmann, *Ginze Yerushalmi*, 262). I removed them since Hoshaya's teaching seems to relate to service rather than to receiving inquiries; see *QE* and the next note.
[10] In the Bologna fragment for *Meg.*, "כשר," fit, instead of "עובד," serve. Stemberger, "Bologna," 249.

Said R. Jonah to him [R. Jeremiah]: I was with you [when you heard this]. He [R. Yohanan] did not refer to serving but to receiving inquiries.

Rav Hoshaya brought the *matnita* of Bar Qappara from the South and recited: And the sages say, "He does not serve in the eight garments of a high priest nor in four garments of an ordinary priest."

3. *Beẓah* 3:4 62a

אתא עובדא קומי ר׳ אימי וסבר מימר, ר׳ יודה ור׳ שמעון—הלכה כר׳ יודה. אייתי רב הושעיה מתנית׳ דבר קפרה מדרומא ותנא: "וחכמ׳ אומ׳. כל שמומו ניכר מערב יום טוב ולא התירו מומחה אלא ביום טוב אין זה מן המוכן". וקיבלה וחזר ביה.

[The Mishnah presents a dispute in the case of a first-born male animal which fell into a pit on a festival day. Rabbi Judah rules that an expert may go down and examine if it has a defect and the owner may bring it up and slaughter it. But R. Simeon says that any animal whose defect was not evident while it is still day is not eligible for slaughter on the festival.]

A case came before R. Immi, and he inclined to say [as the general rule for cases where] R. Judah and R. Simeon [dispute]—the law accords with R. Judah."

Rav Hoshaya brought the *matnita* of Bar Qappara from the South, and recited: And the sages say, "Any [beast] whose defect was not evident prior to the festival, but which an expert permitted only on the festival day—it is not [considered] ready [for slaughter on the festival]."

And he [R. Immi] accepted it and retracted [from his inclination to rule as R. Judah].

In each of these cases, our knowledge changes because a teaching of Bar Qappara's recitation, which was hitherto unknown, is brought by R. Hoshaya from the South. In the first passage, R. Jeremiah's restrictive interpretation of the Mishnah is undermined by the Southern teaching. In the second passage, we hear two traditions attributed to R. Yohanan pertaining to the vestments the priest anointed for war must wear during divination and offering respectively. R. Jonah claims that the teaching concerning offering did not actually address that topic originally,[11] leaving us without a teaching on this topic. Rav Hoshaya brings such a teaching from the South. In these two passages, the scholars mentioned prior to R. Hoshaya's intervention do not respond to the intervention. We do get such a response in the third passage. A case on which R. Judah and R. Simeon dispute in the Mishnah comes before R. Immi; he is inclined to rule according to the former, given the guideline that in disputes between these two sages, one should rule with

---

[11] Frankel, *Einleitung*, 99a, argues there is a scribal error here since R. Jonah and R. Yohanan probably did not overlap.

R. Judah.¹² Again R. Hoshaya intervenes with a text from the South: a version of the Mishnaic dispute, or an addendum to it, records that the majority of sages had an opinion more similar to R. Simeon. In light of this new text, R. Immi retracts his intention to rule with R. Judah.

As with the story of R. Abbahu, the teachings which are introduced in these passages are new not because they had just been composed; they are marked as *matnitot*, "recited teachings," which the Talmud generally takes to represent the positions of sages from the Tannaitic past. What makes these teachings new is that they were not known before, at least in the location in which the discussion is taking place. It took the arrival of a scholar from another region to introduce them into the discussion.

These passages mark the South as a place from which certain pieces of Torah come. It is a great source of teachings not because R. Hoshaya or Bar Qappara, the two scholars named here, are particularly insightful or original themselves, but because R. Hoshaya was exposed to Bar Qappara's great collection of older texts. The collection, in this sense, resides in the South; Tiberian scholars can only encounter it if the texts are brought from the South to Tiberias. These passages effect an orientation to Tiberias precisely because it is not named: it is the implied "here" to which teachings are brought from "there." The Torah we are hearing normally, the passage signals to us, is Tiberian; it is lacking that piece that is brought to it from the South; but even when it is brought to us, to Tiberias, it is still marked as coming from somewhere else.

Knowledge of rabbinic teachings, as it is presented here, is heterogeneous and dynamic: different scholars have different access to different teachings, but there are moments in which access can be gained, through movement, and that access changes the course of the discussion. Part of what creates this image in the passages we have seen until now is the plasticity with which they treat oral texts, almost as if they were books. In the story about R. Abbahu, that plasticity is enhanced by the student's mistaken reference to a treasure. In the phrases invoking R. Hoshaya's introduction of Bar Qappara traditions, it is the use of the verb "bring" in conjunction with a location. The version of these phrases in the Babylonian Talmud is even more suggestive of materiality, as they tell us that "When R. Hoshaya came from Nehardea,¹³ he came and brought a *matnita* in his hand."¹⁴

There is a much larger set of passages reporting the discovery of recited teachings, though they are even less explicit on the mode of transmission than the passages so far discussed. In about eighty instances, the Talmud introduces a recited

---

¹² For the guideline itself, see *Ter.* 3:1 42a; on its application here, see Brandes, "Rules," 250.
¹³ On the connection between Nehardea and the South, see Schwartz, "Southern Judaea and Babylonia," and Lieberman, *YK*, 458 on *Pes.* 5:3 32a, where R. Jonathan tells R. Simlai, "I have a tradition from my fathers that Aggadah may not be taught to a Babylonian or a Southerner, as they are pompous but poor in Torah, and you are a Nehardean who lives in the South, and, furthermore, a minor!"
¹⁴ See e.g. *b. Shab.* 19b, *b. Suk.* 54a, and *b. Beẓ.* 26b. See Schwartz, "Southern Judaea and Babylonia," 189–92, for other instances of this phrase (not just with R. Hoshaya) in the Bavli.

teaching by saying "it was found recited."[15] The function of the phrase is to indicate that the recited teaching in question was discovered at some stage, and that the scholars cited in the discussion preceding the discovery did not have access to that teaching; the newly found teaching then offers a resolution to a problem raised in the discussion, often negating or affirming previous statements.[16] Consider the following example:

Shabbat 3:4 6a (par. *'Avodah Zarah* 3:4 42d)

ר׳ יעקב בר אידי בשם ר׳ יהושע בן לוי: שואלין הילכות המרחץ בבית המרחץ והילכות בית הכסא בבית הכסא.

כהדא: ר׳ שמעון בן אלעזר עאל מיסחי עם ר׳ מאיר. אמ׳ ליה: מהו לקנח? אמ׳ ליה: אסור. מהו להדיח? אמ׳ ליה: אסור.

ולא כן שמואל שאיל לרב, "מהו לענות אמן במקום מטונף", והוא אמ׳, "אסור, ואסור דאמרית לך אסור"?

אשכח תני[17]: שואלין[18] הילכות המרחץ במרחץ והילכות הכסא בבית הכסא.

R. Jacob b. Iddi [said] in the name of R. Joshua b. Levi: One may inquire about the laws of bathing in the bathhouse and the laws of the privy in the privy.

Like this: R. Simeon b. Eleazar went bathing with R. Meir [on the Sabbath]. He said to him, "What is [the law regarding] wiping off?" He said to him, "It is prohibited." He said to him, "What is [the law regarding] rinsing?" He said to him, "It is prohibited."

But did not Samuel ask Rav this [in such a place], "What is [the law regarding] answering 'Amen' in a filthy place," and he said to him, "It is prohibited, and It is prohibited that I tell you it is prohibited"?

It was found recited: One may inquire about the laws of bathing in the bathhouse and the laws of the privy in the privy.

---

[15] The phrase, אשכח תני, is grammatically difficult and vague. My translation follows Moscovitz, *Terminology*, 84, who nonetheless points out the difficulty, that the subject of the verb cannot be the recited teaching (*matnita*) since the verb is in the masculine form. Assis, *Concordance*, 171, believes the phrase is an abbreviated form of a fuller phrase, "[a reciter] was found reciting," pointing to *M. S.* 1:7 53a. Moscovitz argues that in that passage the verb refers to the person who is finding, not to what is found.

[16] Bacher, *Terminologie*, 216; See more below on Moscovitz's interpretation.

[17] Reading with the Genizah fragment (T-S F 17.40; Sussmann, *Ginze Yerushalmi*, 144) and the parallel in *'A. Z.* MS Leiden records here "אשכח תנא תני," which Assis considers the full form of the phrase (above n. 15); but even according to Assis, the text should be emended to "אשכח תניי תני" since תנא is a Babylonian form.

[18] Reading with the Genizah fragment and the parallel in *'A. Z.* MS Leiden reads here "אין שואלין," "one may not ask."

The passage addresses the permissibility of discussing matters of Torah in bathhouses and privies. Two teachings indicate that such discussions are permissible as long as they concern conduct in these places: one teaching presents a general statement to that effect, and another tells a story which shows us that R. Simeon and R. Meir did not refrain from discussing such laws in these places. The Talmud then challenges this position with a story. Samuel asked Rav a question about the laws of the privy in the privy, and Rav answered him but also told him he was prohibited from answering him. At this point in the passage, then, the Talmud has orchestrated an uncertainty: do we follow the first two teachings, which permit discussing these laws in these places, or the last teaching, which prohibits such discussion? This uncertainty is resolved with the statement that a recited teaching was found—of which, it is implied, the sages mentioned until this point were unaware[19]—and that it rules that such discussions are permitted.

A common structure for these passages is the presentation of a hypothesis or a tentative suggestion which is then ruled out or confirmed by the discovered teaching:[20]

m. Yoma 8:1

יום הכיפורים אסור במלכה ובשתייה וברחיצה וביסיכה ובינעילת הסנדל ובתשמיש המיטה. המלך והכלה ירחצו את פניהם והחיה תנעול את הסנדל—דברי ר׳ אליעזר. וחכמים אוסרים.

[On] the Day of Atonement [one] is prohibited from working, eating, drinking, bathing, putting oil, wearing sandals, and having sexual intercourse. The king and the bride may wash their face and a woman who had just given birth may wear sandals—these are the words of R. Eliezer, but the sages prohibit.

Yoma 8:1 44d

הוינן סברין מימר על סופה. אשכח תני על כולהון.

We would think to say [that the attribution to R. Eliezer applies only to] the conclusion [i.e. the last case]. It was found recited for all of them.

---

[19] This is the underlying logic of the passage, at least with respect to Rav and perhaps also with respect to R. Joshua b. Levi (if our assumption is that he would cite Tannaitic support if he had it). One could of course object that Rav may have known about the source and disputed it, but that does not seem to be a possibility the Talmud considers here.

[20] For cases where the suggestion is negated by the discovered teaching see, in addition to the passage discussed above, *Pe'ah* 2:2 17a (both instances), *Kil.* 9:10 32d (for which see below), *'Er.* 2:6 20b, *'Er.* 4:11 22a (both instances), *Yom.* 1:3 39a, *Suk.* 2:5 53a, *R. H.* 3:2 58d, *R. H.* 4:6 59c, *Yev.* 6:1 7b, *Ned.* 3:4 38a, *Naz.* 7:2 56b. Cases where the suggestion is affirmed are not formulated hypothetically in the same way, but see e.g. *Ned.* 2:2 37b and *Ned.* 4:3 38c. Sometimes it is difficult to determine if the statement is formulated tentatively or definitively (from the utterer's perspective); see below n. 25.

The last sentence of this passage in the Mishnah tells us R. Eliezer disputed with the sages, but the scope of the dispute depends on whether the attribution ("these are the words of R. Eliezer") refers to all the permissions specified in the passage—the king, the bride, and the woman recovering from childbirth—or just the last one. The Talmud raises, anonymously, the hypothesis that it is the latter, but we then hear that another recited teaching was discovered, one which makes it clear that the dispute extends to all these permissions.

The passages employing this phrase exemplify both features of Amoraic scholarship discussed in this chapter. First, they are premised on a distinction, even a hierarchy, between positions which have a text to support them and those which do not, showing us the orientation of Amoraic study culture towards textual sources. At the same time, these passages draw attention to the sages' uncertain, uneven, and varying knowledge of rabbinic teachings: they tell us that at a certain point these teachings were unknown, and that when they were still unknown Amoraic scholars were uncertain and even offered misleading suggestions about the issue at hand. These passages seem to portray discovery of recited texts in accidental terms, rather than as the result of deliberate searching for texts.[21] The Talmud does not usually record or present the reactions of Amoraic scholars to such discoveries. In one case, though, we hear that R. Jeremiah criticized R. Haggai about his interpretation of the Mishnah; after he left, R. Haggai found a teaching and said: "If R. Jeremiah heard this teaching, he criticized [me] appropriately!"[22]

Moscovitz writes that "it was found recited" introduces a recited teaching specifically in matters about which there is uncertainty. This is correct for the majority of the instances. The discovered teachings are frequently adduced to answer questions or, as we have seen in the second example above, respond with certainty to what has been presented only tentatively. In many of these instances, however, the statements that precede the discovered teachings are not formulated tentatively, and they do not, on their own, suggest uncertainty.[23] In the first example above, R. Joshua b. Levi seems certain that matters of Torah should be discussed in the bathhouse and the privy, whereas Rav seems certain that they should not; the uncertainty results from the Talmud's juxtaposition of these

---

[21] A rare example of searching for a corroborating text (perhaps like the searching for confirming "counterpart" teachings, e.g. in the story about Issi discussed in Chapter 1 above) is at 'Er. 1:6 19b: "a recited teaching was sought and not found," "איתבעת מתני ולא אישתכחת."

[22] M. S. 1:7 53a, though see the rest of the passage, where R. Ze'ira argues that R. Haggai's interpretation was indeed correct. As mentioned above (n. 15), this passage may not, technically speaking, be employing the phrase "it was found recited"; but even so, it certainly shows the same dynamics of discovery discussed here.

[23] Moscovitz, Terminology, 85 n. 416, offers examples of statements he considers tentative in this context, but with respect to several of them I think the more precise issue is that they are not backed by a text; see e.g. the example adduced here from Kil. 9:10 32d.

positions.[24] There are instances where even that type of uncertainty is absent;[25] consider, for example:

Kil'ayim 9:10 32d

ר׳ סימון בשם ר׳ יהושע בן לוי: לא שנו אלא שק. הא סל לא.

אשכח תני: הסל והשק והקופה מצטרפין בכלאים.

[On *m. Kil.* 9:10: "the sack and the basket [one attached to a strip of wool, the other to a strip of linen] combine into mixed kinds," and therefore may not be carried together.]

R. Simeon [said] in the name of R. Joshua b. Levi: They only recited "sack"—so [we can derive that] a reed-basket does not [combine into mixed kinds].

It was found recited: "The reed-basket and the sack and the basket combine into mixed kinds."

R. Joshua b. Levi derives, from the fact that a ruling in the Mishnah mentions only a sack and a basket, that the ruling does not apply to a reed-basket. There is nothing tentative or uncertain about the way that his teaching is formulated: it is similar to many such derivations from the language of the Mishnah. But the Talmud subsequently reports that another version of the ruling was found, in which a reed-basket is explicitly mentioned. R. Joshua b. Levi's conclusion therefore turns out to be incorrect, and the fact that it was based on speculation rather than firm textual basis is highlighted. The implication is that R. Joshua b. Levi was ignorant of that version, and that had he known it he would not have said what he did. I am pressing the point that the original formulation of the teaching was not tentative because it allows us to consider the destabilizing effect of these passages, the way they undermine confidence in the completeness of the sages' knowledge and replace it with a sense of the fragmentary. These comments showed students how even great scholars were limited by the arbitrary accessibility of rabbinic texts. Views and interpretations we find compelling may turn out to be wrong if a text is found to contradict them.

The composition of these passages shows us the attention the scholars who shaped the Talmud paid to the problem of textual access. In all these cases, the

---

[24] For similar instances where the statement is formulated definitively rather than tentatively and the uncertainty emerges only from a challenge by the Talmud or the citation of a disputed teaching, see *Shevi.* 10:2 39c (par. *Mak.* 1:1 31a), *M. S.* 1:7 53a, and *Yev.* 4:10 6b (par. *Ta'an.* 2:8 66a and *Meg.* 1:3 70d).

[25] In addition to the passage above, see e.g. *Ber.* 7:1 11a and *Ber.* 7:4 11c as well as similar passages in *Yev.* 2:2 3c, *Yev.* 11:1 11c, *Yev.* 15:5 15a, and *San.* 9:1 26d. In all those cases we would not have known that there is any problem with the position until the discovery of the teaching introduced by "it was found recited." See also cases where the discovered teaching confirms statements that are not presented in tentative terms, e.g. *Sot.* 2:2 17d and *Ket.* 5:1 29d.

186   THE RISE OF TALMUD

choice could have been made to omit the question, the tentative suggestion, or the rejected interpretation. In addition to highlighting the fragmentary state of rabbinic textual knowledge, the structure of these passages could serve various pedagogical and literary functions. The preservation of the "obsolete" teachings contributes to the archival impression that the Talmud offers as a text and a learning experience. It simulates for the students the process of discovery and invites them to participate in it. By presenting interpretations that were rejected, these passages offered a lesson in the limits of scholarly analysis. By presenting interpretations that were confirmed, these passages demonstrated the possibility of brilliantly deriving knowledge even in the absence of good sources. When these passages contrasted Tannaitic and Amoraic teachings, they offered a historical interpretation, and therefore a justification, of variance in ruling.

2. Amoraic teachings coming and going

While the passage discussed so far addressed recited teachings, we find similar patterns of representation with Amoraic teachings. There are about eighty unique instances in the Talmud of the phrase "R. so-and-so came [and said] in the name of R. such-and-such."[26] Moscovitz demonstrated that this phrase has a specific function, similar to the one we have seen with "it was found recited": it introduces a text—in this case, an Amoraic teaching—into a discussion in which there was uncertainty or only analysis-based knowledge.[27] To give a few examples:

1. *Megillah* 2:4 73b (par. *Berakhot* 2:3 4d and *Terumot* 1:2 40c)

אמ' ר' יוסה: מסתברא יודה רב חסדא בתרומות דהיא דר' יוסי. אתא[28] ר' חנניה בשם רב חסדא: דר' יוסה היא.

Said R. Yose: It seems reasonable that Rav Hisda would acknowledge that [the teaching] at [*m.*] *Terumot* [1:2] is R. Yose's. R. Hanina came [and said] in the name of R. Hisda: It is R. Yose's.

2. *Yoma* 2:1 39c

תרם והפריחתו הרוח—תפלוגתא דר' יוחנן ודר' חנינה. דאמ' ר' חנינה: קומץ שנתנו על גבי האישים והפריחתו הרוח—בפריחה האחרונה נתכפרו הבעלים ויצאו השיריים ידי מעילה. ר' יוחנן אמ': משיאחוז האור ברובו. מהו ברובו? ברובו שלקומץ או ברוב כל פרידה ופרידה

---

[26] On the number of the instances, see Assis, "Neziqin," 283; and Moscovitz, "Ata r. peloni," 505–7. See below for an alternative translation of the phrase.
[27] Moscovitz, "Ata r. peloni," 510–11.
[28] In MS Leiden for *Ber.*, אתא was deleted and replaced with אמר. The context suggests אתא is the correct version (see the similar passage at *Shab.* 10:1 12b). The parallel in *Ter.* omits the phrase altogether.

אתאמרת? אתא ר' חזקיה ר' יונה ר' בא ר' חייה בשם ר' יוחנן: ברוב כל פרידה ופרידה איתאמרת.

If [in the ritual of removing the ashes from the altar and depositing it on the floor, Lev 6:3], he lifted them and the wind blew them away—[the law is subject to] a dispute between R. Yohanan and R. Hanina. For R. Hanina said, "A fistful [of grain offering] that was put in the fire, and the wind blew it away—in the final blow the owner is atoned for and the remains are released from [liability for] sacrilege. R. Yohanan said, "[The act is considered complete] from the point the flame seizes the great part of it."

What is "the greater part of it"? Was it said concerning the greater part of the [entire] fistful, or the greater part of each and every chunk? R. Hezekiah came [and said in the name of] R. Jonah [who said in the name of] R. Abba [who said in the name of] R. Hiyya [who said] in the name of R. Yohanan: It was said with respect to the greater part of each and every chunk.

3. *'Avodah Zarah* 1:4 39d

ר' יצחק בר נחמן שאל לר' חנינה: יריד עזה מהו? אמ' ליה: הלכת לצור מימיך וראית יש' וגוי שהן שותפין בקדירה ואינו חושש שמא ניער הגוי בקדירה? וקשיא. הוא שאל ליה דא ומגיב ליה דא? אלא בגין דלית ר' חנינא אמ' מילה דלא שמעה מיומוי, בגין כן הוא שאל ליה דא ומגיב ליה דא. אתא ר' יוסי ביר' בון אבא בר בר חנה בשם ר' יוחנן: לא אסרו אלא כגון ירידה שלבוטנה.

R. Isaac b. Nahman asked R. Hanina: What is [the law concerning buying at] the fair at Gaza? He said to him: Have you ever gone to Tyre and seen a Jew and a gentile sharing a pot and he is not concerned about the gentile pouring something into the pot?

And this is difficult. He asked him this, and he responded that? [R. Hanina's answer has nothing to do with R. Isaac's question]. Rather, because R. Hanina never said something he has not heard [from his teachers, and he did not have such tradition on this question], that is why [it happened that] he [R. Isaac] asked this and he [R. Hanina] responded that. R. Yose b. R. Abbin came [and said in the name of] Abba b. b. Hanna [who said] in the name of R. Yohanan: They forbade only likes of the fair at Botnah.

In all these cases, the phrase introduces a teaching of which a previous stage of the discussion was wanting. In passage 1, which continues the discussion we have seen in Chapter 1 on *m. Megillah* 2:4, R. Yose (the Amoraic scholar) has a conjecture about R. Hisda's identification of the ruling in that Mishnah as the words of R. Yose (the Tannaitic sage). He does not have textual evidence to support his conjecture, and the discussion could have ended here. But the Talmud then tells us that R. Hanina arrived with a teaching explicitly attributed to R. Hisda, confirming R. Yose's conjecture with textual evidence. In passage 2, a question arises about the precise meaning of a statement by R. Yohanan; R. Hezekiah's intervention provides a solution to this question attributed to R. Yohanan himself. In passage 3, R. Isaac asks R. Haninah a question which the latter cannot answer because he has not heard an explicit teaching on the matter;[29] R. Yose b. R. Abbin comes and presents a teaching by R. Yohanan which answers the question. In each of these cases, the Talmud could have simply used the normal introductory formula, "Rabbi so-and-so said in the name of Rabbi such-and-such." Instead, by employing this phrase and this structure, these passages dramatize the process of discovery, as they highlight the fact that there was something lacking in the previous stage of the discussion, a source unavailable to its participants, which is now introduced.

At least literally, this phrase also refers to movement: "Rabbi so-and-so *came*." Moscovitz argues that the language of movement is used here figuratively, and no actual move is meant. Pointing to other phrases in rabbinic literature where the verb "come" does not refer to physical movement, he argues that in our phrase the verb refers to the turning point presented by the introduction of the teaching into the discussion, itself an "arrival" of sorts.[30] Moshe Assis, in contrast, has argued that the phrase refers "to the arrival of a scholar to the academies at Tiberias from one of the academies of other towns," positing that each of the scholars said to "come" was either not a resident of Tiberias or had spent extended time away.[31]

Assis's argument puts a lot of weight on problematic Talmudic biographical data; but there are some general considerations that make something like this interpretation attractive. One consideration is that a similar phrase in the Babylonian Talmud, "when R. so-and-so came," does seem to indicate a physical move (even if it is a fictional one).[32] More important, the function of the phrase as introducing textual discovery does not necessarily contradict reading it as a claim concerning movement from one place to another.[33] What the phrase may suggest is that the teaching was not known to some sages precisely because it was preserved only in a different region. The fact that other passages examined in this chapter, such as the reports about R. Hoshaya coming from the South, connect physical travel to the introduction of unknown teachings, seems to support the interpretation that such travel may also be indicated in this more common phrase.

---

[29] Responding with something else to not leave him empty handed; see *Shevi.* 6:1 36c.

[30] See Moscovitz, "Ata r. peloni," 509, 511 and n. 42, and 513. Under this interpretation, the phrase may better be translated with something like "came R. so-and-so in the name of R. such-and-such," as it is the teaching which is arriving.

[31] Assis, "Neziqin," 284–91.

[32] On the Bavli's term, see Redfield, "Redacting Culture."

[33] Though Assis himself does not discuss this function.

There are two cases employing a similar phrase which explicitly mention the geographical factor:

1. *Pesaḥim* 1:7 28a

> ר' יסי מקשי: למה ר' יסי או', "אינה המידה"? ר' יסי—דו שמע דאמ' ר' יוחנן, "מדברי
> ר' עקיבה ומדברי ר' חנינא סגן הכהנים", והוא שמע דבר קפרא אמ', "אב הטומאה
> דבר תורה, ולד הטומאה מדבריהן", ולא שמע דמר ר' יוחנן, "בין זה ובין זה דבר
> תורה". והוא מקשי [...].
>
> אתא ר' חייה בר בא מן צור ואמ' מן שמיה דר' יוחנן: בין זה ובין זה דבר תורה.[...]
> בגין כן ר' יוסי אמ'. אינה היא המידה.

[On *m. Pes.* 1:7, where R. Yose rejects an analogy by R. Meir which permits contamination of pure priest's share during Passover by burning it together with impure priest's share.]

R. Yose [the Amora] raised a difficulty: Why did R. Yose [the Tanna] say, "It is not an [appropriate] analogy?"

R. Yose [the Amora raised this difficulty] because he heard that R. Yohanan said, "[the inference by R. Meir] was from the words of R. Akiba and the words of R. Hanania the prefect of the priests," and he heard that Bar Qappara said that "a source of impurity [imparts impurity] according to the Torah [= Scripture], but a derivative impure object [which received its impurity from that source, imparts impurity only] according to their words [i.e. it is rabbinic]," but he did not hear that R. Yohanan said, "Both this and this [i.e., both primary and derivative impurities, impart impurity] according to the Torah"—and he [R. Yose the Amoraic scholar, therefore] raises the difficulty [concerning R. Yose's statement in the Mishnah . . . .]

R. Hiyya b. Abba came from Tyre and said in the name of R. Yohanan: "Both this and this according to the word of Torah. [. . .] This is why R. Yose said [in the Mishnah], 'It is not an appropriate analogy.'"

2. *Ta'anit* 1:2 64a

> אמ' ר' יוסה לר' חנניה בר אחוי דרב הושעיה: נהיר את כד הוינן קיימין קומי חנותיה דרב
> הושעיה חביבך, עבר ר' זעורה ושאלנן ליה ואמ', "עוד אנא היא צריכה לי", עבר ר' יסא
> ושאלנן ליה ואמ', "עוד אנא היא צריכה לי", ובסופה אתמציית[34] ליה ואמ', "לא שנייא. הל'
> מקום שמזכירין שואלין".
>
> ר' חייה בר בא אתא מן צור ואמ' מן שמיה דר' יוחנן: הלכה. מקום שמבירין שואלין.

R. Yose said to R. Hananya, the son of R. Hoshaya's brother: Do you remember that when we were standing in front of the store of your uncle R. Hoshaya,

---

[34] Correcting את מציית, with Rabinovitz, *STEI*, 290.

R. Ze'ira walked by and we asked him [whether referring to God's gift of rain in prayer may be separated from asking for rain in prayer] and he said, "I too am in doubt about it." R. Yose walked by and we asked him and he said, "I too am in doubt about it," but eventually, it was settled for him and he said, "There is no difference. The law is that where they refer [to the rain] they ask [for the rain].'"

R. Hiyya b. Abba came from Tyre and said in the name of R. Yohanan: The law is that where they refer [to the rain] they ask [for the rain].

Both passages clearly indicate R. Hiyya arrived from Tyre, and both of them present a structure similar to the other passages which feature arrival statements: a question is raised and then resolved by a teaching hitherto unknown. In *Pesaḥim*, the Talmud cites a question or objection from R. Yose, the Amoraic scholar, concerning the words of the Tannaitic R. Yose, and then explains that it was grounded in the Amoraic scholar's lack of familiarity with a pertinent teaching attributed to R. Yohanan; after it reconstructs how the teachings that were available to R. Yose would lead him to formulate this objection, the Talmud tells us that R. Hiyya, one of R. Yohanan's students, came from Tyre with that exact teaching that was previously unavailable to R. Yose. In *Ta'anit*, R. Yose and R. Haninah recall how R. Ze'ira would not answer a certain question they had, and even R. Yose pondered the matter for a while before answering. Here too, R. Hiyya arrives from Tyre and resolves the matter with a teaching attributed to R. Yohanan.

Whether or not we have here instances of the common phrase "Rabbi so-and-so came" with some additions (the preposition "from," the place name, and the word "said"),[35] these passages can teach us about that phrase by showing us how a similar structure can be connected to a scholar's travel. My argument is not that all or any passages employing "R. so-and-so came" are reliable reports about scholars arriving to Tiberias, but rather that they present or imagine the movement of scholars as resulting in the introduction of new texts, and that they draw on the idea of a spatial dispersion of knowledge. Regardless, however, of whether the common phrase alludes to scholars moving from one place to another, it attests to the Amoraic interest in the problem of textual knowledge and the way that textual discoveries animate Talmudic discussions.

While these passages concern scholars coming in and teaching, we also find passages about scholars traveling out and learning. Scattered in the Talmud are several reports by R. Mana, who returns to his base in Tiberias to inform people there of what he has heard in his visit to Caesarea:

---

[35] Assis, "Neziqin," 292, believes it is: for him, Tyre is mentioned because it is not a place of an established academy; for Moscovitz, "Ata r. peloni," 511 n. 42, these differences show that it is not an instance of the common phrase. As Moscovitz emphasized to me (personal communication), the fact that the verb "said" does not appear in in the common Yerushalmi phrase also contrasts it with the other two examples I offered above of traveling scholars: the Bavli's "arrival statements" (which employ "and said") and the passages about Bar Qappara's *matnita* (which employ "and recited").

1. *Demai* 1:3 22b (par. *Qiddushin* 2:8 63a)

אמ' ר' מנא: אזלית לקיסרית ושמעית ר' חזקיה יתיב ומתני, "המקדש בחלקו בקדשי קדשים
ובקדשים קלין אינה מקודשת'—ר' לעזר אמ', 'דברי הכל'. ר' יוחנן אמר, במחלוקת'".
ואמרית ליה: מנן שמע ר' הדא מילתא? ואמ' לי: מן ר' ירמיה.

R. Mana said: I went to Caesarea and heard R. Hezekiah in session teaching, "'If one betrothed a woman with his portion of the holiest sacrifices or the lesser sacrifices, she is not betrothed' (*m. Qid.* 2:8), R. Eleazar said, 'this is everyone's opinion.' R. Yohanan said, 'this matter is under dispute.'"

And I [i.e. R. Mana] asked him [R. Hezekiah], "From whom did you hear this statement?" He said to me, "From R. Jeremiah" [...].

2. *Ḥallah* 1:1 57a (par. *Pesaḥim* 2:5 29b)

ר' יוסי בשם ר' שמעון: תני ר' ישמעאל כן; ר' יונה ר' זעירא ר' שמעון בן לקיש בשם ר'
ישמעאל; אמ' ר' מנא: אזלית לקיסרין ושמעית ר' אחווה בר זעירא אמר[36], "ואבא הוה אמ'
ליה בשם ר' ישמעאל": נאמ' "לחם" בפסח ונאמ' "לחם" בחלה.

R. Yose [said] in the name of R. Simeon [b. Laqish]: Thus is recited by R. Ishmael;

R. Jonah [said in the name of] R. Zeʻira, [who said in the name of] R. Simeon b. Laqish [who said] in the name of R. Ishmael;

R. Mana said: I went to Caesarea and I heard R. Ahava b. R. Zeʻira, and my father said it in the name of R. Ishmael:

It was said, "bread" concerning Passover (Deut. 16:3) and "bread" concerning Ḥallah (Num. 15:18) . . . .

3. *Shabbat* 7:2 10b

בישל בחמי טיבריא מהו? חזקיה אמ': אסור. ר' יוחנן אמ': מותר. אמ' ר' מנא: אזלית לקיסרין
ושמעית ר' זריקן בשם חזקיה, "לחזקיה צריכה ליה פסח שנתבשל בחמי טבריא מהו. תרין
אמורין. חד אמ', 'אסור'. וחרנה אמ'. 'מותר'".

If a person cooked in the hot springs of Tiberias [on the Sabbath], what is [the law]? Hezekiah said "prohibited," R. Yohanan said, "permitted." Said R. Mana: I went to Caesarea and heard R. Zeriqan [say] in the name of Hezekiah: "Hezekiah had a question, 'Passover cooked in the hot springs of Tiberias, what is [its status]? There are two interpreters. One said it is prohibited. The other said it is permitted . . . .'"

4. *Bava Qamma* 9:3 6d

חילפיי אמ': נשבע לו קודם הפסח, אחר הפסח משלם לו חמץ יפה. אמ' ר' מנא: אזלית
לקיסרין ואשכחית לר' חזקיה דדריש לה משום דר' יעקב בר אחא, "אין אית בר נש פליג על
חילפיי, שאין משלם חמץ יפה—הכל מודין בחמץ שמשלם חמץ יפה".

---

[36] Leiden reads "ור' זירא" and omits "אמר"; reading with *Pes.* (though the verb אמר is often implied).

Hilfai said: He takes an oath prior to Passover, and after Passover he must restitute with good leavened food. Said R. Mana: I went to Caesarea and I found R. Hezekiah who expounded in the name of R. Jacob b. Aha, "If there is anyone who disputes Hilfai, that one must not restitute with good leavened food, [know that] everyone agrees, in the case of leavened food that he must restitute with good leavened food."

To these we can add a very similar formulation that concerns a different scholar and a different region:

5. *Pe'ah* 1:6 16c

טבח כהן—חברייא בשם ר׳ יהושע בן לוי: פטר לו שבת אחת. אמ׳ ר׳ יוסי: אזלית לדרומה ושמעית ר׳ חנן אבוי דר׳ שמעון בשם ר׳ יהושע[37] בן לוי, "פטר לו שבת אחת".

A butcher who is a priest—The colleagues [say] in the name of R. Joshua ben Levi: He is exempt for a week. Said R. Yose: I went to the South and heard R. Hanan, the father of R. Simeon, [say] in the name of R. Joshua b. Levi: He is exempt for a week.

These passages, which include all but two instances of this phrase,[38] highlight the mechanisms of transmission. In passage 1, R. Mana tells us that he heard from R. Hezekiah in Caesarea about a dispute between R. Simeon and R. Yohanan; R. Mana inquired what was Hezekiah's source for this dispute, and he replied that he heard about it from R. Jeremiah. In the next stage of the text, not cited here, R. Mana goes on to use this new teaching he learned in Caesarea to understand another teaching by R. Jeremiah. It is worth noting that R. Jeremiah, like R. Mana, is from the Galilee—so when R. Mana is reporting this tradition, he is bringing back a piece of Galilean Torah that was preserved only in Caesarea, but had been missing in the Galilee.[39] Passage 2 presents a series of alternative channels of transmission attributing a teaching to R. Ishmael; R. Mana's report from Caesarea adds one or two additional chains of transmission.[40] A similar case is passage 5, where R. Yose introduces from the South a teaching which we already heard from the colleagues; the added value there might be that the scholar to whom the

---

[37] MS Leiden reads "Simeon b. Levi," but it seems from context that Joshua b. Levi is intended, and that the scribe wrote "Simeon" here because Simeon is mentioned earlier; see Frankel, *Einleitung*, 92a.

[38] The others are *Kil.* 6:3 30c and *Ter.* 8:8 46a (par. *Pes.* 1:7 28a; for the differences between these passages, see Moscovitz, "Parallel Sugiot," 532–3).

[39] The passages cited in the previous note also present Cesarean transmission of Galilean sages.

[40] Two, if R. Mana gives us two alternatives—one that he heard R. Ahava b. Zeira teach it anonymously, and another, that he heard his own father, R. Jonah, teach it in the name of R. Ishmael (thus Frankel, *Einleitung*, 108b–109a). One, if he is reporting that he heard R. Ahava b. Zeira reporting that his father, R. Ze'ira, would teach it in the name of R. Ishmael (thus Lieberman, *YK*, 403, based on the version in *Pesaḥim*). Both options correlate with the second chain of transmission mentioned earlier in the passage.

teaching is attributed, R. Joshua b. Levi, was himself a Southerner.[41] In passage 3, R. Mana seems to relate an alternative version of Hezekiah's opinion preserved in Caesarea—whereas earlier it was recorded that he thought this kind of cooking is prohibited, here he is uncertain.[42] In passage 4, R. Mana brings out R. Hezekiah's attestation about R. Aha's position as evidence that no one disputes the tradition attributed to Hilfai.[43]

In all these cases, R. Mana (or R. Yose) reports he heard one scholar transmitting a teaching attributed to another scholar.[44] As with the passages referring to R. Hoshaya's recited teachings or to the "arrival" of sages, here too what is encountered is not an opinion, but a cited text. This is also the case with another set of passages that pertain not to travel within Palestine, but to arrival from Babylonia:[45]

Berakhot 2:1 4b (par. *Megillah* 2:2 73a)

אמ' ר' זעירא: עד דאנא תמן תמן צריכת לי, וכד סלקת להכא שמעית ר' יסא בשם ר' יוחנן, "אפי' שמען כל היום יצא".

Said R. Ze'ira: When I was there [= Babylonia], this issue was unclear to me, but when I came up here [= Palestine] I heard R. Yose say in the name of R. Yohanan: Even if he heard them [only] through the duration of the day, he has fulfilled his obligation.

Here too, R. Ze'ira's arrival in Palestine exposes him not to the opinion of the sages he meets there, but to teachings they transmit.[46] In another similar case, he learns a different version of a recited teaching that he learned in Babylonia; in yet another case, he juxtaposes a teaching by R. Eleazar he heard in Babylonia with a teaching attributed to the same sage which he now heard in Palestine.[47] There are other examples that do not employ fixed verbal patterns but show the same interests in the way access to teachings varies geographically.[48]

---

[41] See *Ter.* 8:11 46b.
[42] See for this interpretation Tamar, *Mo'ed*, 94–5.
[43] Attributing the clause "is there anyone who disputes Hilfai..." to R. Mana, with Assis, "Nineteen Sugyot," 76.
[44] An apparent exception is at *Dem.* 2:1 22c; but there, R. Mana reports a practice he has observed rather than a ruling he has *heard*; when R. Mana asks R. Isaac about this this practice, the latter attributes it to yet another sage, so in a sense the structure of the double transmission is maintained.
[45] On the trope of Babylonian scholars arriving to Palestine, see Schwartz, "Tension"; Kiperwasser, *Going West*.
[46] Epstein, *IMT*, 294.
[47] *Yev.* 2:3 3d and *Ḥag.* 1:4 76b (par. *Suk.* 4:8 54c). Another instance is at *'Er.* 1:1 18d. On other occasions, R. Ze'ira reports his actions or thoughts in Babylonia without contrasting them with what happened after he immigrated to Palestine: see *Ber.* 7:2 11b, *Yev.* 3:4 4d, *Kil.* 4:8 29c. At *'Er.* 6:8 23d a similar formulation appears with another sage, not with reference to a teaching but as a report of a conversation.
[48] See *Yev.* 1:12 2d (I offer a detailed analysis of the way the passage addresses textual knowledge in Vidas, "Place of Torah," 46–8), *Shevu.* 6:7 37b, and *Beẓ.* 3:4 62a. See Miller, *Sages and Commoners*, for a wealth of passages in the Talmud which mark teachings as belonging to particular localities.

3. "He did not hear"

Despite this recurrent presentation of scholarly knowledge as fragmentary and subject to change, Amoraic commentary on rabbinic teachings generally assumes that sages had access to the same material. In the passages examined above, the implication is that the teaching that was discovered or which arrived was generally unknown, at least in that place. There is, however, a significant number of passages in which Amoraic scholars do argue that specific sages were ignorant of a teaching. In the discussion of the phrase "R. so-and-so came [and said a teaching] in the name of R. such-and-such," I cited the anonymous comment in the Talmud which posits that R. Yose could have only made a certain objection because he "*did not hear*," i.e. did not know, a teaching by R. Yohanan, which was then introduced to him by R. Hiyya arriving from Tyre (*Pesaḥim* 1:7 28a). The phrase "did not hear" is used similarly in about twenty-five passages in the Yerushalmi to argue that a certain teaching betrays ignorance of another teaching.[49] While that comment about R. Yose presents a detailed "source criticism"—it lists two teachings that R. Yose had heard, and one that he had not—such comments are normally simpler:

Berakhot 1:4 3c

ר' יסא כד סליק להכא חמתין גחנין ומלחשין. אמ' לון: מהו דין לחישה? ולא שמיע דמר ר' חלבו ר' שמעון בשם ר' יוחנן; ר' ירמיה ר' חנינא בשם ר' מיישא; ר' חייא בשם ר' סימאי; ואית דאמרין ליה חבריא בשם ר' סימאי: מודים אנחנו לך אדון כל הבריות [...].

R. Yose, when he came up here [= Palestine], saw them bowing and whispering [during the Thanksgiving Blessing of the Amidah prayer]. He said to them, "What is this whispering?"

And he did not hear that R. Helbo said in the name of R. Simeon [who said] in the name of R. Yohanan, [and] R. Jeremiah [said] in the name of R. Hanina [who said] in the name of R. Maysha, [and] R. Hiyya [who said] in the name of R. Simai—and there are those who attributed it to the colleagues [who say] in the name of R. Simai: "We give thanks to you the master of all creatures [...]."

R. Yose, who has just immigrated from Babylonia, is unfamiliar with the Palestinian liturgical practice, so he asks about it when he observes it, and the Talmud explains that he did not know of the teaching, attributed here through three different chains of transmission, which instructs a different, longer version of the Thanksgiving Blessing.[50]

---

[49] Moscovitz, *Terminology*, 337–8; for a list of instances, see Assis, *Concordance*, 556–8.
[50] See Ginzberg, *Commentary I*, 185–7.

This passage is typical of passages employing this phrase. Normally, the comment which states that the sage did not know a certain teaching is not attributed.[51] The teaching that supposedly displays ignorance is normally attributed, though there are four instances where the argument applies to anonymous comments.[52] The teaching of which the sage is said to be ignorant is, in all but one case, an attributed Amoraic teaching; that one instance in which it is a recited teaching is also the one instance where the statement is retracted,[53] though there are other instances which do not employ this specific phrase and speak about a sage being ignorant of a recited teaching.[54]

Why would these passages assume that the sage *did not know* the teaching in question, rather than that he did know it and disagreed with it? An Amoraic scholar may, after all, disagree with another Amoraic scholar. A few types of explanations emerge from these passages. First, just as we have seen in the statements preceding the phrase "it was found recited," the comment "did not hear" follows, in almost half of the instances, teachings expressing uncertainty or doubt: a question, a challenge, or a tentative statement.[55] In other passages, the teaching presents scholarly comments such as correlation, quotation of additional support, and derivation.[56] Only in two instances we find such claims applying to rulings.[57]

Another explanation for why Amoraic scholars may have appealed to ignorance rather than disagreement is geographical factors. We have seen how the phrase is used to suggest that, having just arrived from Babylonia, R. Yose was puzzled by the local liturgy; another passage similarly involves R. Yose and local Palestinian practice. We also have the opposite example: a scholar who immigrates to Babylonia is said to be unaware of a Babylonian teaching. On two occasions, the Yerushalmi comments about teachings attributed to "the rabbis there" that they were unaware of Palestinian teachings; similarly, we hear that the "judges of Nehardea" did not

---

[51] The exceptions are *Shevi.* 4:2 35b and *Ket.* 8:3 32a, where it is attributed to R. Yose, and perhaps *R. H.* 2:7 58a (par. *San.* 1:2 18c), where it is either anonymous or attributed to R. Zevida.

[52] See *Bik.* 1:2 54d (par. *Ḥag.* 2:5 78b, *Ḥag.* 3:2 79a), *Yev.* 15:5 15a (par. *Naz.* 3:7 52d, *San.* 5:2 22d), *Ket.* 2:1 26a, and *Ket.* 13:2 35d (par. *Ned.* 4:2 38c). In that last passage, QE considers the "did not hear" statement to apply to Rav's teaching, and then interprets R. Abbin's statement as a challenge to that argument (since it makes sense Rav would not know a teaching by R. Yohanan); but R. Abbin's statement is connected to the statement after it.

[53] *Shevi.* 4:2 35b.

[54] See *B. B.* 10:6 17c, "if Rav had heard this recited teaching, he would not have said this"; following the emendation in Rabinovitz, *STEI*, 507.

[55] Questions: *Ber.* 1:4 3c (for which see above), *Ber.* 1:5 3d (though the utterance is missing, it is almost certainly a question), *Yom.* 6:7 44a, *R. H.* 1:2 57a (both instances), and *Git.* 5:5 47a; challenges: *Kil.* 6:6 30c, *Shevi.* 5:1 35d, and *Pes.* 1:7 28a (for which see above); tentative statements: *Shevi.* 4:2 35b (even though this is the exception where in the end it is decided that the sage must have known the teaching, the tentativeness may help us explain why the possibility came up in the first place) and *Ḥal.* 3:8 59c.

[56] Correlations and associations: *Bik.* 2:1 64d (par. *Ḥag.* 2:5 78b, *Ḥag.* 3:2 79a), *Ket.* 8:3 32a, *Ket.* 13:7 36b; identification: *Pes.* 7:13 35c; adducing additional support: *Yev.* 15:5 15a (par. *Naz.* 3:7 52d, *San.* 5:2 22d), *Ket.* 13:2 35d (par. *Ned.* 4:2 38c), and *Ket.* 2:1 26a; Halakhic derivation: *Yev.* 5:6 7a.

[57] See *Shevu.* 6:7 37b and probably also *R. H.* 2:7 58a (par. *San.* 1:2 18c), if we take the statement there to refer to the practice of the Patriarch's house. See perhaps also the passage at *R. H.* 2:7 58b (par. *San.* 1:2 18c).

know teachings by R. Yohanan. In another passage, the location of the scholar is not mentioned specifically but the ignorance again relates to the divide between Babylonia and Palestine.[58] The implication might be that the sage is unlikely to have come across the teaching originally taught far away, and that had he heard it he would have not spoken or reacted as he did. To be sure, these factors appear in many other places where Amoraic scholars do not offer such explanations, but they may have contributed to the use of this type of commentary.

These comments draw on the image of the fragmentary Torah to interpret rabbinic teachings. They argue that scholars may ask questions, raise challenges, or make erroneous or incomplete statements because they lack access to or knowledge of pertinent sources. These comments partake therefore in the special kind of canonical interpretation explored in this book: on the one hand, rabbinic teachings are important enough to interpret them and structure intellectual life around them; on the other hand, the resulting interpretation is informed by the notion that these teachings are subject to various imperfections and contingencies.

4. Access to rabbinic teachings in Tannaitic literature

Tannaitic literature does not present this image of a scattered Torah. There are passages which refer to access and discovery, but these are almost entirely confined to the early Tannaitic discourse of *shemu'ot*. Passages that refer to discovery of teachings use the vocabulary specific to these traditions (e.g. *mequbal*, "I have received"), and trace the traditions to the time of the Temple or even more distant past:

1. *m. Pe'ah* 2:6

מעשה שזרע ר' שמעון איש המצפה לפני רבן גמליא'. ועלו ללשכת הגזית ושאלו. אמר נחום הליבלר: מקובל אני מרבי מיישא שקיבל מאבא שקיבל מן הזוגות שקיבלו מן הנביאים הלכה למשה מסיני, "הזורע את שדיהו שני מיני חיטים. אם עשאן גורן אחת נותן פיאה אחת. שתי גרנות. נותן שתי פיאות".

It once happened that R. Simeon, a man of Mitspah, sowed [his field with two kinds of wheat and the case came] before Rabban Gamaliel. They went up to the Chamber of Hewn Stone and inquired [about this]. Nahum the Scribe said: "I have received [this tradition] from R. Me'asha, who received it from father [or: Abba], who received it from the Pairs, who received it from the Prophets, a tradition [given] to Moses at Sinai, that a man who sows his field with two kinds

---

[58] R. Yose: *Suk.* 3:4 53d; moving to Babylonia: *Ber.* 1:5 3d; "Rabbis there": *Pes.* 7:13 35c, *Yev.* 5:6 7a; "Judges of Nehardea": *Shevu.* 6:7 37b; Babylonia/Palestine divide: *Ket.* 10:5 34a.

of wheat, if he made of them one granary, he designates only one *pe'ah*; two granaries, he designates two *pe'ot*.

2. *m. Yadaim* 4:3

וכשבא ר׳ יוסי בן דורמסקית אצל ר׳ אליעזר ללוד אמ׳ לו: מה חידוש היה לכם בבית המדרש היום? אמ׳ לו: נמנו וגמרו—עמון ומואב מעשר עני בשביעית. בכה ר׳ אליעזר ואמ׳: "סוד ייי ליריאיו ובריתו להודיעם". צא ואמור להן, "אל תחושו למנינכם. מקובל אני מרבן יוחנן בן זכיי ששמע מרבו ורבו מרבו הלכה למשה מסיני שעמון ומואב מעשר עני בשביעית".

And when R. Yose b. Durmasqit came to R. Eliezer in Lod, he [the latter] said to him: "What new thing have you had in the study house today?" He said to him, "They voted and decided that Ammon and Moab must give poor tithe in the seventh year." R. Eliezer wept and said: "The secret [*sod*] of the Lord is to those who fear him, and he makes his covenant known to them." (Ps 25:14) Go and tell them: Do not be worried about your vote! I received [this tradition] from Rabban Yohanan b. Zakkai, who heard it from his teacher, and his teacher from his teacher, a tradition [given] to Moses at Sinai, that Ammon and Moab must give poor tithe in the seventh year.

3. *m. Yebamot* 16:7

אמ׳ ר׳ עקיבה: כשירדתי לנהרדעא לעיבור השנה מצאני נחמיא איש בית-דלי ואמ׳ לי, "שמעתי שאין משיאין את האשה בארץ-ישר׳ על פי אחד אלא יהודה בן בבא". נומיתי לו: כן הדברים. אמ׳ לי: לך ואמור להן משמי, "אתם יודעים שהמדינה הזאת משובשת בגייסות ומקובל אני מרבן גמליא׳ הזקן שמשיאין את האשה על פי עד אחד". וכשבאתי והרציתי את הדברים לפני רבן גמליא׳ ושמח לדברייי ואמ׳, "מצינו חבר ליהודה בן בבא".

מתוך הדברים נזכר רבן גמליא׳ שנהרגו הרוגים בתל-ארזא והשיא רבן גמליא׳ הזקן את נשותיהן על פי עד אחד.

R. Aqiva said: When I went down to Nehardea to intercalate the year, I was met by Nehemiah of Bet-Deli and he told me, "I heard that in the Land of Israel they do not allow a woman to marry [another] based on a single testimony [e.g. that the husband was killed], with the exception of R. Judah b. Bava." I told him: "That is the case." He said to me, "Go and tell them in my name: You know that this country is disrupted by invaders, and I received [a tradition] from Rabban Gamaliel the Elder that we allow a woman to marry based on a single testimony." And when I came and presented these words before Rabban Gamaliel, he was overjoyed at my words and said: "We have found a counterpart for Judah b. Bava." And as this was happening, Rabban Gamaliel remembered that men were killed in Tel Arza and Rabban Gamaliel the Elder allowed their wives to marry based on a single testimony.

Like our Talmudic passages, these passages present the discovery of knowledge which is otherwise unknown to the majority of the sages. Here too, the discovery takes place upon the arrival of sages to particular places. But again, these passages are exceptional: they are few in number and refer to a specific type of tradition. They are also exceptional in their specific characteristics. The first passage presents an inquiry, during the time of the Temple, in the Chamber of Hewn Stone, which the sages imagined as the place "from which Torah" *used* "to come forth to all Israel," before the destruction (*t. Sanhedrin* 7:1); in the third passage, R. Aqiva visits Nehardea, a place rarely visited by Tannaitic sages. A further indication of the unusual nature of these passages is that two of them constitute two of the three times that the phrase "a tradition [given] to Moses at Sinai" appears in the Mishnah.

In these passages, the discovery does not present quite a twist in the plot: in two of them it gives a more solid foundation to what is already known through the tradition of a single sage (the third passage) or reasoning (the second passage); the first passage confirms, with Sinaitic authority, what was already presented as the law (*m. Pe'ah* 2:5). To these we can add the story which we have seen in Chapter 1, where Issi the Babylonian discovers a corroborating teaching, even though that discovery does present a certain twist to Issi, who was about to despair of his teaching's authenticity.[59] There are, however, also cases where the discovery prompts a change in approach; consider the following passage:

m. 'Eduyot 1:3

הלל או': מלא הין מים שאובין פוסלין את המקווה. שאדם חייב לומ' כלשון רבו. ושמי אומ': תשעת קבים. וחכמ' אומ': לא כדברי זה ולא כדברי זה. אלא עד שבאו שני גרדיים משער האשפות שבירושלם והעידו משם שמעייה ואבטליון ששלושת לוגים מים שאובין פוסלין את המקווה. וקיימו את דבריהן.

Hillel says "a *hin* of drawn water disqualifies the purifying pool"—[using the word *hin*] because one must use the same formulation as his teacher. And Shammai says: "Nine *kabs*." But the sages say [the law follows] neither the words of this one nor the words of that one, but rather, when two weavers arrived from the Dung Gate in Jerusalem and testified in the names of Shemaia and Avtalion that three *logs* of drawn water disqualify the purifying pool, and they [the sages] confirmed their words.

In this passage, a question which was in dispute between Hillel and Shammai concerning the amount of drawn water which disqualifies a purifying pool is resolved when the true Halakhah is discovered. The Tosefta version emphasizes that Hillel and Shammai's positions themselves are not based on a *shemu'a*, though Hillel's formulation is itself supposedly traditional ("the same formulation as his teacher").[60]

---

[59] See *t. Zev.* 2:17, discussed above Chapter 1, Section 5.
[60] See Rosenthal, "Tradition and Innovation," 372–4.

Here too, the revelation is part of the discourse of *shemu'ot* and Temple-era "testimonies," and here too, the situation is unusual, with the testimony coming from the Dung Gate weavers rather than a sage. This teaching and others like it usually concern the earliest generations of the sages,[61] though we find occasional "discoveries" of tradition among later Tannaitic sages as well.[62] But more commonly, and in contrast with what we have seen in the Talmud, when later Tannaitic sages "arrive" and introduce a twist in the plot, they do not present newly revealed texts, but rather their own arguments.[63]

Gaps in knowledge are rarely invoked concerning sages in Tannaitic literature. A prominent teaching attributes the proliferation of disputes among the sages to the negligence of the students of Shammai and Hillel;[64] but ignorance of tradition is rarely named as a reason for differing rulings. When Tannaitic sages say "they have not heard" a *shemu'a*, in a specific case, their solution is often not to adduce such a *shemu'a*, but rather to derive the law through interpretation or reasoning from what they have heard.[65] As we have seen before, Tannaitic compilations are not always interested in demarcating traditions from what is derived from them, and it is therefore not always clear when a dispute is based on different access to traditional knowledge and when it is based on different positions. Consider the following comparison:

m. Niddah 1:3	*t. Niddah* 1:5
ר' אליעזר אומ'. ארבע נשים דיין שעתן. בתולה ומעוברת ומניקה וזקינה. אמ' ר' יהושע. לא שמעתי אלא בתולה. אבל הלכה כדב' ר' אליעזר.	ר' אליעזר אומ'. ארבע נשים דיין שעתן. בתולה ומעוברת מניקה וזקינה. אמ' ר' יהושע. לא שמעתי אני אלא בתולה.
	אמ' לו ר' אליעזר. אין אומ' מי שלא ראה את החדש יבוא ויעיד אלא למי שראה.[66] אתה לא שמעתה ואנו שמענו. אתה שמעת אחת ואנו שמענו ארבע.
R. Eliezer says: There are four women [for whom] the time [of first seeing the blood] suffices: a virgin, a pregnant women, a nursing woman, and an old woman.	R. Eliezer says: There are four women [for whom] the time [of first seeing the blood] suffices: a virgin, a pregnant women, a nursing woman, and an old woman.
R. Joshua said: I have only heard [this concerning] a virgin. But the law follows R. Eliezer.	R. Joshua said: I have only heard [this concerning] a virgin.

---

[61] *t. San.* 2:13 (par. *t. 'Ed.* 3:1).
[62] e.g. *t. Naz.* 5:1.
[63] Mostly with R. Aqiva: *m. M. S.* 5:8, *m. Ned.* 6:9, *t. Pes.* 1:7, *t. M. Q.* 2:10, 12, and *Sifra Zavim* 5:3 79c; but also with Rabban Gamaliel at *m. 'Er.* 10:10.
[64] *t. Ḥag.* 2:9, *t. Sot.* 14:9, *t. San.* 7:1, cf. *San.* 1:6 19c; and see Rosen-Zvi, "Protocol," 471–3.
[65] *m. Yev.* 8:4, 15:1 (par. *m. 'Ed.* 1:12, *t. 'Ed.* 1:6), *m. Pes.* 9:6, *m. Bek.* 6:8 (*t. Bek.* 4:11), the series of cases in *m. Kar.* 3, *m. Neg.* 7:4, 9:3, 11:7, *m. Par.* 1:1, and *m. Yad.* 3:1.
[66] MS Vienna has "לא ראה," text follows printed edition.

> Said to him R. Eliezer: We do not tell
> someone who did not see the new moon to
> come and testify, but to someone who did
> see. You have not heard and we did hear.
> You have heard one and we heard four.

In the Mishnah, R. Eliezer presents the law with respect to four categories of women. R. Joshua says he only has an explicit tradition with respect to one of the four. It is not clear, in the Mishnah, whether R. Eliezer's teaching is grounded in tradition or not. In the Tosefta version, that is clear. R. Eliezer emphasizes that he did hear the law as he presented it, and argues that R. Joshua's more restrictive tradition presents lack of knowledge rather than evidence to the contrary.[67]

A much-studied passage in the Tosefta (*t. 'Eduyot* 1:1) speaks about the inability to find words of Torah; scholars have suggested many different interpretations of the particular problem to which it refers—that the vast production of unstructured knowledge makes the rabbinic corpus difficult to memorize, that Halakhah may be seen as "one seamless corpus of legal teachings," or that disputing traditions make it so that the law is unclear.[68] Scholars have not proposed that this passage refers to problems resulting from uneven transmission. In any event, the passage presents the problem as having been resolved by the activity of the sages at Yavneh.

The Tannaitic corpus refers, occasionally, to the problems of transmission and access discussed in this chapter; but such references appear primarily among the early generations of Tannaitic sages and in reference to a specific kind of tradition, the *shemu'a*. As the intellectual focus on arguments and reformulation took over the Tannaitic study house, these references, alongside the occupation with specific utterances in general, gradually receded in importance. In the Talmud, we see how such concerns became integral to that intellectual exchange.

Conclusion

To the degree that rabbinic study in the Tannaitic period was oriented around textual knowledge, it was knowledge of Scripture. The Talmud shows us a study culture oriented around knowledge of rabbinic texts as well. But while rabbinic literature presents the scriptural text as accessible and known perfectly by all sages, the Talmud presents the rabbinic textual corpus as scattered, known imperfectly

---

[67] The next sentence in the Tosefta, skipped in the presentation above, seems to parallel the Mishnah's statement that the law follows R. Eliezer, but the sentence is problematic. See Lieberman, *TR*, 257.
[68] See Naeh, "Omanut," 583–4; Fraade, "Polysemy," 19–21; Schremer, "Avot," 306–8; Furstenberg, "Tradition to Controversy," 593–7. Bar-Asher Siegal, "Tosefta Eduyot 1:1," 49, argues that the passage can be read as addressing different problems because it is composed of different sources which had different concerns.

even by some of the most important sages, its availability subject to the contingencies of circumstance. While the passages examined here describe discovery and improvement of knowledge in accidental terms, they mobilize this fragmentation of textual knowledge as a source of scholarly energy. It drives their narrative, provides moments of suspense, and lends dramatic value to their resolutions. It underscores the importance of scholarly exchange, travel, and chance encounters. It serves as a hermeneutic resource to interpret certain statements as resulting from limited access to particular teachings. These passages show us how Amoraic scholarship on rabbinic teachings was not (just) limited by the fragmentation of knowledge: it thrived on it.

6

Variae Recitationes
Comparison of Divergent Texts

We have seen, on several occasions, the Talmud adducing texts which are very similar to each other, but which diverge on a particular point or wording. We may call such texts "variants" or "versions," but because these terms have acquired a specific meaning in the history of scholarship, I will call them, for now, divergent texts. This chapter argues that the Amoraic discussion of such divergences presented a new development in rabbinic scholarship. Much like Greek and Latin scholars compared different copies or editions of the same work, Amoraic scholars compared different recitations of the same teaching, introducing a discourse of "variant readings" with a particular Talmudic inflection into the study of Torah.

In his *Introduction to the Mishnaic Text*, Jacob Nahum Epstein posited that there was a singular, stable, and written text of the Mishnah already during the Talmudic period. An obvious challenge to Epstein's thesis was the numerous times the Talmuds cite what seem to be alternative texts of the Mishnah. In the first chapter of his book, which runs 165 pages, Epstein aimed to demonstrate that these texts do not, in fact, present such alternatives. The chapter opens with one of Epstein's most influential ideas, a distinction between two types of textual difference: "variants" (in Hebrew, *ḥilufei nusḥa'ot*; in German: *Varianten*) and "versions" (*ḥilufei leshonot*; *Versionen*). "Variants" are differences that are caused by errors in the transmission of the text; "versions" are different compositions which adapt the same content, reflecting the different approaches and styles of those who compiled or composed the text. Epstein argued that the divergent texts which the Talmud cites were not variants introduced by error in the course of the Mishnah's transmission. Rather, they were versions, that is, alternative adaptations and formulations, of the same textual materials which the Mishnah itself adapts and formulates. From this distinction between variants and versions also follows a normative distinction in approaching these textual differences: scholars can and should correct the erroneous variants; but they must not correct one version according to another.[1]

The main support Epstein offered for his argument was the way Amoraic scholars, particularly those cited in the Yerushalmi, read divergent texts alongside the Mishnah. Epstein argued that the discussions in the Talmud show us that these

---

[1] Epstein, *IMT*, 1, and many other places—see especially the conclusion of the chapter, ibid., 164–5; and see Sussmann, *Oral Law*, 311 n. 57, for references to other places in Epstein's corpus where the distinction is implicit.

scholars perceived such texts not as alternative texts of the Mishnah, but as its parallels. These scholars may say, for example, that both the Mishnah and the divergent text are necessary to teach us different things, or that they represent different opinions. They never posit that these divergent texts resulted from errors in transmission, and they do not, as a rule, use divergent texts to correct the Mishnah, but rather see them as co-existing with it.

Epstein's argument about the text of the Mishnah has been subjected to a great deal of criticism. Many scholars today do not think that the Mishnah was written in the rabbinic period.[2] The question of writing and orality overlaps only in part with the question of textual stability—uniformity can be achieved through oral transmission as well, but there were problems with other parts of the argument. Epstein claimed, for example, that the divergent texts cited by the Talmud are not found in the Mishnah's manuscripts, but they are sometimes found in other Tannaitic compilations like the Tosefta; this meant, he argued, that these divergences did not occur, and were not perceived, as part of the transmission of the Mishnah. Abraham Rosenthal noted, in contrast, that a significant number of these divergences are reflected in manuscripts or attestations of the Mishnah; he also pointed to cases where the Talmuds present corrections of the Mishnah based on these divergent texts.[3] Similarly, Leib Moscovitz argued that the nature of divergences makes it more plausible that these are variants rather than independent versions (e.g. they present small or phonetic differences).[4] Yaacov Sussmann mounted a thorough critique of Epstein's argument, along these lines and others, pointing also to a problem in its very conceptual scheme.[5]

Epstein makes a clear separation between the composition of the work and its transmission. When R. Judah the Patriarch adapts his sources, these changes are part of the making of the Mishnah; but any change that is made in the process of transmission is by definition erroneous, since the compilation of the work has been completed and the purpose of transmission is the accurate representation of the work as it had been composed.[6] A series of scholars, beginning with E. S. Rosenthal, problematized this distinction.[7] Shamma Friedman challenged

---

[2] See Sussmann, *Oral Law*; but even scholars who give some role to written transmission (Stern, "Publication") do not endorse Epstein's theory.

[3] Rosenthal, "Le-masoret," 34–5.

[4] Moscovitz, *Terminology*, 65 and n. 270, 67 n. 285.

[5] Sussmann, *Oral Law*, 309–17.

[6] To some degree, Epstein qualifies this sharp distinction later in the book, when he speaks of Amoraic emendations as changes of "redaction" (עריכה), the same term he uses for the compositional stage of the Mishnah (as observed by Schremer, "Text Transmission," 399 n. 76). The next chapter addresses Epstein's analysis of emendations.

[7] Rosenthal, "History of the Text," 1–3; see also, in addition to the studies noted below, Schremer, "Text Transmission." Many of these studies have focused on other rabbinic compilations, especially the Bavli, which is not coincidental: the Mishnah is a much stabler text in comparison with the Bavli, and its early association with R. Judah the Patriarch could suggest a definite moment of closure in a way that has no counterpart for the Bavli. But these scholars engaged Epstein's conceptual assumptions in a way that is broadly relevant for our investigation of the Talmud's discourse of textual difference.

Epstein's assumption that the purpose of tradents was the conservative transmission of texts, demonstrating how deliberately creative reworking characterizes transmission both during and after the classical rabbinic period.[8] Vered Noam argued that since the production of all rabbinic texts involves transmission of still earlier texts as well as their reformulation and interpretation, the line between "redaction" or composition of the text and its "transmission" is a construct of scholarship; this line marks what is in fact only a "station" in the text's development as its point of origin and therefore privileges it as representing the text's true form.[9] Peter Schäfer suggested in a programmatic essay that the variation in the manuscripts defies the very identity of rabbinic works, and that our object of study should therefore not be any hypothetical work but rather the manuscripts themselves, as compositions in their own right.[10]

Modernist philology encountered similar challenges in other fields. Bernard Cerquiglini argued that the search for a stable or original text anachronistically applied modern notions shaped by the reproducibility achieved through the printing press, developments in intellectual property law, and historical positivism. The variants that modernist philology saw as errors were in fact the essence of medieval literature.[11] Cerquiglini's essays helped crystallize a movement identified as "new" or "material" philology, which eschewed a search for the hypothesized original work in favor of studying the manuscripts in their own right.[12] More recently, Hindy Najman argued that ancient Jewish textuality did not produce finite "books" which could then be either accurately or creatively transmitted; rather, specific texts were composed and perceived as instances of a process of dynamic development. By privileging certain moments over others, scholarship both misconstrues the nature of these texts and replicates long-standing canonical assumptions.[13]

The discussions of textual divergences in the Talmud have been read as evidence for the state of the Mishnah's text.[14] But if, as the studies just mentioned argue, the configuration of textual difference varies according to approaches and contexts, then we should ask not only what these discussions tell us about the Mishnah, but also what they tell us about the scholars who produced them. How did they perceive the relationship between texts that were similar, but different? What was their purpose in comparing such texts? What do these comparisons tell us about their notions of text? This chapter aims to answer these questions by focusing on the most common phrase used in the Talmud to compare divergent recited teachings.

---

[8] Friedman, "Uncovering," 37; see also idem, *Tosefta*, on Mishnah-Tosefta relationships; and idem, *Talmudic Studies*, 157–71, on the Bavli's text.
[9] Noam, "Development of a Talmudic Sugya," 172–3.
[10] Schäfer, "Rabbinic Literature."
[11] Cerquiglini, *In Praise of the Variant*.
[12] Nichols, "Introduction"; Utz, "Them Philologists."
[13] Najman, "Reading beyond Authority." See also Mroczek, *Literary Imagination*.
[14] In addition to Epstein and critics such as Sussmann (*Oral Law*, especially 314–15 n. 70), see Albeck, "Nushaʾot."

1. "There is a reciter reciting"

There are about two hundred and fifty unique instances in the Talmud of the phrase "there is a reciter reciting (a divergent teaching)." In about fifty-five of those, one of the divergences is recorded in the Mishnah. Consider the following example:[15]

m. Berakhot 5:3

האומר על קן ציפור יגיעו[16] רחמיך. . . משתיקים אותו.

Whoever says [in prayer, in praise of God], "upon a bird's nest your mercies shall reach" . . . they silence him.

Berakhot 5:3 9c (par. *Meg.* 4:9 75c)

ר' פנחס[17] בשם ר' סימון: כקורא תיגר על מדותיו שלהקב"ה. על קן ציפור הגיעו רחמיך ועל אותו האיש לא הגיעו רחמיך.

ר' יוסי בשם ר' סימון: בנותן קיצבה למדותיו שלהקב"ה. עד קן ציפור הגיעו רחמיך.

אית תניי תני "על" ואית תניי תני "עד". מאן דמר "על" מסייע לר' פינחס, ומן דמר "עד" מסייע לר' יוסי.

R. Phinehas [said] in the name of R. Simon: like someone who challenges the dispensations of the Holy One, blessed be he, [saying] upon the bird's nest your mercies reached, but upon that man [i.e. me] your mercies had not reached.

R. Yose [said] in the name of R. Simon: [the teaching speaks] of someone who delimits the dispensations of the Holy One, blessed be he: "until the bird's nest your mercies had reached."

There is a reciter reciting "upon" (*'al*) **and there is a reciter reciting "until"** (*'ad*). The one who says "upon" supports R. Phinehas and the one who says "until" supports R. Yose.

The Mishnah rules that if, while praising God's merciful nature in prayer, someone mentions that God's mercies reach even a bird's nest (alluding to Deuteronomy 22:6–7), they must be silenced. The Talmud offers two explanations for why that prayer might be illegitimate. According to R. Phinehas, R. Simon said that the problem is that such a prayer may be understood as challenging God, who spares birds but not the person praying: "upon the bird's nest, but not upon me." According to R. Yose, R. Simon said that the problem is that the prayer may be understood to limit the capacity of God's mercy by offering an

---

[15] This is also the first example offered in Frankel, *Einleitung*, 19; and Moscovitz, *Terminology*, 65.
[16] MS Kaufmann reflects a correction from "have reached" (הגיעו) to "shall reach" (יגיעו).
[17] Correcting "Isaac," with the parallel from *Meg.*, and as indicated by the rest of the discussion.

example: "until the bird's nest, but not more." The Talmud then proceeds to tell us that there is a divergence in the way the Mishnah's teaching is formulated: according to one reciter, the teaching posits that the illegitimate prayer is "*upon* a bird's nest your mercies shall reach," whereas according to another reciter, it is "*until* a bird's nest your mercies shall reach." The Talmud notes that this small difference—one letter in Hebrew—may decide which of the interpretations is correct: the recitation which has "until" supports R. Yose's explanation, that the prayer is illegitimate because it sets a boundary to how merciful God can be; whereas the recitation with "upon" supports R. Phinehas's explanation, that such prayer suggests God is merciful towards the birds but not necessarily towards the person praying.

The translation I offered for this phrase, "there is a reciter reciting,"[18] requires some discussion since the Aramaic noun which appears in it has been, in my opinion, misunderstood. Scholars have usually interpreted the noun *tannay* (תני)[19] in light of its usage in the Bavli. They suggested it could refer to "a sage from the Tannaitic period," in contrast with an *amora*, a sage from the Amoraic period; to a member of a particular subset of the sages who "arranged" the Tannaitic texts; or to one of the professional reciters entrusted in the rabbinic academies with the memorization and recitation of Tannaitic teachings.[20] With respect specifically to our phrase, Michael Higger wrote that it is difficult to decide whether it refers to the first category or the third category. Moshe Assis argued that Epstein interpreted the phrase as referring to any of the three options, depending on context. Michael Sokoloff's *Dictionary* lists our phrase under the second meaning, that of the arranger of Tannaitic texts. Sussmann wrote that the phrase refers to specialized transmitters.[21]

In an article based on a study of all instances of this noun in the Yerushalmi, I argued that these definitions are premised on distinctions and realities that have been imported either from the Bavli or from the concerns of modern scholarship. There is very little evidence for the existence of professional reciters in late ancient Palestine, where it was the sages themselves who recited teachings in study sessions. Likewise, there is no passage in the Yerushalmi which contrasts *tannay* and *amora* as chronological markers. Finally, the distinction between "sages" and "arrangers" is also not made in the Talmud, where we find *tannay* applying to various

---

[18] I translate the subject and the verb in the singular though it is possible to read them in the plural, "there are reciters reciting." Epstein, *IMT*, 74, offers both singular and plural translations (to Hebrew) without discussion; Friedman, "Ancient Manuscripts," 29, also offers a plural translation; Maman, "R. Hai Gaon's Dictionary," 364 n. 86, shows how the noun has been vocalized in different ways which imply singular or plural.

[19] We find the word spelled in different ways. For clarity, I refer to the word in the Yerushalmi as *tannay* in the singular and *tannayin* in the plural regardless of how the word is spelled in the passage I am discussing.

[20] Sokoloff, *DJPA*, 678, following Epstein, *IMT*, 674–5; See similarly Jastrow, *Dictionary*, 1679–80.

[21] Higger, *Otzar ha-baraitot*, 4.486–7; Assis, *Concordance*, 82–3 n. 757; Sussmann, *Oral Torah*, 341 n. 47.

sages. Instead, I offered a single definition of *tannay* as the figure who shaped a recited text, a given *matnita*.

To the degree that this activity of formulating recited teachings was understood to be tied to a specific period, this term was also tied with that period.[22] As we have seen in Chapter 1, when Amoraic scholars identified anonymous recited teachings, they only named individuals from what we call the Tannaitic era; only Tannaitic-era sages may be the subject of recited teachings, though such teachings may be attributed to early Amoraic sages; and with the exception of two cases, all individuals identified with the noun *tannay* are Tannaitic. But the meaning of the term is not primarily chronological: it refers to a particular function that is also, to some degree, defined chronologically.

We speak of the "writers" of certain texts—books, notes, messages—even when we do not know who that writer might be; the figure is hypothesized from the activity of writing, such that "the writer of the mysterious note" simply means "the person who wrote the mysterious note." Similarly, the noun *tannay* denotes an activity, reciting, that is, the transmission and formulation of the recited teaching (*matnita*) under interpretation. *Tannay* is therefore an interpretive term bound with the text being interpreted, rather than describing people whom the sages encountered or remembered. That is why there is not a single instance of *tannay* in the Yerushalmi which is not connected with a specific text; *tannayin* are always inferred from texts that are cited or implied.[23]

While the Talmud uses *tannay* to discuss various properties of rabbinic teachings, including their legal positions or interpretation of Scripture, the term frequently appears in the context of these teachings' formulation and transmission. When the Talmud refers to a named sage as a *tannay*, it is almost always in order to speak about how that sage *formulated* the words of another sage, often in a way that varies from another version of these words. *Tannay* is used in discussions which explain that one text is composed of two texts reflecting two opinions; in reference to alternative contradictory transmissions of a statement by the same sage; or in commenting on literary features such as the use of particular examples and selection of items in lists. This association with textual activity is also indicated in the verb that is used in our phrase, "recite." This verb normally introduces precise quotations of teachings, rather than paraphrases of positions and opinions, and it is frequently used in passages where the wording a teaching is discussed.

Both "reciter" and "reciting," then, refer to textual activity. This activity involved both transmission and formulation. The root *t. n. y.* has the primary sense of *seconding* or *repetition*,[24] but as we have seen, the term *mishnah*, which features

---

[22] On recent scholarship and factors that challenge the idea that recited teachings go back to the Tannaitic period, see the discussion in the Introduction, and nn. 59–60.

[23] Vidas, "*Tannay*," on the (lack of) evidence for professional reciters, 24–54; on *tannay* not being a period marker, 54–75; on "arrangers," 76–7; and on the sense of *tannay* as a shaper of text, 75–88.

[24] See Sokoloff, *DJPA*, 676–7.

the equivalent Hebrew root, was deployed already in the Tannaitic period in passages that acknowledged sages shaped teachings as they transmitted them.[25] "Recitation" then signifies both the transmission of existing material and the reshaping of it by the reciting sage. As we shall see throughout this chapter, the comparisons introduced by the phrase "there is a reciter reciting" reflect these textual concerns.

2. The emergence of Talmudic "variant readings"

Divergent teachings are ubiquitous in Tannaitic compilations. The Mishnah is replete with disputes, from its very beginning: "From what time do they read out the Shema in the evening? From the time the priests go inside to eat their priest's share, until the end of the first watch—the words of R. Eliezer; but the sages say: Until midnight" (*m. Berakhot* 1:1). With respect to most of these disputes, however, there is no reason to think that what is at stake is the transmission or formulation of texts. When the Mishnah tells us about that dispute between R. Eliezer and the sages, it does not seem to mean that R. Eliezer and the sages were transmitting a teaching that began with the words, "From what time do they recite the Shema in the evening? From the time the priests go inside to eat their priest's share, until..."—and R. Eliezer completed that teaching with "the end of the first watch" whereas the sages completed it with "midnight." These disputes present not alternative formulations of text but rather different positions on the issue at hand.

The passages employing the phrase "there is a reciter reciting" show us a new conversation, in the Amoraic period, about *textual* divergences, that is, divergences stemming from the transmission of texts and resulting in their formulation. When the Talmud tells us that "there is a reciter reciting" differently, it means not (or not only) that two teachings present different positions, but that there seem to be two formulations—two recitations—of the same teaching. To be sure, Tannaitic compilations also occasionally record such textual divergences. We have seen the phrase *ḥiluf ha-devarim*, by which Tannaitic works convey that a certain sage reversed a certain teaching either in terms of its content or in terms of its attributions; with the phrase *omer mi-shemo*, such works sometimes suggest that one sage has a modified or expanded version of a teaching that has been attributed to another sage;[26] there are a few disputes about what a certain sage said;[27] on one occasion, the Tosefta comments that a certain dispute was "not about the law [*halakhah*], but

---

[25] See Chapter 1, Section 5.
[26] Instances where the phrase introduces what could be an alternative version or expansion of the teaching just transmitted include *m. Ber.* 4:7, *m. Pe'ah* 2:4, *m. Avot* 2:8, *m. T. Y.* 3:4–5. Sometimes (e.g. *t. Yev.* 12:11), the phrase introduces answers to objections or questions about a teaching attributed to the sages. But there are places where the relationship between the first teaching and second teaching is much looser—e.g. *Sifra Emor* 10:2 101a and *t. Ter.* 9:9.
[27] *Sifre Zuta Numbers*, 19:3.

about the formulation [*lashon*],"[28] and in another place, it adduces three alternative transmissions of a teaching by Rabban Gamaliel but notes that they all amount to the same point.[29] But those passages are relatively rare; their terminology is not particularly specialized; almost all differences that they note have clear legal implications; and they offer almost no commentary on these divergences, except to note, in those rare cases where they do not find such difference in legal outcome, that the divergence applies to formulation alone.

In the opening of his *Introduction*, Epstein cites what might at first seem to be a significant number of passages which demonstrate that Tannaitic compilations commonly present disputes about the formulation of teachings. Many of Epstein's examples indeed show that these compilations employ different formulations even when they do not dispute the law, but in almost none of these examples do the compilations themselves present the matter in this way. He cites, for example, several Tannaitic disputes "which seem like disputes on the law but in fact are disputes on formulation," drawing on the Toseftan comments noted above—but in most of these cases, it is the Talmud that supplies the information that there is no dispute about the law.[30] Other examples which Epstein cites include variations in terminology that are not juxtaposed at all in the Tannaitic compilations but rather by Epstein himself; disputes about what certain sages said, which clearly and primarily focus on legal position rather than on wording; and passages which present R. Judah the Patriarch as addressing questions of formulation, all coming again from the Talmuds rather than the Tannaitic corpus.[31]

The introductory phrase "there is a reciter reciting" itself calls attention to the textuality of the divergences it presents and sets them apart from other types of disputes we find in rabbinic literature. As we have seen, both the noun "reciter" and the verb "reciting" are associated with transmission and formulation. The attribution of these divergent teachings to anonymous "reciters," *tannayin*, distinguishes them from the normal form of dispute in rabbinic literature, which is attributed to named sages: "Rabbi so-and-so permits, and Rabbi so-and-so prohibits." As Yair Furstenberg showed, that form of presentation was created in the Tannaitic period as a way of preserving and presenting contradictory traditions: attribution resolves the problem of contradiction because it presents teachings as stemming from different sages, each authoritative on his own.[32] In contrast, in the passages discussed in this chapter, the Talmud presents a dispute not by two sages but by

---

[28] *t. Par.* 11:7: לא נחלקו על ההלכה אלא על הלשון.

[29] *t. Kel. B. Q.* 6:17.

[30] Epstein draws mainly on the collection of these divergences at *'A. Z.* 2:7 42a, which alludes also to the same examples noted in the Tosefta.

[31] Epstein discusses disputes that are about formulation rather than law are cited at *IMT*, 1–2; formulation differences that are not juxtaposed in the sources themselves at 2–4; disputes about what sages said at 5–7; and Judah the Patriarch on formulations at 7–25—though with respect to some of those even Epstein concedes that attributing the consideration to Judah himself is "uncertain" (8).

[32] Furstenberg, "Tradition to Controversy."

two *reciters*. The consistency of this attribution shows that it is not accidental, and in some places, we will see in the next section, it may even result from deliberate re-attribution. The use of "reciter" and "reciting" constructs a difference between two textual artifacts, two recitations, an oral version of "some editions" or "some manuscripts" say.

There are other phrases, far less common, which introduce recitation divergences in the Yerushalmi. In a few passages, the Yerushalmi compares what "we have recited," that is, in "our" Mishnah, and what was recited in other *mishnayot*. In ten unique passages, such divergences are introduced with the phrase "we have recited ... R. Hiyya recited [in his version of the *mishnah*] ...," almost always at the beginnings of Mishnaic chapters;[33] and in seven passages, the majority of which are in tractate Shabbat, we find: "we have recited ... [those of] the house of Rabbi [the Patriarch] recited ...."[34] While in these phrases, the divergence is attributed, the use of the verb "recite" on both sides of the comparison emphasizes again the difference in transmission and formulation. The divergences introduced by these formulae and the Talmudic discussions of them generally resemble those that are introduced with the phrase "there is a reciter reciting," except that in the case of attributed recitations we find comments emphasizing the "necessity" of each of the recitations, possibly because they were accorded a higher status.[35] There are other forms of attributed recitation divergences that are handled similarly.[36] We also find the rare phrase "there is a recited teaching which says," which is functionally similar to the phrase investigated here, but highlights the way the latter emphasizes the agent behind the recitation.[37]

3. Typology of divergences and their presentation

While the phrase introducing these divergences calls attention to their specific formulation in a way that was unprecedented in rabbinic literature, the divergences

---

[33] אנן תנינן... תני ר' חייה; *Ber.* 1:1 2a, *Shab.* 1:2 3a, *Pes.* 9:1 36c, *M. Q.* 2:1 81a, *Yev.* 6:1 7b, *Ket.* 8:1 32a, *B. Q.* 1:1 2a, *San.* 4:2 22b, and *'A. Z.* 1:5 39d. There are other references to versions from R. Hiyya's recitations which do not employ this phrase; see for example the passage from *Yev.* 4:10 6b discussed in Chapter 1 above and *M. Q.* 1:10 81a; and there are numerous citations of recited teachings in the name of R. Hiyya that do not involve textual divergence.

[34] אנן תנינן... תני דבי רבי; *Pe'ah* 3:1 17b; *Shevi.* 2:5 33d, *Shab.* 4:1 6d, *Shab.* 7:1 9a, *Shab.* 9:3 12a (par. *Shab.* 19:3 17a), *Shab.* 17:6 16b, *Sheq.* 2:2 46c. Here too there are cases where the contrast is clearly between two diverging formulations, see e.g. *Meg.* 2:3 73a–b, discussed in Chapter 7, Section 3. Epstein (*IMT*, 72–4), argues that the Yerushalmi attributes these recited teachings to R. Judah the Patriarch himself, but the passages he uses to demonstrate this claim do not employ the phrase "of the House of Rabbi." At the same time, the phrase may tell us that neither "our Mishnah" nor these recitations are identical to the R. Judah the Patriarch's Mishnah, but rather that both presented particular versions of it.

[35] On the possibility of higher status, see the discussion below on the comparable phenomenon in Homeric scholarship; on the claim for "necessity," see Chapter 8, Section 2.

[36] See e.g. *Shevi.* 2:8 34a.

[37] מתניתא אמרה; see *Shab.* 9:1 11d (par. *'A. Z.* 3:6 43a and *Qid.* 2:1 62a), and see Moscovitz, *Secondary Terms*, 43.

themselves are diverse. A significant number of them concern exclusively the formulation of the text, with no legal implication or a legal implication that is secondary; these present most distinctively a new sphere of rabbinic scholarly attention. Other divergences introduced by this phrase do not seem to be alternative formulations of the same teaching, at least not at first, and they resemble more or less the disputes we find elsewhere in rabbinic literature. The majority of divergences fall somewhere between these two sets: they can be seen as disputes about the law, but they are presented in a way which invites us to imagine them as alternative transmissions or formulations.

I begin my discussion with the first group, found particularly though not exclusively in discussions of teachings which were included in the Mishnah:[38]

m. Shabbat 11:1–2

הזורק מרשות היחיד לרשות הרבים או מרשות הרבים לרשות היחיד—חייב. מרשות היחיד לרשות היחיד ורשות הרבים באמצע—ר׳ עקיבה מחייב וחכ׳ פוטרים. כיצד? שתי קצוצראות זו כנגד זו ברשות הרבים והמושיט והזורק מזו לזו פטור.

If someone threw [an object on the Sabbath] from a private domain to a public domain, or from a public domain to a private domain—he is liable.

But from a private domain to [another] private domain with a public domain in between—R. Aqiva holds him liable, but the sages hold him exempt.

How so? If there are two balconies, one against the other, in the public domain, and one passes [an object] or threw [an object] from one to the other—he is exempt.

Shabbat 11:1 12d

אית תניי תני "כיצד". אית דלא תני "כיצד".

There is a reciter reciting "how so" [and] there is [a reciter] not reciting "how so."

The Mishnah presents a dispute between R. Aqiva and the sages. R. Aqiva rules that if a person threw, on the Sabbath, an object from one private domain to another but the object passed through the public domain, they are liable for transgressing the prohibition of transporting from private to public domain on the Sabbath. The sages do not hold them liable, because the beginning and end points of the object were both in the private domain. The Mishnah then offers what seems to be an illustration of such a case,[39] where there are two balconies (two private

---

[38] This is expected, as teachings which were included in the Mishnah were likely to be particularly entrenched in the curriculum, perhaps even before Judah included them in his Mishnah, and thus their particular wording was more likely to be have become a subject for discussion.

[39] At least as the Yerushalmi understands it; but in the Mishnah, "how so" might not introduce an example but a qualification, see on this passage Goldberg, *Shabbat*, 202.

domains) facing one another, and someone threw an object from one to the other on the Sabbath (so the object passed through the public domain).

The Talmud cites a divergence in the recitation of this teaching. While one reciter recites the words "how so" between the report about the dispute and the description of the balconies case, another reciter does not recite these words. This is important, since without these words we might think that the balconies case is not necessarily an example of the case in which R. Aqiva and the sages dispute; note that the Mishnah does not tell us how R. Aqiva would rule in the balconies case, and without the words "how so" the teaching might imply that in that case, he agrees with the sages. That is in fact what the Talmud suggests later in this passage: that not reciting "how so" can be correlated with the opinion that R. Aqiva agrees with the sages in the balconies case (because, it is suggested, the balconies are more than ten cubits above the ground). But while this divergence between the reciters may reflect or result in a difference in Halakhic opinions, it is primarily a difference in the shaping of a text: do we or do we not recite the words "how so." It is hard to imagine this kind of dispute recorded in the usual manner in which disputes are recorded in Tannaitic literature.

This is the case also with divergences that unlike this example, do not depend on literary context, but which still primarily concern the wording of the teaching:

Yoma 1:2 39a

תני: ר' או, "אומר אני שלא יטול אלא מחצה". אית תניי תני: ר' או, "אומר אני שיטול מחצה".

היך עבידה? היה שם עור אחד—רבנן אמרי, "נוטל את כולו", ר' או, "אומר אני שלא יטול אלא מחצה". היו שם ארבעה חמשה עורות—רבנן אמרי, "נוטל אחד", ר' או, "אומר אני נוטל מחצה".

[Regarding the part of the sacrifice that the High Priest may take for himself given his privileged status:]

It has been recited: Rabbi [Judah the Patriarch] says: I say he takes **only** a half.

There is a reciter reciting: Rabbi [Judah the Patriarch] says: I say he takes a half.

How does it go? If there was one hide—the sages say, "he [the high priest] takes all of it," and Rabbi [Judah the Patriarch] says: "I say he takes only a half." If there were four or five hides there—the sages say, "he takes one," and Rabbi [Judah the Patriarch] says, "I say he takes a half."

There is no obvious or necessary difference of opinion—or even meaning!—between these two formulations of Judah's teaching. The Talmud's anonymous commentary on this divergence proceeds to suggest how both formulations might make sense, each in a specific scenario. But the divergence itself does not point to a dispute about opinion, ruling, or even a scenario; it relates to the formulation of the teaching transmitted.[40]

There are two other sets of passages in which the centrality of formulation is clear. First are passages in which the phrase does not introduce a citation, but rather is part of a report about how the teaching diverges from the one before it. In the majority of such cases, the Talmud relates that "there is a reciter reciting and switching" the attributions. One teaching presents a dispute in which R. Meir says one thing and R. Yose the other, while the divergent teaching records the same words but with switched attributions. This phenomenon has significant precedent in Tannaitic literature. Epstein considered such switching of attributions to have obvious Halakhic significance because of the so-called rules for deciding Halakhic disputations. But these rules never come up in "there is a reciter reciting" passages, and in none of these "switched attributions" passages does the Yerushalmi treat the question of attribution as obviously implying a Halakhic consequence—in fact, in a number of these passages, the questions of attribution and ruling are clearly separate:[41]

Mo'ed Qattan 3:7 83b (par. Horayot 3:7 48b)

אי-זהו רבו? כל שפתח לו תחילה—דברי ר' מאיר. ר' יהודה או': כל שרוב תלמודו ממנו. ר' יוסי או': כל שהאיר עיניו במשנתו אפילו בדבר אחד. ר' אבהו בשם ר' יוחנן: הל' כדברי מי שהוא או', "כל שרוב תלמודו ממנו". ולמה לא אמ' כר' יהודה? אית תניי תני ומחליף.

Who [counts] as one's teacher? Whoever first opened [his studies] for him—the words of R. Meir. R. Judah said: Whoever most of his learning is from. R. Yose said: Whoever brightened his eyes in his recitation, even with respect to a single thing.

R. Abbahu [said] in the name of R. Yohanan: The law accords with the one who said, "Whoever most of his learning is from." And why did he [R. Yohanan] not say, "The law accords with R. Judah"? There is a reciter reciting and switching.

Similar passages also report switching but it is one of content rather than attribution, or that one reciter records a dispute while another records a unanimous teaching, or that the reciters diverge on the context in which the words appear.[42] In all these passages, again, the Talmud describes the divergence as primarily textual.

---

[40] Other examples of divergences which more clearly relate to formulation include Ber. 1:1 3a (for which see Naeh, "Paschal Lambs"), Pe'ah 7:2 20a, Ḥal. 4:2 59d (which also assumes the literary context in the Mishnah), Suk. 5:1 55a (par. Suk. 5:7 55d), and Ta'an. 4:6 68d; see also Ḥal. 2:4 58c and Ḥal. 4:9 59d (where according to the Talmud there is no difference of opinion).

[41] See similarly Kil. 9:3 32a, Ta'an. 1:3 64a, and Ta'an. 2:10 66b.

[42] "We have recited it disputed, there is a reciter reciting [it] anonymously," Sot. 6:1 20d; the location or scope of the teaching ("there is a reciter reciting even on the first one," etc.), Ned. 5:4 39b (second instance), Qid. 4:8 66a; content switched: Ta'an. 4:4 68b, Ḥag. 2:2 77d (par. San. 6:4 23c).

Another set of passages reports divergences in recitation of very close-sounding words that have the same meaning. There are eight instances of this sort in the Yerushalmi, all relating to the Mishnah.[43] To give one example:

m. Shabbat 5:2

רחלין יוצאות שחוזות כבולות וכבונות.

Ewes may go out [on the Sabbath] exposed [shehuzot; i.e. with their tales up, so that they may be mounted by the males], chained, or clasped.

Shabbat 5:2 7b

אית תניי תני "שחוזות" ואית תניי תני "שוזות". מאן דאמ' "שוזות", מעתדן, כמ' דתימר "שית זונה ונצורת לב". מאן דמר "שחוזות", כמ' דתימ', "אין משחיזין את הסכין".

There is a reciter reciting *shehuzot* and there is a reciter reciting *shozot*.

The one who said *shozot* [formulates the word in the sense of] prepared, like that which you say, "decked out like a prostitute (*shyt zona*), wily of heart" (Prov. 7:10). And the one who said *shehuzot* [formulates the word] like that which you say, "they must not strap (*mashehizin*) the knife" (m. Beẓ. 3:7).

Epstein has shown that both recitations refer to the same verb, though in different dialects or registers.[44] The Talmud does not offer this type of linguistic analysis, but it too assumes that the two words have the same meaning even if they diverge in etymology.[45] Discussions of such divergences offered Amoraic scholars an opportunity to apply their textual erudition; they focus on linguistic, rather than legal, differences.

In contrast with the passages I have discussed so far, the majority of the divergences introduced by our phrase can be read as disputes about opinions or rulings. But there is a feature of these divergences—or, as we shall see, of the Talmud's presentation of these divergences—which, along with the "reciting" language employed in the introductory phrase, lends them the look, if not always the substance, of textual variation. In the majority of the cases the divergences result in relatively small differences of wording. Sometimes, the different teachings are separated by one, close-sounding letter:[46]

---

[43] In addition to the passage reproduced above, see *Ber.* 6:8 10d, *Pe'ah* 8:1 20d, *Kil.* 8:4 31c (par. *Shab.* 5:1 7b), *Shab.* 5:4 7c (the second instance), *Sot.* 6:1 20d (the second instance), *Ket.* 13:3 36a, *'A. Z.* 3:5 43a.
[44] Epstein, *IMT*, 103.
[45] Etymology is used to explain variants also in other kinds of passages; see for example the discussion in *'Er.* 5:1 22b, part of which we saw above in Chapter 4.
[46] In addition to this example, see e.g. *Ber.* 5:3 9c (par. *Meg.* 4:9 75c), discussed above, *Kil.* 7:7 31a, *Shab.* 2:6 5b, *'Er.* 2:1 20a, *Ta'an.* 4:6 68d, *'A. Z.* 2:3 41b.

Terumot 3:4 42a

מימתי תורמין את הזיתים? אית תני תני, "משיטחנו", ואית תני תני "משיטענו".

From what time does one separate olives for the priest's share? There is a reciter reciting, "From the time they are grounded (*misheyitaḥanu*)" and there is a reciter reciting, "From the time they are pressed (*misheyita'anu*)."

While most of the divergences are not so close, in more than half the instances the phrase introduces divergences which apply to only one or two words. The single most common type of divergence is the addition or subtraction of negation.[47] Similarly, we find switches between binaries such as "prohibited" and "permitted," "valid" and "invalid," "liable" and "exempt," etc.[48] Another common category is differences in numbers: one reciter recites "one" or "first," another recites "two" or "second."[49] Let me offer some examples:

Megillah 4:3 75b

אית תני תני, "אין אבילים עולין מן המניין", ואית תניי תני, "אבלים עולים מן המניין".

There is a reciter reciting: "mourners are counted towards [a liturgical] quorum," and there is a reciter reciting: "mourners are **not** counted towards [a liturgical] quorum."

Berakhot 5:4 9c

תני: הפורס את שמע [. . .][50] לא יענה אחר עצמו אמן. ואם ענה הרי זה בור. אית תני תני, "הרי זה בור", ואית תני תני, "הרי זה חכם".

It was recited: "One who leads the Shema [and other liturgical rituals] should not respond 'Amen' after his own [blessing]. And if he responded, then he is a **boor**." There is a reciter reciting: then he is a **boor**. There is a reciter reciting: then he is a **sage**.

Sukkah 3:1 53c

סוכה גזולה—אית תני תני: כשיר, אית תני תני, פסולה.

A stolen Sukkah—There is a reciter reciting: it is **valid**, and there is a reciter reciting: it is **disqualified.**

Pesaḥim 9:6 37a

הפריש פסחו ואבד והפריש אחר תחתיו, לא הספיק להקריב את השיני עד שנמצא הראשון, והרי שניהן עומדין—אית תני תני, "מצוה להקריב את הראשון", אית תני תני, "מצוה להקריב את השיני".

---

[47] See, in addition to the example offered above, e.g., *Ter.* 3:6 42b, *M. S.* 1:3 52d, *Shab.* 6:1 7d, *Yom.* 1:1 38c, *R. H.* 2:6 58a, *Bez.* 4:7 62d, *M. Q.* 3:7 83a.
[48] e.g. *Kil.* 9:9 32d, *Ter.* 9:3 46c–d, *'Or.* 1:1 60d, *Shab.* 1:1 2c, *Pes.* 5:4 32b, *Suk.* 1:4 52b, *B. Q.* 3:4 3d.
[49] e.g. *Ber.* 2:2 4c, *Shab.* 2:5 5a, *Shab.* 8:2 11b, *'Er.* 1:1 18c, *M. Q.* 3:5 82c, *Yev.* 10:1 10d.
[50] I am omitting here a list of other liturgical rituals.

If he designated his paschal lamb [for offering] and it was lost and he designated another one, [and] had not yet offered the second one when the first one was found, and thus both are standing: there is a reciter reciting, "it is a commandment to offer the **first**" [and] there is a reciter reciting, "it is a commandment to offer the **second**."

In other cases, the order of words is switched:

Yoma 5:6 43a

"וכלה מכפר את הקודש". אית תניי תני, "אם כילה כיפר". ואית תניי תני, "אם כיפר כלה".

"When he has finished atoning for the holy place" (Lev 16:20):

There is a reciter reciting: If he has **finished**, he has **atoned**.

And there is a reciter reciting: If he has **atoned**, he has **finished**.

Sanhedrin 2:3 20b

אית תניי תני: הנשים מהלכות תחילה והאנשים אחריהם. ואית תניי תני: אנשים תחילה והנשים אחריהם.

There is a reciter reciting: the **women walk** first and the **men** after them.

And there is a reciter reciting: the **men** first and the **women** after them.

It is true that all these passages point to a difference of opinion, ruling, or scriptural interpretation. But all of them also invite us to imagine two reciters who differ only in a word or two, in a way that suggests both formulate or transmit the same teaching differently.

This is the result of the Talmud's representation of these divergences. In several cases parallel passages from other rabbinic compilations present the same divergences in a different way.[51] Let me offer a few examples:

m. *Yevamot* 12:2	*Yevamot* 12:1 12c
חלצה בלילה חליצתה כשרה.ר׳ אלעזר פוסל.	אית תניי תני: חליצה בלילה כשירה.אית תניי תני: חליצה בלילה פסולה.
If she removed [the sandal] at night her *ḥaliẓah* is valid.	There is a reciter reciting: a *ḥaliẓah* at night is **valid**.
R. Eleazar disqualifies.	There is a reciter reciting: a *ḥaliẓah* at night is **disqualified**.

---

[51] Epstein, *IMT*, 121; see more examples there. Epstein does not use these parallels, as I do here, to argue for a particularly Talmudic pattern of representation.

t. Terumot 3:13	Terumot 3:4 42a
מאימתי תורמין את הזיתים? משיטענו. ור' שמעון או': משייטחנו.	מימתי תורמין את הזיתים? אית תני תני, "משיטחנו". ואית תני תני, "משיטענו".
From what time does one separate olives for the priest's share? From the time they are pressed. R. Simeon says: From the time they are grounded.	From what time does one separate olives for the priest's share? There is a reciter reciting: "From the time they are **grounded**," and here is a reciter reciting: "From the time they are **pressed**."
t. Pesaḥim 8:7	Pesaḥim 9:3 36d
הראשון חייבין עליו כרת והשני אין חייבין עליו כרת. דברי ר'. ר' נתן אומ'. אף השני חייבין עליו כרת. ר' חנינא בן עקביא או'. אם עשו את השני אין חייבין עליו כרת על הראשון. לא עשו את השני חייבין עליו כרת על הראשון.	אית תני תני: על השיני הוא ענוש כרת. על הראשון אינו ענוש כרת. אית תני תני: על הראשון הוא ענוש כרת. על השיני אינו ענוש כרת. ואית תני תני: בין על הראשון בין על השיני אינו [52] ענוש כרת.
For the first one is liable to extirpation and for the second one is not liable to extirpation—the words of Rabbi [Judah the Patriarch]. R. Nathan says: Even for the second, one is liable to extirpation. R. Hanina b. Aqavia says: If they performed the second, they are not liable to extirpation for the first; if they did not perform the second they are liable to extirpation for the first.	There is a reciter reciting: for the **second** he is subject to extirpation, and for the **first** one he is not subject to extirpation. There is a reciter reciting: for the **first** he is subject to extirpation, and for the **second** one he is not subject to extirpation. And there is a reciter reciting: either for the first or for the second he is not subject to extirpation.
b. Megillah 32a	Megillah 3:6 74c
תנו רבנן: פותח ורואה גולל ומברך וחוזר ופותח וקורא. דברי ר' מאיר. ר' יהודה אומ': פותח ורואה ומברך וקורא.	אית תני תני: פותח ורואה גולל ומברך. אית תני תני. פותח ורואה ומברך.
Our rabbis recited: One opens [the scroll] and looks into it, rolls it up and recites the blessing, and then again opens [the scroll] and reads [from the scroll]—the words of R. Meir. R. Judah says: One opens [the scroll] and looks [into it] and recites the blessing and reads [from the scroll].	There is a reciter reciting: One opens [the scroll], looks into it, **rolls it up** and recites the blessing. There is a reciter reciting: One opens [the scroll], looks into it, and recites the blessing.

In all these cases, the Yerushalmi reports a divergence that we find elsewhere in rabbinic literature, but in a different form. Epstein wrote that the Yerushalmi "abbreviates" these disputes; but in several cases the presentation in the Yerushalmi does not actually shorten the teaching, and in none of the cases is the difference in length significant.[53] Further, in only three of the cases that Epstein surveyed,

---

[52] MS Leiden has both "exempt" and "not," and both have been erased by the corrector; the reading here follows Lieberman, *YK*, 510.

[53] Consider the first two examples in the table above. The versions in the Tannaitic compilations clock at seven and nine words, respectively, whereas the Yerushalmi's versions consist of twelve words.

the parallel is in the Mishnah—in the rest of the cases, the parallel is either in the Tosefta or in the Babylonian Talmud, and thus we cannot know for certain that the composers of the Yerushalmi were aware of it.[54] What we can say, however, is that these passages employ a pattern for presenting disputes which diverges from the pattern we find in Tannaitic sources. To be sure, the Yerushalmi's presentation may have various functions—it can, for example, bring out the dispute more clearly, though it does not always do so. But across the board, this pattern has two distinct features. First, as we have seen, it draws attention to the act of recitation and its connotation of transmission and formulation. Second, it presents the divergence as two teachings that are nearly identical in wording, which invites us to consider them as different formulations of the same teaching.

So far, I addressed divergences which consist of a small difference in wording; even in cases where this scope of the divergence is only suggested by the Talmud's presentation, we can nonetheless reconstruct two similar teachings diverging in a limited way. There are, however, cases where such reconstruction is not possible, despite what might at first seem from the Talmud's presentation. Consider the following example:

Qiddushin 4:8 66a (par. *B. B.* 8:6 16b)

היה עומד בצד המוכסין ואמ׳, "בני הוא", וחזר ואמ׳, "עבדי הוא"—נאמן. "עבדי הוא", וחזר ואמ׳, "בני הוא"—אינו נאמן. אית תני תני: נאמן.

If he was standing by the tax collectors and said, "this is my son," and then retracted and said, "this is my slave," he is believed [since we assume that he said "son" at first to avoid taxes on the enslaved person].

If he said, "this is my slave," and then retracted and said, "this is my son," he is **not** believed.

There is a reciter reciting: he is believed.

At first, it might seem that the second reciter (the last line) presents the same teaching as the first reciter (the first two paragraphs) and that they differ on a single word—in the second case offered by the teaching, the first reciter says "not believed" whereas the other says "believed." But the whole point of the teaching is the distinction between the two cases, that it matters whether the person said "son" or "slave" first. If in either case the person is believed, there is no point in distinguishing the two cases; and even if someone wanted to distinguish between the two cases to make the point that both are treated similarly, we would expect

---

[54] On the question of the familiarity of the Amoraic scholars of the Yerushalmi with Toseftan teachings, see Mazeh, "Demai," 20–46.

a different formulation, something like "whether he said 'son' and then 'slave' or 'slave' and then 'son' he is believed."[55]

Similarly, there are instances in which it might seem that the second teaching is an alternative recitation of the first, but on closer inspection it is a response to it. Consider the following passage concerning the vessel into which the "water of bitterness" is poured during the Sotah ordeal:

Sotah 2:2 17d

אית תניי תני: בכלי חרש לא במקידה. אית תניי תני: אפילו במקידה.

There is a reciter reciting: ["The priest shall take holy water] in a clay vessel" (Num 5:17)—[the verse requires the water to be in a unified vessel,] **not** in a disassemblable one.

There is a reciter reciting: **Even** in a disassemblable one.

The first teaching derives from the word "vessel" in the verse that water must be poured into a single, whole vessel, rather than a container composed of discrete, breakable parts.[56] The second teaching rules that the water may be put even into such a disassemblable container. We could, then, imagine that there were two recitations of the same teaching differing in one word, one that said, "in a vessel—*not* in a disassemblable one" and one that said, "in a vessel—*even* in a disassemblable one." But that is unlikely, since the second teaching does not make much sense without the first teaching. There is no reason to include something that we would not think to exclude, and the conclusion regarding the disassemblable container does not work as an independent derivation from the verse.[57] It is possible to see these examples as undermining my interpretation, that the Talmud in these passages, in general, points to a type of variant reading—or at least see these examples as exceptions to that general rule. But it is also possible that the common pattern of presentation of recitation divergences, which does fit the variant reading model, was sometimes used imprecisely, even in cases which did not fit that model well.

As I have mentioned, in the majority of passages the difference between the divergences is limited to one or two words. There is, however, a significant number of instances in which the difference between the two recitations is greater. This is the case, for example, with the following discussion about the high priest's divination using the Urim and Thummim on his breastplate:

---

[55] See similarly *Naz.* 9:3 57d.
[56] Brand, "Li-shemot," 325. See there for alternative interpretations.
[57] See the next instance in *Sot.* there; see also *Pes.* 2:2 29a.

Yoma 7:5 44c

אית תניי תני: הקול היה שומע. אית תניי תני: הכתב בולט.

There is a reciter reciting: He would hear the [heavenly] voice.

There is a reciter reciting: The writing [on the breastplate] would stand out [spelling out the message].

Or this discussion about the time from which one may recite the Shema in the morning:

Berakhot 1:2 3a

אית תניי תני: בין זאב לכלב בין חמור לערוד. ואית תניי תני: כדי שיהא אדם רחוק מחבירו ארבע אמות ומכירו.

There is a reciter reciting: [From the time that it is bright enough to distinguish] between a wolf and a dog, between an ass and a wild ass.

And there is a reciter reciting: [From the time that it is bright enough] for a person to recognize another from four cubits away.

In these passages, the differences between the two recitations in each set are significant: there is very little that is textually common between them. They seem, at first, to be similar to all other disputes in rabbinic literature. But even these divergences *could* be textual: note that these teachings are fragmentary, neither standing on its own. If we had known, for example, that within each set both teachings were responding to an identically formulated question or case description, we could still stipulate that both transmit the same teaching, albeit with a large degree of variance. In the case of the passage from *Berakhot*, for example, the Yerushalmi compares these two teachings one to the other but not to the Mishnah, even though the Mishnah addresses the same subject; only later the Yerushalmi correlates each of the teachings to one of the opinions expressed in the Mishnah, suggesting it sees both of them as related to one another in a way that they are not related to the Mishnah.[58] Still, while we cannot rule out the textuality of these divergences, they seem to be closer to divergences in position alone.

As is the case with other terms and phrases studied in this book, the uniformity of terminology should not be mistaken for uniformity of meaning: the phrase is common enough that it was almost certainly used by different scholars to express different types of analysis, and it may have been introduced to discussions where it was not originally present as part of a standardization of terminology.

---

[58] But it seems unlikely that it is a variant of the recited teaching cited earlier in the passage; see the *derashah* there.

Not all passages, therefore, follow the same pattern. But several factors—the use of "reciter" and "reciting" which highlights transmission and formulation; the passages where the divergences are clearly about literary context and wording rather than opinion or position; and the dominance of divergences that are presented as concerning one or two words—point to a primary meaning of the phrase as introducing a divergence that centers on textual transmission and formulation.

4. The Talmud's commentary on recitation divergences

The majority of passages noting recitation divergences also include commentary.[59] The most striking feature of these comments is what they do not contain: they never posit that one of the teachings is the result of error, and they only rarely present any kind of preference for one of the divergent teachings. There are five passages in which an Amoraic scholar explicitly rejects one teaching in favor of another, all dealing with a specific type of divergence, in which the recitations are flipped;[60] it is also only in an instance of this type that an Amoraic scholar comments that we should not be concerned with the divergence.[61] There are six cases in which Amoraic scholars offer emendations, supporting the text reflected in one of the divergent recitations. But it is not clear if these statements were made in awareness of the divergence, and it is possible that the divergence itself was caused by such corrections rather than being prompted by them;[62] in the next chapter, we will see that the majority of Talmudic emendations are not supported by quotations of recited texts. There are about a dozen passages in which there is a legal ruling in accordance with one of the teachings,[63] but such comments do not dismiss the other teaching as an unreliable text; they merely state that it does not reflect the law.

---

[59] Exceptions include *Shab.* 16:1 15c (though an additional recited teaching cited there supports the position in one of the versions), *'Er.* 1:1 18c (but we have a ruling as one of the variants), *Pes.* 5:1 31d (though each of the recitations is related to another teaching quoted in the passage), *Pes.* 9:6 37a, *Yom.* 5:1 42b, *Yom.* 6:4 43d, *Meg.* 3:5 74b (both instances), *Sot.* 7:5 21d (both instances), *Ned.* 5:4 39b (though the second is explained), *Naz.* 9:3 58a, *Qid.* 4:8 66a, *San.* 1:2 18b, *Shevu.* 2:5 34a, *Hor.* 2:1 46c (which is unusual in other ways as well).

[60] *Kil.* 6:5 30c, *Shab.* 6:10 8c, *Pes.* 3:8 30b, which deal with attribution switching, and *Ta'an.* 4:4 68b, with content switching (appropriately, the Mishnah there also concerns such a switch). These passages seem related: they all employ the phrase "as our recitation," and all but *Shab.* include a mnemonic by R. Yudan to recall which version is the correct one.

[61] See R. Eleazar's rhetorical question at *Bez.* 2:1 61b.

[62] With "it's not here": *Ber.* 1:1 3a, *Ter.* 11:9 48a; with "thus is the recitation": *B. Q.* 2:3 3a, *B. B.* 9:7 17b (both instances), and possibly *Bik.* 3:4 65d. "It's not here" appears also in *Shab.* 11:1 12d (analyzed above), but not as an emendation.

[63] *'Er.* 1:1 18c, *Suk.* 3:1 53c, *Meg.* 1:8 71c (both instances), *Meg.* 3:6 74c, *M. Q.* 3:1 82a, *M. Q.* 3:5 82c, *M. Q.* 3:7 83c, *Qid.* 1:4 60b (where the very function of citing the divergence is to explain a Halakhic ruling the Yerushalmi deems redundant), *B. Q.* 4:6 4c (see Lewy, *Interpretation*, 124). In *Yev.* 8:1 8d and *Shevu.* 4:4 35c the Halakhic rulings seem to be independent of the discussion of the recitation divergence.

The tendency to uphold divergent recitations is evident not only in what these comments lack, but also in how they do address these recitations. The single most common type of comment applies a common Talmudic interpretive technique, to which I return in Chapter 8; it argues that the recitations do not dispute but rather refer to different cases or issues:[64]

Yoma 8:1 44d (par. Ta'an 1:6 64c, Yev. 12:1 12c)

אית תניי תני: יוצאין באמפליא ביום הכיפורים. ואית תניי תני: אין יוצאין. אמר רב חסדא: מאן דמר, "יוצאין", באמפליא של בגד. ומאן דמר, "אין יוצאין", באמפליא של עור.

There is a reciter reciting: One may go out [wearing] *impilia*[65] on the Day of Atonement.

There is a reciter reciting: One may **not** go out.

Rav Hisda said: The one who said "one may go out" [spoke] of cloth *impilia* and the one who said "one may not go out" [spoke] of leather *impilia*.

It is important to stress, however, that the presence of dispute itself was not a problem for Amoraic scholars. The majority of comments on recitation divergences accept that they are disputing even as they uphold both divergences. Such comments include construing the divergence as reflecting a disagreement between sages by associating or identifying a divergent recitation with a different (Tannaitic-era) sage or sages;[66] supporting recitations with a scriptural verse or an explanation of their reasoning;[67] or the statement that each of the recitations supports a position by an Amoraic scholar.[68]

This effort to preserve contradictory or apparently contradictory teachings rather than selecting between them is apparent already in the Tannaitic compilations, but here it takes a different form. In the Tannaitic compilations, the primary mode of preservation is the attribution of conflicting teachings to different sages

---

[64] There are more than sixty instances of this type of comment; see e.g. *Ber.* 5:4 9c (the second instance), *Dem.* 2:3 23a, *Shab.* 2:1 4d, *'Er.* 2:1 20a, *Naz.* 9:3 57d, *Qid.* 2:1 62b, *B. M.* 6:3 11a, *'A. Z.* 2:6 42a. Nineteen of these comments are attributed to Rav Hisda. The significance of this prevalence depends on the significance of attributions, but at the very least we can say Hisda was remembered as associated with this approach. Florsheim, "Hisda," reads these comments alongside other teachings attributed to Hisda in both Talmuds; but as Florsheim says, his conclusions are applicable to Talmudic interpretation in general (48).

[65] A type of inner shoe, usually worn like socks as lining (Goldman, "Roman Footwear," 125); the usual translation of this term in rabbinic literature is "felt shoes" (see e.g. Cohen et al., *Oxford Annotated Mishnah*, 2.56), but I did not use it here because the question is precisely the material of which the *impilia* are made.

[66] In about forty instances (the count includes various kinds of identifications, associations, and correlations, as well as suggestions that are rejected); see e.g. *Ber.* 1:1 3a, *'Er.* 1:1 18c, *Pes.* 2:1 28d, *Yev.* 8:2 9b, *Ned.* 1:3 37a, and *Shevu.* 2:1 33d.

[67] e.g. *Ber.* 4:4 8b, *Or.* 2:1 61d, *'Er.* 1:3 19a, *Pes.* 7:2 34b, *Ket.* 5:6 30b, *Naz.* 7:1 56b, and *San.* 2:3 20b.

[68] See the examples discussed below and n. 71.

already in their initial presentation. The Talmud's general commentarial form and interpretive orientation mean that, like in many other realms, these passages first present the problem of contradiction and only subsequently resolve it. The result is an increased presence of contradiction and variation and a highlighting of the scholarly process of their negotiation. More specifically, the textual nature of these divergences, which I began exploring in the previous section, allows for a different range of problems and solutions which shaped a new scholarly discourse. We have already seen, for example, how the Talmud preserves not only contradictory teachings, but also teachings with minute differences in formulation, by giving those differences significance they may not have had originally.

One could interpret this effort at preservation and the avoidance of pointing to errors in transmission as apologetic or conservative. But while it is true that explicit references to erroneous rabbinic teachings are not very common, the next two chapters address substantial sets of comments that are predicated on the idea that rabbinic teachings circulated in erroneous forms.[69] And while it is of course possible that there was a diversity among Amoraic scholars in approaching the possibility of such errors, to the degree that the attributions tell us something, they suggest that the same sages could make both kinds of commentary: the Talmud attributes to Rav Hisda both the large proportion of comments sustaining recitation divergences and the comment, examined in the next chapter, that the Mishnah contains an erroneous "slip of the tongue."[70] This interpretation of the Talmud's commentary on recitation divergences also does little by way of explaining its specific form.

A more compelling explanation lies in the scholarly and interpretive possibilities that these divergences allowed. The Talmud uses divergences for various ends: to explain the logic behind different rulings, to explore how the law changes according to different cases, to tie different rulings together in a conceptual scheme, to elucidate distinctive perspectives on a particular issue, to explain lack of specificity in Halakhic rulings, and to show how small differences in wording may have significant implications for the matter at hand. Drawing out significance from divergences is more generative than deeming them erroneous.

The previous sections argued that while there is some diversity in the way the phrase "there is a reciter reciting" functions in the Talmud, pervasive patterns in its form and use suggest that it introduces alternative transmissions or formulations of a given teaching. The commentary these passages present does not change this picture; some types of commentary even reinforce it. I mentioned above that one common type of comment posits that each recitation supports a position in an Amoraic dispute. In most of these instances, the dispute concerns the

---

[69] In addition to the passages discussed in the next chapter and in Chapter 8, Section 3, see also the comments discussed in Chapter 3, Section 5.

[70] On the attributions of sustaining comments to Rav Hisda, see n. 64; the comment on "slip of the tongue" is at *Meg.* 2:4 73b (par. *Ber.* 2:3 4d and *Ter.* 1:2 40c).

interpretation of a particular teaching.[71] Consider the very first example I offered in this chapter, from *Berakhot*. R. Phinehas and R. Yose give different interpretations of the Mishnaic teaching about the person who mentions the bird's nest in prayer, and the Talmud comments that each of their interpretations is supported by a recitation of that teaching. If these were not recitations of the same teaching, this type of comment would not make sense. The passage does not say that each Amoraic scholar spoke about a different recitation, but that each recitation supports an alternative interpretation of the teaching in question. In another example, the Talmud has R. Eleazar explaining a teaching with the phrase *kini matnina*, "thus is the recited teaching," whereas R. Yohanan presents an alternative interpretation with the phrase *matnita be-*, "the recited teaching speaks of . . . ."[72] The Talmud's comment in that passage, that these positions are supported by different recitations, necessitates that we understand them as alternative recitations of the same recited teaching, *matnita*, over which R. Yohanan and R. Eleazar disputed.

If we apply the same framework to the common argument that the two recitations address a different case or context, what it posits is that each of the reciters formulated the same teaching based on the case they had in mind, resulting in parallel formulations. It is possible, again, that in some of these cases the language of two recitations is not used so intentionally or precisely: that the argument in some instances is not that the same teaching was recited with small differences in wording by two reciters, but simply that the law makes a distinction between different cases and circumstances. Since most of these comments are not accompanied with much discussion, it is difficult to assess precisely what they mean. But when we do have more of a discussion, it supports the interpretation that the passage points to textual variation:

'*Orlah* 1:1 60c–d

רימין שנטען לשם רימין,[73] בנות הדס שנטען לשם בנות הדס—אית תניי תני, "חייב", אית תניי תני, "פטור".

אמ' רב חסדא: מאן דאמ' "חייב", במקום שרוב משמרין. מאן דאמ' "פטור", במקום שאין הרוב משמרין.

---

[71] In addition to the two examples discussed here, see *Shab.* 5:4 7c (second instance), *Shab.* 7:3 10d, *Ket.* 7:1 31b, *Ned.* 3:1 37d, *'A. Z.* 2:3 41b. While these examples concern teachings included in the Mishnah, the same comment applies to a teaching not included in the Mishnah at *Kil.* 8:1 31b (par. *Shab.* 7:2 9d, *San.* 7:4 24d). See also, though with a different formulation, *Shab.* 11:1 12d, discussed above. In other cases, the Amoraic positions which the recitations purportedly support are not, or not necessarily, interpretive in character: *Ber.* 4:3 8a (*Ta'an.* 2:2 65c), *Ḥal.* 1:1 57b, *Yom.* 1:1 39a (par. *Ḥag.* 2:4 78b). At *Kil.* 7:7 31a, the positions are interpretive, but they apply to a different teaching in the Mishnah than the one to which the recitations attest. In one striking example, the comment says that each recitation supports a *Tannaitic* position (*Git.* 8:4 49c).

[72] *Pe'ah* 7:2 20a.

[73] MSS Leiden and Vatican read "רימון" in both instances. "רימין" following Sirilio (and see e.g. *m. Dem.* 1:1); therefore also changing the verb to the plural.

ר' יוסי בעי: אם במקום משמרין למה לי חישב? אפילו לא חישב. כך אנו אומ', "זית ותאינה עד שיחשוב עליהן"? אלא אפילו מחצה משמרין ומחצה שאין משמרין.

[Tractate ʿOrlah addresses the prohibition to consume the produce of trees in the first three years after they are planted. This prohibition applies only to trees which are planted for their edible produce. This discussion concerns a case where a person planted trees that normally are not planted for their produce, but in this specific case were.]

The jujube which one planted for the jujube [fruit], or myrtle berries which one planted for the myrtle berries—there is a reciter reciting, "it is liable" [to the ʿOrlah prohibition, and] there is a reciter reciting, "it is exempt."

Rav Hisda said: The one who said, "it is liable," in a place where the majority keep [such produce for consumption]. The one who said, "it is exempt," in a place where the majority does not keep [such produce].

R. Yose asked: If [the recitation which holds "liable"] concerns a place where they keep [such produce], why do I need [the specification] that he intended [the planting for the produce]? [He is liable] even if he did not intend [to consume from their produce]. Is this what we say, "olive and fig [he is not liable] unless he intends [to consume] them"? Rather, [the teaching means that such intention makes the trees liable] even in a place where half [of the people] keep [such produce] and half do not.[74]

Rav Hisda offers his typical solution, positing that each reciter speaks of a different case: the one who applies the prohibition addresses a place where these particular species are normally planted for their produce, whereas the one who does not, speaks of a place where such intention is uncommon. R. Yose objects that if that were the case, the reference in the teaching to the planter's intention is redundant; in a place where these species of trees are generally recognized as edible produce trees, intention is irrelevant. This objection assumes that the two recitations are verbally identical except the final word, and therefore both include the reference to the planter's intention. It does not take Rav Hisda's interpretation as a general reference to different rulings in different contexts, but rather as addressing alternative attestations or formulations of the same teaching.

---

[74] I am not reproducing here the final comment in the discussion. The text in both MSS Leiden and Vatican is problematic; see the suggested reconstruction in Elitzur, "Amoraim," 222. For my purpose, it is important to emphasize that the Talmud attributes the teachings to two reciters ("there is a reciter reciting..."; "the one who said..."). If indeed this last comment refers to the "latter," it does not conceive these recitations as parts of the same teaching (as implied by Elijah of Fulda), but rather merely refers to the latter of the two teachings.

5. Recitation divergences and the Amoraic configuration of textual difference

The analysis in the previous sections allows for the following general observations. Amoraic scholars read divergent recitations as alternative attestations of texts, that is, different formulations or transmissions of teachings that had specific wording. They were not, however, interested in placing these recitations in hierarchical relationships with each other or even with a hypothesized original. The aim of these passages is not to arrive at the original or correct text, but to draw out significance from textual difference. At the same time, these passages present each of the recitations as giving us a partial, imperfect picture. Knowing only one recitation might mean we would only know one opinion, where there are two; that we would conflate the application of the teaching in one case with its application in another; or that we would adopt what is only one of the teaching's possible interpretations.

The Talmud's comments were crucial for Epstein in his argument that the Mishnah's text was stable and uniform in the Amoraic period. Because Amoraic scholars did not state that divergences are errors, because they did not correct the Mishnah's text in light of divergent recitations, because they upheld these divergent recitations as parallel to the Mishnah rather than mutually exclusive with it—then these divergences, Epstein argued, are not *variants* of the Mishnah, that is, errors introduced in the course of its transmission, but rather other *versions*, that is, other compositions adapting the same material.

But what Epstein read as evidence of the stability of the Mishnah's text is better read as evidence of Amoraic interpretive practices and interests. This is not just because of the theoretical observation that texts or their meanings are produced by their readers, but also because of specific features of these discussions. First, the patterns that Epstein observed apply to the Amoraic discussion of all divergences: even when they addressed teachings that were not included in the Mishnah, Amoraic scholars upheld both divergences and avoided correcting one based on the other. Since they are not restricted to the Mishnah, these features of the Talmud's discussions could not have stemmed from facts about the Mishnah's circulation.

Second, and more important, these discussions set up the Mishnah and other extant *mishnayot* not as the *attested* texts, but rather as the *attesting* texts. The Talmud does not classify any recitation divergence as attesting to "our Mishnah," or any other *mishnayot*. We never find in these passages phrases like "there is a reciter reciting in *our* Mishnah" or "there is a reciter reciting in the *mishnah* of R. Hiyya." Since regardless of the medium of transmission—writing or oral—it is very unlikely that there was *no* variation in the transmission of these *mishnayot*, we should see this lack of reference to varying attestations as a feature of their definition. Terms such as "we recited," "our Mishnah," "R. Hiyya recited," refer, in the Talmud's presentation, to the unique formulation that defines these recitations: if a teaching is recited differently than it is in "our Mishnah" or in R. Hiyya's *mishnah*, then by definition, that teaching is not in "our Mishnah" or R. Hiyya's *mishnah*. In the passages which speak, for example, about recitation divergences in attribution, the choice of one of these recitations is "as our Mishnah," which assumes the term signals a specific formulation.[75]

This configuration may be related to oral transmission. In written transmission, texts may be classified as attesting to the same work because they are transmitted under the same title and in long form, which allows other aspects of the text to identify it as the same work. An oral study culture focuses on short bits of texts which do not circulate necessarily under a title, and therefore may not classify two different formulations as belonging to the same long-form recitation. At the same time, even in an oral context, Amoraic scholars could have introduced a divergence with a phrase like "there is a reciter reciting in our Mishnah," or indicated in their discussions that the recitations relate to "our Mishnah."[76] They did not do so because they were interested in the way that the Mishnah or similar recitations attested to other teachings, not in how these *mishnayot* were attested by still other recitations. In part, this allowed for the upholding of multiple recitations: placing diverging recitations as transmissions of "our" Mishnah or R. Hiyya's *mishnah* would mean that one of them represented correctly the text shaped by Judah the Patriarch or R. Hiyya. In any case, the distinction that was so important to Epstein, the line between the composition and transmission of a specific "work" or compilation, simply does not figure in these discussions.[77]

The distinction that does seem to inform these discussions, at least to some degree, is the distinction between the Tannaitic and Amoraic period. To the extent that the term "reciter" is chronologically defined,[78] the attribution of these divergences to "reciters" meant that they were seen as reflecting Tannaitic positions; discussions that respond to these divergences with identifications name only Tannaitic-era sages.[79] But this attribution to "reciters" as well as these

---

[75] Above n. 60.

[76] To this observation we can also add Sussmann's observation that these passages do not consistently make terminological distinctions between divergences involving the Mishnah and those that do not. For Sussmann, this means that these passages are only interested in the "general indication that there are disputing *opinions*" (Oral Torah, 315 n. 70, emphasis original). But without discounting the diversity with which the phrase is applied, the analysis in the previous sections suggests that these discussions were generally designed to address textual attestations. The lack of consistent reference to the Mishnah as a compilation is consistent with the Amoraic construction of these divergences, which was not concerned with whether they represented that compilation (regardless of the possibility that in fact they emerged in the Mishnah's transmission, a point on which Sussmann is certainly correct).

[77] For the same reason, accounts which posit the opposite of Epstein, that these variations are necessarily variations "of our Mishnah" (see e.g. Albeck, "Nushaʾot") also miss the mark.

[78] See the discussion above, Section 2.

[79] There are no exceptions to this rule, but there are a couple of instances which complicate it. At *Pes.* 10:3 37d, the phrase introduces what seems like a variation on a statement attributed to R. Joshua b. Levi. At *Shab.* 11:1 12d, Amoraic positions are described as determining the text ("on the opinion of R. Eleazar there is 'how so' here, on the opinion of Samuel there is no 'how so' here"), rather than being supported by the recitations.

identifications both reflect a construction and a judgment rather than facts about these divergences: in an oral culture, where teachings were presented by Amoraic-era agents rather than read from Tannaitic-era copies, it is an interpretive choice to consider these teachings as "recited" teachings. Marking a divergence as Amoraic would lead to an imbalance in authority between the divergences.

The Talmud's discussions of divergences indeed present almost exclusively "versions" in Epstein's terms, but this reflects the approach of Amoraic scholars, their interests and construction of textual difference, rather than facts about the Mishnah's circulation. At the same time, Epstein's distinction between "versions" and "variants" itself assumes the importance of definite moments of redaction or production of "works" and a separation between composition and transmission which were not part of this Amoraic configuration. The next section examines a scholarly tradition that was interested in such a categorization of textual difference, illuminating the distinctiveness of this Amoraic approach.

6. Textual difference in ancient scholarship: the example of Christian biblical scholarship in Palestine

Scholarship in the Greco-Roman world often featured discussions of textual differences based on the collation of manuscripts and editions.[80] These discussions are similar to the Amoraic discussions studied in this chapter not only in the general sense that both are interested in textual divergence, but also in some more specific ways. The Homeric scholar of the third century BCE, Aristarchus, employed etymology in discussing variants much like Amoraic scholars do.[81] But while Aristarchus uses these etymologies to decide between variants, in the Talmud they are employed to justify both divergent recitations. Another possible structural similarity concerns the attribution of textual differences. I have mentioned above that while in most cases, the Talmud cites anonymous recitations, there is a significant number of occasions where it associates recitation divergences with a named authority or institution—R. Hiyya, the House of the Patriarch, and of course "our" Mishnah. Studies on the reception of the Homeric epics noted a similar distinction

---

[80] For various strands of scholarship in Greek, see references below; on Latin scholarship, see Zetzel, *Critics*, 198, who writes that in Latin the discussion of variants was less common than in Greek, though of course still important to certain scholars. See also idem, *Latin Textual Criticism in Antiquity*, 206–39. The Greco-Roman tradition provides a good comparative perspective since it is well developed and well preserved, and since some of it was produced by contemporaries of Amoraic scholars and sometimes in their immediate surrounding. But annotations of variant readings and emendations are also documented, for example, in Akkadian texts and commentaries (see Gabbay, *Akkadian Commentaries*, 72–6; and Worthington, *Akkadian Textual Criticism*, 20–8); and while the culture which produced them was long gone by the time of Amoraic scholars, Gabbay (ibid., 289–304) has shown that the terminology of these commentaries shows surprising convergence with rabbinic terminology.

[81] On Aristarchus, see Schironi, *Best of the Grammarians*, 363–5; on the Talmud's etymologies, see Section 3 above.

in the work of ancient scholars. Didymus, working at the turn of the first century, mentions both anonymous copies and those corrected by individual scholars or produced in certain cities. He shows a clear preference for the latter group.[82] It is possible that Talmudic discussions reflect a similar distinction: it is only in discussions where both recitations have a pedigree that the Talmud states emphatically that both are "necessary";[83] but the hierarchy is much less clear, if it is at all there.[84]

These specific differences reveal a broader difference between Amoraic discussions of textual difference and their counterparts in Greek and Latin scholarship. Whereas, as we have seen, the Talmud rarely shows preference or hierarchy between divergent recitations, Greek and Latin discussions of textual difference were often bound with the pursuit of a correct text. Often, but not always: we will see in this section some important examples where there is discussion of variants without selection or emendation, and in the next chapter, we will see that it is not clear whether Aristarchus appealed to variant readings when he made emendations. But the general picture is clear: Greek and Latin scholars routinely used variants in the correction and preparation of various texts. Readings from copies and editions were used, at least from the time of Didymus, in producing corrected texts of the Homeric epics;[85] they appear in the margins of papyri of Greek drama;[86] and they are discussed by Galen in his commentaries on Hippocrates.[87]

This difference reflects, in part, approaches that precede the Amoraic discourse of divergences. It reflects the long rabbinic tendency to preserve conflicting traditions. It may also reflect Jewish textual practices, or even pervasive ancient textual practices, that are attested in the biblical text: scholars have documented the tendency of scribes to preserve multiple versions by including them in the texts they were writing, which resulted in so-called "double readings," "conflations," or "harmonizations."[88] From this perspective, what might stand out is not the Talmud's inclusive approach, but the selective approach in (some strands of) Greco-Roman literary culture.[89] At the same time, there is an important difference between including multiple versions in a single text—without commentary and often in ways

---

[82] West, *Text and Transmission*, 50–1; Schironi, *Best of the Grammarians*, 65–6.
[83] For examples, see Chapter 8, Section 2.
[84] See also Lieberman's idea of the Mishnah as an *ekdosis*, *Hellenism*, 83–99; and see above Chapter 1, n. 47.
[85] West, *Text and Transmission*, 46–85. See also the studies on Aristarchus cited in the next chapter.
[86] See Johnson, *Readers and Reading Culture*, 185–90.
[87] Hanson, "Galen"; Roselli, "Galen's Practice." More on Galen and textual criticism in the next chapter.
[88] See e.g. Talmon, "Double Readings"; Person, "Scribe as a Performer"; Carr, *Formation*.
[89] In a methodological essay published in 1956, Isac Seeligmann lamented that text criticism of the Hebrew Bible is more limited "per force, not per choice" than criticism of classical (i.e. Greek and Latin) texts, because of the "Near Eastern tendency towards repetitions, variations, and the preservations of every variants that ever came into being," which meant variants continued to circulate side by side in the text itself ("History," 30). This dichotomy is problematic not only because of its orientalist judgment, but also because recent accounts have shown that at least the earliest phases of Greek literature were similar in this respect (e.g. Carr, *Formation*, 13).

which smooth over or minimize the significance of their differences—and the Talmudic discussions which call out textual difference, draw significance from it, and often emphasize the conflicting nature of the different texts.

The rest of this section examines discussions of textual difference by late ancient Christian scholars working in Palestine. My discussion here focuses on Origen, whose work has been foundational for subsequent scholars, though it also draws on Eusebius, Jerome, and Epiphanius. I center on discussions of the New Testament, since discussions of the "Old Testament" introduce additional consideration of issues stemming from the translation of Hebrew to Greek.[90]

A passage from Origen's *Commentary on the Gospel of Matthew* is particularly revealing of his notions of textual difference. Matthew 19:16–22 recounts an encounter between Jesus and a wealthy young man, who asks how he could obtain eternal life. Jesus answers that he must keep the commandments. The young man asks which commandments. Jesus offers a list: "You shall not murder, you shall not commit adultery, you shall not steal, you shall not bear false witness, honor your father and mother. Also, you shall love your neighbor as yourself." The young man replies that he has kept all these commandments and asks what he still lacks. Jesus answers that if he wishes to be perfect, he should sell all his possessions and give the money to the poor (Matthew 19:16–22).

Origen is bothered by the reference, in Jesus's first reply, to the commandment to "love your neighbor as yourself." He argues that fulfilling this commandment amounts to attaining perfection; it is puzzling that Jesus should tell the young man he still needs to do more to become perfect, if he accepted that he fulfilled this commandment. Origen therefore suggests that Jesus did not actually refer to that commandment and that it was added to the list by "someone" who did not understand what was being said. He proceeds to note that the reference to this commandment does not appear in the other gospels which offer an account of this encounter, Mark (10:17–22) and Luke (18:18–23). But neither the exegetical problem, nor these divergent accounts in the gospels, provides sufficient support, according to Origen, for the contention that the reference to that commandment is erroneous:

> Now if there was not disagreement on many other details among our copies, such that not all those of Matthew agree with each other, and likewise in the other Gospels, one might think the person impious who supposes that this command to the rich man was added here and that the Saviour did not say, "You shall love your neighbour as yourself." But it is clear that the differences between the copies have become numerous, either from the shoddy work of copyists, or from the wicked recklessness of some either in neglecting to correct what is written,

---

[90] See, however, n. 108 below, on Origen's approach to the Septuagint.

or even in adding or removing things based on their own opinions when they do correct.[91]

Even though in this case Origen does not document any specific variation in the copies he had of the Gospel of Matthew, he appeals here to the general fact that such copies are discordant, which he presents as the result of various kinds of carelessness or deliberate but misguided "corrections." It is only that state of the copies which allows us to posit, without facing the charge of impiety, that the reference to the commandment is an inappropriate addition.

This passage makes a distinction between two kinds of textual difference, which are conceived and approached differently: the differences between copies of each of the gospels, on the one hand, and the differences between the gospels themselves, on the other. Discussions of the former kind of difference by Origen and other late ancient Christian scholars routinely present them as resulting from error and corruption, and therefore they also routinely involve rejecting one text for another.[92] Origen rejects, for example, copies which have Jesus criticize anger "without a cause" because he thinks Scripture shows that any anger is to be avoided; he finds it unlikely that Barnabas, crucified with Jesus, was himself also called "Jesus Barnabas" as some copies would have it, since "the name of Jesus is not suitable for someone sinful"; and he postulates that "enemies of the church" may be behind copies which have the sun "eclipsed" rather than "darkened" at the moment of the crucifixion.[93] Epiphanius hails "uncorrected copies" (ἀδιορθώτοις ἀντιγράφοις) of the Gospel of Luke, prior to well-meaning but misguided orthodox removal of verses which made Jesus seem weak;[94] and he chastises those who removed the second Jeconiah from Matthew's genealogy because they thought it was a duplicate, and thus, "as though for scholarship's sake," destroyed Matthew's scheme of fourteen generations.[95] While selection and rejection were a substantial aspect of discussions of such differences, they were not the rule. In the majority of passages in which Origen mentions variation in New Testament copies, he does not select between them.[96] He is often content to note variation without offering any commentary, even in passages which concern the specific wording of

---

[91] Origen, *Commentary on Matthew*, 15.14, trans. Heine, 204, except I changed the first sentence to clarify Origen's reference to the differences in the copies. It reads in Greek (ed. Klostermann, *TLG*): Καὶ εἰ μὲν μὴ καὶ περὶ ἄλλων πολλῶν διαφωνία ἦν πρὸς ἄλληλα τῶν ἀντιγράφων, ὥστε πάντα τὰ κατὰ Ματθαῖον μὴ συνᾴδειν ἀλλήλοις, ὁμοίως δὲ καὶ τὰ λοιπὰ εὐαγγέλια, κἂν ἀσεβής τις ἔδοξεν εἶναι ὁ ὑπονοῶν ἐνταῦθα προσερρίφθαι οὐκ εἰρημένην ὑπὸ τοῦ σωτῆρος πρὸς τὸν πλούσιον τὴν ἀγαπήσεις τὸν πλησίον σου ὡς ἑαυτὸν ἐντολήν.
[92] My discussion of references to New Testament textual variants in late ancient Christian scholarship is based on Donaldson, "Explicit Reference."
[93] See the discussions of these passages in Donaldson, ibid., 103–4 (geography and etymology), 352–3 (on anger), 387 (on Barnabas), and 424 (eclipse).
[94] *Ancoratus* 31.4; translation from Kim, *Ancoratus*, 106.
[95] *Panarion* 1.8.4 (ed. Holl, *TLG*), translation from Williams, *Panarion I*, 31.
[96] This observation is based on the passages from Origen's work in the catalog offered by Donaldson, ibid. See also the discussion of Jerome in Letteney, *Christianization*, 210–11.

the text.[97] In one striking example, he offers an interpretation of Romans 5:14 both on the reading that the verse refers to "those who sinned in the likeness of Adam's transgressions" and on the reading that it refers to "those who have *not* sinned" like Adam.[98] Eusebius and Jerome show a similar range of approaches.[99]

But while these scholars' negotiation of differences among copies of New Testament books presents some diversity, it is still distinct from the approach to the other kind of variation, the differences between the gospels themselves. In the passage with which we began, Origen discusses the differences in the gospels' account of Jesus' words to the young man: Matthew includes the reference to the love commandment, whereas Mark and Luke do not. As we have seen, that divergence was not sufficient for Origen to establish that the reference in Matthew is an addition; he appeals to the poor state of the copies to argue that our extant texts do not represent Matthew's words. While, as Amy Donaldson writes, late ancient Christian scholars "at times appear to treat the different Gospels as though they are additional MSS of the same text,"[100] when Origen wants to reject the text of one gospel in favor of the other gospels, he emphasizes that the mistake is not in the gospel itself but in its *copies*.[101] That is because even though the gospels attested to the same words and events, Origen did not attribute divergences between them to error, but rather approached each gospel as an authoritative account worthy of commentary on its own terms.

Another passage from Origen's commentary on Matthew provides a good example. The synoptic gospels offer an account of an incident in which Jesus healed blindness in Jericho (Matthew 20:29–34; Mark 10:46–52; Luke 18:35–43). They diverge on what Jesus said on that occasion, as well as on other details—for example, whether Jesus healed two blind men or one. Origen first relates the "simple" (ψιλῇ) meaning of these passages: if we understand them as accounts of historical events, he argues, we must posit that these accounts refer to three separate incidents involving different blind men; the accounts cannot contradict each other "if we believe the Gospels have been recorded accurately with the cooperation, too, of the Holy Spirit, and that those who wrote them"—that is, the evangelists—"did not err in their recollection."[102] Origen's second solution is addressed to those who seek a "deeper interpretation" (βαθυτέραν διήγησιν); it reads the blind man or men as

---

[97] For Origen, see the passages discussed in Donaldson, ibid., 355, 373, 375, 414. See similarly with Jerome, in the passages discussed in Metzger, "St. Jerome's Explicit References," 180, 183–4, 186; and with Epiphanius, the passages discussed by Donaldson, ibid., 345–6, 427.

[98] Donaldson, ibid., 99–100. See also the variant in the *Commentary on Luke* discussed ibid., 416. On Jerome similarly offering interpretations based on different readings, see ibid., 156–7.

[99] On selection in Jerome and Eusebius, see Donaldson, ibid., 111–12 (on Eusebius) and 158–61 (on Jerome). On lack of selection, in Jerome see ibid., 156–7, as well as Letteney's discussion in *Christianization*, 210–11; Eusebius dismisses the long ending of Mark but nonetheless offers commentary on that ending; Metzger, "Practice," 343–4.

[100] Donaldson, ibid., 264–5.

[101] See the passages discussed in Donaldson, ibid., 362–3, 554.

[102] Origen, *Commentary on Matthew*, 16:12 (trans. Heine, 249).

representing Jews (Israel if one, Israel and Judah if two) who may believe in Jesus's message but are still blind to his divinity. Origen proceeds to offer a detailed interpretation of each gospel's account, paying meticulous attention to minute differences in wording which he reads as indicative of the intention and understanding of each author.[103] Helmut Merkel traced how these and other strategies which Origen developed to address diversity among the gospels were taken up by other late ancient Christian scholars, including Eusebius, Jerome, and Epiphanius.[104]

Putting aside Origen's emphasis on the inerrancy of the evangelists or the role of the holy spirit in the production of the gospels, this distinction between differences among the gospels and differences in their copies may seem intuitive to us. If we treat "the Gospel of Matthew" and the "Gospel of Mark" as discrete literary works that were shaped by different authors, then we may want to use the different copies of these works to reconstruct the text as the author intended it. But this view of the gospels as discrete texts, each having its own textual identity and authority, represented a particular approach to texts and traditions attesting to Jesus's words. Recent scholarship has argued that the gospels were not originally composed or understood as discrete texts, but rather as attestations of "the Gospel" (τὸ εὐαγγέλιον): the singular oral proclamation of the apostolic tradition.[105] The composition of the gospels involved the formulation and reformulation of this singular message, each gospel treating its predecessors as open-source material. Early discussions of events or words recorded in the gospels do not refer to the specific works, but to what Jesus said or did; they do not discuss the "authors" of the gospels, nor comment on the perspective each gospel represents.

Most scholars consider Irenaeus of Lyons (late second century CE) to represent an inflection point.[106] Writing against competing approaches that he deems heretical, he argues for four distinct and authoritative books, written and published by four named authors. But as Annette Yoshiko Reed has shown, even Irenaeus uses the word "εὐαγγέλιον" primarily to describe the singular apostolic message. Likening what he calls the "four-formed" Gospel to the four-faced cherubim of Ezekiel's vision of the divine throne (or Revelation's four creatures), Irenaeus constructs the individual gospels as different "faces" of the Gospel, suggesting its multiplicity is "simply the way in which human believers may come to understand the singular, divine Truth."[107] While Origen and still later ancient scholars certainly

---

[103] Origen, *Commentary on Matthew*, 16.12–13 (trans. Heine, 249–52).
[104] See Merkel, *Widersprüche*, noting Origen's influence on Eusebius, 146, and Jerome, 216–17; Epiphanius shares with Origen the idea that the gospels cannot contradict each other but differs from him by rejecting the allegorical method (172, 180).
[105] Watson, *Gospel Writing*; Larsen, *Gospels before the Book*; Keith, *Gospel as Manuscript*; Rodriguez, *Combining Gospels*. These accounts diverge on various questions, but they are united in treating the notion of the gospels as discrete texts as a construction that has a history.
[106] Pagels, "Irenaeus," 347; Reed, "ΕΥΑΓΓΕΛΙΟΝ"; Larsen, *Gospels before the Book*, 93–6; Rodriguez, *Combining Gospels*, 142–55.
[107] Reed, "ΕΥΑΓΓΕΛΙΟΝ," 37.

responded and contributed to the circulation of the gospels as juxtaposed texts, composed by specific authors, with clear textual identities, they also continued to study them as overlapping accounts, as attestations of the same statements and events.

For our purposes, what is important is that this process results in a distinction between two kinds of textual difference, a distinction that is not characteristic of Amoraic scholarship, but which is analogous to Epstein's distinction between "versions" and "variants." The gospels, like Epstein's versions, present legitimate differences in intention, perspective, and source material, resulting from different adaptations of similar materials by different authoritative figures (the evangelists or Tannaitic-era sages). The differences among the copies are like Epstein's "variants": they are introduced, deliberately or inadvertently, by the transmitters of the text, and they necessarily present errors since the proper purpose of transmission is the accurate representation of the author's work. And much like Epstein's rule is never to correct one version in light of another but only variants, Origen does not correct one gospel in light of another, except through appeal to extant or hypothesized variants in the copies.[108] Above all, the comparison between these approaches illuminates how such distinctions between different kinds of textual difference—including many variations of the modern philological distinction between "higher" and "lower" criticism—are bound with hierarchies of canonicity and authority, even as for modern philologists, this hierarchy is framed in secularized terms which privilege a particular historical moment of origin as defining and stabilizing the text's identity.

Amoraic discussions of recitation divergences are not interested in such hierarchies of textual difference. They present no substantial parallel of Origen's discussions of errors in the copies, but they do present similarities with his discussions of divergences in the gospels. In both cases, for example, scholars address apparent contradictions by positing different referents, or elaborate on different intentions, implications, and complementary perspectives offered by such variations. In both cases, these discussions reflect a transition from textual fluidity (the rewriting of gospels, the reformulation of teachings in the Tannaitic period) to commentary on defined texts.[109] Intriguingly, Matthew Larsen suggested that this

---

[108] While this distinction is related to the specific history and form of the gospels, it seems to represent a broader methodological approach. In the same passage (*Commentary on Matthew*, 15.14 [trans. Heine, 204]), Origen himself relates his approach to the gospels to his approach to the Septuagint. He says he addressed disagreements among copies of the Septuagint by comparing them to the Hebrew and other "editions" (*ekdoseis*) of the Greek, construing them as authoritative texts according to which the copies of the Septuagint may be corrected, much like the erroneous copies of Matthew may be corrected in light of other gospels. On the way that Origen's approach conferred a canonical status on those editions, establishing a particular order on a messier reality of textual variation, see Grafton and Williams, *Christianity*, 129, relying on the work of Dominique Barthélemy; see also Kharanauli, "Origen and Lucian."

[109] Coogan, *Eusebius the Evangelist*, makes the argument that Eusebius' scholarship continues the project of gospel re-writing—but in other means; the same can be said about Amoraic scholarship and the reformulation of rabbinic teachings.

shift in understanding the gospels also involved a shift in understanding the significance of their attribution to individuals, which is similar to some degree to the shift posited in the first part of this book.[110] But in the Talmud, the avoidance of labeling recitations as erroneous is not connected with claims to divine inspiration, and while Origen and others emphasized the harmony of the gospels as opposed to the disagreement of the copies, Amoraic scholars allowed recitations to stand in disagreement. It is difficult to imagine Origen saying that different gospel versions support conflicting interpretations of Jesus' words by later Christian scholars in the way that Talmudic comments posit that divergent recitations support conflicting interpretations by Amoraic scholars.

Both ancient scholarly traditions share an interest in how texts change and diverge in the course of their transmission, and in the significance of small differences in wording. I argued above that Amoraic scholars drew various kinds of interpretive significance from recitation divergences. Adam Kamesar used the term "exegetical maximalism" to describe the way Origen consulted different versions of the Old Testament to expand the possibilities of exegesis,[111] and the same can be said for Origen's discussions of differences among the evangelists and among the copies. At the same time, in comparison to Amoraic scholars, Origen and other Christian scholars more often note variation without commenting on it.[112] Epiphanius explicitly theorized this phenomenon of insignificant variance as a way of maintaining the sense that the biblical text offers a singular message. The context of his discussion is Origen's use of the critical sign known as *lemniscus* in his *Hexapla*:

> Therefore this kind of sign also they attach to the divine words, that when there is found in rare instances in the translation of the seventy-two a dissonant word, neither subtracted from nor added to words similar to it, you may know, because of the two points placed by it, that this was translated by one or two pairs. But they were read in two ways or similarly . . . . In Psalms 71 it says, "And their name is honored before him," but instead of this is put "And their name is honored in his eyes." And so you may find it in many places, where there is nothing taken away or changed but it is the very same (in meaning), though expressed differently, so that it is not foreign to the others; they read both ways.[113]

The phrase appearing in the title of this chapter, *variae recitationes*, was coined by Rosenthal in a foundational essay on the history of the Babylonian Talmud's text.

---

[110] Larsen, "Correcting the Gospel."
[111] Kamesar, *Jerome*, 19.
[112] See n. 97 above; on the infrequent cases where the Talmud notes variation without commentary, see n. 59.
[113] Dean, *Epiphanius' Treatise on Weights and Measures*, 22–3 (translating the Syriac version, which does not differ here in significant ways; see Moutsoulas's edition of the Greek, *TLG*).

236 THE RISE OF TALMUD

Rosenthal signified with this phrase textual differences resulting from the fluid oral transmission of the Bavli. He suggested these were differences in wording, not meaning, a suggestion which was in part inspired by Epiphanius.[114] While this phrase is an apt one for the recitation divergences the Talmud marks with "there is a reciter reciting," Rosenthal is closer in his understanding of textual difference to Epiphanius than to Amoraic scholars. The model of the meaningless variant was also adopted in the first history of rabbinic literature: according to the *Letter of Rav Sherira*, the sages may transmit different formulations of the tradition, but those are identical in meaning; the point of the Mishnah's composition was to ensure that this uniformity of tradition is also reflected in a uniformity of language.[115] Amoraic scholars, in contrast, embraced textual divergences and their significance: it is rare for them to conclude that recitation divergences do not present a meaningful difference.[116] The next section argues these scholars may even have invented some of these divergences.

7. Fictional and functional

Up to this point, I have treated textual divergences as an existing fact which the Talmud reports and discusses—and that is how the Talmud presents it: "*there is* a reciter reciting." But there are indications that some of these divergences may be scholarly fabrications or the result of scholarly exercises.[117] In several places, for example, divergences appear in sequence or proximity and follow a similar pattern even though they are on disparate subjects, which suggests that they might have been created by the composers of those sections in the Talmud. We find, for example, five negation divergences one after the other on a variety of questions on festival day prohibitions in tractate *Bezah*;[118] another series of three "liable" and "exempt" switches on separate issues in tractate *Pesaḥim*, with two others following closely after;[119] in *Ḥallah*, there are three similar reverse-order divergences cited in close proximity.[120] A particularly instructive case is in tractate *Yevamot*, which presents a series of four divergences shortly followed by another series of three, most of which involve switches between a "valid" and an "invalid" *ḥalizah* in various scenarios.[121]

---

[114] Rosenthal, "History of the Text"; the phrase *variae recitationes* appears on 30; Epiphanius is quoted on 26.
[115] Lewin, *ISG*, 18–24.
[116] See e.g. *Shab.* 4:1 6d.
[117] See Hidary, *Rabbis and Classical Rhetoric*, 131–73, on the Talmud's conjuring of hypothetical cases as scholarly exercise in the context of Greco-Roman education.
[118] *Bez.* 4:3 62c.
[119] *Pes.* 5:4 32b and 7:2 34b.
[120] Two at *Ḥal.* 2:4 58c and a third at 4:5 59d.
[121] *Yev.* 12:1 12b–12c.

The second series contains a parallel to the passage we have seen above about footwear on the Day of Atonement:

Yevamot 12:1 12c

חלצה באמפילייא—אית תניי תני: חליצתה כשירה, אית תניי תני: חליצתה פסולה. מאן דאמ', "חליצתה כשירה", באמפילייא שלעור. מאן דאמ', "חליצתה פסולה", באמפילייא שלבגד.

במנעל באמפילייא—אית תניי תני חליצתה כשירה, אית תניי תני: חליצתה פסולה. מאן דאמ', "חליצתה כשירה", כשהיתה באמפילייא שלבגד ומנעל שלעור. מאן דאמ', "חליצתה פסולה", כשהיתה אנפילייא שלעור ומנעל שלעור.

אית תניי תני: יוצאין באמפילייא ביום הכיפורים. ואית תניי תני: אין יוצאין באמפילייא. אמ' רב חסדא: מאן דאמ', "יוצאין", באמפילייא שלבגד, ומאן דאמ', "אין יוצאין", באמפילייא שלעור.

If she performed the ḥalizah ceremony with *impilia*[122]—there is a reciter reciting, "her ḥalizah is valid," there is a reciter reciting, "her ḥalizah is invalid." The one who said "her ḥalizah is valid" [spoke] of leather *impilia*, the one who said "her ḥalizah is invalid" spoke of cloth *impilia*.

If she performed the ḥalizah ceremony with a shoe and *impilia* [lining it]—there is a reciter reciting, "her ḥalizah is valid," there is a reciter reciting, "her ḥalizah is invalid." The one who said "her ḥalizah is valid," when it was cloth *impilia* and a leather shoe, the one who said "her ḥalizah is invalid," when it was leather *impilia* and a leather shoe.

There is a reciter reciting: one may go out in *impilia* on the Day of Atonement. And there is a reciter reciting: one may not go out in *impilia*. Said Rav Hisda: The one who said "one may go out" [spoke] of cloth *impilia* and the one who said "one may not go out" [spoke] of leather *impilia*.

While it is possible that these divergences emerged independently and were joined here by the creator of the passage, it seems more likely, given their similarities, that they formed as a group or at least were gathered and reformulated in connection to each other. We could, for example, take as an indication of originality the fact that the divergence concerning the Day of Atonement is the only one with an attributed response, and postulate that the other divergences were created as a scholarly exercise by applying to the levirate rejection ceremony the same question about shoes.

In some cases, the possibility that the divergence was produced as a scholarly exercise is strongly suggested by the content of the teaching; consider the following example:

---

[122] See n. 65 above.

m. ʿEruvin 3:5

מתנה אדם על עירובו ואומ׳, "אם באו גוים מן המזרח, עירובי למערב, ואם באו מן המערב, עירובי למזרח".

A person may make conditions for his *ʿeruv*, saying: "If gentiles come from the east, my *ʿeruv* is towards the **west**, and if they come from the west, my *ʿeruv* is towards the **east**."

ʿEruvin 3:5 21b

אית תניי תני: במזרח. מאן דמר, "במזרח", אילין טקסיווטי. מאן דמר, "במערב", באילין רומאי.

There is a reciter reciting: "towards[123] the **east**." The one who said "towards the east," [speaks about] those garrison soldiers; the one who said, "towards the west," [speaks] about those Romans.

m. ʿEruvin 3:5

"בא חכם מן המזרח עירובי למזרח. בא מן המערב עירובי למערב".

"If a sage comes from the east my *ʿeruv* is towards the **east**, if he comes from the west my *ʿeruv* is towards the **west** . . . ."

ʿEruvin 3:5 21b

אית תניי תני: במערב. מאן דמר, "במערב", באילין חכימיא. מאן דמר, "במזרח"[124], ברגיל.

There is a reciter reciting: "towards the **west**." The one who said "<u>towards the west</u>," [speaks] about those sages [whom one might want to avoid]; the one who said, "<u>towards the east</u>," [speaks] about a [sage to whom] he is accustomed[125] [and whom he would like to meet].[126]

The Mishnah's teaching allows people to stipulate that their *ʿeruv*, the area in which they may walk and carry on the Sabbath, will extend in a particular direction depending on situations that developed after the Sabbath has entered. It gives two

---

[123] The text, here and in the next example, uses "in" rather than "towards" as the Mishnah text has it; I homogenized them in the translation for clarity.

[124] Switching the order of "מזרח" and "מערב" that appears in the manuscript, see below.

[125] My interpretation here differs from the one offered by Lieberman, "Emendations (F.)," 378–9, who argues that *ragil* refers to someone who holds an administrative position in the rabbinic academy, and because the *ragil* was in charge of fundraising, people would want to get away from him. The word *ragil* commonly describes in the Yerushalmi a person that someone is accustomed to or familiar with (see e.g. *Ber.* 1:2 3a); there is little evidence for the position to which Lieberman refers; and most importantly, there is no evidence for the idea that the *ragil* would be fundraising or that others might want to avoid him. See also the following note.

[126] Both MS Leiden and the Genizah fragment (T-S 16.326; Sussmann, *Ginze Yerushalmi*, 203) have first "the one who said 'towards the east'" and then "the one said 'towards the west.'" My emendation switches the order. The next line in the Yerushalmi, omitted in MS Leiden but found in the fragment, records R. Judah's ruling that if two sages arrived, and he is accustomed to one of them, he should go to that one, and if he is accustomed to both, he can choose (see also *t. ʿEr.* 3:1). It therefore seems more likely that the sage to whom one is accustomed would be the sage that one would want to greet.

examples: a stipulation about gentiles, whom one might want to escape, would mean the *'eruv* would extend in the direction away from the gentiles, such that if they come from the east the *'eruv* extends to the west and vice versa; and a stipulation about sages, whom one might want to honor by coming towards them, would mean the *'eruv* would extend in the direction from which they are coming, such that if they come from the east the *'eruv* extends towards the east.

The Talmud reports that there are alternative recitations of both teachings: in the first example, concerning gentiles, there is a reciter reciting that the *'eruv* should actually extend *towards* the gentiles rather than away from them; and similarly in the second example, concerning the sages, there is a reciter reciting that the *'eruv* should extend *away* from the sages rather than towards them. The Talmud responds to this divergence with its common strategy of positing that each of the alternative recitations addresses a different situation, and that therefore they are not contradictory. It explains that "our" recitation deals with gentiles one would want to escape, whereas the reciter who recited that the *'eruv* extends towards the gentiles was speaking of such gentiles one might seek to honor. Similarly, the Talmud posits, there are indeed sages one might want to advance towards, but also sages one might want to avoid, and the reciter who recited that the *'eruv* extends away from the sages had the latter kind in mind.

These divergences seem more like a scholastic exercise than genuine alternative recitations of this teaching. The point of the teaching is to contrast people you want to seek and people you want to run away from; it is very unlikely that such a teaching would employ "gentiles" as the paradigmatic example for people you seek and "sages" as the paradigmatic example of people you might want to flee. It is much more likely that these divergences were formulated as a scholastic exercise that switched the original teaching's assumptions, shifting the focus away from the specific examples to its underlying logic, while also entertainingly turning on its head the hierarchy between gentiles and sages in rabbinic literature.

Fabrication follows from function; divergences were imagined because they were useful for rabbinic scholarship. It was not, in any of these cases, *necessary* for the arguments made in these passages to be made through a discussion of a divergent text; but that is what makes them interesting and distinctive. Consider the following comparison between the two Talmuds:

m. Beẓah 4:7	
	ואין מלבנין את הרעפים לצלות עליהם.
And one may not heat the tiles in order to roast upon them [on a festival day].	
Beẓah 4:7 62b	b. Beẓah 33b–34a
אית תניי תני: מלבנין. ואית תניי תני. אין מלבנין. אמ' רב חסדא: מאן דאמ', "מלבנין". בבדוקים. ומאן דאמ', "אין מלבנין". בשאינן בדוקים.	"ואין מלבנין את הרעפים". מאי קא עביד? אמ' רבה בר בר חנה אמ' ר' יוחנן: הכא ברעפים חדשים עסקינן מפני שצריך לבודקן.

There is a reciter reciting: One may heat. There is a reciter reciting: One may **not** heat. Said Rav Hisda: The one who said "one may heat" [speaks] of examined [tiles], and the one who said "one may not heat" [speaks] of unexamined [tiles].	"And one may not heat the tiles." What is he doing [that is prohibited]? Rabbah b. b. Hannah said that R. Yohanan said: We are dealing here with new tiles, [and it is prohibited] since he needs to examine them [before heating them].

The Mishnah's prohibition on heating tiles on festival days for the purpose of roasting food is not clear, since labors of food preparation are generally permitted on such days. The Yerushalmi and the Bavli offer the same interpretation for this prohibition, positing that it applies only to tiles which require examination to see if they can withstand the heat, and since they might not—and therefore will not be used in the end for food preparation—their use is prohibited. What is interesting for our purposes is that while in the Bavli, the point is made as a direct interpretation of the Mishnah, in the Yerushalmi the point is made through a discussion of a divergent text. Here too we could consider the divergence fictional;[127] but either way, what we see here is how the analysis of textual divergences functions in constructing and presenting interpretive arguments which could have been made in a different way.

Conclusion

The rise of textual divergences as an object of rabbinic scholarly attention is a distinctly Amoraic development. Divergence characterized rabbinic literature from its earliest stages, but the passages studied here presented new kinds of divergences and new ways of reading them. Scholarly attention was expanded to variance in formulation, to differences that may imply but not explicitly state difference of opinion, and to differences that earlier literary patterns would not have been able to represent. More commonly, the comparison of recitations provided a new framework for understanding differences in legal position as textual in nature. Sometimes, we have seen, this idiom of textual difference was applied imprecisely—but that only shows us the centrality of this framework in Amoraic scholarship.

Amoraic scholars construed recitations as alternative attestations or presentations of the same teaching, much like Greek and Latin scholars compared copies or editions as attestations or presentations of the same text. But there are significant differences in the ways these traditions negotiated textual difference. In contrast with Greek and Latin philologists (and even more so, with their modern

---

[127] The mere omission of the negation would not result in a probable text, at least if the full teaching is as it appears in the Mishnah. See the discussion of similar passages at the end of Section 3 above.

counterparts), Amoraic scholars did not normally posit that textual divergences resulted from errors, and they rarely expressed preference or hierarchies among divergences. Instead, they preferred to see divergences on equal footing, considering them to reflect different opinions, interpretations, or applications. At the same time, these discussions construed each of these recitations as offering a partial perspective, as only one way to recite the teaching in question.

This chapter argued that this discourse of textual difference was not simply a response to facts about the transmission of rabbinic teachings. The fact that the sages did not comment on variants of the biblical text shows us that such comments do not inevitably accompany intensive textual study; the fact that they also did not do so with rabbinic teachings in the Tannaitic period shows us that scholarly attention to textual divergences is not an inevitable result of orality. Perhaps the best indication that Amoraic scholars did not just begrudgingly pursue the analysis of recitation divergences is that they occasionally fabricated them. The particular features of these discussions, such as their tendency to sustain both recitations rather than selecting between them, did not reflect the inherent stability of the Mishnah's text, as Epstein posited, nor was it an apologetic reflex; it reflected, rather, these scholars' interests and aims. Examining these discussions shows us a particular construction of textual difference, one which, in contrast with modern discussions of the same divergences, was not interested in the composition and transmission of a discrete historical "work," the Mishnah. Rather, Amoraic scholars pursued the analysis of textual divergence when they could mobilize it as a productive catalyst for a variety of interpretive aims. The result was an image of the rabbinic tradition as a body of texts reflected through a hundred shards of glass, none offering a full picture, but each equally significant and worthy of scholarly care.

7

It's Not Here

Emendations

Hananya b. Shilamya had the terrifying privilege of teaching the Mishnah to the son of the most prominent scholar of his generation, Rav. The Talmud records a story about one of these lessons, conducted, apparently, outside the family house:

'Eruvin 1:1 18d

חנניה בר שילמיא הוה יתיב מיתנא לחייה בריה דרב. אפיק רב רישיה מן כוותא. אמ׳ ליה: לית כן! אמ׳ ליה: ולא ניתנייה כך? אמ׳ ליה: אתניתיה[1] ואודעיה דלית כן.

Hananya b. Shilamya was sitting and reciting to Hiyya, Rav's son.

Rav stuck his head out the window. He said to him: It's not here!

He said to him: And shall I not recite it to him here?

He said to him: Recite it and inform him that it's not here.

Eavesdropping on the lesson his son was receiving, and hearing a certain bit of the text as it was presented by the teacher, Rav popped his head out of the window and corrected him: "it's not here." This phrase appears in scores of Talmudic passages to offer emendations of the Mishnah and other recited teachings. In this case it is directed, it seems, at a clause in *m. 'Eruvin* 1:1.[2] The Mishnah rules that an entryway to an alley that is wider than ten cubits must be narrowed down (e.g. using fences) in order to permit carrying items within that alley on the Sabbath.[3] It adds, however, the stipulation that if the entryway "has the shape of a doorway, it is not necessary to narrow it down."[4] Rav's windowed interjection relates to that stipulation clause, stating that it does not belong in this passage: "it's not here."

---

[1] MS Leiden: דתניתיה. The emendation follows Lieberman, *YK*, 227.

[2] Though the story is not specific about which part of the Mishnah Rav thought was "not here," it is evident from the rest of the discussion in the Talmud. The version of the story at *b. 'Er.* 2b suggests Rav told the teacher (there, Rav Judah) to recite "should" instead of "should not." The Halakhic outcome is the same, but the Yerushalmi imagines a different type of intervention: Rav explicitly instructs the recitation stays the same but the phrase "לית כאן" be added.

[3] On this passage in the Mishnah, see Fonrobert, "The Place of Shabbat," 440–3.

[4] מבויי שהוא גבוה עשרים אמה ימעט. ר׳ יהודה אומר: אינו צריך. הרחב מעשר אמות ימעט. אם יש לו צורת הפתח, אף על פי שהוא רחב מעשר אמות אינו צריך למעט.

Emendations of this kind were a newly acquired practice among Amoraic scholars. They appear neither in the Tannaitic engagement with rabbinic teachings nor in the sages' study of Scripture, but they are found in significant numbers in the Talmud, applying primarily to recited teachings.[5] The use of emendations introduced a different type of dynamic between text and interpreter. Interpretations of Scripture or of rabbinic teachings may stretch or limit the meaning of the text to the point that, at least from an outsider's perspective, the interpretation may amount to a rejection or blatant modification of the text. But even such far-reaching interpretations are not predicated on the idea that the text is faulty and needs correction. The interpreter accepts the text as it is and works with it to draw out (or in) the desired meaning. Emendations, in contrast, argue that the text as it has been received is wrong.

This chapter explores Amoraic emendations by examining instances of the phrase "it's not here," which introduces emendations in about sixty unique instances in the Talmud.[6] Thirty-seven of these apply to teachings which are included in the Mishnah. There are other phrases for emendations in the Yerushalmi—most notably, the phrase "thus is the recitation," in some of its instances;[7] I chose to examine "it's not here" since it introduces emendations more uniformly.

The most thorough study of Talmudic emendations to date appears, much like with the divergences examined in the previous chapter, in Epstein's *Introduction to the Mishnaic Text*. While Epstein acknowledged that such emendations appear in the Talmuds, he insisted that many of them, and in some sense *all* of them, are not actually emendations, and that they were intended to dispute the rulings in the teachings on which they comment rather than correct these teachings' texts. Epstein meant this in two senses. First, in terms of the reason for the emendations: "the emendations of Amoraic scholars (at least the early ones) . . . are never actual emendations, but rather changes—if one may say that—of composition [or: redaction], the reason and source of which is dissent of opinion."[8] In other words, these statements express a different opinion about the matter at hand rather than claiming that the text is erroneous. Second, Epstein argued, in many cases the intended effect was not a correction of the text but rather a ruling or interpretation of the law.[9] Lieberman agreed with Epstein on this

---

[5] We also find them, though more rarely and in different form, applying to Amoraic teachings; see Or. 1:9 61c (par. 'A. Z. 3:5 43a), where R. Hananya offers, in the name of R. Phinehas, a "corrected" ("מתקנתה") formulation of the dispute between Kahana and R. Yohanan.

[6] See lists in Assis, *Concordance*, 856–9. I discuss instances where the phrase does not introduce emendations below, nn. 12–14.

[7] On "thus is the recitation" (כיני מתניתא), see Epstein, *IMT*, 441–508 who argues the phrase only sometimes offer emendations; Goldberg, "An Interpretive Remark," argues it rarely, if ever, does so. While this phrase does have a variety of functions, many of its instances do seem to offer emendations, especially in light of considerations raised in this chapter.

[8] Epstein, *IMT*, 218. I translated "עריכה" here as "composition" in light of Epstein's comments in the beginning of his book. His point that these are not emendations of errors but rather rejections of the teaching's position is made clearly also ibid., 205.

[9] Epstein, ibid., 205, 262, 266, and other places.

244 THE RISE OF TALMUD

issue.[10] My discussion below suggests that these judgments were in part motivated by imposing modern philological standards on Amoraic scholars, and that they did not sufficiently appreciate the particular form of Amoraic emendations. In his entry on the phrase "it's not here" in *The Terminology of the Palestinian Talmud*, Leib Moscovitz argued against Epstein's idea that the phrase can simply indicate an interpretation of the text, but he also posited, similarly to Epstein, that in some cases the phrase can signal a rejection of the *content*, rather than the wording, of the text on which it comments.[11]

It is true that "it's not here" does not only introduce emendations in the Talmud. Just as we have seen with other phrases and terms, it appears with a certain degree of inconsistency. Sometimes, for example, we find the phrase indicating that a certain principle or interpretation is not applicable in a particular case, without invoking the wording of a teaching at all.[12] In other cases, the phrase does seem to invoke the teaching's wording, but if only those words that are "not here" are removed, the resulting text is senseless.[13] And there are still other instances that, for various reasons, cannot be read straightforwardly as emendations.[14] No other consistent terminological sense, however, emerges from these passages; they simply show us a less specific or non-technical use of this phrase.

The wording of the phrase, "it's not here," and of its longer form, "there is no *x* here but *y*," suggest a reference to a text, in contrast with phrases such as "this is not so" or "and this is not the law" found elsewhere in rabbinic literature. This phrase, then, presents evidence for the development of a distinctive language for emendations among Amoraic scholars. And while the phrase itself may, like all Talmudic terminology, reflect a later formulation, analysis of the comments it introduces also suggests they are emendations: in the large majority of instances, one could reformulate the teaching in question according to the emendation and the result would

---

[10] See Lieberman, *TK*, 2.498 and *TK*, 8.820; the passages Lieberman analyzes in those places are discussed below.

[11] Moscovitz, *Terminology*, 344–5; see also idem, "Women Are (Not) Trustworthy," 128. Moscovitz offers three examples for this sense of the phrase: the instance from '*Er.* with which this chapter opens, discussed more below; an instance in *Sheq.* 6:4 50a (for which see below in the last section); and the instance in *A. Z.* 5:6 45a, for which see n. 13 below. I agree with Moscovitz that the term "is generally used to reject the contents of the statement and not only their wording" (ibid.), but comments employing the phrase normally bind content and wording, and in several cases the emphasis is on wording rather than legal position (more below).

[12] See *Ma'as.* 2:5 49d, *Pes.* 2:2 29a, *Yev.* 14:2 14b, *Yev.* 16:7 16b, *Ket.* 9:7 33b, and perhaps *Ter.* 4:3 42d.

[13] See e.g. "it's not here" comments which negate a distinction that is essential to the teaching's construction, *Meg.* 1:10 72c, *Yev.* 10:1 10d, and '*A. Z.* 5:6 45a (and see the discussion of a similar issue with recitation divergences in Section 3 of the previous chapter). The Yerushalmi raises the issue of the resulting text only once, at *B. B.* 3:3 14a; see Epstein, *IMT*, 217–18. Occasionally, "it's not here" comments seem to aim at a specific element of the teaching but do not use the same word that appears in the teaching (see e.g. *Shab.* 7:2 10c, discussed below).

[14] In two instances the phrase relates to a previous emendation that has been presented (see the second instances of the phrase in *M. S.* 2:1 53a [par. *Shab.* 9:4 12a, *Yom.* 8:1 44d, *Ta'an.* 1:6 64c] and *Or.* 1:2 61a). Five comments in a single passage at *Shab.* 11:2 13a present the primary examples where "it's not here" applies to recited teachings but presents interpretations rather than emendations.

be sensible and grammatical; and we shall see below that "it's not here" comments were motivated by textual considerations and aimed to correct the text. Such comments are attributed to some of the earliest Amoraic scholars, such as Rav and Samuel; the scholar whose name appears most commonly with "it's not here" is Rabbi Yohanan.[15] While there are certainly cases where the Talmud records an alternative solution alongside the emendation, we do not find in the Talmud resistance to "it's not here" emendations *qua* emendations.[16]

1. Emendations as paratextual comments

In the story with which this chapter opened, Rav's interjection is followed by a dialogue between Rav and his son's teacher: the teacher asks Rav whether he should not recite the clause to his son; Rav replies that he should. This instruction that the clause should remain in the recitation has led modern scholars to conclude that here and elsewhere, the phrase "it's not here" does not introduce an emendation to the text, but rather a rejection of the law in question.[17] There are, however, good indications that Rav's comment is, in fact, an emendation. Hananya, after all, understands it that way when he asks, "should I not recite it?" And while Rav does tell Hananya to recite it, he also tells him that he should inform his son that the clause is not here.

Rather than showing us that the phrase does not indicate an emendation, this story teaches us something significant about the form of emendations in Amoraic scholarship. Textual criticism, in both its ancient and modern forms, often marks emendations paratextually, commenting on or marking the "wrong" text, rather than silently producing only the "correct" text. Corrected editions of ancient texts started not from scratch but with a particular copy of the text, on which the critic could make certain markings. When Zenodutus (fl. third century BCE) prepared his edition of Homer, and thought a line was spurious, he marked it in his edition in various ways. Sometimes, he instructed those who would consult his edition that the line should not be written; but he is also credited with inventing a way of marking a line as spurious without rejecting it outright, with a sign termed *obelos*, a horizontal stroke to the left of the line. The line could thus be reproduced, but with a mark that indicated it was problematic.[18] Fausto Montana argued that this creation of an intermediate category between rejection and acceptance of

---

[15] *Pace* Epstein's distinctions (*IMT*, 214, 353) between "early" and "late" scholars. See Sussmann, *Oral Law*, 279 n. 73.

[16] A possible exception is at *Ket.* 4:10 29a–b, but the passage itself requires significant emendations to make even basic sense, so any reconstruction would be of limited reliability.

[17] Epstein, *IMT*, 205 argues it is "a paradigmatic case" from which we can infer that many instances of this phrase "are not emendations of the Mishnah ... but rather a rejection of the Mishnah's legal validity." See also there, 245 and 306, and Moscovitz, *Terminology*, 345.

[18] Montanari, "Homeric Philology," 121–2. See also idem, "Ekdosis," 652–3.

the traditional text allowed the critic to record his judgment without precluding the possibility for other critics to form an opinion of their own—and by doing so prefigured the apparatus of modern critical editions.[19] According to Franco Montanari, Zenodotus' successors, Aristophanes and Aristarchus, abandoned outright deletions altogether and adopted the *obelos* as "the prime tool for expressing cautious doubts on parts of the text," inventing also other signs to indicate a range of textual problems.[20] Closer to the Talmud in place and time, Origen tells us that in his critical examination of his Septuagint copies, he was "not so audacious" so as to remove passages completely, but rather marked them with a similar set of critical signs;[21] Jerome followed with a similar practice.[22]

While those paratextual features rely on writing as a medium, Rav's instruction to Hananya provides an oral parallel to these features: recite the text as you received it, but let the student know that the clause "is not there"—a phrase that states a judgment about the text, not a prescription to do something with the text (like "do not write" or "do not recite"). This mode of presentation had several advantages. The continued transmission of the text as it was received could show that the emended text does not reflect ignorance of the received text but rather a response to it, anticipating objections from those who know the text as commonly received. If, say, Rav told his son's teacher that indeed he should *not* recite that qualification clause, and the son subsequently heard about that clause from his friends as they all passionately discussed their Mishnaic lessons one evening, his conclusion might be that his teacher was ignorant of that part of the Mishnah, and that his instruction was lacking. But if that clause was recited alongside a comment that it does not belong there, the son could tell his friends: yes, I have heard about your qualification clause, but my prominent scholar father said that "it is not here." On the scholarly level, this format marked emendations as opinions or arguments, which allowed other scholars to contest them—and indeed several emendations in the Talmud are contested.[23] By making the scholarly process visible, it also provided scholars with the opportunity to display erudition and judgment through emendation. Finally, such marking exposed students to emendation as a type of commentary: by reciting the teaching with the emendation, Hananya was teaching Rav's son not just something about the passage in question, but also about the possibility that occasionally, teachings in the Mishnah could and should be corrected.

Some of these considerations—in particular, those which pertain to the Halakhic rather than textual question of preserving the text as transmitted—are

---

[19] Montana, "Hellenistic Scholarship," 104. See also Dubischar, "Typology," 551, on "non-destructive criticism."
[20] Montanari, "Homeric Philology," 124.
[21] Origen, *Commentary on Matthew*, 15.14 (trans. Heine 204).
[22] On Jerome, see Letteney, *Christianization*, 160–3.
[23] See *Kil.* 4:4 29b, *Ter.* 11:8 48a (first instance), *Pes.* 2:5 29b (par. *Meg.* 1:11 72d), *Meg.* 3:1 74a, *'A. Z.* 5:6 45a.

raised explicitly in the Talmud, though in a passage addressing a different subject. A discussion at *Shevi.* 1:1 33a concerns prohibitions of agricultural work in the months leading to the sabbatical year. These prohibitions are discussed extensively in Tannaitic compilations, but the Tosefta and the Talmud know of a decree by Rabban Gamaliel (the son of R. Judah the Patriarch) which abrogated them. An anonymous comment in the Talmud asks why the Mishnah's text was not changed to reflect this decree. The passage records three answers: subsequent generations may wish to reverse the decree; like Scripture, the Mishnah can and should record even sections that may no longer be followed in practice; the inclusion of the abrogated law ensures the transmission of the knowledge that it was rejected, so if someone adduces the tradition of the abrogated law in the future, it will be common knowledge that the law is indeed on the books, but it is no longer to be followed.[24] While "it's not here" emendations are different from the notation of an abrogating decree, their commentarial form achieved similar effects to those the Yerushalmi attributes in this passage to the preservation of the abrogated law alongside notation of the decree.

There are good indications that similar considerations were at play in the transmission of Roman legal texts. James Zetzel argued that Roman philological practice, especially its commentarial form, originated in a legal context, since legal texts could not have been changed: even editorial suggestions, therefore, had to be made separately.[25] Kathleen McNamee observed that beginning in the reign of Theodosius—corresponding to the time in which the Talmud was compiled or immediately after it—books were produced with wide margins, deliberately designed to be annotated. McNamee argued that this practice originated in the change of the language of legal instruction from Latin to Greek and its effect on the shape of legal scholarship, but stressed it was quickly adopted in other disciplines.[26] Mark Letteney has recently proposed that this format was part of a new "order of books," originating in Christian practices of theological argumentation which resulted in an increasingly "aggregative" mode of composition, in which texts included even positions, versions, or laws which their authors or compilers rejected.

Letteney's argument on the *Theodosian Code* is particularly important for our purpose. It shows how commentary could negotiate tensions between the legal and scholastic functions or conceptions of the text, as well as the relation of these functions to the preservation of a particular version. He points out that as the *Code* itself states, it included, to begin with, laws which had already been invalidated, trusting its intended audience of "more industrious people" to discern, through their "scholarly effort," such supervened laws.[27] While the Roman Senate specifically

---

[24] See Mazeh, "Uprooting," on this passage and the way it adapts the discussion on inclusion of minority positions in *m. Ed.* 1:5–6.
[25] Zetzel, *Critics*, 25–7.
[26] McNamee, "History of Scholia."
[27] Quotations from the *Theodosian Code*, 1.1.5.

prohibited annotation on public copies of the *Code*, other copies were produced in a format that was designed for personal annotation. Letteney shows how such annotation specifically reflected the discernment its compilers envisaged: the fifth-century commentary, *Summaria antiqua codicis Theodosiani*, added in the margins of a sixth-century copy of the code, frequently presented comments such as "this is no longer in force."[28] These annotations, Letteney argues, participated in a broad culture which increasingly relied on paratextual instruments, including Jerome's use of the *obelos* in textual criticism. While his argument may apply to a somewhat later period—depending on how we date the Talmud—his point about paratextual instruments and aggregative texts illuminates Amoraic practice at the very least because rabbinic textuality is also aggregative.

The Talmud's discussion of the abrogated law in *Shevi'it* and the consideration of Roman legal commentary show us the significance of paratextual or commentarial forms in legal contexts specifically. But as we have seen, such forms characterized ancient textual criticism more broadly. "It's not here" comments, I argued at the beginning of this chapter, were formulated primarily as comments about text, not the law, to the degree that these dimensions can be distinguished where the text in question is also the source of the law. The subsequent sections examine the way these comments addressed textual issues, even when they were bound with legal interests and implications.

2. Emendations and alternative attestations

The majority of emendations in the Talmud do not spell out their reasons.[29] Only a minority of Amoraic emendations are supported by recited teachings which attest to the text for which the emendation argues.[30] Given that no reason for the emendation is usually given, we could have suggested that such alternative teachings do stand behind these emendations; that is, that the statement "it's not here" means "we have a recited teaching in which this word or phrase does not appear." But that seems unlikely. First, because there are some occasions where the Talmud does support an emendation with an alternative recited teaching, and it therefore seems that when such support was available, it was provided. Second, as we have seen in the previous chapter, when Amoraic scholars encountered two alternative recitations they were usually reluctant to choose between them. As far as our

---

[28] Letteney, *Christianization*, 108–11, 163–6, and 207–8.
[29] Epstein, *IMT*, 441.
[30] Among "it's not here" emendations, I count seven resulting in a text that is also documented in a recited teaching quoted in the passage (I note first the three passages discussed below): *Sheq.* 6:4 50a, *Meg.* 2:3 73a, *Git.* 4:8 46a, *Ber.* 1:1 3a; *Ter.* 11:8 48a (second instance), *Shab.* 11:1 12d, and *Ned.* 11:3 42c. There are other instances, of course, where a recited teaching supports the *argument* behind the emendation (see e.g. *Shevi.* 9:6 39a), but that is different than choosing between two extant versions.

evidence goes, then, it seems that multiplicity of attested texts is not what motivated Amoraic emendations, nor was examination of such texts a regular part of the method by which emendations were proposed.

Modern textual criticism prefers emendations that are grounded in extant documents.[31] That was the case with some ancient scholars as well. Galen, for example, repeatedly criticized audacious scholars who changed the text without manuscript support; he emphasized the importance of ancient copies, in part because they were relatively free of such misleading "corrections"; and he preferred ancient versions even when they were difficult or seemed to make less sense.[32] But this approach was not shared by all ancient scholars. Historians of Homeric scholarship debate whether the most prominent Homeric critic in antiquity, Aristarchus, based his emendations on evidence from manuscripts. In her recent comprehensive discussion of this question, Francesca Schironi concludes that while Aristarchus "certainly could (and did) look at manuscripts" in making his edition, the evidence consistently shows that his "main criteria for editorial choices were internal reasons . . . and not the fact that a reading was attested in the majority of manuscripts or in particularly authoritative copies."[33] And we have seen, in the previous chapter, how while Origen recognizes that corrections without documentary basis may present a problem, he nonetheless suggests them based on his judgment, appealing merely to the general corruption in the copies.

The debate about Aristarchus is instructive for our purposes not just for what it tells us about ancient textual criticism, but also for what it shows about its modern students. Montanari, for example, writes that "the idea that the Alexandrian philologists offered only arbitrary conjectures, without any documentary basis and without comparison among copies, has had a number of supporters . . . this tendency . . . leads *recta via* to a (quite unfair) underestimation of the value of the work performed by the Alexandrians."[34] Modern descriptions of ancient scholarly practice, then, were bound with judgments about its quality that reflected the preferences of modern philology. This may be the case, too, with the reluctance of modern Talmudists to see the Talmud's "it's not here" statements as emendations. Lieberman, for example, comments on one such emendation: "it seems clear to me that they did not mean to emend the teaching against all [extant] versions," echoing Lieberman's own methodological principle of avoiding such emendations as much as possible.[35] In other words, perhaps one of the reasons that Epstein and Lieberman resisted reading Amoraic emendations as emendations was that,

---

[31] On the transition in early modern philology from emendations based on conjecture to those based on documented texts, see Grafton, *Scaliger*, 27–8 and 32.
[32] Roselli, "Galen's Practice of Textual Criticism."
[33] Schironi, *Best of the Grammarians*, 74–5.
[34] Montanari, "Homeric Philology," 128. For the opposite position, see West, *Studies in the Text*, 36.
[35] Lieberman, *TK*, 2.498: "ונ״ל ברור שלא כיוונו להגיה את הברייתא כנגד כל הנוסחאות". Compare Lieberman's own methodological statement, ibid., 1.*22: "ורק במקומות מועטים מאד הגהנו את הספר כנגד כל הנוסחאות."

from the perspective of their own twentieth-century standards, such emendations constituted "bad philology", and they wanted to save Amoraic scholars from that charge when it was possible.[36] But the fact that Amoraic emendations do not fit modern standards for emendation does not mean they were not emendations, and again, the fact that only a minority of "it's not here" emendations are supported by attested texts places them in line with emendations made in several ancient philological traditions.

The recognition that Amoraic emendations are neither motivated nor supported by extant texts can also help us understand how the emendations examined in this chapter relate to the discussion of recitation divergences studied in the previous chapter. From the perspective of most modern (and some ancient) configurations of textual criticism, the search for the correct text is bound with the existence of its multiple forms, both in the sense that multiple attestations motivate that search and in the sense that emendations are normally supported by such attestations. From this perspective, emendations seem to stand in contrast with the Talmud's upholding of multiple recitations. But since Amoraic emendations do not normally respond to or engage textual difference, the two sets of comments are not as opposed as it may at first seem. The notion that certain recitations are incorrect does not contradict the notion that certain teachings have multiple legitimate recitations. The difference between the two discussions is a difference of occasion and interest: Amoraic scholars invoked multiple recitations in those cases when they could construe them as equally valid; emendations were offered when a recitation was considered, for the reasons examined below, to be erroneous or imprecise. In both cases, these comments were driven by scholarly utility and function.

3. Why emend?

If emendations were not motivated by textual difference, what problems brought Amoraic scholars to emend the text? Epstein, we have seen, posited that Talmudic emendations stem from disagreements about the law, and this certainly seems correct in many cases. Take, for example, Rav's interjection in his son's lesson: it may well have been motivated by disagreement with the Mishnah's qualification clause, that is, by the position that even if an opening has a "shape of a doorway," one nonetheless must narrow it down to allow carrying in the alleyway. Later on in the passage, R. Yose argues (with the phrase *ke-da'ateh*) that Rav's emendation represents a Babylonian opinion: because Babylonian sages defined "the shape of a doorway" much less strictly than their western colleagues, they considered it less

---

[36] See Epstein's disparaging remarks, *IMT*, 353, on those instances which he does consider emendations.

effective in changing the legal space and therefore thought the qualification clause is "not here."[37]

There are, however, quite a few emendations in the Talmud that cannot be interpreted as resulting from a difference in legal opinion, but rather seem to be motivated by the notion that the text is erroneous. Consider the following example:

m. Megillah 2:4

הכל כשירים לקרוא את המגילה חוץ מחרש שוטה וקטן.

Everyone is qualified to read out the [Esther] scroll [and discharge both themselves and others from the obligation to read it out], except for **the deaf**, the mentally incapacitated, and the minor.

Megillah 2:4 73b (par. *Berakhot* 2:3 4d and *Terumot* 1:2 40c)

רב חסדא אמ׳. לית כאן "חרש". באשגרת לשון היא מתנית׳.

Rav Hisda said: **There is no "deaf" here.** This recited teaching is [recited this way] on account of a slip of the tongue.

The Mishnah accepts recitation of the Esther scroll from everyone except someone who is deaf, mentally incapacitated, or a minor. In the Talmud, Rav Hisda says "the deaf" does not belong here. He does not explain why he thinks so, but he seems to rely on the assumption, made explicit elsewhere in the Mishnah, that "everywhere the sages speak of a deaf person—[they mean] someone who can neither hear nor speak" (*m. Terumot* 1:2). According to this definition, it makes no sense to say a deaf person is not qualified to read the Esther scroll out loud—he cannot speak at all! Rather, Rav Hisda says, the Mishnah features a slip of the tongue: "the deaf, the mentally incapacitated, and the minor" are often mentioned together,[38] and in this case the deaf was wrongly included out of habit.

Rav Hisda's comment does not stem from his disagreement with the law the Mishnah presents. From his perspective, he is not applying a particular interpretation or approach to a legal or other issue with which someone can disagree. He is certainly not ruling, as opposed to the Mishnah, that a deaf person *may* read out the Esther scroll. Rather, Rav Hisda seems to be stating that the text as we have it makes no sense, that it must be an error.[39] While there are no other cases

---

[37] Vidas, "Place of Torah," 57–8.
[38] e.g. *m. 'Er.* 3:2, *m. R. H.* 3:8, *m. Git.* 2:5.
[39] Epstein, *IMT*, 355, offers two options: either Rav Hisda refers to a slip of the tongue by the professional reciter, in which case he intends to emend the error, or he means the slip was by the sage who formulated this teaching, in which case he only means to interpret the Mishnah. This analysis reflects the problem with Epstein's treatment of emendations in general: it is preconceptions about the authority of the Mishnah, rather than the nature of the comment, which determines whether he considers a comment to be an emendation. As I noted in the previous chapter, there is little evidence for the position of the professional reciter in the Yerushalmi; and while Rav Hisda indeed explains why the Mishnah mentions "deaf," he also argues that this mention is "not here."

in the Talmud where a similar explanation of "slip of a tongue" is offered (despite the impression one might get from a certain medieval commentator),[40] the same reasoning seems to underlie several other instances in which "it's not here" is applied to items in a list or a coupling.[41]

Earlier in the same chapter in the Talmud, we find another emendation that seems to argue the text is mistaken:

m. Megillah 2:3

בן עיר שהלך ליכרך ובן כרך שהלך לעיר. אם עתיד לחזור למקומו קורא במקומו. ואם לאו קורא עמהן.

[Town-dwellers are obligated to read the Esther scroll on the fourteenth of the month of Adar; city-dwellers read it on the fifteenth.] **A town-dweller who went to a city**, or a city-dweller who went to a town—if he is going to return home, he reads at home; and if [he is] not [returning home], he reads with them [i.e. the people with whom he is now].

Megillah 2:3 73a–b

ניחא בן כרך שהלך לעיר, שזמנו מואחר. בן עיר שהלך לכרך—ואין זמנו מוקדם?

אמ' ר' יודן: לית כאן "בן עיר שהלך לכרך". ותניי דבית ר' כן: בן כרך שהלך לעיר.

אמ' ר' יוסי: אית[42] כאן. בעתיד להשתקע עמהן.

It is all right concerning the city-dweller who went to the town, for his [reading] time is later [so if he was in the town on the fourteenth, he does not need to read with the town-dwellers that day but rather can read the scroll when he is back home in the city on the fifteenth]. [But] a town-dweller who went to the city—is his time not earlier [how can we say he can read when he returns home to his town, if townsmen have already read the scroll]?

Said R. Yudan: **There is no "a town-dweller who went to a city" here**. And [those] of the House of Rabbi [Judah the Patriarch] recited so: "A city-dweller who went to a town."

Said R. Yose: There is ["a town-dweller who went to a city"] here. [The teaching refers] to [a person] who plans to settle among them.

---

[40] Meiri (on *b. R. H.* 9b) implies he had something like Rav Hisda's comments before him along with "it's not here" at *Or.* 1:2 61a. But "slip of the tongue" does not appear in any extant version of that passage—see Lieberman, *TK*, 2.498 n. 5. It seems more likely it was introduced here by Meiri himself, who liked the phrase and used it frequently (see his discussions at *b. Pes.* 28b and *b. Yev.* 83a).

[41] See e.g. *Or.* 1:2 61a (and the previous note), *Shab.* 6:1 7d, *Shab.* 7:2 10c (discussed below), *Pes.* 1:1 27a, and *Yev.* 13:2 13d.

[42] Correcting "אוף."

The Mishnah, as the Talmud understands it, rules that a town-dweller, who was in a city during the time he was obligated to read out the Esther scroll (on Adar 14th), may read with the city-dwellers (on Adar 15th) unless he plans to return home, in which case he can read with the members of his town in their time. R. Yudan says that the reference to the town-dweller "is not here." While he does not spell out his reasoning, the objection recorded in the Talmud just prior to the emendation suggests, again, that the Mishnah is nonsensical: if the town-dweller was not in the town on the 14th, he had already missed the reading, and we cannot say that he can skip the city reading on the 15th in anticipation of the town's reading on the 14th. Here too, the issue is not a disagreement about the law: R. Yudan is not saying that the town-dweller may not participate in the town's reading, or that his participation would be invalid; he points out that since such a reading had already passed, the Mishnah's formulation projects an impossible reality, by sloppily applying the same stipulation to the city-dweller and the town-dweller. R. Yose sustains the Mishnah's formulation not by adopting its legal position but by offering a new interpretation of its wording, saying that the Mishnah's point is not about whether or not the person plans to return home on time to read the scroll, but rather whether the person intends to relocate. Here, too, then, "it's not here" concerns not a different legal position but the idea that the text as we have it is faulty. Another example comes from *Gittin*:

m. Gittin 4:8

המוציא את אשתו משם אילונית—ר' יהודה או': לא יחזיר. וחכמ' אומ': יחזיר. נישאת לאחר והיו לה בנים והיא תובעת כתובתה—אמ' ר' יהודה: אומ' לה, "שתיקותיך יפה ליך מידיבוריך".

If someone divorced his wife on account of her being an *aylonit* [i.e. of intersex status and unable to bear children]—R. Judah says he may not re-marry her [and the divorce is final], and the sages say he may re-marry her.

If she married another person and she had children and demands her *ketubah* money [saying that after all, she does not have *aylonit* status since she was able to have children, and therefore she deserves the *ketubah* like any divorced woman]—**said R. Judah: He may tell her, "your silence is better for you than your speech."** [He may threaten her that he will invalidate the divorce, since it was premised on the wrong assumption that she was unable to conceive, and if he does so her second marriage may become invalid and her children declared illegitimate.]

Gittin 4:8 46a

"ר' יהודה או': לא יחזיר", ואת אמר כך? אמ' ר' יוחנן: לית כאן "ר' יהודה" אלא "ר' מאיר". ותני כן משום ר' מאיר: אומ' לה, "שתיקותיך יפה מדיבוריך".

"R. Judah says he may not re-marry," and you say this [that R. Judah also says the husband may threaten the wife that he will invalidate the divorce]? Said R. Yohanan: **There is no "R. Judah" here but "R. Meir."** And it was recited so in the name of R. Meir: He may say to her, "Your silence is better than your speech."

An anonymous comment raises a difficulty in the Mishnah. It cannot be that R. Judah says both that the divorce is final and that the man may threaten that he will invalidate the divorce: someone who believes the divorce is final cannot also mention the possibility of its invalidation. To be sure, there are other ways of solving this difficulty, such as positing that R. Judah did not mean that the divorce is final in every situation, but such solutions are not recorded in the Talmud here. Instead, R. Yohanan resolves the problem by emending "R. Judah" to "R. Meir."[43] Here too the emendation is not motivated by a different legal position but by the sense that the text, as we have it, is wrong because it attributes to the same sage statements that cannot logically coexist.

Inconsistency, more broadly construed, is the issue behind a significant number of emendations in the Talmud.[44] In *'Eruvin*, R. Yohanan again emends "R. Judah" to "R. Meir" because a position by R. Judah about reading a long scroll on the top of a roof seems to contradict his principle regarding the use of airspace on the Sabbath. In *Terumot*, he emends a teaching from *Bava Batra* so that the Mishnah presents a consistent approach to oil that was left over in a jar; and in *Megillah*, he offers an emendation to resolve what seems like contradictory presentations of disputes on the selling of synagogues. Another emendation is based on the observation that a case which, in tractate *Yevamot*, is defined as an uncertain case of divorce, seems to be defined in tractate *Gittin* as a case of divorce that, at least in retrospect, is accepted.[45] Even when inconsistency is not marked as a problem, it may still underlie the emendation; consider the following:

m. *Terumot* 10:10

כל הנכבשין זה עם זה מותרים אלא עם החסית.

Any [unconsecrated produce] **pickled** together [with priest's-share produce] is permitted, except for [produce pickled] with allium.

Terumot 10:10 47b

אמ' ר' יוחנן. לית כאן "נכבשין" אלא "נשלקין". כבוש כרותח[46] הוא.

---

[43] Kahana, *Repairing the World*, 437–41.
[44] In addition to the examples noted above, see also *Ber.* 1:1 3a (bringing m. *Ber.* 1:1 into conformity with m. *Pes.* 9:10), *Ter.* 1:8 41a (correcting m. *'Ed.* 2:5 according to m. *Ter.* 1:8), and *Shab.* 2:5 5a (perhaps allowing for the concluding clause of the teaching to stand in harmony with the middle clause).
[45] *'Er.* 10:3 26b, *Ter.* 11:8 48a (first instance), *Meg.* 3:1 74a, and *Yev.* 3:8 5a (par. *Git.* 9:4 50b).
[46] Correcting "ברותה," a graphic error.

Said R. Yohanan: **There is no "pickled" here** but rather "heated in water." Pickled is like boiled.

The Mishnah in *Terumot* presents a series of rulings about whether the consecrated status of priest's-share produce expands to unconsecrated produce that is processed with it. It makes distinctions about the types of process (boiling, pickling, heating in water) as well as about the types of liquid or produce. This teaching presents a general rule about pickling: with the exception of allium, pickling priest's-share produce with unconsecrated produce does *not* expand the sacred status of the former to the latter; therefore, unconsecrated produce that was pickled with priest's-share produce may be eaten by non-priests. This general rule seems to contradict an earlier ruling which prohibits to non-priests unconsecrated olives that were pickled with priest's-share olives or brine in certain cases (*m. Terumot* 10:7). While the contradiction between the general rule about pickling and the earlier ruling about olives is not mentioned by the Yerushalmi, R. Yohanan emends the general rule in *m. Terumot* 10:10, so that it refers to heating in water rather than pickling. Following the emendation is a statement that pickling is like boiling, that is, a process in which the sacred status of priest's-share produce does expand. Epstein reads this as the motive for the emendation: since R. Yohanan considered pickling like boiling, he emended the Mishnah accordingly.[47] But it seems likely that like other examples noted above, this emendation was motivated at least in part by the apparent contradiction in the Mishnah.

We find other cases where, even though a Halakhic motivation or consequence is certainly present, it is also bound with concern for textual precision or removal of errors. Consider the following example:

m. Miqva'ot 9:1

אילו חוצצין באדם: חוטי צמר חוטי פשתן והרצועות שבראשי הבנות. ר' יהודה אומ': של
צמר ושל שיער אינן חוצצין מפני שהמים באים בהן.

[For immersion to be valid, nothing may separate the body of the person immersing from the water, such as clothing]. The following separate [the body from the water] in the case of a person [wearing them, thus rendering the person's immersion invalid]: threads of wool, threads of flax, and the ribbons on the heads of girls. R. Judah says: [threads] of wool and **of hair** do not separate, as the water runs through them.

Shabbat 6:1 7d

שמואל אמ': לית כאן "שלשיער" על דעתיה דר' יהודה, אלא שלצמר. הא ששיער דברי הכל
אין חוצצין.

---

[47] Epstein, *IMT*, 262.

Samuel said: **There is no "of hair" here** in the opinion of R. Judah, but only "of wool." Thus [threads] of hair, according to everyone, do not separate [the body from the water].

The Mishnah presents a dispute between an anonymous position and R. Judah. The anonymous position states that threads of wool and flax, as well as ribbons, count as barriers between a person's body and the immersion water, and therefore wearing them disqualifies the immersion; R. Judah says that threads of wool and hair do not count as barriers. Samuel's argument, in the Talmud, is that "threads of hair" does not belong in R. Judah's statement. He does not offer a reason for this argument, but a close reading of the Mishnah suggests such a reason. The anonymous position, with which R. Judah seems to dispute, mentions threads of wool but no threads of hair. Samuel seems to conclude from this—and perhaps also from the fact that the Mishnah does not mention threads of hair in a similar list in tractate *Shabbat* (6:1), that R. Judah and the anonymous position do not dispute concerning threads of hair.

It is true that Samuel's statement has a clear and explicitly stated Halakhic implication, that threads of hair are not under dispute and that everyone agrees that immersions with them are valid. But this position in itself does not necessitate an emendation: given that the anonymous position in the Mishnah does not mention threads of hair, Samuel could have made the same point by simply clarifying the scope of the dispute. The Bavli records a similar statement, attributed to the same Samuel, which lacks the emendation:

b. Shabbat 57b (MS Budapest)

אמ׳ רב נחמן אמ׳ שמואל: מודים חכמי׳ לר׳ יהודה בחוטי שער.

Said Rav Nahman: Said Samuel: The sages concede to R. Judah with respect to threads of hair.

The Yerushalmi may end in the same place, in terms of the law, but the path it takes is different. When the statement in the Yerushalmi argues that the words "of hair" do not belong in R. Judah's statement, it aims not only to assert that threads of hair are not in dispute. It is also concerned with textual precision: if "threads of hair" are not disputed, then it is redundant for R. Judah's statement to mention them. This emendation is predicated on the idea that the teaching, in its correct form, must be precisely formulated, attributing to the Mishnah the same type of textual economy the sages attributed to Scripture;[48] at the same time, and in contrast with the way the sages approached Scripture, it considers the extant version of the teaching to be flawed.

---

[48] See next chapter.

The following passage similarly combines legal and textual considerations:

m. Gittin 3:7

המלוה מעות את הכהן ואת הלוי ואת העני להיות מפריש עליה מחלקן—מפריש עליהן בחזקת שהן קיימין, ואינו חושש שמא מת כהן או לוי או שמא העשיר העני. מתו, צריך ליטול רשות מן היורשים.

If someone lent money to a priest, a Levite, or a poor person, so that he may separate against it their share [i.e. deducting the sum of the loan money from what the person needs to offer as priest's share, the Levite's share or the poor's tithe], he may separate against it [in this way] with the assumption that they are alive, **and he does not [need to] worry that [in the meantime] the priest or the Levite may have died, or that the poor person may have become rich** [which would invalidate this deduction, since the lender might need to offer a priest's or Levite's share to a living priest or Levite and the poor's tithe to a person who is still poor]. If they died [and he was informed], he needs to take permission from their heirs.

Gittin 3:7 45a

לית כאן "אינו חושש" אלא[49] "אבל חושש הוא שלא יעשיר העני". ותני כן: המלוה מעות את העני והעשיר[50] אין מפרישין עליהן, שאין מפרישין על האבוד.

There is no "he does not [need to] worry" here, rather "but he does [need to] worry the poor person may have become rich." And it was recited so: If he lent money to a poor person and he became rich, he may not separate against it, for one may not separate against what is lost.

The anonymous comment in the Talmud says two things about this passage in the Mishnah. First, that the sentence beginning with "he does not [need to] worry" should be deleted; second, that the teaching should say that the lender must be concerned about the poor person becoming rich. The first element has no legal consequence: given that the previous sentence in the Mishnah already says that the lender may deduct the loan amount from the priest's or Levite's share with the assumption that the priest or Levite he lent to is alive, there is no legal consequence for deleting the words "he does not [need to] worry that the priest or the Levite may have died." The second element does result in a change of legal position: whereas the Mishnah says the lender does not need to worry that the poor person has become rich, the corrected teaching says that the lender must be concerned about this possibility.

---

[49] I am adding אלא, "rather," since that is the common form when "it's not here" offers an alternative text; it may have been skipped here erroneously because of the following "אבל." The analysis I offer above works regardless of this addition.

[50] Reading with medieval testimonia (Mordecai, Or Zarua); MS Leiden here erroneously: את העשיר.

If this emendation was only concerned with legal position, it could have commented only on the part dealing with the poor person: "there is not 'or that the poor person may have become rich' here, but rather 'but he should worry that the poor person may have become rich.'" Instead, the emendation aims both at the redundant negative statement (with which it has no legal disagreement) *and* at the statement about the poor (with which it disagrees). The first element in the emendation seems to be motivated by the sense that the clause "he does not [need to] worry that the priest or Levite may have died" is superfluous—since the previous sentence in the Mishnah has already stated that the lender is entitled to that assumption.[51]

We have seen in this section emendations which cannot be described as motivated by a dissenting opinion or resulting in Halakhic consequence, but rather point to perceived mistakes or imprecisions in the text: items erroneously included in lists, seemingly sloppy formulations, and various kinds of inconsistency. It is true that the majority of emendations in the Talmud do have legal implications, and that in a culture where the source of the law is textually conceived, sharp distinctions between textual and legal considerations are often hard to make. But even those emendations that express a different legal position cannot be reduced to this Halakhic element. First, as we have seen, even emendations that may have stemmed from or aimed at a different Halakhic position could be bound with removal of redundancies, inconsistencies, or imprecise formulations. More broadly, Amoraic scholars had other instruments to limit the legal validity of teachings—identification of the teaching, narrowing its applicability through interpretation, or stating that its legal position is not to be followed. Reducing emendations to the legal position they expressed ignores their specific significance. Above all, this analysis of Amoraic emendations shows that they did not intend to restore a particular historical formulation of recited teachings. Rather, they aimed to produce correct texts, precisely formulated and therefore fit for the exacting analysis to which Amoraic scholars subjected such teachings and reflecting the law as their correctors understood it.

4. Where is "here"?

In its traditional form, both in Greco-Roman antiquity and in the modern era, textual criticism involves discussion of two kinds of texts. On the one hand, there are what we might call the documents: the extant texts available to the scholar, in manuscripts, editions, or quotes in other works. On the other hand, there is the work itself: the poem, philosophical treatise, novel, and so forth, to which such documents attest. The premise of traditional textual criticism is that no document,

---

[51] Lieberman, *TK*, 8.820.

that is, no extant text, perfectly represents the work—otherwise, all we would have to do is present that document accurately. The role of the scholar is to reconstruct the work through critique of the documents.[52] As we have seen in the previous chapter, Amoraic scholars configured textual difference somewhat differently, but their discussions nonetheless imply a similar distinction between "attesting" texts (the equivalent of *documents*) and "attested" texts (the equivalent of *works*), and that they approached recited teachings, including the Mishnah, as attesting to other teachings.[53]

Emendations show the same approach: when these emendations state a phrase is not "here," "here" does not mean "here in the Mishnah" (R. Judah the Patriarch's edition, the attesting text or document), but rather here in the *mishnah*, in the correct recitation of the given recited teaching.[54] Consider, again, the example with which this chapter opened: what allows Rav to say that the qualification clause about the shape of the doorway "is not here" but that one should continue to recite it nonetheless, is a conceptual separation between the teaching as it has been recited, on the one hand, and the correct recitation, on the other hand. He instructs Hananya to continue to recite the clause as it is in "our recitation," the Mishnah, but to inform his son that the clause is not "here," in this *mishnah* to which our recitation attests.

This model can also explain some of the commentary that accompanies textual criticism in the Talmud. In modern text-critical commentary, we may find comments that explain why a particular document "deviated" from the imagined correct work: "this sentence was erroneously skipped because it ends with the same words as the previous sentence"; "this word was incorrectly copied here from a marginal gloss." Such comments describe the document rather than the work. Similarly, when Rav Hisda says, in the passage we have seen above, that the Mishnah's listing of "the deaf" in the context of reading the scroll is a slip of the tongue, he aims to explain how "our recitation" formed even though "deaf" is not "here," in the correct recitation. The same can be said also about the following example:

m. Shabbat 7:2

הצד צבי השוחטו והמפשיטו והמולחו והמעבדו והמחקו והמחתכו.

[Among the archetypal labors prohibited on the Sabbath are] one who hunted a deer, **slaughtered it**, flayed it, salted it, cured it, scraped it, or sliced it . . . .

---

[52] See e.g. Jacob, "From Book to Text," 5 (who uses "books" and "texts" instead of "documents" and "works"): "Philology appeared from the moment when the autonomy of the text in relation to the book was recognized." For the terms I use here see Tanselle, *Textual Criticism*. I am not endorsing myself the utility of these terms for philological practice; for a critique, see Bryant, *Fluid Text*, and the scholarship discussed in the previous chapter, nn. 7–13.

[53] See the discussion in Section 4 of the previous chapter and the examples noted in n. 71 there.

[54] Under this suggestion, *matnita* is used for both the attesting and attested texts, which may seem confusing, but note for example the similar use of εὐαγγέλιον to mark both each gospel and the Gospel to which they attest in Irenaeus, as explained by Reed (see previous chapter, n. 107).

Shabbat 7:2 10c

ר' שמעון בן לקיש אמ': ליח כאן שחיטה. שחיטה תולדת חבורה היא. ולמה[55] תנינתה
עמהון? אלא בגין דתנינן סדר סעודה תנינתה עמהון.

> R. Simeon b. Laqish said: **There is no "slaughtering" here.** Slaughtering is derived from [the archetypal labor] of injuring. And why did we recite it [i.e. slaughtering] among them [these archetypal labors, even though it is a derived labor]? It was only because we have just recited the [labors connected with the] preparation of the meal that we recited it among them.

The Mishnah presents certain labors prohibited on the Sabbath as "archetypal" labors, from which other prohibited labors may be derived. R. Simeon b. Laqish believes that one of those labors, "slaughtering," is not an archetypal labor but a derivative of the archetypal labor of "injuring."[56] Therefore he states that "slaughtering" does not belong in the list of archetypal labors. He—or, more likely, an anonymous comment elaborating on his argument—follows by explaining that the Mishnah mentioned slaughtering because it was going through the labors associated with preparing a meal, rather than being precise about the status of such labors.[57]

This last comment led scholars to conclude that R. Simeon did not intend to emend the text: why explain the appearance of this word if it is to be erased? R. Simeon's comment, they concluded, is an interpretation of "slaughtering" rather than an emendation.[58] But why then would the passage employ "it is not here"? R. Simeon could have simply said that slaughtering is a derivative of the archetypal labor of injuring, and explain it appears here because other meal preparation labors are mentioned. Whoever used "it's not here"—R. Simeon himself or a later formulator—wanted to suggest that the reference to slaughtering is incorrect. Under the model I propose here, R. Simeon argues that the extant text of the teaching, in the Mishnah, is imprecise; in the correct recitation, the reference to slaughtering should not appear on this list, and the reason it appears in the Mishnah was that the formulator (*tannay*) of our recitation got carried away with listing activities connected with meal preparation.[59]

---

[55] Skipping "not" in MS Leiden, with the Academy's edition.

[56] "Injuring" is not mentioned in the Mishnah at all; see the dispute in *Shab.* 2:5 5a, on whether slaughtering is derived from injuring or vice versa.

[57] See the similar explanation earlier in the discussion without connection to emendation, with respect to baking, which should be a derivative of cooking: "because we recited the [labors of] dough, we recited it with them" (*Shab.* 7:2 10b).

[58] Epstein, *IMT*, 291; Assis, *Concordance*, 857 n. 658.

[59] See similarly *Pes.* 8:3 35d, though the comment there speaks at the same time about the shaper of the Mishnah *and* the person speaking in the legal case it conjures.

Positing that "it's not here" statements allude to the correct teaching as abstracted from any particular recitation of it also sheds light on another type of passage which scholars have deemed as not featuring emendations. Moscovitz writes that in addition to emendation, the phrase "it's not here" may point to a negation of the entire text in question. He offers the following example:

m. Sheqalim 6:4

שלושה-עשר שולחנות היו במקדש. שמונה שלשייש בבית המטבחיים שעליהן מדיחין את הקרבים; ושנים במערב הכבש, אחד שלשייש ואחד של כסף: על של שייש נותנים את האברים ועל של כסף נותנים כלי שרת; ושנים באולם מבפנים על פתח הבית, אחד של שייש ואחד שלזהב: על של שייש נותנים את לחם הפנים בכניסתו ועל של זהב ביציאתו, שמעלים בקודש ולא מורידים; ואחד של זהב מבפנים שעליו לחם הפנים תמיד.

There were thirteen tables in the Temple. Eight of marble in the slaughtering place, on which the entrails are rinsed; and two west of the ramp, one of marble and one of silver: on the marble one they place the limbs, and on the silver one they place the vessels; and there were two inside the hall at the Temple doorway, **one of marble** and one of gold: **on the one of marble**, they place the face-bread as it was brought in, and on the one of gold, as it was taken out, for we ascend [when it comes] to holiness, rather than descend; and one of gold, inside, upon which the face-bread is always [presented].

Sheqalim 6:4 50a

תני: על שלכסף. ר' יוסי בשם ר' שמואל בר רב יצחק; ר' חנניה מטי בה משמיה דר' יוחנן: לית כאן "שלכסף" מפני שהוא מרתיח.

It was recited: "**on the one of silver**." R. Yose [said] in the name of R. Samuel b. R. Isaac, [while] R. Hananiah traces it from the name of R. Yohanan: There is no "**of silver**" here, since it heats up [the bread, spoiling it].

The Mishnah enumerates the number of tables placed in the Temple, including a group of tables used for the bread that is replaced once a week. The Talmud's discussion opens with a recited teaching which differs from the Mishnah's teaching in describing one of the tables in that group. Whereas in the Mishnah, the table on which the bread was placed when it was brought in was a marble table, the recited teaching says that it was a silver table. R. Samuel b. R. Isaac and R. Yohanan say that "there is no 'of silver' here," but rather marble, because silver would have heated up the bread and make it spoil.

Moscovitz argues that this statement cannot suggest an emendation since if we erase the words "of silver," there is essentially no teaching left. But the teaching the Talmud cites, "on the one of silver," means nothing on its own: it is clearly cited here as a recitation divergence of the teaching included in the Mishnah, presenting "on the one of silver" where the Mishnah has "on the one of marble" (a parallel teaching of this sort is preserved more fully in the Bavli, b. Men. 99b). The juxtaposition between this teaching and the Mishnah, alongside the word "here," suggest both of these teachings are attestations of the same textual "place." Under the model proposed here, the statement by R. Yohanan and R. Samuel b. R. Isaac means that "here," in the correct recitation, it is "marble," just like we have it in our recitation, rather than "silver," as it is in the alternative recitation. This comment points to the correct text of the work by endorsing one of the documents against another.[60]

The distinction between a *mishnah* and its attestations may also shed light on other broad features of Talmudic emendations. As we have seen, these emendations aimed not to restore an original text that can be traced to a particular moment or sage, but rather to produce a precise text, free of errors and consistent with the law as the scholars making the emendations perceived it. Furthermore, a large majority of these emendations apply to anonymous rather than attributed teachings.[61] This correlation may be incidental, but it is also possible that because anonymous teachings were construed as offering us "the" *mishnah*, the binding recitation in contrast with the opinions of individual sages, scholars were more likely to emend them than attributed teachings.

Emendations stand in tension with the general Amoraic approach to recited teachings as authoritative sources: not only do they reject or reformulate such teachings, but they do so usually without the support of alternative recited teachings. The evidence does not allow for a universal, straightforward solution to this tension, especially since the Talmud never presents clear principles on when emendations may be made. But the distinction between attesting and attested text may again be helpful in reconstructing the model of textual authority at work in these emendations. For those who offered emendations, it was the correct recitation that was authoritative, not the Mishnah or other recited teachings. These latter recitations had to be emended precisely to reflect the authoritative and binding *mishnah*. In other words, the more Amoraic scholars had a notion that what was binding was a *text*, even disagreements about the law had to be expressed as emendations which bridged different opinions and that text.

---

[60] See also *Ned.* 11:3 42c and *Meg.* 1:10 72c.

[61] Among passages employing "it's not here," only eight apply to teachings attributed to individual sages: *Ter.* 1:8 41a (R. Yose's version of the House of Shammai, but here the emendation is connected to the attribution to R. Yose), *Shab.* 2:5 5a (R. Simeon b. Eleazar in the name of R. Eleazar b. R. Zadoq, though it may be motivated by considerations of consistency of the teaching as a whole), *Shab.* 6:1 7d (R. Judah, see above), *Shab.* 7:1 9b (apparently R. Eleazar b. R. Simeon), *Yev.* 13:2 13d (R. Joshua), *Yev.* 13:7 13d (apparently Rabban Gamaliel), *Shevu.* 5:1 36a (Ben Azzai), and *San.* 1:2 18c (R. Meir). I consider emendations of attributions (e.g. the example we saw above from *Git.*, where R. Yohanan emends "R. Judah" to "R. Meir") among emendations of unattributed teachings, since in those cases the attribution itself is unattributed.

Conclusion

Compared with other types of comments explored in this book, emendations are relatively less common, but they are certainly not a negligible phenomenon: they appear in scores of passages in the Talmud. In presenting emendations, Amoraic scholars engaged in a practice widely attested in other Greco-Roman scholarly traditions, introducing a new type of argument to rabbinic scholarship; but in adopting this practice, they also adapted it. As with other traditions of textual criticism, Amoraic emendations were transmitted alongside the received text, thus offering the emendation itself for study and discussion; but this form was achieved through oral presentation rather than graphic annotation. Consultation of extant recited texts rarely motivated or justified Amoraic emendations. Instead, emendations were driven by a desire to make the text sensible, consistent, and precise, as well as to bring it into conformity with the known law (at least according to the perspective of the emending scholar). These motivations relate to broad phenomena of Amoraic scholarship. The exacting interpretive practices to which Amoraic scholars subjected rabbinic teachings, which derived significance from minute verbal details, required teachings without superfluous or imprecise language. And since the source of the law was understood to be textual, in the sages' words, then the correct text also had to reflect the correct law. In some cases, emendations—much like some of the discussions of textual difference analyzed in the previous chapter—served as a new idiom to express and understand disagreements in positions rather than address issues which were primarily textual; but the use of this idiom is itself significant.

The previous two chapters argued that central features of Amoraic scholarship construed knowledge of rabbinic teachings in fragmentary and imperfect terms: the teachings we know represent only a part of an imperfectly known body of teachings, subject to the contingencies of transmission, and some of them were themselves formulated in ignorance of important material; and many of the texts we encounter are only partial attestations of other teachings. I argued that rather than approaching this imperfection as a problem, Amoraic scholars set it up as an opportunity. The emendations examined in this chapter are predicated on an even more negative judgment of extant texts, construing them as erroneous or imprecise. But they also engage more clearly in the scholarly ability to right the wrongs, and therefore reveal more clearly the new interpretive dynamic that is shaped by this construction of rabbinic teachings, one in which the scholar is in a position of superiority over the text.

8
Needy, Lost, and Kind of Divine
Intertextuality, Necessity, and Recontextualization

While previous chapters addressed aspects of Amoraic commentary on rabbinic teachings which are absent or rare in Midrash, this chapter examines interpretive practices which are common to both, and which scholars have aptly highlighted to show continuity between these two realms. My argument is that even here, continuity is only part of the story. Even as Amoraic scholars subjected rabbinic teachings and Scripture to the same interpretive practices, these practices engaged different and even opposite notions of text, in a way that resulted in interpretive claims that sometimes looked and functioned differently.

An argument from the theory of interpretation which has been very influential in the study of Midrash is that interpretive practices are rooted in the ideas interpreters hold about the text. A newspaper article and a poem may have the same exact words, but we would read them differently in each context because we think differently about the nature of these texts. Much of the literature on Midrash in the past decades has been dedicated to uncovering the sages' concepts of Scripture, scriptural language, and the act of interpretation, and to showing how such concepts may have informed their commentary.[1]

Because explicit statements of such hermeneutic concepts are rare in rabbinic texts, scholars normally reconstruct them by analyzing Midrashic interpretive practice.[2] But this methodological necessity does not mean we should assume a singular correlation between interpretive practice and hermeneutic positions: similar or even identical practices may be implicated in different ideas about texts. Modern scholars, after all, have appealed to different hermeneutic frameworks to explain the same Midrashic practice: David Daube, for example, proposed that the Midrashic practice of reading words in a different order than they appear was premised on the idea that the text speaks in a unique divine language, whereas Yakir Paz argued that the same practice was premised on the idea that the Torah was written using the very human rhetorical conventions of the period.[3] If

---

[1] For a clear statement of the approach and its philosophical background, including the example of reading a newspaper or a poem, see Yadin-Israel, *Scripture as Logos*, 1–10. Kugel's discussion of the four assumptions of ancient interpreters (*Traditions*, 14–19) has been extremely influential; see Sommer, "Concepts of Scripture," for a detailed and sophisticated application of that analysis to Midrash. For a recent account of the state of scholarship see Rosen-Zvi, *Mishnah and Midrash*, 311–38. More studies are cited below.

[2] Rosen-Zvi, *Mishnah and Midrash*, 314; Yadin-Israel, *Scripture as Logos*, 10.

[3] Daube, *The New Testament and Rabbinic Judaism*, 411; Paz, *Scribes to Scholars*, 273–306.

the same practice can be interpreted differently by modern scholars, it could also have different meanings in the various ancient contexts in which it was applied.

Furthermore, while ideas about the text have an important role in giving sense to interpretive practices, they are not necessarily the main cause or foundation of these practices. David Stern, for example, suggested that the Midrashic reading of verses in isolation from their context is connected not with a particular concept about Scripture, but with the reading practices through which the sages encountered it. Scripture was not primarily studied by linear reading of whole books, but rather by memorizing bits of heard texts, which amounted to isolated sequences of words.[4] Concepts, therefore, represent not only the assumptions that shape interpretation, but also the conceptualization of existing practices—and therefore, we may find different conceptualizations of the same practice.

The interpretive practices on which this chapter centers are some of the hallmarks of Midrash: intertextual illumination, the marking and interpretation of apparent redundancies, and recontextualizing commentary. In order to show that when these practices applied to rabbinic teachings they were implicated in different notions of text, I first discuss how these practices operate in Midrash, and then turn to their application in the Talmud's commentary on rabbinic teachings, focusing on cases in which ideas about such teachings are made visible with explicit principles, justifications, or distinctive terminology. Concluding from these more explicit but relatively rare examples about the way Amoraic scholars understood these interpretive practices more broadly is by nature speculative, but that is the nature of reconstructing rabbinic hermeneutics more generally. My argument is not that these interpretive practices always differed in significance and form when they applied to rabbinic teachings—they demonstrably did not. Rather, I argue that the application of these practices to Scripture and rabbinic teachings entailed different ranges of form, function, and significance.

1. Intertextuality and the imperfection of the Mishnah

As Daniel Boyarin argued in *Intertextuality and the Reading of Midrash*, the most characteristic aspect of Midrash is the way it produces readings of Scripture by recomposing a textual mosaic of verses from different parts of the Bible.[5] James Kugel posited that this type of reading was premised on an assumption the sages shared with other ancient interpreters, that Scripture is "perfect and perfectly harmonious," a unity which "must speak with one voice," and that therefore, "any biblical

---

[4] Stern, "Jewish Books," 180–7.
[5] Boyarin, *Intertextuality*, 22–38. My use of the term "intertextuality" in my discussion of Midrash follows the important role it has had in the history of scholarship. For a critique of the term, see Najman, *Vitality*, ch. 3.

text might illuminate any other."⁶ This does not mean that the sages viewed the Bible as one homogeneous block and disregarded its textual heterogeneity. Boyarin shows that Midrash thrives on the fissures and gaps within and between biblical verses.⁷ But even in doing so, the sages projected and emphasized an image of a unified Scripture. Azzan Yadin-Israel demonstrated that Ishmaelian Midrashim, for example, personified Scripture as an entity which "recognizes its own interpretive *cruces*, often resolves them, and, more importantly, even when the task is left to the rabbinic reader, he proceeds under the guidance" of Scripture itself.⁸ The Yerushalmi presents an instructive formulation of this interpretive principle:

Rosh ha-Shanah 3:5 58d

תני בשם ר' נחמיה: היתה כאניות סוחר ממרחק תביא לחמה—דברי תורה עניים במקומן ועשירים במקום אחר.

It was recited in the name of R. Nehemiah: "She is like trade ships, bringing her bread from afar" (Prov 31:14)—the words of the Torah are poor in one place but rich in another.

This passage describes the process of solving a problem raised in reading one scriptural passage by reading another, distant passage from Scripture. The words of the Torah may be lacking some things in some places, but the unified whole is a well-stocked trade empire which is able to sustain itself, so it is lacking in nothing.

Scholars such as Christine Hayes and David Stern have observed that the sages use the same strategy, the illumination of texts through other texts, in their interpretation of rabbinic teachings.⁹ But there is a difference between applying this strategy to what is construed as a unity and what is construed as a body of discrete teachings from different sources. We can observe this difference by comparing the passage just cited, from *Rosh ha-Shanah*, to a passage in which two Amoraic scholars debate how to read the Mishnah:

m. Kil'ayim 1:6

הזאב והכלב, כלב הכופרי והשועל, העזים והצבאים, היעילים והרחילים, הסוס והפרד, הפרד והחמור, החמור והערוד—אף-על-פי דומין זה לזה, כלאים זה בזה.

The wolf and the dog, the wild dog and the jackal, goats and gazelles, wild goats and sheep, the horse and the mule, the mule and the donkey, the donkey and

---

⁶ Kugel, *Traditions*, 17; see there, 18–19, for reservations about the connection between this assumption and the idea of divine authorship.
⁷ Boyarin, *Intertextuality*, 39.
⁸ Yadin-Israel, "Authorial Intent," 9.
⁹ Hayes, *Talmuds*, 105; Stern, "Canonization," 240–52.

the wild donkey—though they resemble each other, they are [considered] mixed kinds one with the other.

Kil'ayim 1:6 27a (partial parallel in *Bava Qamma* 5:7 5a)

עוֹף לֹא תְנִיתָהּ? אָמַ' ר' יוֹחָנָן: אַיְיתִיתָהּ מִן דָּבָר דָּלִיָּה, "תַּרְנְגוֹל עִם הַפִּסְיוֹנִי תַּרְנְגוֹל עִם הַטַּוָּוס. אע"פ שֶׁדּוֹמִין זֶה לָזֶה כִּלְאַיִם זֶה בָּזֶה." ר' שִׁמְעֹ' בֶּן לָקִישׁ אֲמַ': מִשְׁנָה שְׁלֵימָה שָׁנָה לָנוּ ר', "וְכֵן חַיָּה וָעוֹף כַּיּוֹצֵא בָהֶן." אָמַ' ר' יוֹנָה:[10] צַרְכָא לַהֲדָא דר' יוֹחָנָן. תְּנִינַן הָכָא חַיָּה וּפֵרְשְׁתָּהּ תַּמָּן, תְּנִינַן בְּהֵמָה הָכָא וּפֵרְשְׁתָּהּ תַּמָּן, עוֹף תְּנִיתָהּ תַּמָּן, אֲתָא וּפֵרְשְׁתָּהּ הָכָא. אָמַ' ר' יוֹסֵי: וְיָאוּת. בָּא לְהוֹדִיעֲךָ שֶׁהָעוֹף אָסוּר בְּכִלְאַיִם.

Fowl—he [the *tannay* of the Mishnah] did not recite [a similar ruling regarding] it?

Said R. Yohanan: I will bring this [ruling] from that [*mishnah*] of Bar Dalya: "a cock with a pheasant, a cock with a peacock—even though they are similar to one another they are [considered] mixed with one another."

R. Simeon b. Laqish said: Rabbi [Judah the Patriarch] recited to us a perfect Mishnah: "[There is one and the same law for the ox as well as any domestic animal with respect to ... mixtures ...], and so too, wild animals and fowl, like them" (*m. B. Q.* 5:7).

Said R. Jonah: There is a need for R. Yohanan's [teaching]. We recited here [in *B. Q.*], "wild animal" but specified it there [in *Kil.*]; we recited domestic animal here, but specified it there; fowl we recited there, and he came and specified it here [in Bar Dalya's version of *Kil.*].

Said R. Yose: And this is appropriate—it comes to tell you that fowl has mixture prohibitions.

The Mishnah in *Kil'ayim* lists animals which, despite their similarity, are considered of different kinds and therefore mixing them constitutes a transgression of the laws of mixture. The Talmud's discussion opens with an anonymous question or statement which points to an apparent lack in this passage: the Mishnah mentions various species but says nothing about kinds of fowl. R. Yohanan says he can "bring this"—i.e. adduce a similar ruling concerning mixture of fowl—from the teachings of Bar Dalya, whose collection of recited teachings is mentioned elsewhere.[11] He proceeds to quote a teaching which is formulated much like the list in the Mishnah, but which specifies the types of fowl that are considered different kinds. R. Simeon b. Laqish responds that there is a place where the Mishnah itself implies a prohibition on the mixture of fowl. In *Bava Qamma*

---

[10] In MS Leiden: R. Yohanan. "R. Jonah" in MS Vatican as well as in citations by R. Isaac of Vienna and R. Samson of Sens. Alternatively, we may correct the second "R. Yohanan" to "Bar Dalya."

[11] e.g. *Pe'ah* 3:7 17d, *Shevi.* 2:6 33d, *Bez.* 2:8 61d.

5:7, the Mishnah explains that even though the Torah may mention, in any of its laws, only an ox, it speaks of other animals as well. That passage in the Mishnah specifically mentions the law of mixtures among the laws that apply broadly no matter which animals are stated explicitly, and it specifically mentions fowl among the categories of animals to which laws apply. Thus, R. Simeon b. Laqish argues, the Mishnah itself indicates a prohibition on the mixture of fowl species. R. Jonah points out that nonetheless, the teaching R. Yohanan quotes is necessary: after all, even if the passage in *Bava Qamma* implies a prohibition on mixing different kinds of fowl, it does not provide us a list of which kinds of fowl are considered different in the way that the Mishnah in *Kil'ayim* provides us for other animals; in order to complete the list in *Kil'ayim*, we still need the teaching adduced by R. Yohanan. R. Yose's comment seems to underscore that in any event, the Mishnah in *Bava Qamma* serves to inform us that fowl is liable to mixture prohibitions.

R. Simeon's argument approaches the Mishnah in the same way the sages approach the Torah.[12] His statement, "Rabbi [Judah the Patriarch] recited to us a perfect Mishnah," remarkably applies to the Mishnah what the sages read in the Psalms about the Torah: "the Torah of God is perfect" (Ps. 19:8, with the adjective *temimah* that appears in most versions of R. Simeon's teaching).[13] The method R. Simeon applies to the Mishnah follows from this description. Much like, as we have seen, the Torah's "poor" passages are replenished by the Torah's "rich" passages, the Mishnah is a self-sufficient text which fills its own gaps, and so we can use the passage from *Bava Qamma* to fill in what we were missing in *Kil'ayim*. There are a few other passages in the Talmud which champion this kind of position. The same R. Simeon is said to have identified other places where Judah teaches us implicitly in the Mishnah something that is only explicitly mentioned in another recited teaching.[14] Another passage records a more dramatic conversation in connection with this approach:

Qiddushin 1:1 58d

חילפיי אמ': אייתיבוני על גיף נהרא, דלא אפיקית מתנית' דר' חייה רבא ממתניתין זרקוני לנהרא! אמרין ליה: והא תני ר' חייה, "סילעא ארבע דינריך". אמ' לון: אוף אנן תנינתה, "כמה תהא הסלע חסירה ולא יהא בה הוניה? ר' מאיר או' ארבע איסרות מאיסר לדינר". אמ' ליה: והתני ר' חייה. . . .

---

[12] Epstein, *IMT*, 287, understands this dispute as part of a broader dispute between R. Simeon and R. Yohanan on the status of the Mishnah; see also Goldberg, "Palestinian Talmud," 310.

[13] "תמימה" in MS Vatican, as well as in the parallel in *B. Q.* according to MS Escorial and a Genizah fragment (Ox. Georg. C. 1(P)(2672); Sussmann, *Ginze Yerushalmi*, 533); and in the instances of the phrase in MS Leiden at *Shab.* and *San.* The other versions (MS Leiden in *Kil.*, *B. Q.*, and *Pes.*) read "שלימה".

[14] See Epstein, *IMT*, 287 and 811, on the phrase "here R. [Judah the Patriarch] recited" attributed in both Talmuds to R. Simeon b. Laqish (though it also appears attributed to R. Yose at *B. B.* 8:5 16b).

Hilfai said: Seat me on the bank of the river. If I cannot derive the *mishnah* of R. Hiyya the great from our Mishnah, throw me to the river!

They said to him: Here, R. Hiyya recited: [one] *sela* [a coin denomination] is [equal to] four *dinar*. He said to them: We, too, have recited [in our Mishnah], "How much may a *sela* be defective without the [transaction being considered] a fraud? R. Meir says, four *issars*, an *issar* to the *dinar*."

They said to him: Here, R. Hiyya recited....

The challenge Hilfai takes upon himself is to derive what is known from the *mishnah* of R. Hiyya using only "our" Mishnah.[15] There follows a series of challenges, all concerning coin denominations, where Hilfai's interlocutors cite information known ostensibly only from teachings recited by R. Hiyya and he demonstrates it can be found in the Mishnah itself. Elsewhere in the Yerushalmi, an allusion to this challenge appears in connection with a different subject of the law.[16] Note that Hilfai does not take upon himself to derive information in the other way, saying that he could also derive anything known from the Mishnah only by using the *matnita* of R. Hiyya. Hilfai, then, seems to be expressing a similar sentiment to that of R. Simeon b. Laqish in *Kil'ayim*: the Mishnah is a complete guide to the law, and everything can be derived from it; other collections are unnecessary.

These passages pit the interpretation of the Mishnah on its own against the use of recited teachings from other collections.[17] R. Simeon's teaching in particular presents a "Scripturalization" of the Mishnah, applying to it the language otherwise used to speak of the Torah's perfection, and using the same principle we have seen the sages emphasized for the Torah, by which what seems lacking in the text in one place is supplied by the text itself elsewhere. The fact that this approach is relatively explicit about its premises allows us to consider the premises of the opposing approach, the one presented here by R. Yohanan: if R. Simeon's reading of the Mishnah reflects the idea that the Mishnah presents Torah-like perfection or completeness, then R. Yohanan's use of Bar Dalya's collection to complete what is lacking in the Mishnah is bound with the idea that the Mishnah is imperfect or incomplete, that it is *not* like the Torah.

R. Yohanan's approach to the problem is just as "intertextual" as R. Simeon's, but in a different sense. The texts R. Yohanan employs, unlike those of R. Simeon, are not conceived as parts of the same text, but rather as two differentiated texts, two

---

[15] On the Bavli's narrative expansion of this tradition, see Rubenstein, *Stories*, 41–61.
[16] *Ket.* 6:7 30d–31a.
[17] Scholars have seen these passages as reflecting early debates between the opponents and defenders of the Mishnah (Halivni, "Reception," 208; Weiss, *Dor*, 3.3). But the illumination of the Mishnah with other teachings persists even in layers of the Talmuds in which the Mishnah's elevated status is well established.

alternative presentations of the tradition, associated with different individuals—Judah the Patriarch and Bar Dalya. R. Yohanan therefore does not claim that these texts amount to a complete and singular unity. The emphasis in R. Simeon's statement is on the design of the Mishnah: Judah "recited to us a perfect Mishnah." R. Yohanan's claim is not that Bar Dalya and Judah somehow collaborated to produce a perfect text which by design solves its own lacks. His claim is rather that Judah's Mishnah left out the issue of fowl (as we find elsewhere in the Yerushalmi, "the reciter has left this out"),[18] and Bar Dalya's *mishnah* did not (it is difficult to know whether Bar Dalya had the full list, and R. Yohanan cites only the part that is different from our Mishnah, or perhaps Bar Dalya's *mishnah* itself just supplemented our Mishnah's list with the case of fowl). Not unlike a modern philologist who claims to have found a manuscript recording the missing part of a text, here R. Yohanan shows us the benefit of his erudition, of knowing multiple editions: it is only through the act of scholarship that we can get the full picture, since the texts themselves are lacking.

For David Halivni, Hilfai's insistence on deriving laws from the Mishnah alone represented the approach that the Mishnah should be read using the same principles applied to Scripture, whereas his interlocutors' emphasis on the importance of other *mishnayot* represented the opposition to this approach.[19] Stern, in contrast, argued that the sages' juxtaposition of the Mishnah with other sources is an example of how their reading of rabbinic teachings was similar to their reading of Scripture, since "what was canonized was the tradition in its entirety, not any specific literary work."[20] Both of these accounts capture something correct: the sages' illumination of the Mishnah with other recited teachings certainly bears similarity to the reading practices we find in Midrash. But precisely because these practices now applied to tradition in its entirety and variety, they took on a different significance.

This type of explicit discourse about the perfection or sufficiency of the Mishnah is unusual. The phrase "perfect Mishnah" appears only in one other passage.[21] But these passages may provide a conceptual framework for scholarly practices we find throughout the Talmud, in which the Mishnah is constantly read alongside and supplemented by other recited teachings. These exceptionally explicit passages allow us to see this much wider phenomenon as reflecting the idea that the Mishnah, unlike the Torah, is incomplete, and that because it cannot supply its own lacks, it requires scholars to take a different reading strategy, completing it using other texts.

---

[18] *Meg.* 3:1 73d and *Shevi.* 7:3 37c.
[19] Halivni, "Reception," 208.
[20] Stern, "Canonization," 242.
[21] *Shab.* 14:1 14b (par. *Pes.* 7:11 35a and *San.* 8:2 26a), where R. Simeon argues against R. Yohanan's qualification of the Mishnah, positing that it is "perfect" or "complete" in the sense that it is exhaustive and final.

2. "Necessary" or "needy"?

The fundamental task of Midrash, Ishay Rosen-Zvi writes, "is to show that there is nothing superfluous in Scripture."[22] While the sages present a diversity of approaches to this issue—there are certain particles and grammatical phenomena from which Aqivan Midrashim derive meaning and Ishmaelian Midrashim do not. But the marking of textual details as apparently redundant, and the derivation of meanings from such redundancies, is characteristic of Midrashic interpretation as a whole. Kugel described this approach as the "doctrine of 'omnisignificance,'" whereby "nothing in Scripture is said in vain or in rhetorical flourish," which he saw as deriving from the perfection of Scripture.[23] Yadin-Israel argued that at least for the Ishmaelian Midrashim, the hermeneutic markedness of redundancies is "not so much motivated by the assumption that Scripture is perfect as by the assumption that Scripture is an intentional teacher, a view that ultimately leads back to the attempt to establish Scripture as the lead agent of interpretation."[24] Paz has shown that the discourse on redundancies has a counterpart in Homeric scholarship, in which "redundant words, which do not add information, are considered a fundamental flaw and attest to the author's poetic limitations."[25] This feature of Midrash intersects with the phenomenon examined in the previous section because the problem of apparent redundancy often arises from reading together two distant verses which say similar things.

When modern scholars have argued that the sages expanded Midrashic approaches to rabbinic teachings, they have often focused on the way that the Talmuds apply to these teachings a similar assumption of verbal economy. A long-standing view has attributed this approach particularly to the Bavli or even its latest layers.[26] Hayes argued that the difference between the Talmuds on this question is more a difference of degree.[27] There is a variety of interpretive practices which can be related to this approach, and here I focus on a small but significant subset of them. I center on what I call "necessity claims," arguments that a teaching or a particular part of a teaching is "necessary." Such claims thematize the issue of verbal economy in a way that passages which lavish attention on textual detail do not.[28]

---

[22] Rosen-Zvi, *Mishnah and Midrash*, 274.
[23] Kugel, *Traditions*, 17.
[24] Yadin-Israel, *Scripture as Logos*, 51.
[25] Paz, *Scribes to Scholars*, 107.
[26] On this approach as a characteristic of the Bavli or the late Bavli, see e.g. Frankel, *Einleitung*, 28a–31b; Goldberg, "Babylonian Talmud," 331; Cohen, "Biqoret." Since we are talking about a variety of interpretive phenomena, the argument that some of them appear in the Yerushalmi does not negate the conclusions that others are unique to certain strands of the Bavli. The issue, especially with Frankel and Goldberg, is over-generalization as well as the judgment that such readings deviate from the "plain" sense of the text.
[27] Hayes, *Talmuds*, 225. See also Kretzmer-Raziel, "Talmudic Stam," 624, 642, and 653.
[28] A good example of the challenges of a broad inquiry is the passage Hayes uses to demonstrate that the Yerushalmi presents the hermeneutics of verbal economy. Hayes writes that the Bavli passage in b. ʿA. Z. 6b, which makes a necessity claim, has a Yerushalmi parallel that "simply lacks the introductory and concluding term צריכא/צריכי" (225), referring to a passage in ʿA. Z. 1:1 39b which she analyzes on

These claims address different kinds of apparent redundancy: they may address textual duplication or excess (e.g. two verses or teachings which say similar things, or words which are superfluous in the eyes of the interpreter); or they may address teachings which are apparently trivial given a broadly held principle. I focus on the former type, necessity claims which address apparent textual excess, since they engage more directly with notions of textual design.[29]

The most common way the sages speak about the "necessity" of rabbinic teachings is with terms or phrases based on the root *tz. r. kh*, denoting "need." As Rosen-Zvi notes, even though Midrash so often demonstrates that there is no textual excess in Scripture, the sages only rarely apply this terminology to biblical verses. This difference may be telling. It may show that rhetorically, with respect to Scripture, what needs demonstration is not *that* verses are necessary, since that may (or even must) be taken for granted, but rather *how* they are necessary. The relative avoidance of "need" with respect to Scripture may also be connected to the negative association with this terminology. More frequently, classical Midrashic works apply such terms to the reader of Scripture (*ma ani tzarikh*, "why do I need" to be taught this) or the homily (*eino tzarikh*, "it," the homily, is not necessary since the same information may be derived more directly from another verse).[30] If avoidance of "need" is the result of circumspection, it was not absolute: "need" is sometimes used with respect to scriptural verses,[31] and as we have seen in the passage in *Rosh ha-Shanah*, the Talmud may even say that the Torah is "poor" in certain places.

In the Yerushalmi, the language of "need" or "necessity" has a broad range of functions. Some of these functions only partially overlap with concerns of textual economy and therefore will not concern us here. These include indicating that a certain sage was in doubt about an issue (*tzerikhah leh*, "it is wanting for him") and determining the meaning of a certain teaching (*la tzurkha dela*, "it is only required" given a particular case or viewpoint). There are about forty instances in which the Yerushalmi says about a certain teaching, "therefore it was needed/necessary to

---

p. 71. While it is fair to say that in these passages, both Talmuds derive significance from each element of the Mishnah, their comments proceed from opposite premises. The Bavli, at least on the level of presentation, begins with the premise that some of the prohibitions in the Mishnah are redundant because they can be derived from other prohibitions; its purpose is therefore to establish the difference between these prohibitions to demonstrate that each is necessary. The Yerushalmi begins with difference: in each pair one ruling is reasonable and the other is not, so the unreasonable ruling must be explained. The Yerushalmi does not point to redundancy in the text, and therefore does not aim to demonstrate the necessity of each teaching. The Bavli does record a parallel discussion to the Yerushalmi earlier on that page (the discussion beginning with *bi-shelama*, the equivalent of the Yerushalmi's *niḥa*), but that passage does not make a necessity claim.

[29] On these different types of redundancies in Midrash, see Rosen-Zvi, *Mishnah and Midrash*, 278–82.
[30] For "*ma ani tzarikh*," see e.g. *Sifre Deuteronomy* §31, §230; *Mekhilta de-Rabbi Simeon* on Ex 12:13, 21.11. On "*eino tzarikh*," see Rosen-Zvi, "Structure and Reflexivity," 281–5.
[31] e.g. in the Yerushalmi: *Pe'ah* 7:7 20c, *Shevi.* 10:2 39c (par. *Mak.* 1:1 31a), *Yev.* 6:3 7c.

say," but the large majority of these passages do not address redundancy that arises from textual excess.³²

In the previous section, I distinguished between comments that illuminate a text with what is conceived as part of the same text, on the one hand, and comments which draw on two texts that are understood to be distinct from each other, on the other. This distinction applies in the case of necessity claims as well. When such claims are made about parts of a single rabbinic teaching or about two teachings within the Mishnah, they function like they do with Scripture. Just as often, however, these claims are made concerning two differentiated rabbinic texts: statements attributed to different sages or alternative recitations of a teaching. In those cases, I argue, such claims emphasize the partiality and insufficiency of the teachings involved.

In a significant number of instances, necessity claims in the Talmud respond to apparent redundancy arising from a single teaching. Consider the following example:

m. Pe'ah 2:1

ואלו מפסיקין לפיאה: הנחל והשלולית, ודרך היחיד ודרך הרבים, ושביל הרבים ושביל היחיד והקבוע בימות החמה ובימות הגשמים.

The following divide [a field] for [the purpose of] *pe'ah*: A stream and a pond, and a private road and a public road, and a public path and a private path, fixed in [both] the summer season and the rainy season.

Pe'ah 2:1 16d

מכיון דתנינן "דרך היחיד", "ודרך הרבים" מה צורכה? אתא³³ מימר לך אפי' דרך הרבים אינו מפסיק³⁴ לאילן אלא גדר. מכיון דתנינן "שביל היחיד", "שביל הרבים" מה צורכא? להוציא את הקבוע בימות החמה ואינו קבוע בימות הגשמים.

Since we have recited "private road," what is the need for "and a public road"? It comes to tell you that even a public road does not divide for trees, only a fence. Since we have recited "private path," what is the need for "public path"? To exclude one which is fixed in the summer season but not in the rainy season.

The Talmud asks why the Mishnah mentions both "private" and "public road" and similarly "private" and "public path": surely, if private paths and roads constitute

---

³² "לפום כן צרך מימר". The majority of these correct mistaken interpretations or respond to objections that the teaching is redundant given a broadly held principle; see e.g. Ber. 2:3 4d, Shevi. 1:6 33b. The exceptions which do address "textual" redundancy are Shevi. 9:1 38c, Shab. 11:4 13a (discussed below), Yev. 9:3 10b. 11 instances of the phrase concern Scripture; for examples see previous note.
³³ Correcting אנא.
³⁴ Correcting מפסיד.

divisions in the field, we could deduce that their more substantial public equivalents constitute such divisions. In the first case, the Talmud provides the answer that mentioning public roads is necessary since later on in the Mishnah we hear that none of the aforementioned dividers apply to tree plantations (*m. Pe'ah* 2:3). If only private roads would have been mentioned in our list, we might have concluded that since public roads are more substantial they do present a division in the case of trees. Similarly, it is necessary to mention public paths since the Mishnah proceeds to exclude seasonal paths, and if public paths were not mentioned explicitly, we might have concluded that since they are more substantial, seasonal public paths do constitute a division.

As scholars have pointed out, this kind of interpretation applies a particular sense of verbal economy to the text.[35] The Mishnah may simply try to offer an exhaustive list, or in other similar cases merely offer several examples for the sake of stylistic variety; the inquiry into what each and every element in the list teaches us rests on the assumption that the Mishnah is speaking very precisely and that it is designed to be studied for all that it might imply. In other words, the sages here approach the Mishnah like they approach Scripture. A different kind of redundancy, in tractate *Shabbat*, is addressed in a way which might strike modern readers as particularly far-fetched:

m. Shabbat 11:4

הזורק בים ארבע אמות פטור. אם היה רקק מים ורשות הרבים מהלכת בו—הזורק בתוכו ארבע אמות חייב. וכמה הוא רקק מים? פחות מעשרה טפחים. רקק מים ורשות הרבים מהלכת בו—הזורק בתוכו ארבע אמות חייב.

Someone who throws [something the distance of] four cubits into the sea is exempt.

If there was a shallow pool of water and a public domain passed through it—someone who throws [something a distance of] four cubits into it is liable. How much is shallow water? Less than ten hand-breadths [deep].

[If there was] a shallow pool of water and a public domain passed through it—someone who throws [something a distance of] four cubits into it is liable.

Shabbat 11:4 13a

ולמה תנינתה תרין זימנין? ר׳ חנניה בשם ר׳ פינחס: בשהיו שני רקקים. אחד הרבים מהלכין בו ואחד אין הרבים מהלכין בו אלא כשהן נדחקין. שלא תאמ׳, הואיל ואין הרבים מהלכין בו אלא כשהן נדחקין, אינו רשות הרבים אלא רשות היחיד. לפום כן צרך מימר רשות הרבים הוא.

---

[35] Hayes, *Talmuds*, 92–4.

And why did we recite it [the stipulation about a shallow pool] twice? R. Hananya [said] in the name of R. Phinehas: [The Mishnah refers to a case] in which there were two pools; one through which the public would walk and the other through which the public would not walk except when pressed. Lest you say that, since the public do not walk through it except when pressed, it is not the public domain but rather a private domain, therefore it was necessary to say that it is the public domain.

The Mishnah repeats, almost verbatim, the ruling about throwing an object on the Sabbath in a shallow pool of water. Modern commentators have suggested that this duplication shows that this unit was composed of different layers.[36] In the Talmud, R. Phinehas says that both instances of the rulings are necessary. The second teaching, he argues, refers to a pool through which people walk only when pressed. It was necessary to include it since we might have thought that because the public does not normally use this pool, it does not count as the public domain, and therefore throwing an object there does not violate the Sabbath transporting laws.

In both examples we have seen, Amoraic scholars aim to defend the integrity and precision of the Mishnah, which in turn, as we have seen with the emendations studied in the previous chapter, also justifies their exacting methods of reading it. This type of necessity claim is certainly similar to those we find in Midrash. It is not, however, the only type of necessity claim in the Yerushalmi, and it is not as common as one might think (in part because it is more common in the Babylonian Talmud). Among the passages in the Talmud which employ the language of necessity, there are only ten such examples, including the two instances quoted above.[37]

The other type of necessity claim which is relevant for our purpose concerns differentiated teachings. In five passages—including the passage analyzed above concerning Bar Dalya's list of mixed kinds—the claim applies to two divergent texts attributed to different recitations:[38]

m. Shabbat 1:2

לא ישב אדם לפני הספר סמוך למנחה עד שיתפלל.

One may not sit down in front of the barber near [the time of] the afternoon prayer unless they have already prayed.

---

[36] Goldberg, *Shabbat*, 224–5.
[37] See *Kil.* 3:3 28d, *Kil.* 6:6 30c, *Shevi.* 9:1 38c, *Ter.* 2:1 41b, *Ḥal.* 4:3 59d, *Yev.* 10:1 10d, *Git.* 8:10 49d, and *San.* 3:4 21b.
[38] In addition to the examples from *Kil.* And *Shab.*, see *Pe'ah* 3:2 17b, *M. Q.* 2:1 81a, *'A. Z.* 1:5 39d (the last two share the same structure and wording with the passage at *Shab.*, in a way that suggests literary dependence among the three passages).

Shabbat 1:2 3a

אנן תנינן: סמוך למנחה. תני ר' חייה: סמוך לחשיכה. מתני' צריכה למיתניתיה דר' חייה,
מתניתיה דר' חייה צריכה למתני'. אילו תנא ר' חייה ולא תנינן אנן, הוינן אמרין לא אמר אלא
חשיכה—הא מנחה לא. הוי צורכה למתני'. או אילו תנא ר' חייה ולא תנינן אנן, הוינן אמרין
כולהן דתנינן "מנחה", מנחה, וכלהן דתנינן "חשיכה", חשיכה. מן מה דתנינתה "מנחה"
ותנתה ר' חייה רובה "חשיכה", הדא אמרה אפילו חשיכה דתנינן דבתרה מנחה היא.

We have recited [in the Mishnah], "near [the time of] the afternoon prayer." R. Hiyya recited [in his *mishnah*]: "near [the time of] nightfall."

Our Mishnah needs the *mishnah* of R. Hiyya, and the *mishnah* of R. Hiyya needs our Mishnah. If R. Hiyya recited [what he did], and we did not recite [what we did], we would say he only refers to nightfall, not the afternoon prayer. Thus, there is a need for our Mishnah. Or, if we recited [what we did], but R. Hiyya did not recite [what he did], we would say that in all those [cases] where we recite "nightfall," [the reference is only to] nightfall. From the fact that we have recited "the afternoon prayer," and R. Hiyya the Great recited "nightfall," it means that even the "nightfall" which we recite later on [in *m. Shab.* 1:3] is [at the time of] the afternoon prayer.

The anonymous teaching presented in the Mishnah prohibits a person from sitting for a haircut close to the time of the afternoon prayer unless they had already prayed. Another version of this teaching, recited by R. Hiyya, records "nightfall" rather than "afternoon prayer." The Talmud's first comment on this divergence assumes that these two versions are formulations of the same ruling. Each formulation, the Talmud argues, provides only a partial perspective on the law, but both are necessary. If we had only R. Hiyya's version but not "our" version, we would have thought that the prohibition only applies at nightfall—at the conclusion of the afternoon prayer—when in fact it applies already at the time of that prayer's beginning. R. Hiyya's version is also necessary. It teaches us that "afternoon prayer" and "nightfall" are equivocal, and therefore when the Mishnah later teaches that "a tailor may not go out with his needle [on Friday] close to nightfall" (*m. Shabbat* 1:3), we know that the ruling also applies even during the time of the afternoon prayer.

In eight other passages, necessity claims apply to two explanations of a ruling:[39]

m. Yoma 1:1

שבעת ימים קודם ליום הכיפורים מפרישין כהן גדול מביתו ללשכת הפרהדרין.

Seven days before the Day of Atonement, they separate the high priest from his house to the councilors' apartment [in the Temple complex].

---

[39] In addition to the passage from *Yom.*, see *Dem.* 6:12 25d, *M. S.* 1:2 53a, *R. H.* 2:9 58b, *Yev.* 1:1 3c, *Git.* 1:5 43d, *B. Q.* 1:1 2b, and *Shevu.* 4:12 35d.

Yoma 1:1 38a–c

ר' בא בשם ר' יוחנן שמע לה מן הדא: "כאשר עשה ביום הזה"—אילו שבעת ימי המילואים.
"צוה יי"—לדורות [...]. [...] פירש בן בתירה: שמא יבוא על אשתו נידה וידחה כל שבעת. [...]

אשכחת אמר: מה⁴⁰ דאמ' ר' יוחנן צריכה לבן בתירה, מה דאמ' בן בתירה צריכה לר' יוחנן.
אילו אמ' ר' יוחנן ולא אמרה בן בתירה, הוינן אמרין ישמש מיטתו וישן לו בלשכת פלהדרין.
הוי צורכה להיא דאמ' בן בתירה. אילו אמ' בן בתירה ולא אמ' ר' יוחנן, הוינן אמרין יפרוש
ממיטתו וישן לו בתוך ביתו. הווי צורכה להיא דאמ' ר' יוחנן וצורכה להיא דאמ' בן בתירה.

R. Abba in the name of R. Yohanan derived it [the Mishnah's ruling] from this [verse]: "As has been done today" (Lev. 8:34)—this is the seven days of ordination [of Aaron], "which the Lord commanded" (ibid.)—for the following generations [and therefore much like Aaron was separated for seven days, so does the high priest need to be separated for seven days] ....

Ben Betera interpreted [the ruling]: Lest he has intercourse with his wife while she is menstruating, and he would be unfit [because of the impurity he contracted] all seven days. [...]

You therefore say, that what R. Yohanan said needs Ben Betera, and what Ben Betera said needs R. Yohanan. If R. Yohanan said [his explanation] and Ben Betera did not say his, we would have said he [the priest] may have sexual intercourse, but he must sleep in the councilors' apartment. Thus the need for that which Ben Betera said. If Ben Betera said [his explanation] but R. Yohanan did not, we would have said he [the priest] must abstain from sex, but he may sleep in his own house. Thus the need for that which R. Yohanan said [since like Aaron, the priest may not sleep in his home], and the need for that which Ben Betera said.

Ben Betera and R. Yohanan offer explanations for the ruling that the high priest must be separated in a particular room for a week prior to the Day of Atonement.[41] R. Yohanan traces a scriptural source for this separation. He argues that Leviticus 8:34 tells us that the procedures followed by the first priest, Aaron, must be followed by all subsequent generations. Since Aaron was instructed to spend seven days in the tent (Lev 8:33), the high priest must similarly spend seven days in the Temple complex. Ben Betera explains that the separation is meant to prevent the priest from having sexual intercourse with his wife, since, should she be menstruating, he would contract impurity and be disqualified from service in the Temple during the Day of Atonement.

The Talmud's comment assumes that the law requires both that the priest be separated from his wife and that he sleeps in the Temple complex rather than in his home. It may be drawing on the Mishnah's language, which indicates both that the

---

[40] Correcting מאן, here and in the next instance; see the similar formulation at R. H. 2:9 58b.
[41] Ben Betera's teaching also appears at t. Yom. 1:1.

priest is separated for seven days from "his home," which can mean "his wife," and that he must spend seven days in the Temple complex. The anonymous comment argues that the explanations by R. Yohanan and Ben Betera each captures only one of these aspects. If the reason for the separation is the concern about contracting impurity, then as long as the priest does not sleep with his wife he may stay home; if the separation is modeled on the procedure followed by Aaron, then the priest must spend the seven days in the Temple (as Aaron did in the tent). Both explanations, this comment argues, are required for the law to be understood fully.

There are important differences between the first set of necessity claims examined above, which apply to parts of a single teaching or the same collection of teachings, and these necessity claims, which apply to teachings attributed to different sages. First, these necessity claims do not address the same problem. This is apparent in the way they are presented. In all instances where necessity claims apply to a single teaching, they are presented as answers to objections concerning textual redundancy: "Why did we recite it twice?"; "What is the need for 'and a public road'?" In contrast, none of the necessity claims which apply to two differentiated texts respond to such objections. The necessity claims of the first kind, like their Midrashic counterparts, address, as we have seen, the possibility that there is a flaw in the text because it repeats itself or contains superfluous elements. It is hard to conceive how such a concern could lie behind the necessity claims of the second kind. The passage from *Shabbat* does not seem to imagine that R. Hiyya added "nightfall" to the Mishnah's "afternoon prayer" or vice versa—nor does it seem to posit that the formulators of these texts were aware of each other's versions. Likewise, in the second example, the explanations of R. Yohanan and Ben Betera are presented separately, as two alternative answers to the same question, rather than as potentially redundant components of the same text. The problem these necessity claims address is different: given that the two teachings agree on the law but present it or explain it differently, why do we need both? These passages do not aim to defend a text's perfection or deliberate design.

Correspondingly, these two sets of passages make different claims. Necessity claims of the first kind argue that a reciter deliberately included certain examples or teachings—much like what Midrash argues about Scripture. If the second set of passages was making such an argument, it would imply that the pairs of sages collaborated, or that at least one of them knew of the other and deliberately added his words to explain or express the ruling fully. But this does not seem to be the point. Instead, the Yerushalmi argues that each teaching captures only part of the ruling, and therefore both are required for a full appreciation of the law and its reasoning. A phrase found in many of these passages emphasizes the way the texts are wanting, the way they are in *need* of each other: "our Mishnah needs the *mishnah* of R. Hiyya, and the *mishnah* of R. Hiyya needs our Mishnah."[42] This

---

[42] Here and in its other occurrences, the phrase could also mean: "Our Mishnah *is needed* by the *mishnah* of R. Hiyya, and the *mishnah* of R. Hiyya *is needed* by our Mishnah." The order in which the "need" is demonstrated does not necessarily lead to one translation or the other. While the "neediness"

phrase is never used in the other set of passages. These claims, then, highlight not the deliberate design of rabbinic teachings or their perfection, but rather their imperfection. The fact that in the Bavli the first type of necessity claim is much more common than the second, even in comments concerning rabbinic teachings, shows that the Yerushalmi's approach is not an inevitable response to the characteristics of rabbinic teachings.[43]

This fragmentary construction also implies a different role for the scholar. While Midrashic interpretation may imply that the true meaning of Scripture is revealed only through the work of the homilists, the emphasis, as Yadin-Israel argued, is on the agency of Scripture. To use the language in the passage from *Rosh Ha-Shanah*, it is the Torah itself which brings its bread from far away. In the absence of such rhetoric concerning rabbinic teachings, and given phrases which emphasize their mutual "neediness," the implication of these passages is that only the scholar, with his erudition, can bring about the complete understanding of the law that was until now scattered in parts.

3. Recontextualization and fragmentation

I use the term "recontextualization" to refer to a broad range of comments which argue that a teaching should be read with a different referent—a different case or a different text—than it was assumed to have had until that point. Such commentary, we shall see, applies both to teachings which circulated independently and to teachings which circulated already embedded in a particular literary context. We have encountered such comments throughout the preceding chapters. The previous section, for example, analyzed the Talmud's discussion of the Mishnah's repetition of the ruling on shallow pools. At first, the Talmud assumes both instances refer to the same situation, which raises the question of why both instances are necessary. R. Phinehas solves this problem by suggesting that the second teaching refers to a specific case of a pool which the public would walk through only when pressed. As I noted in Chapter 6, the single most common response the Talmud offers to recitation divergences is such recontextualizing commentary.

---

of the texts is more pronounced in the translation I chose, the statement highlights the way the teachings need each other under both translations.

[43] In tractate *'Eruvin*, for example, "necessity" applies only once to two differentiated teaching (b. 'Er. 40a), but many times to two parts of the Mishnah or a single teaching (b. 'Er. 3a, 35a, 66b, 70a, 84a) or to teachings attributed to the same sage (23a, 23b, 39b, 49a, 57b, 74b, 77a, and see especially 55a–b, where the issue is raised explicitly). In tractate *Qiddushin*, we find one case where a necessity claim applies to two *baraitot* (b. Qid. 24a), and there are a couple of cases where such claims address teachings attributed to different sages (59b, 74a); but more often, such claims apply to a single passage in the Mishnah (50b, 60b, 64b, 65a, 79a), a single Amoraic teaching (43b, 66a), or teachings of the same sage or set of sages (7a, 13b, 75a, 60b). On *zerikhuta* and the anonymous layer of the Bavli more broadly, see Cohen, "Biqoret"; Blankovsky, *Reading Talmudic Sources*, 117–20.

We have seen, for example, how the apparent contradiction between the recitation which permits wearing *impilia* on the Day of Atonement and the recitation which prohibits it was addressed by positing different referents: the teaching which permits refers to *impilia* of cloth, while the teaching which prohibits refers to *impilia* of leather.[44] There are several common phrases used to introduce such comments in the Yerushalmi: "it was said concerning..." (*le/be... ita'amrat*), "let it be solved" (*tipater*), "the recited teaching [speaks] of..." (*matnita be-*) and its abbreviated form (*be...*), "to [different] sides," (*li-ẓedadin*), and "I sustained it..." (*qiyamtiah*); others are explored below.

Scholars often refer to such comments as *oqimtot* (singular: *oqimta*). The term derives from verbal forms used for some recontextualizations in the Babylonian Talmud, though the noun itself was coined later. Various definitions have been offered for *oqimtot*, and while the term is frequently applied to the Yerushalmi, discussions of the phenomenon have normally relied on the Bavli. Here, I use the term as a shorthand for the most common type of recontextualizing comment in the Talmud: the qualification or argument that the teaching applies only in a particular case or set of cases. Such qualifications appear already in the Tannaitic corpus, but while Tannaitic qualifications are normally presented in the same voice of the teaching, seemingly as a clarification of its scope,[45] their Talmudic counterparts are more frequently presented as discrete comments which aim to sustain teachings in light of objections.[46]

There are few aspects of Talmudic commentary that have generated as much scholarly discussion as *oqimtot*, especially those in the Bavli and those which argue that seemingly general rulings apply only to very narrow cases. Much of the modern debate on the way that the Talmuds ignore the "plain sense" of the Mishnah has focused on them; and they therefore contributed to the idea that the Talmuds offer non-contextual and non-literal reading of rabbinic teachings, much like the sages do with Scripture.[47] As is the case with Midrash, some scholars suggested *oqimtot* are pseudo-interpretations. Menachem Fisch, for example, argued that the *oqimta* is a self-conscious exercise in anti-traditionalism, employed by later generations to address teachings that no longer seemed viable to them through "interpretations" that are in fact blatant rejections.[48]

---

[44] *Yom.* 8:1 44d (par. *Ta'an* 1:6 64c, *Yev.* 12:1 12c).

[45] See especially the very common phrase, "In what [cases] are these things said," e.g. in *m. B. Q.* 1:2, cited below.

[46] The difference is of degree, and there is a significant number of Tannaitic qualifications which are presented as commentary and respond to an objection (see e.g. *t. Ket.* 7:11, *m. Pes.* 1:1) or harmonize contradictory sources (see e.g. *m. Sheq.* 4:7, *m. 'Ar.* 8:5, *t. M. S.* 4:5, *t. Shab.* 8:2, and *t. M. Q.* 1:8).

[47] See e.g. Gafni, *Mishnah's Plain Sense*, 146–7, on Schorr's attack on the Talmuds' *oqimta* for *m. Sot.* 9:3; and see ibid., 97, on the *oqimtot* and the idea, attributed to Elijah of Vilna, that the Talmud attends to the *derash* (as opposed to "plain sense") of the Mishnah.

[48] Fisch, "Parshanut." Reichman, "Okimta," suggests the *oqimta* works like a Peircean abduction, deriving the ostensibly "surprising" teaching's meaning not through interpretation of the teaching itself, but from generally known principles.

In a recent book dedicated to the *oqimta* in the Bavli, Itamar Brenner argued against such judgments that we should take seriously the interpretive function of *oqimtot* and reconstruct the hermeneutic approaches which they reflect. Brenner opposes *oqimtot* with what he terms "literal" or "philological" interpretation. "Literal" interpretation aims to understand the original meaning of the text based on its wording; it is "philological" when it criticizes the current form of the text and seeks to restore its original form. The *oqimta*, in contrast, is "non-literal" interpretation. Instead of aiming at the text's original meaning, it seeks to give sense to the text in particular frameworks—scholastic exercise, legal application, and the promotion of certain values. In contrast with a "philological" approach, it defends the integrity of the text as it is. Though both kinds of interpretation are found in the Bavli, it is the *oqimta*-style, "non-literal" interpretation, which is more dominant. What justifies the *oqimtot* is the "religious-divine" authority of the sources which they uphold. In all these senses, Brenner argues, the Bavli's interpretation of rabbinic teachings is like the Midrashic interpretation of Scripture.[49] I agree with Brenner that we must take seriously the claim of *oqimtot* to be interpretations (though I think that sometimes, they were proposed with a wink). While his study focuses on the Bavli, I engage with it here in detail because it presents a rich theory of the hermeneutics underlying *oqimtot*, and because my interpretation of the way they work in the Yeurshalmi goes in the opposite direction, emphasizing the difference, rather than convergence, between recontextualizing commentary on Scripture and rabbinic teachings.

It is certainly the case that Midrash presents what can be described as *oqimtot* as well as other recontextualizing commentary on biblical verses.[50] Rosen-Zvi writes that what allows for such non-contextual readings in Midrash is the sages' notion of the nature of Scripture: "the linear reading, one verse after the other, is according to them only one possibility which does not exhaust all the meanings held by the sacred text."[51] With rabbinic teachings, I argue, recontextualizing commentary interacts with a different set of conceptions or constructions: the Talmud binds such commentary with a critique of the transmission and composition of the text that the sages do not apply to Scripture.[52] Amoraic scholars constructed rabbinic

---

[49] See Brenner, *Okimta*, 24–30, on "literal" and "non-literal" interpretations as well as on the similarity between *oqimtot* and scriptural interpretation; see also 159–60. On "divine-religious" authority, see ibid., 44. On the contrast between "philology" and *oqimtot*, see ibid., 71–3 and esp. 107–30.

[50] Recontextualizing commentary on verses is commonplace; it is sometimes introduced with marked terminology, for example, with the phrase, "if it does not concern *x*, teach it concerning *y*"; see e.g. *Pes.* 2:2 28d. In a few places in his survey of Midrash, Rosen-Zvi aptly uses the term *oqimta* to describe Midrashic recontextualizing commentary: see *Mishnah and Midrash*, 416–17 (on Mekhilta de-Rabbi Ishmael, Kaspa §20), 276–7 (Mekhilta de-Rabbi Ishmael, Neziqin §10), and 308–9 (Sifra, Sherazim, 1:2).

[51] Rosen-Zvi, *Mishnah and Midrash*, 327.

[52] We do find rabbinic passages about biblical disorder, but they do not explain such disorder as the result of error, but rather as a sign of divine authorship, or, alternatively, as a feature of conventional (but deliberate) literary rhetoric. For the former explanation, see Moss, "Disorder"; for the latter, see Paz, *Scribes to Scholars*, 273–306. The main point of these passages is that the order of appearance is not

teachings as fragments in the sense that they are lost. They posited that these teachings separated from their original context in the process of transmission, and that they now circulated without crucial contextualizing detail or were embedded in a misleading context. The aim of recontextualizing commentary, in this framework, is to restore the original context or referent of the teaching.

I mentioned above Stern's suggestion that the Midrashic interpretation of verses in isolation from their context stems from the way that the sages encountered Scripture, primarily as memorized bits of text. With respect to rabbinic teachings, a similar argument can be made even more forcefully. After all, while the sages recognized scriptural verses had a literary context in the Bible even when they chose to transcend or ignore it, many rabbinic teachings circulated without a definite context. The only rabbinic compilation the Talmud comments on as such is the Mishnah. Other teachings are cited as short bits of text. In some cases, it would appear teachings circulated without any context at all—in one passage, Amoraic scholars debate whether a certain teaching, which defines a kind of ladder as having more than three rungs, was said in the context of Sabbath laws, impurity laws, or property laws.[53] We also have evidence that the transposition of teachings from one case to another or from one literary context to another was a widespread phenomenon, indeed one of the central ways in which rabbinic literature and law developed.[54] The Talmud itself, we shall see, comments on the phenomenon. In other words, one could say that whereas Midrash fragments Scripture by taking verses out of context, Amoraic scholars read rabbinic teachings as fragments because they were, already, fragments, puzzle pieces that moved from one context to another.

But the Talmudic discourse studied here cannot be explained only in terms of the facts of rabbinic transmission; it presents a particular hermeneutic approach. Recontextualizing commentary is not simply a response to a lack of context: it is not only that many recontextualizations apply to teachings that the sages encountered in the Mishnah, a literary context they knew well; it is also that recontextualizations more generally assume a certain referent or context for a teaching and argue against it. Talmudic representations of the process in which

---

necessarily determinative for the order of meaning—see the similar point made about the Mishnah at Dem. 5:1 24c and see Mazeh, "Demai," 174–5.

[53] Shab. 3:6 6c and B. B. 3:6 14b.

[54] This phenomenon has many aspects and works differently in various levels and layers. Albeck emphasized how essential it is for the systematic development of Halakhah already in the Mishnah—see his *Untersuchungen*, e.g. 5–10; and with respect to the Talmuds in *Talmud*, 452–522. Weiss's studies (e.g. *Talmud in Its Development*), though focused on the Bavli, offer important theoretical insights on the connection between this phenomenon and the development of the Talmudic genre. With respect to the Yerushalmi, the phenomenon has most often been discussed in relation to the duplication of passages (Moscovitz, "Formation," 673–5), which by definition relates to the late stages of the Yerushalmi's development or even to its transmission in writing, but here too the phenomenon is deep and varied—see Sussmann, "Ve-shuv," 90–1; and esp. Mazeh, "Demai," 85–197.

rabbinic teachings were transmitted or composed have been analyzed by scholars interested in the information they provide us on the formation of the rabbinic corpus: passages where Amoraic scholars say, for example, that a teaching was appended to the wrong context, have been used by scholars such as Chanoch Albeck to demonstrate that teachings "wandered" from one context to another. But such discussions by Amoraic scholars are not, or not only, reports on the realities of transmission: they are often the result of these scholars' own analysis of the text, motivated by interpretive considerations such as resolving contradictions or addressing redundancies. While these passages may certainly provide us with useful information on how rabbinic teachings were composed, circulated, and embedded in literary sequences, they also show us how Amoraic scholars construed these processes and mobilized them in service of their own scholarly agenda.

Faulty transmission and recontextualization

In Chapter 5, we have seen that the Talmud sometimes uses "arrival statements" to show that there is a definite tradition on a question that was until that point answered through speculation. Occasionally, we find such arrival statements supporting recontextualizing interpretations by offering a different version of the teaching on which the question arose:

'Avodah Zarah 1:4 39d

ר' בא בריה דר' חייה בר בא בשם ר' יוחנן: אם היה פונדק מותר.

ר' זעירא בעי: ביריד אסור ובפונדק מותר? דילמ' בפרגמטיא אמרה ר' יוחנן.

אתא ר' בא בריה דר' חייה בר בא בשם ר' יוחנן: אם היה פונדק מותר בפרקמטיא.

[The discussion in general concerns restrictions on participation of Jews in trade fairs dedicated to Greco-Roman deities].

R. Abba son of R. Hiyya b. Abba [said] in the name of R. Yohanan: If it was an inn, it is permitted.

R. Ze'ira asked: in the case of the fair it is prohibited and in the case of the inn it is permitted? Perhaps R. Yohanan was speaking with respect to goods.

R. Abba son of R. Hiyya b. Abba came [and said] in the name of R. Yohanan: If it was an inn it is permitted in goods.

Shabbat 1:10 4b

ר' אחא ר' תנחום בר חייא בשם ר' שמעון בר': חמין שהוחמו כל צורכן מותר להחזירן על גבי כירה שאינה קטומה.

ר׳ זעירא בעי: לשהות אסור ולהחזיר מותר? דילמ׳ לא איתאמרת אלא על פסח.

אתא ר׳ אחא בשם ר׳ שמעון בְרֵיבִי: פסח שנצלה כל צורכו מותר להחזירו על גבי כירה שאינה קטומה.

R. Aha [said] in the name of R. Tanhum b. Hiyya [who said] in the name of R. Simeon b. Rabbi: Hot water that was sufficiently heated, it is permitted to place it back on a stove which has not been covered with ashes.

R. Ze'ira asked: To leave it is prohibited, but to place it back permitted? Perhaps it was actually said concerning the Passover offering.

R. Aha came [and said] in the name of R. Simeon b. Rabbi: A Passover offering that was roasted sufficiently, it is permitted to place it back on a stove which has not been covered with ashes.

In both passages, R. Ze'ira objects that a certain teaching seems inconsistent with other known laws on the subject, and suggests a recontextualizing interpretation: in the first case, the teaching speaks not just of an inn but specifically about trade goods in an inn;[55] in the second case, the teaching speaks not of hot water but of the Passover offering.[56] In both cases, R. Ze'ira's interpretation is conveniently confirmed by arrival statements which present the allegedly correct version of the teaching with its proper context. R. Simeon b. Rabbi's teaching was circulating with the wrong wording, and originally indeed concerned the Passover offering and not hot water;[57] R. Yohanan's teaching was transmitted only partially, and originally referred not just to the inn but specifically to goods at the inn. There is a difference between the two cases in the fault of transmission these passages implicitly allege: R. Yohanan's teaching on the inn was transmitted intact but lost a crucial specification; R. Simeon's teaching was mistakenly transmitted with reference to water sufficiently heated rather than to an offering sufficiently roasted. But in both cases, the claim is that the referent of a teaching was lost or corrupted in transmission, and that R. Ze'ira's interpretation restored the original as confirmed by supposedly more reliable texts.[58]

---

[55] While the structure of this passage is clear, R. Ze'ira's precise point is not. From context, the point seems to be that trading at the inn is permitted because it does not benefit specifically from the fair's tax benefits; see Safrai, "Fairs," 148. R. Ze'ira may refer to "goods which entered the city prior to the fair," as his very similar *oqimta* later in the passage reads; others suggested that the text be emended so it reads "trader" rather than "goods," or that R. Ze'ira is speaking about "goods" as opposed to slaves (Rabinovitz, *STEI*, 558; Krochmal, *Jerusalem*, 93).

[56] On this issue, see Wald, "Food for the Sabbath."

[57] The next unit in the Mishnah discusses the Passover offering—it is possible that the Talmud is making the claim that this is why the subject of the teaching was switched.

[58] Other examples include an additional instance in each of the passages discussed above, and since all involve a similar structure—an objection from R. Ze'ira, followed by his interpretation, and then an arrival statement—they themselves show us evidence of "transferring" of teachings from context to context (R. Ze'ira is also involved in a similar passage in *Ter.* 10:10 47b).

I noted above Brenner's argument that, in contrast with what he defines as "literal" interpretations, *oqimtot* do not aim to restore the text's original intention.[59] Here, though, we see how R. Ze'ira's *oqimta* is justified by adducing the supposedly original form of the text. It is useful to contrast the claim made by this kind of passage with another set of claims which similarly present what seems like the innovative result of interpretation as the recovery of something that was once known and lost. We have seen that kind of justification in Mishnah *Yadaim*, and the Yerushalmi too sometimes deploys the argument, "thus was the tradition in their hand, but they had forgotten it." But those passages speak about the restoration of a once-known law, not any specific teaching. Several of them bind such restoration with claims to trans-historical continuity of tradition from the Sinaitic revelation. They argue that, precisely because it is not the contribution of a specific sage, it can always be restored with sufficient intellectual effort.[60] Here, the restoration aims at what a specific sage said in a specific utterance.

This emphasis is even clearer in two other sets of examples. First, in several passages, Amoraic scholars invoke the teaching's original moment of instruction to show that it had a different referent and to criticize other scholars for omitting or mistaking that referent:

Yevamot 8:3 9c–9d (par. *Qiddushin* 3:12 64c and 4:1 65c)

רב הונא אמ': אין ממזר חי יותר משלשים יום. ר' זעירא כד סלק להכא שמע קלין קריין, "ממזירא" ו"ממזרתה". אמ' לון: מהו כך? הא אזילא ההיא דרב הונא, דרב הונא אמ', "אין ממזר חי יותר משלשים יום."

אמ' ליה ר' יעקב בר אחא: עמך הייתי כד אמ' ר' בא רב הונא בשם רב, "אין ממזר חי יותר משלשים יום. אימתי. בזמן שאינו מפורסם." הא אם היה מפורסם חי הוא.

Rav Huna said: **A *mamzer* does not live for more than thirty days.** R. Ze'ira, when he came up here [to Palestine], heard voices saying, "*mamzera*," and "*mamzerta*" [referring to living individuals as *mamzerim*]. He said to them [the local sages], "What is this? Here goes that [teaching] of Rav Huna."

Said to him R. Jacob b. Aha: I was with you when R. Abba b. Rav Huna said in the name of Rav: "A *mamzer* does not live for more than thirty days. In what cases? When his status is not publicized"—therefore, if his status is publicized, he does live.

This passage first introduces us to Rav Huna's teaching that *mamzerim*, offspring of illegitimate unions whom the Torah prohibits from marrying other Jews, do not

---

[59] See above n. 49.
[60] See the passages discussed above in Chapter 5, Section 4, and Chapter 4, nn. 93–5. In *Pe'ah* 2:6 17a (par. *Ḥag.* 1:7 76d) the discussion concludes with an anonymous question that is skeptical of such claims that laws once known were forgotten.

live for more than thirty days.[61] We then hear that when R. Zeʻira moved from Babylonia to Palestine, he heard people calling various individuals *mamzerim*, which, if we take it seriously as a descriptor of those individuals' genealogical status, seems to undermine Rav Huna's teaching: here we have living adult *mamzerim*. R. Jacob b. Aha responds that he was present when R. Zeʻira heard that teaching from Rav Huna's son, and on that occasion, it was made clear that the teaching only applies to *mamzerim* that are not known (and therefore people may unwittingly marry them), while the individuals R. Zeʻira heard called out are, by definition, known to be *mamzerim*. The passage emphasizes that the teaching has been circulating in a missing form—seemingly because R. Zeʻira did not understand or left out the important qualification which was made at the time of instruction, and was therefore misunderstood.[62]

Two passages in tractate ʻ*Orlah* give us a bit more detail on how a teaching may have assumed a misleading context. In both passages, R. Yose attributes to R. Yohanan the teaching that "roots have no significance"; R. Zeʻira asks him if he heard this explicitly from R. Yohanan and proceeds to explain how R. Yose may have gotten the teaching wrong. In the first passage, R. Zeʻira suggests to R. Yose, "you were studying tractate ʻ*Orlah*, and this issue [of roots] in *Bikkurim* was mentioned, and he [R. Yohanan] said, 'roots have no substance'"—and because of that R. Yose mistook the teaching to be about ʻ*Orlah*.[63] In the second passage, R. Zeʻira suggests R. Yose may have mistakenly derived this teaching "from the line (*shita*)" of R. Yohanan, by assuming that the logic R. Yohanan applies in one case can be applied to another.[64] This passage records the argument that an Amoraic scholar sloppily conflated the general context of the lesson with the specific context of the teaching, or erroneously produced a teaching about a particular case through misapplication of R. Yohanan's ruling in other cases.

While the passages studied in this section emphasize the original utterance of the sage, they themselves present the fluid textuality they ostensibly resist. First, they seem to have been produced through the transpositions characteristic of rabbinic literature, which apply to various situations the same structures and sometimes words. The first two passages, about R. Zeʻira, follow exactly the same pattern: R.

---

[61] On this passage, see Koren, "Persons," 161–91; Kiperwasser, *Going West*, 47–51.

[62] There are other instances where such reports work to offer a particular context or referent to a teaching—see *Taʻan*. 4:7 69c (par. *Meg*. 1:3 70c, *Yev*. 6:6 7d) on whether Rabbi Judah's attempt to abolish the 9th of Av concerned specifically a 9th of Av that coincided with the Sabbath, and *Yom*. 1:1 38d (par. *Meg*. 1:9 72b and *Hor*. 3:4 47d) on whether R. Yohanan's teaching on the priest's vestment was about serving or receiving inquiries. At *Shevi*. 5:5 36a, R. Judah reports that R. Tarfon let them eat arum following Sukkot, and R. Yose corrects him that it was after Passover. The phrase works to offer other kinds of corrections in *M. Q*. 3:5 82c and in the other instance in the *Taʻan* passage cited above.

[63] ʻ*Or*. 1:1 60d: אמ' ר' זעירא לר' יסא. בפירוש שמעתנה מן דר' יוחנן או בערלה הויתון קיימין ואתדכרת הדא מילתא בביכורין ואמ'. שרשין אין בהן ממש. Cf. also *B. B*. 2:12 13c. My interpretation follows Elijah of Vilna; other commentators have an opposite understanding of the original and mistaken context, but the structure of the argument is the same.

[64] ʻ*Or*. 1:5 61a: אמ' ר' זעירא לר' יוסי. בפירוש שמעתנה מן ר' יוחנן או מן שיטתיה. See Lieberman, *TK*, 2.818.

Ze'ira raises a problem, offers a solution, and the solution is confirmed by an arrival statement citing a different version of the same teaching. The passages invoking the original context of the teaching apply the same phrase, "I was with you," in different contexts. The two passages in which R. Ze'ira criticizes R. Yose seem to be two versions of the same story. Furthermore, by offering recontextualizations, these arguments continue the process of changing the context of teachings through other means, even if they do so through commentary rather than reformulation, and even as they claim to restore the teaching's lost context.

The number of passages which argue that teachings circulate in a missing or misleading form is not insignificant, but the large majority of recontextualizing comments in the Talmud do not appear with such justifications. It is therefore possible that these passages do not tell us much about the phenomenon of recontextualizing commentary in general. But it is also possible that these passages reveal the hermeneutic framework that is at work even when such justification is absent. Before considering this possibility further, I look at comments in the Yerushalmi which probe the literary context of teachings.

"It was not said about this, but about that"

There is nowhere in the Talmud an account of the process by which rabbinic teachings came to be included in compilations or otherwise attached one to the other—though there are bits and pieces: we have seen, for example, in Chapter 1, discussions of how teachings became anonymized; another example is the reference to Sinaitic traditions "embedded in the *mishnah*" (*Pe'ah* 2:6 17a and parallels). In this section, I study comments which argue that a teaching should have a different textual referent, and which therefore call into question the process by which the teaching acquired its current referent. These statements resemble the recontextualizing comments examined above, since offering a different textual referent almost always means the teaching applies to a different case, but they target more specifically the way the teaching was appended to other teachings or the order in which teachings appear. The most common phrase used in the Talmud for such comments is "it was not said about this but about that," which appears in eleven passages:[65]

m. Bava Qamma 4:3

שור של ישרא' שנגח שור של נכרי פטור. ושלנכרי שנגח לשור של ישרא', בין תם ובין מועד, משלם נזק שלם.

---

[65] In addition to the three passages analyzed below, see *Pe'ah* 4:9 18c, *Pe'ah* 7:2 20a, *Dem.* 2:4 23a, *Ḥal.* 1:4 57d, *'Er.* 4:5 22a, *'Er.* 5:6 22d, *Ned.* 3:2 38a, and *'A. Z.* 4:11 44b. Another phrase with a similar function is "the teachings are here" (שמועתא הכא/כאן)—see *Shevi.* 3:2 34c (par. *M. Q.* 1:2 80b), and *Ter.* 10:1 47a (par. *'Or.* 2:8 62a and *'A. Z.* 5:2 44d), and Moscovitz, "Shemu'ata Kan."

The ox of a Jew who gored the ox of a gentile, he [the Jewish owner] is exempt. But [the ox] of a gentile who gored the ox of a Jew, whether it is unattested [to be prone to goring] or attested, he [the gentile] pays full damages.

Bava Qamma 4:3 4b

ר׳ אבהו בשם ר׳ יוחנן אמ׳: כדיניהן. אמ׳ ר׳ לא: לא על הדא איתאמרת אלא בהדא דתני ר׳ חייה, "שור שלגוי שנגח שור שלגוי אחר חבירו. אע״פ שקיבל עליו לדון כדיני יש׳ בין תם בין מועד משלם נזק שלם", על הדא אתאמרת, ר׳ אבהו בשם ר׳ יוחנן, "כדיניהן".

R. Abbahu said in the name of R. Yohanan, "It is in accord with their laws."

Said R. Hila: It was not said about this [*matnita*] but about that [*matnita*] that R. Hiyya recited, "An ox belonging to a gentile which gored an ox belonging to another gentile, his fellow: even if he accepted upon himself to be judged according to Jewish law, whether the ox was unattested or attested, he must pay full damages"—on this it was said: R. Abbahu [said] in the name of R. Yohanan, "it is in accord with their laws."

The Mishnah presents two rulings. First, if a Jewish-owned ox gored a gentile-owned ox, the Jewish owner is exempt from paying damages to the gentile; second, if a gentile-owned ox gored a Jewish-owned ox, then the usual rule, which would have the owner of the goring ox pay full damages only if the ox was attested to goring in the past (and therefore should have been guarded more carefully), is suspended, and the gentile owner must pay full damages whether the ox has been attested or not.

The Talmud records R. Yohanan's comment that the Mishnah's ruling is "according to their laws"—i.e. the gentiles' laws. It is unclear which of the Mishnah's rulings this comment aims to explain. Maimonides takes it to provide a reasoning for the first rule: "the ox of a Jew who gored the ox of a gentile ... he is exempt—for the gentiles do not hold liable a person for damages his animal caused, and we judge them according to their own laws."[66] But the majority of commentators on the Yerushalmi take R. Yohanan's statement to refer to the latter part of the Mishnah: since gentile law makes no distinction between an unattested ox and an attested ox, the gentile must pay full damages even if the ox was unattested.[67]

The next statement in the Talmud, by R. Hila, argues that R. Yohanan's teaching was not said in connection with these teachings in the Mishnah at all. Rather, it refers to a different teaching, recited by R. Hiyya. That teaching does not discuss a gentile-owned ox goring a Jewish-owned ox, but rather a gentile-owned ox goring

---

[66] Maimonides, *Book of Torts*, Property Damages 8:5 (Ma'agarim).
[67] See e.g. Lewy, *Interpretation*, 112. See Furstenberg, "Competition to Integration," 48 n. 80, who refers to *Digest* 9:1 to confirm that Roman law indeed made no such distinction.

another gentile-owned ox. It rules that even if the parties agree to be judged according to Jewish law, full damages are paid whether the ox was attested or not. A version of this teaching in the Tosefta explains that this is because "there is no 'unattested' and 'attested' in the damages of a gentile."[68] Under R. Hila's explanation, R. Yohanan's teaching makes the same point: since gentile law does not make this differentiation between "attested" and "unattested," it does not apply to gentiles even if they litigate their case through Jewish courts.[69]

R. Hila's comment not only reflects a different understanding of R. Yohanan's teaching; it also draws our attention to how appending that teaching to this passage in the Mishnah determines its meaning and, by disputing this context, makes that connection a topic of discussion. There are two possibilities for understanding R. Hila's comment and others of its kind. As I mentioned in the introduction to this section, some scholars have seen such comments as evidence that teachings circulated without a fixed textual context. If we apply this approach here, R. Hila is either reporting that he learned R. Yohanan's comment in connection with R. Hiyya's teaching rather than with the Mishnah, or he is responding to doubts about the comment's proper context and suggests it was said about R. Hiyya's teaching.

A second possibility is that this statement is not just a reflection of the way R. Yohanan's teaching was circulating, but rather an interpretive argument about this teaching. Under this possibility, R. Hila encountered R. Yohanan's teaching, much as we do in the Talmud, as a comment about the Mishnah's ruling. Based on his own analysis, he decided that this context is mistaken, and that in fact R. Yohanan's teaching should be interpreted in relation to R. Hiyya's ruling. While under both possibilities, the passage highlights the way a teaching may be seen as a fragment placed in multiple contexts, it is only under the second possibility that this presentation is a construct imposed by an Amoraic scholar on the text.

In the case of this passage, there are two factors supporting the first possibility. First, we cannot assume that R. Hila encountered the teaching in the way we do in the Talmud, so it may well be that he has learned it as a comment on R. Hiyya's teaching or not appended to any teaching at all; when he then heard R. Yohanan's teaching presented as a comment on the Mishnah, he corrected that association with the statement "it was not said about this, but about that." Second, R. Hila's statement is not explicitly presented as motivated by interpretive concerns, so it is possible he is simply reporting the way he learned the teaching. At the same time, the Yerushalmi often does not report such interpretive motivations, and in this case, we could easily supply one: the argument may be that R. Yohanan's explanation is more apt in a case that does not involve Jewish owners.

---

[68] *t. B. Q.* 4:2: שאין תם ומועד בנזקי הגוי.
[69] On the different conceptions the passage presents of the relationship between non-Jews or non-Jewish law and Jewish law, see Furstenberg, "Competition to Integration," 47–51.

In other passages we find such statements presented explicitly as answers to objections and addressing teachings that Amoraic scholars encountered in a textual context they certainly knew well—the Mishnah.[70] Consider the following example:

m. Nedarim 5:1

השותפים שנדרו הנייה זה מזה אסורין ליכנס לחצר. ר' אליעזר בן יעקב אומ': זה נכנס לתוך שלו וזה נכנס לתוך שלו. שניהן אסורין מלהעמיד ריחיים ותנור ומלגדל תרנגלין.

היה אחד מהן מודר מחבירו הנייה, לא ייכנס לחצר. ר' אליעזר בן יעקב או': יכול הוא לומ' לו, "בתוך שלי אני נכנס ואיני ניכנס בתוך שלך". כופין את הנודר שימכור את חלקו.

Joint owners who vowed not to benefit one from the other are prohibited from entering the courtyard [they share]. R. Eliezer b. Jacob says: This one enters his own [part], and that one enters his own. Both are prohibited from setting up a mill or an oven or raising chickens.

If one of them was prohibited by vow to benefit from his fellow, he may not enter the courtyard. R. Eliezer b. Jacob says: He may say to him, "I am entering my own, and I am not entering yours." We compel the vower to sell his share.

Nedarim 5:1 39a

"בתוך שלי אני נכנס ולא בתוך שלך", ואת אמר "כופין"? לא על הדא איתאמרת אלא על הדא, "היה אחד מהן מודר מחבירו הנייה לא ייכנס לחצר",[71] עליה "כופין את הנודר[72] שימכור חלקו". באומ' "הנייתי עליך", אבל באומ' "הנייתך עלי" לא בדא.

"I am entering my own, and I am not entering yours"—and you say, "we compel"? It was not said about this, but about that: "*If one of them was prohibited by vow to derive benefit from his fellow*"[73]—on this [it was said] "we compel the vower to sell his share," with respect to the one who said "my benefit is prohibited to you," but not with respect to the one who said "your benefit is prohibited to me."

---

[70] In addition to the two passages from *Ned.* analyzed below, see also *'Er.* 4:5 22a (with Lieberman, YK, 286), and *Pe'ah* 7:2 20a, as reconstructed in Maimonides (in his Mishnah Commentary) and Lieberman, TK, 2.172.

[71] The underlined passage represents my emendation. See n. 73.

[72] Correcting מוכר.

[73] MS Leiden quotes here the next unit in the Mishnah (*m. Ned.* 5:2, "I enter my fellow's, not yours") as the new referent of the statement "we compel the vower to sell his share." This does not seem right, given the conclusion of the Yerushalmi here and the comment in the discussion of that next unit that in that case "compel" is not recited. Lieberman, TK, 7.435, notes that some medieval testimonia lack any reference and concludes that the reference in MS Leiden is an erroneous addition; he writes that the point of the Yerushalmi is that the ruling "we compel" is part of the sages' words, not R. Eliezer's. Moscovitz ("Double Readings," 217–18 n. 230) agrees that the reference to *m. Ned.* 5:2 is erroneous but argues that the phrase "it was not said about this, but about that" requires an alternative reference; he suggests it is the very first case of the Mishnah, "the joint owners who vowed not to benefit are prohibited from entering the courtyard." But this seems incorrect as well—how can the statement "we compel the *vower*" refer to a case where both parties vowed? My emendation is close to Lieberman's interpretation but reflects Moscovitz's point that some reference is required; my analysis below further supports this reading.

The Mishnah discusses two cases concerning joint owners of a property with a shared courtyard. In the first case, both owners vowed not to benefit from one another, and the anonymous ruling is that even though they both own the courtyard, they may not enter it since that constitutes benefiting from each other's property. R. Eliezer b. Jacob's dissent argues that each owner may enter his own part. In the second case, only one of the owners was prohibited by vow to derive benefit from the other. The anonymous ruling is again that he may not enter the courtyard, and again R. Eliezer b. Jacob disputes the ruling and says he, the person prohibited by vow, may enter his part since he is merely benefiting from his part of the property. The Mishnah then adds that "we compel the vower to sell his share."

The Talmud records an objection to this last clause in the Mishnah. This objection first assumes that this last sentence is part of R. Eliezer b. Jacob's dissenting view. If it is possible for the one prohibited by vow to enter his own share, why should we compel a sale of the property? The Talmud concludes that the lines must be switched, and the statement "we compel" does not belong in R. Eliezer b. Jacob's words, but in the anonymous position before it. The result of this shift is a ruling which highlights the contrast between the different parties of the case: "If one of them *was prohibited by vow* (*mudar*) to benefit from his fellow, he may not enter the courtyard. We compel the *vower* (*noder*) to sell his share." This change also allows the Yerushalmi to explain the conceptual distinction behind the Mishnah's ruling. When the Mishnah describes the case where only one of the joint owners was prohibited from benefiting, it uses the word *mudar* ("prohibited by vow") rather than *noder*. This is a case where Justin is prohibited from benefiting from Carlos not because Justin vowed not to benefit from Carlos, but because Carlos vowed Justin may not benefit from him. In the last clause, the Mishnah identifies the person forced to sell as the *noder*, vower, the person making the vow (our Carlos). Forcing a person to sell, the Yerushalmi concludes, makes sense only in such cases where there is a distinction between *noder* and *mudar*. A joint owner may restrict himself from benefiting from a shared property. But if he restricts his fellow owner from benefiting from that property—even though the vow is valid, and his fellow owner is prohibited by the vow from entering their shared courtyard—the vowing owner must sell his share. Otherwise, joint owners could restrict their fellow owners from using shared property without consequences.

One could argue that this passage only makes a claim about how the Mishnah should be interpreted, that all it says is that the clause "we compel the vower to sell" should be read as part of the words of the anonymous sages. But there are good reasons to think that the claim is not only that these words were misinterpreted, but also that they are misplaced. First, the phrase "it was not said about this but about that" usually describes two discrete teachings that have been matched together, as we have seen above with R. Hila's comment on R. Yohanan's teaching. In such cases, the argument is clearly that the match was a mismatch; here, too, then, the comment likely draws on the notion of the Mishnah as a composite text, and one that could have been mis-composed. Moreover, there are other phrases the Talmud could use if it were merely making a point about how to interpret this unit in the Mishnah. Earlier in the same discussion, the Talmud raises a similar question about the last sentence in the Mishnah's discussion of the previous case, "They are both prohibited from setting up a mill or an oven or raising chickens." The Talmud asks if this prohibition is in reference to R. Eliezer b. Jacob's ruling (and therefore applies only in the case where each joint owner may go into the courtyard) or to the sages' words (and therefore part of the majority opinion). The sensible conclusion is the former: "For whom was this needed? For R. Eliezer b. Jacob."[74] A similar statement could have been made with respect to the teaching about compelling the sale—"for whom was it needed? For the sages."[75] The use of the phrase "it was not said about this but about that" seems to indicate that the Talmud is making the additional point that the teaching is misplaced—it should have been presented as part of the sages' words.

In the passage just examined, the change in location posited by the Talmud is small: a switch in the order of two teachings. Later in the same tractate we find another instance of the phrase which argues for a very different new referent:

m. *Nedarim* 10:1–2

נערה מאורסה—אביה ובעלה מפירים נדריה. היפר האב ולא היפר הבעל, היפר הבעל ולא היפר האב—אינו מופר. אין צורך לומ' שיקם אחד מהן.

מת האב לא ניתרוקנה רשות לבעל. מת הבעל ניתרוקנה רשות לאב.

A betrothed girl—her father and her husband may nullify her vows. If her father nullified and the husband did not nullify, [or] the husband nullified and the father did not nullify—it is not nullified. And there is no need to say that if one of them [explicitly] upheld [the vow, that the other may not subsequently nullify it].

If the father died, [his] authority is not transferred to the husband. If the husband died, [his] authority is transferred to the father.

Nedarim 10:1 41d

איתא חמי: היפר האב אין מופר, ואת אמר הכין?

לא על הדא אתאמרת אלא על הדא: היפר האב את חלקו. לא הספיק הבעל להפר עד שמת, האב מיפר חלקו שלבעל. אמ' ר' נתן: זו דברי בית שמי. אבל דברי חכמ' אין צורך להפר בשלא הקם. אבל אם הקם אינו יכול להפר.

---

[74] למי נצרכה? לר' אליעזר בן ר' יעקב. For the emendation adding למי see Rabinovitz, *STEI*, 403.
[75] See *Shab.* 7:2 10d for a similar discussion of a *matnita* (cf. *t. Shab.* 12:1) which presents an anonymous ruling, a disputing ruling, and then another anonymous ruling, and the Talmud comments the last ruling "was needed only for the sages."

Come and see: If the father nullified it [and the husband did not nullify] it is not nullified, and you say this?

It was not said about this, but about that: If the father nullified his portion, and the husband did not nullify before he died, the father may nullify the husband's portion. Said R. Nathan: These are the words of the House of Shammai. But the words of the sages are that there is no need to nullify if he did not uphold it [explicitly], but if he did uphold it he may not nullify.

According to rabbinic law, a man may nullify the vow of his daughter or wife. The Mishnah here stipulates that in the case of a betrothed girl—a minor still living in her father's house but already engaged to be married—both her father and her husband must nullify the vow for it to be considered null. The Mishnah adds that obviously, if one of the men explicitly upheld the vow, it may not be nullified by the other. According to the Yerushalmi's commentators,[76] the Talmud takes issue with this supposedly superfluous statement: if we were already told that both men need to nullify, why does the Mishnah need to state that if one of them explicitly upheld the vow, the other may not nullify? The answer is that these words were said with respect to another recited teaching which is not included in the Mishnah. That teaching mentions a possible case in which the husband upheld the vow shortly before his death. The Talmud's point is that we may have thought that since, as the Mishnah says later, when the husband dies, his authority transfers to the father, the latter may nullify the vow even if the former explicitly upheld it. The Mishnah therefore had to teach specifically that explicit upholding hinders the nullification. This interpretation of the Talmud's passage is not without difficulties,[77] but regardless of the exact point it makes, its structure is clear, and the passage shows us how Amoraic scholars recontextualized a Mishnaic statement by arguing that its literary referent is not its immediate context in the Mishnah, but rather an altogether different teaching.

---

[76] e.g. *PM* and Shapira, *Noam Yerushalmi*.

[77] While none of the problems with this interpretation is decisive on its own, they add up. First, this interpretation attributes to the Yerushalmi an odd reading of the Mishnah, according to which the statement "if one of them upheld," which avoids specifying whether it was the husband or father who upheld the vow, applies only to a case where the husband upheld it. It is also unusual for the Yerushalmi to make an objection based on redundancy when the Mishnah itself says "and there is no need to say" (such an objection is recorded at *b. Ned.* 67a, but the Bavli in general is more prone to mark redundancies in the Mishnah). In other instances when the phrase "come and see" is used to mark an ostensible redundancy, it is explicitly marked (see Pe'ah 8:7 21a and Ta'an. 1:6 64c). While this interpretation is also reflected in the lemma of the Mishnah cited in our texts, lemmata are later and often erroneous—see Epstein, *IMT*, 941–5; Sussmann, "Introduction," 31 n. 208. A possible alternative is that the Yerushalmi objects to a perceived contradiction between the first and second units in the Mishnah: how could the Mishnah say that "if the father nullified and the husband did not it is not nullified" and then say that "if the husband died his authority is transferred to the father"—after all, the husband has not nullified? The solution is to suggest that the latter statement (the authority transfer) refers to a more specific case. See *t. Ned.* 6:2 which offers a qualification of the same statement.

Modern scholars mined passages employing the phrase "it was not said about this, but about that" for evidence about rabbinic processes of literary composition. Albeck and Weiss, in particular, read them alongside other evidence to demonstrate that rabbinic teachings "wandered" from one context to another.[78] But as we have seen, Amoraic statements that teachings were "not said about this" are not simply indications that these teachings circulated without a definite literary context. Amoraic scholars applied such statements to teachings that were embedded in a context they knew well. Their use of these statements to resolve objections suggests that they are arguments grounded in analysis rather than statements of fact about these teachings' transmission. Hanan Mazeh insightfully writes that understanding these statements as interpretive arguments is not inconsistent with positing that the context of rabbinic teachings was in fact fluid: "it is natural for a scholar who is used to teachings transferring from one context to another ... to suggest that a particular teaching should be appended to a different source or a different part of a source."[79] But while for Mazeh, this point supports the use of such passages for reconstructing Talmudic compositional processes, we should also consider what they teach us about Amoraic notions of rabbinic texts and how these notions informed and justified Amoraic interpretations. These passages show us that Amoraic scholars considered that rabbinic teachings may circulate in misleading contexts, a view which may indeed have been grounded in what they knew about how rabbinic teachings circulated. They developed analytical instruments that allowed them to dislodge teachings from their current context based on interpretive considerations and regardless of the facts about how those specific teachings were transmitted.

The connection between these passages and compositional practices further underscores that they make claims about these teachings' composition rather than simply about their interpretation. In my analysis of the passage from *Nedarim* 5, I observed a difference between the phrase "it was not said about this" and another claim used in the passage which does not make a claim about the passage's composition ("for whom was it needed? For R. Elazar b. Jacob"). A similarly illuminating contrast is with passages employing the phrase *al ... hushva*, "it goes back to" or "it refers to." Such passages address clauses in the Mishnah with ambiguous references:

---

[78] Albeck, *Introduction to the Talmud*, e.g. 452–3, 460 (on comments in the Yerushalmi in particular; see the chapter as a whole for discussions of similar statements in the Bavli); Weiss, *Talmud*, 281–300 (on the Bavli).

[79] Mazeh, "Demai," 125. In his analysis of specific passages, Mazeh concludes that Talmudic discussions are motivated by "authentic doubt" about a teaching's context rather than "interpretive concerns" (ibid., 157, 166, 177). While I may have chosen different words (after all, for Amoraic scholars "interpretive concerns" may be just as "authentic" of a reason to doubt a teaching's context), I do not disagree with these conclusions, but consider other cases to be clearly motivated by interpretation (Mazeh's only example employing "our" phrase is more similar to the first example given here).

m. Bava Qamma 2:2

והבהמה מועדת לאכל פירות וירקות. אכלה כסות או כלים, משלם חצי נזק. במי דברים אמורים? ברשות הניזק, אבל ברשות הרבים פטור.

The domestic animal is presumed to do harm by eating fruit and vegetables, but if it ate clothes or vessels, he [the animal's owner] pays half damages.

In which [case] are these words said? [When the damage was done] in the domain of the damaged party, but in the public domain, he [the owner] is exempt [from paying].

Bava Qamma 2:2 3a

ריש-לקיש אמ': על הראשונה הושבה. ר' יוחנן אמ': על כולה הושבה.

R. Simeon b. Laqish says: It refers to the first [clause]. R. Yohanan says: It refers to all of it.

R. Simeon and R. Yohanan debate the reference of the Mishnah's qualification, which exempts the owner of an animal from paying damages it caused by consumption in the public domain. R. Simeon argues it refers only to the first case described in the Mishnah, of normal damages caused by an animal by eating fruit or vegetables. R. Yohanan argues the qualification applies to all that preceded it, and so it applies even in the unusual case where the animal ate clothes or vessels. What is at stake here is not the composition of the passage, but how to read an ambiguous text. Neither R. Yohanan nor R. Simeon question the unity of this literary unit. Passages employing "it was not said about this, but about that," in contrast, rarely result in a reading of a singular text: they usually argue for unmatching or matching two distinct literary units, or state that the order of the text is inappropriate. The next set of examples similarly shows how Amoraic scholars viewed rabbinic texts as compilations.

"Two reciters" and recontextualization

The last kind of scholarly technique I introduce in this chapter brings us full circle back to the issue of anonymous texts examined in Chapter 1. In eleven passages in the Talmud, we find the argument that a certain recited teaching or two units in the Mishnah are a composite of multiple formulators, "two reciters" or occasionally "three reciters."[80] These passages break apart what until that point was assumed to be a single unit. Consider the following example:

---

[80] In addition to the passages discussed in the main text, see *Ter.* 8:8 46b (par. *Pes.* 1:7 28b), *Shevi.* 2:3 33d, *Shevi.* 7:7 37c, *Shab.* 10:4 12c, *'Er.* 1:7 19b (see Lieberman, *YK*, 236–7), *Meg.* 1:1 70a and 70b, *Ned.* 2:4 37c, and *Shevu.* 3:1 34b. In other instances, the phrase does not argue a teaching is composite but

m. Pesaḥim 1:7

ר' חנניה סגן הכהנים או': מימיהם שלכהנים לא נמנעו מלשרוף את הבשר שניטמא בוולד הטומאה עם הבשר שניטמא באב הטומאה אף-על-פי שמוסיפין לו טומאה על טומאתו.

הוסיף ר' עקיבה: מימיהן שלכהנים לא נמנעו מלהדליק את השמן שניפסל בטבול יום בנר שניטמא בטמא מת אף-על-פי שמוסיפין לו טומאה על טומאתו.

אמ' ר' מאיר: מדבריהם למדנו ששורפים תרומה טהורה עם הטמאה בפסח. אמ' לו ר' יוסי: אינה היא המידה.

מודה ר' אליעזר ור' יהושע ששורפין זו לעצמה וזו לעצמה. ועל מה נחלקו? על התלויה ועל הטמאה. שר' אליעזר אומ' תישרף זו לעצמה וזו לעצמה. ור' יהושע או' שתיהם כאחת.

R. Hananiah, prefect of the priests, says: "Never in their days did the priests avoid burning flesh that became impure through [contact] with a derivative of impurity with flesh that became impure through [contact] with a [primary] source of impurity, even though they [thus] added [further] impurity upon its impurity."

R. Aqiva added: "Never in their days did the priests avoid kindling oil that has been disqualified through [contact] with the day-immersed person [whose purification process will only be completed when the day passes] in a lamp that became impure through [contact] with a person who contracted corpse impurity, even though they [thus] added [further] impurity upon its impurity."

Said R. Meir: From their words we learned that one [may] burn pure priest's share with impure [items in that status] in Passover.

Said R. Yose: This is not a [valid] inference.

R. Eliezer and R. Joshua agree[81] that one [must] burn each on its own. And in what did they dispute? [In the case] of uncertain [priest's share] and impure [items of that status], in which R. Eliezer says each should be burned on its own, and R. Joshua says they may be burned as one.

Pesaḥim 1:7 27d–28a

אמ' ר' יוחנן: מדברי ר' עקיבה מדברי ר' חנניה סגן הכהנים.

ר' שמעון בן לקיש אמ': מדברי ר' אליעזר ומדברי ר' יהושע.

---

rather more generally that teachings which had been thought to represent the same position (because they are both anonymous or because both are attributed to the same sage) are in fact contradictory and therefore do not need to be harmonized (see e.g. *Qid.* 1:2 59c).

[81] MS Kaufman has the singular form, "מודה," but that form might signify the plural (see Friedman, *Tosefta*, 113–14). Later in the Yerushalmi's discussion the version is "R. Eliezer concedes to R. Joshua" (*Pes.* 1:7 28a).

אמ' ר' זעירא קומי ר' יסי: על דעת' דר' שמעון בן לקיש ניחא. על דעת' דר' יוחנן,[82] מה בא ר' ליעזר ור' יושוע לכאן? אמ' ליה: תניין אינון.

Said R. Yohanan: [When R. Meir said, "From their words," he meant] from the words of R. Aqiva [and] from the words of R. Hananiah, prefect of the priests.

R. Simeon b. Laqish said: [No, he meant] from the words of R. Eliezer and from the words of R. Joshua.

Said R. Ze'ira before R. Yose: It is all well on the opinion of R. Simeon b. Laqish. On the opinion of R. Yohanan, why would R. Eliezer and R. Joshua come here?

He said to him: These are [different][83] reciters.

The Mishnah offers two statements, from R. Hananiah and R. Aqiva, about the conduct of the priests in disposing of impure *sancta*; these are followed by R. Meir who derives an additional ruling from "their words." In the Talmud, R. Yohanan suggests "their" words means the preceding words, those of R. Hananiah and R. Aqiva, whereas R. Simeon says it is the opinions of R. Joshua and R. Eliezer discussed later. While R. Yohanan's opinion might seem intuitive, given that R. Meir's statement follows directly the statements of R. Hananiah and R. Aqiva, R. Ze'ira objects to it: if "their words" means the words of R. Hananiah and R. Aqiva, why are R. Eliezer and R. Joshua mentioned here, seemingly in relation to R. Yose's critique of R. Meir? R. Yose (now the Amoraic scholar, rather than the one mentioned in the Mishnah) replies to R. Ze'ira that there are two reciters—that is, this passage is composed of two different teachings formulated by two different people, which resulted in its apparent inconsistency.

This scholarly technique too is premised on the notion that rabbinic teachings circulate as fragments which appear to us not in their original context but rather in composite, uneven sequences. The way it fragments the text is well captured by the phrase used for similar comments in the Bavli, "Break it! Whoever recited this did not recite that."[84] This Bavli phrase also resembles a phrase used by the Tosefta, "whoever said this did not say that"[85] in passages employing the Midrashic technique of positing multiple speakers, and it is illuminating to compare the two.[86] In both cases, the sages take a sequence that seems to be speaking in a singular voice and break it. But the Midrashic technique divides speech among characters,

---

[82] MS Leiden reads: "all is well on the opinion of R. Yohanan. On the opinion of R. Simeon b. Laqish..."—but the names must be switched.

[83] Or "two," according to the common form of the phrase.

[84] See e.g. *b. Shab.* 92b: "תברה מי ששנה זו לא שנה זו." Cf. Friedman, *BM VI*, 381, who translates more broadly: "it breaks it" or "it is a contradiction," so that it fits a broader range of the cases. But as Leib Moscovitz emphasized to me (personal communication), the Bavli phrase is not fully equivalent to the Yerushalmi phrase, as not all the Yerushalmi passages concern contradictions.

[85] "מי שאמר זה לא אמר זה" (*t. Sot.* 2:2–3).

[86] On this unusual Midrashic technique, see Mazeh, "Speaker-Splitting Technique."

not formulators. It is used, for example, to clarify where reported speech ends and narration resumes; or to produce from a single statement a dialogue among characters. It is not used to argue that the biblical text represents conflicting sources because it was formulated by different people. Arguments about multiple reciters, in contrast, are making claims about those who formulated the Mishnah and other texts rather than the speakers in them.[87] In the passage above, the speakers in the Mishnah are clear: R. Hananiah, R. Aqiva, R. Meir, and so forth. When R. Yose says that there are multiple reciters, he refers to the sages who are telling us about these speakers, the sages who shaped the words of these named speakers and composed the teachings, or different parts of the teaching, included in the Mishnah. The technique is similar to other scholarly analyses which posit that what is now presented as a single text is a composite work of different authors. We find such an argument, for example, in Galen's analysis of the *Nature of Man* attributed to Hippocrates—though the analysis there is different in significant ways: Galen posits a genuine Hippocratic composition was joined with a text from his student Polybus and many other still lesser sources by someone who was interested in selling the book at a higher price.[88]

While some modern scholars have seen in the positing of multiple reciters a "radical" conclusion or one which goes against the dominant characteristics of Talmudic interpretation,[89] there is no evidence in the Yerushalmi that Amoraic scholars saw the technique as an aberration. "Two reciters" arguments are attributed to some of the most prominent scholars in the Talmud. No objection is recorded to the very use of this technique, though of course we find disagreements about its application in specific passages, as with any type of analysis in the Talmud.[90] It is true that the technique is not as common as other solutions to contradictions, but it does relate to other phenomena which are very common: for example, the solution that two divergent recitations represent the words of different sages (which we have seen in Chapter 6), or the identification of anonymous components of the Mishnah as the words of a particular sage (which we have seen

---

[87] This is also clear in other instances: see e.g. *Shevi.* 2:3 33d.
[88] Hanson, "Galen," 33; Hankinson, "Galen," 150–3.
[89] See e.g. Weinberg, *Seride 'esh*, 4.242. On the idea that this technique opposes the Talmuds' interpretive orientation, see my discussion of Brenner's position below.
[90] There are six cases in which one sage's "two reciters" argument (not necessarily of the prevalent kind examined here) is followed by another sage's statement that the teaching is from a "single reciter" (חד תני). In none of them is the opposition formulated in a way that implies that the technique itself is problematic. It is true that at *Shevi.* 7:7 37c, the counter argument, attributed to R. Ze'ira, is phrased: "I can solve it [the contradiction in the Mishnah] as [stemming from] a single reciter" (according to the emendation by *PM*, cf. Epstein, *IMT*, 242 n. 3), which could be taken to mean that one should avoid positing two reciters if a different interpretation is available; but "I can solve it [in an alternative way]" is used throughout the Yerushalmi against various kinds of argument—in one case, instructive for our purposes, R. Simeon b. Laqish says he can interpret a passage using an identification rather than an *oqimta* (*Kil.* 8:1 31b [par. *Qid.* 3:5 64a]). The other instances of "single reciter" responses are *'Er.* 1:7 19b (see Lieberman, *YK*, 236–7), *Meg.* 1:2 70b, *Sot.* 8:5 23a, and *Ned.* 2:4 37c, in addition to *Ned.* 1:1 36c–d discussed below. At *'Er.* 8:9 25b the argument appears without a "two reciters" argument before it; R. Mana there coordinates the different positions in a similar way to the earlier instance in *'Er.*

in Chapter 1). While "two reciters" arguments posit divisions in what was considered a unity, these strategies overlap: in the passage in *Pesaḥim*, for example, a few lines below R. Yose's argument that the Mishnah is of two reciters, we hear that R. Yohanan identified the latter part of the Mishnah as the words of R. Simeon.

The following example allows us to compare such arguments to *oqimta*-style recontextualizations:

Nedarim 1:1 36c–d

"'איסר' זו שבועה. 'מבטא' זו שבועה.

אם אומר את איסר זו שבועה, חייב על כל איסר ואיסר ועל כל שבועה ושבועה. אם את אומר אין[91] אסר מין שבועה, חייב על זה בפני עצמו ועל זה בפני עצמו."

"אסר זו שבועה" ותמר "אם או' את" כן?

אמ' ר' אלעזר: תרין תניין אינון.

אמ' ר' ירמיה: חד תניי הוא. אמרו בלשון נדר את תופסו בלשון נדר. אמרו בלשון שבועה את תופסו בלשון שבועה. "אסר הרי הוא על ידיי". את[92] תופסו בלשון נדר. "אסר ואיני טועמו". את תופסו בלשון[93] שבועה.

"'Bind' (*isar*; Num 30:2) refers to oath; 'utterance' (Num 30:6) refers to oath. If you say 'bind' refers to oath, one is liable for each and every 'bind' and for each and every oath. If you say 'bind' is not a kind of oath, one is liable for each kind on their own."

[You say] "'bind' refers to oath"—and [then] you say, "if you say" that [and consider the possibility that it does not]?

R. Eleazar said: These are two reciters.

R. Jeremiah said: It is a single reciter. If one said it [i.e. the commitment to "bind"] with a vow formulation you treat it as a vow formulation, if one said it with an oath formulation you treat it as an oath formulation. "This bind is upon me," you treat it as a vow formulation. "This is a bind, and I shall not taste it," you treat it as an oath formulation.

The recited teaching which opens this passage responds to the wording in Numbers 30:2, "when a man makes a vow to the Lord or swears an oath, binding himself in a bind, he shall not break his word." Vows and oaths are two well-established categories of self-imposed commitments in rabbinic law, but this

---

[91] Adding "not" with QE; see also Benovitz, *Shevuot III*, 45. See later in the Yerushalmi where the first option is described as "bind is a kind of oath," which seems to show that the distinction is not between "oath" and "kind of oath."
[92] Correcting MS Leiden, which reads "אם" both here and the next "את."
[93] Correcting "במקום."

teaching is focused on other elements of the biblical chapter, the "bind" (*isar*) mentioned after the oath as well as "expression" mentioned later in Numbers 30:6. It first interprets these words as just another way to refer to oaths, but then considers that interpretation as only one of two possibilities (perhaps in a way that is intended to reject the first).[94] The Talmud objects to this apparent inconsistency, and R. Eleazar resolves the issue by positing two reciters: the first part of the teaching was formulated by someone who understood the bind as an oath, while the second teaching was formulated by someone who wanted to compare the two interpretations and their implications. R. Jeremiah argues that the teaching is the work of a "single reciter," and he posits not two different formulators but two different cases.[95] The sage who formulated this teaching thought that a "bind" may be considered either an oath or a vow, depending on whether this term is used as part of typical vow or oath formulations.[96] The first part of the teaching is speaking of a case where the person used the term as part of an oath formulation, which is why it treats "bind" as an oath; the second part of the teaching speaks of consequences in both cases.

This passage presents two alternatives to resolve the contradiction: R. Eleazar employs the "two reciters" technique, while R. Jeremiah offers an *oqimta* of the first part of the teaching. Brenner considers passages in the Bavli which similarly oppose *oqimtot* and "two reciters" arguments.[97] While Brenner's focus is on the Bavli, and on passages that are unusual, even in the Bavli, for expressing explicit (though not unambivalent) preference for *oqimtot*, his discussion is important for our purposes since he leverages those passages to make a broad argument about an inherent opposition between these two types of comments. "Two reciters" arguments, according to Brenner, represent a "philological emendation" of the text, whereas *oqimtot* present an "interpretation." The former attempt to restore the original text and its sense, whereas the latter offer a sense for the text as it is and defend its integrity; the former are unusual in the Bavli, whereas the latter are typical of its hermeneutics. As Brenner notes, a similar opposition is also implied (with different emphases) by other modern scholars who attended to these two kinds of comments.[98] If we apply this model to our passage, there is a wide gap between the notions of text and interpretation posited by R. Eleazar and R. Jeremiah. For R. Eleazar, the teaching is a composite text, a misleading combination of two

---

[94] Benovitz, *Shevuot III*, 52–4.
[95] For other instances of such arguments, see above n. 90; the other instance in *Ned.* is also attributed to R. Jeremiah.
[96] On the development of the idea that *isar* is a vow, see Benovitz, ibid.
[97] See *b. Qid.* 63a–b and *b. Men.* 55a. Brenner, *Okimta*, 107–19, distinguishes between the former passage and its Yerushalmi counterpart at *Qid.* 3:6 64b and does not attribute to the Yerushalmi the preference found in the Bavli, but he joins Epstein (*IMT*, 241) in reading the "two reciters" argument into the Yerushalmi passage which does not have it. On Brenner's interpretation of the Yerushalmi here see also above, Chapter 1 n. 43.
[98] Brenner, *Okimta*, ibid., and see his comments on other scholars at 184–5 n. 10.

sources, which must be dissected into two; R. Jeremiah defends the integrity of the text as it is and seeks to make sense of its current form.

But it is possible to interpret this passage without positing such a gap. As I have argued, "two reciters" arguments are not an aberration in the Talmudic hermeneutic landscape; and as we have seen in the previous sections, recontextualizing comments could be bound with the idea that the current form of the text is misleading, that it was wrongly matched with a teaching or case in the process of its transmission. Arguments that a teaching is the work of "two reciters" or that a teaching "was not said about this but about that" have similar notions of text and interpretation: in both cases, the text is seen as misleadingly or erroneously composed of originally independent teachings; in both cases, the interpreter aims to recover the teaching's original meaning by separating it from its context. We can read R. Jeremiah's *oqimta* along similar lines, bringing it closer to R. Eleazar's "two reciters" argument. Both scholars argue that the teaching is composite. For R. Eleazar, the teaching is composed of two discrete statements, from two different individuals, addressing the same issue. For R. Jeremiah, the teaching is also composed of two discrete statements, but from a single individual, addressing two different issues. Both posit that the text must be dissected to be interpreted correctly.

We have seen that in a significant number of cases, Amoraic scholars offered recontextualizing commentary which probed the transmission and composition of rabbinic teachings. Such cases may show us the hermeneutic framework that informed recontextualizing commentary more broadly, even when these processes were not explicitly invoked. They may suggest that when Amoraic scholars posited that a teaching has a context or referent which is not apparent in its wording, they were arguing that the teaching has lost key details or has been misplaced in the process of transmission. In cases where a teaching is cited without any context, this approach takes advantage of and responds to the already isolated form of the quotation; in cases where such commentary applied to teachings embedded in a literary context, it relied on the notion that the sequencing could be erroneous.

Still the passages explored here, and the way they bind interpretation with a construction of rabbinic teachings as fragments, are important in their own right, regardless of what they tell us about recontextualizing commentary more broadly. They show us, again, that even when similar interpretive practices were applied to Scripture and rabbinic teachings, these practices interacted with a different range of hermeneutic ideas, and they significantly enrich our view of Amoraic notions of text and interpretation.

There are two ways in which modern scholarship has missed the hermeneutic peculiarity of these comments. First, as we have seen in other cases in this book, the hermeneutic premises of these comments were transparent to modern scholars because, to some degree, they shared them. Albeck and Weiss took "it was not said about this" comments (and their Babylonian counterparts) as evidence for the reality of "wandering" teachings, and, more important, as an inspiration for their own search for the "original" context of rabbinic teachings.[99] "Two reciters" arguments had a similar modern afterlife. In their commentary on the passages examined above, Shamma Friedman and Moshe Benovitz praise their Amoraic predecessors for using "source criticism" and apply similar arguments themselves.[100] Epstein referred to this technique as "a great rule" for reconstructing the history of the Mishnah and frequently used the phrase "two reciters" and its equivalents in his own voice.[101] In his early work, Halivni justified his interpretation of Amoraic statements by claiming that the Talmud's "forced" interpretations were premised on errors in transmission and composition, much like Amoraic scholars did.[102] But as recent studies have emphasized, the dissection of composite texts and the search for the reliable text behind faulty or fragmentary forms present a particular approach to texts rather than the "plain reading" of them.[103]

The second way modern scholarship missed the hermeneutic significance of such Amoraic comments was by construing them as aberrations or even failures of Talmudic hermeneutics. I have mentioned above Stern's argument that the sages' commentary on rabbinic teachings projects a unified body of "oral Torah." He provides an illuminating analysis of a passage from the Babylonian Talmud that negotiates different teachings on the recitation of the Shema. The passage ends with a couple of "two reciters" comments which claim that there are conflicting reports on the positions of R. Meir and R. Eleazar. Stern concludes that these comments represent a failure of the Talmud's project of harmonization, and that this project is "virtually impossible because the tradition is by definition inconsistent, fragmentary, unsystematic."[104] But these comments are not a failure of the Talmud's interpretation; they are a part of it. As we have seen, Amoraic scholars employed "two reciters" arguments even when other options were available. The fact that these scholars applied such arguments to rabbinic teachings and not to Scripture was not because the rabbinic tradition was inherently more inconsistent or fragmentary than Scripture, but because they construed these bodies of text in different ways. When we do not neutralize or naturalize these methods, we can see how these comments reflect a particular construction of rabbinic teachings, and how they fit a diverse but observable pattern of fragmentation in ancient Talmudic scholarship.

---

[99] See especially the way Albeck's discussion moves from cases where the Talmuds themselves report such transposition (*Introduction to the Talmud*, 452–64) to his own claims about such transpositions in the lion's share of the chapter (464–92).

[100] Friedman, *Tosefta Atiqta*, 115, on *m. Pes.* 1:7, and Benovitz, *Shevuot III*, 54, on *Ned.* 1:1 36c–d.

[101] "Great rule": *IMT*, 238; for Epstein using "two reciters" in his own voice, see, for example, his foundational discussion of Mishnaic source criticism at *IMT*, 2–3. See also Weinberg, *Seride 'esh*, 483–5.

[102] Halivni, *Introductions*, 145–54. This argument is the origin of the name of his commentary series, *Sources and Traditions*, distinguishing between the true "sources" and their faulty or lacking "traditions."

[103] Najman, "Traditionary Processes"; "Configuring the Text." For a phenomenology of the fragment in the modern philological imagination, see Gumbrecht, *Powers*.

[104] Stern, "Canonization," 248–50, referring to *b. Ber.* 2b–3a.

Conclusion

The preceding chapters argued that a construction of rabbinic teachings as imperfect or fragmentary attestations informed a series of practices and tropes in Amoraic commentary that are absent or rare in Midrash: discussions of access to texts and their discovery, analysis of textual pluriformity, and emendations. This chapter, in contrast, explored practices that the sages applied in both realms of interpretation. I argued that when such practices were applied to rabbinic teachings, they could be embedded in that same construction of rabbinic teachings as imperfect or fragmentary, which provided conceptual and rhetorical settings different from those associated with these practices when they applied to Scripture.

Amoraic scholars engaged in intertextual illumination and necessity claims in a way that emphasized that rabbinic teachings imperfectly and incompletely capture the law; and they offered recontextualizing comments which argued that teachings lost their proper context through errors of transmission and composition. In the previous chapter, I suggested that the interpretive practices examined in this part of the book present a particular interpretive dynamic, one in which the scholar claims a privileged vantage point over the interpreted text. The comparison presented in this chapter with Midrashic practices underscores this observation. In Midrash, Scripture is normally presented as the active agent or as a text deliberately designed to juxtapose verses and suggest multiple contexts, guiding the passive interpreter to the proper reading. Most of the passages studied here, in contrast, present the scholar as the agent who restores the text's proper context or joins together fragmentary texts to offer a complete picture. Observing the differences between these two realms of interpretation does not mean losing sight of the similarity between them, nor denying that practices migrated from one realm to another, or that in both cases they stemmed from the same culture of learning. It allows us, instead, to paint a rich picture in which similar practices acquired different meanings or overtones as they were applied to different kinds of text.

Conclusion
The More Humane Letters

The first Talmud allows us to trace the rise of textual scholarship on rabbinic teachings. In the middle of the third century CE, following a standardization of the rabbinic curriculum and the promulgation of the Mishnah, Amoraic scholars took on commentary on these teachings, in their specific formulation, as an end in itself. This new body of scholarship drew, in some ways, on Midrash, but it also departed significantly from it, introducing new areas of inquiry and interpretive practices that were rare or absent in the rabbinic study of Scripture. The distinctive features of the study of rabbinic teachings did not result inevitably from the nature of these teachings, or even from the fact that they were now approached as texts. What is striking about the new scholarly apparatus we see in the Talmud is how, through interpretive engagement, Amoraic scholars came to develop a new conception of the sages' words.

Part I argued that Amoraic scholarship pursued and produced a new understanding of rabbinic teachings as shaped by individuals. Changes in citation formulae reflected an interest in distinguishing the "authors" and "tradents" of teachings. Identification of anonymous teachings read Tannaitic anonymity against its grain, employed an authorial construct to attribute such teachings, and insisted that the identity of the sage behind the teaching is crucial for understanding it. The unprecedented and pervasive application of the term *de'ah*, "opinion," to rabbinic teachings presented a new emphasis on the way these teachings reflected the individual minds that shaped them, and *ke-da'ateh* claims demonstrated individual inclinations by noting patterns in sages' teachings. Amoraic scholars developed the term *shita*, "line," as part of a new attribution-based comparative reading method, possibly employing a tabular visualization; the phrase *meḥalefa shitateh* functioned to project hypothetical distinctive profiles for individual sages and reinforce the sense of individual patterns even where those seemed to break down. Talmudic narratives and images engaged in a new debate about the significance of attribution, some invoking a well-attested ancient motif of textual immortality to articulate a newly individuated sense of rabbinic teaching.

Part II argued that Amoraic scholarship was interested in raising and solving textual problems predicated on a construction of the extant corpus of rabbinic teachings as fragmentary or imperfect. Recurring patterns in Talmudic passages presented rabbinic teachings as scattered texts to which scholars had limited, unpredictable, or variable access; they drew on this image to leverage moments of textual discovery for literary, pedagogical, and intellectual effects, or to analyze how certain teachings reflect only partial knowledge of other teachings. Discussions of divergent recitations compared them as alternative attestations of teachings the way other traditions of scholarship compared copies or editions; this comparison allowed Amoraic scholars to examine new kinds of divergences, such as minute differences in wording, but it also affected a new, textualized understanding of divergences which hitherto were understood to concern the law. The novel use of emendations combined a judgment of extant teachings as erroneous with a view of the corrected text as precisely formulated. This construction of rabbinic teachings informed even those interpretive practices which, in Midrash, were connected with an emphasis on completeness and deliberate design: intertextual illumination and claims about necessity were sometimes employed to emphasize the incompleteness of rabbinic teachings, and recontextualizing commentary was at times presented as restoring the context which teachings lost in the process of composition or transmission.

Recognizing this elaborate and innovative body of scholarship offers us a different perspective on the Yerushalmi as well as the intellectual history of the Talmuds. It is still common to present the first Talmud in terms of what it lacks in comparison with the later Bavli. Jacob Neusner concluded that "the sages of the Talmud of the Land of Israel seek certain knowledge about some few, practical things."[1] In his recent *History of the Talmud*, David Kraemer quotes Neusner approvingly and expands on the Yerushalmi's "penchant for brief questions and deliberations followed by clear answers, its failure to take the next logical analytical step, and its preference for the teachings of tradition above conclusions suggested by mere human reasoning."[2] This depiction of the Yerushalmi and its focus on "certainty" stems from a contrast with the tendency in the Bavli to present elaborate dialectical argumentation in which all contrasting positions are justified, without deciding the matter for one side or another.[3]

While the observation of differences that inform this comparison is fair, using it as a central criterion for depicting the Yerushalmi results in a mischaracterization. Certainty and practical interests are not identical. Positing that the scholars cited in the Yerushalmi are interested in "practical things" misses the purpose of the vast and elaborate commentary that constitutes that Talmud. The chapters above demonstrate how identifications of anonymous teachings, comments on consistency and inconsistency, discussions of access, comparisons of divergent texts, and emendations were often disconnected from any conclusion about law or ritual. Even when the Talmud does draw such conclusions from these types of comments, the same conclusion could have been drawn or stated much more directly without

---

[1] Neusner, *Judaism in Society*, 110–11.
[2] Kraemer, *History*, 120, 123–4.
[3] See Boyarin, *Border Lines*, 151–201, for an exploration of the rhetorical and epistemological aspects of this feature of the Bavli.

them. The analysis of Halakhah was certainly one of the functions of Talmudic scholarship, but the aim that emerges from the specific nature of these discussions is the scholarly analysis of rabbinic texts.

The argument that the Yerushalmi favors "tradition" over "human reasoning" relies on passages in which the Talmud prefers positions that are documented in text as opposed to analytical inferences; we have seen, in Chapter 5, how this preference shapes passages employing arrival statements or the phrase "it was found recited." It is not clear to me that such discussions promote "certainty" or avoid "troubling" questions; the Bavli's confidence in the power of reasoning can be interpreted as less troubling in comparison with the Yerushalmi's representation, which, on the one hand, uses traditional texts to undermine reason, but on the other hand, presents tradition as poorly known and subject to a fraught transmission. Be that as it may, the very contrast between "tradition" and "human reasoning" misses the ways, observed throughout this book, in which the Yerushalmi construes rabbinic tradition as a thoroughly human product.

At stake, however, is not only the character of the Yerushalmi; it is also the significance of the development of scholarship on rabbinic teachings. I noted how the rise of commentary on rabbinic teachings has been explained, following mainly the Bavli, as a process of "Scripturalization," which led to overlooking some of this commentary's most distinctive features as well as to describing the Yerushalmi as a less mature or developed instance of this commentary. In other works, the development of scholarship on rabbinic teachings plays a secondary or tertiary role. Abraham Weiss's account of the transition from the Tannaitic to the Amoraic period focuses almost exclusively on the emergence of the *sugyia*, the literary form characteristic of the Talmuds, and especially the appearance of elaborate back-and-forth argumentation, the Talmuds' "give and take."[4] For Kraemer, similarly, the most significant development in the Amoraic period was "the turn ... to argumentation as a form worthy of preserving and supplementing";[5] when he comes to describe what was innovative about the Yerushalmi as a compilation, he emphasizes its qualities in terms of a Talmudic "genre," characterized by "the citation of opinions, the record of disputes, the working out of differences, and engaged interpretation and extension of a received canonical text."[6]

The increased emphasis on argumentation and the rise of the *sugyia* as a literary form are certainly important developments in the story of both Talmuds.[7] But the near exclusive attention to these developments may reflect the traditional focus

---

[4] Weiss, *Amoraim*, 7–23. Weiss notes the interpretation of rabbinic teachings as an important aspect of this give-and-take, but he does not discuss the nature of this interpretation, and what defines the transition for him is the rise of dialectical literary structures and argumentation.

[5] Kraemer, *History*, 97.

[6] Kraemer, ibid., 124.

[7] For studies of the design of the Yerushalmi *sugyia*, see Introduction, n. 71.

in the Jewish curriculum on the Mishnah and the Bavli, to the exclusion of other Tannaitic compilations and the Yerushalmi.[8] The Tannaitic Midrashim already present an emphasis on give-and-take and dialectical argumentation, even if in a different form.[9] Long, dialectical *sugiyot* are more prominent in the Bavli, and centering them in the definition of the Talmudic genre leads to the teleological judgment that the Yerushalmi presents an undeveloped instance of that genre. What is shared by both Talmuds, and what distinguishes them from other rabbinic compilations more than any other element, is the type of commentary on rabbinic teachings which they present; this commentary also informs the specific form which dialectics and argumentation take in the Talmuds, even as it is shaped by those elements. As we have seen, the Yerushalmi attests both to the intricate development of this commentary and to its transformative effect.

The textualization of the study of rabbinic teachings intensified a process which began earlier, in the middle of the second century with the rise of Midrash: the process by which the sages became primarily textual experts.[10] Sages in the Tannaitic period developed textual scholarship on Scripture, but their study of Halakhah focused on the analysis of cases, concepts, and principles rather than on the interpretation of earlier rabbinic texts. Amoraic scholars had various interests, including principles and concepts, but they pursued them first and foremost through the interpretation of words.

Seth Schwartz wrote that "rabbis were emphatically not normal elites or sub-elites of the eastern part of the Roman Empire," that attempts to equate them with recognizably Roman groups such as "sophists, philosophers, *iurisprudentes*" have mostly failed because "the sages combined elements of all of these functions in a way that no one else in the Greco-Roman world did."[11] While Schwartz is certainly correct about the diversity of roles we find associated with the sages, Amoraic scholars, at least as they are represented in the Talmud and the Midrashim, pursued these roles largely through textual expertise. Recognizing the epistemic primacy of textual expertise does not mean denying the sages' legal or ritual interests and their involvement in shaping practice and norms.[12] These Halakhic aspects of rabbinic scholarship presented continuities with earlier perceptions of the Torah even as they expanded them. And the combination of legal and textual concerns was not

---

[8] See Fraade, "Polysemy," for critique of the Bavli-centric neglect of argumentation and dialectic in the Halakhic Midrashim.

[9] Weiss, *Amoraim*, 7 and 119–21, concedes that argumentation is frequent in the Halakhic Midrashim and posits a similarity between their composition and the Bavli's. But he also argues that the existence of give-and-take in these Midrashim does not undermine the opposition he draws between Tannaitic and Amoraic literature because it is short and does not digress. This argument leaves us again with the emphasis on the long, digressive *sugiya*. See also Halivni's idea that the Bavli's creators are the "successors" of the Halakhic Midrashim (*Midrash*, 3, 93–104).

[10] Mandel, *Origins*, 289–305.

[11] Schwartz, *Imperialism*, 163.

[12] Furstenberg, "The Rabbinic Movement," argues the rabbis should be understood as provincial Roman jurists; see the critiques published alongside that article.

unique to rabbinic scholarship: James Zetzel has argued that in the Roman scholarly tradition, philological, ritual, and legal expertise were closely bound.[13]

The cultivation of specifically textual expertise among Amoraic scholars aligns with what we know of other elites in the Roman Empire, where, according to William Johnson, "elite intellectuals became focused upon, even obsessed with, certain types of philological scholarship."[14] As we have seen throughout the preceding chapters, Christian scholars working in close geographical and chronological proximity to Amoraic scholars developed their own elaborate tradition of textual scholarship. This book examined several points of similarity and difference between Amoraic and Greek and Latin scholarship: in discussions of attribution, and more important, in the interpretive significance of the connection between individuals and texts; in discussions of textual difference; and in the form and method of emendations. A more precise determination of the degree to which Amoraic scholarship on rabbinic teachings was shaped by the specific character of Greco-Roman scholarship requires a more detailed comparative study, of the kind that has been undertaken on Midrash.[15] The differences are significant; but at the same time, the consideration of commentary on rabbinic teachings removes or qualifies several contrasts that appear when we only focus the comparison on rabbinic scriptural interpretation. If Amoraic scholars were competing for prestige and persuasion in settings where textual expertise was greatly valued, we can consider how the development of these new interpretive practices allowed them to claim some of the same types of critical philological expertise in which other elites excelled, while maintaining the unique status of the Hebrew Scriptures as insulated from such inquiries.

The analysis in this book suggests that commentary on rabbinic teachings differed from Midrashic hermeneutics not only in its interpretive practices and notions of text, but also in how it configured the interpretive dynamic between the text and its interpreters. As Azzan Yadin-Israel emphasized, Midrashic texts attribute agency to Scripture and passivity to its interpreters. Scripture *teaches*, the sages *hear*; Scripture, as the active agent of interpretation, guides its readers to the proper meaning of the verses and to the proper methods of reading.[16] The use of this rhetoric is not all-encompassing: some Midrashic terminology presents the sages as active interpreters, and Yadin-Israel contrasts the rhetoric of passivity with a famous story in the Bavli which portrays R. Aqiva's interpretation of Scripture in very active terms.[17] Ishay Rosen-Zvi argued that there are good reasons not to

---

[13] Zetzel, *Critics*, e.g. 26, 58, 123–5.

[14] Johnson, *Readers and Reading Culture*, 179. On the increasingly important role of intellectual, and particularly textual, expertise in religious traditions in the Roman urban context, see Wendt, "Intellectualizing Religion." On Roman religion and literature beyond the concept of "Scripture," see MacRae, *Legible Religion*.

[15] See Introduction, nn. 68–69.

[16] Yadin-Israel, *Scripture as Logos*; idem, "Authorial Intent."

[17] Yadin-Israel, "Authorial Intent," 17–22.

take the Midrashic rhetoric of passivity at face value, pointing, for example, to Moshe Halbertal's argument that in cases where the sages say they were compelled by Scripture to say certain things, they do so ironically, knowing full well that the statement is the result of their own interpretation.[18] In another essay, Halbertal argued that common Midrashic literary structures which posit interpretive alternatives emphasize the role of the interpreter.[19] At the same time, the fact that the rhetoric of passivity is found in commentary on Scripture and not in commentary on rabbinic teachings is significant, and may illuminate some of the differences in practice between these two realms of interpretation.

The types of comments which the sages avoided in Midrash but pursued in their analysis of rabbinic teachings set up an interpretive dynamic where scholars have more agency and even a superior vantage point over the texts on which they comment. This dynamic, I argued above, is particularly visible in the types of commentary examined in Part II: comments on the way teachings reflect the limited knowledge of the scholars who shaped them, the comparison of divergent texts which posit that each of the teachings is just one way to recite the tradition, and emendations which point to errors in teachings. But we can also observe it in the comments examined in Part I. Whereas anonymity in Tannaitic teachings is a claim to broad acceptance, Amoraic identifications routinely make the point that anonymous teachings represent the individual perspective of the sages who shaped them; *ke-da'ateh* comments similarly argue that teachings which make claims about the law reflect the individual characteristics and viewpoints of the sages to whom they are attributed. This interpretive dynamic stands in marked contrast to the image of the passive interpreter taking cues from the text. While Midrashic interpretation exhibited its own forms of bold creativity, this difference may suggest that Amoraic scholars developed these reading strategies in part because they offered them a new type of interpretive position that was not quite possible in the interpretation of Scripture.

Modern Talmudic scholarship often presents itself as a departure from traditional modes of scholarship, including those found in the Talmuds themselves.[20] But throughout this book, we have observed continuities between Amoraic and modern scholarly practices. There is no better example than the foundational work of the "father of research of the exact Talmudic science,"[21] Jacob Nahum Epstein's *Introduction to the Mishnaic Text*.[22] Epstein draws on Amoraic notions of texts and

---

[18] Rosen-Zvi, "Joining the Club"; Halbertal, "It Could Not Be Said."
[19] Halbertal, "The Language of Midrash."
[20] See Gafni, *The Mishnah's Plain Sense*, and the English summary in idem, "Reception."
[21] This somewhat pleonastic epithet of Epstein, אבי המחקר של המדע התלמודי המדויק, was coined by Lieberman (*Siphre Zutta*, 135). Defending himself against Epstein's criticism of his thesis on the Caesarean origins of tractate *Neziqin*, which was published posthumously by Epstein's student E. Z. Melamed, Lieberman insisted that the "idle words" of this criticism would never have been published had "the father of research of the exact Talmudic science" prepared the publication himself.
[22] On *IMT*, see Mayer, "The Greatest Book"; and Fuchs, "On 'Introduction.'"

interpretive methods when he identifies sections of the Mishnah as stemming from individual sages, when he considers the way the Mishnah was shaped by its purported redactor, when he constructs his theory about "versions" and "variants," and when he posits "two reciters" behind a single teaching. But we have also seen other examples, such as Albeck's and Weiss's project of redeeming teachings from their misleading contexts.

These convergences show us the enduring legacies of Amoraic concepts and practices on the long history of Talmudic scholarship—for better or worse. They also disturb neat distinctions between "traditional" and "critical" or "ancient" and "modern" forms of reading. The pervasiveness of these converging elements and their connection to other aspects of Amoraic commentary argue against positing that they represent a departure from "typical" Talmudic hermeneutics, or that they reflect an Amoraic division between "literal" and "non-literal" exegesis.[23] Throughout this book, we have seen that examining these overlaps allows us to consider how these scholarly practices were predicated on specific hermeneutic positions and agendas which modern philologists have taken for granted because, to a large degree, they shared them: the tracing of texts to individuals, and the understanding of extant texts as fragments or corrupt forms which scholarship should restore to their complete or original context. But the comparison with modern Talmud scholarship or even historicist European philology more broadly also allows us to assess what distinguished the Amoraic forms of such discussions. It highlights the different balance Amoraic scholarship struck in negotiating the tension between the reconstruction of a particular historical meaning and other aims for which the significance of such reconstruction may be suspended or limited.

On the one hand, much like historicist philology, Amoraic scholarship was interested in tracing texts to individuals and considered attributions to limit or allow certain types of interpretation, since its purpose was to understand specific utterances by specific individuals. It considered aspects of rabbinic teachings that were shaped by contingency and individuality to be essential and worthy of commentary, rather than setting them aside. In this sense, Amoraic commentary on rabbinic teachings diverged from Midrash, in which there is less of a distinction between the interpreter's truth and the text's meaning, and from the Tannaitic engagement with rabbinic tradition, in which even positions that the sages did not see as legally binding were updated according to new paradigms in the analysis of

---

[23] Weinberg, *Seride 'esh*, 4.235–89, presents such separation to defend the Talmuds from their modern detractors. When the role of the sages as community leaders required them to develop new laws, they had to ground them in the Mishnah through non-literal or "*derash*" interpretation; but the same scholars also engaged in literal, "*peshat*" interpretation, in which they employed "the method of scientific criticism in all its rules and principles" (243). From a different perspective, Brenner, *Okimta*, suggests that "philological" commentary exists in the Bavli, but contrasts it with the *oqimtot*; see Chapter 8 n. 49 and 98.

Halakhah. As I argued above, Amoraic scholars thrived on the critical disposition such discussions allowed.

On the other hand, these tendencies were balanced with other aims, not only in those moments in which this commentary resembles Midrash or Tannaitic engagement with the tradition, but even more strikingly when it aligns more with historicist inquiries. In their discussions of attribution, Amoraic scholars did not normally reject teachings as inauthentic, but rather aimed to place teachings in a stunningly diverse library, extending the community of teaching and learning through time by producing distinctive profiles for individual sages. The purpose of their comparisons of recitation divergences was not to determine which text was first, but rather to draw out significance from alternative meanings, positions, or applications. In their emendations, these scholars did not aim to restore a particular historical form of the text, but rather to establish the text as it should be, precisely formulated and fit for exacting reading strategies. We have seen how this blending of historicist and non-historicist aims led to misappreciations in modern evaluations of these aspects of Amoraic commentary; but while the tension between these aims may be evident in that commentary itself, their juxtaposition and interconnection show that this tension need not be considered as a contradiction between two mutually exclusive approaches.

The title of this conclusion is the English equivalent of a Latin phrase, *literae humaniores*, best known nowadays as a name for the Classics course at the University of Oxford. The phrase draws on the humanistic idea of *studia humanitatis*, from which we get the modern "humanities." The primary sense of these terms is that the studies in question are those most appropriate for the cultivation of a human being, but these terms were sometimes understood to make a distinction (though not necessarily an opposition) between studies of "human" and "divine" texts.[24] It is in this sense that I borrow the term to describe the rabbinic study not of Scripture but of rabbinic teachings, the more humane letters: the close examination of texts shaped by the achievements, limitations, circumstances, and individualities of those who created them, which, for precisely that reason, presents us with the opportunity to encounter their humanity as well as our own.

---

[24] On *studia humanitatis* in contrast with *studia divinitatis*, see Kohl, "Changing Concept," 188, 192. On *literae humaniores* in contrast with studies of sacred texts or theology, see Vale, *Renaissance*, 90–1.

Bibliography

Ahuvia, Mika. "Reimagining the Gender and Class Dynamics of Premodern Composition." *Journal of Ancient Judaism* 14 (2023): 321–54.
Albeck, Chanoch. *Introduction to the Mishnah*. Jerusalem, 1967 (Heb.).
Albeck, Chanoch. *Introduction to the Talmud, Babli and Yerushalmi*. Tel Aviv, 1969 (Heb.).
Albeck, Chanoch. "Nusḥa'ot ba-mishnah shel ha-amorai'm." *Abhandlungen zur erinnerung an Hirsch Perez Chajes*. Vienna, 1933, 2.1–28.
Albeck, Chanoch. *Shisha sidre mishnah*. Tel Aviv and Jerusalem, 1952–9.
Albeck, Chanoch. *Studies in the Baraita and the Tosefta and Their Relationship to the Talmud*². Jerusalem, 1969 (Heb.).
Albeck, Chanoch. *Untersuchungen über die Redaktion der Mischna*. Berlin, 1936.
Alexander, Elizabeth Shanks. "The Orality of Rabbinic Writing." *The Cambridge Companion to the Talmud*, ed. C. E. Fonrobert and M. Jaffee. Cambridge, 2007, 38–57.
Alexander, Elizabeth Shanks. *Transmitting Mishnah: The Shaping Influence of Oral Tradition*. Cambridge, 2006.
Alexander, Philip. "'Homer the Prophet of All' and 'Moses Our Teacher.'" *The Use of Sacred Books in the Ancient World*, ed. L. V. Rutgers et al. Leuven, 1998, 127–42.
Amit, Aaron. "The Homilies on Mishnah and Talmud Study at the Close of Bavli Bava' Metsi'a' 2 and Yerushalmi Horayot 3: Their Origin and Development." *Jewish Quarterly Review* 102 (2012): 163–89.
Amir, Abraham. *Institutions and Titles in the Talmudic Literature*. Jerusalem, 1977 (Heb.).
Ashkenazi, Samuel. *Yefe mar'eh*. Venice, 1590.
Assis, Moshe. "A Fragment of Yerushalmi Sanhedrin." *Tarbiẓ* 46 (1977): 29–90 (Heb.).
Assis, Moshe. "And Even Regarding Rabbi . . . It Is Not Difficult." *Studies in Memory of the Rishon Le-Zion R. Yitzhak Nissim*, Vol. II, ed. M. Benayahu. Jerusalem, 1985, 49–66 (Heb.).
Assis, Moshe. "Commentaries on Nineteen Sugyot in Yerushalmi Baba Kamma." *Saul Lieberman Memorial Volume*, ed. S. Friedman. New York and Jerusalem, 1993, 65–78 (Heb.).
Assis, Moshe. *Concordance of Amoraic Terms, Expressions and Phrases in the Yerushalmi*. Jerusalem and New York, 2010 (Heb.).
Assis, Moshe. "More on the Question of the Redaction of Yerushalmi Neziqin." *Tarbiẓ* 83 (2013): 191–294 (Heb.).
Assmann, Jan. "Schrift, Tod, und Identität: Das Grab als Vorschule der Literatur im alten Ägypten." *Schrift und Gedächtnis: Archäologie der literarischen Kommunikation I*, ed. A. Assmann et al. Munich, 1983, 64–93.
Azar, Moshe. "Lepikak in Rabbinic Hebrew." *Leshonenu* 74 (2012): 109–23 (Heb.).
Bacher, Wilhelm. *Die Exegetische Terminologie der Jüdischen Traditionsliteratur*. Leipzig, 1905.
Bacher, Wilhelm. *Tradition und Tradenten in den Schulen Palästinas und Babyloniens: Studien und Materialien zur Entstehungsgeschichte des Talmuds*. Leipzig, 1914.
Bakhos, Carol. "Rabbinic and Patristic Interpretations of the Bible." *The Routledge Handbook of Jews and Judaism in Late Antiquity*, ed. C. Hezser. London, 2023, 290–306.
Balberg, Mira. *Blood for Thought: The Reinvention of Sacrifice in Early Rabbinic Literature*. Oakland, 2017.
Balberg, Mira. *Fractured Tablets: Forgetfulness and Fallibility in Late Ancient Rabbinic Culture*. Oakland, 2023.
Bar-Asher Siegal, Michal. *Jewish-Christian Dialogues on Scripture in Late Antiquity*. Cambridge 2019.
Bar-Asher Siegal, Michal. "Tosefta Eduyot 1:1: On the Fear of Losing Torah and the Redaction of Tannaitic Materials." *Land and Spirituality in Rabbinic Literature*, ed. S. Fine and S. Schick. Leiden, 2022, 38–50.

Barthes, Ronald. "The Death of the Author." Trans. S. Heath, *Image-Music-Text*. New York, 1977, 142–8.

Baum, Armin Daniel. "Content and Form: Authorship Attribution and Pseudonymity in Ancient Speeches, Letters, Lectures, and Translations—A Rejoinder to Bart Ehrman." *Journal of Biblical Literature* 136 (2017): 381–403.

Baum, Armin Daniel. *Pseudepigraphie und literarische Fälschung im frühen Christentum: mit ausgewählten Quellentexten samt deutscher Übersetzung*. Tübingen, 2001.

Baumgarten, Albert. "R. Yohanan and Resh Lakish on Anonymous Mishnayot." *Jewish Law Association Studies 2*, ed. B. S. Jackson. Atlanta, 1986, 75–88.

Becker, Hans-Jürgen. *Die grossen rabbinischen Sammelwerke Palästinas: zur literarischen Genese von Talmud Yerushalmi und Midrash Bereshit Rabba*. Tübingen, 1999.

Be'eri, Nurit. *Exploring Ta'aniot: Yerushalmi, Tractate Ta'aniot—Forming and Redacting the Traditions*. Ramat Gan, 2009 (Heb.).

Benovitz, Moshe. *BT Shevu'ot III: Critical Edition with Comprehensive Commentary*. New York and Jerusalem, 2003 (Heb.).

Benovitz, Moshe. "Transferred 'Sugyot' in the Palestinian Talmud: The Case of Nedarim 3:2 and Shevuot 3:8." *Proceedings of the American Academy for Jewish Research* 59 (1993): 11–57.

Berkovitz, Abraham J. "Beyond Attribution and Authority: The Case of Psalms in Rabbinic Hermeneutics." *Rethinking "Authority" in Late Antiquity*, ed. A. J. Berkovitz and M. D. Letteney. New York, 2018, 57–77.

Berzon, Todd S. "The Double Bind of Christianity's Judaism: Language, Law, and the Incoherence of Late Antique Discourse." *Journal of Early Christian Studies* 23 (2015): 445–80.

Blankovsky, Yuval. *Reading Talmudic Sources*. Leiden, 2020.

Blidstein, Yaakov. "The Concept of Oral Law in R. Sherira's Epistle." *Da'at* 4 (1980): 5–16 (Heb.).

Blum, Rudolf. *Kallimachos: The Alexandrian Library and the Origins of Bibliography*. Trans. H. H. Wellisch. Madison, 1991.

Boch, Yehoshua. *Talmud yerushalmi: masekhet rosh ha-shanah 'im perush or la-yesharim*. Jerusalem, 2011.

Bokser, Baruch M. *Post Mishnaic Judaism in Transition: Samuel on Berakhot and the Beginnings of Gemara*. Chico, 1980.

Bokser, Baruch M. and Lawrence H. Schiffman. *Yerushalmi Pesahim*. Chicago, 1994.

Börno, Maria and Sean Coughlin. "Galen on Bad Style (*kakozēlía*): Hippocratic Exegesis in Galen and Some Predecessors." *Technai* 11 (2020): 145–75.

Boyarin, Daniel. *Border Lines: The Partition of Judeo-Christianity*. Philadelphia, 2004.

Boyarin, Daniel. *Intertextuality and the Reading of Midrash*. Bloomington, 1990.

Brand, Joshua. "Li-shemot kelei ha-ḥeres ba-mishnah." *Leshonenu* 8 (1936): 322–6.

Brandes, Yehuda. "The Beginnings of the Rules of Halachic Adjudication." PhD Dissertation, Hebrew University of Jerusalem, 2002 (Heb.).

Brandes, Yehuda. "The Canonization of the Mishnah." *Journal of Ancient Judaism* 10 (2019): 145–80.

Bregman, Marc. "Pseudepigraphy in Rabbinic Literature." *Pseudepigraphic Perspectives: The Apocrypha and Pseudepigrapha in Light of the Dead Sea Scrolls*, ed. E. G. Chazon and M. E. Stone. Leiden, 1999, 27–41.

Bröcker, Ludwig O. "Die Methoden Galens in der literarischen Kritik." *Rheinisches Museum für Philologie* 40 (1885): 415–38.

Bryant, John. *The Fluid Text: A Theory of Editing and Revision for Book and Screen*. Ann Arbor, 2002.

Carr, David McLain. *The Formation of the Hebrew Bible: A New Reconstruction*. Oxford, 2011.

Cerquiglini, Bernard. *In Praise of the Variant: A Critical History of Philology*. Trans. B. Wing. Baltimore, 1999.

Chin, Catherine Michael. "Rufinus of Aquileia and Alexandrian Afterlives: Translation as Origenism." *Journal of Early Christian Studies* 18 (2010): 617–47.

Clements, Ruth. "Origen's Hexapla and Christian-Jewish Encounter." *Religious Rivalries and the Struggle for Success in Caesarea Maritima*, ed. T. Donaldson. Waterloo, Ontario, 2000, 303–29.

Cohen, Avinoam. "Biqoret hilkhatit le-'umat biqoret sifrutit be-sugyot ha-talmud." *Asupot* 3 (1989): 331–446.

Cohen, Shaye J. D. "The Rabbi in Second-Century Jewish Society." *The Cambridge History of Judaism*, ed. W. Horbury et al. Cambridge, 1999, 922–90.

Cohen, Shaye J. D., Robert Goldenberg, and Hayim Lapin (eds). *The Oxford Annotated Mishnah: A New Translation of the Mishnah with Introductions and Notes*. New York, 2022.

Coogan, Jeremiah. *Eusebius the Evangelist: Rewriting the Fourfold Gospel in Late Antiquity*. Oxford, 2023.

Coogan, Jeremiah. "Tabular Thinking in Late Ancient Palestine: Instrumentality, Work, and the Construction of Knowledge." *Knowledge Construction in Late Antiquity*, ed. M. Amsler. Berlin, 2023, 57–81.

Crawford, Matthew R. *The Eusebian Canon Tables: Ordering Textual Knowledge in Late Antiquity*. Oxford, 2019.

Dalton, Krista. "Rabbis as Recipients of Charity and the Logic of Grammarian Piety." *Journal for the Study of Judaism* 53 (2021): 94–130.

Daube, David. *The New Testament and Rabbinic Judaism*. London, 1956.

Dean, James Elmer. *Epiphanius' Treatise on Weights and Measures*. Chicago 1935.

Derrida, Jacques. "Signature, Event, Context." Trans. S. Weber and J. Mehlman, *Limited Inc.*, ed. G. Graff. Evanston, 1988, 1–23.

Dilley, Paul. "The Invention of Christian Tradition: Apocrypha, Imperial Policy, and Anti-Jewish Propaganda." *Greek, Roman, and Byzantine Studies* 50.4 (2010): 586–614.

Dohrmann, Natalie B. "Jewish Books and Roman Readers: Censorship, Authorship, and the Rabbinic Library." *Reconsidering Roman Power: Roman, Greek, Jewish and Christian Perceptions and Reactions*, ed. K. Berthelot. Rome, 2020, 417–41.

Donaldson, Amy. "Explicit References to New Testament Variant Readings among Greek and Latin Church Fathers." PhD Dissertation, University of Notre Dame, 2009.

Dubischar, Markus. "Typology of Philological Writings." *Brill's Companion to Ancient Greek Scholarship*, ed. F. Montanari et al. Leiden, 2015, 545–99.

Ehrlich, Uri. "The Ritual of Lending a Shoulder: Distribution and Signification in Talmudic Times." *Hebrew Union College Annual* 75 (2004): 23–35.

Ehrman, Bart. *Forgery and Counterforgery: The Use of Literary Deceit in Early Christian Polemics*. Oxford, 2013.

Elitzur, Yoel. "'Al 'amoraim' le-raglei har tavor." *Sinai* 101 (1988): 220–4.

Elitzur, Yoel. "מידה in Mishnaic Hebrew and the Last Passage in the Tractate Avoth." *Sha'are Lashon: Studies in Hebrew, Aramaic, and Jewish Languages Presented to Moshe Bar-Asher*, ed. A. Maman et al. Jerusalem, 2007, 19–30 (Heb.).

Elon, Menachem. *Jewish Law: History, Sources, Principles*. Trans. M. J. Sykes. Philadelphia, 1994.

Epstein, Jacob N. *Introduction to Amoraitic Literature: Babylonian Talmud and Yerushalmi*. Jerusalem, 1962 (Heb.).

Epstein, Jacob N. *Introduction to the Mishnaic Text*.[3] Jerusalem, 2000 (Heb.).

Epstein, Jacob N. *Introduction to Tannaitic Literature: Mishna, Tosephta and Halakhic Midrashim*. Jerusalem, 1957 (Heb.).

Epstein, Jacob N. "To 'Emendations on the Jerushalmi.'" *Tarbiz* 2 (1931): 241–3 (Heb.).

Even-Shoshan, Avraham. *Milon Even-Shoshan*, ed. M. Azar. Tel Aviv, 2003.

Feintuch, I. Zvi. *Versions and Traditions in the Talmud*, ed. D. Sperber. Ramat Gan, 1985 (Heb.).

Felix, Yehuda. *Talmud yerushalmi: masekhet shevi'it*. Jerusalem, 1980.

Fiano, Emanuel. *Three Powers in the Heaven: The Emergence of Theology and the Parting of the Ways*. New Haven, 2023.

Finkelstein, Louis. *Sifre on Deuteronomy*. Berlin, 1939, repr. Jerusalem 1993 (Heb.).

Fisch, Menachem. "Parshanut dehuqah ve-teqstim meḥayvim: ha-oqimta ha-amora'it veha-fiolosofia shel ha-halakhah." *New Streams in Philosophy of Halakhah*, ed. A. Ravitzky and A. Rezenak. Jerusalem, 2008, 311–44 (Heb.).

Flemming, Rebecca. "Commentary." *The Cambridge Companion to Galen*, ed. R. J. Hankinson. Cambridge, 2008, 323–54.

Florsheim, Joel. "Rav Ḥisda as Exegetor of Tannaitic Sources." *Tarbiẓ* 41 (1972): 24–48 (Heb.).
Fonrobert, Charlotte Elisheva. "The Place of Shabbat: On the Architecture of the Opening Sugya of Tractate Eruvin (2a–3a)." *Strength to Strength: Essays in Honor of Shaye J. D. Cohen*, ed. M. L. Satlow. Providence, 2018, 437–54.
Foucault, Michel. "What Is an Author?" Trans. J. Harari, *The Foucault Reader*, ed. P. Rabinow. New York, 1984, 101–20.
Fraade, Steven. "Moses and the Commandments: Can Hermeneutics, History, and Rhetoric Be Disentangled." *The Idea of Biblical Interpretation*, ed. H. Najman et al. Leiden, 2004, 399–422.
Fraade, Steven. "Rabbinic Polysemy and Pluralism Revisited: Between Praxis and Thematization." *AJS Review* 31 (2007): 1–40.
Frankel, Zacharias. *Einleitung in den Jerusalemischen Talmud*. Breslau, 1870 (Heb.).
Frankel, Zacharias. *Hodegetica in Mischnam librosque cum ea conjunctos Tosefta, Mechilta, Sifra, Sifri: Pars prima: Introductio in Mischnam*. Leipzig, 1859 (Heb.).
Friedman, Shamma. "Fragments of Ancient Manuscripts for Tractate *Bava Metiza*." *Ale Sefer* 9 (1981): 5–55 (Heb.).
Friedman, Shamma. "Ha-shem gorem." *These Are the Names: Studies in Jewish Onomastics*, ed. A. Demsky. Ramat Gan, 1999, 51–77 (Heb.).
Friedman, Shamma. *Talmud Arukh: BT Bava Meziʻa VI*. Jerusalem, 1990 (Heb.).
Friedman, Shamma. *Talmudic Studies: Investigating the Sugya, Variant Readings and Aggada*. Jerusalem, 2010 (Heb.).
Friedman, Shamma. *Tosefta atiqta: pesaḥ rishon*. Ramat Gan, 2002.
Friedman, Shamma. "Uncovering Literary Dependencies in the Talmudic Corpus." *The Synoptic Problem in Rabbinic Literature*, ed. S. J. D. Cohen. Providence, 2000, 35–57.
Friedman, Shamma. "Zacharias Frankel and the Study of the Mishnah." *From Breslau to Jerusalem: Rabbinical Seminaries: Past, Present, and Future*, ed. G. Meron. Jerusalem, 2009, 39–73 (Heb.).
Fuchs, Uziel. "On 'Introduction to the Text of the Mishnah': Reflections 50 Years Later and Towards a New Edition." *Jewish Studies* 38 (1998): 365–76 (Heb.).
Furstenberg, Yair. "From Competition to Integration: The Laws of the Nations in Rabbinic Literature within Its Roman Context." *Dine Israel* 32 (2018): 21–58 (Heb.).
Furstenberg, Yair. "From Tradition to Controversy." *Tarbiẓ* 85 (2018): 587–641 (Heb.).
Furstenberg, Yair. "The Invention of the Ban against Writing Oral Torah in the Babylonian Talmud." *AJS Review* 46 (2022): 131–50.
Furstenberg, Yair. "The Literary Evolution of the Mishnah." *What Is the Mishnah? The State of the Question*, ed. S. J. D. Cohen. Cambridge, 2022, 98–125.
Furstenberg, Yair. "The Rabbinic Movement from Pharisees to Provincial Jurists." *Journal for the Study of Judaism* 55 (2023): 1–43.
Gabbay, Uri. *The Exegetical Terminology of Akkadian Commentaries*. Leiden, 2016.
Gafni, Hanan. *The Mishnah's Plain Sense: A Study in Modern Talmudic Scholarship*. Tel Aviv, 2011 (Heb.).
Gafni, Hanan. "The Reception of the Mishnah in the Modern Era." *What Is the Mishnah? The State of the Question*, ed. S. J. D. Cohen. Cambridge, 2022, 489–509.
Gafni, Isaiah. "Between Babylonia and the Land of Israel: Ancient History and the Clash of Ideologies in Modern Jewish History." *Zion* 62 (1997): 213–42.
Geiger, Joseph. *Tents of Japheth: Greek Intellectuals in Ancient Palestine*. Jerusalem, 2012 (Heb.).
Ginzberg, Louis. *A Commentary on the Palestinian Talmud I*. New York, 1971 (Heb.).
Gluska, Yitzhak. "Leshon tefilat ha-ʻamidah shel ḥol le-fi ha-nusaḥ shebe-seser rav saʻadyah gaʼon." *Masʼat Aharon*, ed. M. Bar-Asher et al. Jerusalem, 2010, 102–25.
Goldberg, Abraham. *Commentary to the Mishna Shabbat*. Jerusalem, 1976 (Heb.).
Goldberg, Abraham. "The Babylonian Talmud." *The Literature of the Sages I*, ed. S. Safrai. Assen, 1987, 323–66.
Goldberg, Abraham. *The Mishnah Treatise Eruvin*. Jerusalem, 1986 (Heb.).
Goldberg, Abraham. "The Palestinian Talmud." *The Literature of the Sages I*, ed. S. Safrai. Assen, 1987, 303–18.

Goldberg, Abraham. "The Purpose and Method in Rabbi Judah Hannasi's Compilation of the Mishna." *Tarbiẓ* 28 (1959): 260–59 (Heb.).
Goldberg, Abraham. *Tosefta Bava Kamma: A Structural and Analytic Commentary*. Jerusalem, 2001 (Heb.).
Goldberg, Abraham. "כיני מתניתא" ('The Mishnah Should Be Read in the Following Way'): An Interpretive Remark or a Different Reading?" *Sha'are Lashon*. Vol. II: *Rabbinic Hebrew and Aramaic*, ed. A. Maman et al. Jerusalem, 2007, 82–7 (Heb.).
Goldman, Norma. "Roman Footwear." *The World of Roman Costume*, ed. J. L. Sebesta and L. Bonfante. Madison, 1994, 101–29.
Gumbrecht, Hans Ulrich. *The Powers of Philology: Dynamics of Textual Scholarship*. Urbana, 2003.
Grafton, Anthony. *Forgers and Critics: Creativity and Duplicity in Western Scholarship*. London, 1990.
Grafton, Anthony. *Joseph Scaliger: A Study in the History of Classical Scholarship*. Oxford, 1983.
Grafton, Anthony, and Megan Williams. *Christianity and the Transformation of the Book: Origen, Eusebius and the Library of Caesarea*. Cambridge, MA, 2006.
Gray, Alyssa. *A Talmud in Exile: The Influence of Yerushalmi Avodah Zarah on the Formation of Bavli*. Providence, 2005.
Green, Peter. *Ovid: The Erotic Poems*. New York, 1982.
Green, William S. "What's in a Name?—the Problematic of Rabbinic 'Biography'." *Approaches to Ancient Judaism I*, ed. W. S. Green. Chico, 1978, 77–96.
Gross, Simcha. "Editorial Material in the Babylonian Talmud and Its Sasanian Context." *AJS Review* 47 (2023): 51–76.
Halbertal, Moshe. "If the Text Had Not Been Written, It Could Not Be Said." Trans. R. Neis, *Scriptural Exegesis: The Shapes of Culture and the Religious Imagination*, ed. L. Lieber and D. Green. Oxford, 2009, 146–61.
Halbertal, Moshe. *People of the Book: Canon, Meaning, and Authority*. Cambridge, MA, 1997.
Halbertal, Moshe. "The Language of Midrash." *To Be of the Disciples of Aharon: Studies in Tannaitic Literature and Its Sources in Memory of Aharon Shemesh*, ed. D. Boyarin et al. Tel Aviv, 2021, 367–80 (Heb.).
Halevy, Isaak. *Dorot Harischonim: Die Geschichte und Literatur Israels: Theil IIa*. Frankfurt, 1901 (Heb.).
Halivni, David Weiss. *Introductions to "Sources and Traditions": Studies in the Formation of the Talmud*. Jerusalem, 2009.
Halivni, David Weiss. *Midrash, Mishnah, and Gemara: The Jewish Predilection for Justified Law*. Cambridge, MA, 1986.
Halivni, David Weiss. "Safke de-gavre." *Proceedings of the American Academy of Jewish Research* 46/7 (1980): 67–83.
Halivni, David Weiss. "The Reception Accorded to R. Judah Hanasi's Mishnah." *Jewish and Christian Self-Definition*, ed. E. P. Sanders et al. Philadelphia, 1981, 2.204–12.
Halton, Thomas P. *Jerome: On Illustrious Men*. Washington, DC, 1999.
Hammer, Reuben. *Sifre: A Tannaitic Commentary on the Book of Deuteronomy*. New Haven, 1986.
Hankinson, Robert J. "Galen the Hippocratic: Textual Analysis and the Practice of Commentary." *Hippocratic Commentaries in the Greek, Latin, Syriac and Arabic Traditions*. Leiden, 2021, 147–66.
Hanson, Ann. "Galen: Author and Critic." *Editing Texts/Texte edieren*, ed. G. W. Most. Göttingen, 1998, 22–53.
Hauptman, Judith. *Rereading the Mishnah: A New Approach to Ancient Jewish Texts*. Tübingen, 2005.
Hayes, Christine. *Between the Babylonian and Palestinian Talmuds: Accounting for Halakhic Difference in Selected Sugyot from Tractate Avodah Zarah*. New York, 1997.
Hayes, Christine. "'Halakhah le-Moshe mi-Sinai' in Rabbinic Sources: A Methodological Case Study." *The Synoptic Problem in Rabbinic Literature*, ed. S. J. D. Cohen. Providence, 2000, 61–117.

Hayes, Christine. *What's Divine about Divine Law? Early Perspectives.* Princeton, 2015.
Haynes, Christine. "Reassessing 'Genius' in Studies of Authorship: The State of the Discipline." *Book History* 8 (2005): 287–320.
Havlin, Shelomo Z. "Al 'ha-ḥatimah ha-sifrutit' ke-yesod ha-ḥaluqah li-tequfot ba-halakhah." *Researches in Talmudic Literature* (Heb.). Jerusalem, 1983, 148–92.
Heine, Ronald. *The Commentary of Origen on the Gospel of Saint Matthew.* Oxford, 2018.
Heinemann, Isaac. "On the Development of Technical Terms for Biblical Interpretation." *Leshoneu* 15 (1947): 108–15 (Heb.).
Henshke, David. "Eimatay yoshevim ba-sukah? Le-shiḥzurah shel mishnah rishonah." *Atara L'Haim: Studies in the Talmud and Medieval Rabbinic Literature in Honor of Professor Haim Zalman Dimitrovsky*, ed. D. Boyarin et al. Jerusalem, 2000, 87–104.
Henshke, David. "Is Reciting 'Shema' a Biblical Commandment? The Babylonian 'Amoraim' versus the Anonymous Redactors of the 'Sugya.'" *Sidra* 31 (2016): 33–57 (Heb.).
Henshke, David. *The Original Mishna in the Discourse of Later Tanna'im.* Ramat Gan, 1997 (Heb.).
Hezser, Catherine. *Form, Function, and Historical Significance of the Rabbinic Story in Yerushalmi Neziqin.* Tübingen, 1993.
Hezser, Catherine. *The Social Structure of the Rabbinic Movement in Roman Palestine.* Tübingen, 1997.
Hidary, Richard. *Dispute for the Sake of Heaven: Legal Pluralism in the Talmud.* Providence, 2010.
Hidary, Richard. *Rabbis and Classical Rhetoric.* Cambridge, 2018.
Higger, Michael. *Otzar ha-baraitot.* New York, 1938–48.
Hirshman, Marc. *A Rivalry of Genius: Jewish and Christian Biblical Interpretation in Late Antiquity.* Trans. B. Stein. Albany, 1996.
Hirshman, Marc. *The Stabilization of Rabbinic Culture 100 C.E.–350 C.E.* Oxford, 2009.
Hoffmann, Philippe. "What Was Commentary in Late Antiquity? The Example of the Neoplatonic Commentators." *A Companion to Ancient Philosophy*, ed. M. L. Gill and P. Pellegrin. Oxford, 2006, 597–622.
Inowlocki-Meister, Sabrina. "From Text to Relics: The Emergence of the Scribe-Martyr in Late Antique Christianity (Fourth Century–Seventh Century)." *Journal of Early Christian Studies* 32 (2024): 403–30.
Jacob, Christian. "From Book to Text: Towards a Comparative History of Philologies." *Diogenes* 47 (1999): 4–22.
Jacobs, Andrew. *Epiphanius of Cyprus: A Cultural Biography of Late Antiquity.* Oakland, 2016.
Jacobs, Andrew. *The Remains of the Jews: The Holy Land and Christian Empire in Late Antiquity.* Stanford, 2004.
Jacobs, Louis. *Structure and Form in the Babylonian Talmud.* Cambridge, 1992.
Jacobs, Martin. *Die Institution des jüdischen Patriarchen: eine quellen- und traditionskritische Studie zur Geschichte der Juden in der Spätantike.* Tübingen, 1995.
Jaffee, Martin. "Oral Torah in Theory and Practice: Aspects of Mishnah-Exegesis in the Palestinian Talmud." *Religion* 15 (1985): 387–410.
Jaffee, Martin. "Rabbinic Authorship as a Collective Enterprise" *The Cambridge Companion to the Talmud*, ed. C. E. Fonrobert and M. S. Jaffee. Cambridge, 2007, 17–37.
Jaffee, Martin. *Torah in the Mouth: Writing and Oral Tradition in Palestinian Judaism 200 BCE–400 CE.* Oxford, 2001.
Jastrow, Marcus. *A Dictionary of the Targumim, the Talmud Babli, and Yerushalmi, and Midrashic Literature.* London, 1903.
Johnson, William. *Readers and Reading Culture in the High Roman Empire: A Study of Elite Communities.* New York, 2010.
Kahana, Menahem. "On the Fashioning and Aims of the Mishnaic Controversy." *Tarbiẓ* 73 (2004): 51–81 (Heb.).
Kahana, Menahem. *Sifre on Numbers: An Annotated Edition.* Jerusalem, 2011–15 (Heb.).
Kahana, Menahem. *Sifre Zuta on Deuteronomy: Citations from a New Tannaitic Midrash.* Jerusalem, 2002 (Heb.).

Kahana, Menahem. "The Halakhic Midrashim." *The Literature of the Sages II*, ed. S. Safrai et al. Assen, 2006, 3–105.

Kahana, Menahem. "The Relations between Exegeses in the Mishnah and Halakhot in the Midrash." *Tarbiz* 84 (2015): 17–76 (Heb.).

Kahana, Menahem. *Tiqqun olam (Repairing the World): Babylonian Talmud Tractate Gittin, Chapter 4*. Jerusalem, 2020 (Heb.).

Kahana, Menahem. "וכולה מתניתין—Who Were the Abbreviators of Mishnayot in the Tannaitic Midrashim?" *Tarbiz* 88 (2022): 5–40 (Heb.).

Kamesar, Adam. *Jerome, Greek Scholarship, and the Hebrew Bible: A Study of the Quaestiones Hebraicae in Genesim*. Oxford, 1993.

Katz, Menahem. "Division into Sugyot in the Yerushalmi: Redactional Trends and Their Significance." *Studies in the Redaction and Development of Talmudic Literature*, ed. A. Shemesh and Aaron Amit. Ramat Gan, 2011, 68–86 (Heb.).

Katz, Menahem. *Jerusalem Talmud, Tractate Qiddushin: Critical Edition and a Short Explanation*. Jerusalem, 2016 (Heb.).

Keith, Chris. *The Gospel as Manuscript: An Early History of the Jesus Tradition as Material Artifact*. New York, 2020.

Kellner, Menachem. *Maimonides on the "Decline of the Generations" and the Nature of Rabbinic Authority*. Albany, 1996.

Kharanauli, Anna. "Origen and Lucian in the Light of Ancient Editorial Techniques." *From Scribal Error to Rewriting: How Ancient Texts Could and Could Not Be Changed*, ed. A. Aejmelaeus et al. Göttingen, 2020, 15–52.

Kim, Young Richard. *Epiphanius: Ancoratus*. Washington, DC, 2014.

Kiperwasser, Reuven. *Going West: Migrating Personae and Construction of the Self in Rabbinic Culture*. Providence, 2021.

Kister, Menahem. "A Contribution to the Interpretation of Ben Sira." *Tarbiz* 59 (1990): 303–78 (Heb.).

Koren, Yedidah. "The Persons Who May Not 'Enter the Congregation' in Rabbinic Literature." PhD Dissertation, Tel Aviv University, 2021.

Kosman, Admiel. "'Shitta' as a Method of Study—Its Formation and Pattern of Acceptance in the Academies of Eretz Israel and Babylon." *Sidra* 7 (1991): 103–23.

Kosovsky, Moshe. *Concordance to the Talmud Yerushalmi*. Jerusalem, 1979–2002.

Kraemer, David. *A History of the Talmud*. Cambridge, 2019.

Kraemer, David. *The Mind of the Talmud: An Intellectual History of the Bavli*. New York, 1990.

Kretzmer-Raziel, Yoel. "The Talmudic *stam* as an Evolutionary Phenomenon." *Tarbiz* 86 (2019): 611–62 (Heb.).

Krochmal, Abraham. *Yerushalaim ha-Benuyah*. Lemberg, 1867.

Krueger, Derek. *Writing and Holiness: The Practice of Authorship in the Early Christian East*. Philadelphia, 2004.

Kugel, James L. *Traditions of the Bible: A Guide to the Bible as It Was at the Start of the Common Era*. Cambridge, MA, 1998.

Kugel, James L. "Two Introductions to Midrash." *Prooftexts* 3 (1983): 131–55.

Lampe, Geoffrey W. H. *A Patristic Greek Lexicon*. Oxford, 1969.

Landes, Isaac M. "The Transmission of the Mishnah and the Spread of Rabbinic Judaism, 200–1200 CE." PhD Dissertation, Princeton University, 2023.

Lange, Armin. "Rabbi Meir and the Severus Scroll." *"Let the Wise Listen and Add to Their Learning" (Prov. 1: 5)*, ed. C. Cordoni and G. Langer. Berlin, 2016, 51–74.

De Lange, Nicholas. *Origen and the Jews: Studies in Jewish-Christian Relations in Third-Century Palestine*. Cambridge, 1976.

Lapin, Hayim. "Institutionalization, Amoraim, and Yerushalmi Šebi'it." *The Talmud Yerushalmi and Graeco-Roman Culture III*, ed. P. Schäfer. Tübingen, 2002, 161–84.

Lapin, Hayim. *Rabbis as Romans: The Rabbinic Movement in Palestine, 100–400 CE*. New York, 2012.

Lardet, Pierre. *Saint Jérôme: Apologie contre Rufin*. Paris, 1983.

Larsen, Matthew. "Correcting the Gospel: Putting the Title of the Gospels in Historical Context." *Rethinking "Authority" in Late Antiquity*, ed. A. J. Berkovitz and M. D. Letteney. New York, 2018, 78–103.
Larsen, Matthew. *Gospels before the Book*. New York, 2018.
Leibner, Uzi. "Settlement Patterns in the Eastern Galilee: Implication Regarding the Transformation of Rabbinic Culture in Late Antiquity." *Jewish identities in Antiquity*, ed. I. L. Levine and D. R. Schwartz. Tübingen, 2009, 269–95.
Letteney, Mark. *The Christianization of Knowledge in Late Antiquity: Intellectual and Material Transformations*. Cambridge, 2023.
Levine, Lee I. "The Status of the Patriarch in the Third and Fourth Century: Sources and Methodology." *Journal of Jewish Studies* 47 (1996): 1–32.
Lewy, Israel. *Interpretation des I.–VI. Abschnittes des päläst. Talmud-Traktats Nesikin*. Breslau, 1895–1914, repr. Jerusalem, 1970.
Lichtheim, Miriam. *Ancient Egyptian Literature: A Book of Readings*. Vol. 2: *The New Kingdom*. Berkeley, 1976.
Lieberman, Saul. "Emendations in Jeruschalmy." *Tarbiẓ* 2 (1931): 106–14 (Heb.).
Lieberman, Saul. "Emendations on the Jerushalmi (F.)." *Tarbiẓ* 4 (1933): 377–9 (Heb.).
Lieberman, Saul. *Hayerushalmi Kiphshuto²*, ed. M. Katz. New York and Jerusalem, 2008 (Heb.).
Lieberman, Saul. *Hellenism in Jewish Palestine²*. New York, 1962.
Lieberman, Saul. *On the Yerushalmi*. Jerusalem, 1929 (Heb.).
Lieberman, Saul. *Siphre Zutta (The Midrash of Lydda)*. New York, 1968 (Heb.).
Lieberman, Saul. *The Talmud of Caesarea: Jerushalmi Tractate Nezikin*. Supplement to *Tarbiẓ* 2 (1931): 1–108 (Heb.).
Lieberman, Saul. *Tosefta Ki-fshuta: A Comprehensive Commentary on the Tosefta*. New York and Jerusalem, 1955–88 (Heb.).
MacRae, Duncan. *Legible Religion: Books, Gods, and Rituals in Roman Culture*. Cambridge, MA, 2016.
Maman, Aharon. "The Remnants of R. Hai Gaon's Dictionary *Kitāb al-Ḥāwi* in the Adler and Taylor-Schecter Geniza Collection." *Tarbiẓ* 69 (2000): 341–421 (Heb.).
Mandel, Paul. *The Origins of Midrash: From Teaching to Text*. Leiden, 2017.
Mandel, Paul. "The Tosefta." In *The Cambridge History of Judaism* 4, ed. S. T. Katz. Cambridge, 2006, 316–35.
Mansfeld, Jaap. *Prolegomena: Questions to Be Settled before the Study of an Author or a Text*. Leiden, 1994.
Martens, Peter W. *Origen and Scripture: The Contours of Exegetical Life*. Oxford, 2012.
Mayer, Yakov Z. *Editio Princeps: The 1523 Venice Edition of the Palestinian Talmud and the Beginning of Hebrew Printing*. Jerusalem, 2022 (Heb.).
Mayer, Yakov Z. "From Material History to History Context: The 'Vatican Ebr. 133' Manuscript of the Palestinian Talmud." *Zion* 83:3 (2018): 277–321 (Heb.).
Mayer, Yakov Z. "The Greatest Book of Our Time: On the Scholarly Work of Jacob Nahum Epstein." *Katharsis* 28 (2017): 102–11 (Heb.).
Mazeh, Hanan. "'He Who Said This Did Not Say That': The Origin and Development of the Speaker-Splitting Technique in Rabbinic Midrash." *Jewish Studies* 51 (2016) 1–30 (Heb.).
Mazeh, Hanan. "Tractate Demai of the Palestinian Talmud: Interpretation, Halakha and Social Dynamics in the Amoraic Period." PhD Dissertation, Ben Gurion University, 2020 (Heb.).
Mazeh, Hanan. "'Uprooting from the Mishnah'—Halakhic Complexity and Legal Changes in the Eyes of Sages in the Palestinian Talmud." *Judaism, Sovereignty and Human Rights* 4 (2018), 54–84 (Heb.).
McNamee, Kathleen. "Another Chapter in the History of Scholia." *Classical Quarterly* 48 (1998): 269–88.
Meir, Ofra. "Questions or Answers: On the Development of the Rhetoric of the 'Mahaloket' (Conflict of Opinions) in the Palestinian Rabbinic Literature (Part I)." *Dappim: Research in Literature* 8 (1992): 159–86 (Heb.).
Melamed, Ezra Z. *Introduction to Talmudic Literature*. Jerusalem, 1973 (Heb.).

Merkel, Helmut. *Die Widersprüche zwischen den Evangelien: ihre polemische und apologetische Behandlung in der Alten Kirche bis zu Augustin.* Tübingen, 1971.
Metzger, Bruce. "St. Jerome's Explicit References to Variant Readings in Manuscripts of the New Testament." *Text and Interpretation,* ed. E. Best and R. McL. Wilson. Cambridge, 1979, 179–90.
Metzger, Bruce. "The Practice of Textual Criticism among the Church Fathers." *Studia Patristica* 12, ed. E. A. Livingstone. Berlin, 1975, 340–49
Miller, Stuart. *Sages and Commoners in Late Antique 'Erez Israel: A Philological Inquiry into Local Traditions in Talmud Yerushalmi.* Tübingen, 2006.
Montana, Fausto, "Hellenistic Scholarship." *Brill's Companion to Ancient Greek Scholarship,* ed. F. Montanari et al. Leiden, 2015, 60–183.
Montanari, Franco. "Alexandrian Homeric Philology: The Form of the *Ekdosis* and *Variae Lectiones.*" *Epea Pteroenta: Beiträge zur Homerforschung,* ed. M. Reichel and A. Rengakos. Stuttgart, 2002, 119–40.
Montanari, Franco. "*Ekdosis*: A Product of the Ancient Scholarship." *Brill's Companion to Ancient Greek Scholarship,* ed. F. Montanari et al. Leiden, 2015, 637–72.
Morlet, Sébastian, "Aux origines de l'argument patristique? Citation et autorité dans le Contre Marcel d'Eusèbe de Césarée." *On Good Authority: Tradition, Compilation, and the Construction of Authority in Literature from Antiquity to the Renaissance,* ed. R. Ceulemans and P. de Leemans. Turnhout, 2015, 69–94.
Moscovitz, Leib. "Ata r. peloni." *Mehqere Talmud III: Talmudic Studies Dedicated to the Memory of Professor Ephraim E. Urbach,* ed. Sussmann and D. Rosenthal. Jerusalem, 2005, 505–18.
Moscovitz, Leib. "Between Casuistics and Conceptualization: On the Term Ameru Davar Ehad in the Palestinian Talmud." *Jewish Quarterly Review* 91 (2000): 101–42.
Moscovitz, Leib. "Double Readings in the 'Yerushalmi'—Conflations and Glosses." *Tarbiz* 66 (1997): 187–221 (Heb.).
Moscovitz, Leib. "On the Aggadic 'Foreign Bodies' in the Yerushalmi." *Tarbiz* 64 (1995): 237–58 (Heb.).
Moscovitz, Leib. "Parallel Sugiot and the Text-Tradition of the Yerushalmi." *Tarbiz* 60 (1991): 523–49 (Heb.).
Moscovitz, Leib. "Shemu'ata Kan: Towards the Resolution of a Terminological Crux in the Talmud Yerushalmi." *Envisioning Judaism: Studies in Honor of Peter Schäfer,* ed. R. Boustan et al. Tübingen, 2013, 487–500.
Moscovitz, Leib. "Sugyot Muhlafot in the Talmud Yerushalmi." *Tarbiz* 60 (1991): 19–66 (Heb.).
Moscovitz, Leib. *Talmudic Reasoning: From Casuistics to Conceptualization.* Tübingen, 2002.
Moscovitz, Leib. "The Formation and Character of the Jerusalem Talmud." *The Cambridge History of Judaism.* Vol. IV: *The Late Roman-Rabbinic Period,* ed. S. T. Katz. Cambridge, 2006, 66–77.
Moscovitz, Leib. *The Terminology of the Yerushalmi: The Principal Terms.* Jerusalem, 2009 (Heb.).
Moscovitz, Leib. *The Terminology of the Yerushalmi: The Secondary Terms.* Jerusalem, 2025 (Heb.).
Moscovitz, Leib. "'Women Are (Not) Trustworthy'—Toward the Resolution of a Talmudic Crux." *Studies in Josephus and the Varieties of Ancient Judaism,* ed. S. J. D. Cohen and J. Schwartz. Leiden, 2007, 127–40.
Moss, Candida. "The Secretary: Enslaved Workers, Stenography, and the Production of Early Christian Literature." *Journal of Theological Studies* 74 (2023): 20–56.
Moss, Yonatan. "Disorder in the Bible: Rabbinic Responses and Responsibilities." *Jewish Studies Quarterly* 19 (2012): 104–28.
Moss, Yonatan. "Noblest Obelus: Rabbinic Appropriations of Late Ancient Literary Criticism." *Homer and the Bible in the Eyes of Ancient Interpreters,* ed. M. Niehoff. Leiden, 2012, 245–67.
Mroczek, Eva. *The Literary Imagination in Jewish Antiquity.* Oxford, 2016.
Mroczek, Eva. "Truth and Doubt in Manuscript Discovery Narratives." *Rethinking "Authority" in Late Antiquity,* ed. A. J. Berkovitz and M. D. Letteney. New York, 2018, 139–60.
Münz-Manor, Ophir. "The Liturgical Performance of Identity." *The Routledge Handbook of Jews and Judaism in Late Antiquity,* ed. C. Hezser. London, 2023, 386–97.

Naeh, Shlomo. "Did the Tannaim Interpret the Script of the Torah Differently from the Authorized Reading?" (Heb.). *Tarbiẓ* 61 (1992): 401–48 (Heb.).
Naeh, Shlomo. "Omanut ha-zikaron: mivnim shel zikaron ve-tavniot shel teqst be-sifrut Hazal." *Mehqere Talmud III: Talmudic Studies Dedicated to the Memory of Professor Ephraim E. Urbach*, ed. Sussmann and D. Rosenthal. Jerusalem, 2005, 543–89.
Naeh, Shlomo. "The Eating of Paschal Lambs Is Not Recited." *To Be of the Disciples of Aharon: Studies in Tannaitic literature and Its Sources in Memory of Aharon Shemesh*, ed. D. Boyarin et al. Tel Aviv, 2021, 251–76 (Heb.).
Naeh, Shlomo. "The Script of the Torah in Rabbinic Thought (A): The Traditions Concerning Ezra's Changing of the Script." *Leshonenu* 70 (2008): 125–43 (Heb.).
Naeh, Shlomo. "The Structure and Division of 'Torat Kohanim' (A): Scrolls." *Tarbiẓ* 66 (1997): 483–515 (Heb.).
Naeh, Shlomo. "'Talmud Yerushalmi' of the Academy of Hebrew Language." *Tarbiẓ* 71 (2002): 569–603 (Heb.).
Naeh, Shlomo. "Three Comments of the Text of the Jerusalem Talmud and Its Meaning." *Leshonenu* 74 (2012): 195–215 (Heb.).
Najman, Hindy. *Past Renewals: Interpretative Authority, Renewed Revelation and the Quest for Perfection in Jewish Antiquity*. Leiden, 2010.
Najman, Hindy. "Reading beyond Authority." *Rethinking Authority in Late Antiquity*, ed. A. J. Berkovitz and M. D. Letteney. New York, 2018, 17–30.
Najman, Hindy. *Scriptural Vitality: Rethinking Philology and Hermeneutics*. Oxford, forthcoming.
Najman, Hindy. *Seconding Sinai: The Development of Mosaic Discourse in Second Temple Judaism*. Leiden, 2003.
Najman, Hindy. "The Vitality of Scripture within and beyond the 'Canon.'" *Journal for the Study of Judaism* 43 (2012): 497–518.
Nautin, Pierre. *Origène: sa vie et son œuvre*. Paris, 1977.
Neis, Rachel Rafael. *The Sense of Sight in Rabbinic Culture: Jewish Ways of Seeing in Late Antiquity*. Cambridge, 2013.
Neuschäfer, Bernhard. *Origenes als Philologe*. Basel, 1987.
Neusner, Jacob. *Judaism in Society: The Evidence of the Yerushalmi*. Chicago, 1983.
Newman, Hillel. "A Patristic Perspective on Rabbinic Literature." *The Classic Rabbinic Literature of Eretz Israel: Introductions and Studies*, ed. M. Kahana et al. Jerusalem, 2018, 681–704 (Heb.).
Newman, Hillel. "Jerome and the Jews." PhD Dissertation, Hebrew University of Jerusalem, 1997 (Heb.).
Nichols, Stephen G. "Introduction: Philology in a Manuscript Culture." *Speculum* 65 (1990): 1–10.
Niehoff, Maren. *Jewish Exegesis and Homeric Scholarship in Alexandria*. Cambridge, 2011.
Nisbet, Robin G. M., and Niall Rudd. *A Commentary on Horace: Odes Book III*. Oxford, 2004.
Noam, Vered. "'The Later Rabbis Add and Innovate': On the Development of a Talmudic Sugya." *Tarbiẓ* 72 (2003): 151–75 (Heb.).
Novick, Tzvi. "Scripture as Rhetor: A Study in Early Rabbinic Midrash." *Hebrew Union College Annual* 82-3 (2014): 37–59.
Novick, Tzvi. "Tradition, Scripture, Law, and Authority." *The Literature of the Sages: A Revisioning*, ed. C. E. Hayes. Leiden, 2022, 64–92.
Nunlüst, René. "Aristarchus and Allegorical Interpretation." *Ancient Scholarship and Grammar*, ed. S. Matthaios et al. Berlin, 2011, 105–17.
Pagels, Elaine. "Irenaeus, the 'Canon of Truth,' and the Gospel of John: 'Making a Difference' through Hermeneutics and Ritual." *Vigiliae Christianae* 56 (2002): 339–71.
Paz, Yakir. *From Scribes to Scholars: Rabbinic Biblical Exegesis in Light of the Homeric Commentaries*. Tübingen, 2022.
Peirano, Irene. "Authenticity as an Aesthetic Value: Ancient and Modern Reflections." *Aesthetic Value in Classical Antiquity*, ed. I. Sluiter and R. Rosen. Leiden, 2012, 215–42.

Peirano, Irene. *The Rhetoric of the Roman Fake: Latin Pseudepigrapha in Context.* Cambridge, 2012.

Person, Raymond F. "The Ancient Israelite Scribe as Performer." *Journal of Biblical Literature* 117 (1998): 601-9.

Pfeiffer, Rudolf. *History of Classical Scholarship: From the Beginnings to the End of the Hellenistic Age.* Oxford, 1968.

Porter, James. "Hermeneutic Lines and Circles: Aristarchus and Crates on the Exegesis of Homer." *Homer's Ancient Readers: The Hermeneutics of the Greek Epic's Earliest Exegetes,* ed. R. Lamberton and J. J. Keaney. Princeton, 1992, 67-114.

Rabinovitz, Zeev Wolf. *Sha'arei torat erez Yisrael.* Jerusalem, 1940.

Rapoport, Solomon. *Erekh Millin: Opus Encyclopaedieum.* Prague, 1852 (Heb.).

Rebillard, Éric. "A New Style of Argument in Christian Polemic: Augustine and the Use of Patristic Citations." *Journal of Early Christian Studies* 8 (2000): 559-78.

Redfield, James Adam. "Redacting Culture: Ethnographic Authority in the Talmudic Arrival Scene." *Jewish Social Studies* 22 (2016): 29-80.

Reed, Annette Yoshiko. "ΕΥΑΙΓΓΕΛΙΟΝ: Orality, Textuality, and the Christian Truth in Irenaeus' 'Adversus Haereses'." *Vigiliae Christianae* 56 (2002): 11-46.

Reed, Annette Yoshiko. "Pseudepigraphy, Authorship, and the Reception of 'the Bible' in Late Antiquity." *The Reception and Interpretation of the Bible in Late Antiquity,* ed. L. DiTommaso and L. Turcescu. Leiden, 2008, 467-90.

Reed, Annette Yoshiko. "Textuality between Death and Memory: The Prehistory and Formation of the Parabiblical Testament." *Jewish Quarterly Review* 104 (2014): 381-412.

Reichman, Ronen, "The Talmudic Okimta and Its Logical Structure: A Contribution to the Systematic Research into Talmudic Legal Hermeneutics." *Jewish Studies Quarterly* 2 (2005): 129-47.

Reynolds, L. D. and N. G. Wilson. *Scribes and Scholars: A Guide to the Transmission of Greek and Latin Literature³.* Oxford, 1991.

Richardson, Ernest Cushing. "Jerome's Apology for Himself Against the Books of Rufinus." *A Select Library of the Nicene and Post-Nicene Fathers of the Christian Church* 2-3, ed. P. Schaff and H. Wace. New York, 1906.

Riggsby, Andrew M. *Mosaics of Knowledge: Representing Information in the Roman World.* Oxford, 2019.

Rodriguez, Jacob. *Combining Gospels in Early Christianity.* Tübingen, 2023.

Rollston, Chris A. "Ben Sira 38:24-39:11 and the 'Egyptian Satire of the Trades': A Reconsideration." *Journal of Biblical Literature* 120 (2001): 131-9.

Roselli, Amneris. "Galen's Practice of Textual Criticism." *From Scribal Error to Rewriting: How Ancient Texts Could and Could Not Be Changed,* ed. A. Aejmelaeus et al. Göttingen, 2020, 53-72.

Rosen-Zvi, Assaf and Ishay Rosen-Zvi. "Tannaitic Halakhic and Aggadic Methodology." *Tarbiz* 86 (2019): 203-32 (Heb.).

Rosen-Zvi, Ishay. "A Protocol of the Yavnean Academy? Rereading 'Tosefta Sanhedrin' Chapter 7." *Tarbiz* 78 (2009): 447-77 (Heb.).

Rosen-Zvi, Ishay. *Between Mishnah and Midrash: The Birth of Rabbinic Literature.* Ra'anana, 2020 (Heb.).

Rosen-Zvi, Ishay. "Introduction to the Mishnah." *The Classic Rabbinic Literature of Eretz Israel: Introduction and Studies,* ed. M. Kahana et al. Jerusalem, 2018, 1-64 (Heb.).

Rosen-Zvi, Ishay. "Joining the Club: Tannaitic Legal Midrash and Ancient Jewish Hermeneutics." *Studia Philonica* 17 (2005): 153-60.

Rosen-Zvi, Ishay. "Like a Priest Exposing His Own Wayward Mother: Jeremiah in Rabbinic Literature." *Jeremiah's Scriptures: Production, Reception, Interaction, and Transformation,* ed. H. Najman and K. Schmid. Leiden, 2017, 570-90.

Rosen-Zvi, Ishay. "Structure and Reflectivity in Tannaitic Legal Homilies, or: How to Read Midrashic Terminology." *Prooftexts* 34 (2014): 271-301.

Rosen-Zvi, Ishay. *The Mishnaic Sotah Ritual: Temple, Gender and Midrash.* Trans. O. Scharf. Leiden, 2012.

Rosen-Zvi, Ishay. "'Who Will Uncover the Dust from Your Eyes?': Mishnah Sotah 5 and R. Akiva's Midrash." *Tarbiẓ* 75 (2006): 95–127 (Heb.).
Rosenthal, Avraham. "Le-masoret girsat ha-mishnah." *Saul Lieberman Memorial Volume*, ed. S. Friedman. New York, 1993, 29–48.
Rosenthal, Avraham. "Torah she-bel 'al peh ve-torah mi-sinai—halakhah ve-ma'aseh." *Meḥqerei Talmud II*, ed. M. Bar-Asher and D. Rosenthal. Jerusalem, 1993, 448–89.
Rosenthal, David. "'Al derekh tipulam shel ḥazal be-ḥilufei nusaḥ ba-miqra." *Sefer yitsḥak aryeh zeligman*, ed. Zakovich and A. Rofé. Jerusalem, 1983, 395–417.
Rosenthal, Eliezer Shimshon. "The History of the Text and Problems of Redaction in the Study of the Babylonian Talmud." *Tarbiẓ* 57 (1988), 1–36 (Heb.).
Rosenthal, Eliezer Shimshon. "Tradition and Innovation in the Halakha of the Sages." *Tarbiẓ* 63 (1994): 321–74 (Heb.).
Rubenstein, Jeffrey L. "Criteria of Stammaitic Intervention in Aggada." *Creation and Composition: The Contribution of the Bavli Redactors (Stammaim) to the Aggada*, ed. J. L. Rubenstein. Tübingen, 2005, 417–40.
Rubenstein, Jeffrey L. "Some Structural Patterns of Yerushalmi Sugyot." *The Talmud Yerushalmi and Graeco-Roman Culture III*, ed. P. Schäfer. Tübingen, 2002, 303–13.
Rubenstein, Jeffrey L. *Stories of the Babylonian Talmud*. Baltimore, 2010.
Rubenstein, Jeffrey L. *The Culture of the Babylonian Talmud*. Baltimore, 2003.
Rubenstein, Jeffrey L. "The Talmudic Expression 'Rabbi X Following His Reasoning, Said,'" *Sidra* 10 (1994): 111–29 (Heb.).
Rustow, Marina. *Heresy and the Politics of Community: The Jews of the Fatamid Caliphate*. Ithaca, 2008.
Safrai, Zeev. "Fairs in the Land of Israel in the Mishnah and Talmud Period," *Zion* 49 (1984): 139–58 (Heb.).
Satlow, Michael. *Creating Judaism: History, Tradition, Practice*. New York, 2006.
Schäfer, Peter. *The Jewish Jesus: How Judaism and Christianity Shaped Each Other*. Princeton, 2012.
Schäfer, Peter. "Research into Rabbinic Literature: An Attempt to Define the Status Quaestionis." *Journal of Jewish Studies* 37 (1986): 139–52.
Schäfer, Peter and Hans-Jürgen Becker. *Synopse zum Talmud Yerushalmi*. Tübingen, 1991–8.
Schironi, Francesca. *The Best of The Grammarians: Aristarchus of Samothrace on the* Iliad. Ann Arbor, 2018.
Schofer, Jonathan. *The Making of a Sage: A Study in Rabbinic Ethics*. Madison, 2005.
Schott, Jeremy. "Plotinus's Portrait and Pamphilus's Prison Notebook: Neoplatonic and Early Christian Textualities at the Turn of the Fourth Century C.E." *Journal of Early Christian Studies* 21 (2013): 329–62.
Schremer, Adiel. "Avot Reconsidered: Rethinking Rabbinic Judaism." *Jewish Quarterly Review* 105 (2015): 287–311.
Schremer, Adiel. "Between Text Transmission and Text Redaction: Fragments of a Different Recension of TB Mo'ed-Qatan from the Genizah." *Tarbiẓ* 61 (1992): 375–99 (Heb.).
Schremer, Adiel. "'What God Has Joined Together': Predestination, Ontology, and the Nature of the Marital Bond in Early Rabbinic Discourse." *Diné Israel* 30 (2015): *139–61.
Schremer, Adiel, and Benjamin Katzoff. "Inseparable Considerations: The Origins, Redaction, and Text of the Baraita about the Script of the Torah in Tosefta Sanhedrin 4:7." *Jewish Studies: Internet Journal* 22 (2022): 1–21 (Heb.).
Schwartz, Joshua. "Southern Judaea and Babylonia." *Jewish Quarterly Review* 72 (1982): 188–97.
Schwartz, Joshua. "Tension between Palestinian Scholars and Babylonian Olim in Amoraic Palestine." *Journal for the Study of Judaism* 11 (1980): 78–94.
Schwartz, Seth. *Imperialism and Jewish Society: 200 B.C.E. to 640 C.E.* Princeton, 2001.
Schwartz, Seth. *Were the Jews a Mediterranean Society? Reciprocity and Solidarity in Ancient Judaism*. Princeton, 2010.
Secunda, Shai. "The Talmud of Babylonia," *Oqimta* 10 (2024): 347–77.
Seeligmann, Isac L. "Studies in the History of the Biblical Text." *Textus* 20 (2000): 1–30.

Shapira, Chaim. "'Beit Hamidrash'—Concept and Institution in the Period of the Mishna and Talmud." *Proceedings of the World Congress of Jewish Studies* 12 (1997): 45–60 (Heb.).
Shapira, Joshua Isaac. *No'am yerushalmi*. Vilnius, 1863–9.
Shashar, Yitzhak. "The Jerusalem Manuscript 5702.24 (Sassoon 507) and Its Place in the Formation of the Tiberian Textus Receptus." PhD Dissertation, Hebrew University of Jerusalem (Heb.), 1983.
Shemesh, Aharon and Moshe Halbertal, "The Me'un (Refusal): The Complex History of Halakhic Anomaly." *Tarbiẓ* 82 (2014): 377–93 (Heb.).
Shilat, Yitzhak. *Hakdamot ha-Rambam la-Mishnah*. Jerusalem, 1992.
Simon-Shoshan, Moshe. "The Tasks of the Translators: The Rabbis, the Septuagint, and the Cultural Politics of Translation." *Prooftexts* 27 (2007): 1–39.
Skehan, Patrick and Alexander Di Lella. *The Wisdom of Ben Sira*. New Haven, 1987.
Smith, Andrew. *Boethius: On Aristotle's On Interpretation*. London, 2010.
Sokoloff, Michael. *A Dictionary of Jewish Palestinian Aramaic of the Byzantine Period*[3]. Ramat Gan, 2017.
Sommer, Benjamin D. "Concepts of Scriptural Language in Midrash." *Jewish Concepts of Scripture: A Comparative Introduction*, ed. B. D. Sommer. New York, 2012, 64–79.
Sorabji, Richard. *The Philosophy of the Commentators, 200–600 AD: A Sourcebook*. London 2004.
Speyer, Wolfgang. *Bücherfunde in der Glaubenswerbung der Antike*. Göttingen, 1970.
Speyer, Wolfgang. *Die literarische Fälschung im heidnischen und christlichen Altertum*. Munich, 1971.
Steiner, Richard. "A Jewish Theory of Biblical Redaction from Byzantium." *Jewish Studies: An Internet Journal* 2 (2003): 123–67.
Stern, David. "The First Jewish Books and the Early History of Jewish Reading." *Jewish Quarterly Review* 98 (2008): 163–202.
Stern, David. "On Canonization in Rabbinic Judaism." *Homer, the Bible, and Beyond*, ed. M. Finkelberg and G. Stroumsa. Leiden, 2003, 227–52.
Stern, David. "The Publication and Early Transmission of the Mishnah." *What Is the Mishnah? The State of the Question*, ed. S. J. D. Cohen. Cambridge, 2022, 444–70.
Stern, Sacha. "Attribution and Authorship in the Babylonian Talmud." *Journal of Jewish Studies* 45.1 (1994): 28–51.
Stern, Sacha. "The Concept of Authorship in the Babylonian Talmud." *Journal of Jewish Studies* 46 (1995): 83–195.
Stern, Sacha. "Rabbi and the Origins of the Patriarchate." *Journal of Jewish Studies* 54 (2003): 193–215.
Sussmann, Yaacov. "A Halakhic Inscription from the Beth-Shean Valley." *Tarbiẓ* 43 (1973): 88–158 (Heb.).
Sussmann, Yaacov. *Ginze Yerushalmi*. Jerusalem, 2020 (Heb.).
Sussmann, Yaacov. "Introduction." *Talmud Yerushalmi: According to MS Or. 4720 (Scal. 3) of the Leiden University Library with Restorations and Corrections*. Jerusalem, 2005, ט-לי.
Sussmann, Yaacov. "Masoret-limud u-masoret-nusaḥ shel ha-talmud ha-yerushalmi—le-veirur nushao'teiah shel yerushalmi masekhet sheqalim." *Researches in Talmudic Literature*. Jerusalem, 1983, 12–76.
Sussmann, Yaacov. *Oral Law Taken Literally: The Power of the Tip of a Yod*. Jerusalem, 2019 (Heb.); pagination cited according to the original publication in *Mehqere Talmud III: Talmudic Studies Dedicated to the Memory of Professor Ephraim E. Urbach*, ed. Sussmann and D. Rosenthal. Jerusalem, 2005, 209–384.
Sussmann, Yaacov. "Ve-shuv li-yerushalmi neziqin." *Talmudic Studies I*, ed. Sussmann and D. Rosenthal. Jerusalem, 1990, 55–134.
Talmon, Shemaryahu. "Double Readings in the Massoretic Text." *Textus* 1 (1960): 144–84.
Tamar, Issachar. *'Alei tamar: Yerushalmi seder mo'ed I*, ed. A. Z. Rabbinovitz. Alon Shevut, 1992.
Tanselle, Thomas G. *A Rationale of Textual Criticism*. Philadelphia, 1989.
Theodor, Julius and Chanoch Albeck. *Bereschit Rabba: mit kritischem Appart und Kommentar*. Berlin, 1903–36, repr. Jerusalem, 1965.

Thomas, Samuel. "Eternal Writing and Immortal Writers: On the Non-Death of the Scribe in Early Judaism." *A Teacher for All Generations: Essays in Honor of James C. VanderKam*, ed. E. F. Mason et al. Leiden, 2012, 573–88.

Utz, Richard. "Them Philologists: Philological Practices and Their Discontents from Nietzsche to Cerquiglini." *The Year's Work in Medievalism* 26 (2011): 4–12.

Veltri, Giuseppe. *Eine Tora für den König Talmai: Untersuchungen zum Übersetzungsverständnis in der jüdisch-hellenistischen und rabbinischen Literatur*. Tübingen, 1994.

Vessey, Mark. "The Forging of Orthodoxy in Latin Christian Literature: A Case Study." *Journal of Early Christian Studies* 4 (1996): 495–513.

Vidas, Moulie. "A Place of Torah." *Talmudic Transgressions: Engaging the Work of Daniel Boyarin*, ed. C. E. Fonrobert et al. Leiden, 2017, 22–73.

Vidas, Moulie. *Tradition and the Formation of the Talmud*. Princeton, 2014.

Vidas, Moulie. "What Is a *tannay*?" *Oqimta* 7 (2021): 21–96.

Viezel, Eran. "'David Wrote the Book of Psalms Through [al-yedei] Ten Elders' (BT, Bava Batra 14b–15a)." *Oqimta* 10 (2024): 161–85 (Heb.).

Viezel, Eran. "Moses' Role in the Writing of the Torah in Rabbinic Literature and in Transition to the Middle Ages." *Jerusalem Studies in Jewish Thought* 24 (2015): 29–53 (Heb.).

De Vries, Benjamin. *Studies in the Development of the Talmudic Halakah*. Tel Aviv, 1962 (Heb.).

Wald, Stephen. "'For He Has Benefited from the Holy Sabbath': Restrictions on the Preparation of Food for the Sabbath." *Sidra* 19 (2004): 47–75 (Heb.).

Watson, Francis. *Gospel Writing: A Canonical Perspective*. Grand Rapids, 2013.

Weinberg, Jehiel Jacob. *Seride 'esh: she'elot u-teshuvot, hidushim u-ve'urim*. Jerusalem, 2003.

Weiss, Abraham. *Studies in the Literature of the Amoraim*. New York, 1962. (Heb.).

Weiss, Abraham. *The Talmud in Its Development*. New York, 1954 (Heb.).

Weiss, Isaac Hirsch. *Dor Dor we-Dorschaw*[6]. Vilnius, 1911 (Heb.).

Weiss, Moshe. "A Study of Talmudic Terminology." *Tarbiz* 51 (1982): 543–65 (Heb.).

Wendt, Heidi. "Intellectualizing Religion in the Cities of the Roman Empire." *Urban Religion in Late Antiquity*, ed. A. Lätzer-Lasare et al. Berlin, 2020, 97–121.

Wertheimer, Abraham and Abraham Lis. *Piske ha-rid, berakhot ve-shabbat*. Jerusalem, 1992.

West, Martin. *Studies in the Text and Transmission of the Iliad*. Leipzig, 2001.

Williams, Frank. *The Panarion of Epiphanius of Salamis: Book 1*[2]. Leiden, 2009.

Williams, Meaghan Hale. *The Monk and the Book: Jerome and the Making of Christian Scholarship*. Chicago, 2006.

Wilson, Adrian. "Foucault on the 'Question of the Author': A Critical Exegesis. *Modern Language Review* 99 (2004): 339–63.

Wollenberg, Rebecca Scharbach. "'A King and a Scribe Like Moses': The Reception of Deuteronomy 34:10 and a Rabbinic Theory of Collective Biblical Authorship." *Hebrew Union College Annual* 90 (2019): 209–26.

Wollenberg, Rebecca Scharbach. "The Book That Changed: Narratives of Ezran Authorship as Late Antique Biblical Criticism." *Journal of Biblical Literature* 138 (2019): 143–60.

Wollenberg, Rebecca Scharbach. *The Closed Book: How the Rabbis Taught the Jews (Not) to Read the Bible*. Princeton, 2023.

Worthington, Martin. *Principles of Akkadian Textual Criticism*. Berlin, 2012.

Yadin-Israel, Azzan. "Authorial Intent: Human and Divine." *Talmudic Transgressions: Engaging the Work of Daniel Boyarin*, ed. C. E. Fonrobert et al. Leiden, 2017, 3–22.

Yadin-Israel, Azzan. "Halakhic Midrashim and the Canonicity of the Mishnah." *What Is the Mishnah? The State of the Question*, ed. S. J. D. Cohen. Cambridge, 2022, 425–43.

Yadin-Israel, Azzan. *Scripture and Tradition: Rabbi Akiva and the Triumph of Midrash*. Philadelphia, 2015.

Yadin-Israel, Azzan. *Scripture as Logos: Rabbi Ishmael and the Origins of Midrash*. Philadelphia, 2004.

Yeivin, Israel. *Introduction to the Tiberian Masorah*. Missoula, 1980.

Yuval, Israel. "The Orality of Jewish Law: From Pedagogy to Ideology." *Judaism, Christianity, and Islam in the Course of History: Exchange and Conflicts*, ed. L. Gall and D. Willoweit. Munich, 2016, 237–59.

Zetzel, James. *Critics, Compilers, and Commentators: An Introduction to Roman Philology, 200 BCE–800 CE*. New York, 2018.

Zetzel, James. *Latin Textual Criticism in Antiquity*. New York, 1981.

Zipor, Moshe. *Tradition and Transmission: Studies in Ancient Biblical Translation and Interpretation*. Tel Aviv, 2001 (Heb.).

General Index

For the benefit of digital users, indexed terms that span two pages (e.g., 52–53) may, on occasion, appear on only one of those pages.

Aaron, 179, 277–78
Ahuvia, Mika, 23–24
Albeck, Chanoch, 46–47, 282–83, 294, 301–2, 309–10
Albeck, Shalom, 7–8
Alexander, Elizabeth Shanks, 10, 175
annotation in margins, 102, 247–48
anonymization of teachings, 44, 46, 47–48, 75, 287
anonymous teachings, 24, 35–76, 305–6
    in Amoraic sources, 40, 49, 309
    as authoritative position, 41–45, 49–50, 52, 140–41
    as indication of an individual's position, 39–40, 41, 45–46, 48–51, 75, 140–41, 309
    as indication of majority position, 39–40, 45–46, 48–51, 67, 309
    relation to attributed/individual teachings, 39–40, 41–45, 49–50, 60–61
    in Tannaitic sources, 39–40, 41–44, 49–50, 140–41, 304, 309
    see also attributions; demonstrations of identifications; identifications of teachings
Aristarchus, 70n.128, 71–72, 74–75, 228–29, 245–46, 249–50
Aristophanes, 245–46
Aristotle, 68–69
arrival statements, 43–44, 190, 283, 284, 286–87, 306
Asaph (biblical figure), 27
Assis, Moshe, 14, 188, 206
Assmann, Jan, 150, 151, 153
associations
    between anonymous and attributed teachings, 22–23, 38–39, 60–61, 65
    between casuistic and explicit legal teachings, 88–89
    between teachings and sage's biography, 85
    between teachings attributed to the same sage, 80–82, 84, 85, 92
attributions, 21–22, 23–24, 35–36, 39–40, 71–72, 130–31, 160, 163–64, 304, 310
    Amoraic, 2–3, 32–33, 163–64
    changes to, 46–47, 69, 117–18, 160n.92
    divergences in, 226–27

early Christian, 74, 234–35
emendations of, 254, 262
fixity of, 145
in Greek and Latin writings, 68–75
honor of, 140–41
mistakes in, 69, 153–54
post hoc determination of, 63–64
reliability of, 15, 22–23
role of Halakhic positions in, 23–24, 30, 70–71, 74
switched, 213, 221n.61
Tannaitic, 30–31, 32–33, 39–40, 61–68, 74, 75, 153
vs. identifications, 35–36, 61
see also anonymous teachings; citations; identifications of teachings
Aulus Gellius, 68–70, 71
authorial consistency, 21–22, 24, 38, 56, 57, 59–60, 72–73, 77, 82, 85, 96–97, 98, 99, 102, 105–7, 114, 123–24, 128, 304
    Greco-Roman, 69–73
    lack of, 98, 102–3, 105–7, 108–9, 110, 111, 114, 115–16, 117–18, 119–20, 121, 123–24, 128
    see also inconsistency
    Tannaitic notions of, 105, 124
    see also individuation
authorial constructs, 63, 65, 67–68, 71, 72, 304
authorship
    collective, 15, 23–24, 74, 133
    see also majority teachings
    early Christian notions of, 22, 27–28, 68–69, 73–74
    Greco-Roman notions of, 22, 23–24, 68–75
    individual, 21–22, 24, 29, 33, 133–34, 161–62
    modern notions of, 22–23, 24, 71, 74–75, 116
    rabbinic notions of, 3, 30–31, 123–24, 133–34, 145, 164–65, 304
    of Scripture, 24–28

Babylonia, 7–8, 86, 137, 193, 194, 195–96, 285–86
Babylonian Talmud, 3–4, 15, 16–17, 52, 107, 203n.7, 206–7, 235–36, 271–72, 278–79, 280–81, 300–1, 305, 306–7

GENERAL INDEX

Barthes, Roland, 22
Benovitz, Moshe, 301–2
Berkovitz, A. J., 27
books and codices, 104, 170–71, 177–78, 181, 204, 247
　see also writing
Bosker, Baruch, 82
Boyarin, Daniel, 265–66
Brenner, Itamar, 281, 285, 300–1

Caesarea, 176–77, 190, 191–93
Callimachus, 68–69
canonicity, 6–7, 8–9, 12, 69, 71, 196, 234, 270
　see also Scripture
Cerquiglini, Bernard, 204
Chamber of Hewn Stone, 100, 159, 196–98
Chin, Mike, 73, 74
Christianity, 13–14, 22, 23–24, 25–26, 27–28, 68–69, 73, 103–4, 170, 177, 228, 247, 308
Cicero, 151–52
citations, 30–33, 36
　Amoraic period, 9–10, 21–22, 31, 32–33, 123–24, 138
　ethics of, 130–35, 137, 140, 153
　and immortality, 144–50, 158, 164, 165, 304
　Tannaitic period, 5–6, 31, 32–33, 138, 153, 159
　see also attributions
Clement of Rome, 70n.128
contradictions, 49, 107, 108–9, 111, 115–16, 117–18, 119–20, 222–23, 234–35, 255
　see also authorial consistency, lack of; inconsistency; recited teachings, divergent

Daube, David, 264–65
David, 144–45, 147–49, 151
demonstrations of identifications, 52–57, 64, 67
Didymus, 73–74, 228–29
Dinarchus, 68–69
Dionysius of Halicarnassus, 68–69, 70n.129, 71
Donaldson, Amy, 232

Ebionites, 177
Egypt, 150
Ehrlich, Uri, 131
Eleazar the Priest, 154–56
Elijah, 152–53
emendations, 242–63, 304–6, 311
　as changes to content/legal ruling, 243–44, 246–47, 250–51, 255–56, 258
　as changes to form/text, 243–44, 248, 251–52, 253, 254, 256, 258, 260
　paratextual, 245, 263
　of recited teachings, 221, 242–43, 245–46, 262
　textual support for, 248–50

Enoch, 152–53
Epiphanius, 13–14, 177–78, 230, 231–33, 235–36
Epstein, Jacob N., 35–36, 46–47, 52, 140–41, 154, 202–4, 206, 209, 214, 217–18, 226, 227, 228, 234, 243–44, 249–51, 255, 301–2, 309–10
Esther (biblical figure), 154–55
Eusebius, 13–14, 103, 230, 231–33
evil eye, 86
Ezekiel (biblical figure), 27
Ezra (biblical figure), 25–26, 152–53

Fisch, Menachem, 280
Foucault, MIchel, 22–23, 56, 68–69
Fränkel, David, 121
Friedman, Shamma, 203–4, 301–2
Furstenberg, Yair, 28–30, 174, 209–10

Galen, 68–69, 72–73, 74–75, 229, 248–49, 297–98
Ginzberg, Louis, 112
Goldberg, Abraham, 46–47
gospels, 103, 177, 230–35
Greek and Latin scholarship, 22, 23–24, 35, 68–75, 151–52, 169, 170–71, 202, 228, 240–41, 308
Greek language, 48n.47, 99, 103, 152n.72, 247
Green, William, 35

Halakhah, 6, 23–24, 29, 30, 178, 200
　and attributions/identifications in the Talmud, 40–52, 60–61
　and attributions in the Tannaitic corpus, 30, 61–64, 95–97, 153–54
　and emendations, 246–48, 250–58
　rules to decide disputes in, 46n.40, 52, 180–81
　and textual difference, 210–21
　and textual expertise, 307–8
　see also Index of Halakhic Subjects
Halbertal, Moshe, 308–9
Halivni, David, 8, 270, 301–2
Hayes, Christine, 266, 271–72
Herodotus, 68–69
Higger, Michael, 206
Hippocrates, 72, 229, 297–98
Homer, 22n.2, 68n.110, 70n.128, 71–72
Homeric scholarship, 13–14, 71–72, 228–29, 245–46, 249, 271
honor, 132–34, 137, 141, 143–44, 164
Horace, 132

identifications of teachings, 33, 35, 39–48, 68–71, 74, 82–83, 113, 227–28, 305–6
　demonstration of, 52–57, 64, 67

role of in interpretation, 57–61
significance of, 35–39
Tannaitic, 61–68
Tannaitic vs. Amoraic, 61, 65, 67–68
see also anonymous teachings; individuation
inconsistency, 69, 98, 102–3, 104–7, 110, 111, 115–16, 120, 121, 128–29, 254, 258, 302, 305–6
see also authorial consistency, lack of; contradictions; recited teachings, divergent
individuation, 2, 21–30, 45–46, 47, 52, 75–76, 77, 130–31, 137, 156, 164
see also identifications of teachings
interpolations, 5–6, 69–70
intertextuality, 24–25, 172–73, 265, 304–5
Irenaeus of Lyon, 233–34
Isaiah (biblical figure), 27
Isocrates, 151–52

Jacobs, Louis, 26
Jaffee, Martin, 21, 22, 28, 33, 70–71, 164–65
Jeremiah (biblical figure), 26–27
Jerome, 13–14, 22, 73–75, 151–52, 230, 231–33, 245–46, 247–48
Jesus, 230–33, 234–35
Job, 26, 107–8
Johnson, William, 308
Joseph of Tiberias, 177–78
Joshua (biblical figure), 26, 155, 160–61
Judah the Patriarch, 1, 7–8, 9, 42–45, 46–49, 203–4, 210n.34, 227
see also Mishnah, compilation of

Kahana, Menahem, 28–29, 170
Kamesar, Adam, 235
knowledge, rabbinic notions of, 22, 77–78, 160–61, 165, 169, 178, 190, 194, 199–201
Kosovsky, Moshe, 14
Kraemer, David, 11, 305, 306
Kugel, James 265–66, 271

Landes, Yitz, 9
Lapin, Hayim, 9–10
Larsen, Matthew, 234–35
law, Rabbinic., *See* Halakhah
law, Roman, 52n.64, 247–48, 288n.67, 307–8
Lella, Di, 152–53
Letteney, Mark, 247–48
Letter of Rav Sherira, 7–8, 175, 235–36
Lieberman, Saul, 136–37, 243–44, 249–50

Maimonides, 288
majority teachings, 39–40, 49–52, 57, 59–60
see also authorship, collective

manuscripts, 102, 203–4, 209–10, 228–29, 249
Masoretic lists, 102
master-disciple relationships, 31, 130–41, 157
see also teachers, godlike status of
Mazeh, Hanan, 294
McNamee, Kathlee, 247
memorization, 4–5, 102, 162, 170–71, 172, 200, 206, 265, 282
see also orality
Merkel, Helmut, 232–33
Midrash, 1–2, 6–7, 13–14, 24–25, 100, 264–66, 270, 271–72, 278–79, 280–82, 297–98, 303, 307–9
Aqivan, 6–7, 271
Ishmaelian, 265–66, 271
modern study of, 264–66, 271–72, 308–9
Tannaitic, 9–10, 306–7
techniques of, 24–25, 102, 169, 271–72, 278–79, 282, 297–98
Mishnah, the 4
authority of, 8, 11, 41, 50, 262
canonization/promulgation of, 6–11, 203–4, 226, 304
compilation of, 1, 6–8, 11, 12, 46–49, 140–41, 202–4
see also Judah the Patriarch
divergent texts, 202–3, 205–6, 226–27
emendations of in the Talmud, 203, 251–52, 253, 254, 255, 259, 260, 261–62
(im)perfection of, 265, 278–79
precise formulation of, 175, 207, 256, 258, 262, 263, 274, 275
see also recited teachings; teachings
mishnah, 8–9, 11–12, 16n.73, 207–8, 259, 262
of an individual sage, 64–68, 226–27, 268–70, 276, 278–79
Montana, Fausto, 245–46
Montanari, Franco, 245–46, 249–50
Moscovitz, Leib, 14, 80–82, 88, 107, 184–85, 186, 188, 203, 243–44, 261–62
Moses, 24–25, 26, 28, 78, 89, 152–53, 154–56, 158–59, 160–61
Moss, Candida, 23–24

Naeh, Shlomo, 102
Najman, Hindy, 204
necessity claims, 271–74, 275, 276, 278–79, 303, 304–5
see also redundancies, interpretation of
Nehardea, 195–96, 197–98
Neis, Rafael, 143–44
Neusner, Jacob, 305
New Testament. *See* gospels
Noam, Vered, 203–4

GENERAL INDEX

obelos, 245–46, 247–48
oqimta, 279–82, 285, 299, 300–1
orality, 4–5, 6–7, 68, 104, 145, 153, 164–65, 170–71, 172, 174, 177–78, 181, 203, 226–28, 233, 235–36, 241, 246, 263, 265
  see also writing
Origen, 13–14, 69–70, 70n.126, 70n.130, 73–74, 103, 230–35, 245–46, 249
Ovid, 151–52, 153

Pamphilus, 74
Paul, 69–70, 70n.130
Paz, Yakir, 264–65, 271
Peirano, Irene, 71
Pharisees, 28
philology
  Greco-Roman, 68–69, 169, 240–41, 247, 249–50
  modern, 3, 169, 204, 234, 249–50, 269–70
  modern, Talmudic 3, 202–4, 227, 235–36, 243–44, 249–50, 267, 309–11
piyyutim, 24, 152–53
Plautus, 68–70, 71
Polybus, 297–98
Psalms, 145, 147–48, 149

Rapoport, Solomon, 7–8
recited teachings, 11–12
  anonymous, 49, 51, 207, 209–10, 228–29, 262
  authority of, 11–12, 50
  discovery of new, 178, 193
  divergent, 204, 205–6, 208–26, 228–29, 234–36, 239, 240–41, 248–49, 250, 261–62, 279–80, 304–5, 311
  emendations to, 221, 242–43, 245–46, 262
  precise formulation of, 256, 258, 260, 262–63
  regional, 178, 181, 193, 194
  see also Mishnah; teachings
reciters, 24, 47–48, 206–10, 220–21, 227–28, 251n.39
  multiple, 117–18, 295, 309–10
reciting/recitation, 24, 45–46, 67–68, 170–71, 207–10, 220–21, 259
redaction, 203–4
redundancies, interpretation of, 265, 271–73, 275, 278, 293
  see also necessity claims
Reed, Annette Yoshiko, 152–53, 233–34
Rosenthal, Abraham, 203
Rosenthal, David, 170
Rosenthal, E. S., 29–30, 203–4, 235–36
Rosen-Zvi, Ishay, 27, 28–29, 271, 272, 281–82, 308–9
Rufinus, 73–74

Samaritans, 103
Samuel, 26
Saracens, 139–40
Schäfer, Peter, 203–4
Schironi, Francesca, 249
Schott, Jeremy, 74
Schwartz, Seth, 143–44, 149, 307–8
Scripturalization of the Mishnah, 1–2, 3–4, 8, 10n.47, 175, 246–47, 256, 268, 269, 270, 273, 274, 278–79, 280–81, 306
  see also canonicity
Scripture, 1–6, 11, 24–28, 72–73, 169–71, 172–73, 178, 200–1, 243, 256, 264–66, 271, 272, 281–82, 308–9
  see also Torah
Septuagint, 170
Sinai, 89, 156–58, 162, 196–98, 285
Sokoloff, Michael, 206
Solomon, 148–49, 151
standardization of the rabbinic curriculum, 9, 12–13, 174–75, 304
Stern, David, 12, 170–71, 265, 266, 270, 282, 301–2
Stern, Sacha, 22
student-teacher relationships, 31, 130–41, 157
study house, 9–10, 144
Sussmann, Yaacob, 203, 206, 227n.77

tables
  in ancient Christian scholarship, 103–4
  possible use of in ancient Talmudic scholarship, 100–4, 127
Tannaitic period, 5–6, 11–12, 227–28
  anonymous teachings in, 39–40, 41–44, 49–50, 140–41, 304, 309
  associations in compared to the Amoraic period, 92
  citations in, 5–6, 31, 32–33, 138, 153, 159
  discovery of new traditions in, 196
  identifications of teachings, 61–68
  Midrashim in, 9–10, 306–7
  notions of attribution and authorship in, 21–22, 28, 32–34, 39–40, 61–68, 74–75, 140–41, 153, 174
  notions of authorial consistency in, 105, 124
  textual interpretation in, 171
  transmission in, 30–31, 32–33
Targum, 25–26
teachers, godlike status of, 135–36, 143–44
  see also master-disciple relationships
teachings
  corrections to, 174, 202–3, 221, 226
    see also emendations
  discovery of new, 188, 190, 196

fragmentary nature of, 185–86, 200–1, 263, 279, 297–98, 301–3, 304–5, 310
reformulation of, 5–6, 24, 28–30, 33–34, 63–64, 65, 75–76, 174–75, 202, 203–4, 207–8, 226, 234–35, 237, 244–45, 262
regional, 188, 190, 192–93, 194–96, 198–99
see also Mishnah; recited teachings
Temple (Jerusalem), 27, 29–30, 148–49, 151, 169, 196, 197–98, 261, 276–78
terminology, Talmudic, 14
inconsistent or diverse usage 15, 38–39, 220–21, 244
see also Index of Terms and Phrases
textual criticism, 13–14, 245–46, 247–50, 258–59, 263
Theodosius, 247–48
Theophilius, 70n.131
Thomas, Samuel, 152–53
Tiberias, 1, 156–57, 176–78, 181, 188, 190, 191
Torah, 2–3, 4–5, 24–26, 147
fragmentary nature of, 178, 181, 192–93, 196, 200–1
oral, 4–5, 164–65, 302
perfection of, 268, 269
study and teaching of, 2–3, 16n.73, 89–92, 156–58, 160–61, 164–65, 178
Tosefta, 6–7, 10n.48, 11–12, 47, 52–53, 61n.87, 140–41, 203
tradents, sages as, 21, 28–29, 30, 33–34, 117, 120, 124, 133–35, 145, 158–59, 161, 162, 203–4, 304
transmission, 24, 28, 75–76, 105–6, 116, 117, 123, 133–34, 162, 163, 164, 203–4, 207–8, 209–10, 220–21, 235, 282–83
chain of, 21, 24, 31–33, 67, 79–80, 123, 156–61, 192–93, 194
changes to teaching during, 116, 117, 203–4, 207–9, 216

errors in, 169, 202–4, 207, 223, 226, 234, 284, 285–86, 301–2, 303, 306
face-to-face, 31–32, 33, 163–65, 174–75
mechanisms of, 192–93
oral, 171n.14, 172, 203, 227, 235–36
Tannaitic notions of, 30–31, 32–33
verbatim, 171–72, 174, 207, 246
see also Mishnah, precise formulation of; recited teachings, precise formulation of
travel between rabbinic academies, 188, 190, 193, 194, 195–96, 197–99
see also recited teachings, regional; teachings, regional
Tyre, 189, 190

variants 169–70, 202, 203, 204, 208, 214, 219, 222–23, 224, 226, 228–29, 231–32, 234–35, 241
versions, 169, 170–71, 202, 203, 207, 226, 228, 234
visualization, 102, 127, 161, 304

Weiss, Abraham, 294, 301–2, 306, 309–10
Wollenberg, Rebecca, 25–26, 170–71
writing, 4–5, 26, 104, 145, 147–48, 151–53, 164–65, 170–71, 172, 203, 207, 226–27, 245–46
and immortality, 150
see also books and codices; orality

Yadin-Israel, Azzan, 173–74, 265–66, 271, 279, 308–9
Yavneh, 171, 200

Zenodutus, 245–46
Zetel, James, 247, 307–8
Zipor, Moshe, 169

Index of Rabbinic Terms and Phrases

For the benefit of digital users, indexed terms that span two pages (e.g., 52–53) may, on occasion, appear on only one of those pages.

Tannaitic Compilations

אל תקרי... אלא (do not read... but...), 170
אני אפרש (I shall specify/explain), 172–73
דבר (word, deed, rabbinic teaching), 78–79, 149–50
   במה דברים אמורים (in what [cases] are these words said), 280n.45
   דברי היחיד; דברי הרבים (the words of the individual [sage]; the words of the many/majority [of sages]), 39–40
   דברי רבי פלוני, וחכמים אומרים (the words of R. so-and-so, but the sages say), 39–40
   הוסיף רבי פלוני (R. so-and-so added), 177n.1
   חילוף הדברים, (switching the words/statements), 208–9
כיוצא בו (similarly), 93
לא נחלקו על... ועל מה נחלקו... על (They did not dispute concerning... but rather, concerning what did they dispute? Concerning....), 30, 63
מדרש (*midrash*, advanced study or teaching), 16–17
מודה רבי (R. so-and-so concedes/agrees), 95–96
מי שאמר זה לא אמר זה (whoever said this did not say that), 297–98
מידה (measuring instrument, rule; also figuratively), 124–28
משנה (*mishnah*, recitation), 8–9, 64–68
סתם (unspecified), 39n.17
עד שבא רבי פלוני ולימד (until R. so-and-so came and taught), 198–99
צרך (need, necessity), 272
   אינו צריך (it [the homily] is not necessary), 272
   מה אני צריך (why do I need), 272
רואה אני את דברי רבי פלוני (I prefer the words of R. so-and-so), 47n.42
רבי פלוני אומר משמו (R. so-and-so says in his name), 208–9
רבי פלוני בשם רבי אלמוני (R. so-and-so in the name of R. such-and-such), 30
שמועה (ancient tradition), 28–29, 134n.11, 171
שמע (hear, in the sense of receiving a tradition), 199–200
תלמוד (*talmud*, Torah study or advanced form thereof), 16–17

Talmud Yerushalmi

אולפן (received instruction, ≠recited teaching, ≠opinion), 79–80
אשגרת לשון (a slip of the tongue), 223, 251–52, 259
אמרו דבר אחר (they said one thing), 88
איתא חמי (come and see), 293n.77
אתא רבי פלוני (R. so-and-so came/arrived), 186–90
אתיא כרבי פלוני (it goes like/as [i.e., conforms with] R. so-and-so), 38, 84
בשם גרמיה (in his own name), 34n.56, 120–24
דעה (*de'ah*, rabbinic opinion or personal inclination), 77–80, 102–3, 160–61, 304
   לא מן דעתיה (not based on his own opinion), 79–80
   על דעתיה דרבי פלוני (on the opinion of R. so-and-so), 79n.8, 82n.17
   רבי פלוני כדעתיה (R. so-and-so [said this] according to his opinion), 80–97, 102–3, 104, 106–7, 113, 250–51, 304, 309
דרבי פלוני היא ([this teaching] is R. so-and-so's), 35–36, 53–54, 93n.39
זו דברי רבי פלוני אבל דברי חכמים (this [teaching] is the words of R. so-and-so's, but the words of the [majority of] sages are...), 51–52
זעירא (junior, also in the hierarchical sense), 137–38
יחיד, יחידאה (an individual sage), 41
משום יחיד אני שונה אותה (I recite it in the name of an individual), 51–52
יכיל אנא פתר לה (I can interpret it/resolve it), 298n.90
ירדו לה בשיטת רבי (they approached it in the line of R. so-and-so), 60–61, 84
חכמים שהם בשיטת רבי פלוני (the sages [teaching] in R. so-and-so's line), 38

336 INDEX OF RABBINIC TERMS AND PHRASES

לא על הדא איתאמרת אלא על הדא (it was not said about this but about that), 287–95, 301–2

לא שמיע (he did not hear), 194–96, 199

לית כאן... אלא (it's not here; there is no... but...), 242–63

על... הושבה (it refers to...), 294–95

משנה/מתניתא (mishnah, recitation/recited teaching), 11, 24, 48–49, 207–8, 226–27, 259
אית מתניתא אמרה, 210

משנה שלימה שנה לנו רבי (Rabbi [Judah the Patriarch] recited for us a perfect/complete mishnah), 267, 268, 269–70

משניות, 9n.35, 48–49, 69n.120

כיני מתניתא (thus is the recitation), 223–24, 243

מתניתא ב... (the recited teaching speaks of...), 223–24, 279–80

מתניתא דר׳ פלוני (the recited teaching is of R. so-and-so's), 35–36, 177n.1, 178, 179, 180–81, 276

מתניתן; כמתניתן (our recitation; as our recitation= the Mishnah), 11, 221n.61, 226–27, 269, 276, 278–79

על... הושבה (it refers to...), 294–95

עמך הייתי (I was with you...), 285–86

צרך, צרצורכא (need, necessity), 271

לא צורכא דלא (it was not needed except for), 272–73

למי נצרכה (for whom was it needed), 294

לפום כן צרך מימר (it was therefore needed/necessary to say), 272–73, 275

צריכא לה (it was wanting for him/he was in doubt about it), 272–73

ר׳ פלוני בשם ר׳ אלמוני (R. so-and-so in the name of R. such-and-such), 30

שיטה (line or row, also figuratively, the sage's line of teaching), 60n.85, 84, 98–104, 286, 304

מחלפה שיטתיה דר׳ פלוני (R. so-and-so's line is switched), 104–29, 291, 304

שמועה, שמועתא (received teaching), 79–80, 134n.11

בעל השמועה (the master of the tradition), 161–62

מרה דשמועתא (the master of the tradition) 161–62

שמועתא הכא/כאן (the teachings [ought be taught] here), 287n.65

תוספתא (additional teaching), 177n.1

תלמוד (talmud, Torah study or advanced form thereof), 16–17

תני (recite), 24, 207–8

אנן תנינן... תני ר׳ חייא (we recited... R. Hiyya recited...), 210, 266, 275–76

אנן תנינן... תני דבי רבי (we recited... R. Hiyya recited...), 210

אשכח תני (it was found recited), 41, 181–86, 306

מאן תנא... רבי פלוני (who recited [this teaching]? R. so-and-so), 35–36

תני רבי פלוני (R. so-and-so recited), 9n.35

תניי (reciter), 206–7, 260, 267

אית תני תני (there is a reciter reciting [a divergent teaching]), 202–41

אית תניי תני ומחלף (there is a reciter reciting and switching [the teachings/attributions]), 213

חד תנייא (a single reciter), 298n.90

ערק תנייה מינה (the reciter has left it out), 269–70

תניין אינון; תרין תניין אינון (these are two reciters; there are [different] reciters), 295–301

Index of Halakhic Subjects

For the benefit of digital users, indexed terms that span two pages (e.g., 52–53) may, on occasion, appear on only one of those pages.

adulteress (suspected; =*sotah*), 44–46, 94, 110–11, 219
androgynous people, 111–12
aylonit, 253–54

blessings, 55–56, 194, 216
book of Esther, reading of, 58–59, 251–53

circumcision, 111–12

damages, 287–89, 295
Day of Atonement, 126–27, 183, 222, 236–37, 276–78, 279–80
deafness, 58, 251–52
divorce, 36, 37–38, 40, 59, 87–88, 93, 108–9, 118–19, 125–26, 127–28, 253–54

'eruv, 94, 111–12, 120–21, 135–36, 238–39
eunuchs, 108–9
execution, 110–11

gentiles, 187, 238–39, 287–89

ḥaliza, 108–9, 112–13, 118n.70, 216, 236–37

idols, 141–43
immersion, 89, 111–12, 121, 255–56
inadvertent transgressions, 30

ketubbah, 253

leaven, 59–61, 112
leprosy, 112–13

mamzer, 285–86
marriage and betrothal, 36, 37–38, 40, 41, 59, 93, 95–96, 109, 125–26, 197, 253–54, 292–93
menstruation, 82–83, 199, 277–78
mental incapacity, 58, 77–78, 118–19, 251

mixed kinds, 89, 185, 266–68

new year, 139
Nazirites, 114–15, 146
Ninth of Av, 109

offerings, 124–25, 126–27, 172, 212
    festal, 89–92
    first fruits, 55–56, 89–92, 224–25
    grain, 44–46, 114–15, 124–25, 186–87
    pilgrimage, 89–92
    purification, 118–19

Passover, 87, 122–23, 191–92, 215–16, 283–84
pilgrimage festivals, 126–27
prayer, 21, 89–92, 122–23, 189–90, 194, 205–6, 275–76
priests, 29–30, 44–46, 89, 94, 179–81, 192, 219, 276–78, 296–97
priests' share (*terumah*), 38, 59, 60–61, 62, 64–65, 81, 82–83, 189, 215, 254–55, 257
property ownership, 108–9, 153–54
purity, 29–30, 62–63, 64–65, 89, 112–13, 118–19, 126–27, 173–74, 189, 277–78, 296–97

Sabbath, 54, 56–57, 79, 81, 111–12, 116–17, 182, 211–12, 214, 238–39, 242, 254, 259–60, 274–75
sabbatical year, 89, 179, 197, 246–47
Samaritans, 59–61
Shema, 39–40, 58–59, 89, 132–33, 208, 215
Sukkot, 56–57, 122–23, 215

Temple, the, 44–45, 55, 125, 126–27, 261, 276–78
tithes, 89, 94, 197

vows, 36–38, 71, 89, 93, 114–15, 290–93, 299–300

widows, 40, 89, 134–35, 197

Index Locorum

For the benefit of digital users, indexed terms that span two pages (e.g., 52–53) may, on occasion, appear on only one of those pages.

Hebrew Bible

Genesis
17:10, 111–12
29:2–3, 100

Exodus
15:26, 58–59
23:17, 111–12
29:29, 179

Leviticus
6:3, 187
8:33, 277
8:34, 277
11:13, 89
14:14, 113
16:16, 44–45
16:20, 216
19:18, 110

Numbers
6, 146
6–9, 78n.5
12:3, 78
15:18, 191
19:2, 172
30:2, 89, 299–300
30:6, 299–300
31:21, 154

Deuteronomy
4:2, 102n.13
4:9, 162
4:9–10, 157–59
6:4, 58
16:3, 191
19:14, 154
21:3, 172
22:6–7, 205–6
25:7–10, 113
26: 3–10, 55

2 Samuel
8:15, 148–49

Jeremiah
1:1, 27
49, 27

Ezekiel
23:48, 110

Obadiah
1, 27

Psalms
19:8, 268
25:14, 197
39:7, 161
61:5, 144, 145
62:9, 109, 109n.47
68:6, 109
79, 27
119:97, 66
122:1–2, 148

Proverbs
1:23, 27
7:10, 214
10:7, 150
21:3, 148
20:6, 163
21:3, 148
31:14, 266

Song of Songs
7:10, 146

Ecclesiastes
8:1, 176

Esther
2:22, 155

1 Chronicles
2:54, 149–50
17:11–12, 148

Pseudepigrapha and Apocrypha

1 Enoch
92:1, 152n.70

Sirach
13:6–7, 136–37
39:9–10, 152–53
44:14–15, 152–53, 152n.72

Rabbinic Literature

Mishnah

Berakhot
1:1, 208, 254n.44
2:3, 39–40, 58
4:3, 21
4:7, 208n.26
5:3, 205
6:2, 55–56

Pe'ah
2:1, 273
2:3, 273–74
2:4, 208n.26
2:5, 198
2:6, 32n.54, 159, 196

Demai
1:1, 225n.74
3:6, 95n.41

Kil'ayim
1:3, 65n.103
1:6, 266
2:7, 89, 93n.39
2:11, 47n.44
3:7, 141n.33
6:5, 89
7:4, 89
9:10, 185

Shevi'it
4:2, 61n.88
5:3, 179
7:1, 179
10:8, 97n.43

Terumot
1:2, 186, 251
1:8, 254n.44
2:4, 38, 38n.14
2:6, 38
4:7, 43n.29
5:2, 93n.38
8, 95
10:2, 81
10:7, 255
10:10, 254, 255
11:1, 38, 38n.14

Ma'aser Sheni
2:4, 63n.95
3:6, 30n.45
3:10, 105n.27
5:8, 65n.103, 199n.63

Ḥallah
4:9, 64, 65n.104

'Orlah
2:1, 43n.29, 82–83
2:11, 59

Bikkurim
1:6, 55

Shabbat
1:2, 157, 275
1:3, 97n.43, 276
3:3, 81
5:2, 214
6:1, 256
7:2, 259
7:3, 54
8:1, 54
10:5–6, 95
11:1–2, 211
11:4, 274

'Eruvin
1:1, 242
1:2, 141n.33
3:2, 251n.38
3:4, 120
3:5, 238
3:7–8, 94
4:5, 95n.41
7:11, 78n.3
10:10, 199n.63

Pesaḥim
1:1, 280n.46
1:6, 29–30, 65n.103, 89, 177n.1
1:7, 82–83, 124n.85, 128n.97, 189, 296, 302n.100
3:3, 43n.29
3:4, 43n.29
6:1–2, 105n.27
9:6, 173n.22, 199n.65
9:10, 254n.44
10:4, 77n.2

Sheqalim
4:6, 128n.97
4:7, 47n.42, 125n.90, 280n.46
6:4, 261

Yoma
1:1, 276
8:1, 183

Sukkah
3:15, 77n.2

INDEX LOCORUM   341

   4:1, 57
   5:1, 56

Beẓah
   3:7, 214
   4:7, 239
   5:4, 89, 107n.38

Rosh ha-Shanah
   3:8, 251n.38
   4:4, 138n.23

Ta'anit
   1:2, 122

Megillah
   2:3, 252
   2:4, 58–59, 187–88, 251
   3:4, 79

Ḥagigah
   2:1, 78n.6

Yevamot
   4:10, 40, 43, 53–54
   8:3, 105n.27
   8:4, 173n.22, 199n.65
   12:2, 216
   15:1, 199n.65
   15:6–7, 95
   16:7, 197

Ketubbot
   1:6–7, 95
   2:2, 95n.41, 96
   13:3–5, 47n.42

Nedarim
   1:2, 36n.8
   2:4, 39n.17
   4:3, 78n.3
   5:1 290
   5:2, 290n.73
   6:1, 65n.103
   6:9, 199n.63
   7:3, 37–38
   8:7, 36, 37–38
   9:6, 65n.103
   10:1–2, 292

Nazir
   1:2, 115
   2:1, 114
   2:2, 115

Sotah
   1:5, 110
   2:2, 94

   5:2, 89
   6:1, 43n.29
   6:3, 43n.29
   9:3, 280n.47
   9:9–15, 7–8n.27

Gittin
   2:5, 251n.38
   2:6, 77n.2
   3:3, 106n.37
   3:7, 257
   4:8, 253
   7:4, 106n.37

Qiddushin
   2:8, 191

Bava Qamma
   1:2, 280n.45
   2:2, 295
   4:3, 287
   5:7, 267–68

Bava Meẓi'a
   8:9, 77–78

Bava Batra
   1:2, 78n.3
   9:1, 47n.42
   9:2, 95n.41
   9:7, 95n.41
   10:7, 93

Sanhedrin
   3:4, 65n.102
   6:3, 110

Shevu'ot
   1:4, 126
   6:3, 47n.42

'Eduyot
   1:3, 198
   1:4–6, 39n.18
   1:5–6, 247n.24
   1:8, 63n.95
   1:12, 199n.65
   2:1, 65n.103
   2:5, 254n.44
   2:8, 92
   3:10, 92
   6:2, 105n.27
   6:3, 126
   8:1, 65n.103
   8:7, 32n.54, 159n.90

'Avodah Zarah
   2:5, 169n.4

Avot
 2:5, 31n.48
 2:8, 208n.26
 2:12, 21
 4:7, 78n.6
 4:20, 147n.55
 5:11, 78

Menaḥot
 2:1, 95n.41
 3:4, 124–25
 6:1, 45n.34
 12:3, 114–15, 115n.61

Ḥullin
 2:6, 125n.89

Bekhorot
 5:3, 78n.3
 6:8, 199n.65
 7:2, 98n.2

'Arakhin
 2:3, 57
 8:5, 47n.42, 280n.46

Temurah
 3:1, 30n.45

Karetot
 3, 199n.65
 3:7–9, 140n.28, 171n.19
 3:10, 105n.27
 4:2–3, 30
 5:4–8, 95

Kinnim
 3:6, 78n.6

Kellim
 5:4, 78n.3
 5:5, 97n.43
 17:6, 78

Oholot
 16:1, 173

Nega'im
 7:4, 199n.65
 9:3, 199n.65
 10:6–7, 98n.2
 11:7, 199n.65
 14:9, 113

Parah
 1:1, 28n.38, 39n.17, 95n.41, 172, 199n.65

Miqva'ot
 2:2, 121
 9:1, 255
 9:6, 141n.33

Niddah
 1:3, 28n.38, 199
 6:13, 82–84
 10:5, 95n.41
 Tevul Yom
 3:4–5, 208n.26
 Yadaim
 3:1, 199n.65
 4:3, 32n.54, 105n.27, 159n.90, 197

Tosefta
Berakhot
 5:9, 78
 5:30, 30n.45
 6:2, 78

Demai
 1:9, 47n.42
 2:22–24, 97n.43
 3:1, 32n.54
 3:10–11, 53n.71

Kil'ayim
 1:2, 65n.103
 3:10, 47n.42

Shevi'it
 8:3, 47n.42

Terumot
 3:13, 216
 9:9, 208n.26
 10:2, 31n.48
 Ma'aserot
 2:20, 140n.32

Ma'aser Sheni
 2:1, 62, 64
 2:12, 65n.102
 4:5, 47n.42, 280n.46
 4:6, 47n.42

'Orlah
 1:8, 32n.54

Shabbat
 2:13, 63n.93
 8:2, 280n.46
 8:10, 54
 9:13, 31n.48
 12:1, 292n.75
 14:16, 31n.48
 15:9, 30n.45
 15:17, 140n.32

'Eruvin
 3:1, 240n.127

Pesaḥim
 1:7, 64n.99, 64–65, 65n.103, 199n.63

3:8, 31n.48
5:4, 30n.45
8:7, 216

Sheqalim
1:8, 53n.71
2:10, 64n.99
3:9, 64n.99

Yoma
1:1, 173n.22, 277n.41

Sukkah
4:14, 57n.79

Ta'anit
3:8, 149–50

Megillah
1:6, 31n.48
3:16, 140n.30, 140n.32

Mo'ed Qattan
1:8, 280n.46
2:10, 65n.103, 199n.63
2:12, 199n.63
2:14, 65n.103

Ḥagigah
2:9, 199n.64

Yevamot
3:31, 28n.38
11:6, 140n.30, 140n.32
11:8, 140n.32
11:8–9, 140n.30
11:9, 140n.32
12:11, 208n.26
12:15, 140n.32
13:4, 47n.42, 126n.92

Ketubbot
3:8, 53n.71, 61n.87
7:11, 280n.46
12:4, 30n.45

Nedarim
4:6, 89
5:1, 65n.103
6:2, 293n.77
6:3–4, 64n.99

Nazir
5:1, 32n.54, 161n.99, 199n.62

Sotah
2:2–3, 297n.85
2:6, 45n.36
5:9, 78
7:12, 78n.6
14:9, 199n.64

15:1, 47n.42
15:4, 7–8n.27

Gittin
2:6, 140n.32
5:7–9, 140n.30
6:6, 140n.32
6:7, 140n.32
6:9, 140n.32
7:11, 98n.3

Bava Qamma
4:2, 289n.68
6:18, 141n.33
6:21, 140n.32
9:31, 32n.54

Bava Meẓi'a
10:4, 53n.75

Bava Batra
5:7, 140n.32
11:10, 98n.3

Sanhedrin
2:13, 199n.61
3:8, 78n.6
4:7, 25n.20
4:8, 32n.54
5:1, 78n.6
7:1, 197–98, 199n.64
7:4–5, 171n.17
7:6, 78n.6
7:9, 78n.6
8:6, 78
12:10, 140n.32

'Eduyot
1:1, 200
1:4, 39n.17
1:6, 199n.65
3:1, 199n.61

Horayot
2:1, 173n.23

Menaḥot
4:5, 47n.42
8:3–4, 45n.34

Ḥullin
7:1, 78n.4

Bekhorot
4:11, 199n.65
4:16, 141n.33

'Arakhin
1:13, 57n.79
5:15, 65n.102

Me'ilah
  1:20, 47n.42

Kelim Bava Qamma
  6:15, 140n.32
  6:17, 209n.29

Kellim Bava Meẓi'a
  4:5, 63n.93
  4:15, 61n.88
  6:7, 140n.32
  11:3, 61n.88

Oholot
  4:14, 32n.54
  14:4, 140n.32
  15:12–13, 174n.25
  18:18, 132n.5

Nega'im
  1:2, 32n.54, 140n.32
  2:11, 64n.100
  5:3, 140n.32

Parah
  3:3, 141n.33
  11:7, 209n.28
  12:18, 64n.99

Tohorot
  7:7, 173n.22

Miqva'ot
  6:14, 141n.33

Niddah
  1:5, 199
  3:6, 173n.22
  5:2, 88

Zevaḥim
  1:8, 173n.22
  2:17, 66, 198n.59
  4:1, 125n.87
  9:5, 140n.32

Yadaim
  2:16, 32n.54

Mekhilta de-Rabbi Ishamel

Pisḥa §14, 173n.23
Pisḥa §16, 141n.33, 150n.61
Neziqin §10, 281n.50
Kaspa §20, 78n.5, 281n.50
Shabbata §1, 77n.2

Mekhilta de-Rabbi Simeon
  Ex 12:13 21.11, 272n.30

Sifra
Nedava 11:1, 95n.41
Ḥova 2:5, 95n.41
Sheraẓim 1:2, 281n.50
Zavim 5:3, 65n.103, 199n.63
Emor 10:2, 208n.26
Be-har 1:1, 28n.37

Sifre Numbers
  §23, 106n.37
  §31, 141n.33
  §46, 78n.5
  §101, 78
  §115, 97n.43
  §134, 78n.6
  §139, 173n.23
  §140, 155n.79, 173n.23
  §157, 154

Sifre Zuta Numbers
  19:3, 208n.27

Sifre Deuteronomy
  §31, 272n.30
  §38, 47n.42, 150n.60
  §48, 173n.23
  §161, 16n.73
  §188, 153
  §230, 272n.30
  §306, 16n.73
  §317, 100
  §324, 150n.61
  §356, 169n.3

Talmud Yerushalmi
Berakhot
  1:1 2a, 210n.33
  1:1 3a, 213n.40, 221n.63, 222n.67, 248n.30, 254n.44
  1:2 3a, 132n.8, 220, 238n.126
  1:2 3b, 31n.49, 89n.34, 89
  1:4 3c, 194, 195n.55
  1:5 3d, 195n.55, 196n.58
  2:1 4b, 131, 132, 137, 138, 141, 144, 146, 148, 193
  2:2 4c, 215n.49
  2:3 4d, 41n.22, 52n.62, 52n.66, 53n.68, 58, 186, 224n.71, 251, 273n.32
  2:6 5b, 137n.22
  2:8 5d, 59n.84
  4:1 7a, 146n.52
  4:1 7b, 109n.49, 118n.71
  4:1 7c, 1n.2, 108n.42
  4:3 8a, 224n.72
  4:4 8b, 222n.68

5:1 8d, 108n.43
5:1 9a, 162n.101
5:3 9c, 205, 214n.46
5:4 9c, 215, 222n.65
6:2 10b, 53n.73, 55
6:8 10d, 214n.43
7:1 11a, 185n.25
7:2 11b, 106n.36, 193n.47
7:4 11c, 185n.25
9:1 13a, 100n.12

Pe'ah
1:1 15b, 35n.2, 85n.26, 89, 160n.95
1:1 15c, 69n.121
1:1 15d, 132n.9, 134n.11
1:6 16c, 192
2:1 16d, 273
2:2 17a, 183n.20
2:6 17a, 160n.94, 285n.60, 287
2:6 17b, 177n.1
3:1 17b, 210n.34
3:2 17b, 275n.38
3:5 17c, 59n.83
3:7 17d, 267n.11
4:9 18c, 287n.65
4:11 18c, 50n.56, 53n.73
5:2 18d, 39n.16
5:2 19a, 106n.33
5:3 19a, 105n.23
6:2 19d, 104n.22, 105n.23, 107n.38
7:2 20a, 213n.40, 224n.73, 287n.65, 290n.70
7:7 20c, 272n.31
8:1 20d, 214n.43
8:7 21a, 293n.77

Demai
1:3 22b, 31n.50, 191
2:1 22c, 193n.44
2:1 22d, 89n.34
2:3 23a, 222n.65
2:4 23a, 35n.2, 53n.71, 287n.65
3:2 23b, 35n.4, 53n.73
3:4 23c, 38n.15
4:6 24b, 103n.16
4:6 24c, 84n.25
5:1 24c, 41n.22, 59n.84
5:9 24d, 108n.42, 118n.69
6:6 25c, 89n.34
6:12 25d, 276n.39
7:4 26b, 106n.31
7:6 26b, 59n.82, 158n.88

Kil'ayim
1:6 27a, 267
1:7 27a, 109n.49

1:9 27b, 86n.28
1:9 27d, 38n.13
2:5 27d, 34n.56, 124n.84
2:7 27d, 93n.39
2:10 28b, 35n.2
3:1 28c, 169n.4
3:3 28d, 275n.37
4:4 29b, 246n.23
4:7 29c, 89, 93n.39
4:8 29c, 193n.47
4:9 29c, 117n.63
5:7 30a, 85n.27
6:3 30c, 192n.38
6:5 30c, 221n.61
6:6 30c, 195n.55, 275n.37
7:7 31a, 214n.46, 224n.72
8:1 31b, 224n.72, 298n.90
8:4 31c, 214n.43
9:3 32a, 213n.41
9:4 32b, 137n.22
9:9 32d, 215n.48
9:10 32d, 183n.20, 184n.23, 185

Shevi'it
1:1 33a, 246–47
1:6 33b, 160n.95, 273n.32
2:3 33d, 47n.45, 295–96n.80, 298n.87
2:5 33d, 210n.34
2:6 33d, 267n.11
2:8 34a, 210n.36
2:10 34b, 84n.25, 103n.16
3:2 34c, 287n.65
3:3 34c, 132n.8
4:2 35b, 195n.51, 195n.53, 195n.55
5:1 35d, 79–80, 195n.55
5:3 35d, 178
5:5 36a, 286n.62
6:1 36c, 132n.5, 188n.29
7:1 37b, 59n.84
7:3 37c, 270n.18
7:4 37c, 138
7:6 37c, 124n.84
7:7 37c, 295–96n.80, 298n.90
8:5 38a, 108n.43
8:5 38b, 107n.38
8:7 38b, 52n.66
9:1 38c, 273n.32, 275n.37
9:1 38d, 106n.31
9:6 39a, 248n.30
10:2 39c, 185n.24, 272n.31

Terumot
1:2 40c, 53n.68, 58, 186, 224n.71, 251
1:8 41a, 262n.61
2:1 41b, 275n.37

Terumot (cont.)
  2:6 41d, 38n.14, 106n.30
  3:1 42a, 47n.45, 52n.63, 52n.64, 52n.66,
     53n.69, 181n.12
  3:4 42a, 215, 216
  3:6 42b, 215n.47
  4:3 42d, 52n.61, 244n.12
  4:11 43b, 82n.17
  5:2 43c, 93n.38
  7:5 44d, 111n.52, 120n.76
  7:7 45a, 85n.27
  8:4 45c, 35n.2
  8:5 45c, 162n.100
  8:5 45d, 162n.100
  8:8 46a, 192n.38
  8:8 46b, 295–96n.80
  8:11 46b, 193n.41
  9:3 46c–d, 215n.48
  9:7 46d, 35n.4
  10:1 47a, 287n.65
  10:2 47a, 81
  10:10 47b, 254, 284n.58
  11:1 47c, 47n.45, 53n.75
  11:1 47d. 106n.30
  11:2 47d, 31n.49
  11:8 48a, 246n.23, 248n.30, 254n.45
  11:9 48a, 221n.63

Ma'aserot
  1:5 49a, 158n.88
  1:8 49b, 52n.62, 52n.66, 53n.69
  2:5 49d, 244n.12
  3:1 50b, 47n.45

Ma'aser Sheni
  1:2 52c, 120n.76, 122n.78, 123n.83, 276n.39
  1:3 52d, 215n.47
  1:7 53a, 53n.69, 182n.15, 184n.22, 185n.24
  2:1 53a, 244n.14
  4:12 55b, 47n.45
  5:1 55d, 69n.120
  5:14 56d, 103n.16

Ḥallah
  1:1 57a, 81, 191
  1:1 57b, 224n.72
  1:2 57c, 105n.28, 106n.31
  1:4 57d, 287n.65
  2:2 58c, 85n.27, 89n.34, 89, 103n.15, 105n.29,
     107n.38
  2:3 58c, 108n.43
  2:4 58c, 213n.40, 236n.121
  3:1 59a, 60n.85
  3:5 59c, 85n.27, 86n.28
  3:8 59c, 195n.55
  4:2 59d, 213n.40
  4:3 59d, 275n.37
  4:5 59d, 236n.121
  4:9 59d, 213n.40
  4:9 60b, 65n.104, 89n.34, 103n.15, 105n.29

'Orlah
  1:1 60c, 89
  1:1 60c–d, 224
  1:1 60d, 85n.27, 99n.8, 215n.48, 286n.63
  1:2 60d, 105n.28, 106n.37
  1:2 61a, 105n.23, 105n.28, 118n.70, 120n.76,
     244n.14, 252n.40, 252n.41
  1:5 61a, 59n.84, 99n.8, 286n.64
  1:6 61b, 118n.68, 120n.76
  1:9 61c, 243n.5
  2:1 61d, 43n.29, 53n.70, 82–83, 222n.68
  2:8 62a, 287n.65
  2:11 62b–c, 38n.15, 59n.83, 60
  2:11 62c, 41n.22, 52n.62
  3:9 63b, 53n.75

Bikkurim
  1:2 54d, 195n.52
  1:5 64a, 53n.70, 53n.75, 89
  1:6 64b, 55
  1:7 64b, 52n.61
  2:1 64d, 195n.56
  2:11 65c, 47n.44
  3:4 65d, 221n.63

Shabbat
  1:1 2b, 82n.17
  1:1 2c, 38n.15, 105n.28, 117n.66, 215n.48
  1:2 3a, 32, 132n.4, 156, 158, 161, 162, 210n.33,
     276
  1:3 3b, 105n.23, 105n.28, 109n.49
  1:4 3c, 85n.27
  1:4 3d, 160n.95
  1:6 4a, 35n.2
  1:10 4b, 283
  2:1 4c, 60n.85
  2:1 4d, 222n.65
  2:3 4d, 31n.49
  2:5 5a, 215n.49, 254n.44, 260n.56, 262n.61
  2:6 5b, 214n.46
  3:3 5d, 81
  3:3 6a, 38n.13
  3:4 6a, 182
  3:6 6c, 38n.13, 59n.82, 282n.53
  4:1 6d, 210n.34, 236n.117
  5:1 7b, 214n.43
  5:2 7b, 214
  5:4 7c, 214n.43, 224n.72
  6:1 7d, 215n.47, 252n.41, 255, 262n.61
  6:3 8b, 53n.73, 105n.23, 105n.28
  6:10 8c, 221n.61

7:1 9a, 210n.34
7:1 9b, 41n.22, 262n.61
7:2 9d, 224n.72
7:2 10b, 53n.75, 59n.84, 105n.28, 191, 260n.57
7:2 10c, 244n.13, 252n.41, 260
7:2 10d, 292n.75
7:3 10d, 224n.72
8:1 11a, 54, 87, 176
8:2 11b, 215n.49
8:6 11b, 106n.31
9:1 11d, 210n.37
9:3 12a, 210n.34
9:4 12a, 244n.14
10:1 12b, 186n.28
10:4 12c, 295–96n.80
10:6 12c, 111n.51
11:1 12d, 211, 221n.63, 224n.72, 228n.80, 248n.30
11:1 14d, 47n.45
11:2 13a, 244n.14, 274
11:4 13a, 273n.32
12:3 13d, 108n.43
12:5 13d, 104n.22, 106n.33, 111n.51
13:5 14a, 105n.23, 111n.51
14:1 14b, 270n.21
14:3 14c, 80n.10, 86
14:4 15a, 32, 164n.105
16:1 15c, 6–7n.21, 49n.50, 221n.60
16:5 15d, 59n.82
17:6 16b, 210n.34
19:3 17a, 210n.34
19:3 17b, 112n.53

'Eruvin
1:1 18c, 106n.34, 108n.42, 215n.49, 222n.64, 222n.67
1:1 18d, 193n.47, 242
1:3 19a, 222n.68
1:5 19a, 117n.63
1:6 19b, 69n.120, 184n.21
1:7 19b, 295–96n.80, 298n.90
2:1 20a, 85n.27, 93n.38, 214n.46, 222n.65
2:4 20a, 106n.30
2:6 20b, 183n.20
3:1 20c, 35n.4, 53n.75
3:4 21a, 111n.52, 121
3:5 21b, 60n.85, 238
3:7 21b, 79–80, 106n.31
4:1 21d, 79–80
4:5 22a, 287n.65, 290n.70
4:11 22a, 183n.20
5:1 22b, 135, 214n.45
5:6 22d, 287n.65
6:8 23d, 52n.63, 57n.80, 193n.47
7:2 24b, 116

8:6 25a, 106n.31, 107n.38
8:9 25b, 298n.90
10:3 26b, 117n.66, 254n.45
10:7 26b, 35n.2
10:15 26d, 105n.23

Pesaḥim
1:1 27a, 89n.34, 252n.41
1:3 27c, 106n.31
1:4 27c, 112n.54
1:6 27d, 89
1:7 27d–28a, 296
1:7 28a, 82–83, 189, 192n.38, 194, 195n.55, 296n.81
1:7 28b, 295–96n.80
2:1 28c, 120n.76
2:1 28d, 222n.67
2:2 28d, 281n.50
2:2 29a, 220n.58, 244n.12
2:5 29b, 81, 191, 246n.23
3:3 30b, 43n.29
3:8 30b, 221n.61
4:1 30d, 47n.46
5:1 31d, 53n.75, 221n.60
5:3 32a, 102n.13
5:4 32b, 31n.50, 215n.48, 236n.120
5:4 32c, 89n.34
5:7 32c, 85n.27, 89n.34
7:2 34b, 222n.68
7:6 34c, 38n.15
7:10 35a, 60n.85
7:11 35a, 270n.21
7:11 35a–b, 105n.28, 117n.66, 118n.72, 120n.75
7:13 35c, 195n.56, 196n.58
8:3 35d, 260n.59
8:8 36b, 84n.21
9:1 36c, 210n.33
9:3 36d, 216
9:6 37a, 84n.25, 103n.16, 215, 221n.60
9:11 37a, 35n.4
10:1 37a, 54
10:1 37c, 87, 176
10:3 37d, 228n.80

Sheqalim
1:6 46b, 53n.71
2:2 46c, 210n.34
2:5 47a, 130n.1, 149
3:2 47c, 87, 176
4:5 48a, 117n.65
5:1 48c–d, 7–8n.27
6:4 50a, 244n.11, 248n.30, 261
7:6 50d, 105n.28, 108n.41

Yoma
1:1 38a–c, 277
1:1 38c, 215n.47
1:1 38d, 179, 286n.62
1:1 39a, 224n.72
1:2 39a, 212
1:3 39a, 183n.20
2:1 39c, 84n.24, 112n.53, 186
2:3 39d, 53n.69
5:1 42b, 221n.60
5:6 43a, 216
6:4 43d, 221n.60
6:7 44a, 195n.55
7:5 44c, 220
8:1 44d, 183, 222, 244n.14, 280n.44

Sukkah
1:4 52b, 89n.34, 215n.48
2:5 53a, 183n.20
2:7 53a, 106n.31, 108n.43
3:1 53c, 215, 222n.64
3:4 53d, 196n.58
4:1 54b, 160n.95
4:8 54c, 193n.47
5:1 55a, 56, 213n.40
5:7 55d, 213n.40

Beẓah
1:1 60a, 106n.31
1:1 60b, 31n.50
1:4 60c, 47n.45
1:7 60d, 106n.35, 118n.68
1:8 60d, 53n.75, 59n.84
2:1 61b, 221n.62
2:8 61d, 267n.11
2:10 61d, 38n.13
3:1 61d, 105n.23, 111n.51
3:4 62a, 180, 193n.48
4:3 62c, 236n.119
4:7 62b, 239
4:7 62d, 105n.23, 215n.47
5:2 63a, 109

Rosh ha-Shanah
1:2 57a, 195n.55
2:6 58a, 215n.47
2:7 58a, 195n.51, 195n.57
2:7 58b, 162n.100, 195n.57
2:9 58b, 276n.39, 277n.40
3:2 58d, 183n.20
3:5 58d, 266
4:4 59b, 139
4:6 59c, 183n.20

Ta'anit
1:1 63a, 103n.15, 117n.65
1:1 63d, 106n.31, 109n.49
1:1 64a, 169n.5
1:2 64a, 106n.31, 108n.41, 122, 189
1:3 64a, 213n.41
1:6 64c, 222, 244n.14, 280n.44, 293n.77
1:7 64d, 109
2:2 65c, 224n.72
2:8 66a, 40, 42, 185n.24
2:10 66b, 213n.41
4:1 67c, 108n.42, 109n.49, 118n.71
4:2 68a, 169n.3
4:4 68b, 213n.42, 221n.61
4:6 68d, 213n.40, 214n.46
4:6 69b, 109
4:7 69c, 286n.62

Megillah
1:1 70a, 295–96n.80
1:1 70b, 47n.46, 295–96n.80
1:2 70b, 298n.90
1:3 70c, 286n.62
1:3 70d, 40, 42, 185n.24
1:7 71b, 41n.22, 51n.60, 53n.75
1:8 71b–c, 25n.20
1:8 71c, 222n.64
1:8 71d, 170n.8
1:9 72a, 104n.22
1:9 72b, 179, 286n.62
1:10 72c, 139n.27, 244n.13, 262n.60
1:11 72d, 246n.23
2:1 73a, 85n.26
2:2 73a, 193
2:3 73a–b, 210n.34, 248n.30, 252
2:4 73b, 53n.68, 58, 186, 224n.71, 251
3:1 73d, 51n.60, 270n.18
3:1 74a, 246n.23, 254n.45
3:4 74a–b, 79
3:5 74b, 221n.60
3:6 74c, 216, 222n.64
4:3 75b, 215
4:9 75c, 205, 214n.46

Mo'ed Qattan
1:2 80b, 287n.65
1:10 81a, 210n.33
2:1 81a, 38n.15, 117n.66, 210n.33, 275n.38
3:1 81c, 89n.34
3:1 82a, 222n.64
3:5 82b, 89, 138n.23
3:5 82c, 215n.49, 222n.64, 286n.62
3:5 82d, 137n.22
3:7 83a, 215n.47
3:7 83b, 213
3:7 83c, 131, 132, 137, 138, 141, 144, 146, 148, 222n.64

Ḥagigah
1:1 76a, 112n.53
1:4 76b, 193n.47
1:7 76d, 160n.94, 285n.60
1:8 76d, 177n.1
2:1 77a, 35n.4
2:2 77d, 213n.42
2:4 78b, 224n.72
2:5 78b, 195n.52, 195n.56
3:2 79a, 195n.52, 195n.56

Yevamot
1:1 2d, 193n.48
1:1 3c, 276n.39
2:2 3c, 185n.25
2:3 3d, 193n.47
3:4 4d, 105n.28, 193n.47
3:8 5a, 254n.45
3:9 5a, 134n.12, 134n.13
4:1 5c, 59n.83
4:10 6a, 31n.50, 31, 69n.121, 117n.65, 117n.66
4:10 6b, 40, 42, 48, 185n.24, 210n.33
5:6 7a, 195n.56, 196n.58
6:1 7b, 183n.20, 210n.33
6:3 7c, 272n.31
6:4 7c, 104n.22, 112n.53
6:6 7d, 286n.62
7:3 8a, 132n.5
7:5 8b, 106n.37, 120n.76
8:1 8d, 53n.75, 222n.64
8:1 9a, 112n.53
8:2 9a, 138n.23
8:2 9b, 222n.67
8:3 9c–9d, 285
8:4 9d, 108n.43, 109n.46
9:3 10b, 273n.32
10:1 10d, 215n.49, 244n.13, 275n.37
10:3 10d, 78n.4, 103n.15, 105n.29
10:3 11a, 140n.31
10:9 11b, 134n.12, 134n.13
11:1 11c, 185n.25
11:7 12b, 106n.30, 111n.52
12:1 12b–c, 237n.122
12:1 12c, 216, 222, 237, 280n.44
12:2 12d, 105n.28, 107n.38, 112, 118n.70
12:4 12d, 59n.83
13:2 13d, 252n.41, 262n.61
13:7 13d, 262n.61
13:11 14a, 59n.83
13:12 14a, 53n.68
14:2 14b, 244n.12
15:5 15a, 134n.12, 134n.14, 185n.25, 195n.52, 195n.56
15:9 15b, 57n.80
16:7 16b, 244n.12

Ketubbot
1:1 24d, 109
1:2 25b, 128n.95
1:4 25c, 53n.68
2:1 26a, 195n.52, 195n.56
3:6 27d, 84n.24
3:8 27d, 51n.60, 53n.71, 53n.75, 61n.87
4:10 29a–b, 245n.16
5:1 29d, 185n.25
5:5 30a, 87
5:6 30b, 222n.68
6:1 30c, 50n.56
6:7 30d–31a, 269n.16
7:1 31b, 224n.72
8:1 32a, 210n.33
8:3 32a, 195n.51, 195n.56
8:8 32c, 160n.95
9:2 33a, 89
9:7 33b, 244n.12
10:5 34a, 196n.58
11:5 34c, 158n.88
12:3 35a, 137n.22
13:2 35d, 195n.52, 195n.56
13:3 36a, 214n.43
13:7 36b, 195n.56

Nedarim
1:1 36c–d, 298n.90, 299, 302n.100
1:3 37a, 222n.67
2:1 37b, 89
2:2 37b, 183n.20
2:4 37c, 295–96n.80, 298n.90
3:1 37d, 224n.72
3:2 38a, 287n.65
3:3 38a, 183n.20
4:2 38c, 195n.52, 195n.56
4:3 38c, 85n.27, 183n.20
5:1 39a, 290
5:4 39b, 213n.42, 221n.60
8:2 40d, 105n.28, 106n.30, 119n.74
8:2 40d–41a, 118n.67
8:7 41a, 37
10:1 41d, 292
11:1 42c, 107n.38
11:3 42c, 248n.30, 262n.60

Nazir
1:1 51a, 49n.50
2:1 51d, 114, 117n.65
2:9 52a, 111n.51
3:5 52c, 111n.51, 118n.68
3:7 52d, 195n.52, 195n.56
4:3 53b, 89n.34
5:4 54b, 106n.36
7:1 56b, 222n.68

Nazir (cont.)
  7:2 56b, 183n.20
  7:2 56c, 60n.85
  9:3 57d, 222n.65
  9:3 57d, 219n.56
  9:3 58a, 221n.60

Sotah
  1:5 17a, 105n.23, 110
  2:1 17d, 45n.36
  2:2 17d, 185n.25, 219
  2:2 18a, 94
  3:6 19b, 45, 79n.7
  4:3 19c, 59n.83
  5:2 20a, 117n.65
  5:2 20c–d, 107
  5:5 20d, 26n.27
  6:1 20d, 42n.25, 43n.29, 213n.42, 214n.43
  7:5 21d, 221n.60
  8:2 22d, 53n.73
  8:5 23a, 177n.1, 298n.90
  9:2 23c, 104n.22, 107n.38, 112n.53
  9:15 24c, 69n.121

Gittin
  1:1 43b, 108n.42
  1:5 43d, 84n.22, 276n.39
  2:2 44b, 84n.22
  2:4 44b, 38n.15
  3:7 45a, 53n.73, 257
  4:4 45d, 117n.65
  4:8 46a, 248n.30, 253
  5:5 47a, 195n.55
  6:1 48a, 108n.42
  6:6 48b, 117n.63
  7:1 48c, 107n.38, 118
  7:4 48d, 105n.28, 106n.37, 112n.55
  8:2 49b, 108n.41, 108n.44, 117n.65
  8:4 49c, 224n.72
  8:7 49c, 140n.31
  8:9 49c–d, 89n.34
  8:10 49d, 275n.37
  9:4 50b, 53n.69, 254n.45
  9:6 50c, 117n.64, 120n.76, 122n.78

Qiddushin
  1:1 58c, 112n.53
  1:1 58d, 268
  1:2 59c, 295–96n.80
  1:4 60b, 222n.64
  1:6 60d, 84n.25, 103n.16
  1:7 61a, 32, 132n.4, 156, 158, 161, 162
  1:7 61c, 134n.11
  2:1 62a, 210n.37
  2:1 62b, 222n.65
  2:8 62d–63a, 120n.76, 122n.78

  2:8 63a, 31n.50, 123n.83, 191
  3:4 64a, 60n.85
  3:5 64a, 298n.90
  3:6 64b, 47n.43, 300n.97
  3:9 64b, 105n.28, 106n.30, 118n.67, 119n.74
  3:12 64c, 285
  3:12 64d, 31n.49, 108n.42, 117n.65
  4:1 65c, 285
  4:6 65d, 82n.17
  4:8 66a, 213n.42, 218, 221n.60

Bava Qamma
  1:1 2a, 210n.33
  1:1 2b, 276n.39
  1:4 2c, 53n.75
  2:1 2d, 128n.96
  2:2 3a, 111n.51, 120n.76, 295
  2:3 3a, 221n.63
  2:5 3a, 53n.75
  3:3 3c, 103n.16
  3:4 3d, 215n.48
  4:3 4b, 288
  4:4 4b, 59n.83
  4:6 4c, 222n.64
  5:1 4d, 132n.8
  5:7 5a, 267
  6:5 5c, 104n.22, 105n.23, 107n.38
  9:3 6d, 191

Bava Meẓi'a
  2:11 8d, 132n.6
  6:3 11a, 222n.65

Bava Batra
  2:12 13c, 286n.63
  3:6 14b, 135n.15, 282n.53
  8:5 16b, 268n.14
  8:6 16b, 218
  9:6 17a, 137n.22
  9:7 17b, 221n.63
  10:6 17c, 195n.54

Sanhedrin
  1:1 18b, 139n.27
  1:2 18b, 221n.60
  1:2 18c, 162n.100, 195n.51, 195n.57, 262n.61
  1:6 19c, 199n.64
  2:3 20b, 216, 222n.68
  3:3 21a–b, 138
  3:4 21b, 275n.37
  4:2 22b, 210n.33
  5:2 22d, 134n.12, 134n.14, 195n.52, 195n.56
  5:3 22d, 112n.54
  6:3 23c, 105n.23, 110
  6:4 23c, 213n.42
  7:4 24d, 224n.72

INDEX LOCORUM

7:9 25c, 53n.75
8:2 26a, 105n.28, 117n.66, 118n.72, 120n.75, 270n.21
9:1 26d, 185n.25
11:3 30b, 136

Makkot
1:1 31a, 185n.24, 272n.31

Shevu'ot
1:4 33a, 127
2:1 33d, 111n.52, 222n.67
2:5 34a, 106n.31, 109n.49, 221n.60
3:1 34b, 106n.33, 295–96n.80
3:4 34c, 89n.34
4:4 35c, 222n.64
4:12 35d, 276n.39
5:1 36a, 262n.61
6:1 36d, 112n.53
6:2 37a, 106n.31, 108n.42, 109n.45, 117n.65
6:7 37b, 193n.48, 195n.57, 196n.58
8:1 38c, 128n.96
8:3 38d, 106n.31, 117n.65

'Avodah Zarah
1:1 39b, 271–72n.28
1:4 39d, 187, 283
1:5 39d, 210n.33, 275n.38
2:3 41a, 162n.100
2:3 41b, 214n.46, 224n.72
2:4 41c, 106n.30
2:6 42a, 222n.65
2:7 42a, 209n.30
3:4 42d, 182
3:5 43a, 214n.43, 243n.5
3:6 43a, 210n.37
3:7 43b, 117n.65
3:8 43b, 142
4:4 44a, 89n.34, 117n.65
4:11 44b, 287n.65
5:2 44d, 287n.65
5:6 45a, 244n.11, 244n.13, 246n.23
5:8 45a, 52n.62, 59n.83, 60

Horayot
1:2 45d, 118
1:5 46b, 38n.15
2:1 46c, 221n.60
3:3 47b, 111n.52
3:4 47c, 104n.22
3:4 47d, 179, 286n.62
3:7 48b, 132n.6, 213
3:8 48c, 6–7n.21, 9n.35, 16n.73, 49n.50, 147n.55, 177n.1, 178n.7

Niddah
1:4 49b, 31n.50, 31, 69n.121, 117n.65, 117n.66

2:3 49d, 38n.15
3:2 50c, 117n.65
3:2 50d, 89n.34

Talmud Bavli

Berakhot
2b–3a, 302n.104

Shabbat
19b, 102n.14
46a, 50n.54
57b, 256
87a, 25n.17
92b, 297n.84

'Eruvin
2b, 242n.2
3a, 279n.43
23a, 279n.43
23b, 279n.43
35a, 279n.43
39b, 279n.43
40a, 279n.43
49a, 279n.43
53a, 137n.21
55a–b, 279n.43
57b, 279n.43
66b, 279n.43
70a, 279n.43
74b, 279n.43
77a, 279n.43
84a, 279n.43

Pesaḥim
28b, 252n.40
42b, 88n.32

Sukkah
54a, 102n.14

Beẓah
26b, 102n.14
33b–34a, 239

Rosh ha-Shanah
9b, 252n.40

Ta'anit
2b, 123n.81

Megillah
9a, 170n.8
15a, 155n.81, 155n.82
31b, 25n.17
32a, 216

Mo'ed Qattan
18b, 109n.47

Ḥagigah
14a, 161n.99

Yevamot
  15b, 50n.56
  17b, 50n.54
  42b, 50n.54
  83a, 252n.40
  96b–97a, 130n.1

Nedarim
  67a, 293n.77

Nazir
  66b, 160n.92

Sotah
  49b, 7–8n.27

Qiddushin
  7a, 279n.43
  13b, 279n.43
  24a, 279n.43
  30a, 157n.87
  43b, 279n.43
  50b, 279n.43
  58a, 158n.88
  59b, 158n.88
  60b, 158n.88
  63a–b, 47n.43, 300n.97
  64b, 158n.88
  65a, 158n.88
  66a, 158n.88
  74a, 158n.88
  75a, 158n.88
  79a, 158n.88

Bava Qamma
  102a, 43n.30

Bava Mezi'a
  33a–b, 6–7n.21

Bava Batra
  14b–15a, 26n.27
  145b, 161n.99

Sanhedrin
  21b–22a, 25n.20
  22a, 109n.47
  86a, 48–49, 49n.53, 141n.33
  89a, 27

'Avodah Zarah
  6b, 271–72n.28
  7a, 43n.30

Menaḥot
  55a, 300n.97
  99b, 261–62

Ḥullin
  104b, 155n.82

Niddah
  19b, 155n.82

Midrash Rabbah
Genesis Rabah
  1, 25n.15
  2:5, 150n.61
  9:5, 169n.5
  20:5, 100n.12
  20:6, 117n.66
  20:12, 169n.5
  44:4, 100n.12
  65:2, 109n.47
  68:4, 109n.47
  70:8, 100n.10
  82:10, 149n.59
  94:9, 169n.5
  100:10, 93n.40

Ecclesiastes Rabbah
  2:8:1, 9n.35
  3:11:2, 100n.12

Lamentations Rabbah
  2:16, 147n.55
  5:2, 27n.31

Leviticus Rabbah
  2:6, 100n.12
  8:1, 109n.47
  29:8, 109n.47

Numbers Rabbah
  5:2, 155n.82

Pesiqta de-Rav Kahana
  12.5, 147n.55
  13.2, 27n.34

Pesiqta Rabbati
  §2, 147n.56

Tanḥuma
  ba-midbar §22, 155n.82

Minor Tractates
Avot de-Rabbi Nathan
version A 34.25 / version B 37.28, 26n.26

Kallah
  §25, 155n.83

Greek and Latin Sources

Aristotle
Poetics, 1459a–b, 68n.110

Aulus Gellius
Attic Nights
3.3.1–14, 68n.113, 70n.129
3.3.13, 69n.121

Cicero
De Officis
3:4, 152n.67

Diogenes Laertius
Lives of the Philosophers
3.57, 70n.127

Galen
De Dignoscendibus Pulsibus
4, 72n.140

In Hippocratis Epidemiarum III
1.4, 72n.137

In Hippocratis Prognosticum
1:4, 72

Herodotus
Histories
2.117, 68n.110

Horace
Odes
3:30 1–2, 152n.65
3:30 6–13, 152n.65

Isocrates
Antidosis, 151n.64

Ovid
Amores
1.15, 152n.66

New Testament

Matthew
19:16–22, 230
20:29–34, 232–33

Mark
10:17–22, 230
10:46–52, 232–33

Luke
18:18–23, 230
18:35–43, 232–33

Romans
5:14, 231–32

Ancient Christian Sources

Epiphanius
Ancoratus
31.4, 231n.95

Panarion
1.8.4, 231n.96
30.3.8–4.1, 177n.3
30.6.7–9, 177n.5
30.15.3, 70n.126

Eusebius
Ecclesiastical History
6.25.11–4, 70n.124

Jerome
Adversus Rufinus
2.11, 73

On Illustrious Men
11, 152n.68
15, 70n.128
25, 70n.129, 70n.131
64, 152n.68
75, 177–78n.6

Origen
Commentary on Matthew
15.14, 231n.92, 234n.109
16.12, 233n.103
16.12–13, 233n.104

Rufinus
Origen's Commentary on the Epistle of the Romans
epilogue, 74